Cognitive Behavior Therapy with Children

APPLIED CLINICAL PSYCHOLOGY

Series Editors: Alan S. Bellack, *Medical College of Pennsylvania at EPPI, Philadelphia, Pennsylvania,* and Michel Hersen, *University of Pittsburgh, Pittsburgh, Pennsylvania*

HANDBOOK OF BEHAVIOR MODIFICATION WITH THE MENTALLY RETARDED
Edited by Johnny L. Matson and John R. McCartney

THE UTILIZATION OF CLASSROOM PEERS AS BEHAVIOR CHANGE AGENTS
Edited by Phillip S. Strain

FUTURE PERSPECTIVES IN BEHAVIOR THERAPY
Edited by Larry Michelson, Michel Hersen, and Samuel M. Turner

CLINICAL BEHAVIOR THERAPY WITH CHILDREN
Thomas Ollendick and Jerome A. Cerny

OVERCOMING DEFICITS OF AGING: A Behavioral Approach
Roger L. Patterson

TREATMENT ISSUES AND INNOVATIONS IN MENTAL RETARDATION
Edited by Johnny L. Matson and Frank Andrasik

REHABILITATION OF THE BRAIN-DAMAGED ADULT
Gerald Goldstein and Leslie Ruthven

SOCIAL SKILLS ASSESSMENT AND TRAINING WITH CHILDREN
An Empirically Based Handbook
Larry Michelson, Don P. Sugai, Randy P. Wood, and Alan E. Kazdin

BEHAVIORAL ASSESSMENT AND REHABILITATION OF THE TRAUMATICALLY BRAIN DAMAGED
Edited by Barry A. Edelstein and Eugene T. Couture

COGNITIVE BEHAVIOR THERAPY WITH CHILDREN
Edited by Andrew W. Meyers and W. Edward Craighead

TREATING CHILD-ABUSIVE FAMILIES
Intervention Based on Skills-Training Principles
Jeffrey A. Kelly

Cognitive Behavior Therapy with Children

Edited by

Andrew W. Meyers

Memphis State Univesity
Memphis, Tennessee

and

W. Edward Craighead

Pennsylvania State University
University Park, Pennsylvania

Springer Science+Business Media, LLC

Library of Congress Cataloging in Publication Data

Main entry under title:

Cognitive behavior therapy with children.

(Applied clinical psychology)
Bibliography: p.
Includes index.
1. Behavior therapy. 2. Cognitive therapy. 3. Child psychotherapy. I. Meyers, Andrew W., 1949- . II. Craighead, W. Edward. III. Series.
RJ505.B4C63 1983 618.92'89142 83-16116
ISBN 978-1-4757-9735-0 ISBN 978-1-4757-9733-6 (eBook)
DOI 10.1007/978-1-4757-9733-6

Originally published by Plenum Press, New York in 1984
Softcover reprint of the hardcover 1st edition 1984

To my parents: Bea and Lou
A. W. M.

To my family: Linda, Benjamin, and Wade.
W. E. C.

Contributors

Jeanne Brooks-Gunn The Infant Laboratory, Educational Testing Service, Princeton, New Jersey and College of Physicians and Surgeons, Columbia University, New York, New York

Louis Burgio Department of Psychology, University of Notre Dame, Notre Dame, Indiana

Bonnie W. Camp Department of Pediatrics and Psychiatry, University of Colorado Medical School, Denver, Colorado

Robert Cohen Department of Psychology, Memphis State University, Memphis, Tennessee

W. Edward Craighead Department of Psychology, The Pennsylvania State University, University Park, Pennsylvania

David S. Glenwick Department of Psychology, Fordham University, Bronx, New York

Robert J. Hall Department of Educational Psychology, Texas A & M University, College Station, Texas

Leonard A. Jason Department of Psychology, De Paul University, Chicago, Illinois

Mary Beth Johnston Department of Psychology, University of Notre Dame, Notre Dame, Indiana

Philip C. Kendall Department of Psychology, University of Minnesota, Minneapolis, Minnesota

Robert E. Kennedy Department of Psychology, Davidson College, Davidson, North Carolina

Barbara K. Keogh Special Education Research Program, Graduate School of Education, University of California, Los Angeles, California

Daniel S. Kirschenbaum Department of Psychology, University of Wisconsin—Madison, Madison, Wisconsin

Avigdor Klingman Department of Counseling, University of Haifa, Haifa, Israel

Alan J. Litrownik Department of Psychology, San Diego State University, San Diego, California

Wendy S. Matthews Department of Pediatrics, University of Medicine and Dentistry of New Jersey—Rutgers Medical School, Piscataway, New Jersey

Andrew W. Meyers Department of Psychology, Memphis State University, Memphis, Tennessee

Barbara G. Melamed Department of Clinical Psychology, College of Health Related Professions, University of Florida, Gainesville, Florida

Patricia Morison Department of Psychology, University of Minnesota, Minneapolis, Minnesota

Rosemery O. Nelson Department of Psychology, University of North Carolina at Greensboro, Greensboro, North Carolina

Arnold M. Ordman Department of Psychology, University of Wisconsin—Madison, Madison, Wisconsin

Roberta Shockley Ray Department of Psychology, University of Denver, Denver, Colorado

Richard N. Roberts Kamehameha Educational Research Institute, Honolulu, Hawaii

Robert Schleser Lewis College of Arts and Letters, Illinois Institute of Technology, Chicago, Illinois

Lawrence J. Siegel Department of Clinical Psychology, College of Health Related Professions, University of Florida, Gainesville, Florida

Hillary Turkewitz Greater Lawrence Psychological Center, Inc., 36 Lawrence Street, Lawrence, Massachusetts

Thomas Whitman Department of Psychology, University of Notre Dame, Notre Dame, Indiana

Preface

Recent estimates (Hallahan & Kauffman, 1978) indicate that over 4.7 million children, 7.3% of the child population under the age of 19, are labeled emotionally disturbed, mentally retarded, or learning-disabled. Moreover, many of these children remain unserved or are inadequately served. The past decade has produced an increasing concern with the mental health needs of these children and their families. This trend had as much impact in behavior therapy as it did in any other branch of the helping professions. Behavioral work with children, with its emphasis on skill development and environmental modification, helped to build into child psychotherapy a true preventive mental health orientation. The ease of delivery and application of behavioral procedures allowed parents and other caregivers to become meaningfully involved in the clinical process, and so facilitated therapy gains and the maintenance and generalization of those gains.

Perhaps the most significant change in behavior therapy in the 1970s was the move beyond interventions derived strictly from learning theories to applications based on knowledge from a variety of psychological research areas. The cognitive mediational activities of the client have received special attention, and this book presents the conceptual, methodological, and clinical issues in contemporary cognitive behavior therapy with children.

The chapters that follow review the experimental cognitive behavioral work with children and include descriptions of cognitive behavioral preventive mental health interventions and cognitive behavioral interventions for specific child behavior problems. Because these presentations attempt to integrate academic and applied orientations, both the scholar and the practitioner can benefit from the contributions. The book is designed for use in graduate-level cognitive behavior therapy practica and child therapy courses, and in advanced undergraduate courses covering cognitive behavior therapy, child clinical, and child and family counseling.

As in any work of this scope, many people deserve our appreciation. However, a special note of thanks is in order for Sylvia Watson and Esther Strause for their aid in the preparation of the manuscript. We would also like to thank Leonard Pace, formerly of Plenum Press, for his assistance in the development and preparation of this book.

Andrew W. Meyers
W. Edward Craighead

Contents

CHAPTER 3

CHAPTER 4

CHAPTER 6

CHAPTER 7

CHAPTER 10

CHAPTER 11

1

Cognitive Behavior Therapy with Children

A HISTORICAL, CONCEPTUAL, AND ORGANIZATIONAL OVERVIEW

Andrew W. Meyers and W. Edward Craighead

ORGANIZATIONAL OVERVIEW

Cognitive behavior therapy with children is a relatively new and rapidly developing area of clinical psychology. In a recent survey of employment in APA-approved clinical psychology programs, Klesges, Sanchez, and Stanton (1982) found that 40% of the new faculty described their theoretical orientation as cognitive behavioral and an additional 18% described themselves as behavioral; both of these percentages exceeded any other specific theoretical preference. In their recent survey sampling clinical psychologists of Division 12 of APA, Norcross and Prochaska (1982) reported that behavior modification and family therapy involving children were among the most rapidly increasing therapy activities. It is likely that this increased emphasis will continue, because the youngest group of therapists (less than 10 years of postdoctoral experience) spent a greater percentage of their time engaged in these recently developed approaches than did the more experienced therapists.

The purposes of this book are (1) to provide a broader conceptual base and empirical foundation for cognitive behavior therapy with chil-

Andrew W. Meyers • Department of Psychology, Memphis State University, Memphis, Tennessee 38152. **W. Edward Craighead** • Department of Psychology, The Pennsylvania State University, University Park, Pennsylvania 16802.

dren, and (2) to provide descriptions of cognitive behavioral clinical procedures and critical reviews of their applications to children's problems. This chapter begins that process by fitting cognitive behavior therapy with children into a conceptual and historical perspective and by presenting the organizational structure of the book within its stated purposes.

HISTORICAL AND CONCEPTUAL PERSPECTIVE[1]

The treatment of childhood academic and mental-health problems was initiated in the United States by Lightner Witmer, who established the first Psychological Clinic at the University of Pennsylvania in 1896. Many of his clients were children with learning difficulties; his interventions were directive, educational, and based on principles from perception and learning; and he empirically evaluated treatment effectiveness. Thus, in many ways Witmer may be legitimately claimed as a forerunner of contemporary behavior therapy. Most historical accounts of behavioral interventions with children begin, however, with the work of John B. Watson (1924) and his colleagues Rosalie Rayner (Watson & Rayner, 1920) and Mary Cover Jones (1924a,b), who studied the effects of conditioning on the development and alleviation of fear in children. In addition, historical accounts of behavior therapy usually note the Mowrers' (Mowrer & Mowrer, 1938) development of the "bell-and-pad" procedure for the treatment of enuresis. Although the work of these contributors was substantial (e.g., Watson's emphasis on methodological behaviorism and the Mowrers' procedure still the treatment of choice for enuresis), the directly traceable history of child behavior therapy begins with the clinical application of operant procedures in the late 1950s and early 1960s. Behavioral interventions with children developed rapidly thereafter, and as Ross (1981) noted, some 70 articles had been cited by Gelfand and Hartmann (1968) in the first thorough review of this field. Ross's recent book contains nearly 500 references, which he claims to represent "but a fraction of the available literature" (Ross, 1981, p. 5).

The aforementioned and oft-cited case histories (Watson & Rayner, 1920; Jones, 1924b) were virtually ignored until a later era for a number of reasons. First, as with clinical psychology in general during the first

[1]Appreciation is extended to *School Psychology Review* for permission to reprint most of the material in this section which appeared previously in "A Brief Clinical History of Cognitive-Behavior Therapy with Children" by W. E. Craighead, *School Psychology Review*, 1982, *11*, 5–13.

half of this century, the prevailing approach to the treatment of psychological problems was Freudian or psychoanalytic. The influence of this school of thought was so pervasive that when Arnold Gesell, a prominent leader of the Child Guidance Movement, appealed in 1938 to professionals to pay more attention to behavioral procedures, his advice went unheeded (cf. Ross, 1981). When mental-health professionals did finally begin to break from the psychoanalytic influence, they turned to the nondirective model of client-centered therapy espoused by Carl Rogers (1951); this slant particularly characterized developments in school counseling. Thus, by the early 1950s psychologists, psychiatrists, and social workers approached children's problems primarily from a psychoanalytic perspective, while school counselors tended to employ a client-centered model.

School psychologists, the other major professional group that has concerned itself with the interface between academic and clinical childhood problems, historically have focused on assessment and intervention in intellectual disorders. When assessed educational and learning deficits have clearly produced behavioral dysfunctions, educationally oriented programs have been designed by school psychologists to produce both academic and behavioral change. Otherwise, these professionals have referred behaviorally disordered children to school counselors or other mental-health professionals for clinical intervention.

Although psychodynamically oriented psychotherapy, with its emphasis on the therapist–patient relationship, was the prevailing model for clinical intervention, its general therapeutic effectiveness began to be questioned in the 1950s and early 1960s. This was especially evident within the emerging behavior therapy movement (Eysenck, 1960, 1966; Skinner, 1953; Ullmann & Krasner, 1965). Within the child-clinical area, Levitt's two milestone critiques (1957, 1963) of primarily psychodynamic psychotherapy concluded that there were few if any data to support its effectiveness. It was into this arena that child behavior therapists marched, reinforcers in hand, in the 1950s.

CLINICAL BEHAVIOR THERAPY WITH CHILDREN[2]

Behavior therapy with children began in earnest during the latter half of the 1950s. At that time, the primary focus was on the application of operant conditioning, which more recently has been called applica-

[2]For an extensive discussion of the history of behavior modification, including cognitive-behavioral procedures, the reader is referred to Kazdin (1978b).

tion behavior analysis. Perhaps because of the appropriateness of the procedures, but at least partially because of the characteristics of the population and the sociology of the treatment of behavioral dysfunctions, early applications were with severely disordered children. It was with these forgotten and difficult clients, for whom traditional therapies are least appropriate and effective, that behavior therapists, were at least tolerated, if not welcomed.

The initial clinical application of applied behavioral analyses can be traced to a few centers, with programs such as the following characterizing the period. Bijou and his colleagues and students (Baer, Wolf, and Risley, to mention only a few) at the University of Washington used operant programs to improve performance on academic tasks, to increase skills in children with motor deficits, and to decrease inappropriate social behaviors. At UCLA, Lovaas (who had been trained at Washington), extending the work of Ferster and DeMyer (1961, 1962), attempted to decrease the stereotypic and self-destructive behaviors of autistic children while teaching them appropriate social behaviors and language (Lovaas, 1967; Lovaas, Koegel, Simmons, & Long, 1973). Many intervention programs were developed in educational settings in the mid-1960s, for instance, the work of Becker and his colleagues at the University of Illinois at Urbana-Champaign (they were partially influenced by Bijou, who moved to Illinois in 1965), the work of Baer, Wolf, Risley (who moved from the University of Washington to the University of Kansas in the mid-1960s), and others at the University of Kansas. This early work and the collaboration of these colleagues resulted in the introduction of the *Journal of Applied Behavior Analysis,* with its first volume published in 1968. This journal served as an outlet for the publication of clinical applications of behavioral programs for children and, through the publication of influential papers (e.g., Baer, Wolf, & Risley, 1968), largely defined the domain and direction of applied behavioral analysis for the next decade. It was also an outlet for the more conceptual research that developed in parallel to the clinical work, for example, research on generalized imitation (cf. Burgess, Burgess, & Esveldt, 1970).

Except for the clinical work with modeling procedures and forms of systematic desensitization for the treatment of anxiety and phobias (Gelfand & Hartmann, 1968; Graziano, 1971), behavior therapy with children in the 1960s focused on applications of operant procedures. This focus is apparent from O'Leary and O'Leary's (1977) list of clinical procedures in educational settings:

A. Procedures to increase behavior:
   1. Praise and approval

2. Modeling
3. Shaping
4. Passive shaping
5. Token reinforcement programs
6. Programmed instruction
7. Self-specification of contingencies
8. Self-reinforcement
9. Establishment of clear rules and direction

B. Procedures to decrease behavior:
1. Extinction
2. Reinforcing behavior incompatible with undesired behavior
3. Soft reprimands
4. Time-out from reinforcement
5. Relaxation
6. Gradual presentation of fearful stimuli *in vivo*
7. Desensitization
8. Response cost
9. Medication (recommended as a prompt in conjunction with behavior modification programs)
10. Self-instruction
11. Self-evaluation

Even though some of the procedures bear labels that currently are listed as cognitive-behavioral (e.g., self-reinforcement, self-instruction, self-evaluation), they were, except for self-instruction, generally conceptualized within a traditional behavioral or applied learning-theory perspective.

BEHAVIOR THERAPY UNDERGOES A CHANGE IN THE 1970s

Gradually, behavior therapy increased its involvement with less severely disturbed children such as those seen in outpatient clinics and children in nursery schools and day-care centers. This expansion was accompanied by an increased concern with internal thought processes as both *targets* and *mechanisms* of change. In addition, in educational settings there was a shift from an emphasis on the modification of attentive and disruptive motor behaviors to a concern with educational tasks that involve cognitive or thinking skills (cf. Lahey & Drabman, 1981).

The material that follows provides a brief description of the major factors that led to the shift from primarily operant to more cognitive behavioral interventions.[3] These shifts toward cognitive behavior therapy with children paralleled and interacted with similar changes that were occurring in behavior therapy with adults.

Factor 1: Cognitive Psychology

Cognitive psychology made its impact on behavior therapy with children through three avenues. The first was a cognitive information-processing explanation of modeling effects. The second was the employment of the cognitive developmental language literature in the conception and application of self-instruction training. Third was the development of clinical procedures based on the problem-solving literature.

Modeling

Modeling, or observational learning, is a label for the process whereby an individual learns by viewing another's behavior. In this process, learning may occur without the individual performing the overt behavior or receiving direct consequences for emitting the behavior. Much of the conceptual and clinical work with modeling procedures has been conducted with children, and modeling procedures have been used both to teach children new responses and to modify the frequency of previously learned behaviors (Bandura & Walters, 1963; Rosenthal & Bandura, 1978).

Because modeling research was developed within a learning framework and because behavior therapy was viewed by many as the clinical application of principles of learning, modeling procedures have been identified historically with behavior therapy (cf. Craighead, Kazdin, & Mahoney, 1981). By 1969, however, Bandura's explanation of modeling effects had become more cognitive in nature. He suggested that the major factors that influenced observational learning were processes of attention, retention, motor reproduction, and incentive and motivation. The cognitive processes (attention and retention) were drawn largely from an information-processing model of cognitive psychology. This viewpoint ushered in a cognitive explanation for a portion of behavior therapy procedures with children. Bandura's explanation of modeling and his discussion of the role of symbolic cognitive processes in behav-

[3]It must be noted that there are many childhood problems—for instance, self-injurious behaviors—for which operant procedures used alone remain the treatment of choice (Forehand & Atkeson, 1981; Ross, 1981). Additionally, operant and cognitive procedures are not incompatible and, in fact, may ultimately be most effective when they are fully integrated (Craighead, Meyers, Craighead, & McHale, 1982).

ior change (Bandura, 1969a) became major springboards for the development of cognitive behavior therapy. Due to both the influence of the *model* as well as the influence of the *modeler*, it subsequently became more acceptable to employ findings from other areas of psychology (in addition to learning) in order to develop and explain clinical procedures. Soon thereafter various other behavior therapy procedures were interpreted both from an information-processing and a more general cognitive viewpoint (cf. Mahoney, 1974).

Self-instruction Training

Self-instruction training was developed in the early 1970s by Meichenbaum. During generalization tests of operantly conditioned "healthy talk" by schizophrenic patients, Meichenbaum observed that they repeated aloud the experimental instructions before they emitted the trained responses. These observations led him to speculate that individuals could be taught to produce internally generated self-statements and to talk to themselves in a self-guiding fashion; he called such interventions self-instruction training (Meichenbaum, 1974a, 1975, 1977).

In conceptualizing the mechanisms of change in self-instruction training, Meichenbaum (1974a, 1975) turned to the language-development branch of cognitive developmental psychology. In particular he drew from the writings of Luria (1961) and Vygotsky (1962), who had suggested that during development, the child's behavior is at first under the verbal control of the social environment (adults), and that only gradually does the child learn to control his or her own behavior, first by overt speech and then by covert speech. Based on such a model, Meichenbaum and Goodman (1971b) developed a self-instruction program to teach impulsive children how to control their behavior. The experimenter modeled the overt behavior and the appropriate self-statements, and subsequently the child imitated the target behavior while first self-instructing aloud, then whispering, and finally covertly rehearsing the self-statements. Since this initial successful application, self-instruction training has been further evaluated as a successful treatment procedure for impulsive children and has been employed to decrease aggression, reduce hyperactivity, reduce fears, improve academic performance, and train social competence in children (Craighead, Wilcoxon-Craighead, & Meyers, 1978; Kendall & Williams, 1981). Self-instruction training has also been used as an effective treatment for adult disorders as diverse as anxiety, aggression, pain, social skills deficits, and schizophrenia (Meichenbaum, 1977).

In addition to Meichenbaum's initial reliance on relevant subsections of the language-development literature for the development of self-instruction training, investigators and clinicians in subsequent applications have seen the necessity of delving more extensively into the cognitive developmental literature in order to apply appropriately cognitive behavior therapy procedures (see Chapter 3, Cohen & Schleser). The relevance of cognitive developmental psychology is clearest in the area of social skills training, where the appropriate target behaviors and level of intervention can be partially defined from the social cognition literature (Combs & Slaby, 1977; Furman, 1980; Gresham, 1981).

Problem-Solving

Problem-solving as a clinical procedure was introduced into behavior therapy in 1971 by D'Zurilla and Goldfried. Based on the general problem-solving literature, they suggested the following steps for its use in clinical practice: (1) develop a general orientation or set to recognize the problem, (2) define the specifics of the problem and determine what needs to be accomplished, (3) generate alternative courses of action that might be used to resolve the problem and achieve the desired goals, (4) decide among the alternatives by evaluating their consequences and relative gains and losses, and (5) verify the results of the decision process and determine whether the alternative selected is achieving the desired outcome.

Problem-solving, like modeling, has been associated historically with the learning literature; however, it has most frequently been explained from an information-processing model in cognitive psychology (cf. Mahoney, 1974, pp. 199–212). Even phenomenological interpretations have been offered, and indeed, Gestalt psychology research has employed a problem-solving paradigm for a century or so (Riopelle, 1967). Because of its development from the cognitive psychology literature in problem-solving and its focus on internal thought processes as the mechanism of change, clinical problem-solving is usually classified as a cognitive behavioral procedure.

As compared with clinical research with adults, the clinical use of problem-solving with children is even more obviously related to cognitive psychology. The first, most extensive, and most successful application of problem-solving with children took place in the early 1970s by Spivack, Shure, and their associates at Hahnemann Medical College. These investigators developed treatment programs and assessment instruments designed to teach and evaluate three types of social problem-solving thinking: alternative thinking—generation of numerous solutions to interpersonal problems; means–end thinking—sequential planning of the step-by-step process necessary to reach a desired goal; and consequential thinking—ability to see the consequences that occur as a result of emitting a particular behavior or sequence of behaviors. In a large-scale application, this problem-solving program was found to improve performance on specific measures of problem-solving skills, to facilitate adjustment in kindergarten children, and to prevent maladaptive behavior when these children entered first grade (Spivack & Shure, 1974). Subsequent prevention programs have combined the Hahnemann program with the D'Zurilla and Goldfried (1971) recommendations. At the University of Connecticut, Allen, Chinsky, Larcen, Lochman, and Selinger (1976) reported the effects of such a combined program with third- and fourth-grade children, and at the University of Rochester, Gesten, Flores de Apocada, Rains, Weissberg, and Cowen (1979), employed a similar social problem-solving program with second- and third-grade children. In the main, these latter studies replicated the Hahnemann findings that children can be taught problem-solving skills; however, the positive relationship between these learned skills and adjustment in the classroom was only partially replicated.

These programs, with their emphasis on the modification of thinking processes as mechanisms for producing both behavioral and cognitive changes, illustrate clearly the interface between cognitive behavior therapy and cognitive developmental psychology. The obvious relationship between the types of thinking employed in the problem-solving package and cognitive developmental levels of children (cf. Flavell, 1977), the failure to replicate effects of problem-solving training across age levels, and subsequent research investigating the relationships between problem-solving skills and childhood psychopathology (see Chapter 14, Kirschenbaum & Ordman), all underscore the necessity for increased interaction between cognitive developmental and clinical cognitive behavioral psychologists.

Factor 2: Self-control

A second major factor that led to the birth of cognitive behavior therapy was the development of self-control clinical interventions. Self-control procedures have been a part of the contemporary behavioral armamentarium from the beginning. Skinner (1953), for example, argued that individuals control their own behaviors in the same fashion that they control others' behaviors. According to his operant model, however, the behavior can, by proper analysis, ultimately be accounted for by external factors. Based on this operant viewpoint, Ferster, Nurnberger, and Levitt (1962) described a seminal self-control program for weight control. In the mid-1960s Goldiamond (1965), working first with stutterers and then with other problems as varied as academic performance and marital discord, played a major role in the extension of self-control procedures conceptualized according to an operant model. In fact, many authors still offer operant explanations for the effectiveness of self-control procedures (e.g., Brigham, 1978; Cantania, 1975).

During the late 1960s, however, alternative and more cognitive explanations of self-control procedures began to develop. In a popular paper, Homme (1965) spoke of coverants, which he defined as operants of the mind, and suggested procedures based on an operant model for modifying convert events—that is, thoughts. Although Homme's paper had an operant slant, it served the heuristic role of triggering a number of clinical investigations of self-control programs designed to change behavior by modifying covert thought processes (cf. Mahoney, 1974).

The increasing significance of the role of internal factors in self-control and the more widespread use of self-control procedures in clinical intervention were supported by an influential series of papers by Kanfer in the early 1970s (1970, 1971; Kanfer & Karoly, 1972). His division of self-control into the components of self-monitoring, self-evaluation, and self-reinforcement is still widely accepted. Concurrently, investigators such as Bandura and Mischel at Stanford were conducting clinically relevant laboratory studies designed to assess the effect of self-control on factors such as modeling and delay of gratification (Bandura, 1971b; Mischel, 1974). Clinical applications of self-control, especially with habit disorders such as overeating and cigarette-smoking (cf. Craighead, Brownell, & Horan, 1981), increased rapidly in the early 1970s. These advances in clinical applications and conceptual research resulted in summary books by Thoresen and Mahoney (1974; Mahoney & Thoresen, 1974) and Goldfried and Merbaum (1973).

The major conceptual issue that developed in the self-control literature was the disagreement over the role of internal and external factors in effecting self-controlled responses. Although this issue remains unresolved (Jones, Nelson, & Kazdin, 1977), many clinicians and experimental investigators have argued for the importance of internal controlling variables and thereby have placed self-control within the cognitive behavioral framework (Mahoney & Arnkoff, 1978). Significantly, it was partially in his resolution of this issue that Bandura developed the notion of reciprocal determinism, which maintains that individuals (including their cognitive processes) and environments reciprocally interact to affect each other. Reciprocal determinism is a major component of Bandura's *Social Learning Theory* (1977b) and of cognitive behavior therapy in general.

Much of the early self-control work was done with adults, but applications with children began in earnest in the mid-1970s. It was during this time that self-control began to be conceptualized as more cognitive in nature, so many of the papers frequently summarized under the label of cognitive behavior therapy were actually conducted under the rubric of self-control. The presentation and discussion of that clinical work and research are in the various chapters of this volume.

Factor 3: Cognitive Therapy

Cognitive therapy developed relatively independently of the two previously discussed factors. Although there is no monolithic model of cognitive therapy, there is one distinct assumption that is fundamental to all cognitive therapies: that maladaptive cognitive processes produce psychological disorders, which are, therefore, best alleviated by the modification of those cognitive processes. Of this approach to therapy, Ellis and Beck are the two major exponents who have had an effect on cognitive behavior therapy. Their approaches to cognitive therapy were developed almost exclusively in the clinical rather than the laboratory setting. Even though many similarities exist between these cognitive therapies and Meichenbaum's self-instruction training, described earlier, Meichenbaum developed his procedures independently and from different influences.

Within his rational-emotive approach to therapy, Ellis (1962) maintained that people engage in maladaptive behaviors and/or feel bad because they engage in illogical and irrational thought processes. That is, it is not what individuals say or do that upsets them, but it is how they think about the things that they say or do. The focus in therapy is on changing these maladaptive ways of thinking. Similarly, Beck (1976) maintained that psychological disturbance occurs because people engage in maladaptive cognitions (such as inappropriate, irrational, and illogical self-statements) which are reflections of their assumptions and beliefs about themselves and the world. Although it is in many respects similar to the rational-emotive therapy of Ellis, Beck's cognitive therapy places greater emphasis on the modification of fundamental irrational assumptions and beliefs rather than the specific self-statements *per se*.

Most evaluations of cognitive therapy have been conducted with adults, with whom it appears to be especially effective in the treatment of depression (cf. Rehm, 1981). In the conceptual sections of reports of clinical research with children, however, investigators have frequently alluded to the work of Ellis and Beck and their colleagues. Thus, while at this point cognitive therapy's influence on the treatment of children is less directly traceable than that of cognitive psychology or self-control, it appears not to be a trivial one. In fact, Beck's popularization of the term "cognitive therapy" has been a major factor in the development of the name "cognitive behavior therapy."

SUMMARY AND OVERVIEW

Our brief review of historical and conceptual developments in child behavior therapy implicitly brings us to the creation of this book. Both the tremendous growth in theory, research, and application in child clinical psychology and the revolutionary developments in behavior therapy with children have served to prompt this edited work.

This broader behavioral model, which encompasses cognitive, affective, and other mediational influences, has enabled child clinicians to offer a more comprehensive accounting of behavioral phenomena and, potentially, to develop more effective behavior change strategies (see Bandura, 1977b; Kendall & Hollon; 1979). The present contributions come at a moment when these new theoretical influences and applied orientations must be recognized and the existing and ever-growing body of empirical evidence in child cognitive behavior therapy must be summarized.

As mentioned earlier, a number of influences have shaped this model of cognitive behavior therapy with children. These include Bandura's (1969a) work on modeling, Meichenbaum's (1977) research on self-instruction behavior, clinical applications of problem-solving (e.g., Spivack & Shure, 1974), work on self-control by Kanfer (1970) and others, and the development of cognitive therapies by Ellis (1962) and Beck (1976). Bandura's (1977b) social learning theory presents a framework for many of these recent developments in child behavior therapy. While social learning theory emphasizes the role played by vicarious, symbolic, and self-regulatory processes, Bandura has also recognized the reciprocal nature of deterministic influences. Bandura's reciprocal determinism argues that personal variables, behavior, and environment interact to determine one another, which indicates that evidence from development, learning, cognition, sensation and perception, and social psychology is all relevant for a comprehensive understanding of human behavior and the process of behavior change.

These influences have provided fertile ground for the growth of cognitive behavior therapy, and this intervention perspective has shown vigorous development over the last decade. It has become increasingly obvious that all active social, developmental, and learning influences on human behavior must be considered if we are fully to enrich the cognitive behavior therapy model. Our contributors attempt to achieve this enrichment by recognizing the influence on human behavior of a wide variety of factors. Each of these reviews presents an appraisal of and status report on a research or clinical problem area of child clinical psychology. The contributed chapters are designed to enable one to develop a fuller understanding of cognitive behavior therapy and cognitive behavioral intervention strategies and to crystallize the vital research issues in these areas. Such an understanding should allow cognitive behavioral child clinicians to build a foundation for the design and implementation of the integrative experiments that must be done if the cognitive behavioral model is to continue to progress.

Two contributions serve as examples of this integrative effort. Cohen and Schleser, in their chapter on cognitive developmental contributions to child cognitive behavior therapy (Chapter 3), emphasize the importance of a consideration of the child's cognitive abilities in any cognitive behavioral intervention effort. The evidence from their research program indicates that the child's ability to use cognitive strategies determines his or her performance on self-instruction training tasks. Cohen and Schleser go on to suggest that the thorny question of generalization of behavior change in cognitive behavior therapy may be closely related to the sophistication of the child's cognitive strategies. Only more cognitively sophisticated children may be able to profit from more effortful metacognitive interventions thought to facilitate generalization of behavior change.

The second example is Kirschbaum and Ordman's integration of cognitive behavioral interventions with children and community-based prevention programs (Chapter 14). They argue that large-scale community interventions, based on cognitive behavioral methods, which emphasize the development of individual behavioral and mediational strengths, hold great promise for fulfilling a true prevention function.

ORGANIZATION OF THE BOOK

The chapters in the present volume are divided into three sections: a conceptual framework, methodological issues, and clinical problems. A theoretical and empirical foundation for both viewing and eventually expanding cognitive behavior therapy with children is provided in the conceptual framework section. The chapters in this section examine the current and potential contribution to clincial intervention of research on children's social development, cognitive development, and family systems. These chapters delineate how empirical findings in other substantive areas may relate both conceptually and practically to cognitive behavior therapy interventions with children.

After our brief historical review of the development of child cognitive behavior therapy, Matthews and Brooks-Gunn trace the role of children's social development in deviance. They assert that early interactions among the child, caregivers, and larger social systems set the stage for later interactions and relationships, and that an understanding of this social development is necessary to conceptualize deviance adequately. Matthews and Brooks-Gunn then review social development through family, peer, and social systems and through the development of specific social behaviors of imitation, aggression, empathy and conformity.

The next chapter, by Cohen and Schleser, examines cognitive developmental contributions to child clinical practice. Then Turkewitz, in her chapter on the contribution of family systems to child behavior problems, argues that behavior therapists must integrate behavioral and family systems theory to develop a comprehensive view of the child. She reviews three theories of family interaction that conceptualize the identified problem child as an agent of family tension reduction and increased marital stability. Turkewitz also stresses the importance of research examining the relationship between family interaction patterns and child psychopathology and of research on the effects of children's behavior on parents and other caregivers.

The methodological issues section includes two chapters—one, a review of cognitive behavioral assessment with children, and the second, a discussion of the different loci for cognitive behavioral intervention. Each of these chapters provides an overview of theory and research in the area relevant to clinical intervention. The first, by Roberts and Nelson (Chapter 5), reviews cognitive behavioral assessment issues and assessment strategies. Basic issues in cognitive behavioral assessment include the recognition of developmental processes, the identification of appropriate targets for intervention, the assessment of cognitive processes as both independent and dependent variables, and the recognition of the interaction between cognitive-verbal and motor systems. Roberts and Nelson also outline a comprehensive set of cognitive and behavioral assessment strategies for both academic and social domains. Tha authors place special emphasis on the assessment of changes in cognitive processes as a function of treatment.

Glenwick and Jason, in the second chapter in the methodology section, examine alternatives to traditional treatment formats. They describe traditional treatment as a passive mode, relying on one-to-one and small-group delivery and directed toward clients with identified disorders. Alternative interventions are conducted at levels beyond the individual. This active model assumes a preventive stance and often employs paraprofessionals in a consultation format to work with the family, schools, community organizations, and the media. Glenwick and Jason stress the importance and impact of using the natural environment and natural change agents in both assessment and treatment (see Kirschenbaum and Ordman's chapter for an application of this alternative intervention model).

The final section of the book examines the psychological dysfunctions of childhood. Each chapter is organized around a specific problem area. The chapters include a description of the problem, a brief historical perspective of the development of relevant therapy procedures, a description of contemporary clinical intervention strategies, and a review of the relevant evaluation literature.

Keogh and Hall, in their chapter on learning disabilities, argue that the inconsistent performance of learning-disabled children suggests that these children can benefit from cognitive training. They rely on evidence that learning-disabled children show no impairment in learning general life functioning skills (possibly reflected in IQ scores) but perform poorly on learning tasks in the decontextualized school situation (reflected in achievement test scores). This decontextualized learning requires the development and application of organizational and retrieval strategies, areas where Keogh and Hall find learning-disabled children deficient. The authors review a variety of cognitively based problem-solving interventions with learning-disabled children and find inconsistent but promising evidence for these programs.

The chapter on cognitive behavioral interventions with mentally retarded children by Whitman, Burgio, and Johnston (Chapter 8) examines research in five areas. Work with mentally retarded children in the areas of self-regulation skills, cognitive strategy use, correspondence training, and the related area of self-instruction has yielded positive results; evidence on problem-solving interventions with this population is less encouraging. Whitman, Burgio, and Johnston argue for an examination of the importance of individual characteristics, nature of the target tasks, and types of training available in designing any intervention program—an argument also made by Cohen and Schleser in their cognitive development chapter.

Litrownik's chapter examines diagnostic and etiological confusion over psychotic children and traces the history of intervention with such populations. He finds that psychoanalytic efforts with such children have been generally ineffective and that behavioral interventions, while successful, have demonstrated poor maintenance and generalization of behavior change problems. Based on evidence that psychotic children display information-processing deficits, Litrownik suggests that application of cognitive training strategies designed to develop controlling rather than content skills should be beneficial. Litrownik draws from related research areas to outline psychotic children's development of these self-management skills within a problem-solving model.

In their chapter on social skills (Chapter 10), Kendall and Morison suggest that social skill development is central to the peer interaction that forms the basis of future socialization. They further suggest that the development of competent social skills may enable the child to overcome or withstand family and other social problems. The authors review behavioral and social-cognitive interventions for social skill development and conclude that both behavioral and cognitive components must be considered.

Melamed, Klingman, and Siegel's chapter on childhood anxiety emphasizes the development of individualized cognitive behavioral interventions for children's response to stressful events. Employing medical and dental situations as stress prototypes, these authors review informational, modeling, desensitization, and self-control interventions. While some promising outcomes are reported, Melamed *et al.* found few studies that attempted to match interventions to specific fear-eliciting factors and child characteristics. They recommend that intervention strategies consider the child's cognitive ability, fear-relevant belief systems, style of coping with threat, and prior experience with the stressful situation. An example of such an intervention program is presented.

Camp and Ray detail the problem of aggression among children. Their review indicates that childhood aggression is a prevalent problem, stable over time, and predictive of later adolescent and adult adjustment problems. Further, their examination of previous intervention efforts with aggressive children finds little controlled research support or, in the case of behavioral parent training, questionable maintenance and generalization of treatment gains. This material and their data on cognitive deficits in aggressive boys led Camp and Ray to their self-instruction, problem-solving-based Think Aloud program, described in the chapter. After reviewing evaluations of Think Aloud, Camp and Ray stress the importance of environmental support for cognitive change and suggest promising methodological and content changes in their training program.

Kennedy's chapter on delinquency (Chapter 13) documents the significant role played by adolescents in the American crime problem. He reviews operant interventions with the juvenile delinquent population and finds specific treatment gains but resistance to the treatment and, as with operant work with other problem areas reviewed here, poor long-term followup. These problems and evidence that delinquents show deficits in problem-solving, impulse control, expectation of conventional goal achievement, and ability to adopt the perspective of others suggest that cognitive training programs with this population may be beneficial. Kennedy finds strong data-based support for problem-solving training with delinquents but only limited support for self-instruction interventions, self-management programs, and training in perspective-taking. He argues for the assessment of specific cognitive deficits in aggressive populations and the development of training programs for these specific deficits.

As noted earlier, Kirschenbaum and Ordman's chapter on the community application of cognitive behavioral preventive mental health strategies serves as a conclusion to the clinical problems sections of the book.

In this initial chapter, we have traced the roots of cognitive behavioral work with children and have outlined the contents of the remainder of the book. In the chapters that follow, the contributing authors present a comprehensive review of contemporary child cognitive behavior therapy.

2

Social Development in Childhood

Wendy S. Matthews and Jeanne Brooks-Gunn

From the moment of birth, a child is enmeshed in a social milieu, a network that, ideally, will offer security, love, and intimacy but will also require the acquisition and maintenance of an entire repertoire of social behaviors deemed appropriate by a particular group or culture. Social development encompasses the task of growing up within a social system such that one is able to behave in that system's socially accepted ways (Lewis, 1982). Traditionally, the study of social systems has fallen under the purview of anthropologists or sociologists, the study of interpersonal relationships has been a major focus of clinicians, and the study of social behaviors (e.g., aggression, empathy) has captured the attention of social and developmental psychologists. The past few years have heralded the emergence of interpersonal relationships and social knowledge as relevant topics of inquiry for developmentalists of all persuasions (cf. Hinde, 1974; Lewis & Brooks-Gunn, 1979; Youniss, 1980).

Although we cannot do justice to all topics related to a child's social development, we shall attempt to provide a conceptual framework in which to examine relationships and social behavior as the key aspects of social development.

SOCIAL SYSTEMS AND RELATIONSHIPS

All would agree that the establishment of social relationships is central to healthy, adaptive functioning. Thus, among the goals of early

Wendy S. Matthews • Department of Pediatrics, University of Medicine and Dentistry of New Jersey—Rutgers Medical School, Piscataway, New Jersey 08854. **Jeanne Brooks-Gunn** • The Infant Laboratory, Educational Testing Service, Princeton, New Jersey 08541, and College of Physicians and Surgeons, Columbia University, New York, New York 10032.

childhood are entering into and maintaining relationships and developing the capacity to negotiate new relationships continually within an ever-expanding social system. By "relationships," we mean shared social systems, at least some of which should be enduring over time and characterized by feelings of love and intimacy. Formerly, the concept of love was taboo among social scientists, who deferred to poets for its illumination. They preferred instead to discuss behaviorally defined concepts such as attachment and dependency. But since Harlow's 1959 article, "Love in infant monkeys," emotions have constituted a lively area of study and the abstract terminology of love has taken its place in the literature.

To define relationships more concretely, Hinde (1976) has listed numerous dimensions: content, diversity, quality, frequency, patterning, and reciprocity. Each of these aspects contributes to the complexity of relationships that arise from interactions with others in the social environment. Each aspect is accessible to study through the observation of interactions. Cognition also is mentioned as a factor, since the meaning of a relationship and the ability to interact in a complementary fashion with another individual is partially determined by one's cognitive skills or one's cognitive stage of development. So relationships can be defined not only by dimensions of interactions but also by developmental phenomena, as we shall see when considering the origins of relationships.

Finally, the characteristic of multiplicity must be considered since relationships are embedded in social systems that expand as the child grows. Some of the primary networks of which the child becomes a part are the family, peer group, school, community, and such larger networks as ethnic, cultural, regional, or national groups. Childhood relationships tend to be studied primarily within the family and peer systems, for it is here that they first evolve.

The Family System

Origins of Social Systems

The infant is born into a social system. Immediately, he or she is somone's baby, someone else's cousin, grandchild, or namesake. In most cases, the first social system is defined by the family, which confers a family name upon the infant,[1] introduces him or her to relatives and

[1]Kinship is critical for the definition of the child's social network. For example, when a sample of pregnant teenagers were asked after whom their baby would be named, they indicated that one half of the male babies and only 8% of the female babies would be

friends, and provides a place for the child in the community at large through religious ceremonies and secular celebrations. What do infants bring to this process? A psychobiologist might claim that infants are born a gregarious lot, prepared by evolution to mesh their activities and needs with those of the persons whose environment they share. A learning theorist might contend that infants are born asocial, *tablae rosae* among an array of *tablae plenae,* who in turn have been primed by their own social histories to cuddle, reject, abuse, and confuse the newly arrived individual. A cognitive theorist might declare that it is not until infants can differentiate between themselves and others that they may truly enter into a social system.

Research evidence is accumulating on previously unrecognized neonatal capabilities and indicates that the human infant enters the world well prepared to assume a place in a social system. With the first wail and gasp, the infant may appear totally tuned in to itself and no one else. But this is not the case. Even prior to birth, infants are responsive to their mothers' heart beat, voice, and a variety of externally produced sounds. At birth, whatever discomforts neonates might suffer are made known to their social environment through their limited yet effective repertoire of cries, facial expressions, and body movements. Adjustment to the social system can emerge so smoothly that it might seem as if human infants are predisposed to respond to other people. For just within the infant's visual range (approximately 8 to 12 inches, the distance between its mother's breast and the infant's face), the nursing infant finds total responsiveness: nurturance, warmth, and a lively, attentive pair of eyes. The structural features of the caregiver's face happen to be those to which the infant's visual apparatus is most attuned: pattern, movement, contrast, and three-dimensionality. And the human voice is the sound to which infants are most likely to respond. Together, these characteristics carry a virtual guarantee that the caregiver will have considerable appeal to the infant (Lewis & Brooks-Gunn, 1974; Schaffer, 1971). Combined with other recent revelations, this phenomenon of the inherent attractiveness of social stimuli suggests that infants are prepared from the start to respond to members of their own species. For example, research shows that the newborn infant can discriminate and

---

named after the children's fathers (first, middle, or given name). Among the adolescents who did not marry the father of their child, those who had named the child after him found that their partner was more involved with the child over the first five years of life than were fathers with children not named after them (Furstenberg, undated). Gutman (1977) has suggested that naming was especially important in slave cultures where fathers were likely to be separated from their children. The taking of the father's name may have provided historic continuity and a sense of kinship in the face of possible separation.

turn toward his or her own mother on the basis of olfactory cues from her lactating breast (as opposed to another mother's breast) in the first week of life (Macfarlane, 1975). They can accommodate to their mothers' nursing by developing a synchronic pattern of bursts and pauses in sucking response (Kaye, 1977), and can be soothed or alerted on the basis of touch and voice cues (Condon & Sander, 1974; Korner & Thoman, 1970). If all these phenomena were not enough, adults too seem "primed" to accept social engagement with an infant. The infant's protruding cheeks and forehead, large head and eyes, and general quality of "babyness" somehow engage the adult more dramatically than adults features do (Fullard & Reiling, 1976; Lorenz, 1970).

Integration into a Social System

To be prepared for social interaction at the time of birth does not, however, mean that one exhibits intentional social behavior at birth. Nevertheless, parents treat their child as though this were true. Consider the caregiver's response to a neonatal stretch: "Oh, look, she wants her daddy," or to a cry: "Not even 2 days old, and he is complaining already!" From the moment of birth, parents can be seen reacting to their infant as though he or she had social motives and intentions. As Lozoff, Brittenham, Trause, Kennell, and Klaus (1977) explained, "They perceive the infant's presocial smile, eye contact, and reflexes such as the grasp as interactive indications of recognition, affection, or appreciation" (pp. 2–3). Thus, from birth, parents enter into a relationship with their child, laying the foundation for later social exchange.

Take, for example, Macfarlane's (1977) observations in the delivery room. From the moment an infant opens its eyes, the parents greet him or her as a person, that is, in a social manner ("Hello baby, is that really you?"). Within the first interactions, the mother and infant begin intricate visual, tactile, and auditory interactions, which focus attention on specific interlocking behavior patterns. These early patterns appear to unite the mother and infant in a social interaction that develops later into a social relationship between them (Klaus & Kennell, 1977; Lewis, 1982).

By 3 weeks of age, mothers and infants are engaged in clearly describable reciprocal interactions. As Brazelton, Tronick, Adamson, Als, and Wise (1975) have observed, in the course of the interaction, mutual attentional and affective involvement occur in a sequence of dyadic phases including an initiation, mutual orientation, greetings, play-dialogue, and, eventually, disengagement. The cyclical quality of approach–withdrawal, attention–nonattention underlying this sequence of social events is made possible both by the caregiver's sensitivity to the cues of the infant's involvement and by the infant's active participation in the maintenance or discontinuance of the exchange (Stern, 1977). This kind of rhythmic interaction and rudimentary turn-taking is being increasingly recognized as a basis for later social and linguistic communication (Bates, 1976; Stern, 1977).

Asynchrony in early social interchange has been associated with a number of etiological factors. Even prior to conception, factors might be at work that will render the parents of the child ill-suited to the task of caregiving. Teenage pregnancy, psychosis, and drug or alcohol addiction are but a few of the conditions placing an expectant mother at risk for parenting problems and the child at risk for maladjustment. Physiological factors affecting the fetal environment can have profound implications, too. For example, hormone medications to prevent spontaneous abortions can have the effect of androgenizing the fetus, leading to the development of ambiguous sex characteristics, which, if not corrected, may lead to problems in later sex-role identification. Exposure to viral infections such as rubella can lead to physical deformities and retardation. Smoking during pregnancy may lead to low birth weight, with its associated complications of higher risk for morbidity, learning disorders, and affective delays (Drillien, 1964). The birth process itself may affect the child's adjustment and transition into a social system. A heavily sedated mother delivers a sedated infant with whom interaction is postponed or hazy. A Caesarean or premature delivery frequently involves the early separation of mother and infant as well as affecting maternal state. Postdelivery factors such as maternal depression, high anxiety, physical discomfort, and lack of social support systems can result in impaired interactions (cf. Barnett, Leiderman, Grostein, & Klaus, 1970; Nuckolls, Cassel, & Kaplan, 1972), as can the inattentiveness, unattractiveness, or irritability of the infant. For example, premature infants who smiled late or who exhibited reduced responsivity were found to have mothers who were less likely to interact with them (Cohen & Beckwith, 1979; Field, 1979; Field, Ting, & Shuman, 1979). Even as mundane a matter as a hospital's rooming-in policy can affect early interactions: infants who room-in and who are thus exposed to a single primary caregiver are less likely to cry and more likely to establish a day–night rhythm quickly than are infants whose first days are spent mostly in a traditional hospital nursery (Sander, Julia, Stechler, & Burns, 1972).

Whatever the cause or causes, a recognition of the "normal" social developmental process in which harmonious relationships occur is necessary if we are to recognize or understand deviance. It is important to realize that early interactions based on maternal, child, and "system" characteristics set the stage for later interactions and, ultimately, relationships.

The Emergence of Interactions

By 3 months of age the child should be firmly entrenched within the family system. By this time, parents usually have established definite perceptions of their child based partially on their infant's individual characteristics and partially on their own expectations and belief systems. A basic individual characteristic attributed to infants is temperament, also known as "behavioral style" or "primary reaction pattern." Several researchers have identified dimensions of an infant's behavioral style, such as sociability, distractibility, intensity of mood, activity, and persistence (Carey, 1970, 1927; Thomas & Chess, 1977). With the use of temperament scales developed by these researchers, one can devise profiles of infants that reflect their individual qualities. Or, one can group them together and classify them as "easy" or "difficult" based on their ratings on specific dimensions. Infants who are "difficult" will experience different maternal interaction patterns and less time in interaction with their mothers than will "easy" babies (Brooks-Gunn & Lewis, in press). For example, mothers are less apt to vocalize to handicapped infants who are more active and distractible (Brooks-Gunn & Lewis, 1982a). High-risk infants often fall under the classification of "difficult." Frequently unable to modulate their responses to those of others, they might find stimulation of any kind aversive, even social stimulation, especially in the first few months of life. These infants may have very frustrated mothers. Seeing their infants averting their gaze, becoming fussy, or even becoming drowsy (all ways to reduce the stimulation level; Field *et al.*, 1979; Field, Dempsey, & Shuman, 1981), the mothers often have difficulty adjusting to the fact that they cannot interact with their infants as they would like. Sometimes, they develop irrational beliefs about their own failure to engage their infants as they think they should, decreasing their overall amount of interaction or becoming less responsive to their infants' needs as a result. Sometimes, they blame or resent the infant for his or her difficultness. Several intervention programs have been developed in order to help mothers of premature infants interact more effectively with their children (Cohen & Beckwith, 1979; Field *et al.*, 1981).

It is possible for perceptions alone to influence interactions. For example, responding to sex-role perceptions, mothers of 3-month-old girls are more likely to talk to them and to respond verbally to their babbling than are mothers of 3-month-old boys, despite the fact that there is no difference in the verbal behavior of boys and girls at that age (Lewis, 1972). Mothers of babies who were sick at birth treat their infant more carefully and interact with them less at 3 months of age, when they are completely well, than are mothers of 3-month-old babies who were healthy at birth. It is as though the parents believed the children were still fragile or sick long after recovery (Fox & Lewis, 1981).

In the second half of the first year, mother–infant interactions become more consistent, predicting later interactive styles (Ainsworth, Blehar, Waters, & Wall, 1978; Lewis & Coates, 1980). At the same time, interactions with others in addition to the primary caregiver acquire importance. Infants interact differentially with father and mother, recognize siblings and other salient figures, and respond to strange adults differently from the way they respond to familiar adults. The social network has begun to be differentiated. Parents accelerate this process by the manner in which they interact with their children: Fathers are more likely to focus on play activities, mothers on caregiving and nurturance (Lamb, 1976). The child, recognizing that interaction patterns are unique to specific individuals, can utilize this information and differentiate among persons. Additionally, interactive differences, if tied to roles (i.e., mother versus father, parent versus day-care personnel, adult versus child) can teach the infant about the various functions of persons, thus contributing to a developing social knowledge. For example, by 18 months of age, sex, age, and familiarity are dimensions of the social world that the child can and does utilize to differentiate among others (Brooks-Gunn & Lewis, 1978). When infants' responses to the approach of various strangers and to pictures of various persons are examined, between 9 and 18 months of age, they exhibit more positive responses to children and infants as compared with adults, to women as compared with men, and to parents as compared with other adults.

The Emergence of Relationships

The second half of the first year also heralds the formation of an attachment style. Using the ethologically oriented perspective of Bowlby (1969), Ainsworth and her colleagues (Ainsworth & Bell, 1970; Ainsworth *et al.*, 1978) developed a system for observing infants' and toddlers' (12- to 18-month-olds) responses to their mother and to a stranger in a variety of situations such as having the mother separate from and reunite with her child alone in a room, and so on. Three types of infants have been identified: securely attached, insecurely attached, and ambivalently attached. Not only are the response styles descriptive of the infants' behavior, but they also predict later emotional adjustment, self-concept, and special interactions characteristic of the infants (Ainsworth *et al.*, 1978). In fact, attachment and interaction are more predictive of later functioning than other infancy skills, such as cognition or discrete behaviors (Kagan & Moss, 1962; Schaeffer & Bayley, 1963). For example, in studies of normal infants, early infant intelligence scores do not predict later functioning whereas maternal education and maternal responsivity to an infant's behavior do (Lewis & Coates, 1980).

Thus, if we are concerned about child adjustment and later relationships, the classification of an infant's attachment system in infancy provides important information. Twelve-month-olds who are insecurely or ambivalently attached may be at risk for later difficulties such as impaired relationships with peers, further difficulties with their mother, and deficits in ego strength (Sroufe & Waters, 1979).

Relationships and the Concept of Self

The interaction patterns developed primarily with parents in the first six months of life lay the groundwork for the emergence of relationships with these people in the second half of the first year. This phenomenon was illustrated by the attachment relationship described earlier. Hinde (1976) conceptualized relationships in terms of various interactive dimensions and cognitive abilities. Yet another element involves social cognition, or the knowledge of self. The young infant may be interacting with others in an organized fashion, but until he or she has acquired a concept of self, truly reciprocal relationships in the sense we have described are not possible (Lewis, 1982). The young infant must first distinguish between self and others by learning that the self is separate from other people. This occurs probably around 3 to 6 months of age, the age at which Mahler, Freud, and Spitz suggested the self was differentiated. At 8 to 9 months of age, rudimentary knowledge that one exists across space probably develops. Like object permanence, self-permanence allows children to conceptualize themselves as separate from others and lays the groundwork for self-identity (Lewis & Brooks-Gunn, 1979). After this time, infants rapidly accumulate knowledge about themselves relevant to such social categories as age, sex, size, competence, and effectance, and, as evidenced by their recognition of visual self-representations and facial features, they come to view themselves as unique persons (Brooks-Gunn & Lewis, 1978, 1982b).[2]

[2]All humans, at least in Western society, recognize themselves (particularly their faces) as represented in mirrors and pictures, with the exception of children under 8–24 months of age, mentally retarded persons who are functioning at an age equivalent of less than 2

By preschool, persons like one's self are preferred (especially in terms of same-sex and same-age persons), constancy develops, and self categories are added at a rapid rate. The child's growing sense of self is necessary, but not sufficient, for the development of relationships (Lewis, 1982; Youniss, 1980), which require for their initiation and maintenance the negotiation of two separate and distinct selves. At the same time, as Mead, Cooley, and Sullivan, among others, have pointed out, it is through the development and experience of relationships that the child's notion of self is enhanced.

In anticipation of becoming part of a social system even before his or her entrance or participation in it, the infant has not only to activate a repertoire of interactive styles and skills based on individual qualities such as temperament and perceptual skill, but must also contend with the idiosyncracies of his or her family system. Within the family system, the child moves from interaction with other social beings to the development of relationships with significant others. In the process of interacting, he or she develops a social awareness of and accommodation to others that will carry over to other social systems. In addition, the infant comes to differentiate the social world into broad categories of familiar-unfamiliar, like-unlike, self–other, the latter distinction providing the foundation for an evolving self-identity within a social world.

The Peer System

Developmental psychology has underestimated the importance of peers in the development of social behavior. Their counterparts in anthropology, clinical child psychology, comparative psychology, and personality provided the rationale for assigning the peer system a relatively large role in the socialization of children.

Anthropology's interest in peers stems from the fact that most tribal or transitional cultures are composed of extended families. Cousins, siblings, and other child relatives offer a peer group that is highly visible and may be quite distinct from the adult group. Whiting and Edwards (1973) have described peer and adult interactions in children from six different cultures (including Kenya, Okinawa, India, the Phillipines,

years, and persons with severe affective disorders (Cichetti & Sroufe, 1978; Lewis & Brooks-Gunn, 1979). Recent studies suggest that the self-distortions common among psychotic patients are not due to perceptual problems, since patients have no perceptual difficulties with nonsocial objects (Traub & Orbach, 1964). Anorexia nervosa can be regarded as a case of bodily distortion in which patients perceive themselves as being heavier than they are, in spite of the ability to judge others' bodies fairly accurately (Garner, 1981; H. Bruch, 1978).

Mexico, and Orchard Town, U.S.A.). In most cultures studied, older children care for younger children. Small groups of children often perform specific duties learned from peers. Across cultures, the amount and importance of peer interaction vary: Most notably for our concerns, peer interactions are least frequent in single-house, nuclear-family cultures such as ours. If early peer involvement is less common in our society, it may not be surprising that psychologists have often downplayed its importance. Parents in Western cultures commonly seem to believe that peer relationships in the early years are unnecessary; in a study of Princeton (New Jersey) mothers, only 20% provided any peer contact for their infants and toddlers, and many felt that peer relationships had no impact until later childhood (Lewis, Young, Brooks, & Michaelson, 1975). Clinical psychologists in suburban settings, however, must often confront the consequences of isolation from peers in cases of withdrawal and social avoidance among their young clients. Working patterns in the 1980s may alter these views or at least provide more opportunity for peer interaction. While the decrease in birth rate and the increase in one-child families make the formation of sibling and cousin peer groups even less likely than in previous decades, the increase in the number of single and working mothers should increase the number of young children in group care settings. Thus, two sets of normative peer groups may coexist—sibling peer groups and day-care peer groups.

The idea that the peer system may be as important as the family system vis-à-vis support and socialization has, until recent years, leaned heavily on the classic studies of Anna Freud and Harry Harlow. Following World War II, Freud and Dann (1952) described the amazing closeness of a group of young children who, while living together in a concentration camp, lost their parents and came to rely exclusively on one another for nurturance and affection. When brought to England after the war, the children refused to interact with others. Only with a great deal of patience and encouragement did they eventually form attachments with their caregivers. Their responsivity to one another and displays of protection and concern suggested that peers could very well provide for many of the needs usually thought to be the province of parents. In a radically different context, Harlow demonstrated that motherless monkeys, when reared in groups of peers, could grow up to be effective adults and could demonstrate appropriate social behavior (Harlow, 1969). Harlow, willing to go out on a limb and describe primate relationships in terms of love, also referred to the substitution of peers as love objects for the young.

Several theorists have also discussed the importance of the peer system for socialization. For example, Sullivan (1953) not only contrasted and compared the peer and adult systems, determined that the social reality of peers is reciprocal while that of adults and children is not. The presence or absence of reciprocity may lead to very different functions of relationships within each of the two systems (Youniss, 1980). Piaget also provided new insights (which will be discussed later) into the establishment of peer relations.

Given the view that peers can play a significant role in the development of social behavior and that their role differs from that of the family, we shall discuss several topics—the definition of a peer, the origins of peer relationships, the development of perspective-taking and empathy in peer contexts, aggression in peer groups, and the emergence of friendship. Before turning to these topics, a word on the importance of the peer group for the clinician might be in order. In any attempt to evaluate children's ability to cope, adaptations in the family, in school, and with peers are typically assessed. For example, these are the arenas for adjustment identified by Achenbach and Edelbrock (1981). However, information on adaptation with peers is limited by the fact that adults commonly do not have access to peer–peer interactions outside the classroom and family settings. Like most instruments, the Child Behavior Profile (Achenbach, 1978; Achenbach & Edelbrock, 1979) uses parent and teacher judgments to assess peer adjustment. As has been found in the Educational Testing Service's Institute for the Study of Exceptional Children, by the time children are 6, their parents may not even know who their children's best friends are. When asked whom their child would invite to a birthday party, mothers failed to name many of the "guests" listed by their children (M. Lewis, personal communication). Techniques such as sociometrics involve children's responses to other children (e.g., "Whom would you most like to play with on the playground?") but are cumbersome tools for the assessment of the individual child. Disruptions in peer relationships may be the adjustment problem most difficult to uncover, especially in shy, withdrawn children (parents and teachers are informed mainly about aggressive acts involving other children, either by the parents or those aggressed against).

What Is a Peer?

The meaning of "peer" probably varies culturally and subculturally. With children in America, peer has been construed as same-age playmate, probably because of our educational practice of fairly strict age groupings in school. But in situations where there are lower concentrations of children or where children's movements are restricted (villages, rural communities, apartment buildings), a peer group may have a five-year age range or be divided into three general groups—toddlers, children, and adolescents. Rather than age, the function of a peer may be a more important definitional characteristic. Peers may fulfill a variety of functions, including (but not limited to) play, friendship, learning of skills, practicing of roles, competition, and cooperation. In some circumstances, peers may fulfill traditional parenting functions—care and protection. In the main, peers tend to serve different functions from those of adults, and these functions define a peer more than does actual age. As an example, Edwards and Lewis (1979) asked 3- to 5-year-old children to decide with which of three persons (as represented by pictures that they could identify as "little children," "big children," and "parents") they would like to play, learn, or share, and from whom they would receive help. The children preferred to play with the same-age child, to receive help from the adult, and to share with the older child. We suspect that with increasing age, the young children would exhibit more variability in the function–social object relationship, reflecting the diversity of roles in which persons may engage.

One function often considered to be the exclusive province of adults is that of educating, but peers may also play an important educating role. In Harlow's study (1969), for example, the primate peers played an active role in socializing other monkeys. The effectiveness of older children as teachers or role models for younger children is increasingly recognized, as is the imitation and idolization of older by younger children. The child clinician can use this phenomenon therapeutically in providing peer therapy, self-help, and social support groups analogous to those used with adults in the treatment of alcoholism, drug addiction, child abuse, and a wide range of other adjustment problems.

Origins of Peer Interaction

After a lull of nearly five decades, interest in peer interactions in infancy has been revived. In the 1920s and 1930s, several large observational studies of infants and toddlers in play groups were reported (Bridges, 1933; Buhler, 1930). After Piaget suggested that peer interactions did not occur until after the child had acquired a certain level of cognitive functioning, and Bowlby hypothesized that the mother–infant relationship was the only one of importance in the first 18 months of life, investigations of early peer interaction subsided. In the 1970s, interest was renewed, primarily because the infant's capabilities in other aspects of development were shown to be more sophisticated than was previously supposed (Lewis & Rosenblum, 1975). From these studies, early peer relationships may be described as follows.

In the first months of life, infants exhibit a visual interest in one another, just as they do for objects, people, and mirror images (Bridges, 1933; Vincze, 1971). Shortly thereafter, if given the opportunity, they will move beyond mere looking and make contact with other babies. By the sixth month, the looking-and-touching infant who takes the initiative of adding a coo or a gurgle to his or her repertoire of peer-directed behaviors might even be able to elicit a smile response from the agemate. As a result, he or she might go so far as actively to seek the responsive peer out, mobilizing toward and reaching out for him or her (Durfee & Lee, 1973).

So far, the behaviors described—looking, touching and reaching—are also elicited by objects and other persons. To demonstrate that the behaviors are related specifically to peer contact, differential use needs to be demonstrated. It is not until approximately the ninth month that such differences are observed and that infant–infant interaction may be described as unique. At this time, the infant's interaction may be considered social in nature: Infants are seen offering and taking objects and playing reciprocal games such as rolling a ball back and forth (Bronson, 1975). By 12 months of age, infants have been shown to interact differentially with adults and peers, strangers and familiar persons (Lewis *et al.*, 1975). In a series of studies, these investigators found that about 50 out of 64 infants offered a toy to their mothers and to their same-age peers, but only 15% did so to unfamiliar adult females (in this case, the other infants' mothers). Thus, the adult female strangers were ignored, while peers were engaging in as much toy social interaction with one another as with their mothers. Interestingly, over 67% took a toy from a peer as compared with 25% from the mother and only 11% from the adult female. In a second study in which 12-month-olds were observed "playing" with a familiar and an unfamiliar peer on two occasions, infants were more likely to interact with, to imitate, and to show more positive affect toward their friends than toward the strangers (Lewis *et al.*, 1975).

Mueller and colleagues (Mueller & Brenner, 1977; Mueller & Lucas, 1975), using a framework like that used by Piaget, have described the development of early peer relationships in terms of three stages. In the first stage, the 1-year-old focuses on object-centered contacts when interacting, with interest being maintained by the action on the object around which the interaction is taking place (not the reverse). In the second stage, toddlers actively initiate interactions, seemingly in terms of the contigencies that children receive from one another. Children respond to a social initiation by a peer in a variety of ways and attempt to keep the interaction going. While in Stage I, the behavioral sequences that maintained an interaction were rigid and formalized and the interchange usually ended with a single response, in the second stage, the interchange might be more extensive, involving a child's laughing at a peer's antics, joining in, or acting silly, all of which can prove engaging for the peer and prompt a sequential response. By Stage III, the interchanges are complementary and reversible, with role-switching occurring for the first time.

Opportunities to practice social skills blossom in the preschool and kindergarten years. For children in day-care settings, academic demands lie dormant and curricula strive above all to introduce children into a nonfamilial setting that has a relatively fixed routine and is primarily social in nature. For children not enrolled in day-care, especially if a younger sibling has not arrived on the scene, the mother might provide for more outside contacts, for example, by brief visits to neighors with children. By preschool, children are able to become mutually engaged in complex social exchanges for extended periods of time, can readily accommodate to the social behavior of a peer, and form important relationships with them (Garvey & Hogan, 1973).

By school age, the same progression from interaction to relationship that had occurred within the family system during the early years gradually recurs within the peer system. Children begin to realize that the children with whom they share social encounters ("momentary physical interaction"; Rubin, 1980) can actually assume long-term mutually supportive roles in their social experience. The developing social awareness that makes this transition possible is described by Selman (1976) by four successive stages. In Stage 0, a friend is someone to play with, someone who happens to be engaged in the right activity at the right time. In Stage 1, (usually between 6 and 9 years of age) a friend is someone to please you, to offer you support and goodwill, with no reciprocity required or even considered; in Stage 2 (usually between 9 and 12), a friend is someone who scratches your back while you scratch his or hers, a reciprocal but transient arrangement. By Stage 3, the friendship is enduring across time and situation, is mutually satisfying, and is dependent to some degree on the psychological compatibility of its members. A child's interpersonal success depends in part on his or her cognitive skills in conceptualizing a social relationship and in part on his or her emotional resources in accommodating to the demands it entails and the affective investment it requires. Children with histories of rejection and scorn, for whatever reason, are among those at risk for later psychiatric problems. The failure to function adequately within a peer system represents the loss of a support system that, in amount of time, similarity of interests and activities, and prevalence in one's daily routine, can surpass even one's family system in its impact on one's psychological adjustment.

SOCIAL BEHAVIOR

Social behaviors are those behaviors that individuals direct toward others. Common ways in which children may conduct themselves toward others are empathically, aggressively, conformingly, coyly, jealously, cooperatively, competitively, submissively, assertively, avoidingly, etc. The process by which a child acquires social behaviors involves a complex interrelationship among many factors.

First, *individual characteristics* of the child, such as temperament, personality, intelligence, and motivation, contribute to his or her social development by affecting both other individuals' views of or behavior toward the child and the child's own perspectives of the values, intentions, and beliefs of others. Specific cognitive skills, such as memory, attention, information-processing skills, problem-solving abilities, associative learning skills, imagery, and representation, also prove relevant to social functioning.

Second, *age-related social cognitions* affect the acquisition of social behaviors. There is an underlying dynamic quality to the child's unique characteristics that complicates and enriches considerably the process of social development. For example, in adapting to their environments, children advance through a variety of intellectual stages in their understanding of the social environment. As Damon (1977) observes, "A child's social knowledge develops in a predictable, age-related manner. That is, the child makes progressive reorganizations . . . in principles that structure various aspects of his social knowledge" (p. 35). The regular, progressive developmental reorganizations in the child's social perceptions and behaviors correspond to the cognitive reorganizations typical of the various cognitive stages through which the child passes. For example, by the 18th month the child has achieved rudimentary categorization skills, accurately differentiating between circles and squares, red and blue, etc. These primitive classification skills extend into the social sphere as well: They can differentiate mother from father and infants from adults (Brooks-Gunn & Lewis, 1978). As shall be seen repeatedly, cognition affects social perceptions and behaviors throughout childhood (and beyond).

Third, *situational factors* often determine an individual's behavior. A child who would ordinarily be disinclined to behave aggressively might do so when confronted with the aggression or hostility of others, as would be the case in a child clamoring to the defense of a younger sibling under attack.

Fourth, *behaviors* themselves can influence one's social development. The young boy with little opportunity to transgress and a lengthy record of good behavior might come to view himself as well-behaved and conduct himself accordingly. A girl with a burning desire to play baseball and a record as the first girl to participate in her community's Little League may generalize this "boy-like" behavior and behave in a boy-like manner in a host of situations unrelated to baseball.

Fifth, the *culture* within which the child grows has an impact on the child's social behaviors as well. For example, the child is more likely to behave competitively in a culture that encourages competition than in one that disparages it.

Finally, the *models* to which the child is exposed influence social development by providing the child with spontaneous demonstrations, illustrations, or verbal accounts of the ways in which one might respond to a variety of situations. The effectiveness of the model will vary according to characteristics of the model (e.g., age, sex, general similarity to the observing child, consequences of the behavior) as well as characteristics of the child (e.g., cognitive capacity to learn, affectability, motivational state, attention toward model). A highly anxious child might be inattentive to those around him or her and might therefore be impervious to the model's potential influence. On the other hand, the anxiety-ridden child may be overly dependent on the actions of models for cues about how to behave but insensitive to the contingencies associated with the observed behavior. Having observed the social conduct of those around them, children might reproduce, or imitate, these behaviors.

In discussing the acquisition of social behavior, we shall focus on several behaviors that are most often studied by developmental psychologists and have implications for clinicians working with children. These include imitation, aggression, empathy, and conformity.

Imitation

Imitation represents a powerful means of acquiring competence in dealing with one's social world. As Yando, Seitz, and Zigler (1978) define it, imitation is "the motoric or verbal performance of specific acts or sounds that are like those previously performed by a model (p. 4)." Terms such as "modeling" or "observational learning" are aspects of the same phenomenon.

Theorizing on the development of imitation skills, Piaget (1962b) has posited a number of stages through which the child passes. At first, imitation is merely a reflexive activity: since even a blind child smiles, one can hardly point to the early smile of an infant as an outcome of the imitative rather than a reflexive process. A second stage, which Piaget termed "imitation by training," occurs when the model repeats the child's immediately preceding response, thus initiating a sequence of imitations first by the model, then by the baby, *ad infinitum*. By 5 months of age, the infant can systematically imitate the actions of others, as long as the activities were previously within his or her range of skills and had actually been performed (Meltzoff & Moore, 1975). The ability to imitate previously unknown acts does not emerge, according to Piaget, until approximately 9 months of age, precisely the time infants begin to pay special heed to their peers.[3]

After a period of consolidation of imitative skills, the child eventually achieves a cognitive level that permits the internalization, or representation, of the modeled act, so that he or she may not actually imitate it for some time thereafter. Piaget's oft-cited example of this dramatic new skill involves the first temper tantrum ever witnessed by his impressionable young 16-month-old child, Jacqueline. During a visit to their home, a little friend of Jacqueline's "screamed as he tried to get out of a playpen and pushed it backwards, stamping his feet" (1962b, p. 63). The next day, the previously tantrum-free Jacqueline proceeded to scream, stamp her feet, and shake her playpen. With her newly acquired cognitive capacity of representation, Jacqueline could begin the limitless expansion (for better or for worse) of her social repertoire.

Rather than await an occasion in which to exhibit or test newly acquired behaviors, young children create these occasions in fantasy play. In fact, preschoolers in a playroom with a peer will spend as much as 50% of their play time in fantasy (Matthews, 1978).

When the representational skills evidenced in fantasy play emerge, the range of individuals with whom the children can interact in a socially meaningful way is not confined to the stimulus properties of their play partners alone, for fantasy permits the partners to transcend the role of the 4-year-olds they are and instead to become parents, fire fighters, doctors, or any one of the many characters they encounter in their daily lives. Beyond the behavioral effect of providing an opportunity for the acquisition social repertoires through the process of imitation, this unique aspect of the fantasy situation has multiple cognitive, social, and affective consequences. It can, literally, put them in another's shoes and thereby facilitate their understanding of that other individual. For example, in an investigation of the sex-role portrayals of young children (Matthews, 1981, p. 981) a pair of 4-year-old play partners was observed playing house. Morgan was the daddy and Jeff the mommy:

[3]Recent research questions the assumption that true imitation emerges in the first half of the first year; what has been considered early imitation may be due to generalized arousal rather than the performance of a specific act. Novel imitation may occur much later (Waite & Lewis, 1979).

MORGAN: I'll work for awhile, in my office.
JEFF: And I'm the mommy, and I'll help you, okay?
MORGAN: No, no. You're the mommy. You help David [the baby], okay?

In such interactions, the child's endeavors to arrive at an understanding of the perspectives of others are laid bare. Areas of current concern become apparent, and hypotheses are easily drawn by the skilled observer about the sources of conflict or confusion for the child. For example, a child may be attempting to sort out why his or her father or mother is so infrequently involved in the family routine. By frantically "running errands," "rushing to the office," or "cleaning up the home," all in fantasy, the child may arrive at an understanding of father's or mother's unavailability for nurturance and support. The play of young children has been described by Sears (1947) as "an open sesame, a psychological x-ray into the motivation systems of young children" (p. 191). To a large extent, therapists of young children utilize this characteristic of play in achieving an understanding of key conflict areas of their young clients. In play therapy, not only is the child's perspective on his or her current situation brought to light, but coping strategies are too. They can be identified and used to advantage. The therapist can even direct the fantasy in such a way that social behavior can be modified. For example, Lazarus (1977) helped a child with an intense fear of dogs construct a fantasy to aid in his adjustment. Noting the boy's enthusiastic interest in sports cars, he engaged the child in a series of fantasy episodes: First, the child was speeding down the highway in his Alpha Romeo; shortly thereafter, his car sped past a small dog, then a large dog; eventually, he pulled his Alpha into a sidewalk cafe where a large dog approached and sniffed at his heels. After several sessions of emotive imagery, Lazarus reported, the boy's attitudes toward dogs had improved markedly, and after one year, no trace of his former phobia remained.

The coping effects of fantasy play have long been recognized. Erikson, in 1950, concluded that "child's play is an infantile form of the human ability to deal with experience by creating model situations and to master reality by experiment and planning" (1950, p. 195). In fantasy, a child can make up for all the defeats, sufferings, and frustrations that befall young children, and can even acquire the skills necessary to prevent their recurrence.

In the brief description of the fantasy play of Morgan and Jeff given above, significant observations of the social interaction styles of the play participants can be made. For example, Morgan, by stating who he is and what he is about to do, is in effect controlling the social sequence. Jeff, by offering himself as a role complement, exhibits an accommodating style, presumably because, for now, he wants to assure the maintenance of the interaction. In the light of Jeff's magnanimous concession to play "mommy," Morgan is willing to seek agreement too ("okay?") although not yet ready to surrender his control over the situation ("No, you help David"). As Sullivan (1953, p. 198) stated, the interaction process is ideally a reciprocal one: "Integration in an interpersonal situation is a reciprocal process in which (1) complementary needs are resolved, or aggravated; (2) reciprocal patterns of activities are developed or disintegrated; and (3) foresight of satisfactions, or rebuff, of similar needs is facilitated." The complexity of the social interaction process lies in the fact that all participants must devise a shared order in it. Without a working consensus or when the consensus breaks down, social interactions cease and social development meets an obstacle.

In fantasy play, children deal not just with the here-and-now but embellish former social situations and lingering concerns and in so doing "work them through," as Freud would have said. To test this assumption, Gilmore (1966) aroused children's fears about a forthcoming initiation ceremony and then observed the effect of his manipulation on their play with stress-related and stress-unrelated toys. Generally, he found that when the stress reaction was not incapacitatingly high (resulting in an avoidance reaction to the anxiety-rousing play materials), the stressed children seemed to prefer to play with toys relevant to the fearful situation. Burstein and Meichenbaum (1979) also found evidence for fantasy as a possible forum for the development of coping strategies. Children scheduled for hospitalization for such minor surgery as tonsillectomies were tested and/or observed for their level of anxiety, defensiveness, and play patterns one week prior to surgery, the night before surgery, and one week following surgery. Those who appeared least anxious prior to their hospitalization emerged as the most distressed by their surgery. In a seven-month follow-up, these investigators were able to identify two classes of children within their sample: the "defenders," who were prone to deny common problems, showing *less* anxiety about their impending hospitalization, and the "worriers," who tended to face up to their problems, as seen in the frequency of their stress-related play. As Bernstein and Meichenbaum suggest, the latter group of children went through "the work of worrying," reviewing through fantasy play possible scenarios related to their hospitalization, repeating reassurances that had been offered by their parents, and in general, accommodating to their situation so that when it occurred they appeared better prepared to handle it. Their multiple play rehearsals seems to have served them well, since seven months following surgery they continued to express less distress over the incident.

Aggression

Within the peer system, aggression is a behavior that often interferes with the working consensus, sometimes disrupting the process of social development and necessitating a referral to a mental health practitioner. Early aggressiveness is not necessarily dysfunctional and might actually serve an adaptive function. Waldrop and Halverson (1975) point to a correlation between aggressive and affiliative behaviors in early peer relations and noted that a group of peer-oriented 2½ year olds whom they described as "active, vigorous, assertive, expressive, aggressive, and not fearful or withdrawn," were among the more socially-at-ease at the age of 7½.

In study by Matthews (1972), conducted with Zazzo of the University of Paris, a positive relation between early aggression and sociability was hypothesized. The findings showed that the most popular preschool children were among those who behaved most aggressively as well as most socially in a free-play situation. Their aggressiveness was not characterized by hostility or anger but rather by social interest and vivacity, qualities that seemed to draw others to them as social partners.

These findings suggest that any operational definition of aggression might vary with age or situation. For example, in the early years, aggression may include behaviors associated with sociability or popularity. Grabbing a toy at 24 months of age may be coded as an aggressive act in spite of the fact that it may not be perceived as such by the relatively egocentric 2-year-old and might actually increase frequency of contact with others. A slap on the back may be an expression of friendship under some circumstances or hostility in others.

Aggression seems to peak at about 4 or 5 years of age, gradually declining thereafter. Barrett's (1976) study of aggression and prosocial behaviors, conducted with children ranging in age from 7 to 8 years, failed to show a relationship between aggression and sociability, suggesting that aggression in the school-age children has lost its positive social potential. A developmental change in young children's egocentricity—or embeddedness in their own perspective, as described by Piaget—has been called upon to explain the reduction in aggressive behaviors in school-age children. With an increasing cognitive ability to take the perspective of the other, children become more empathic, considering how the other might feel if aggressed against. The early *enactive* role-taking of the preschool child is replaced by *representational* role-taking, "the general ability and disposition to 'take the role' of another person in the cognitive sense, that is, to assess his response capacities and tendencies in a given situation" (Flavell, 1968, p. 1). It is not that children are indifferent to the perspective of others before school-age: The ability to take the perspective of the other, as we shall see, has its roots in the earliest cognitive accomplishments and social relationships.

Aggression is one of the few social behaviors for which sex differences are reported in study after study. During infancy, aggression as measured by grabbing toys and hitting does not seem to be sex-typed (Brooks-Gunn & Lewis, 1978). By 2½ to 3 years of age, however, boys are more likely to engage in physical aggression than are girls, and boys are more aggressive to other boys while girls are more likely to aggress equally against boys and girls (Fagot, 1980). Socialization seems to play a role, since girls' aggressive acts were more likely to be ignored than were the boys' aggressive acts. If girls do not elicit the expected response from their peers, they may decrease their aggressive acts while boys, receiving responses from peers, continue this behavior.

Other studies of older children also report differences in aggression. In a cross-cultural study examining children in Kenya, Okinawa, India, the Phillipines, Mexico, and the United States, boys exhibited more verbal and physical aggression than girls, although neither exhibited much direct assault (Whiting & Edwards, 1973). Large cross-cultural differences were also found, suggesting that aggression may be more acceptable in some cultures than in others. That girls may be able to express aggression if they find it appropriate is demonstrated in a series of classic studies by Bandura and his colleagues. One group of children was exposed to an aggressive adult model who abused a BoBo doll—punching it, knocking it down, jumping on top of it—and another group of children was exposed to a nonaggressive model who played peacefully. After the children had observed the model, they were left alone in a playroom, and the boys observing the aggressive adults played aggressively while the girls were less likely to do so. However, the girls, when offered a reward for performing as many of the model's acts as possible, acted as aggressively as the boys (Bandura, Ross, & Ross, 1961).

If girls are able to initiate aggressive acts and exhibit them early in life, and if we assume that they are learning not to be aggressive, how is this occurring? Parents are likely to encourage or at least tolerate aggressiveness in their sons more than in their daughters, with this being valid today as well as earlier (Brooks-Gunn & Matthews, 1979; Sears, Maccoby, & Levin, 1957). This is true inside as well as outside the home:

Sons are encouraged to fight back in neighborhood peer relations by their parents more than girls are. Additionally, peers may differentially reinforce aggressive responses, as with Fagot's (1980) young girls whose aggressive responses were ignored. Finally, teachers allow boys much more latitude than girls in acting out and negative behavior in the classroom (Fagot, 1977).

Sex differences in aggressive behavior also have a hormonal component. Androgen, which is present in greater amounts in boys during the prenatal period and after sexual maturity begins, has been shown to be related to aggression in humans and other primates (Brooks-Gunn & Matthews, 1979).

Finally, aggression is the behavioral problem most mentioned by teachers as descriptive of classroom functioning and is the most frequent presenting problem in clinic referrals (Achenbach & Edelbrock, 1981).

Childhood aggression is not only a major behavioral problem when is occurs, but is also predictive of adult maladaptive behavior. For example, one antecedent of adult schizophrenia in young males is aggressiveness (Watt, 1978), while early acting-out behavior (usually measured in terms of aggression) is related to adult criminality (Robins, 1966). In general, antisocial child behavior (fighting, truancy, arrests, drinking) is a necessary but not sufficient condition for adult substance abuse (Robins, 1978; Kellam, Brown, & Fleming, 1982). In a large epidemiological study of the entire first-grade population of a community, aggressiveness in the first grade was related to substance abuse in the teenage years (Kellam *et al.*, 1982).

Empathy

Empathy is an aspect of social knowledge and involves one individual's awareness of or sensitivity to another individual's experiences, thoughts, and feelings. The ability to take the perspective of another does not necessitate actually having shared a particular experience, but requires only that the person be able to imagine how the other individual might view a given situation, what he or she might think in the course of the experience, and how he or she might feel (Lewis & Brooks-Gunn, 1979). In the socialization of children, adults often stress the mutuality of feelings; for example, if a toddler pulls another's hair, the caregiver invariably questions the youngster about how he or she would feel in similar circumstances, sometimes even giving a slight tug of the locks to emphasize the point.

The origins of empathy are predicated upon aspects of the early caregiver–infant relationship. By responding sensitively to a child's needs, a caregiver provides not just relief to the child, but information as well. Statements such as "You want your bottle" or "You're so mad at that dolly for falling out of your crib" or "I love you" identify emotions for the child, provide labels for his or her feelings, and in so doing make them more accessible to the child's growing recognition of them. In a study of 1-year-olds, Lewis and Michalson (1983) examined mother's labeling their 1-year-olds' affective behavior in a free-play situation. Within a 15-minute observation period, 30% of the 120 mothers who participated in the study provided their children with such information. Thus, empathy is demonstrated in early adult–child interactions in which one member of the dyad is able to demonstrate and encourage such behavior. The child's own experience of empathy, however, must await the emergence of his or her concept of self, as differentiated from other, which occurs toward the 18th month of life.

Piaget and others have hypothesized a much later age for engaging in empathic skills, reasoning that empathy depends on the ability to "decenter," to take the perspective of the others in such a way that one can accurately assess the other's "response capacities and tendencies in a given situation" (Flavell, 1968, p. 1). However, more recent evidence, both experimental (Masangkay, McCluskey, McIntyre, Sims-Knight, Vaughn, & Flavell, 1974) and anecdotal (Borke, 1972; Hoffman, 1975), suggests that perspective-taking skills are present as early as 2½ years of age if not earlier. Hoffman, providing a developmental account of empathy, sees precursors to empathy in infants' stress reactions to the cries of another infant, as if what is happening to the others were happening to them. At this stage, according to Hoffman, the empathic response is "a learned response in early childhood . . . in which cues of pain and displeasure from another or from his situation evoke associations with the observer's own past pain, resulting in an empathic affective reaction" (p. 613).

The next stage in the development of empathy comes when children achieve the recognition of the other individual as a separate entity. Yet, they might still be unable to comprehend a state (thought, perception, or need) in the other that might be different from their own. So, their first response would be to assume that the other feels as they might feel. Eventually, by about 2 or 3 years of age, the awareness of inner states independent of their own begins to set in. Then by 6 to 9 years, they can generalize their awareness beyond the immediate situation and utilize this awareness, sociocognitively, in developing an understanding of their social environment.

Difficulties in taking the perspective of the other appear to be related to empathy deficits underlying participation in delinquent behaviors.

Comparing nondelinquent with deliquent youths, Chandler (1973) found marked deficits in the deliquent subjects' ability to differentiate their own and others' points of view. A common mistake was for them to assume that others possessed information that was in fact available only to themselves. To address their social egocentrism, Chandler developed an intervention program in which the youths would be trained specifically to adopt the roles or perspectives of others. Chandler accomplished this by encouraging the subjects to develop and portray dramatic skits dealing with events experienced by persons their own age. Each participant would have the opportunity to portray every role in the plot, with video recordings of each portrayal made and reviewed. In an 18-month period following intervention, the subjects of the experimental training program, as a group, committed approximately half the number of deliquencies as did the placebo or control groups. As a result of the study, Chandler concluded that "sociocognitive operations for the effective solution of important human interaction problems" (p. 332) appear to be necessary for socially competent and appropriate behavior.

Elardo, Caldwell, and Webb (1976) noted that at an early age, failures in social competence seem to be associated with a lack of empathy. In middle childhood, those children who had difficulty taking the perspective of others exhibited behavior problems as well. In comparison with children who had developed or were in the process of developing role-taking skills, they were more disruptive in the classroom, less respectful, less patient, less attentive, and less likely to understand what was learned in class; also, they were less likely to be chosen by their peers as work partners. Elardo *et al.*, citing Piaget, made the point that the relationship between empathy and social competence is a reciprocal one. Children with poor social competence not only have deficits in their ability to assume accurately the perceptions of others, but also are excluded from developing social perspective-taking skills through the social learning situation inherent in peer relations. This suggests that role-taking might be only a single facet of an intervention strategy, another being the provision of social interaction opportunities. Whatever the intervention, the development of empathic skills appears necessary for full participation in one's peer group, and ultimately in society as a whole.

Conformity

The child's acceptance and understanding of authority outside the home involves a number of important dilemmas to be confronted and lessons to be learned. Each child must make an individual accommodation to it. For children whose self-concept is not well defined and whose confidence has been undermined, a social strategy known as conformity can predominate in their responses to the social environment. Conformity can involve the actual acceptance of the groups of norms: The child's behaviors or beliefs will actually change toward those of a group as a response to real or imagined group pressure. However, conformity can also involve compliance only with group norms, with the child behaving as the group wants without really believing in what he or she is doing.

Studies (e.g., Berndt, 1979) have shown that susceptibility to antisocial conformity follows a developmental age trend, increasing between the third and ninth grades and eventually declining. Comparing conformity to parents with conformity to peers, Berndt seems to have hit upon two separate reference groups, each of which is heavily implicated in the child's identification but in very distinct ways. In third grade, the children were more apt to conform to the parental reference group than to peers. By sixth grade, the children maintained a conformity to their parents' wishes and demands but also had begun to pay heed to those of their peer reference group, with few conflicts arising between the two referent group requirements. However, by ninth grade, peer conformity predominated and often conflicted with the parents' demands. As Berndt explains, given the rise in antisocial conformity, it would not be surprising that parental and peer group demands conflict with one another. In addition, the active independence from parents that most adolescents seek would tend to distance them from their parents and, by default, push them toward their peers.

The reasons for children's conformity probably do not differ from those for adults. First, they might actually share the goals of the group to which they conform. In Sherif's classic study, children, all of whom sought to acquire prizes in a tournament of competitive team events, increased their in-group solidarity primarily by accentuating their distance from their rival team by means of conformity to a series of hostile and eventually combative encounters (Sherif, Harvey, White, Hood, & Sherif, 1961). Second, the child might have a strong need to be liked and might worry considerably about the idea of rejection by his or her peer group. In 1950, Berenda, studying conformity in children through the Asch conformity situation (Asch, 1940), found that children were more likely to conform to the judgments of peers than to those of their teacher. Higher status with the teacher was not enough to override their need to be liked.

Another motive of conformity has to do with the need to be correct. Children look to those around them for cues regarding how to behave and what to believe in. In order to reduce the risk of being wrong, they look to their peers, whom they assume to be correct in specific matters.

The relationship of conformity and the development of deviant behavior may be illustrated by the substance abuse literature, focusing on adolescents (Kellam *et al.*, 1982). Both perceived levels of use of drugs among one's peer group (marijuana, alcohol, and so on) and actual use of substances as reported by parents related to an adolescent's future use of drugs. Being attached more to peers than to parents is also related to substance use in teenagers, again suggesting the importance of conformity, especially to peer values (Jessor & Jessor, 1978).

SUMMARY

When we progress developmentally through the various social systems to which individuals must accommodate, it becomes apparent that an individual's social development is an ongoing process that begins at birth and continues throughout life. Because the early social systems comprising the family and the peer group predominate in childhood and because these systems provide the foundation for later social development within subsequently encountered systems, they have been the main focus of the present chapter.

Broader social systems such as the school or the culture also exert their influence over the child's social development. For example, a social institutions's policy with regard to racial integration can have a profound effect on the individual child's competence, sensitivity, or intolerance in interracial social interactions. An in-depth account of the effects of these larger systems is beyond the purview of this chapter, but the possible impact of these systems on the social behavior of the developing child should be considered.

With a multiplicity of factors in mind, the social development of a child can be placed in context and can be viewed as an interactive phenomenon of which the child is but a part.

3

Cognitive Development and Clinical Interventions

Robert Cohen and Robert Schleser

INTRODUCTION

Achenbach (1978b) noted that the vast majority of research on child psychopathology is influenced more by adult treatment models than by a developmental perspective. He asserted that children must be considered in terms of developmental progressions along physical, social, and cognitive dimensions. Researchers and practitioners alike need to become more aware of "normal" developmental sequences and to understand the relationship of their interventions to the current and future states of the changing child.

The purpose of the present chapter is to highlight some general parameters of childhood cognitive development with an eye toward integrating this work with cognitive behavioral intervention strategies. The contemporary historical isolation of developmental psychology interests from concerns of child-clinical interventions makes this task formidable. Thus, the reader is warned at the outset that the picture to be drawn is quite sketchy. Certainly a variety of components of development (i.e., social development, physical development) must be explored and integrated as well. Other chapters in this volume will provide some of this information.

We begin with the assumptions that (1) the child is an active problem-solver; (2) every situation involves the discrimination, extraction, and analysis of information plus the directing and planfulness charac-

Robert Cohen • Department of Psychology, Memphis State University, Memphis, Tennessee 38152. **Robert Schleser** • Lewis College of Arts and Letters, Illinois Institute of Technology, Chicago, Illinois 60616.

teristic of an active problem-solver; and (3) the problem-solving styles and abilities undergo developmental change. This is an interactionist position involving developmental change. It is a rejection of extreme empiricist positions that focus on the content of experiences, as well as a rejection of extreme nativist positions that focus on the biological and genetic programming of the individual.

Any educational or clinical context aimed at altering thought and/or behavior can be conceptualized as a learning situation. Bransford (1979) proposed that learning situations have four critical components: characteristics of the learner, the nature of the material to be mastered, the activities employed in the setting, and the criterion measures or standards. These four components are operating whether we are teaching math skills, cultivating table manners, or trying to train a hyperactive child to behave more adaptively. The point of contact between these applied contexts and the work by cognitive developmental psychologists, of course, lies in the characteristics of the learner. With our interactionist position noted above, a variety of questions become relevant. How should we expect children of different ages to respond to different intervention activities (e.g., rehearsal, role-playing, self-instructions, response cost contingencies)? What tasks and behaviors should be targeted for instruction? What combinations of tasks, activities, and individual developmental differences can we expect to lead to what forms of criterial behaviors?

Three contemporary theoretical orientations are consistent with the theme of the child as an active problem-solver, and these are presented next. This will be followed by a selective review of the research literature on cognitive development, a presentation of our research, and a concluding section offering further directions for the integration of these developmental and clinical domains.

THEORETICAL ORIENTATIONS TO COGNITIVE DEVELOPMENT

Information-Processing Approaches

Bower (1975) provided an excellent review of information-processing approaches to the study of cognition. These approaches have several characteristics in common. A computer model is adopted; the question of human cognition becomes, "What must a computer know in order to produce behavior x?" Information from the environment is abstracted from sensory systems and "flows" through a variety of proposed information-processing components (e.g., sensory buffers, short-term memory, long-term memory). The information is transformed and analyzed at each step; feedback and feedforward loops among the components influence these transformations and analyses. Planfulness and purpose are built into the system by proposing an executive system. The executive—containing sets of elementary information-processing rules—constructs, executes, and monitors the flow of information in the service of the completion of a hierarchy of goals and subgoals.

In recent years, information-processing approaches have been applied to the study of cognitive development (Klahr & Wallace, 1976; Siegler, 1978a). The key to these approaches for cognitive development lies in the nature of rules. It is assumed that the child's behavior is rule governed. What changes with development is the nature of the rules. These rules may relate to particular aspects of the stimulus context that are differentiated and encoded (as stressed by Siegler, 1978b) or they may relate to the ordering of goals and subgoals—planfulness (as stressed by Klahr, 1978). In fact, the rules may delineate any relevant aspect of the processing of information.

Social Learning Theory

Contemporary social learning theorists (Bandura, 1977b; Rosenthal & Zimmerman, 1978) reject a conceptualization of behavior as simply the result of some combination of individual characteristics and environmental influences. Rather, all three factors are viewed as existing within a mutually interdependent network—a set of reciprocal determinants (Bandura, 1977b). Thus, cognitions, beliefs, and expectations influence behavior and vice versa; behavior, in part, determines the nature of the environment (e.g., a school gym set up for a basketball game versus a dance) and vice versa; and cognitions determine the psychological definitions of the environment and its potentialities, and vice versa.

Learning takes place either directly (through the association of behaviors and consequences) or through modeling. The direct consequences of behavior, or reinforcements, are not conceptualized in the more traditional fashion that ignores (or even precludes) awareness of the contingencies on the part of the actor. Rather, consequences of behavior explicitly carry information and function to provoke the individual into formulating and testing hypotheses. Thus, reinforcement serves to influence the probability of a response to the extent that the reinforcement elicits cognitions or thoughts that mediate the association between stimulus context and behavior.

The vast majority of human learning occurs observationally through modeling. New behaviors can be acquired by observation of the behaviors and the consequences of those behaviors. Observational learning is aided greatly by the symbolic abilities of humans. These abilities allow for the abstraction and representation of information and provide an efficient means for retaining that information. Here again, the concept of reinforcement differs from traditional operant accounts of learning. From a social learning perspective, the anticipation of reinforcement may serve as a stimulus to direct attention to a model's behavior; thus, reinforcement may facilitate learning but it is not a necessary condition.

Self-regulatory processes have a central role in social learning theory. Individuals are selective about the aspects of the environment to which they will attend. Cognitive supports and self-reinforcement for behaviors also function to provide elements of self-control and influence. This issue of self-control is best summarized by Bandura's (1977a) concept of self-efficacy, which has played an important role in contemporary behavioral clinical psychology. Self-efficacy refers to a belief that one can perform the behaviors necessary for a given outcome in a specific situation. This competency belief is separate from knowledge about what behavior is needed to produce the outcome.

In summary, social learning theory places a great deal of emphasis on vicarious, symbolic, and self-regulatory processes (Bandura, 1977b). Cognitive development is important to the extent that changes in cognitive functioning influence changes in these processes. For example, with development, children become more facile and experienced with manipulating symbols and, thus, better able efficiently to represent, manipulate, and retain observational experiences. Also with development, one would expect to see changes in the attentional processes, retention processes, motor reproduction processes, and the motivational processes that underlie observational learning.

Piaget

Certainly the most influential individual in the field of cognitive development has been Jean Piaget. Piaget advocated a structuralist position on cognitive development. Developmental change reflects changes in underlying cognitive structures that serve as cohesive frameworks for organizing knowledge and cognitive functioning. The nature of these structures is described in logical-mathematical terms, and the nature of change in these structures in qualitative. That is, at different developmental periods, a reorganization of thought occurs in such a way that a distinctly different individual emerges at each period.

Two types of developmentally invariant processes are hypothesized: organization and adaptation. Organization is the assumption that the individual's cognitive structures are interrelated and interdependent. Change in one part of the cognitive system produces change throughout the system. Adaptation refers to coping with new experiences and consists of assimilation and accommodation. Assimilation is the fitting of aspects of the new experience into existing cognitive structures, thus providing meaning to the new experience; accommodation is the altering of existing cognitive structures to meet the demands of the new experience. Organization and adaptation are complementary processes, as are assimilation and adaptation. The evocation of one implies the activation of the other.

Moderate disequilibrium is the condition for optimal cognitive growth. That is, experiences that are moderately discrepant from those completely comprehensible to the existing capacities (or cognitive structures) of the individual generate the most cognitive change. It is a basic assumption in Piaget's theory that the individual will strive to reduce these states of cognitive disequilibrium and move toward higher and higher states of adaptability.

Piaget proposed four sequentially invariant stages of cognitive development: sensorimotor (0–2 years), preoperations (2–7 years), concrete operations (7–11 years), and formal operations (11 years and up). The rate of passage through these stages is individualistic. A brief description of these stages follows. The reader is directed to Ginsburg and Opper (1969) for an initial exposure to Piaget's theory, and to Flavell (1963), Baldwin (1980), and/or Brainerd (1978) for more extensive accounts.

The names of the stages denote the nature of the existing structures. The sensorimotor infant understands his or her world physically, that is, in terms of actions performed on objects. The infant has no symbolic representation of the world; understanding consists of concrete actions such as touching, viewing, tasting, etc. During the preoperational period, the child begins developing symbolic representations of the world and thus structuring knowledge on a conceptual plane. The thought of the preoperational child is characterized as egocentric; the child is unable to take different perspectives in a given situation, either perceptually or socially. Thus, this child is relatively less influenced by feedback than older children. Likewise, this child has difficulty in decentering thought. The child locks onto a salient perceptual feature and is unable to consider multiple dimensions. As a final distinguishing characteristic, the preoperational child has difficulty reasoning with subordinate and superordinate categories. Confronted with three horses and five cows and asked, "Are there more cows or more animals?" the preoperational child typically responds with "more cows."

With the attainment of concrete operational structures, the child succeeds on tasks that defeated the younger child ("succeeds" in an adult sense of the word). The concrete operational child comprehends the nature of conservation. That is, certain properties of objects are invarient despite state-changing transformations. For example, the child knows that the amount of water doesn't change when poured into a differently shaped vessel nor does the total weight of a rock change when it is broken into pieces. In addition, this child is very good at cognitively manipulating and systematically classifying objects in the world.

The formal operational adolescent can reason beyond the immediate objects in the world. Hypothetical situations can be fully comprehended. Systematic deductive thinking is also characteristic of formal operational thought. This individual not only can understand complex verbal propositional problems, but knows how to generate relevant information to satisfy problems. Adolescent idealism and rebellion make a great deal of sense when one considers that for the first time the individual can conceive of the range of possibilities for situations in the world.

The concrete operational child is not a preoperational child plus something else, nor can we add something to the head of the concrete operational child to make a formal operational adolescent. These people live in different realities; they view the world in qualitatively different ways. These stages, then, represent discontinuities in the course of development. This is not a denial of continuities of cognitive change within a stage nor a claim that all cognitive processes change together; it is a denial of a deficit model of development in favor of a difference position. The young child is not illogical or lacking in logic; rather, the logical rules governing thought are different.

Summary of Theoretical Orientations

Each of the three theoretical positions—information-processing, social learning theory, and Piaget—have certain strengths and limitations. Information-processing approaches explain well the coding and organization of environmental input and the roles played by beliefs and expectations in those processes. Social learning theory provides an excellent analysis of the impact of an extremely wide variety of experiential events and the role played by cognitive skills. Piaget offers a global analysis of cognitive change that governs complex thought across a tremendous range of intellectual phenomena.

The differences among these approaches are considerable. The internal capacities of the child are characterized differently—from rules to skills to logical structures. The relative impact of experience and the nature of change vary. Reliance on hypothesized invariant sequences of development also differentiate the theories.

The point to be stressed here is that all three approaches emphasize an active organism engaged in problem-solving activities; there is presumed to be a dynamic relationship between the characteristics of the knower and what is to be known. Thus, each of the theories qualifies as an appropriate interpretive tool based on our interactive position. We are certainly not suggesting that these theories are interchangeable nor that they are totally complementary. Although the differences among these theories are important and have critical implications for research and practice, we feel that useful work can be performed by accepting the critical "active organism" assumption and agreeing to respect differences in theoretical orientations. As a concrete example, the first author of this chapter is a developmental psychologist aligned with the Piagetian perspective, while the second author is a clinical psychologist who adheres to a social learning framework. Our collaborative research had produced numerous heated discussions and, we believe, some interesting applied-developmental data.

COGNITIVE DEVELOPMENT

General Overview

Through the course of childhood, two major shifts in cognitive development have been identified. White (1965) described the extensive literature on the "5 to 7 shift." Dramatic changes in thinking and reasoning occur from preschool to elementary-school children on such tasks as transposition, inference tasks, discrimination learning, and problem-solving (see White, 1965). This period of change, of course, corresponds to the change from preoperations to concrete operations noted by Piaget.

The cognitive abilities of the preschool child may best be described as qualitative in attitude (Flavell, 1977). There is a strong reliance on perceptual experience over conceptual inferences. This distinction can be clarified for the reader in terms of perceptual illusions, for example, the Müller-Lyer. The two lines within the arrows look to be of different lengths. However, you can prove to yourself with the use of a measuring stick that the appearance is misleading and the two lines are of equal length. The preschooler does not possess the logical thought for these conceptual inferences; the preschooler's logic dictates to "rely on what you see." In a similar way, the preschooler tends to focus on states of objects rather than on the transformations or processes that intervened between those states; there is little integration between past states and present states of a situation.

The elementary school child (approximately 7–11 years old) exhibits a quantitative attitude toward intellectual problems. There is the belief (and ability) that many problems have precise solutions that can be arrived at with appropriate measurement and logic (Flavell, 1977). Thus, this child relies on conceptual inferences and focuses on state-producing transformations. In essence, this child is planful; there is a solution and there is a strategy for arriving at the solution.

As a brief digression, it should be explicitly stated that the young preschooler is not hopelessly bewildered. There is an unfortunate tendency to overly stress the lack of planfulness in the 2- to 7-year-old. To reiterate, this child is not illogical; the rules of logic are different from those of the older child. Also, perhaps not so obviously, an individual can often get along exceptionally well in day-to-day endeavors with a reliance on perceptual here-and-now experiences!

A second, less extensively documented period of dramatic change occurs roughly in the 9- to 11-year-old range (see Neimark, 1975). This change corresponds to the concrete-to-formal operational shift. As mentioned previously in the brief account of Piaget's theory, the elementary-school child does a fine job of analyzing and manipulating what is present and concrete. The adolescent goes beyond this; in fact, the adolescent is more likely to approach a problem from a consideration of what is possible than what is real. Thus, as explained by Flavell (1977), the thought of the school-aged child represents an empirical-inductive approach while that of the adolescent represents hypothetical-deductive reasoning. Flavell also notes, as does Neimark (1975), that although this abstract, deductive reasoning ability emerges with adolescence, it is by no means a universal accomplishment either within or across cultures.

Complementing these dramatic discontinuities in thinking are changes in a wide variety of cognitive processes such as attention, perception, memory, communication, planfulness, and problem-solving. The purpose of the remainder of this section is to highlight some of these changes with a selective review of the research literature. At the outset three points must be emphasized. First, only research on normal child populations will be considered. Second, the omission of certain areas represents the biases and interests of the authors rather than any statement concerning the relative importance of any process or any set of findings. Third, discussion of any cognitive process in isolation is done purely for ease of presentation. It should be taken as a basic assumption that these processes are interrelated and interdependent.

The Development of Attention

An analysis of the process of attention is a good springboard for the purposes of this chapter. The study of attention highlights the active nature of the individual. The human organism is continually bombarded with sensory stimulation across multiple sensory channels. Some information must be selectively attended to while other information must be ignored or rejected. Another feature of the concept of attention that makes it appealing as a starting point is its relevance for both basic developmental researchers and practitioners. The development of the ability to attend to stimuli selectively lies at the heart of issues such as problem-solving and self-control.

Attention may be erroneously conceptualized as a component in cognitive processing. As suggested by Pick, Frankel, and Hess (1975), attention is better conceptualized as a process— a process of selectivity in the service of other activities such as perception, memory, learning, or motivation. Ross (1980) proposed that the ability to focus on and selectively attend to information occurs through three overlapping but sequential states. Until about age 3, the child's attention is captured by salient aspects of a situation while other aspects are excluded. Perceptual features dictate this saliency. In the second stage, roughly between the ages of 3 and 12, the child attempts to shift among features or dimensions of stimuli, in essence trying to analyze too much. The child who is an extreme case of this may appear to be highly distractible. The preadolescent demonstrates true selective attention, able to extract relevant information while ignoring or rejecting the irrelevant.

The progression described by Ross (1980) is supported by findings from numerous studies using an incidental learning paradigm. The child is told to remember certain central information and later is asked to recall this material as well as irrelevant or incidental information in the stimuli. This research (e.g., Druker & Hagen, 1969) typically reveals an increase with age in the amount of central information recalled; the amount of incidental information recalled increases until about the age of 12 and then declines. The school-aged child, then, is actively sorting and classifying information—what we expect from concrete operational children. The formal operational adolescent starts with a goal and generates a plan to glean information; this individual attends quite selectively to the world on the basis of the task at hand.

An area of interest related to the study of the development of attention is the study of cognitive style. Children who respond slowly and accurately are termed "reflective," while those responding quickly and inaccurately are termed "impulsive." These styles have been alternatively conceptualized as resulting from differences in decision processes, motivation, and standards of performance (Kagan, 1976; Kagan, Rosman, Day, Albert, & Phillips, 1964) and as being due to different information-processing stimulus analyses (detail versus global analyses; Zelniker & Jeffrey, 1976).

Children tend to become more reflective with age. Piagetian level correlates with cognitive style, concrete operational children being more reflective than preoperational children (Cohen, Schleser, & Meyers, 1981). Drake (1970) found that reflectives scan more and do so more systematically than impulsives. Finally, several researchers have found that children can be made more reflective by training them in the use of a verbal self-control strategy (e.g., see Craighead, Wilcoxon-Craighead, & Meyers, 1978).

Memory Development

A cornerstone to any analysis of cognitive development must be the study of memory abilities. Kail (1979) noted that memory functions as an important contributor to a variety of behaviors involved in many aspects of the individual's functioning. This being the case, numerous cognitive processes would fall under the rubric of "memory." Of particular relevance to the present chapter, Flavell (1971) characterized memory as applied cognition. That is, memory becomes the focal point whenever analyses occur involving the storing and retrieving of information in the service of particular environmental demands. All three theories outlined above emphasize the representation and manipulation of information. Thus, a discussion of the development of memory and memory abilities qualifies as a good starting point for an account of cognitive development.

A commonly used distinction in the research on memory abilities is between short-term and long-term memory. Short-term memory is a limited capacity buffer that retains items for brief periods of time. Long-term memory involves the relatively permanent and enduring storage of knowledge and experiences. Interestingly, little developmental change occurs in short-term memory capacity (e.g., on a digit serial recall test, the average 3-year-old recalls about three items, the average 7-year-old recalls about five items, and the average 12 year-old recalls about seven items). Dramatic developmental changes occur on tasks requiring long-term memory. These changes reflect differences in how information is stored and retrieved. As a framework for a discussion of these changes, we will use Flavell and Wellman's (1977) three categories of memory phenomena: knowledge, strategies, and metamemory. These categories correspond to Brown's (1975) distinction of memory as knowing, memory as knowing how to know, and memory as knowing about knowing. The majority of the following review is derived from Flavell (1977) and Kail (1979).

Knowledge, or Memory as Knowing

Cognitive phenomena associated with this category of memory involve the role played by prior knowledge on the storage and retrieval of specific information. Children, like adults, are not passive machines making copies of environmental input to be automatically discharged at some later point in time. Rather, current information is elaborated and organized in reference to the knowledge base and cognitive capacity of the individual. Flavell (1977) and Kail (1979) discussed two lines of research as examples of this phenomenon: research on constructive memory and memory research from a Piagetian perspective.

Constructive Memory. If master chess-players and amateurs are asked to remember and reconstruct a random arrangement of chess pieces on a chessboard, they perform equally poorly. However, if the display conforms to an arrangement potentially found in a chess game, the reconstructions of the boards by the master chess-players are far more accurate than those of the amateurs (Chase & Simon, 1973). To the master chess-player, the nonrandom board represents a meaningful configuration—meaningful because of acquired and integrated knowledge of the game. Thus, memory processes in the service of knowing are active, constructive processes.

The examination of the development of constructive memory has relied on several experimental techniques: intrusions in the recall of prose (Brown, Smiley, Day, Townsend, & Lawton, 1977), cued recall of prose as a function of providing the cues either explicitly or having them merely implied (Paris & Lindauer, 1976), and frequency of false recognition of sentences that were not presented but whose meaning could be inferred from the set of contextually related sentences that were presented (Paris & Carter, 1973). Taken together, these studies suggest that, with development, implicit semantic relationships are more likely to be detected and derived. Thus, children, like adults, will spontaneously elaborate and integrate information, this elaboration and integration increasing with age as internal networks of semantic relations increase.

How does this constructive process relate to the ability to retain information? Paris and Upton (1976) presented an interesting analysis of this relationship. Stories were read to 5-, 8-, and 10-year-olds, followed by questions that tested both explicit and implied information in the story. Then the child was asked to recall the story. For all ages, a strong positive relationship existed between the accuracy of inferences recognized and the amount of recall of the story, with this relationship increasing with age. Thus, retention of information and the understanding of implied semantic relationships were related, and this relationship became stronger with development.

Piaget and Memory. We all know that memory deteriorates with time—we forget and we distort. Piaget and Inhelder (1973) discussed instances of memory actually improving over time. From Piaget's theoretical perspective, memory as a cognitive process always operates in relation to the cognitive structures of the individual. Thus, in cases of the cognitive structures critical for the memory task having changed developmentally, we should witness an improvement in the recall of that material.

To assess this proposition, Piaget and Inhelder (1973) presented 10 sticks of varying lengths to children 3–8 years of age. The sticks were presented in a serial order of longest to shortest. One week following this presentation, the children were asked to draw the sticks from memory. Knowledge of seriation predicted the accuracy of the drawings; young children (3–4) drew lines of about equal lengths, 4- to 5-year-olds drew assortments of different lengths (some with two sizes and some with three) and did not produce a seriated order, and the older children reproduced the array accurately. Six to eight months later, the children were again asked to draw the array they had seen. Interestingly, 75% of the children produced more accurate (i.e., more seriated) drawings than they had one week after presentation. Of those children who were classified as transitional to concrete operations (i.e., abilities between preoperations and concrete operations), 90% demonstrated improvement.

This finding has been replicated and extended by several researchers (see Liben, 1977). Liben (1975) showed 8-year-olds a stimulus (a crane) incorporating the concept of verticality (i.e., the wire on the crane hangs by a true vertical, not necessarily perpendicular to the ground). Two weeks later children drew pictures. Three months after the initial session, half of the children received training on the concept of verticality. Two months following training, the children again drew the crane. Of those receiving training, 40% had improved drawings, while only 14% of the untrained children improved. Providing experiences to children who do not fully comprehend but are transitional to full knowledge of the concept underlying the experiences presumably led to cognitive growth. This cognitive growth in turn influenced memory for the reconstruction of an experience that occurred prior to the training.

Strategies, or Memory as Knowing How to Know

Strategies are goal oriented, planful behaviors (Flavell, 1970); strategies devised to facilitate memory are called mnemonic strategies. Mnemonic strategies entail any potentially conscious, voluntary act employed to facilitate the remembering of information. Examples are rehearsing a telephone number prior to making the call, leaving notes for oneself, and devising codes for the organization and recall of information (e.g., ROY G BIV for the colors of the rainbow).

Developmental research on the use of mnemonic strategies constitutes the largest segment of research in the field of memory development. Again with a heavy reliance on Flavell (1977) and Kail (1979), research in this area will be presented under the headings of rehearsal and organization. It will be shown that prior to about 6 years of age the use of strategies is rare and unsystematic, that 6- to 9-year-olds are an interesting transition group who can be provoked to employ strategies but often do not do so spontaneously, and that relatively mature strategic behavior emerges consistently with 10-year-olds.

Rehearsal. Flavell, Beach, and Chinsky (1966) assessed the amount of spontaneous rehearsal of 5-, 7-, and 10-year-olds. The child's task was to point to the subset of the pictures to which the experimenter had pointed, from a set of seven pictures. The experimenter, trained in lip-reading, recorded the amount of rehearsal during a 15-second delay between presentation and responding. Across the ages tested, spontaneous rehearsal increased from 10% to 60% to 85% of the children. Even retesting 5-year-olds on five consecutive days failed to lead to much spontaneous rehearsal (Glidden, 1977).

Can we turn children into successful rehearsers? Keeney, Cannizzo, and Flavell (1967) trained a group of nonrehearsing 6- to 7-year-olds to rehearse. Training not only led to rehearsal in 75% of these children, but it also improved their recall. Following training and recall, the children were given three additional recall trials during which they were told that they could whisper and rehearse as before or they could choose not to. Interestingly, 59% of the children (10 out of 17) chose not to continue rehearsing. All of the children in the study who were initially spontaneous rehearsers continued rehearsing. This finding of the successful training of a strategy but the lack of its maintenance is a critical issue and will be expanded later.

Organization. Rehearsal strategies are but one type of mnemonic strategy. With rehearsal, the individual is applying a "brute-force" plan. A variety of more conceptually oriented memory strategies have been investigated, in which the individual searches for meaningful associations to aid in the storage and/or retrieval of information. The organization of the to-be-remembered material along semantic category lines has been extensively studied by developmental psychologists.

Moely, Olson, Halwes, and Flavell (1969) presented 5- to 11-year-olds with a set of pictures to be recalled. The pictures could be classified into such categories as animals, furniture, clothing, and vehicles, although they were displayed in a random arrangement. The children were allowed to rearrange the stimuli in any fashion prior to recall. Based on a derived clustering measure, the amount of spontaneous organization increased with age; 5- to 9-year-olds showed little clustering, 10- to 11-year-olds showed a great deal of categorization. This spontaneous organizational behavior of the older children was equaled by the younger children after they were given a brief training session. Increases in the number of items recalled accompanied the training as well.

Kobasigawa (1974) examined the use of semantic categories under different retrieval instructions. Six-, eight-, and eleven-year-olds were presented 24 items, three each of eight semantic categories. Large cards pictorially representing the categories were shown during presentation, and the relationship between the items and the cards was noted for the child. Three retrieval conditions were tested: free recall with no cues available, cued recall with the category cue cards present, and directive cued recall with items being solicited by the experimenter through the use of each category cue card in turn. The number of items recalled was very high and was comparable across all ages in the directive cued condition. Recall was much lower in the other conditions and increased with age. Only the 11-year-olds in the cued condition equalled the performance of the children in the directive cued condition. Note the now familiar pattern: Older children spontaneously use mnemonic aids; younger children often can use them but do not do so spontaneously.

Kobasigawa (1974) further examined the performance of children at each age who actually used the cue cards in the cued condition (33% of the 6-year-olds, 75% of the 8-year-olds, and 90% of the 11-year-olds). The 11-year-olds used the cues more efficiently than the younger children. That is, the older child would stay with the cue until the domain was exhausted; the younger child used the cue cards to retrieve a single item, then used the next cue. Thus, 6-year-olds did not use the conceptual cues, 11-year-olds consistently and spontaneously did, and 8-year-olds recognized the value of the strategy but employed it inefficiently.

It is interesting to note the parallels in development between rehearsal strategies and organization strategies. Both go from no use, to "can use but do not" (a so-called production deficiency), to mature use. Rehearsal seems to be mastered somewhat earlier than the organization strategies, which is not surprising given the nature of the strategy and the cognitive requirements.

Flavell (1977) noted that although the spontaneous use of any particular strategy is important, the key to the development of memory is the ability to select and monitor strategies to meet the demands of the situation. This ability is examined in the next section.

Metamemory, or Memory as Knowing about Knowing

How do you know when some mnemonic aid is called for in a situation? What strategy is best to employ? How does one assess the ongoing use of a mnemonic plan? Such questions concerning the awareness of a need to remember, the recognition of one's strengths and limitations, the influence of task variables, and the monitoring of one's strategic behavior, have been the domain of a relatively new and exceedingly popular research area known as metamemory.

Appel, Cooper, McCarrell, Sims-Knight, Yussen, and Flavell (1972) showed sets of pictures to 4-, 7-, and 11-year-olds with instructions either to remember the items or to look at the items. Recall of the items followed these instructions. Only the 11-year-olds behaved differentially as a function of instruction, remembering more items in the *remember* condition. The 7-year-olds in the *remember* condition engaged in more labeling of the items but did not recall any more items than did those in the *look* condition. This pattern of increased awareness of engaging in something extra when memory is called for has been substantiated in other studies using different methodologies (see Kail, 1979, Chapter 3). Once again, we note the progression of lack of planfulness, inefficiency, and mature planfulness in children from preschool to preadolescence.

This pattern is reiterated when examining the child's self-assessment of memory facilities. One way to determine this assessment is to ask the children to predict the length of a series of pictures that they feel they can serially recall (i.e., "Can you remember these two?, these three?" etc.). This predicted span can then be compared with their actual recall span. Preschoolers are significantly unrealistic in their predictions, second- and third-graders are a little more realistic, and fourth-graders are maturely realistic, approximating the performance of adults (Flavell, Friedrichs, & Hoyt, 1970; Yussen & Levy, 1975).

A number of task variables have been studied in terms of metamemory. Children 6 years of age know that the length of a to-be-remembered list influences memory, but they fail to recognize that lists of equal lengths may not be equally difficult to remember (Kreutzer, Leonard, & Flavell, 1975). Similarly, Moynahan (1973) found that third- and fifth-graders were aware that a list of semantically clusterable items is significantly easier to memorize than a list of nonclusterable items, while first-graders were not. Third- and fifth-graders, but not kindergarteners and first-graders, knew that verbatim recall would be more difficult than paraphrasing (Kreutzer *et al.*, 1975). Finally, 8-year-olds but not 4- or 6-year-olds varied their study habits based on a variety of stated retention interval times (Rogoff, Newcombe, & Kagan, 1974).

The last area of metamemory development to be reviewed is the self-monitoring of memory. Flavell *et al.* (1970) noted that second- and fourth-graders were better than kindergarteners at knowing when to terminate study prior to a recall task. Masur, McIntyre, and Flavell (1973) gave a multiple trial picture recall task to first- and third-graders and to adults. After each recall trial, the subject was allowed to select one-half of the pictures to study. The third-graders and adults selected for study items that they had not recalled on the recall trial; first-graders selected about as many recalled items as unrecalled items. Thus, with age, the individual can better monitor ongoing memory strategies both in assessing adequate study time and in distributing study time.

Both Flavell (1977) and Kail (1979) noted that the relationship between metamemory and the use of memory strategies is not well known. Certainly there is a causal relationship between one's analyses of the task, self-abilities, and strategy, and the use of the strategy. Clearly both these self-analyses and this use undergo significant and parallel developmental changes. Yet the link between the two is not well documented (e.g., Cavanaugh & Borkowski, 1980). Knowing about strategies will not unequivocally lead to the use of strategies. More information is required concerning the factors leading to the acquisition of metamemory knowledge and how this knowledge functions to guide strategic behavior.

Summary and Conclusions

In the previous section, the processes of selective attention and memory were briefly reviewed. Much of the discussion involved the interrelationship of these processes with other cognitive activities, more specifically, with what might be termed "higher-order" functions such as planfulness or problem solving. A useful generalization from this review is that the general strategic capacity of children will direct the operation of their cognitive processes; the operation of the processes in turn will influence the overall strategic performance of the child.

The preschool, preoperational child is not particularly planful when confronted with problem-solving situations. Attention is captured by salient perceptual features of the situation; strategies for systematically categorizing information are not typically invoked. This is a here-and-now mentality.

The concrete operational child recognizes the usefulness of strategic behavior. The difficulty for this child seems to be in the directing of this awareness. Situations are attended to in excess, often to the detriment of detail; a clear realization of the use of mnemonic activity must be present in order to provoke the child to use it.

The formal operational adolescent demonstrates highly selective attention. The problem-solving situation is attacked in a deductive fashion; that is, relevant information is sought rather than merely uncovered. Strategies are invoked quite naturally and immediately, with a tremendous flexibility in the application of strategies as the situation warrants.

In summary, whether one conceptualizes developmental change in terms of information processing rules, social learning cognitive skills, or Piagetian structures, a three-step sequence of problem-solving and strategy application emerges. First, the individual uses a less adaptive, more immediate approach to solution. Next, there is a period of instability during which external contingencies often dictate cognitive applications. Finally, a third period of more mature, better adaptive reasoning emerges. This maturity brings with it a flexibility in strategy selection and application. The timetables of this three-step progression for different strategies are, or course, different. The interdependence of these strategies and their influence on the acquisition of new strategies are in need of investigation.

APPLICATION

To this point we have considered cognitive development quite broadly. The title and introduction of this chapter suggested the promise of implications of this work for applied realms. This promise is currently more of a firm expectation than a well-formulated reality. In the present section we provide our research that begins to integrate the fields of cognitive development and child-clinical psychology along the lines suggested in the introduction.

Over the past four years, in collaboration with Andrew Meyers and others, we have examined the use of self-instruction interventions with children. These cognitive behavior modification interventions began with the work of Meichenbaum and Goodman (1971b), and were derived from a number of sources that recognized the important relationship between internal speech and problem-solving performance. Several authors suggested that verbal mediation of problem-solving behavior follows a pattern of development similar to those of attentional and memorial processes. The developing child is seen as passing through stages in which he or she (1) does not use verbal mediation to regulate behavior (Reese, 1962); (2) can use but does not spontaneously produce appropriate verbal mediation (Flavell *et al.*, 1966); and, (3) can produce verbal mediation, but does not comprehend the nature of the task in order to produce the most relevant mediators (Bem, 1970). Poor problem-solving performance can result from a deficiency at any one of these stages of development.

Luria (1961) and Vygotsky (1962) further suggested that verbal mediation of behavior followed a developmental progression from external to internal speech. They noted that internalization of verbal control is essential in the development of voluntary control of overt behavior. The influence of these various sources is clearly reflected in Meichenbaum and Goodman's (1971b) initial work, in which impulsive children rehearsed first overtly and then covertly a set of self-statements designed to remediate specific developmental strategy deficits.

The literature on self-instruction interventions is quite extensive (see Craighead *et al.*, 1978, and Meichenbaum, 1977, for reviews) and is considered in other chapters of this volume. As a starting point for a presentation of our research, it is important to note that the literature on self-instructions consistently demonstrates the efficacy of this technique for the training of a wide variety of skills; findings related to the generalization of self-instruction training have been equivocal (e.g., see Meichenbaum & Asarnow, 1979).

Generalization of training is certainly an important issue; it is rarely the case that one wishes to alter behaviors in a single context or situation. We feel that the equivocal generalization findings reported in self-instruction research (indeed, child-clinical research in general) are due to an incomplete or inadequate conceptualization of the intervention setting. The conceptualization we favor, of course, is that of Bransford (1979): characteristics of the learner, nature of the material, activities employed, and criterion measures.

Four studies will be reported. In the first three (which are presented in greater detail in Cohen & Meyers, in press), normal children served as subjects. Three aspects of the intervention setting were examined, using self-instruction: the effect of Piagetian-defined cognitive level (a "characteristic of the learner" issue), content of the self-guiding statements (a "nature of the material" issue), and delivery procedure for the instructions (an "activities" issue). Findings from these studies were applied to clinical populations and are presented in the last study.

In our first project (Schleser, Meyers, & Cohen, 1981), the content of the instructional package was varied for same-aged groups of Piagetian-defined preoperational and concrete operational children. In one condition, the child rehearsed a specific set of self-guiding statements—that is, the content of the statements was explicitly tailored to meet the demands of the training task. In another condition, the child rehearsed a set of general self-guiding statements. These statements were designed to be relevant to a wide variety of problem-solving tasks. In addition to a no-training control group, two didactic control groups were formed. Children assigned to these groups listened to but never overtly rehearsed either the specific or the general self-instruction statements.

Children who rehearsed the specific-content self-instructions demonstrated the greatest gains on the training task; the general-content instructions led to modest but not significant gains. On a generalization task, only children who rehearsed the general self-instructions improved their performance significantly. Concrete operational children outperformed preoperational children on both tasks, with the effects of training the same for both groups. Finally, children in the didactic control groups performed no better than did children in the no-training group.

Each of the major factors investigated influenced the outcome of the self-instruction training. Specific self-guiding statements aided performance on the task whose demands it mapped; these instructions did not aid the child on a different task. The general-content instructions did not immediately aid performance on a training task but did foster generalization. Concrete operational children performed at higher levels than preoperational children, an individual difference not assessed in previous self-instruction research. Finally, the active involvement of the child through the rehearsal procedure was quite beneficial relative to the more passive listening procedures.

On reflection, involvement may be conceptualized as active in a physical sense or active in a cognitive sense. The rehearsal procedure of previous self-instruction research and of the study above is certainly active in a physical sense but may not be particularly active (especially for concrete operational children) in a cognitive sense. In a second study, we further varied the delivery procedures of the instructions while keeping constant the content of instructions (specific content).

Preoperational and concrete operational children were trained using the traditional five-step, overt-to-covert fading procedures or using a directed-discovery procedure. The directed-discovery procedure used a Socratic approach. Through a programmed set of questions, the child was led to "discover" the same set of self-guiding statements rehearsed by the children in the other self-instruction group. Both self-instruction groups experienced significant improvement on the training task, with the concrete operational children being more successful overall than the preoperational children. On a generalization task, only the concrete operational children in the directed-discovery condition demonstrated significant gains.

Relevant to the issue of active cognitive involvement, we believe that the directed-discovery procedure models more for the child than just a set of self-guiding statements. Strategy generation and application are also systematically put on display. The concrete operational children have the cognitive ability to benefit from this display. Unlike the preoperational child, the concrete operational child can separate form from content and realize the benefits from this abstraction. Thus, the concrete operational child recognizes the benefit of the directed-discovery procedure apart from its benefit to the particular content of that procedure. The preoperational child focuses on the content and gleans the specific self-guiding information, but does not generalize the strategy beyond the training task.

An important consideration remains. Given that preoperational and concrete operational children both generalize from a general but not specific content of instructions (Experiment 1), and given that only concrete operational children generalize from a specific-content, directed-discovery procedure, what happens when these children receive a general-content intervention delivered through a directed-discovery procedure?

Nichol, Cohen, Meyers, and Schleser (1982) combined the general-content instructions of the first study and delivered them to same-aged preoperational and concrete operational children using a directed-discovery procedure. As in the second experiment, only the concrete operational children demonstrated significant generalization of training.

Taken together, these three experiments document the active nature of the child during learning. When considering the generalization of training, it is imperative that the learning context be constructed so as to engage the child optimally. In terms of the parameters investigated here, the preoperational child is best influenced by the rehearsal of a general set of statements that can easily be mapped onto a variety of tasks. Procedures more demanding than rehearsal (such as directed discovery) seem to be less beneficial, while procedures less demanding (such as listening only) are not engaging enough. The concrete operational child is best influenced by the demanding-strategy generation and application procedure of directed discovery. For this child, the procedure subsumes the particular content of the intervention.

Our initial work presented above demonstrates the utility of our approach to self-instructions for fostering generalization using laboratory tasks and nonclinical populations. As a more applied example of our approach, we close this section with an experiment that extends the above findings to more clinically relevant populations.

Schleser, Meyers, Thackwray, and Cohen (1981) assessed the effects of specific-content rehearsal, general-content rehearsal, and specific-content directed-discovery treatments on impulsive fourth-graders. Each child was seen four times and received a math task along with the assigned self-instruction procedure. At the conclusion of the fourth session, each child was assessed on a similar math test plus a variety of other academic tasks, using the Peabody Individual Achievement Test (PIAT). Children receiving the specific-content self-instructions improved only on the math test and the PIAT math subtest. Children in the general-content self-instruction group experienced gains on PIAT spelling, general information, and total test scores. Children in the directed-discovery group improved significantly on all of these plus the PIAT reading recognition subtest.

These results indicate that, unlike preoperational children, impulsive fourth-graders possess the requisite cognitive abilities to benefit from the more demanding directed-discovery procedure. In addition, there are multiple approaches to programming in generalization, and the various approaches differentially affect the breadth of generalization. Finally, these results suggest the need to fit the type of intervention employed to the goals of training. If the goal of training is to improve performance on a particular task in a particular situation, the faded rehearsal of a task-specific strategy is adequate. However, if the goal of training is to produce generalized improvement in behavior, more demanding training procedures such as faded rehearsal of a general strategy or directed discovery are the treatments of choice.

SUMMARY, IMPLICATIONS, AND DIRECTIONS

In this chapter we have attempted an initial interface between the fields of developmental psychology and child-clinical psychology. More specifically, we have tried to demonstrate the relevance of cognitive developmental research for interventions with children. Obviously, we have discussed scant portions of these two very rich domains. This being the case, our goal has been to provoke some additional union of these fields. In closing, several points are stressed.

1. Descriptions of the child's executive functioning have taken many forms: elementary information-processing rules, cognitive structures, cognitive skills, metacognition. The theoretical bases underlying these conceptualizations will certainly have an impact on treatment and research activities. Yet each of these formulations emphasizes an active participant model of the individual. A child, like an adult, is an interpreter and not a mere recorder of experience. Children at different cognitive levels will in fact view the world differently. Simple dilution of adult treatment models for use with children is not satisfactory. Needless to say, this active participant position (from all three theoretical orientations) points to the inadequacy of strictly using chronological age as an assessment of cognitive functioning.

2. Much of what is involved in clinical work can be viewed as prompting an individual to adopt different strategies for mediating behavior. Recall the Keeney *et al.* (1967) finding that 6- and 7-year-old nonrehearsers could be taught to rehearse but stopped using rehearsal following training. Kennedy and Miller (1976) replicated this study with one additional component: One group of nonrehearsers receiving rehearsal training also received feedback concerning the effectiveness of the strategy. These children continued to employ the strategy beyond training, while those not receiving feedback did not. Thus, the provision of metamemorial information facilitated the maintenance of the strategy. To reiterate the often-cited sequence—strategy use develops through lack of use to a transition phase to mature use. Interventions should differ for children who lack a particular strategy and for children who have the strategy but fail to apply it. The developmental timetables for different strategies will vary as well. Thus, practitioners must be aware of the developmental implications of the strategies they are training in terms of the child's position both in the sequence of strategy use and with relation to other prerequisite skills and strategies.

3. Not only do we want our interventions to continue in use (a maintenance issue), but we also want them to apply in appropriate similar contexts (a generalization issue). A variety of plans to foster generalization have been offered. Kendall (1977) proposed four politices. First, he advocated the use of contingent incentives along with self-instruction training. He also recommended designing the training session to resemble the potential generalization settings as closely as

possible. Third, the content of self-instructions should be "child-produced" in style. Fourth, Kendall advocated the use of conceptual over concrete instructions (the same distinction we made concerning specific versus general content).

Bransford (1979) suggested that a good way to promote the generalization of a concept is to train the concept in multiple contexts. Thus, providing a child with multiple tasks to exercise a strategy should promote generalizaion better than restricting training to just one task.

Finally, our research suggests that perhaps we should take Kendall (1977) and Bransford (1979) a step further—not only give mutiple tasks, conceptual rules, etc., but also give the child training in the adaptation of a strategy. Demonstrate for the child how to analyze similarities and differences and the effects of these analyses on the strategy to-be-applied.

The reader should note that this discussion of generalization presupposes adherence to the issues presented in the first two points. The strategy one adopts to foster generalization will be dictated directly by assessments of cognitive functioning from a developmental perspective.

4. An obvious but often overlooked distinction must be made: the distinction between a technique and the interpretation of the effects of that technique. It is often the case that one inappropriately implies the other. To say that operant conditioning works to change a child's behavior does not mean that the child is best conceptualized as an S–R organism. No theory of cognition, to our knowledge, denies that behavior is influenced by environmental contingencies. Rather, the interpretation of the effects involves a recognition of the individual's capacities in interaction with those contingencies. If a child's behavior is modified through operant conditioning, we would choose to analyze those effects in terms of the individual's recognition of (hypotheses about) the environment and his or her behavior in that environment.

5. Related to point number 4, we feel that the role allocated to speech in the self-control of behavior is somewhat exaggerated. Much of cognition involves nonverbal thought. Like Flavell (1977), we would urge investigation of the nonverbal components that underlie self-control. Self-instruction researchers acknowledge that strategies become automatic when truly internalized. What produces this automaticity? What is the nature of this fluid control? What besides talking to oneself is involved? How does the automatic control of a set of strategies influence the acquisition of novel strategies?

6. As a final point, we are advocating a significant new direction in the research and treatment of children. How many child-clinical research projects are performed with a single age group and/or a single

target group? How many articles are there in the child-clinical literature that examine developmental sequences? We suspect that there are very few. Traditional child-clinical research is valuable. We contend that an equally valuable direction would be what we would term developmental-clinical research. Acknowledgment of age-related trends in relation to treatment modes and intervention outcomes would prove to be of invaluable service to the child clinician or educator.

4

Family Systems

CONCEPTUALIZING CHILD PROBLEMS WITHIN THE FAMILY CONTEXT

Hillary Turkewitz

Recurring clinical observations of the family's negative impact on the process and outcome of child psychotherapy led to the development of a family therapy model proposing that ongoing family interactions are the major determinant of a child's behavior. The widespread acceptance of this model is reflected in the recent explosion in the number of conferences and publications on marital and family therapy (Gurman & Kniskern, 1978). The growth in the field is also reflected in the increasing number of research investigations of the relationship between childhood behavior problems and family interaction patterns. Unfortunately, much of this research has not been tied to specific family theories (Olson, 1970).

This chapter provides a summary of the major theories that relate child problems and family context. A review of the literature highlights research evidence that is directly relevant to the theories outlined. The potential for integration of the theories is discussed, and the clinical implications of a family systems perspective are presented.

FAMILY THEORIES

Although the basic tenet of all systems theories is that the family or interpersonal context (rather than intrapsychic factors) is the critical vari-

Hillary Turkewitz • Greater Lawrence Psychological Center, Inc., 36 Lawrence Street, Lawrence, Massachusetts 01840.

able determining an individual's behavior, there are several major schools of family systems theorists. These schools differ with regard to the emphasis placed on the nature of communication, the structure of the relationships, and the level of individual functioning. Three major perspectives—the communication theories developed at the Mental Research Institute in Palo Alto, Murray Bowen's family theory, and Salvador Minuchin's model of structural family therapy—are presented.

The development of social learning or behavioral theories of family functioning has not been characterized by the emergence of various schools. Those aspects of social learning theory particularly relevant to family interactions are reviewed, as are the major contributions of Gerald Patterson and his associates at the Oregon Research Institute.

Communication Theories

The communication or interactional model of family systems is exemplified by the work of Gregory Bateson, Jay Haley, Don Jackson, Virginia Satir, and Paul Watzlawick. The family is conceptualized as a rule-governed system; distress is frequently caused by a conflict over what the rules are and who is to make them (Haley, 1963; Jackson, 1965). A struggle over the definition of the relationships can affect every family interaction, since (a) all behavior is communicative—"One cannot not communicate" (Watzlawick, Beavin, & Jackson, 1967, p. 49), and (b) every communication has a "command" aspect, which defines the nature of the relationship. The content of communication is labeled the "report" aspect.

A family's interaction can become dysfunctional when the members confuse the report and command levels of communication; they argue about content when the conflict lies in the relational aspect of communication. An example of this confusion is the adolescent son and his father who have endless, unproductive arguments about the completion of chores, when the actual source of conflict is their disagreement about authority, or who is to set the rules. Many family rules, such as those regarding the degree of parental authority, should change over time. A family's inability to negotiate a change in these rules can be reflected in the development of behavioral or emotional problems in one of its members. These problems, or "symptoms," are viewed as important albeit indirect forms of communication.

As well as having communicational value, a child's symptomatology is viewed as serving the function of maintaining stability in the family system. Child problems are seen as providing an outlet for family stress or a shift in focus away from marital tensions (Harbin, 1977).

Vogel and Bell (1968) argued that a disturbed child is often serving the role of a scapegoat; parents can externalize their marital conflict by focusing negative feelings and blame on the child. It has been posited that behavior that amplifies deviance on one level of the family system (e.g., symptoms in a child), often serves to inhibit deviance on another level (e.g., marital conflict; Hoffman, 1971). This interdependence of family problems has been conceptualized as a homeostatic process. Family members react to one another in ways that maintain the status quo. As an example, consider a family in which the parents maintain interpersonal distance from each other through arguments about their acting-out child. If the child's behavior changes and the parents are threatened by the prospect of greater intimacy, they can subvert that change by ignoring the progress or placing greater stress on the child. Similarly, a child who enjoys a close relationship with one parent by virtue of siding with that parent during marital arguments can attempt to instigate conflict if the parents move toward reconciliation. This latter example indicates that communication theorists do not view the child solely as a passive victim of family conflict. In contrast to a view of child psychopathology as resulting from a linear causal chain moving from parents to child, these theorists posit circular causality and reciprocal influences in the process of the development of family conflict.

Another key concept of communication theorists is that of metacommunication, or the process of stepping back from the ongoing interaction and talking directly about the communication. It is argued that if struggling family members do not metacommunicate, their interactions can become increasingly confused. Ambiguous and/or conflicting messages are likely to lead to an exacerbation of behavior problems. The "double bind" (Bateson, Jackson, Haley, & Weakland, 1956) is offered as the classic example of a pathology-inducing interactional sequence. An individual is repeatedly exposed to a contradictory communication and is prevented from commenting on the contradiction. A pathological response (e.g., psychotic behavior) is viewed as one way of escaping the bind.

In addition to the importance of communication clarity and consistency, the need for appropriate problem-solving skills has been emphasized. Watzlawick, Weakland, and Fisch (1974) detailed the major ways in which problems are mishandled: Action is not taken when necessary, primarily because the family denies the existence of a problem; action is taken when it should not be, either because the individuals fail to see that change is impossible or because they have unrealistic expectations; and action is taken at the wrong level, often because the family members are focused on the content of their disagreements rather than on the process of their relationships and the way these relationships are defined.

Bowen's Family Theory

The major interactional concept of Bowen's family theory is that the triangle is the basic "building block" of emotional systems (Bowen, 1966, 1976). The triangle is viewed as the most stable relationship; it is predicted that the members of a dyad threatened by anxiety and instability will move to involve a third party. When the dyad consists of spouses and they draw one of their children into a triangle, emotional or behavioral problems often result. Once the dysfunctional triangle is established, family conflict intensifies as the parents react negatively to each other's emotional investment in the child and the child struggles for a favorable or comfortable position in the triad. The alliances shift continually, as does the composition of the conflictual dyadic relationship (Kerr, 1981). A symptomatic child is seen as potentially serving the function of regulating distance between his or her parents by becoming a go-between (Byng-Hall, 1980).

The similarity between the foregoing analysis and aspects of communication theory is clear. A major distinguishing aspect of Bowen's theory is the emphasis he places on the "differentiation of self." *Differentiation* refers to the degree to which an individual's emotional responses and intellectual functioning are independent. A poorly differentiated individual is one whose affective or emotional reactions interfere with his or her intellectual functioning and problem-solving. The degree of differentiation of an individual will affect the degree of fusion or individuality maintained in his or her family relationships. Poorly differentiated spouses will experience more anxiety in marriage because their marriages tend to be characterized by extreme dependency, in which a move toward independence by either spouse will often lead to an immediate negative reaction. The four mechanisms these spouses use to reduce marital tension are: distancing from one another; engaging in intense overt conflict to regulate closeness and distance; having one spouse compromise him- or herself to a submissive position; and/or focusing on a child. It is the last strategy that will often result in behavioral problems in the child. Couples who do not focus on, or "triangle" in, other family members can maintain a highly conflictual marital relationship without having a negative impact on the children.

Bowen stresses the etiological significance of the quality of the relationship with one's family of origin, arguing that unresolved issues often interfere with successful functioning in the nuclear family and lead to psychopathological problems. He describes a multigenerational transmission process, through which similar interactional styles and levels of interpersonal differentiation are transmitted across generations.

Minuchin's Model of Structural Family Therapy

A basic axiom of structural family therapy is that a change in family structure contributes to behavior change (Minuchin, 1974). While communication and Bowen's theories focus on sequential interactions, Minuchin's model places much more emphasis on structure, or spatial patterning in families (Steinglass, 1978). The lack of clear, well-defined boundaries between different subsystems in the family is viewed as a major determinant of child problems. In particular, the need for boundaries clearly separating the parent and child generations is stressed.

A second destructive structural configuration, often occuring in the context of diffuse boundaries, is the existence of rigid alignments. Common dysfunctional coalitions include stable coalitions, detouring coalitions, and triangulation (Aponte & VanDeusen, 1981). All three of these coalitions can be viewed as "triangles," in Bowen's theory. A stable coalition is an inflexible alliance between two family members against another. In distressed families this coalition often occurs between a parent and child, thus violating the marital subsystem boundary. In a detouring coalition, parents submerge their conflict by aligning with each other either to attack (e.g., as a scapegoat) or to help their child. Triangulation involves hostile parents demanding that the child choose sides between them.

A specific model of structural family therapy describing families with psychosomatic children has been proposed (Minuchin, Baker, Rosman, Liebman, Milman, & Todd, 1975). The four primary transactional characteristics of families with psychosomatic children are: enmeshment, or intrusion and lack of privacy; overprotectiveness; rigidity in interactional patterns; and a lack of conflict resolution. It is argued that these characteristics encourage somatization. In describing a circular causal model, Minuchin *et al.* noted that the child's initial input to the development of the psychosomatic problem is in the form of a physiological vulnerability. Once the illness develops, the child is reinforced for symptomatic behavior through the reduction in family conflict that occurs when the parents "detour" their marital tension to deal with the child. The child's involvement in parental conflict is seen as a key factor supporting the symptom. The ability to regulate family stability and conflict and the reinforcing value of parental attention are powerful motivational variables. A child's symptom is viewed as both system maintained and system maintaining.

In all families, the major influence on functioning is the quality of the structure of the system; such characteristics as cohesiveness and the definition or clarity of the subsystem hierarchy are of particular importance. When the current structure is inadequate or when the family is stressed, a key variable predictive of adjustment is the level of flexibility or rigidity displayed (Aponte & VanDeusen, 1981).

Behavioral Theory of Family Interactions

The importance of the family has always been assumed by behavioral theorists, in that the child's behavior is viewed as the result of contingencies operating in his or her social environment (Wilson & O'Leary, 1980). Most applications of social learning theory to child problems focus solely on ways in which the parents act upon the child, rather than on ways in which the child and parents interact with each other. The major concepts include the importance of consistent positive reinforcement for appropriate behavior, the potentially negative effects of punishment, the process of behavior shaping, and the necessity for a careful analysis of the parental behaviors that are serving as both discriminative stimuli and maintaining consequences for problem child behavior. In addition to social learning through direct consequences, vicarious learning through modeling is posited to be an important determinant of behavior patterns.

The introduction of the concepts of reciprocity and coercion marked a shift from a sole focus on parent-initiated attempts at change to an emphasis on interaction in the family system (Patterson & Reid, 1970; Patterson, Cobb, & Ray, 1973). Reciprocity is defined as the tendency for two individuals to exchange pleasing and aversive behaviors, or to reward and punish each other, at similar rates. The coercion process involves the family members' use of aversive stimuli rather than positive reinforcement strategies to effect changes in each other. The coercion process can be initiated by a demand for immediate behavior change that is met with noncompliance (Patterson & Hops, 1972). Once the process is initiated, two factors increase the likelihood of an escalation of family conflict. The aversive control strategy will be reinforced by the immediate desired response obtained—for example, the parent pays attention to the child when he or she screams, or the children stop fighting when the parent screams. In addition, as noted above, the aversive stimuli are likely to be exchanged at a reciprocal rate, so that a child experiencing frequent punishment is likely to be increasingly punitive toward his or her parents.

The relationships between family members are shaped through mutual training (Margolin, 1981). Child problems and family conflict are viewed as the result of a counterproductive training process in which family members use misguided behavior-change or problem solving-strategies.

Comparative Review of Family Theories

There are clear similarities among the theories presented. In the three systems theories, the child's problems are viewed as functional in the family system, either as a means of communication, a stabilizing factor, or a mechanism for reducing marital tensions. In addition, these theoretical approaches underscore the significance of anxiety or conflict in the marital relationship in the etiology and/or maintenance of child problems. While this view is not inconsistent with behavioral theory, the latter does not explicitly address the influence of the parent-to-parent relationship. All of the theorists discuss the concept of reciprocal influences and child effects on interaction, in terms of circular causality, the interdependence of behavior in members of a triangle, and reciprocity.

Both communication and behavioral theorists discuss faulty change strategies and problem-solving techniques. Watzlawick *et al.*'s (1967) discussion of the difficulties created by unrealistic expectations is clearly similar to cognitive behavioral theorists' descriptions of the negative impact of irrational assumptions (Gurman, 1978). The similarity between these two schools is apparently increasing, as more recent developments in family theory have involved the integration of behavioral and systems concepts (Alexander, Haas, Klein, & Warburton, 1980; Linehan & Rosenthal, 1979).

The communication theory is distinct from the other approaches in the emphasis placed on family rules, power struggles over who is to set rules, and the dysfunctional communication and problem-solving style of families with problem children. Minuchin's model stresses the need for clear boundaries around the marital subsystem and highlights particular patterns of dysfunctional parent–child alliances. Bowen introduced the concept of triangles as stable interacting systems. He also stressed the intrapsychic functioning of the individual, apparently drawing on psychoanalytic theory and applying it cross-generationally (Gurman, 1978). The behavioral theorists focus on both social learning and strategies of control, outlining a coercive process and highlighting heightened aversiveness and negativity as etiological and exacerbating factors in child problems.

As noted in the introduction, much of the research on family interaction patterns is not tied to explicit theoretical formulations. Those studies that do address significant theoretical issues or that directly test the validity of particular concepts are included in the following review. No controlled research projects have investigated the communication theorists' concept of family rules, or Bowen's concepts of triangles, differentiation of self, and the transmission of transactional styles across generations. Thus, the following areas will be reviewed: the function or role of the child's problem in the family, the relationship between marital discord and child problems, family interactions associated with child problems, and child effects on family interaction.

THE ROLE OF CHILD PROBLEMS IN THE FAMILY

The most dramatic evidence indicating that children can become involved in a "detouring" process that reduces parental anxiety is found in Minuchin, Rosman, and Baker's (1978) study of chemical changes that occur during children's observations of and interactions with their parents. The authors measured the level of free fatty acids (FFA) in the blood of both parents and children during a sequence of problem-oriented discussions. The level of FFA is an indication of emotional arousal; increased levels lead to acidosis in diabetic children. The responses of families with psychosomatic diabetic children (those whose diabetes could not be controlled with insulin) were compared with those of familiies with controlled diabetics, with and without behavioral problems. The psychosomatic children had a much higher increase in FFA levels when observing their parents' conflicts through a one-way mirror. Of particular interest are the observations that when the psychosomatic child was brought into the room with the parents, (a) the parents stopped interacting with each other and focused almost exclusively on the child, and (b) the parent with the higher FFA level showed a decrease in this level, while the child's FFA level continued to rise. The families of controlled diabetics did not display these patterns. Thus, the introduction of the child into the interaction resulted in a decrease in the parents' emotional arousal, to the detriment of the child's physical state.

Structural family therapists have discussed their clinical observation that when the child's problem improves, the marital conflict surfaces (Liebman, Minuchin, & Baker, 1974; Stanton & Todd, 1976). Currently there are no research data supporting this observation. Oltmanns, Broderick, and O'Leary (1977) reported no significant changes in marital satisfaction following treatment of child problems. However, a difficulty in applying these data to an analysis of the structural model (which plagues most attempts to integrate the family interaction research) is the difference in diagnostic categories of the samples. Oltmanns *et al.* did not specify the percentage of psychosomatic children in their sample, but noted that most of the children would have been labeled as unsocialized aggressive or withdrawn. Detouring could be expected to occur more often in families with a physically ill child, particularly in the form of concern about the illness.

Evidence consistent with the view that some children serve as family scapegoats is provided by those studies that find a tremendous overlap and/or a lack of significant differences between the rates of clinic and nonclinic children's problem behavior (Bugental, Love, & Kaswan, 1972; Lobitz & Johnson, 1975). (Throughout this chapter, the term "clinic" will be used to describe those children or families in therapy at child guidance, mental health, or psychological centers; nonclinic families are those drawn from a general community or school population.) Eyberg and Johnson (1974) found that 41% of referred children displayed rates of deviant behavior that were below the norm. Observational data suggest that the deviant or aggressive behavior of the referred child may be no different from that of his or her siblings (Arnold, Levine, & Patterson, 1975; Patterson *et al.*, 1973). These data indicate that the process by which one particular child is referred for therapy, or identified as the "patient," is not simply a function of disturbed behavior. Vogel and Bell (1968) discussed several hypotheses regarding this selection process: Birth order or physical appearance may play an important role in some families, or one of the children may display behavior that is of particular significance to either parent—for instance, if achievement-related issues present a conflict in the marriage, an underachieving or extremely bright child may be focused upon.

Parents' perceptions of a child's behavior, rather than behavioral ratings, are the best predictor of whether a child is brought to a child clinic; these perceptions and behavioral ratings are not highly correlated (Lobitz & Johnson, 1975). It has also been reported that clinic parents overestimate the frequency of their child's problem behavior (Martin, 1977), and that parents' attitudes regarding their child's problem do not necessarily change even when the child's behavior changes significantly (Peed, Roberts, & Forehand, 1977). Some of the differences found between parents' reports and observational data could be due to methodological variables—for example, biased self-report to obtain clinic services or sampling bias resulting from brief observations during which the child does not engage in the low-frequency, severe behaviors that affect parents' attitudes. There are several possible explanations for these findings, in addition to methodological considerations and the theory of scapegoating. Clinic parents may have a lower tolerance for a child's acting out (Shepherd, Oppenheim, & Mitchell, 1966), may lack information regarding normal development, or may lack basic child-management skills. The existing data do not indicate the causal variables. However, the importance of familial factors is underscored by the evidence concerning physiological changes in psychosomatic children and their parents and by the finding that referral decisions and parental attitudes are not always determined by child behavior.

THE RELATIONSHIP BETWEEN MARITAL DISCORD AND CHILD PROBLEMS

The foregoing discussion centered on the possibility that the development of behavioral or emotional problems in children reflects a family's need to increase stability or reduce tension in the marital relationship. A review of the literature will demonstrate, however, that in many families there is a significant association between child psychopathology and marital dissatisfaction. Thus, while child problems may serve to maintain stability, they are often associated with an increased, rather than decreased, level of marital discord.

In families with young children, relationships have been found between parents' self-reports of their marital satisfaction and school personnel's identification of problem children (Love & Kaswan, 1974), observer ratings of deviant child behavior (Johnson & Lobitz, 1974), and mothers' ratings of their children (Emery & O'Leary, 1979; Klein & Shulman, 1980; Porter & O'Leary, 1980). Interviewer ratings of marital dissatisfaction were significantly related to parents', teachers', and physicians' global ratings of child adjustment (Whitehead, 1979); to mothers' reports of child problems (Rutter, Yule, Quinton, Rowlands, Yule, & Berger, 1974); and to observers' ratings of boys' aggressiveness (McCord, McCord, & Howard, 1961). Parents of clinic children report significantly less satisfaction with their marriages than do parents of nonclinic children (Oltmanns *et al.*, 1977; Wolff & Acton, 1968).

Adolescents whose parents experience marital discord have been found to exhibit more behavior problems (Duncan, 1971; Rutter, Graham, Chadwick, & Yule, 1976) and report lower self-esteem (Matteson, 1974). Undergraduate students who rated their parents' marriage as unhappy also rated themselves as more rebellious (Balswick & Macrides, 1975); depression inventory scores of undergraduate women were significantly related to their ratings of their parents' degree of conflict (Schwarz & Zuroff, 1979).

There is some reason to be cautious in interpreting results from studies using only one data source (usually the parent), since Rutter *et al.* (1974) found a significant relationship only between mothers' reports of marital satisfaction and child problems, and not between mothers' marital reports and teacher ratings. In addition, the data from undergraduates are less compelling than are those from younger children, since such data are based on retrospective reports easily subject to bias. However, it is clear that the argument for a significant relationship between marital discord and child problems has been supported with several data sources (e.g., parents, teachers, children) and various assessment methods (e.g., interview, questionnaire, observation).

Parameters of the Relationship between Marital Discord and Child Problems

Type of Conflict and Type of Child Problem

Porter and O'Leary (1980) studied the correlations between maternal ratings of child behavior problems and maternal reports of (a) the frequency of overt marital hostility and (b) overall marital satisfaction. They found that the report of overt hostility was a better predictor of child problems than was the measure of marital satisfaction. Consistent with this finding, Rutter and his associates reported that child problems were more highly associated with marital tension and overt hostility than with apathy and indifference (Rutter *et al.*, 1974) or lack of warmth (Rutter, 1975). However, a study by Emery and O'Leary (1979) yielded contradictory results, in that the general marital satisfaction measure was correlated with the ratings of behavior problems, but the measure of overt hostility was not.

Although some investigators found that marital conflict was associated with anxiety-related problems in children (e.g., Whitehead, 1979), a clear majority of the research reveals marital conflict to be predictive of aggression, delinquency, conduct disorder, and acting-out behavior.

Age and Sex of the Child

As can be seen from the preceding review, there is evidence of the relationship between discord and child problems in studies of children of all ages. Investigators who have studied age effects directly have not found differences between age groups (Emery, 1981). There are fairly consistent findings, however, regarding sex differences, indicating that boys demonstrate more problems than girls (Block, Block, & Morrison, 1980; Emery & O'Leary, 1979; Porter & O'Leary, 1980; Rutter, 1971).

Theoretical Explanations

Before discussing theoretical explanations of the relationship between child problems and marital discord, an examination of a potentially significant mediating variable is in order. One could argue that the psychopathology of a parent, which frequently covaries with marital discord, is the factor accounting for the observed relationship. Rutter (1971) examined this possibility and found that when there was a good marriage, significant psychopathology of a parent was not related to child problems. He concluded that marital discord was the more important factor in determining the existence of child problems. Emery, Neale, and Weintraub (cited in Emery, 1981) replicated this finding in families with a parent who displayed an affective disorder. However, marital discord was not the mediating variable in families with a schizophrenic parent. Thus, with the exception of schizophrenia, available evidence indicates the primary significance of the interactional variable (marital discord) rather than the intrapersonal one (psychopathology of a parent).

The data on the relevance of open conflict and the frequent occurrence of acting-out problems are consistent with the behavioral theory of modeling. Hostile spouses who fight in front of their children provide aggressive models. Emery (1981), in reviewing this literature, noted evidence that boys are more likely to imitate aggressive behavior than are girls; this sex difference in modeling effects may account for the research indicating a stronger relationship between discord and conduct problems for boys than for girls.

Minuchin's description of triangulation is also consistent with the data on open conflict, since the parents in these marriages are more likely to prompt the child actively to "take sides." There is clearly not a one-to-one relationship between open hostility and child problems, since not all children from such marriages display problems. Perhaps a combination of modeling effects and triangulation increases the likelihood of acting out. No research investigations currently address this possibility.

The modeling hypothesis proposes an indirect effect, in the sense that the critical factor is observational learning, not changes in interpersonal relationships. Another hypothesis regarding indirect effects is that knowledge of marital conflict is stressful to the child, regardless of the nature of the parent–child interactions. Emery and O'Leary (1979) found that a measure of boys' perceptions of marital conflict was a better predictor of parent-rated child behavior problems than was the parents' report of marital dissatisfaction. Awareness of conflict could induce anxieties regarding anticipated loss, presumed responsibility for the conflict, and the safety of oneself and one's parents.

The hypothesis of triangulation supposes a direct effect, positing that marital conflict produces a change in parent–child relations. Another form of direct effect would be differences in discipline practices between satisfied and discordant couples. Rutter (1975), in reviewing research on the impact of varying methods of discipline, concluded that the only two factors consistently associated with increased aggression or acting out were (a) the frequency of punishment and (b) inconsistency between parents.

It has been reported that marital hostility is related to a high use of punishment and a low use of reasoning (Dielman, Barton, & Cattell, 1977). Johnson and Lobitz (1974) found a significant relationship between self-reports of marital satisfaction and observations of parents' negative behavior. In an interesting analogue study, Zussman (1980) found that giving a parent a cognitive task that competed with attending to the children resulted in an increase in criticism and punishment to toddlers and a decrease in positive interactions with preschoolers. If a parent distracted by a neutral task becomes more negative, it is certainly possible that a parent concerned or preoccupied with marital stress would do the same. It is also likely that children would escalate the intensity of their acting out in the presence of a distracted or unattending parent. In this scenario, both parent and child would be contributing to the coercion process that Patterson and Reid (1970) described.

In a study of retrospective reports of early socialization experiences, it was found that parental disagreement on child discipline, and not the level of general parental disagreement, discriminated between clinic and nonclinic children (Oleinick, Bahn, Eisenberg, & Lilienfeld, 1966). Block *et al.* (1980) found that the degree of agreement in child-rearing practices reported when children were 3 years old was a significant predictor of boys' autonomy and appropriate affect one year later and of their task orientation four years later. It is likely that ongoing discord is often associated with disagreements about child rearing. Block *et al.* found that the level of these disagreements was significantly associated with martial status (i.e., divorced or together) 10 years later. Thus, inconsistency or disagreement between parents and frequency of punishment, which are the two child-rearing factors that have a demonstrated association with acting-out problems in children (Rutter, 1975), are correlates of marital discord.

A clear relationship has been demonstrated between marital conflict and certain child problems. An increase in aggressive, acting-out behaviors may reflect a modeling process. Boys may demonstrate more effects because they imitate aggressive models. It is also possible that boys play a different role in marital conflict, or that the perceived threat of loss of father (since father is more likely to leave the children's home than mother in the event of a divorce) affects boys more than girls. However, it would certainly be premature to conclude that girls are not reactive to marital discord. The absence of a strong demonstrated relationship between girls' problems and discord could be due to (a) greater societal sanctions against acting out in girls and more difficulty in measuring anxiety-related problems—for example, Whitehead's (1979) finding that girls in discordant homes were rated as more sensitive and high strung than boys; (b) differences in the clinic referral process for boys and girls—for example, greater teacher attention to boys' acting out; and (c) a delay in the effect on girls—for example, Schwarz and Zuroff's (1979) data on increased depression in female undergraduates from discordant homes.

In sum, in addition to modeling, the direct relational processes and indirect stress effects that have been hypothesized to account for the findings include anxiety about threatened loss; stress induced by feelings of responsibility; pressure to choose between parents, or triangulation; a coercion process in which a child increases demands on a negative, preoccupied parent; and inconsistent punitive discipline practices.

FAMILY INTERACTION RESEARCH

The research comparing interaction patterns in families with children who have different diagnostic labels has been thoroughly reviewed by several authors, who covered both substantive findings and methodological issues (e.g., Doane, 1978; Frank, 1965; Jacob, 1975; Olson, 1972; Riskin & Faunce, 1972). Hence, the following discussion is not an exhaustive review, but highlights findings relevant to the theories that have been presented.

Given the number of studies that have been conducted, particularly since the 1950s, relatively few reliable, consistent differences have been found. Although the research has become increasingly sophisticated, serious methodological problems interfere with a clear-cut interpretation of much of the data. There are major difficulties that arise when comparing across studies, and even across groups within studies, that are caused by poorly defined, potentially unreliable, and overly general diagnostic criteria. Additional potential sources of bias include measures without demonstrated reliability or validity, interviewers or raters who are not blind as to diagnostic label, uncontrolled and/or unreported group differences in age and sex of child, differences between families who agree to participate in research and those who do not (Wild, Shapiro, & Abelin, 1974), and the negative effects on parents of being observed with regard to their child's pathology (Schopler & Liftin, 1969). The problems noted necessitate caution in interpreting the data. Nevertheless, certain findings have been replicated in sufficiently well-designed studies so that conclusions can be drawn with a reasonable degree of certainty.

Communication Patterns

Clarity

The research indicates that families with a schizophrenic child have less clear communication patterns than do controls, in terms of attentional adequacy, acknowledgment, and a focus on others' opinions (Jacob, 1975). Comparisons involving less seriously disturbed children do not reveal consistent differences. Similarly, much of the research that has been designed to investigate the concept of the "double bind" (Bateson *et al.*, 1956) as pathology-inducing has also yielded nonsignificant differences between groups (e.g., Beakel & Mehrabian, 1969; Haley, 1968). While there is some evidence regarding ambiguity in communication that can be interpreted as indirect support of the double bind concept, serious efforts to operationalize and validate the concept have been fraught with difficulties and null results (Mishler & Waxler, 1965; Olson, 1972). In summary, communication theorists' predictions regarding greater ambiguity in the interactions of families with problem children have been confirmed only in correlational studies of families with a schizophrenic member. Given the lack of significant contrasts in less disturbed families, the question must be raised as to whether the differences observed in families with a schizophrenic child reflect a common family process or the effect a psychotic child would have on any interaction. Some research that has been conducted supports the latter interpretation—that is, that a child's effect is the determining variable (Liem, 1974). It is most likely that the observed correlation is determined by both parent and child effects.

Negative and Positive Interactions

The prediction that clinic families will be more negative and less positive in their communication patterns than nonclinic families has received more consistent support in the literature than has any other communication-related hypothesis (Doane, 1978; Jacob, 1975; Linehan & Rosenthal, 1979; Riskin & Faunce, 1972). For example, Alexander (1973) found more defensive (dogmatic, threatening, controlling) and less supportive (empathic) communication in the families of delinquent youths. Snyder (1977) found that families with problem children displayed twice as much negative behavior as did families without a problem child, and that the higher rates were observed in both the problem child and his or her parents. Given that increased negativity and aversiveness are likely outcomes of a coercion process, these data are consistent with such a concept. Also relevant is Snyder's finding that in verbal interactions of families without a problem child, an aversive consequence decelerated the rate of displeasing behavior. In problem families, however, an aversive consequence increased the probability of a recurrence of displeasing behavior. These data indicating an "exchange" of aversive consequences in problem families suggest reciprocity of negative behaviors. Studies of marital interaction have indicated a similar process, in which distressed couples are apparently more likely to reciprocate aversive behaviors than are nondistressed couples (Gottman, Notarius, Markman, Bank, Yoppi, & Rubin, 1976).

In addition to the observed difference in response to aversiveness, Snyder found that although members of families without a problem child provided pleasing consequences for positive behavior and aversive consequences for negative behavior, members of problem families did not consistently respond to each other in this way. Thus, nonproblem families interact in a manner consistent with a successful behavior-shaping process. Positive affect is reinforced and likely to increase. Problem family members, on the other hand, exchange aversive behaviors, so that in these systems it is negative affect that is likely to increase.

Problem-Solving and Decision-Making

Nonclinic families have demonstrated more efficient problem-solving, as indicated by time taken to make a decision (Ferreira & Winter,

1965), time needed to complete an experimental task (Mossige, Pettersen, & Blakar, 1979), and amount of information exchanged in problem-solving discussions (Ferreira & Winter, 1968).

Additionally, nonclinic family members apparently compromise more with each other. Using the Revealed Differences Technique (Strodtbeck, 1951), an investigator determines individual family member's opinions or preferences and then asks the family to make a group decision. The percentage of group decisions that match an individual's preferences indicates the degree to which there is a more even distribution of accomodation (and therefore, compromise) across family members (Ferreira & Winter, 1965; Mead & Campbell, 1972).

The previously discussed finding of increased aversiveness in families with a problem child is relevant to problem-solving, in that the negative behavior observed often occurs within the context of a problem-solving task. It can be concluded that clinic families, when faced with a problem, are less efficient, less accommodating, and more negative than nonclinic families. Vincent, Weiss, and Birchler (1975) reported that spouses in unhappy marriages demonstrated productive problem-solving skills when interacting with strangers but not with each other, indicating that the faulty problem-solving in distressed families is a function of the interactional process in the system, and is not a skill deficit in any of the members.

Parental Dominance Patterns

Decision-making tasks have frequently been employed to study dominance patterns. Given clinical lore regarding the "lethal" combination of a dominant mother and passive father, much research has been directed toward investigating the pathological effects of this constellation. The evidence does not support this long-standing clinical hypothesis; the most frequent finding is of no differences in dominance patterns between families with and without a problem child (Doane, 1978; Duncan, 1971; Rutter, 1975). However, Gassner and Murray (1969) reported an interesting interaction between parental dominance and the sex of the problem child. They too found no overall differences in paternal/maternal dominance or dominance discrepancy. They did find, though, that within the clinic sample, the boys were from mother-dominant homes while the girls were from father-dominant homes. Given that (a) many of the nonclinic children also came from homes where the opposite-sex parent was dominant, and (b) the clinic parents displayed greater hostility, the authors hypothesized that the combination of cross-sex dominance and overt hostility is a key precipitant of the child problems. They propose that if parents are overtly hostile, it becomes more difficult to identify with the same-sex role model if that model is submissive in the marriage. The resulting sex-role conflict would then increase the likelihood of child problems.

Family Structure

There is evidence indicating a lack of hierarchical ordering in family interactions in clinic families. Schuham (1972) found that nonclinic parents talked significantly more than their children but that this parent–child difference did not exist in clinic families. Similarly, Murrell and Stachowiak (1967) found that more statements were addressed to the parents than to the two children present in nonclinic families, but not in the clinic sample. Consistent with Minuchin's hypothesis regarding the need for boundaries, it appears that clinic families may lack a parental subsystem of heightened status. A demonstration of hierarchical differences between clinic and nonclinic families, in addition to these data indicating a parental subsystem in only the nonclinic group, would provide considerably more support for the hypothesis.

There is conflicting evidence regarding the nature of coalitions. In support of the structural model, Schuham (1970) reported more father–mother coalitions in nonclinic families, and more father–child coalitions in families with a disturbed child. Alexander (1973), however, found less father–child and mother–child supportiveness in the problem families. One difference between these investigations is that Schuham studied children with a diagnosis of incipient psychosis; Alexander studied delinquents. One would expect different coalition patterns between these diagnostic groups. Replications are needed, but the existing data indicate that cross-generational coalitions and the lack of a united parental subsystem are potentially troublesome interaction patterns.

CHILD EFFECTS ON FAMILY INTERACTIONS

As noted earlier, all four of the major family theories assume interdependence of behavior patterns, or circular causality. However, this theoretical stance is not reflected in the research on child problems and family interaction. Most of the research designed specifically to study child effects has focused on infants (Bell, 1979), life cycle changes, and handicapped children (Lerner & Spanier, 1978), rather than on children with emotional or behavioral problems.

The research on family conflict is correlational and thus could be interpreted as evidence for adult, child, or reciprocal effects. The data have primarily been interpreted, however, in terms of adult effects. Some investigators have studied the effects that schizophrenic children have on adults other than their own parents (e.g., Liem, 1974). However, the discussions of this research are also limited by a unidirectional model of effects, in this case from child to parent.

Dell (1980) outlined four types of explanation for the findings of different interaction patterns in families with problem children: (a) etiological—faulty communication causes pathology; (b) responsive—faulty communication reflects a reaction to pathology; (c) situational—communication is determined by the demand characteristics of the research setting; and (d) transactional—communication is the result of complex feedback loops and interdependent forces. He views the first two explanations as naive; he clearly favors the transactional model, although he stresses the difficulty, if not impossibility, of testing this model. One would need to operationalize a large number of variables in very complex ongoing interactions and then face the task of observing these interactions over a long period of time.

Bell (1979) noted that although progress in science is typically marked by the simplification of phenomena, progress in the study of parent–child interactions is represented by an increasingly complex view of the phenomenon. Progress is marked by a heightened awareness of the multiplicity of reciprocal influences that are operating on a family at any one time (Margolin, 1981). This complex view is welcomed, as it is a necessary starting point for the development of a clinically significant understanding of family functioning.

EVALUATION OF FAMILY THEORIES

Summary of Research

In order to clarify the degree of empirical support available for the various conceptualizations, this summary of the literature is organized around the previously presented theories.

Systems Theories

As noted, an important commonality of systems theories is the understanding of a child's problem as functional for the family system. This view is supported by the evidence indicating that parental views of a child's problem and a child's referral for psychotherapy are not always determined by actual behavior. The concept of scapegoating is consistent with data indicating no differences in acting out-behavior between the referred child and his or her siblings. Minuchin's data on anxiety reduction in parents of psychosomatic children highlight the use of a child as a detour from conflictual issues. The data on the relationship between marital discord and child problems can also be interpreted as support for the view that a child's problem is a functional response, the function being to maintain stability in a threatened marriage.

Communication Theory

The general assumption that communication patterns are significant correlates of child problems was supported by the research indicating less clarity, less efficiency, more negativeness, and less support in problem families. However, only the first two findings are specifically predicted by communication theory. As Riskin and Faunce (1972) pointed out, one of the problems plaguing family interaction research is an overabundance of abstract concepts that are not easily subject to operational definitions. The theoretical concepts of double bind, homeostasis, and family rules fall into this category. Attempts made to study the double binding communication sequence have not succeeded in validating the concept. No research has directly addressed the concepts of homeostasis or rules.

Structural Family Theory

The data on the lack of hierarchical organization and the existence of cross-generational coalitions in clinic families provide an argument for the importance of subsystem (i.e., parent–sibling) boundaries. As noted earlier, the specific concept of detouring is supported by research with psychosomatic children.

Behavioral Theory

The hypothesis regarding a coercion process is supported by the consistent observation of more negative and less positive behavior in clinic families. The observation that families with a problem child reciprocate negative interactions, while families without a problem child apply contingent positive consequences, provides further support of behavioral concepts. The relationship between marital discord and child problems is not predicted by behavioral theory. However, the observation that conduct disorders are the problem most often associated with discord is consistent with the concept of vicarious learning (modeling) effects.

Bowen's Family Theory

As noted previously, the major constructs in Bowen's theory have not been investigated in controlled research. The previously noted point regarding abstract concepts applies equally well to Bowen's constructs of triangles and the differentiation of self. His hypothesis regarding the impact of relationships with the family of origin would be somewhat easier to test, although much of the relevant data would be retrospective.

Relevance of Family Theories to Different Clinical Problems

The foregoing summary highlighted those theoretical constructs that have the most empirical support. However, the goal was not to choose one "best" theory. Rather, a productive approach to theory evaluation is to identify which concepts are relevant to differing family constellations and problems and to integrate the approaches so as to account for as wide a scope of family experience as possible.

The Context of Theory Development

Communication, structural, and behavioral theories have been developed in the context of clinical work with different client populations. Communication theory, including the concepts of the pathological impact of inconsistent, unclear interaction patterns, was developed in the context of work with families having a schizophrenic member. Minuchin's structural concepts, such as enmeshment (or overprotection) and detouring through concern for a child, were developed out of his observations of families with physically ill, psychosomatic children. Patterson, who introduced the concept of coercion to behavioral family approaches, was working with conduct-disorder, aggressive children. It is not surprising that the theories best fit the family patterns of the populations with whom the theorists were interacting. For example, Minuchin's concept of detouring seems most applicable to families with withdrawn, anxious, or psychosomatic children, since the parents can unite over concern for the child. On the other hand, the behavioral theory regarding coercion seems most applicable to families with conduct-disorder or acting-out children, in which reciprocal aversive, commanding interchanges are common.

Research Comparing Different Diagnostic Groups

Most investigators do not find differences between families with children of different diagnostic labels, either in personality characteristics of parents (e.g., Block, 1969) or in specific interaction patterns (e.g., no difference in information exchanged; Ferreira & Winter, 1968). Isolated findings of differences across groups have not been replicated and at times have been in direct conflict; for instance, Duncan (1971) and Hetherington, Stouwie, and Ridberg (1971) present opposite findings on the degree of open conflict in families of social subcultural delinquents as opposed to other forms of delinquency.

It could be argued that if research has not demonstrated differences between diagnostic groups, then family interactions may not be an important factor in the development of child problems. However, this conclusion does not seem warranted, given (a) the evidence on differences between clinic and nonclinic families, found for a variety of child problems; and (b) the existence of methodological problems that make it difficult to obtain significant contrasts—for example, unreliable diagnostic labels. Additionally, there is a dearth of studies designed to test specific, theory-related predictions such as those addressed in the questions noted earlier. As the issue of differential family patterns is crucial to the refinement of both theory and clinical intervention, these studies should be of high priority to family interaction researchers.

Integration of the Family Theories

Another high-priority area of study is the integration of the different theories in an effort to increase understanding of the development of problems within a family. It is likely that some constructs are more valid and useful when applied to the incipient stages of family conflict, while other concepts explain the exacerbation or maintenance of the problem. For example, consider the following process and the way in which the concepts of communication (C), structural (S), behavioral (Be), and Bowen's (Bo) theories are applied. A young couple experiences a conflict over the rules for their relationships (C), primarily because of vastly different family interaction patterns in their families of origin (Bo). To avoid direct conflict over these rules, their communication pattern becomes increasingly indirect and unclear (C), which leads to inefficient problem-solving (C, Be). This lack of problem-solving skills results in counterproductive demands for immediate change that are not met and in a process of coercion (Be). They have a child in an attempt to increase sharing and positive feelings between them (Bo). This child eventually becomes involved in their arguments, both because they enlist him or her as an ally (S) and because the child has learned that it is possible to gain privileges by allying with one parent and then the other (e.g., child effect). The parents begin to fight about the child and how to discipline him or her, rather than about their original relationship conflict (C, S, Bo). This fighting results in inconsistent and punitive discipline, which increases the child's acting out (Be), which increases their fights about the child and so on.

Such an integrative approach, although not yet empirically validated, provides a more complete picture of family process. This analysis elucidates several potential areas for clinical intervention, for example, rule conflicts, child management, parent–child coalitions. A therapist working from this integrative perspective would be able to conduct a comprehensive assessment and then make an educated decision about when to intervene on the various problems in this family.

OUTCOME RESEARCH

Although both the number and quality of family therapy outcome studies are increasing, the research primarily consists of demonstrations of the effectiveness of a particular strategy or technique. As these demonstrations do not clarify the theoretical issues that are the focus of this chapter, this research will not be reviewed here. Rather, those studies bearing directly upon the importance of family context in child therapy will be reviewed. The interested reader can consult Gurman and Kniskern (1978), Linehan and Rosenthal (1979), and Masten (1979) for recent reviews of outcome literature.

Marital Discord and the Outcome of Child Therapy

Clinical observations of the negative impact of marital discord on progress in child therapy have been reported frequently (e.g., Cole & Morrow, 1976; Kent & O'Leary, 1976; Patterson *et al.*, 1973). Cole and Morrow (1976) discussed two patterns in maritally distressed couples that impeded the implementation of a group parent-training program: (a) lack of agreement between parents on the behavioral goals of treatment, and (b) the lack of follow-through on assigned tasks. Working with parents of developmentally disabled children, Clark and Baker (1979) also found that unhappy spouses were less likely to carry out training programs.

Reisinger, Frangia, and Hoffman (1976) observed less generalization of effects of a skill-training program in mothers who noted marital difficulties during the course of training. Using experimental games, Santa-Barbara and Epstein (1974) classified parents' interactions as cooperative, competitive, dominant/submissive, or mixed. They studied recidivism rates of child problems at a follow-up contact 14 months after therapy and found that the lowest recidivism was in the families of cooperative parents. Although Oltmanns *et al.* (1977) found no relationship between pretreatment level of marital discord and therapy outcome, the fact that their sample was not seriously distressed could have mitigated the effect. The conclusion drawn must be tempered by the dearth of controlled studies, but the available evidence supports the claim that marital discord is a counterproductive influence on child treatment.

Involvement of Fathers and Siblings in Therapy

Although there are data indicating that involvement of fathers does not affect therapy outcome (Martin, 1977), the majority of research demonstrates that the father plays an important role in treatment efficacy (Gurman & Kniskern, 1978). The major finding is that families are less likely to drop out of therapy if the father attends sessions (Cole & Magnussen, 1967; LeFave, 1980; Ross & Lacey, 1961).

Patterson (1973) presented case study data that support the inclusion of siblings in therapy. Home observations indicated that the referred child's sibling was a major stimulus for aggressive behavior. In terms of impact on the referred child, there are no comparative outcome studies investigating the relative merits of including or excluding siblings. However, Klein, Alexander, and Parsons (1977) presented compelling data indicating that including siblings in therapy does have a positive impact on the siblings. Three years following termination of a short-term behavioral family systems therapy for delinquents, court records revealed that the rate of court contacts for siblings in therapy was half that of siblings in the control group and one-third that of siblings in an "eclectic-dynamic" church counseling program. Thus, it may be important to involve siblings in therapy, both to reduce potential precipitants of problem behavior and to affect therapeutically the siblings themselves.

Individual versus Family Therapy

Love, Kaswan, and Bugental (1972) compared two parent-involved treatment programs with individual child therapy and found a greater improvement in academic performance to be associated with parent involvement. However, the child therapy was not significantly different from family therapy in its effect on social behavior in school. Working with hospitalized adolescents, Wellisch, Vincent, and Ro-Trock (1976) found that family therapy resulted in significantly fewer rehospitalizations and a quicker return to school or work.

In a review of the literature on training in problem-solving, Urbain and Kendall (1980) noted that the success of family-oriented approaches indicates the importance of including significant others when training children in cognitive behavioral skills. However, at present there is not sufficient outcome research comparing individual and family therapy to substantiate a claim for the superiority of either modality (Masten, 1979).

CLINICAL RECOMMENDATIONS

This discussion raises clinical issues that should be considered in child treatment and, predictably, underscores the value of including family members in therapy.

Initial Assessment and the Structure of Therapy

The evidence reviewed indicates several important assessment questions that can best be answered by seeing a child with his or her entire family. The following list is not intended to be exhaustive, but is presented to highlight particularly important variables.

1. Is the parental report of the severity of the child's behavioral or emotional problem accurate?

2. Is the child's behavior different from that of his or her siblings? If not, what are some of the parents' reasons for referring only one child (e.g., is it denial of or embarrassment about multiple family problems, or faulty perceptions)?

3. What are the differences between the problem child's experiences and those of his or her siblings? What are some of the factors leading to the development of problems in this particular child? Why would the parents have treated this child differently? Are they continuing to do so? Do the siblings react differently to family stress?

4. What is the quality of the sibling relationships? Are the siblings eliciting problem behavior or excluding the referred child from their subsystem?

5. How do family members communicate with one another? Are they clear and direct? Do they provide verbal or nonverbal positive reinforcement? Can they process their own interactions? Do the spouses display hostility in front of the children? Are attempts made either to engage a child in the conflict or to defuse tension by focusing on a child? What are the children's reactions to marital conflict?

6. Are the family subsystems hierarchically arranged? Are the parents appropriately supportive of each other's authority or are there counterproductive cross-generational alliances?

Decisions regarding initial interventions and the structure of therapy (or whom to work with and when) will necessarily be dependent on the information obtained during the family assessment sessions.

When to Work with the Parents Alone

If the parents have overstated the severity of their child's problem and the child's behavior is in the normal range, one could choose to see the parents alone, to determine the reason for the referral and intervene accordingly. The parents might need to be educated regarding child development norms to reevaluate realistically their expectations of their child, to structure leisure time more effectively so as to increase their freedom for social pursuits, or to address issues or tensions in the marital relationship that were being displaced on the child.

The decision regarding when to focus directly on any marital problems that exist is a difficult one. Should the therapist work on marital and child problems simultaneously? If not, where should the primary initial focus be? Data that directly address this decision-making process are not available. Given the evidence indicating that marital discord impedes follow-through on child management tasks, the therapist might decide to see the parents without the children and focus on the marriage early in therapy. However, many parents will be highly resistant to this intervention. They may deny the existence of marital tension, but even if they recognize that a problem exists, they may not be ready for marital therapy. The parents' expected treatment contract is that the therapist will provide help for their child. The therapist often needs to meet some of these expectations, through a focus on the child's problems, before focusing on the marriage.

Thus, in deciding when to work with the parents alone, the therapist needs to consider such factors as the parents' expectations, both of therapy and their child; the severity of marital distress; and the parents' willingness and ability to work productively on marital issues.

When to Work with the Entire Family Unit

Family sessions would be necessary if the assessment questions regarding siblings revealed either emotional, behavioral, or interpersonal problems in the sibling subsystem. However, an argument can also be made for including siblings even if particular problems are not observed during the initial assessment. There is some evidence indicating that clinic boys engage less in cooperative play with their siblings than do nonclinic boys (Mash & Mercer, 1979). While this lower level of cooperation may not be immediately apparent or be presented as an initial problem, it could interfere with progress in therapy.

The development of the systems approach to schizophrenia has been described as a progression from a focus on the individual to the broader social context. The initial discovery was that "schizophrenics had mothers." After several years the discovery was made that "schizophrenics had fathers, too." The next change in conceptualization involved the link between a discordant marriage and child symptomatology (Haley, cited in Napier & Whitaker, 1978). The interpersonal context has been broadened to include siblings, in theory, but researchers have not paid sufficient attention to the sibling subsystem.

Siblings have been omitted from almost all observational family interaction research. The complexity of measuring dyadic and triadic interactions would certainly discourage the addition of more people. However, potentially critical information is lost. Murrell and Stachowiak (1967) found that older siblings in clinic families received more attention than older siblings in nonclinic families (whether they were the identified clients or not). These data indicate that older siblings may serve a different function in problem families, and a "nonproblem" older sibling in these families may be at risk to develop problems.

The argument that one can achieve primary prevention through including siblings is supported by these data. A clearer demonstration of this possibility, noted in the discussion on outcome research, is the impressive reduction in court contacts for siblings of delinquents involved in family therapy (Klein *et al.*, 1977). Unfortunately, there are no data indicating when it would be advisable to exclude siblings. Possible situations in which sibling involvement be contraindicated include a withdrawn referred child who might not speak at all in the presence of hostile siblings, an overly close alliance of parents and siblings against the problem child that might best be broken by several sessions with the parents and problem child alone, and an adolescent referred child who presents problems that may be inappropriate topics for discussions with much younger siblings—for example, sexual acting out.

Targets for Treatment

As in any clinical situation, targets for treatment necessarily depend on the clients' presenting problem and particular strengths and weaknesses. However, the family interaction literature points to certain patterns among problem families that will frequently need to be addressed in therapy. Several treatment targets have been discussed in the preceding section on assessment and initial structuring, and they will not be covered here. These include parental expectations, marital discord, and sibling relationships.

The importance of improved problem-solving skills and enhanced communication (particularly with regard to aversiveness and positiveness) has been indicated by the interaction research. Improved communication was judged to be important to all families in therapy by 85% of the respondents to a survey of family therapists (Olson, 1970). Families with problem children may actually need to learn "better than average" problem solving skills because, by the time they get to therapy, they share fewer values and opinions than do nonclinic families. It has been reported that clinic family members are less likely to agree on such topics as household chores, admired famous people, desired family activities, and solutions to hypothetical family conflicts (Ferreira & Winter, 1965; Mead & Campbell, 1972; Schuham, 1972). Thus, they are frequently confronted with differences that must be resolved.

Training in child-management skills will often be useful, given that parents of problem children are more negative, less positively reinforcing, and more inconsistent than parents of nonclinic children. While some of this behavior may be the result of marital discord, the therapist should not assume that successful marital therapy will automatically result in appropriate child-management skills.

Maintenance of Gains in Therapy

Systems theory predicts that positive changes in one individual will not be maintained unless the family system is prepared for and accepts that change. The prediction of this process is based on two major concepts: the problem as functional for the system, and homeostasis. Two examples of this process are (1) A fearful child who stayed at home might be missed by his or her mother when the child loses that fear.

Unless mother is provided with another source of activity and emotional support, the conditions that contributed to and/or maintained the fearful behavior will still exist, and it is likely to reappear. (2) A father's aggressive over-involvement in struggles with his delinquent son allow him to gain authority and status in relation to his wife. If the spouses do not successfully negotiate the power and status issues between them, the father may continue his aggressive interactions with his son, even if the boy starts to change his behavior. To ensure maintenance of change, the therapist must be able to predict the potential impact of any behavior changes and prepare for anticipated negative reactions. It is easier to make these predictions in the context of family therapy, but it is possible and advisable to do so when working with a client individually. In individual therapy, the therapist can help prepare the client for potential negative reactions or counterproductive maneuvers on the part of family members.

Questions Remaining

The process and outcome research on family interaction and family therapy have clarified several major issues, as discussed in this chapter. However, important questions remain.

Theoretical issues include: What family interaction patterns are associated with what types of child problems? What variables mediate the relationship among parental psychopathology, marital discord, and child problems? Why do certain children in a family develop problems while others do not?

Clinical questions include: When should one conduct individual as opposed to family therapy? What is the most effective way of interrupting destructive coalitions? When and how should one intervene with siblings?

In spite of these unanswered questions, it is clear that theory and research on family systems have had a major impact on the delivery of psychological services to children. Further integration of empirically validated theoretical constructs and research addressing theoretical and clinical issues such as those noted above would ensure a continued positive impact on these services.

SUMMARY

The major thesis of this chapter is that emotional and behavioral problems of children are frequently best understood and most effectively treated within the family context. Four theoretical conceptualizations of the relationship between child psychopathology and family interactions were presented: communication theory, Bowen's family theory, Minuchin's model of structural family therapy, and behavioral family theory. All of these approaches highlight the importance of examining the reciprocal influences that family members exert on one another. The majority of the theorists posit that a child's problems are in some way functional within the family system—for instance, in reducing the parents' anxiety or in maintaining stability for the marriage. The theories differ in the relative emphasis placed on such factors as communication styles, rules for family interactions, hierarchical arrangements and boundaries between parental and sibling subsystems, child-management and/or problem-solving skills, and coercive behavior-change strategies.

Process research relevant to the major theoretical approaches was presented. While the degree of empirical support for the specific constructs varies, there is a growing body of research supporting the general argument regarding the importance of family systems. Evidence to be considered includes decreases in parents' physiological arousal when the symptomatic child is included in the interaction, the observation that referred children may not behave differently from peers or siblings, heightened aversiveness and counterproductive behavior-shaping in families with problem children, and the relationship between marital discord and child problems.

Clinical recommendations were offered, based on the family theories and outcome research. A strong argument was made for working with the entire family, at minimum, to conduct a comprehensive assessment. Once this assessment is completed, the therapist will be able to decide who should be involved in therapy and will be better equipped to design and implement effective interventions for the child and family.

Acknowledgments

The author would like to thank Sue Geiss and Bea Porter for their insightful and helpful editorial comments.

5

Assessment Issues and Strategies in Cognitive Behavior Therapy with Children

Richard N. Roberts and Rosemery O. Nelson

ASSESSMENT ISSUES

The Role of Developmental Processes in Cognitive Behavior Therapy

Frequently, the targets of intervention with children involve processes that are in continuing stages of development. Thus, whether one assesses cognitive tempo, social problem-solving, or academic problem-solving, competence is frequently defined within the context of developmental levels that are associated with a given mental or chronological age. The developmental progressions of many of the skills assessed in cognitive behavioral intervention programs have several assessment and treatment ramifications.

First, identification of problems must occur in the context of developmental levels. For example, normative data on the Matching Familiar Figures Test (Kagan, Rosman, Day, Albert, & Phillips, 1964) show that children become more reflective as they grow older; that is, response time per item increases and total number of errors decreases (Messer, 1976). A reflective or impulsive score on this test, therefore, can be determined only in relation to the child's age. Similarly, Kassinove, Crisci, and Tiegerman (1977), using their inventory to assess rational or irrational thinking, found a general decrement over time in children's

Richard N. Roberts • Kamehameha Educational Research Institute, Honolulu, Hawaii 96817. **Rosemery O. Nelson** • Department of Psychology, University of North Carolina at Greensboro, Greensboro, North Carolina 27412.

irrational ideas. Thus, the absolute number of irrational ideas cannot be judged a problem without reference to the child's age.

Second, the goal of treatment should be consistent with the developmental level of the child. Thus, developmental norms are useful not only in determining that the child has a problem but also in determining what the treatment goals should be. The success of the treatment can be evaluated, in part, by how well the child learns to behave in ways approporiate to his or her chronological age.

Third, the sequence of intervention steps can be planned in accordance with a developmental model. For example, much of the work with self-instructional training (e.g., Meichenbaum & Goodman, 1971b) was based on Luria's model of the development of verbal control of motor behavior (Luria, 1959). In another example, Sawin and Parke (1979) found that the general tone and specific verbal content must be tailored to developmental levels. In a final example, work on cognitive development by Flavell and by Piaget (Flavell, Beach, & Chinsky, 1966; Piaget & Inhelder, 1956) was related to treatment outcome by Cohen, Schleser, and Meyers (1981). Cognitive level (preoperational versus concrete operational) was found to be strongly related to conceptual tempo and was predictive of overall performance on the Matching Familiar Figures Test (Kagan *et al.*, 1964).

Last, since children do change with age, experiments must be carefully designed so that improvements can be clearly attributed either to the intervention program or to maturation. In research with children, maturation can pose a forceful threat to the internal validity of interventions.

Identification of Target Behaviors and Evaluation of Treatment Outcomes

In behavioral assessment in general, selection of target behaviors frequently involves a value judgment by the therapist and client (Myerson & Hayes, 1978). A large number of philosophical and empirical guidelines have been proposed, however, to influence that value judgment, as previously summarized by Nelson and Hayes (1979). Among the philosophical guidelines are (a) behavior should be altered if it is dangerous to the client or to others in the environment, (b) target behaviors should be selected to maximize the client's reinforcers (Krasner, 1969), (c) desirable behaviors whose frequency should increase are preferred over undesirable behaviors whose frequency should decrease (McFall, 1976), (d) target behaviors should maximize the flexibility of the client's repertoire to achieve long-term individual and social benefits

(Myerson & Hayes, 1978), and (e) optimal rather than average levels of performance should be sought (Foster & Ritchey, 1979). Among the empirical guidelines are (a) the collection of normative data (Kazdin, 1977b); (b) the use of task analysis and of developmental norms (Hawkins, 1975); (c) subjective ratings by community volunteers regarding which behaviors and which rates thereof are important (Wolf, 1978); (d) a behavioral-analytic model in which situations are identified, possible responses are enumerated and evaluated, and measurement items and their scoring are determined (Goldfried & D'Zurilla, 1969); (e) the "known groups" method (McFall, 1976), by which specific behaviors are identified that differentiate two established groups; (f) a components analysis in which different response parameters are experimentally manipulated and their relative effects empirically determined (Mullinix & Galassi, 1981), (g) regression equations to determine which specific behaviors best predict to important criteria (Cobb, 1972); and (h) experimental intervention in which it is shown that intervening with one specific target behavior produced greater change in an important global measure than intervening with a second specific target behavior (Kupke, Calhoun, & Hobbs, 1979).

The manner in which target behaviors have been selected in cognitive behavior therapy with children has been criticized by Hobbs, Moguin, Tyroler, and Lahey (1980). They regret that target behaviors are frequently alterations in scores on psychometric instruments, like the Matching Familiar Figures Test (Kagan *et al.*, 1964), instead of observed change in actual target behaviors relevant to the referral problem. In some sense, their statement presents another philosophical guideline. Research is needed to show whether cognitive or motor target behaviors (or which particular cognitive or moter target behaviors) produce maximal treatment effectiveness. The answers may vary for different types of children. In an example with motor target behaviors, it was found that oppositional and aggressive behaviors decreased more when the target behavior was an increase in solitary play than when the target behavior was an increase in cooperative social play (Wahler & Fox, 1980). In an example with more cognitive target behaviors, it was found that teacher ratings of self-control and of hyperactivity improved more when conceptual directions were used within self-instructional training than when concrete directions were used (Kendall & Wilcox, 1980). Similar research is needed on the circumstances in which cognitive versus motor target behaviors are preferred.

Only a few of the empirical guidelines described above have been used to select target behaviors within cognitive behavior therapy. Camp (1977) assessed aggressive and normal boys on several measures of IQ, academic achievement, cognitive response style, verbal ability, and the use of self-guiding speech. A discriminant function analysis correctly classified 88% of the cases. Those variables contributing to the aggressive classification included poor vocabulary, immature and irrelevant private speech, and impulsive response style. Camp asserted that young aggressive boys differ from their normal counterparts in their failure to use verbal mediational processes in situations when they would be facilitative. Through this known groups comparison method, a target for cognitive and behavioral change was identified. Programs such as "Think Aloud" (Camp, Blom, Hebert, & van Doorninck, 1977) have addressed the identified deficit by teaching verbal-mediational strategies to aggressive children and have found a concomitant decrease in aggressive behavior.

In another example using the known groups comparison method, Havertape and Kass (1978) examined spontaneous private speech of learning disabled children and normal peers in a series of academically related tasks. Differences in problem-solving strategies between the two groups were reflected in their coded private speech. Important differences were found in the children's ability to read the problem, understand the required operations, and arrive at a solution using logical and efficient steps. The verbal behavior exhibited in the target situation provided valuable information with respect to appropriate targets of intervention. Although Havertape and Kass did not develop a treatment program based on these identified deficits, other programs for learning disabled children have addressed similar deficits and found significant changes in academic achievement (Feinberg & Roberts, 1983; Kauffman & Hallahan, 1979).

A final example of the known groups comparison is a recent study by Forman (1980b), which compared self-statements of aggressive and nonaggressive children. Both groups of children were presented with aggression-provoking vignettes and asked to describe appropriate courses of action. Aggressive children responded with more irrational thoughts, more aggressive statements, and more negative evaluations of the children in the vignettes than did nonaggressive children.

In addition to the known groups method, another empirical strategy that has been used to identify appropriate target behaviors has been multiple regression procedures. As an example, Roberts (1981), in a naturalistic study, identified verbal and motor behaviors predictive of success in an academic task. Here achievement test scores, IQ scores, and coded verbal (e.g., task-irrelevant, task-relevant, reading aloud) and motor activity (e.g., on-task, off-task) displayed during a reading task were entered into a regression equation to predict task performance on the reading task. On the whole, motor behaviors were more predictive than verbal ones. Off-task behavior was the best overall predictor and was negatively correlated with success. The category of "irrelevant verbalizations" was the best predictor from the verbal activity score and was also negatively correlated with success.

It has been emphasized that, in applied research, the clinical or social significance of treatment outcome should be evaluated in addition to or instead of statistical significance (Kazdin, 1977b; Wolf, 1978). Some of the empirical guidelines described above are useful not only for determining initial target behaviors but also for evaluating the clinical or social significance of treatment outcome. As an example of the use of normative data to evaluate the clinical significance of a cognitive behavioral treatment for impulsivity, Kendall and Wilcox (1980) compared the pre- and post-test scores of impulsive children on the Self-Control Rating Scale with the mean scores of 110 randomly selected children. Clinical significance of treatment was determined by both the direction and magnitude of the change. Did the treatment produce changes that placed deviant children within normal limits (the mean plus or minus one standard deviation)? Only the Matching Familiar Figures error and latency measures and teacher ratings of hyperactivity reached clincial significance for those children in the conceptual training group. None reached significance for the control group.

It has been suggested that social validation procedures might also be used to evaluate the relative social acceptability of various effective intervention programs. For example, parents and teachers might find programs that emphasize self control more acceptable than programs that emphasize external control. For another example, the benefits gained should be evaluated in relation to the energy expended so that the cost-effectiveness of the program can be determined. For example, is it more cost-effective to develop cognitive behavioral programs that require one-to-one therapist–student contact or programs that can serve groups of students?

In summary, more systematic efforts are needed in cognitive behavior therapy with children to select initial target behaviors, to evaluate the clinical significance of treatment outcome, and to determine the social acceptability of effective treatment programs. A number of empirical guidelines to accomplish these goals have been proposed by Kazdin (1977b), Nelson and Hayes (1979), and Wolf (1978).

Assessment of Cognitive Processes as Independent or Dependent Variables

Cognitive processes do not easily lend themselves to direct measurement. Rather, these processes must be indirectly assessed either through those overt verbalizations frequently referred to as private speech, through self-report measures that may assess attributional processes, or through tasks such as Kagan's Matching Familiar Figures Test (Kagan *et al.*, 1964) that measure cognitive tempo or response style.

In some instances, private speech or self-speech is considered an independent variable and in other cases, a dependent variable. Many self-instructional training programs, for instance, directly modify a child's ongoing verbal monologue as an independent variable and assess the effects on overt motor responding (Camp, Blom, Hebert, & van Doorninck, 1977; Douglas, Parry, Marton, & Garson, 1976; Kendall & Finch, 1978; Meichenbaum & Goodman, 1971b), on both motor and verbal responding (Kendall & Finch, 1979; Roberts & Mullis, 1983), or on a child's attributional processes (Bugental, Whalen, & Henker, 1977; Bugental, Collins, Collins, & Chaney, 1978).

Kendall and Korgeski (1979) have called for assessment of verbalizations as one method of validating treatment mechanisms. Thus, changes in verbal monologues pre- to post-treatment would indicate that the treatment procedure had affected the child's use of private speech as a mediating independent variable. Kendall and Finch (1979) compared verbalizations at pretest, post-test, and follow-up for impulsive children who either received a cognitively based treatment or were in a no-treatment control group. Many of the coded verbalizations did not differ by group or by trial. Impulsive children who received treatment, however, increased in on-task verbalizations at post-test, but this increase was not maintained at follow-up. Using impulsive first-grade children, Roberts and Mullis (1983) conducted a component analysis of self-instructional training. Training was academically relevant to arithmetic tasks. Children were videotaped during pre- and post-testing, and verbal and motor behaviors were coded from the videotapes. Children who received behavioral modeling, verbal modeling, and self-instructional training significantly and equally improved their academic performance at post-test. Children who received instructions only and no-treatment controls did not improve. Motor behaviors categorizable as on-task/off-task were not affected by treatment. Of importance to the present discussion, there were no changes in the use of verbalizations for any of the groups.

The assessment of private speech of children involved in cognitive behavioral treatment programs is a dependent measure that is frequently neglected. This is particularly unfortunate since the majority of outcome-oriented self-instructional training studies mention Luria's (1959) research on verbal control of motor behavior as a theoretical mechanism facilitating change. For example, if a cognitive behavioral program for impulsivity is effective in teaching a child verbal strategies to modify motor activity, then post-treatment measures should be taken on verbalizations and motor behavior to determine how both may have been affected. There are few naturalistic studies that provide information on private speech as it occurs in normal and clinical populations for comparative purposes. Those studies mentioned above are a beginning attempt to collect these important data. Other studies (Kohlberg, Yaeger, & Hjertholm, 1968; R. N. Roberts, 1979; Zivin, 1979) provide additonal data on private speech from a developmental perspective.

Attributions and expectations that children bring to an intervention program are another important variable to be assessed. The child is seen as an active participant who brings to the program a set of beliefs and rules about his or her ability to affect the environment (Bandura, 1977b). These beliefs or attributions may be assessed as independent variables—their effect on performance measures such as task persistence or response style is observed—or as dependent variables—the effect of a given environmental manipulation on a child's attributions of causation and personal effectiveness is assessed. In an example of attribution as an independent variable, Bugental *et al.* (1977) studied the impact of initial expectations held by impulsive and hyperactive children on the differential effectiveness of two programs. One program emphasized external control (social reinforcement), and the other emphasized internal control (self-instructions). Both programs differed from many previous studies of attributional effects because Bugental *et al.* introduced the programs into the regular classroom rather than using an analogue task or setting. The attributional measure consisted of a structured interview in which the children were asked to describe the causal factors in school success and failure. Here is an example from the interview (p. 879):

> If you get a bad grade on a test, what makes that happen?
> a) not studying
> b) the teacher doesn't like you
> c) bad luck

Results indicated that children who were low in perceived causality (external locus of control) tended to perform more accurately in the social reinforcement program, whereas children with high perceived causality (internal locus of control) tended to perform more accurately in the self-control (self-instructional) program. Attributional style, then, may be one factor to consider in developing individually and group-administered programs. As the authors state, "Change strategies (behavioral management, educational programs, psychotherapy, medical intervention) have implicit attributional textures which interact with the attributional network of the individual to influence treatment impact" (p. 881).

In another example of attributions as an independent variable, the manner in which a child labels a task may exercise considerable control over the child's persistence at that task. Masters and Santrock (1976) investigated the effects of self-produced evaluations and affective responses on children's persistence in a motor task. When the children labeled the task as fun or easy, they continued working longer than they did if they labeled it as difficult or not fun.

In an example of attribution as a dependent variable, Bugental *et al.* (1978) assessed changes in attributions and behavior six months after termination of treatment. Children who had received self-control training significantly increased their perceptions of personal control, while children who had received social reinforcement training were rated by their teacher as being less hyperactive or impulsive on the Conners Teacher Rating Scale (Conners, 1969). Thus, self-control training may affect personal beliefs or attributions and have less of an effect on overt behavior. Social reinforcement training, however, because it is tied to specific environmental cues (teacher presence, classroom setting), may serve to inhibit inappropriate behavior in that setting when the teacher is present.

The Relationship between Verbal and Motor Behavior

The relationship between measures of cognitive activity such as attributions, personal beliefs, and private speech and measures of motor behavior is not always clear or easy to assess. What is clear is that it is necessary to assess several modes of behavior in order to understand more completely the relationships that exist among verbal reports, overt motor activity, and physiological states (Cone, 1979).

Several examples serve to illustrate these relationships. Craddock, Cotler, and Jason (1978) compared systematic desensitization to cognitive rehearsal with speech-anxious children. Self-report and behavioral measures of anxiety were taken pre- and post-training. On the self-report measure, the cognitive rehearsal group improved more than either the systematic desensitization group or a no-treatment control group. On the behavioral measure, the three groups improved equally.

Peterson and Shigitomi (1981) provide another good example of measurement in their study of the use of coping techniques to minimize anxiety in hospitalized children. Dependent measures included behavioral observation, self-report questionnaires, questionnaires completed by nurses and parents, and physiological measures such as blood pressure. Measurements across behavioral, cognitive, and physiological domains demonstrated the relative independence of these response modes as they related to changes in anxiety levels. Changes in one domain were not predictive of changes in other domains. Additionally, treatment conditions (coping strategies versus modeling) did not consistently affect specific domains in any differential way.

One goal of cognitive behavioral intervention programs is to increase children's ability to report veridically and evaluate their own performance situation as well as to self-monitor accurately mood, affective experience, and physiological state. Another goal is to manipulate systematically cognitive variables as change agents and to assess their effect on cognitive and behavioral repertoires. A common assessment question with respect to both goals is the degree to which behaviors in one repertoire (verbal or motor) correspond to behaviors in the other. First, correlations among repertoires cannot be assumed unless specific training has been accomplished, and second, verbal control of motor behavior cannot be assumed without similarly specific training (Roberts & Dick, 1982).

Israel (1978) has conceptualized these two situations as two forms of correspondence training: a saying–doing sequence, and a doing–saying sequence. The saying–doing sequence teaches the child to state what he or she will do and then to carry out that activity in precommitted fashion. The doing–saying sequence reinforces the child for accurately reporting behaviors once those behaviors have already occurred. Both sequences of training have implications for assessment in cognitive behavioral programs with children.

If an intervention program trains children to commit themselves verbally to a given activity (e.g., "I will slowly and carefully work on this problem in a step-by-step fashion" or "When Johnny calls me a bad name, I will walk away from him"), an effective program must reinforce correspondence between the emission of such statements and successful completion of the motor activities they involve. Few cognitive intervention programs have assessed this type of correspondence or investigated the differential effectiveness of training correspondence as the first step in a training program. An anecdotal account of the first author's experiences with self-instructional training will serve to highlight the importance of this correspondence issue. A 5-year-old girl, quite impulsive and also educably mentally handicapped, was being trained to talk herself through simple "T" and "L" mazes. After several trials in which the first author modeled the procedure of stopping the pencil at the intersection or corner, looking for the correct turn, and going slowly within the lines to the goal, the girl was allowed to try the first maze. She imitated the verbal strategies quite well, but they had no correspondence to her motor behavior. She stated "I must go slowly" as her pencil raced across the page, and she executed a perfect right turn with the pencil as she said "I have to turn left here." It was only after correspondence between the label and the behaviors was reinforced that the directions came to serve as discriminativve stimuli for the appropriate responses.

Robin, Armel, and O'Leary (1975) observed similar behavior in teaching children to print letters using self-instructional training. Children were not explicitly trained in correspondence, though they were trained in the use of self-instructions. The authors report that although children employed correct self-instructions, they were frequently observed to make simultaneous incorrect writing responses. This prompted the authors to suggest that the children's verbal and motor response systems were often functionally independent.

Several studies have reported the necessity for correspondence training to enhance the effectiveness of cognitive behavioral programs, but only a few studies have systematically assessed correspondence as either an independent or a dependent variable. Karoly and Dirks (1977) investigated the relative efficacy of a say–do sequence (intention) versus a do–say sequence (reporting) in developing self-control with preschoolers in a self-control analogue-type task. Children who received either type of training showed an increase over baseline performance in verbalizations and play with the game. Importantly, reinforcement of verbalizations alone did not produce an increase in self-control activity. Correspondence between saying and doing increased only when a snack was made contingent on matching verbal report to actual performance.

Similarly, Rogers-Warren and Baer (1976) demonstrated that modeling and reinforcement of any report of the target behavior (sharing) increased *reports* of the behavior for preschool children. Modeling and reinfocement of only true reports increased both the reports of sharing *and* the actual behavior.

What implications do these studies of correspondence training have for assessment in cognitive behavior programs? The results of these studies may shed light on the issue of appropriate theoretical models for conceptualizing the bases for cognitive behavioral interventions. It seems clear that verbal behavior and motor behavior are two relatively independent repertoires. It cannot be assumed that one stream automatically or developmentally exerts control over the other. Thus, Luria's model (1959) for the verbal control of motor behavior may have little relevance for theory-building in cognitive behavioral programs. Meichenbaum and Goodman (1979) discussed Luria's model as a useful heuristic for developing a training sequence that progressed from verbal modeling, to overt self-instruction, and finally to covert self-instruction.

Perhaps a more appropriate model for the relationship between self-instructions and motor activity is an interactional one in which both streams of behavior are seen as somewhat independent, with the potential to influence each other under appropriate training conditions (R. N. Roberts, 1979; Roberts & Dick, 1982).

Another assessment question raised by this correspondence issue involves the identification of those instances in which cognitive behavioral programs may be contraindicated. There may be occasions in which more direct training techniques are more appropriate than a cognitive behavioral approach. A study by Higa, Tharp, and Calkins (1978) provides such an example. In a Luria-type task, kindergartners and first- and second-graders were taught to respond to colored lights by either pushing or not pushing a telegraph key. Some children were taught to verbalize after they had been taught the motor response (silent-verbal condition), while others were taught to verbalize concurrent with training in the motor response (verbal-silent condition). Results indicated that verbalizing interfered with acquisition of the motor response for kindergarteners and first-graders, but it did not affect second-graders' performance. The authors interpret their results within the context of a dual-task performance model. Learning two tasks simultaneously is more difficult than learning one task at a time. In many self-instructional training programs, children are, in fact, asked to learn a verbal and motor response simultaneously. For cases in which verbal-motor correspondence does not exist or in which a child has difficulty veridically reporting ongoing or past behavior, it may be advantageous to establish firmly the motor behavior prior to introduction of the verbal stream. Systematic assessment of these issues over time can only help to specify more clearly the mechanisms and procedures most conducive to change.

Maintenance and Generalization of Treatment Effects—A Promise Unfulfilled

One initial hope of researchers in cognivitve behavior therapy with children was that procedures developed within this context would enhance both long-term maintenance of behavior change and generalization from specific training tasks to a wider class of behaviors. As several authors have suggested (Meichenbaum & Asarnow, 1979; Roberts & Dick, 1982), evidence is lacking in both these important areas. Meichenbaum and Asarnow (1979) have stated that "Evidence for treatment generalization . . . especially across response modes and settings is less convincing [than evidence for treatment efficacy] and often equivocal" (p. 15).

This chapter will not review the evidence for or against maintenance or generalization but rather will address the question of how researchers and practitioners should assess these very important areas. A recent review of the literature on social-cognitive problem-solving interventions with children (Urbain & Kendall, 1980) indicated that the majority of studies in this area did not collect any follow-up data to measure even the briefest maintenance effects. For example, of the 14 studies Urbain and Kendall review involving training in social-cognitive problem-solving, only 4 reported any follow-up data. Of the 9 studies involving self-instructional training and social behavior, 5 reported follow-up data. Twelve studies of training in perspective-taking were reviewed, and here, only 2 studies reported follow-up data. Thus, the first problem for assessing maintenance in a training study is the inclusion of a follow-up period in the design so that the effects of training may be evaluated along this dimension.

The second problem involves the interaction of developmental changes with dependent variables used to assess maintenance. As discussed earlier, many of the variables studied in cognitive behavioral programs change through development across time. Thus, any measurement of maintenance must take into account changes in behavior that can be attributed to maturation alone. Known groups comparisons and norm-based assessment provide one answer to the assessment of changes in subjects that are attributable to developmental variables. If, for instance, a researcher studied the effects of self-instructional training on 5-year-old impulsive children and maintenance was assessed on several measures of cognitive tempo six months after termination of treatment, then one would expect children in both the experimental and control conditions to be less impulsive since impulsivity decreases as a function of age (Messer, 1976). Maintenance of treatment effects must outweigh this expected decrement, and the norms for comparison with the average child should be based on the average chronological age of the subjects at the time the follow-up data are collected.

The third problem is that the selection of appropriate variables to measure maintenance effects is not as easy as it might appear at first. Most studies reviewed by Urbain and Kendall (1980), for example, that did employ a follow-up measure used both a behavioral measure (either a teacher checklist or some direct observational measure) and a measure of cognitive problem-solving style. Since most cognitive behavioral procedures directly address both of these domains in treatment, both domains must be assessed at treatment termination and at follow-up. Several studies, however, did not include measures of cognitive variables at termination or follow-up. Bornstein and Quevillon (1976), for example, measured only on-task behavior in their study of the effects of self-instructional training in overactive preschool boys. Not only does the assessment of only one domain make it difficult to assess active components in the treatment package, but in this case, it also makes it difficult to assess how children in this study may have differed from children in the study by Friedling and O'Leary (1979), which failed to replicate Bornstein and Quevillon's findings.

Both domains should be assessed at follow-up to help interpret treatment effectiveness. A dilemma for the researcher develops when both domains are assessed but only one yields significant differences. If both variables yielded significant differences at posttest, the conclusion that the nonsignificant variable at follow-up and the domain that it represents were not affected by treatment is not certain.

An additional problem in the assessment of maintenance effects is oriented less toward outcome and more toward process than those mentioned above. Little is known regarding environmental variables that maintain and support treatment changes over time. More research is needed in the identification of environmental variables that are supportive of a given change. There are few reports in the literature that examine naturally occurring incidents of maintenance of target behaviors (e.g., Perri & Richards, 1977), and much work remains to be done regarding the development of methodologies and procedures for selecting appropriate variables to study this question. At present, we have little information about (a) differences in post-treatment environments in those cases where maintenance effects were found or how (b) subject population by treatment–post-treatment environment interactions have affected the maintenance of post-treatment cognitive behavioral changes. This, indeed, is a rich area for further research.

Assessing generalization of treatment effects presents an equally complex problem. There are at least three sets of variables that must be addressed to determine the generality of treatment effects. These include subject variables, training variables, and task variables. A subject's skill level can be assessed pre- and post-treatment on tasks for which there is a reasonable assumption of the independent variable having some effect on performance in that task. It is important to assess which skills are established in the child's repertoire and which are not.

If prerequisite skills are missing, a child may benefit from training in very limited ways, but generalization to other stimulus conditions may be greatly reduced. The recent trend toward training children in a more general problem-solving set has been the result of attempts to enhance generalization by teaching broader classes of skills in the training itself. Kendall and Wilcox (1980) and Feinberg and Roberts (1983) both found conceptual self-instructions to be more effective than concrete self-instructions in several measures of generalization. Kendall and Wilcox (1980) defined conceptual self-instructions as those "worded more globally and abstractly [than concrete self-instructions] in such a way they could apply to a wide range of situations" (p. 83). One implicit assumption in this conceptual or metacognitive training is that skills cluster together in such a way that when children learn the skill in the context of one task, that skill can be employed in the context of a second task. Impulsive children, for example, are more likely than nonimpulsive children to have deficits in such areas as problem-solving (Ault, 1973), verbal mediation (Camp, 1977), and information-seeking (Finch & Montgomery, 1975). As Messer (1976) has discussed, these deficits are correlational and are predictive of a class of children but not of the individual case. Impulsive children rarely exhibit across-the-board deficits in any of these mentioned areas. Perhaps generalization would be enhanced if more data were available on the topography of those skills that do cluster to form naturally occurring response classes. Meichenbaum (1977) has called for this type of assessment of cognitive skills in what he has termed a "cognitive ethology." There is a crucial information gap in the assessment of skill deficits. Specific data are needed to enhance our understanding of the covariation of behaviors within and across verbal and motor repertoires, skills that functionally and topographically form response classes, and cognitive behavioral skills that serve as keystone behaviors and predict a child's ability to engage in those other tasks that call for more advanced skills or skills represented in the same response class (e.g., Wahler, 1975). As this ecological assessment of skill repertoires becomes possible, cognitive behavioral researchers and therapists will be in a better position to predict generalization across skills.

This ecological assessment is needed with respect not only to subject variables but also to task variables and training variables. Belmont and Butterfield (1977) discuss the necessity of a component analysis of a task in order to define clearly what skills are needed to complete it. Tasks may form natural clusters around those crucial skills required for success. For example, the Matching Familiar Figures Test (Kagan *et al.*, 1964) and the Porteus Mazes (Porteus, 1955) are two measures frequently employed to study generalization of training with impulsive children (e.g., Kendall & Wilcox, 1980). Although impulsive children frequently do poorly on both tests, little is known about whether the tasks tap the same deficit. Knowledge of this nature can only enhance understanding of the processes involved in generalization.

Finally, training variables can greatly affect generalization. Are the independent variables those most likely to effect change in the identified skill deficits? Obviously, the skill taught must match the identified skill deficit if generalization is to occur. However, without information on specific skill deficits for given populations as they relate to skills necessary to complete a task, generalization, in the language of Stokes and Baer (1977), becomes a matter of training and hoping. As the knowledge base in these areas increases, so will the ability to predict when and how generalization occurs.

ASSESSMENT STRATEGIES

Cognitive Assessment in Academic Problem-Solving

One arena in which cognitive behavioral programs have been used with increasing frequency is that of academic remediation. Many academic tasks lend themselves, for example, to the systematic step-by-step problem-solving characteristics of self-instructional methods. To demonstrate the practical utility and theoretical relevance of cognitive behavioral approaches, both the cognitive and behavioral elements in a given program must be assessed. This section discusses methods that have been used to assess the cognitive aspects of available programs, particularly from the perspective of cognitive measures being independent variables. Cognitive measures are rarely employed in this setting as dependent variables. A later section describes the behavioral measures.

When the cognitive aspects of a program are assessed, several options are available. First, one may assess the ongoing overt verbalizations of a child during an academic problem-solving situation. Most cognitive behavioral programs introduce overt verbalizations as an independent variable by asking the child systematically to talk to him- or herself through a task. The manner in which children are to employ the self-instructions presents interesting assessment questions and may lead to differential outcomes. Some studies have required the child to employ self-instructions in a somewhat rote fashion, in which the child learns to label invariant steps in a problem-solving process. Robin *et al.* (1975), for instance, taught children to employ self-instructions in this manner to remediate letter-writing deficiencies. Similarly, Roberts and Mullis (1983) taught children to verbalize specific steps in solving arithmetic problems. Malamuth (1979) taught fifth-grade poor readers to use specific task-oriented self-instructions to impove their reading skills.

Douglas *et al.* (1976) argued against teaching children a rote set of self-instructions. Rather, in their work, hyperactive children were taught to verbalize strategies in their own words; reasonable strategies were accepted even when they differed from those of the trainer. Thus, the authors believed that they not only modeled specific strategies but also reinforced a more general problem-solving set. Meichenbaum and Asarnow (1979) have called this type of training "metacognitive training" after the work by Brown and others (Brown, 1975; Campione & Brown, 1977) in metacognitive development. The aim here is to teach the child how to think about thinking. In this model, Brown, Campione, and Murphy (1977) suggest that children be taught:

> the ability to stop and think before attempting a problem, to ask questions of oneself and others, to determine if one recognizes the problem, to check solutions against reality by asking not "is it right" but is it reasonable, to monitor attempts to learn to see if they are working or worth the effort.

Training within this model raises a number of assessment questions. It is much easier to teach a child a given strategy and then, to assess whether the child verbalizes it at the appropriate time and in the appropriate sequence than it is to assess whether a child has been taught a problem-solving set and whether the child employs that set. Whether the child is employing a specific strategy or a more general problem-solving strategy is important in answering *process* questions regarding the active elements in a cognitive behavioral program and in assessing correspondence between type of strategy employed and motor behaviors exhibited by the child.

To answer *outcome* questions, the major measures are the child's improvement on the academic task given specific versus more general problem-solving strategy training, maintenance of behavior change, and degree of generalization from one task to another as a function of the type of training.

As mentioned earlier, Kauffman and Hallahan (1979) have suggested that the child's overt verbalizations may be used to monitor the child's problem-solving strategies and to correct either misapplications of rules or incorrect rules themselves. Thus, trainers, experimenters, or teachers might systematically ask a child to employ overt self-instructions at specific checkpoints to make overt the presumed covert process. This technique has been suggested by others (e.g., Meichenbaum, 1977), but it has not been systematically employed in the literature.

The question of the presumed correspondence between overt and covert processes leads to the second general approach to the assessment of cognitive processes in academic tasks. This option continues to measure overt behavior but does so with different intent. The overt behavior is seen as a sign of the assumed underlying cognitive process (Mahoney, 1974; Meichenbaum, 1977). What is measured is not so much the overt behavior itself but what is referred to frequently as cognitive style.

Standardized measures such as the Matching Familiar Figures Test (Kagan *et al.*, 1964) and the Kansas Reflectivity–Impulsivity Scale for Preschoolers (Wright, 1972) may be used as independent measures to divide children into groups by response style (e.g., reflective or impulsive), or they may be used as dependent measures to assess the effect of a training program on response styles. Impulsivity has been related to academic achievement (Messer, 1976). Several studies have reported improvements in academic performance as a function of altering impulsive response style (Kendall & Finch, 1976, 1978). Improvements were noted in teacher reports of listening attentively, completing work on time, and beginning work promptly.

Another assessment of cognitive style infrequently employed is a standard measure of intelligence. Intelligence is correlated with cognitive response style (Messer, 1976) and represents a global measure of a child's problem-solving ability. Roberts and Tharp (1980) correlated children's use of private speech in an academic reading task with IQ as measured by the WISC-R. They found strong negative correlations between IQ and evaluative and strategy-type statements. The authors suggest that some forms of verbalizations commonly employed in self-instructional training programs are not those typically used in the natural environment by high-achieving, high-IQ children. Other studies may use IQ as a screening measure or as a dependent measure. Meichenbaum and Goodman (1971b) used WISC Performance IQ scores as dependent measures to assess the effectiveness of one of the early self-instructional programs for impulsivity.

Cognitive Assessment in Social Problem-Solving

Social problem-solving has received considerable attention with cognitive behavioral intervention programs. In many cases, cognitions are not directly assessed and the emphasis is more directly placed on the measurement of a targeted overt behavior. Bornstein and Quevillon (1976), for example, assessed on-task behavior in determining treatment effectiveness for self-instructional training in overactive preschool boys. Snyder and White (1979) assessed school attendance, frequency of impulsive behaviors, and performance in daily living requirements as yardsticks for treatment effectiveness in a cognitive behavioral program for behaviorally disturbed adolescents. In both cases there was neither independent assessment of the use of self-instructional procedures by the children once a training was terminated nor attempts to measure changes in the cognitive domain as a function of treatment.

In contrast, the "Think Aloud" program developed by Camp, Blom, Hebert, and van Doorninck (1977) assessed changes in both the cognitive and behavioral domains in a program aimed at aggressive 6- to 8-year-old boys. In addition to teacher checklists, selected WISC-R subtests, the WRAT reading test, and a subtest from the Illinois Test of Psycholinguistic Abilities, response style on the Matching Familiar Figures Test was also measured. Children were also administered an abbreviated version of the Preschool Interpersonal Problem Solving Test (PIPS; Shure & Spivack, 1974b) to assess changes in problem-solving as a function of the social training received. This test is described in more detail below. Children who received training in the "Think Aloud" program generated more solutions to the problems as a function of training, but these solutions tended to be more aggressive than those of normal controls or aggressive controls, neither of whom had received that training. The authors conclude that the training program seemed "to have loosened their [aggressive children in experimental condition] tongues but failed to assist them toward developing enough constructive alternatives" (p. 165). Nonetheless, the training program was effective to the degree that aggressive children, at post-test, achieved scores similar to the normal controls that differentiated them from aggressive controls in a discriminant function analysis. These types of multiple assessments across several modalities provide very important data both to determine treatment effectiveness and to validate mechanisms of change.

Shure and Spivack (1974b) developed the PIPS test as a measure of interpersonal cognitive problem-solving skills that mediate social adjustment. The PIPS test is designed to elicit as many different solutions as possible to two types of interpersonal problems: (a) obtaining a toy from another child, and (b) avoiding mother's anger after having damaged something of value. A second similar measure is titled the "What Happens Next Game" (WHNG) and is designed to elicit as many different consequences as possible to two different behaviors: (a) taking a toy from another child, and (b) taking something from an adult without first asking. Both measures were used by Shure and Spivack in two related studies (1979, 1980) that taught interpersonal problem-solving to preschool and kindergarten children. The measures yielded data on children's ability to generate alternative solutions and to engage in consequential thinking. These skills were then related to overt social adjustment. This, again, is an example of the use of cognitive assessment to determine treatment effectiveness as well as treatment processes.

An additional test developed by Shure and Spivack (1972) is the Means–End Problem Solving Test (MEPS). Children are confronted with a series of stories portraying hypothetical problems with interpersonal themes. Only the initial situation and the final outcome are presented. The child is then asked to generate the middle of the story. This test appears to differentiate among groups of emotionally disturbed and normal boys (Shure & Spivack, 1972). Emotionally disturbed children tended to generate fewer responses, and those generated tended to more impulsive and aggressive than those of their normal peers (Shure & Spivack, 1972).

There are a number of other measures that have been developed to assess social cognition, such as the Chandler Bystander Cartoons (Chandler, 1973) and the Feffer Role-Taking Task (Feffer, 1959). In the former, the child is asked to tell a series of stories based on cartoon sequences from the perspective of the main character. The test, therefore, is viewed as a measure of the child's ability to take another perspective. The Feffer Role-Taking Task is similar in content and intent. It asks the child to tell a story about a picture, while sequentially taking the role of each person in the story.

While measures such of those developed by Chandler (1973) and Feffer (1959) typically have moderately acceptable psychometric characteristics, they are used infrequently in cognitive behavioral programs. One reason may be that the roots of cognitive behavior therapy lie at least in part in behavioral methodology, in which behavior is generally viewed as a sample rather than as a sign of enduring traits or personality characteristics. Measures such as those described above do not necessarily violate this assumption, but they are more associated with traditional personality assessment techniques. Cognitive behavior therapists in both research and practice are faced with the task of developing cognitive assessment devices that will help to answer questions regarding treatment mechanisms and to relate changes in the cognitive domain to concomitant changes in the behavioral domain.

Behavioral Assessment in Academic and Social Problem-Solving

Most children are referred for treatment because of problem behaviors, sometimes acts of commission, such as hyperactivity or aggression, and sometimes acts of omission, such as social withdrawal or inadequate academic performance. To demonstrate that cognitive behavior therapy techniques produce useful changes, these problem behaviors must be directly assessed (Hobbs *et al.*, 1980). The remainder of this section is a review of three types of measures of behavior that have been used in evaluating the effectiveness of cognitive behavior therapy with children: checklists and rating scales, academic performance, and behavioral observations. Their uses in the child cognitive behavior therapy literature are summarized, and critiques and suggestions for further use are provided.

The appropriate criteria by which to evaluate the quality of these various behavioral measures has been the subject of some debate. Some cognitive behavioral researchers argue that psychometric criteria are appropriate for behavioral measures, and thus include psychometric data in their presentation of assessment issues (Craighead, Meyers, Craighead, & McHale, 1982; Kendall, Pellegrini, & Urbain, 1981). The present authors and others (Hobbs *et al.*, 1980) argue that psychometric criteria are not appropriate to evaluate behavioral measures for two reasons. First, psychometric theory is based on the model that an observed score is the result of a true score plus measurement error. Consistency (as in reliability and validity procedures) is the hallmark of a good assessment device because more of the stable true score is being measured than is measurement error. Behavior and cognitions, however, are thought to be subject to modification. Therefore, inconsistent scores on an assessment device may be due to actual changes in behavior or cognition rather than to a device of poor quality (Nelson, Hay, & Hay, 1977). Second, psychometrics involves data from groups of subjects. Even if a device is reliable and valid for a group, it cannot be assumed that it will be reliable and valid for an individual (Nelson, 1981). Thus, alternative strategies to psychometrics may be needed to evaluate the quality of behavioral and cognitive assessment techniques—for example, treatment validity or idiographic psychometrics (Nelson, 1981).

The quality of the behavioral measures presented next is not evaluated. These measures are presented because they have been used in recent cognitive behavior research with children. For each measure, it is noted whether the measure was "sensitive" to treatment effects. In each study mentioned, some statistically significant effects were reported. If significant effects were obtained when using the described measure, it is noted that the measure was "sensitive" to treatment effects. If significant effects were obtained on other measures but not on the described measure, it is noted that the measure was "insensitive" to treatment effects. No significant changes may have occurred in the described measure because the treatment did not affect the response being measured, or because treatment did affect the response but the measure failed to reflect these changes adequately.

Rating Scales and Checklists

Through rating scales and checklists, the opinions of significant others are sought about a child's status, generally pre- and post-treatment. Both rating scales and checklists contain a list of brief behavioral descriptions. In rating scales, the *degree* to which the item is descriptive of a particular child is recorded by marking a particular point along the rating scale. In checklists, the items are generally marked in all-or-none fashion, as either descriptive or not descriptive of a particular child.

Ratings by Teachers. Frequently, teachers are asked to evaluate hyperactive or impulsive children with rating scales and checklists pre- and post-treatment to assess the effects of cognitive behavior therapy with children. The rating scales and checklists vary in their degree of specificity—that is, how closely they measure the construct for which the child was originally referred. In other words, some devices purport to measure only impulsivity or hyperactivity, whereas others purport to measure a more general adjustment or maladjustment. Examples of specific or narrow rating scales and checklists follow.

The abbreviated or short form of the Conners Rating Scale (Conners, 1969) has frequently been used to measure hyperactivity. It contains 10 items such as "restless or overactive" or "disturbs other children" that the teacher rates on a four-point scale. This scale was sensitive to treatment effects in a study by Kendall and Wilcox (1980) but was insensitive to possible effects in studies by Douglas *et al.* (1976) and by Bugental *et al.* (1977). The psychometric properties of the Conners Rating Scale are summarized by Kendall *et al.* (1981).

Another specific rating scale is the Impulsive Classroom Behavior Scale (Weinrich, 1975, also cited in Kendall & Finch, 1978), which consists of nine five-point items that supposedly describe impulsive children. This scale revealed treatment effects in a study by Kendall and Finch (1978). This same study also used another specific rating scale, which failed to reveal treatment effects. This scale is the Locus of Conflict Scale (Armentrout, 1971) and is scored for internalization, externalization, and total maladjustment.

A final specific rating scale was developed by Kendall and Wilcox (1979) for the explicit purpose of assessing self-control or impulsivity. It is a 33-item seven-point rating scale; sample items include: "Does the child interrupt inappropriately in conversations, or wait his or her turn to speak?" and "Does the child grab for the belongings of others?" This rating scale revealed treatment effects in a study done by Kendall and Wilcox (1980).

Broader teacher checklists were used by Glenwick and Barocas (1979) and were relatively insensitive to treatment effects. These two checklists were the 11-item AML Behavior Rating Scale (Cowen, Dorr, Clarfield, Kreling, McWilliams, Pokracki, Pratt, Terrell, & Wilson, 1973), which measures aggressions (A), moodiness (M), and learning difficulties (L), and the 28-item Classroom Adjustment Rating Scale (Clarfield, 1974), which also assesses aggression, moodiness, and learning difficulties, as well as the teacher's knowledge of, liking for, and overall adjustment rating of the student.

A teacher's questionnaire was used by Meichenbaum and Goodman (1971b, Study 1) to assess children's self-control, activity level, cooperativness, and likability. This questionnaire consisted of 10 incomplete statements, each followed by three forced-choice alternative completions, and was insensitive to treatment effects.

A broad teacher rating scale is the Hahnemann Preschool Behavior Rating Scale (cited in Shure & Spivack, 1979, 1980). It consists of seven nine-point items that assess impatience, emotionality, and dominance/aggression. This scale revealed treatment effects in studies by Shure and Spivack (1979, 1980).

A last broad checklist is the School Behavior Checklist (Miller, 1972), which consists of 96 items in a yes–no format and is designed to assess aggression, withdrawal, and prosocial behavior. When portions of this checklist were used by Camp, Blom, Hebert, and van Doorninck (1977) to evaluate treatment effectiveness, no differences were found on total subscales, but there were improvements on individual items.

Checklists and rating scales were used in a creative way by Camp, Blom, Hebert, and van Doorninck (1977) and Kendall and Wilcox (1980) to evaluate clinical or substantive significance, respectively, as well as statistical significance. Camp, Blom, Hebert, and van Doorninck (1977) compared the treated aggressive boys with both an untreated control group of aggressive boys and an untreated control group of normal boys. The clinical hope was that after treatment, the aggressive boys would receive checklist scores similar to those of the normal boys. Similarly, Kendall and Wilcox (1980) compared the scores that children referred for poor self-control received after treatment on the Conners Rating Scale and on the Self-Control Rating Scale with scores received by normal nonreferred children. Again, the clincal hope was that treatment would help the children referred for problem behaviors to score as did the normal children. The scores for children who were taught conceptual self-instructions did fall in the normal range after treatment.

Ratings by Other Adults. Finally, rating scales have been used by adult assessors other than teachers. Glenwick and Barocas (1979) had parents of target children complete the Parents Rating Scale (a modification of the Werry–Weiss Peters Activity Scale), a 31-item three-point rating scale covering out-of-school behavior and concentrating on hyperactivity (Werry, 1968). This measure, however, proved to be insensitive to treatment effects. Kendall and Finch (1978) had unit personnel in a residential treatment center as well as teachers complete pre- and posttreatment the Locus of Conflict Scale, but no significant effects were found on the staff ratings. Kendall and Wilcox (1980) had therapists complete a 13-item five-point scale assessing each child's degree of improvement in several areas, such as restlessness and distractibility. There were significant differences among groups on this measure, although therapists were aware of the children's experimental conditions. Other checklists for parents to describe their children are the Child Behavior Profile (Achenbach, 1978a; Achenbach & Edelbrock, 1979) and the Parent Questionnaire (Connors, 1973). Although each has adequate psychometric properties, they have not been widely used in cognitive behavior therapy with children.

Evaluation of Rating Scales. A concern about the use of rating scales or checklists to evaluate the effects of a cognitive behavior therapy program is the validity or accuracy of such scales or checklists. In other words, do the scales or checklists accurately measure any changes that have occurred in the child's behavior?

Rating scales have been shown to be more subject to bias than are observational strategies. It has generally been found that experimentally induced bias affected global ratings but not systematic or direct observation. For example, Kent, O'Leary, Diament, and Dietz (1974) found that global ratings were biased by expectations that children's disruptive behavior had either decreased or not changed from a baseline to a treatment phase. Shuller and McNamara (1976) found that global ratings were biased by the assignment of different trait labels (hyperactive, aggressive, and normal) to the same videotaped child. Cunningham and Tharp (1981) found that global ratings were influenced by the amount and type of off-task behavior shown by peers sitting adjacent to the target child. In an exception in which very specific items constituted the rating scale, Siegel, Dragovich, and Marholin (1976) found that neither ratings nor observations were biased by differential expectations from one videotaped child being diagnosed as "extremely hyperactive" or as experiencing "circumscribed fears of fire and the dark."

Thus, one suggestion to improve the accuracy of rating scales is to use items describing specific behaviors. Cronbach (1970) provides other such suggestions: include more than two points in the rating scale, clearly define the anchor points of the scale items, and use raters, perferably several, who have extensive experience with the person being evaluated.

Attempts have been made to validate psychometrically checklists or rating scales by comparing data produced by them with observational data. For example, Kendall and Wilcox (1979) compared teachers' ratings of 110 children on the Self-Control Rating Scale with observers' codings of the child's off-task verbal behavior, off-task physical behavior, off-task attention, out-of-seat behavior, and interruptions. The correlation between the rating scale and the total score of the behavioral observations was 0.18. Even if the obtained correlation had been higher, caution must be exercised against extrapolating from group psychometric data to the validity of a particular measure in evaluating treatment changes produced in a specific child. That is, even if a rating scale correlates well with behavioral observations for a group of children, the relationship between the scale and the observations may not be strong for a particular child.

Behavioral observations seem to have an advantage over checklists or rating scales in assessing specific behavior changes. Checklists or rating scales, however, may have an advantage in assessing the raters' general or more global reaction to the changes that treatment has produced. The reaction of these "consumers" of treatment change is important in assessing the clinical or substantive significance of changes that have occurred and possibly in maintaining those changes. The reactions of significant others are included in the social validation of treatment outsome (Kazdin, 1977b; Wolf, 1978). In conclusion, the ideal strategy is probably to use *both* observational and more global measures of change.

Peer Opinions. When cognitive behavior therapy programs are directed toward children's interpersonal skills (for example, decreases in aggression or in impulsive behavior patterns), the opinions of peers may be sought, as well as those of adults. There are three common ways of obtaining peer opinion (Kane & Lawler, 1978). First is peer nomination, in which a child is asked to name a specific number of peers to fulfill a particular function. Either positive or negative functions may be specified. Peer acceptance is measured by specifying positive functions—for example, naming three children whom you would like to have sit near you, to have work with you, or to have play with you. Peer rejection is measured by specifying negative functions—for example, naming three children whom you dislike. Peer acceptance and rejection are not simple opposites. When both measures are taken, the negative correlation between them is at best moderate (Hartup, 1970). The peer nomination procedure is simplified, especially for younger children, by providing photographs of their peer group from whom to select nominations (Moore & Updegraff, 1964). A second way to obtain peer opinion is by peer ratings, in which each child rates every other group member on a given set of characteristics or skills. A third way is peer rankings, in which each child ranks all other group members from best to worst on some characteristic or behavior. The psychometric properties of these means of obtaining peer opinion are reviewed by Kane and Lawler (1978); Van Hasselt, Hersen, Whitehill, and Bellack (1979); and Kendall *et al.* (1981). Of particular concern is the lack of good correspondence between peer opinion and behavioral data. For example, Greenwood, Walker, Todd, and Hops (1979) found correlations ranging from 0.19 to 0.29 between positive peer nominations and different categories and settings of behavioral observations.

An example of a study that employed a peer rating procedure, as well as behavioral observations, to assess the effects of a cognitive behavior therapy program to reduce social withdrawal is provided by Gottman, Gonso, and Schuler (1976). The peer rating procedure was sensitive to treatment effects, as were aspects of the observation procedure (distribution of interactions, but not total amount of interaction). A quantitative relationship between rating and observation procedures was not reported.

Measuring Academic Performance

Poor academic performance is frequently among the reasons for children being referred for treatment. In such cases, measurement of academic performance is an appropriate dependent measure.

Several studies have evaluated the effects of self-instructional training (Meichenbaum & Goodman, 1971a), sometimes in combination with contingency management procedures, on academic performance. These studies vary in two major ways. The first variation is whether the training task consisted wholly of academic materials, partly of academic materials, or wholly of nonacademic materials. In the first category, children with writing deficiencies were taught to use self-instructions while printing letters in a study by Robin *et al.* (1975). In the second category, Varni and Henker (1979) trained children to self-instruct while using their Sullivan reading and arithmetic texts as well as during tasks involving the Porteus Mazes (Porteus, 1955) and the Matching Familiar Figures Test (Kagan *et al.*, 1964). Similarly, only some of the training tasks used by Malamuth (1979) involved reading. Also, only some training groups received self-instructional training applied to academic tasks in the study by Glenwick and Barocas (1979). In the third category, self-instructions were taught using nonacademic materials (e.g., Douglas *et al.*, 1976; Egeland, 1974).

The second way in which these studies vary is whether the measure of academic performance is standardized or "home-made." Standardized measures were used by Egeland (1974), who found that impulsive children who were taught a search strategy improved more on the Gates–MacGinitie Reading Comprehension Subtest than did impulsives who were taught to delay responding or who were in the control group; no significant differences were found on the Vocabulary Subtest or on the Stanford Achievement Test. Standardized measures were also used by Douglas *et al.* (1976), who demonstrated that the self-instructional group improved more than the control group on the Oral Reading and Oral Comprehension Subtests of the Durrell Analysis of Reading Difficulty, but not on the Listening Comprehension or Spelling Subtests of the Durrell or on the Arithmetic Subtest of the Wide Range Achievement Test. Also using standardized measures, Glenwick and Barocas (1979) found that the self-instructional groups improved more than the control group on the Reading and Arithmetic Substests of the Wide Range Achievement Test, but not on the Spelling Subtest. Using a single-subject design, Varni and Henker (1979) reported improvements for three boys in their reading and arithmetic performances in the Sullivan workbooks during the self-reinforcement phases of the study. Nonstandardized measures were used by Malamuth (1979), who found that children who received self-instructional training improved more on reading a story and answering questions about it than did a control group. Similarly, a nonstandardized writing test was used by Robin *et al.* (1975), who reported that the self-instructional group had better post-test letter-writing scores than either a direct training or a control group when letters used during self-instructional training were employed; no generalization occurred to nontrained letters.

It seems that to increase the possibility of demonstrating change produced by self-instructional training, it would be advisable to use at least some academic materials during training, preferably materials related to the measures of academic performance. These measures would then be *sensitive* to any changes that might occur. Other dissimilar measures could also be employed, but perhaps as measures of generalization rather then direct change. The greater the relationship between the dependent measure and the training task, the greater the chance is of detecting any effects that occurred. The issue of generalization across tasks is also important, but it is an issue different from that of determining whether the treatment was effective at all.

"Home-made" measures may be more sensitive to treatment effects if "home-made" materials are used in training. The advantage, however, of standardized measures is that the resultant scores are meaningful because they can be compared with normative data (Nelson, 1980). Thus, either "home-made" or standardized measures can demonstrate statistically significant differences between groups, but substantive or clinical significance can be shown in addition by the standardized measures. To borrow Carver's terminology, standardized tests may serve both "edumetric" and psychometric purposes; that is, they may assess both the individual's gain as a function of education and the individual's relation to a norm group (Carver, 1974).

Behavioral Observations

The least inferential assessment method is behavioral observation. Observers record behaviors, either as they occur or subsequently from audio or video tape. These observations may occur either in the criterion situation itself or in an analogue situation.

Analogue Situations. Although the criterion situation may be the child's school or home, observational data are sometimes collected for the sake of convenience in an analogue situation, for example, the clinic or laboratory. The behavior that is observed should be of the same topography as the criterion behavior. Given the situation-specificity of behavior, however, concerns about whether the behavior that is observed in the clinic or laboratory would also occur in the home or classroom setting are legitimate.

Sometimes, observations occur while a child is performing experimental tasks that are not the criterion or referral behaviors. The child's performance on the Matching Familiar Figures Test (Kagan *et al.*, 1964) or on a resistance-to-temptation task (see Kendall & Williams, 1982) may be observed in the laboratory. These tasks, however, are generally far removed from the original referral problem or criterion behavior. Inferences are sometimes made that impulsivity or self-control is being measured. To fall into the category of direct behavioral observation, a minimal qualification is that the criterion behavior must be directly observed, even if a laboratory or clinic analogue situation is used.

A variety of behaviors have been observed in analogue situation. Blechman, Olson, and Hellman (1976) assessed family problem-solving skills pre- and post-treatment by coding on-task problem-solving behavior and off-task antagonistic behavior. Similarly, Robin, Kent, O'Leary, Foster, and Prinz (1977) assessed parent–adolescent problem-solving skills pre- and post-treatment by coding the following: defining the problem, listing options, evaluating solutions, and agreeing on possible solutions. A different target behavior, impulsivity, was observed in a clinical setting by Kendall and Finch (1976). They coded "switches," that is, shifts from one behavior to another when the former was not completed, for three targeted areas: topics of conversation, games played, and rules of play. Responses to verbal assaults were observed in an analogue setting by Goodwin and Mahoney (1975); hyperactive impulsive boys were subjected to verbal aggression, while their responses were coded as coping or noncoping, using a time-sampling observation procedure. Finally, hyperactive boys were observed by Varni and Henker (1979) in a clinic setting while they worked on arithmetic and reading assignments; measures included the children's accuracy on these academic tasks as well as their hyperactive behaviors (off-task and gross motor). While role-playing does not seem to have been used to assess the effectiveness of cognitive behavior therapy techniques on children's social skills, role-playing is a possible analogue assessment device (Bornstein, Bellack, & Hersen, 1977).

Behavioral Observations in the Classroom. Whereas observations in analogue setting involve observing criterion behaviors in noncriterion settings, behavioral observations in the classroom involve observing criterion behaviors in a criterion setting. For children who are impulsive or hyperactive, a frequently observed classroom behavior is on-task behavior, generally measured by a time-sampling procedure (Bornstein & Quevillon, 1976; Friedling & O'Leary, 1979; Meichenbaum & Goodman, 1971b; Varni & Henker, 1979). Caution must be exercised, however, in not equating improvements in on-task behavior with improvements in academic accuracy. Being on-task and completing work correctly seem to be somewhat independent behaviors (e.g., Hay, Hay, & Nelson, 1977). If the goal is improved academic accuracy, then the correctness of work should be directly assessed as well as or instead of assessing on-task behavior.

For children who are withdrawn or aggressive, a suitable target behavior to observe is social interaction with peers. Hyperactive impulsive boys who had difficulty coping with verbal aggression were observed in their classroom pre- and post-treatment by Goodwin and Mahoney (1975), as well as in the analogue setting, as previously described; aggressive, destructive, and hyperactive behavior was observed, using a time-sampling procedure. Similarly, the aggressive behavior of emotionally disturbed children was observed in their classrooms using a time-sampling procedure to assess the effectiveness of the Turtle Technique (Robin, Schneider, & Dolnick, 1976). (The Turtle Technique is a self-control procedure that teaches a child to relax and to withdraw into a "shell" instead of making aggressive responses.) The classroom social interactions of socially withdrawn children were scored on a time-sampling procedures by Gottman, Gonso, and Schuler (1976). While the total interaction scores did not differentiate the experimental and control groups, the distribution of the interactions to popular versus unpopular peers did.

Comments on Behavioral Observations. Most of the reported observational systems are "home-made" systems, designed to assess specific behaviors that are the focus of treatment. Some observational systems have achieved a more formal status, primarily because they have been used many times in research projects. Some of these formal systems are described by Kendall *et al.* (1981). They include the O'Leary, Kaufman, Kass, and Drabman (1970) and the Patterson code for home observations (Jones, Reid, & Patterson, 1975). The O'Leary code was used by Anderson, Fodor, and Alpert (1976) to compare the effectiveness of alternative methods of training self-control. Since these formal codes frequently contain several behaviors, they may be relatively insensitive as a dependent measure. The data accumulated using these codes, however, are useful for a variety of purposes. For example, the psychometric properties of these codes have been investigated, and clinical or substantive significance can be examined by comparing present data with normative data collected in previous uses of the code (Nelson & Bowles, 1975).

Users of behavioral observation systems should be aware of some potential problems surrounding their use, namely, reactivity of observees, the relationship between observer accuracy and agreement, and the variables that can influence observer agreement (see reviews by Kent & Foster, 1977, and Wasik & Loven, 1980). Given observable precautions, however, observational data seem quite robust.

The data collected in the studies described above were generally collected by independent trained observers. Another alternative is to have people already in the criterion setting collect observational data, such as teachers, parents, or residential staff. If such participant observers are used, the data-collection system will need simplification. Time-sampling procedures are too complex when people have additional duties to perform. Simpler alternatives include frequency counts and spot-checks. As an example of the former, Snyder and White (1979) had teachers record absences from class and had staff members record completion of specific tasks (e.g., cleaning one's room) and observed instances of impulsive behavior (e.g., aggression, stealing, property destruction, drug abuse). As an example of the latter, Kubany and Sloggett (1973) describe a spot-checking system that is convenient for teachers to use; when a timer rings, the teacher observes a specific student and records the student's behavior that is occurring at that instant. These convenient observational systems could serve as an alternative to teacher checklists or rating scales to provide a more direct measure of the criterion behavior in the criterion setting.

CONCLUSION

This chapter reviews several cognitive and behavioral assessment techniques that have been used predominantly to measure the outcome of cognitive behavior therapy programs for children's academic and social skills. While methodological investigations of the quality of behavioral measures have only a brief history, the history of methodological investigations of the quality of cognitive measures is even briefer. Therefore, in addition to issues discussed earlier, several questions or paths for future research can be outlined.

A first concern is that cognitions cannot be assessed directly. Instead, assessed verbal or motor behaviors are sometimes are taken as signs of an underlying cognitive process. The "sign" approach presents a number of difficulties (Goldfried & Kent, 1972), among them being the necessity of inference (from motor to cognitive behavior) that is difficult to validate empirically and the assumption that the underlying process (cognitions) cause generalized responding (across situations). Cognitive assessors must at least be aware of these difficulties if they are to find solutions.

A second issue is determining for which children and for which problem behaviors various treatment strategies should be used—namely behavioral, cognitive, or cognitive behavioral approaches. A step was made in this direction by Bugental *et al.* (1977), who evaluated the differential effectiveness of two treatment approaches (social reinforcement on self-instructions) for hyperactive and impulsive children with differing attributional systems (internal versus external). More of this differential assessment is needed to maximize treatment effectiveness.

Finally, the mechanisms of change in cognitive behavioral programs merit further examination. Simply because a cognitive behavioral program was implemented and because behavior change occurred does not mean that the program or all of the components of the program caused the change. Assessment is important in identifying and measuring independent variables as well as dependent variables.

6

Locus of Intervention in Child Cognitive Behavior Therapy

IMPLICATIONS OF A BEHAVIORAL COMMUNITY PSYCHOLOGY PERSPECTIVE

David S. Glenwick and Leonard A. Jason

LOCUS OF INTERVENTION: INTRODUCTION AND DEFINITION

The present chapter considers the locus of intervention taken by research and clinical endeavors in child cognitive behavior therapy, with particular emphasis on (a) the implications one's chosen locus of intervention may have on outcome and (b) the possibilities for thoughtful selection of locus of intervention to improve the efficacy of treatment efforts. For present purposes the term *locus of intervention* is defined broadly, encompassing not only the question of *where* to intervene but also the following related issues: (a) when, (b) at what target levels, (c) with what types of populations, (d) with what kinds of training and support personnel, and (e) toward what ends and target behaviors. As will become evident, such a wide-angle view is necessary in discussing locus of intervention because of its inextricable relatedness to these other issues.

Locus of intervention and its ramifications will be explored through consideration of two models of service delivery and action-oriented research—the traditional model and the community model. The next section of the chapter will discuss the essential characteristics of the tradi-

David S. Glenwick • Department of Psychology, Fordham University, Bronx, New York 10458. **Leonard A. Jason** • Department of Psychology, De Paul University, Chicago, Illinois 60614.

tional model as well as the major criticisms that have been directed against it. Following this, the hallmarks of the community model will be outlined, with the model being presented as a reasonable supplement to the traditional approach. The third part of that section will conclude with a brief critique, from a community model perspective, of child cognitive behavior modification projects conducted to date. In the final and lengthiest section of the chapter we will explicate the potential benefits of the community model for child cognitive behavior modification, demonstrating, we hope, that, while the traditional model has its place in dealing with psychopathology, a broader community-based approach is also needed.

CHILD COGNITIVE BEHAVIOR MODIFICATION AND MODELS OF SERVICE DELIVERY

The Traditional Model

Most human services in our society can be regarded as being purveyed through a traditional model or delivery system, the salient features of which include (a) a one-to-one or small-group format, with a therapist treating either a single patient/client or a small group of patients/clients at a time; (b) a late treatment focus, directed toward persons with already identified and often longstanding disorders; and (c) a passive-receptive stance, whereby mental health professionals wait for patients/clients to arrive at their hospitals, clinics, or offices (Zax & Cowen, 1976).

In the past 20 years, several limitations of this model have been noted that have produced considerable dissatisfaction with it among many human service professionals. First, given the passive-receptive stance and one-to-one or small-group emphasis of the model, professional personnel can never hope to meet the ever-increasing demand and need for services (Albee, 1967; Cowen, 1973). This need is illustrated by the finding that 30% of elementary school children had identifiable school adjustment difficulties (Glidewell & Swallow, 1969). A second criticism leveled at the traditional model concerns the mixed success achieved in demonstrating the efficacy of psychotherapy in producing maintenance and generalization of behavior change (e.g., Rimland, 1979; Shapiro, 1971; Smith & Glass, 1977), particularly with well-entrenched disorders. Third, although the highest rates of psychopathology are consistently found in the lowest socioeconomic strata (Dohrenwend & Dohrenwend, 1969), traditional therapists have devoted a disproportionate amount of their time to the treatment of higher-income groups (Zax & Cowen, 1976).

A fourth and final criticism of the traditional model has come from those who point out the implied authoritarian stance of some therapies grounded in this model, with an unequal distribution of power and influence between one person labeled "the healer" or "the expert" and the other, who is in a "one-down" position, labeled "the patient" (Rappaport, 1977). In addition to the philosophical implications of such a relationship, its practical limitations in certain contexts, in terms of its view of our ability to learn to act as our own personal healers and scientists, have been noted (Mahoney, 1974; Rappaport, 1977).

The behavioral approach to the etiology and amelioration of psychological problems has stressed characteristics—particularly its reliance on objective, measurable data; its foundation in experimentally rooted clinical procedures (Mahoney, Kazdin, & Lesswing, 1974); and its attention to overt and covert behaviors rather than to any inferred underlying "disease"—that differentiate it from such other perspectives as the medical and psychoanalytic models of dysfunction. Unfortunately, behaviorists have tended, with respect to their orientation to service delivery, to follow the traditional service approach. MacDonald, Hedberg, and Campbell (1974) found 98% of the articles in four major behavioral journals to be person-centered in their delivery approach—that is, the studies intervened predominantly at the individual or small-group level. Furthermore, as Nietzel, Winett, MacDonald, and Davidson (1977) have noted, a majority of these person-centered interventions have focused on the remediation of deficits as their sole objective, with little attention paid to such goals as prevention and the building-in of competencies.

The Community Model

In the search for a broader model to address these dissatisfactions with the traditional approach, a paradigm known as the *community model* has been developed over the past two decades (Heller & Monahan, 1977; Zax & Specter, 1974). In contrast to the traditional orientation, the community model adopts an active approach (i.e., enters community settings to deliver services and assist in mounting interventions in the immediate locale) and seeks to extend greatly the reach of services and interventions (e.g., through consultation and the use of paraprofessionals). Most individuals in distress do not seek out mental-health professionals (Gurin, Veroff, & Feld, 1960). Consequently, consultation to professional caregivers (e.g., physicians, welfare department workers) and others (e.g., hairdressers, bartenders) who have extensive contact with persons in distress can play an important role in addressing problems in the community (Caplan, 1964; Cowen, Gesten, Boike, Norton, Wilson, & DeStefano, 1979). In addition, since paraprofessionals appear to be at least as effective as professionals in treating a wide variety of behavior problems (Durlak, 1979), delegating at least some traditional direct-service roles to paraprofessionals can free professionals to engage in such other activities as consultation, supervision and training, and development, evaluation, and dissemination of programs.

The community model can itself be viewed as consisting of two somewhat differing variations—the community mental health and the community psychology (or preventive psychology) perspectives (Jason & Glenwick, 1980b). Both perspectives adopt a seeking, proactive stance; utilize the services of paraprofessionals; and, through consultation, strengthen the abilities of natural helpers in the community. The community mental health orientation, though, retains some ties to the traditional model in that it, too, is primarily person-centered, tending to concentrate on individuals experiencing either incipient or entrenched problems. As an example, youngsters in elementary school might be identified as evidencing early signs of social or behavioral maldevelopment; within a community mental health approach, these target children could be treated by paraprofessionals or the teachers could be offered consultation services.

In contrast, the community/preventive psychology strand of the community model broadens the scope of interventions to incorporate those that are primarily preventive in nature and that focus on environments and person–environment matches as well as on individuals and groups (Felner, Jason, Moritsugu, & Farber, 1983; Jason & Glenwick, 1980a,b). Primary preventive approaches are those directed toward either (a) increasing the possibilities that children from high-risk populations (e.g., children whose parents are schizophrenic) do not develop dysfunctions, (b) preventing the onset of specific maladaptive behaviors (e.g., cigarette smoking), (c) building in competencies and strengths (e.g., interpersonal problem-solving skills), or (d) helping individuals cope with milestone transitions (e.g., marriage, school entrance).

While person- or group-centered preventive interventions may serve to reduce the number of mental-health casualties, environmentally targeted projects appear to possess even greater potential for promoting healthy development in youngsters. That is, interventions aimed at organizations, communities, or societies have the possibility of positively influencing the numerous children within these social systems. At the organizational level of intervention, for example, projects can be mounted to alter any of the following dimensions of a particular setting:

(a) its inanimate features (e.g., resources, physical design, lighting), (b) inhabitant characteristics (e.g., resident stability, staff–client ratios), (c) its natural contingencies, and (d) its social climate (Jason & Glenwick, 1980a).

Community- and society-level interventions might focus on such targets as (a) macro-systems (e.g., energy, transportation, education, or corrections systems within a community or a society); (b) formal and informal supports (e.g., voluntary associations, self-help groups); (c) the mass media; (d) executive, judicial, and legislative processes; and (e) economic conditions (e.g., the impact of unemployment on family functioning) (e.g., Everett, 1980; Milan & Long, 1980; Neitzel *et al.*, 1977; Winett, 1980). When participating in interventions at these levels, community psychologists may adopt a variety of roles and strategies ranging from consultation, data gathering, and conflict mediation to social activism and confrontation.

The community psychology approach has most frequently been embraced by nonbehaviorally-oriented theorists and practitioners (see Glenwick & Jason, 1980, for discussion of the reasons for this). However, the theoretical framework represented by community psychology is indeed eminently compatible with the behavioral paradigm's empirical approach. While the former offers us new lenses through which to examine relatively unexplored goals and consequences of intervention, the latter provides a potent technology for bringing about behavior change. In recognition of the potential of community psychology and behaviorism to contribute to each other's growth and to the amelioration of social problems, an attempt to synthesize the two has occurred in recent years. The result—an integration of community psychology's philosophy and behaviorism's methodology and procedures—has come to be called *behavioral community psychology* and has already begun to demonstrate conceptual, heuristic, and practical promise in such areas as mental and physical health, education, environmental preservation and resource conservation, and criminal justice (Glenwick & Jason, 1980; Martin & Osborne, 1980; Nietzel *et al.*, 1977).

With respect to locus of intervention, we see how the "community" in the community model represents much more than merely the setting for our interventions. It represents a comprehensive way of thinking about a host of dimensions related to the ways in which we conduct research and offer services. The community model and child cognitive behavior modification might at first glance appear to be rather strange bedfellows. However, as we hope to show in the remainder of this chapter, community psychology and the subdiscipline of behavioral community psychology could well prove to be very compatible mates to child cognitive behavior modification, opening up uncharted areas for application and investigation.

Child Cognitive Behavior Therapy: A Critique of the Traditional Model

The bulk of child cognitive behavior therapy projects to date can be seen as falling under the traditional model of intervention. That is, in the majority of cases (a) it is a professional clinician or researcher who delivers the intervention; (b) training of child subjects or clients usually occurs on a one-to-one or small-group basis; (c) the intervention most often occurs in an artificial environment (e.g., a laboratory or research trailer) rather than natural settings (Karoly, 1977); (d) training is frequently on artificial, "non-real-world" tasks; and (e) for the most part, target youngsters are selected on the basis of already displaying a deficit of some duration, being labeled "hyperactive," "impulsive," "aggressive," "learning-disabled," and the like.[1]

Given this rather limited intervention scope, it is not surprising that the general conclusion of reviews on child cognitive behavior therapy has consistently been that, while findings to date have been encouraging, evidence for maintenance and generalization is considerably weaker (Abikoff, 1979; Karoly, 1977; Meichenbaum, 1979a; Meichenbaum & Asarnow, 1979). Not only do gains typically fail to transfer to other areas of cognitive functioning (i.e., fail to generalize across response modes) and to other settings (e.g., the classroom), but they also tend to dissipate over time. Such failures of maintenance and transfer, we believe, result not from any inherent deficiency in cognitive behavior therapy techniques but at least partly from the manner in which interventions are generally conducted—the locus of intervention and related aspects of service delivery.

In the following sections we will suggest how incorporation of the community model of service delivery might add to the effectiveness and scope of cognitive behavior modification with children. Five interrelated lines of thought deriving from the model will be considered: (a) prevention and early intervention (b) use of paraprofessional and natural

[1]While it is true, as Karoly (1977, p. 236) argues, that cognitive, and self-control training has predominantly "employed non-clinical populations," these populations still, though not necessarily severely disturbed, tend to be tagged as displaying a particular problem behavior and have therefore been singled out for intervention from a yet larger population.

change agents, (c) utilization of the ecology of the natural environment, (d) attention to individual diversity and cultural relativism, and (e) focus on systems-level change.

IMPLICATIONS OF THE COMMUNITY MODEL FOR CHILD COGNITIVE BEHAVIOR MODIFICATION

Prevention and Early Intervention

In recent writings on child cognitive behavior modification, there has been increasing mention of its potential for prevention and early intervention (e.g., Little & Kendall, 1979; Peterson, Hartman, & Gelfand, 1980; Urbain & Kendall, 1980). The hope espoused by such authors is that by intervening early in the course of problem development (known as early secondary prevention) or, ideally, by building in cognitive competencies, social skills, and problem-solving abilities before deficits have arisen (primary prevention), we will be able to cut down on the later flow of identified "casualties" requiring intervention for well-entrenched dysfunctions. Thus, Peterson *et al.* (1980), for instance, point out, with reference to health psychology, how child cognitive behavior modification could be incorporated into preventive interventions having a wide array of target behaviors, such as obesity and smoking prevention and outreach work by nurses in schools to teach children about medical and hospital procedures. Similarly, Little and Kendall (1979) speculate on how verbal self-instruction programs in the first grade, when covert self-guiding speech is present in most normal children, might decrease the behavior problems of children who otherwise could become candidates for the labels of "impulsive, "hyperactive," "aggressive," or "delinquent."

High-risk Populations

While cognitive behavior modification's potential for prevention has understandably outstripped its realization, several interesting projects in a preventive vein have been conducted with normal children who are at high risk (e.g., as assessed by screening measures or family history data) for various disabilities or problem behaviors. An illustration is provided by Hartman's (1979) work with symptom-free but high-risk high-school students. His group-behavioral-training emphasized the general applicability of self-management strategies and included stress inoculation, social skills training, anxiety management, and progressive relaxation. (See Chapter 14, this volume, for a detailed discussion of this area.)

Transitions and Milestones

An area related to intervention with high-risk children is that of research with youngsters about to undergo significant developmental milestones or life transitions. A focus on potentially stressful transitions (e.g., school entrance, graduation from high school, the birth of one's first child) can be a useful way of acting preventively to build in coping skills that can be employed in future life transitions (Jason, 1980b). In an inner-city school program, Jason and Burrows (1983) taught high-school seniors relaxation, cognitive restructuring, and problem-solving techniques, which were applied to several transitions involving either family, peer, school, or work issues. The intervention produced gains in feelings of self-efficacy, rational beliefs, and use of cognitive restructuring, as well as easier disengagement from family and formal social supports. One of the advantages of such projects is that, compared with research on high-risk groups (in which individuals are selected and designated as being at risk), interventions concentrating on transitions and milestones can frequently be conducted on entire populations (e.g., all pupils beginning kindergarten in a given school) without children having to be singled out for special individual or small-group treatment.

Crises and Stresses

Yet a third group of studies with a preventive flavor has directed its attention to the crises and stresses experienced by all youngsters (e.g., dental visits, hospitalizations). The pioneering work on this topic (e.g., Melamed & Siegel, 1975; Melamed, Hawes, Heiby, & Glick, 1975) involved peer-coping modeling films to reduce fear arousal and disruptive behavior during dental treatment. More recent writings (e.g., Klorman, Hilpert, Michael, LaGana, & Sveen, 1980; Peterson *et al.*, 1980) have called for a broader coping-skills approach, including such cognitive components as stress inoculation, self-verbalization, self-control desensitization, relaxation, imagery, cognitive restructuring, and anxiety management. Coping-skills packages have been successfully employed by Peterson *et al.* (1980), and Siegel and Peterson (1980) in health-care settings. (See Chapter 14, this volume.) Such packages would seem worthy of further research not only for their preventive potential but also for the likely ease with which they might be taught to and used by natural change agents (e.g., dentists, physicians, nurses, teachers).

Paraprofessionals and Natural Change Agents

Paraprofessionals

The past 15 years have seen a noteworthy burgeoning of the use of paraprofessionals—persons who have not received "postbaccalureate formal clinical training in professional programs of psychology, psychiatry, social work, and psychiatric nursing" (Durlak, 1979, p. 80)—as direct service providers. In a review of 42 studies on the comparative effectiveness of paraprofessionals and professionals, Durlak (1979) found that paraprofessionals achieved clinical results equal to those of professionals in 28 projects and results superior to those of professionals in 12 projects; the strongest evidence tended to come from interventions directed at the modification of specific target problems. He concluded (1979, p. 85) that "professional mental health education, training, and experience are not necessary prerequisites for an effective helping person."

Several factors—including their enthusiasm, lack of prejudgments, and ability to establish rapport and empathy with helpees (Zax & Cowen, 1972)—have been hypothesized as possibly accounting for the positive outcomes often produced by paraprofessionals. However, this remains a matter of speculation requiring research attention (and, given behaviorists' methodological skills, amenable to study from a behavioral perspective). Furthermore, there is a need for more and better-controlled investigations with children and adolescents, as well as further study of selection, training, and supervisory procedures and of the process of paraprofessional intervention (Durlak, 1979; Seidman & Rappaport, 1974). Nonetheless, the literature to date is certainly encouraging, not only with respect to the impact of paraprofessionals on those with whom they work but also on themselves as well. Paraprofessionals, particularly college students, participating in a wide array of projects (e.g., public school settings, mental hospitals, crisis intervention, and delinquency prevention) have been shown to derive considerable psychological benefit from their helping role (Gartner & Riessman, 1977). This finding that people providing services to others in need often reap rich emotional and practical rewards themselves has been dubbed the "'helper' therapy principle" by Riessman (1965). Thus by thoughtfully selecting high-risk and target populations to function not only as helpees but as helpers, we might significantly increase the potency of out interventions.

Several models have been advanced to capitalize on paraprofessionals' skills and geometrically expand the utilization of available resources in a cost-effective manner. For instance, Seidman and Rappaport (1974) have proposed the "educational pyramid," a system in which a professional supervises several graduate students or experienced subprofessional mental health workers, who themselves train a number of paraprofessionals (e.g., undergraduates, retirees, high-school students, housewives) to work with high-risk and other target populations. The educational pyramid is essentially a subtype of the "vertical supervision" approach (sometimes referred to as "umbrella" or "hierarchical supervision") employed in many clinical settings (Glenwick & Stevens, 1980).

The educational pyramid and vertical supervision paradigms emphasize the role of the professional as supervisor and trainer of and consultant to students and paraprofessionals. Through the use of these models, the professional can broaden the scope and distribution of direct services to a community and, in addition, devote more of his or her attention to such alternative functions as program developer and evaluator and community consultant (Glenwick & Stevens, 1980). These paradigms are also useful as action-oriented research strategies exploring the impact of paraprofessionals not only on various target populations but also on the social systems in which the target populations are embedded (Seidman & Rappaport, 1974). Through the use of paraprofessionals, change can occur at a systems level as well as an individual level, with paraprofessionals enhancing the preventive potential of human service organizations.

With a few exceptions (e.g., Finch, Wilkinson, Nelson, & Montgomery, 1975; Hartman, 1979), the potential of using paraprofessional for child cognitive behavioral interventions has gone largely unrecognized. This oversight is unfortunate in that, carefully scripted and thoughtfully ordered and organized, many child cognitive behavior modification programs would appear to be well suited and easily adaptable for supervised use by paraprofessionals. That paraprofessionals can be effective in teaching youngsters cognitive self-instruction techniques was shown by Moore and Cole (1978), who, by means of modeling, role-playing, and close supervision, trained undergraduate volunteers to work successfully with hyperactive children aged 8–12. Finally, we might briefly mention Watson and Hall's (1977) use of housewives to administer pre- and post-test measures to hyperactive boys who were trained in self-control. However, the actual instruction of the youngsters was done by psychology and counseling graduate students; a logical next step would be to train housewives and other nonprofessional groups to function as instructors.

Natural Change Agents

Parents and Teachers. In addition to encouraging the use of paraprofessionals, the community model has also emphasized the importance of significant others in the natural environment as supporters of desired behaviors. This emphasis has stemmed from a recognition of (a) the strengths already present in the natural environment and a wish to capitalize on them, and (b) the interrelationships and transactions that exist between an individual's behavior and the network of systems of which the individual is a part (Rappaport, 1977). Such a perspective is quite compatible with behaviorism's own (a) attention to the environmental antecedents to, and consequences of, a person's behavior; (b) awareness of the fact that, for a behavior to occur with any significant frequency, the environmental setting must usually function to promote it actively; and (c) recognition of the importance of the social learning produced by observation of the behavior of significant others.

With respect to children, the two major adult natural change agents influencing their development are obviously parents and teachers. A group of correlational studies has investigated the relationship between children's self-control and various aspects of parental and teacher behavior in laboratory and field settings. This research can be seen as laying the foundation for the utilization of parents and teachers as instructors in self-control. Youngsters' cognitive styles, for example, have been shown to be related to those of their parents (Matekunas, 1973; McKim, 1979) and teachers (Yando & Kagan, 1968). Additionally, mothers of high- and low-self-control children have been found to differ in their interactional (e.g., structuring and control) behaviors (Ross & Karoly, 1977), as have the mothers of reflective and impulsive children (Campbell, 1973; McKim, 1979).

Because of this body of research, as well as the theoretical grounds outlined earlier in this section, recent writings (e.g., Karoly, 1977; Meichenbaum, 1979c; Urbain & Kendall, 1980) have called for greater involvement of natural change agents in child cognitive behavior modification. As Meichenbaum (1979c) comments, the importance of assessing and involving both the situational context and significant others becomes apparent once we consider that interpersonal behavior is a bidirectional process. Similarly, Urbain and Kendall (1980) assert, with respect to social/interpersonal cognitive problem-solving skills, that treatment of children's home problems within the family context and with the inclusion of significant others should enhance the learning and application of such skills. (See Chapter 4, this volume, for a detailed discussion of family systems.)

One role for parents and teachers with regard to self-regulation involves the possibility of helping children distinguish between those situations that call for reflective as opposed to automatic behavior, and vice versa. Self-verbalization, as Lloyd (1980) points out, may interfere with a youngster's performance on those academic tasks (e.g., decoding in reading) in which automaticity rather than reflectivity is important. By instructing children in various attack strategies, adults can enable them to approach problems flexibly and to decide which strategy is appropriate for a given task.

The actual body of cognitive behavioral studies involving parents and teachers in the intervention process is small but suggestive. For example, an examination of the relative effectiveness of parents and teachers as change agents was conducted by Glenwick and Barocas (1979), who compared five groups of impulsive fifth- and sixth-graders. In the first group, the parents and teachers of impulsive children were trained in verbal self-instruction by the experimenters; in the second group, just the teachers of impulsive pupils were given the training by the experimenters; in the third group, just the parents of impulsive youngsters were taught; in the fourth group, the experimenters directly trained a group of impulsive children themselves; and the fifth group of impulsive youngsters served as an assessment control group. In those groups involving parents and/or teachers, the adults were instructed in ways of training, prompting, monitoring, and reinforcing their children's use of verbal self-regulation and problem-solving in the home and school settings. The training took place in eight one-hour-long sessions held over four weeks. As hypothesized, the group of youngsters in which two sets of natural change agents—parents and teachers—were involved generally showed superior gains and maintenance on a variety of cognitive, achievement, and behavior measures compared with the other four groups.

Similarly, parents and/or teachers have also been successfully involved in the intervention process in cognitive behavioral projects directed at children's nighttime fears (Graziano & Mooney, 1980), "acting out" behaviors (Thoresen, Thoresen, Klein, Wilbur, Becker-Haven, & Haven, 1979), hyperactivity (Douglas, Parry, Marton, & Garson, 1976), aggressiveness (Bash & Camp, 1977; Camp, Blom, Hebert, & van Doorninck, 1977), interpersonal cognitive problem-solving skills (Shure & Spivack, 1979; Spivack & Shure, 1974), and self-management abilities

(Hartman, 1979). (See also Chapters 12 and 13, this volume.) This group of studies has demonstrated that the cognitive behavioral approach is one that nonprofessionals can learn and carry out with children of various ages and developmental levels. Since a clinician or researcher can spend only a limited amount of time with a particular youngster or group of youngsters, the use of natural change agents represents a means of affecting a child's life when the child is outside the clinic or experimental setting. While the studies to date are indeed promising, they constitute only the first steps of what is possible. Three aspects of this line of research warrant further investigation in the years ahead. First, there is a need for close monitoring of parents and teachers (e.g., through diary-like journal records, videotapes, behavioral observations, and interviews) to examine how and to what extent they actually implement the cognitive procedures they are taught. This might provide us with a deeper understanding of the reasons for and the mechanisms underlying their effectiveness and enable us to use the results in designing programs.

Second, most of the interventions with natural change agents, even those of a preventive bent, have concentrated on identified target or high-risk youngsters. By such means as parent-education classes and teacher-training curricula and in-service programs, natural change agents could learn to train "normal" child populations in cognitive behavioral strageties. Thus, cognitive problem-solving and self-control procedures could come to be seen as valuable ways of fostering the personal effectiveness and sense of self-efficacy (Bandura, 1977a) of youth through all phases of maturation and development.

Third, the topic of stress reactions in parents, teachers, and others who work with children deserves more attention than it has received. For instance, many teachers report experiencing stress from a variety of sources, with their reactions to such stress ranging from physical (e.g., peptic ulcer, cardiovascular diseases) to psychological (e.g., depression, anxiety) to behavioral (e.g., deterioration in work performance and interpersonal relationships) (Kyriacou & Sutcliffe, 1977). Teachers and parents, Meichenbaum (1979c, 1980c) points out, face many situations in which coping skills and self-control techniques would aid in the reduction of stress. Perhaps by providing cognitive behavioral skills to teachers, parents, and other adults who serve on the front lines with children, we can prevent the development of "burnout" and other stress reactions, thereby improving adults' general feelings of satisfaction and effectiveness and indirectly benefiting the children with whom they work. Recent encouraging work by Forman (1981, 1982) in training urban teachers and school psychologists in stress inoculation procedures suggests that such an approach warrants trial applications with other high-stress groups involved with youngsters, such as juvenile justice personnel, welfare department workers, and pediatric unit staff.

Peers. Besides parents and teachers, peer groups constitute another potent source of influence on children, particularly in the adolescent years. Peers' therapeutic effectiveness has been documented in numerous behavioral studies based on operant and social learning paradigms and utilizing normal, retarded, learning-disabled, and emotionally disturbed youngsters as change agents (see McGee, Kauffman, & Nussen, 1977, for a comprehensive review). The duties of the peer change agents have included pinpointing target behaviors, modeling appropriate behaviors, developing a battery of reinforcement and extinction techniques, delivering differential reinforcement, and collecting data on target behaviors.

In their catalog of recommendations for the programming of generalization, Stokes and Baer (1977, p. 364) strongly endorse the use of peer tutors, not only because of their effectiveness but also because peers constitute "stimuli [who] are likely to be found in generalization settings," (e.g., classrooms and neighborhoods) and not just in the training settings. Other writers of a more cognitive orientation (e.g., Kendall, 1977; Meichenbaum, 1977) voice similar thoughts concerning the use of peers as natural change agents and models in cognitive behavioral interventions. Kendall (1977) suggests that having youngsters interact with one another during self-instructional training could (a) promote generalization to other interpersonal settings and (b) be particularly beneficial for children displaying difficulty in the control of verbal and/or physical aggression.

Child cognitive behavioral projects utilizing peers in various roles and formats have begun to appear in the literature. Most of the early research consisted of laboratory studies in which the primary question being explored was the effect of reflective child models on the cognitive style of impulsive youngsters. Cohen and Przybycien (1974), for instance, had sociometrically selected high-status peers model reflective verbal and behavioral cues for fourth- and sixth-grade impulsive youngsters, resulting in increased reflectivity in the impulsive children. Focusing on the peer model rather than on the observer, Toner, Moore, and Ashley (1978) reported that first- and second-graders who served as rule-following models for peers later showed greater self-control themselves on a resistance-to-temptation task. This finding reminds us that, when choosing and employing peers as cognitive behavioral trainers, we should look at the effects of the intervention on both trainers and trainees (representing another application of Riessman's 1965 "helper" therapy principle discussed earlier in this chapter.)

Several recent studies (Barkley, Copeland, & Sivage, 1980; DeLange, Lanham, & Barton, 1981; Graziano & Mooney, 1980; Hartman, 1979; Henker, Whalen, & Hinshaw, 1980; Kendall & Zupan, 1981) have incorporated peer groups as an integral part of their interventions. For example, child support groups were included in Graziano and Mooney's (1980) work on nighttime fear reduction, and Hartman's (1979) self-management program with high-risk teenagers was conducted in a group format.

Henker *et al.* (1980) involved peers at numerous stages of their intervention study. The goal of their project was to alter the target children's causal attributions by providing them with a greater "sense of personal control over and responsibility for the direction of the sessions" (Henker *et al.*, 1980, p. 24). Groups of three boys formed triads and stayed together throughout the duration of the program. The boys were regarded by the experimenters as consultants, with their input being sought in determining target behaviors and in eliciting and enhancing the children's natural problem-solving strategies (as well as in teaching each other new strategies). Peer monitoring, role-playing of interpersonal situations, and group "rap sessions" were other means by which the power of peers was tapped.

Also working with hyperactive youngsters, Barkley *et al.* (1980) used cognitive behavior modification and self-control procedures with a special classroom of six hyperactive boys. During group-activity sessions, the teachers and boys modeled verbal self-instructions on a variety of academic and social problems. While some gains were produced in the special classroom, no generalization to the boys' regular classroom occurred.

In a comparison of group versus individual treatment of youngsters in grades three through five, Kendall and Zupan (1981) found that the two formats produced a similar degree of improvement on such variables as teachers' ratings of self-control and a role-taking test. Thus, although a group treatment condition might be expected, because of its greater interpersonal context, to be superior to one-on-one training (in addition to being more economical), such superiority remains to be demonstrated.

In summary, empirical evidence for peers' effectiveness in child cognitive behavioral interventions has been somewhat less solid than might have predicted on the basis of theoretical grounds and previous operant research. Speculating on possible reasons for this, we might highlight the need to attend to what happens in the children's lives outside the peer-group-training sessions. In those studies that have not resulted in positive changes or generated transfer of training, there has usually been less than adequate attention to the "real world," since researchers have based expectations for generalization more on a leap of faith than on concrete programming. Recognizing that generalization is not an automatic process, DeLange *et al.* (1981) suggest that a buddy system outside of the peer-group sessions might facilitate peer support and positive reinforcement, thereby encouraging the use of newly acquired skills in real-life situations. By enlisting the natural environment as an ally rather than ignoring it, we might improve the odds for maintenance and transfer to occur. It is to this topic that we turn next.

The Ecology of the Natural Environment

Introduction to the Ecological Perspective

With our society's heightened concern with environmental preservation, the terms "ecology" and "ecological" have been much in vogue during the past decade. For community psychology, the ecological orientation is one that focuses on the transactions—the bidirectional impact—between a person and his or her environment (including the various social groupings and physical settings constituting the environment) (Hobbs, 1966, 1979). Rather than labeling either persons or environments as "inadequate" in isolation from one another, the ecological perspective examines the fit between persons and environments to determine the degree to which the two are in harmony with each other (Rappaport, 1977). Thus, from this viewpoint a person and his or her behavior, as well as any changes in that behavior, cannot be understood independently of the context, settings, and systems of which he or she is a member.

The implications of the ecological approach for action vary according to the biases of the particular community theorist. A representative, though perhaps somewhat extreme, example of a nonbehavioral community psychologist's stance is Rappaport's (1977, pp. 2–3) assertion that "the ecological viewpoint [emphasizes] . . . the creation of alternatives by locating and developing existing resources and strengths, rather than by looking for weaknesses of people and/or communities." A broader conception is conveyed by Kelly's (1971, p. 897) statement that the ecological perspective focuses on "assessing a natural setting and then redesigning the context surrounding a social problem so that a specific community problem is altered as the host environment is changed."

For behaviorally oriented community psychologists, the implications of the ecology viewpoint range from (a) assessment of current environments and behavior–environment fits to (b) modification, by rearrangement of antecedent and consequent stimuli, of existing environments to alter their impact on individuals and groups to (c) utilization of existing interactional patterns to link individuals with settings that can promote desired behavior changes (Jason & Glenwick, 1980a,b). (This last function is referred to by Jason & Glenwick, 1980a, as the "matchmaking" role of the behavioral community psychologist.)

The primary value of the ecological approach for child cognitive behavior modification is that it reminds one of the need to take into account continually the influence of the environment on the behaviors, both public and private, of those children whom we are addressing in our interventions (as well as the reciprocal influence of children on environments). Eager to redress behavior analysts' traditional disregard of cognitive events, cognitive behaviorists may perhaps have gone overboard at times by acting as if (a) the environment within which our target children function is an irrelevant factor and (b) our programs can be successful without consideration of behavior–environment relations. Perhaps it is time to examine how an ecological perspective and an awareness of behavior–environment transactions can be profitably incorporated into cognitive interventions. In the following pages we will outline some of the ecological approach's implications for the assessment, training, and generalization aspects of child cognitive behavior modification.

Assessment

Naturalistic, Descriptive Assessment. With respect to assessment, an ecological orientation points the way toward the observation of children within their various settings as a means of understanding how private speech, self-management procedures, and cognitive strategies are employed in the natural environment. In addition to providing a base on which to ground theory, such observation can aid us in strengthening our interventions by building on the strengths already existing in children and their environments. Several writers (e.g., Meichenbaum, 1980c; O'Leary, 1980) have recognized the potential value of gathering data of this type. Karoly (1977, p. 250), for instance, calls for a "greater emphasis on assessment of supportive and disruptive environmental forces [and] study of naturally occurring episodes of self-management," as well as identification of "social systems that differentially generate self-management systems in children."

While several studies (e.g., Ross & Karoly, 1977) have looked at youngsters' use of private speech during the performance of structured or "contrived" situations, others have focused more on how self-regulation is employed by children in their everyday activities and settings. Thus, in an early project Meichenbaum (1971b) found that, in a free-play context, impulsive preschoolers used more self-stimulating private speech than did reflective youngsters, whereas reflective preschoolers employed more self-guiding private speech. More recent research by Meichenbaum (Meichenbaum & Goodman, 1979) has investigated the private speech of 2- and 3-year-olds at home as well as that of nursery school children.

Assessment of Interventions. The ecological point of view also suggests the need to assess whether and how problem-solving and self-instructional skills are functionally applied following training. That is, it is important to supplement our use of standardized "artificial" measures with attention to *in vivo* behaviors as dependent variables. As Hobbs, Moguin, Tyroler, and Lahey (1980, p. 160) state, child cognitive behavior modification "generally [has] not focused on behavior observed in the home or school setting but on altering performance on psychometric instruments . . . related to global referral problems [such as] hyperactivity or impulsivity."

The necessity of examining whether our interventions influence behavioral adjustment has been echoed by others, such as Urbain and Kendall (1980), who advocate research on the validity of social-cognitive measures to determine whether there is a correlation between these instruments and behavior in the natural environment. Such research is especially desirable because in several studies a significant correlation has not always been demonstrated between such instruments, on the one hand, and interpersonal behavior and successful problem-solving, on the other hand (Meichenbaum, 1979a). An increased focus on real-world target behaviors would enable us better to answer such questions as (Urbain & Kendall 1980, p. 138) "Does the treatment . . . return deviant children to within normal limits on outcome measures?" To date, normative comparisons of this type are rare in the cognitive behavioral literature. A flavor of the types of socially relevant, naturalistic target behaviors that can be included as dependent variables in child cognitive behavioral interventions is conveyed by Snyder and White (1979). After training a group of aggressive and delinquent institutionalized adolescents in self-instructional techniques, Snyder and White looked at the youths' impulsive behaviors (defined by drug-taking, physical aggression, stealing, and property destruction), class absences, and social/self-care responsibilities. (For a more detailed discussion of assessment issues, the reader should consult Chapter 5, this volume.)

Social Validation. Social validation is a form of assessment that has enjoyed increasing popularity in recent years in the behavioral literature and that is quite congruent with an ecological approach. As outlined by Wolf (1978), social validation involves obtaining information (e.g., through interviews and rating scales) from clients/consumers, referral agents, caregivers, and significant others regarding: (a) the social significance of the goals, (b) the appropriateness (e.g., ethics, costs, practicality) of the procedures, and (c) the social importance of the effects. Although operationalized somewhat differently, Kazdin (1977b, p. 429) also emphasizes the desirability of a social validation process to demonstrate that therapeutic changes are truly "clinically or socially important for the client." Two methods, social comparison (a normative comparison process) and subjective evaluation (perceptions of clients/ consumers by significant others), are advanced by Kazdin (1977b) as ways of accomplishing this.

While several studies involving social validation measures have appeared in the operant behavior literature (e.g., Forehand, Wells, & Griest, 1980), social validation components have, unfortunately been almost entirely absent in cognitive behavioral studies. Citing this deficiency, Hobbs *et al.* (1980, p. 161) argue for the "evaluation of the importance of change by referral sources and significant others in the natural environment in the form of parent and teacher ratings as well as child self-reports." While social validation is not without its dangers—such as the potential for undue maintenance of the status quo and fostering of conformity—it can be a useful tool in helping cognitive behaviorists tailor their interventions to the needs, values, and practices of consumers and other community groups. By designing programs whose goals, procedures, and results are acceptable to such populations, we can increase the chances for their support and adoption (Wolf, 1978), thereby enhancing our likelihood of effecting meaningful change in the many natural environments where children find themselves.

Training and Generalization

Training on "Real-World" and Interpersonal Tasks. As with assessment, so too with regard to training itself does an ecological perspective highlight the need for our interventions to address tasks and problems that have meaning to children in their everyday affairs. While "relevance" was generally not emphasized in early work in child cognitive behavior modification (see Hobbs *et al.*, 1980), researchers are increasingly heeding the calls of cognitive behavioral theorists (e.g., Kendall & Finch, 1979; Meichenbaum, 1979a, 1980c; Urbain & Kendall, 1980) to incorporate socially oriented material into our training regimens and to train "directly and explicitly on the skills and tasks that are to be learned, and not on some presumed 'underlying' deficit" (Meichenbaum & Asarnow, 1979, p. 30). Doing so should enhance both the learning that occurs during training (by engaging the child's interest and attention) and the transfer of skills that occurs to times and places outside of training (by making the training setting and tasks not too dissimilar to the child's usual environment and activities).

Several curricula (i.e., sequential lessons) comprising principally social situations and relevant cognitive tasks have been designed (e.g., Bash & Camp, 1977; Wilson, Hall, & Watson, 1978a,b). Examples of the kinds of relevant material that have been included as training matter in cognitive behavioral projects are classroom assignments, such as arithmetic, writing, and social studies problems (e.g., Bornstein & Quevillon, 1976; Glenwick & Barocas, 1979; Robertson & Keeley, 1974); home and neighborhood activities, such as following a recipe or putting up a tent (e.g., Glenwick & Barocas, 1979); and interpersonal problems (e.g., Camp *et al.*, 1977; Snyder & White, 1979).

The modification of pupils' classroom behavior has posed an especially difficult challenge for cognitive behaviorists. Although improvements in behaviors have occasionally been reported (e.g., Kendall & Finch, 1978), these have been mainly on teachers' ratings rather than on behavioral observations. In most cases, classroom behavior has either not been included as a dependent variable or has failed to show postintervention change (Hobbs *et al.*, 1980). Such negative results are, though disappointing, actually not that surprising when one realizes that classroom "survival" skills (e.g., not bothering classmates, paying attention, following teacher's instructions) have rarely been part of the training regimen. Recognizing this, several researchers (e.g., Abikoff, 1979; Barkley *et al.*, 1980; Douglas *et al.*, 1976) have recommended that our interventions explicitly focus on reducing impulsive behavior and increasing task-oriented classroom behavior if these particular social and self-control behaviors are to undergo positive change. Possible strategies for accomplishing these goals include adapting our self-instruction procedures to deal directly with such behavior and/or supplementing cognitive training with such adjuncts as reinforcement contingencies (Glenwick & Barocas, 1979).

While interpersonal problem-solving has until lately been a relatively secondary target (in comparison with nonsocial cognitive material) of cognitive behavior modification, it has a longer and deeper niche within the fields of developmental and community psychology (e.g., Anderson & Messick, 1974; McClure, Chinsky, & Larcen, 1978; Ojemann, 1967). However, most developmental and community psychologists working on social problem-solving have not incorporated behavioral techniques into their interventions. Only recently have we begun to see increased receptivity by each group toward what the other may have to offer it. An example of a group of nonbehaviorally oriented community psychologists being open to cognitive behavior modification is provided by Gesten, Flores de Apodaca, Rains, Weissberg, and Cowen (1979), who have combined Meichenbaum's self-regulatory speech procedures and Spivack and Shure's interpersonal problem-solving approach. One hopes that the future will see a continuing rapprochement between cognitive behaviorists and nonbehavioral child-oriented psychologists in the creation of programs for developing youngsters' social competence. (For further discussion, see Urbain & Kendall, 1980; and Chapters 10 and 13, this volume.)

Utilization of Environmental Supports for Maintenance and Transfer. The ultimate objective of cognitive behavioral interventions is to provide persons with the skills necessary to manage their behavior effectively, and thus to be able to successfully act on their environments. In this way, behavior change might be "portable," that is, not dependent on external environmental supports for its maintenance over time and its transfer to other settings. However, though the end to which we strive may be "power to the person" (Mahoney & Thoresen, 1974), we can still enlist the environment as a means toward reaching that end.

The possible advantages of combining cognitive and environmental approaches as a way of establishing enduring and broad-based self-control skills in children have been remarked on by several recent commentators (e.g., Glenwick & Barocas, 1979; Meichenbaum, 1977, 1980c; O'Leary, 1980; Urbain & Kendall, 1980). As O'Leary (1980, p. 92) states, "Adult-controlled reinforcement of children's accurate and appropriate use of new cognitive skills . . . , maintenance of reasonable contingencies for the target behaviors . . . , joint determination of the problem and the goal, and sharing of global achievement are probably necessary adjuncts of cognitive training."

To combine cognitive and external reinforcement procedures, a fading procedure similar to that generally used in self-control interventions (e.g., Drabman, Spitalnik, & O'Leary, 1973; Turkewitz, O'Leary, & Ironsmith, 1975) could be adopted with cognitive training programs (Meichenbaum, 1979c). That is, both internal and external control could be employed in the early stages of an intervention, with external techniques being utilized to reinforce the children's use of the target cognitive techniques in both the training environment and such other environments as the home and school. For example, as Kendall (1977) remarks, youngsters could be reinforced for correspondence between their self-instructions and actual behavior, with such external rewards gradually faded (Kendall & Finch, 1979) as the target children became proficient in the cognitive procedures.

Antecedent stimuli, as well as consequences (e.g., response-cost, social and concrete reinforcement), can also be capitalized on to enhance generalization. Stimulus cues and discriminative stimuli could be incorporated into training procedures so that children can be encouraged to use the particular cognitive strategies in those situations deemed appropriate (Glenwick & Barocas, 1979; Lutzker, 1980; Robertson & Keeley, 1974). Oral reminders given by teachers and parents, as well as verbal and nonverbal cue cards, can function as prompts for youngsters' utilization of the cognitive techniques when they are faced with problems and assignments at home and school.

Concerning generalization, the unique potential of an ecological perspective lies in its call for examination of (a) those behavior settings (Barker, 1968) in the natural environment where cognitive skills are already being successfully used by youth and (b) factors (e.g., social climate [Moos, 1974] physical design, characteristics of inhabitants) that facilitate the display of such skills. Illustrative of the type of questions deriving from this orientation are: How can we encourage the creation of more such settings? Does class size (and subgroup size within a classroom) make a difference in the development of pupils' problem-solving abilities? If an impulsive pupil is placed in a group containing a large number of reflective youngsters, will his or her cognitive style change?

It would appear that environmental supports to cognitive training should be most acceptable to adult change agents and be most effective when they are part of the natural flow of children's environments, thereby providing minimal disruption of parents' and teachers' routines and, one hopes, creating minimal resistance. Thus, one possible sequence in utilizing environmental supports might be to begin by capitalizing on those environmental strengths that are already in place (e.g., a naturally reinforcing teacher who also reasons out loud when solving problems at the blackboard), to then rearrange these natural environmental supports if necessary (e.g., having such a teacher verbally prompt and socially reinforce his or her pupils' use of verbal self-instruction when doing their classwork), and to introduce artificial supports (e.g., response-cost procedures, material reinforcers) on an "as-needed" basis.

The Natural Environment and the Development of Causal Attributions. One of the desired outcomes of cognitive training and self-control programs is an increase in target children's ability to view themselves as causal agents rather than as being subject to the whims of environmental control. It is postulated (e.g., by Henker *et al.*, 1980; Kendall & Finch, 1979; Meichenbaum, 1980c) that such an increase should lead to a boost in youngsters' self-esteem and sense of self-efficacy, with a consequent rise in their willingness to persist on novel tasks and attempt new actions. By establishing a positive emotional attitude toward cognitive instruction and an increase in feelings of volitional control, we can hope to produce not only positive outcomes in training but, more importantly, greater generalization in the child's use of cognitive and self-control strategies outside of training.

These hypotheses are based on a series of studies demonstrating that children's attributional styles and task performance affect each other in important ways (Bugental, Whalen, & Henker, 1977; Bugental, Collins, Collins, & Chaney, 1978; Diener & Dweck, 1978; Dweck, 1975). This group of studies has several implications for the implementation of cognitive interventions in natural settings. The first is the desirability of assessing target youngsters' "natural" attributional styles before beginning an intervention program (as well as reassessing them post-treatment), in order to determine (a) how to tailor our programs for a particular child or group of children and (b) whether our programs succeed in altering youngsters' attributional styles.

A second inference is that even "luck" attributors, or those who feel "helpless," can be aided in developing "effort" attributions and self-instructional skills. Such children, however, because of their natural styles and/or the natural environments to which they are accustomed, might at first feel more at ease with and respond more quickly to a program having an emphasis on contingent social reinforcement (since the attributional assumptions of such a program may better fit their initial attributional styles). The development of a sense of self-control in such youngsters may require a shaping and fading process to decrease reliance on external contingencies and increase comfort with self-management procedures (Bugental *et al.*, 1977, 1978).

Henker *et al.*'s (1980) program with hyperactive boys was one explicitly aimed at enhancing the target children's sense of themselves as causal agents. Besides extensively involving the boys themselves as project "consultants," Henker *et al.* (1980, p. 25) focused on increasing their "ascriptions of personal control over behaviors and their outcomes" by training in self-management skills and moderate use of external reinforcers (e.g., to increase accurate self-evaluation by the boys).

It should be noted that even if the training setting is one that actively nurtures the enhancement of volitional control, generalization to the target children's natural environments could still pose a formidable challenge, for both methodological and "political" reasons. By "political" we refer here to the distribution of power, that is, the control of behavior and of access to reinforcement in adult–child relationships. Many natural environments in which children spend time are ones in which external control (through both aversive and positive means) by adults is the norm. Through such histories of conditioning, the inhabitants—parents, teachers, and other adult natural change agents, as well as the children themselves—may have established an equilibrium in which they are accustomed to the children being in a "helpless," "one-down" position. Such conditions might well generate considerable resistance and anxiety toward interventions geared to increasing children's decision-making power and ability. To overcome such obstacles and assist all involved parties in seeing the potential virtues of the target children's becoming more independent (yet still socially responsible) would require methodological ingenuity (e.g., regarding the promotion of generalization), consultation skills, and sensitivity to contingencies affecting the behavior of all members of the system in question.

The Natural Environment and the Training of Metacognitive Processes. Partly in reaction to the often disappointing results to date in achieving generalization, theorists have recently emphasized the desirability of instructing youngsters in "metacognitive processes" (i.e., thinking about thinking, knowing about knowing) or "executive functioning" (Meichenbaum, 1979a, 1980a,c; Meichenbaum & Asarnow, 1979). Included under this heading are such components of problem-solving as analyzing and characterizing the problem at hand, reflecting on what one knows or does not know that may be necessary for a solution, devising a plan for attacking the problem, and checking or monitoring one's progress (Meichenbaum, 1980a). Through training in these "superordinate skills," youngsters could be prevented from becoming "'welded' to specific strategies and tasks" and from employing "only domain-specific knowledge and skills" (Meichenbaum, 1980a, p. 87).

Natural change agents would seem to have much to offer in the provision of metacognitive instruction to children. When faced with a problem, many adults probably already employ a metacognitive approach toward its solution, though it may be an implicit one that has gone underground and receded from conscious awareness. By helping parents, teachers, and other adults recognize these metacognitive processes and become more proficient in their use, we can hope to encourage them to aid their children in developing such processes as well (Meichenbaum & Asarnow, 1979). Once adults have learned to think in terms of metacognitive strategies, they can assist youngsters to approach classroom assignments, household problems, interpersonal difficulties, etc., in the same fashion—that is, with an awareness that the process by which a solution or decision is reached may be more important than the outcome. The youngsters themselves might even be enlisted by us in this process to help (e.g., through prompting and reinforcement) the adults in their environment to adopt more effective and humane metacognitions.

Generalization and the Natural Environment: Some Concluding Thoughts. In considering generalization, one is reminded of the aphorism that "there is no such thing as a free lunch." There is rarely such a thing as free generalization, and when it is "free" it is often difficult to explicate its occurrence or replicate the results. Therefore, systematic programming of generalization would appear to be a better approach than "train and hope" (Stokes & Baer, 1977). The operant behavioral literature has already produced the beginnings of a technology of generalization (Stokes & Baer, 1977); cognitive behaviorists would do well to consult this literature, as well as to consider the suggestions for generalization advanced by cognitive behavioral researchers and theorists (e.g., Kendall, 1977; Meichenbaum, 1977). Training across multiple natural settings (Kendall & Finch, 1979; Meichenbaum, 1980a) and teaching "subjects to cue their . . . natural communities to reinforce their desirable behaviors" (Stokes & Baer, 1977, p. 364), for instance, could well enhance our ability to utilize the natural environment to promote generalization across settings, persons, responses, and time.

Finally, it is striking that the most promising directions for increasing the impact of cognitive behavioral interventions appear to be (a) inclusion of environmental supports, on the one hand, and (b) attention to such higher-order "mentalistic" constructs and cognitions as metacognitive processes, internal attributions, and feelings of volitional control, on the other hand. These approaches might, at first glance, seem to derive from differing orientations, one being externally based and the other innerdirected. However, as we have attempted to show, the differences between them might well turn out to be more apparent than real if we can, by adopting an ecological perspective, mobilize already existing strengths and create new ones in the natural environment to assist children in becoming more effective persons through the development of internal controls, cognitive competencies, and a greater sense of self-esteem.

Individual Diversity and Cultural Relativism

One of the salient values deriving from the ecological orientation of a community psychology model is a respect for cultural heterogeneity and individual diversity. In Rappaport's (1977, p. 3) words, "An ecological viewpoint implies that differences among people and communities may be desirable, and the resources of society should not be allocated on the basis of a single standard of competence." Thus, the broad range of variations that exists among individuals and cultural subgroups with regard to the ends toward which they strive, the ways of transacting with their environments to attain those ends, and their styles of living need to be appreciated and, in most cases, tolerated and nurtured by psychologists working in natural settings (Rappaport, 1981; Rappaport, Davidson, Wilson, & Mitchell, 1975). In evaluating persons and environments, therefore, it becomes crucial to determine the match between them—that is, how well a given individual or subgroup is able to act to meet its needs and how well the environment conduces toward a meeting of those needs.

For child cognitive behavior modification, such an appreciation for cultural and individual diversity possesses not only ethical implications but practical and methodological ones as well. The major ethical implication would appear to be that our purpose in mounting cognitive training programs should be to provide youngsters with an array of cognitive strategies that they can utilize flexibly to achieve a combination of self- and societally determined objectives that are functional within their particular cultural contexts. As Kendall (1977) comments, the aim of verbal self-instruction programs is not to turn out youngsters who are meek, overly compliant, inhibited, and unspontaneous. Cognitive training should be a tool for promoting diversity and innovation rather than fostering cultural conformity and homogeneity.

Unfortunately, individual and cultural differences, as well as cognitive developmental variables, have often been ignored in cognitive training programs (Copeland, 1981; Karoly, 1977; Kendall, 1977; Kendall & Finch, 1979). Such neglect may well have resulted in our interventions being less potent than they might otherwise be, since in basic research on self-regulation, such subject variables as "age, sex, ethnic background, cognitive style, causal attributions, and motivational orientations have all been found to be differentially predictive of success" (Karoly, 1977, p. 250). Consequently, by adapting our approach to fit the personal and cultural style (e.g., in language and vocabulary) of the target child or group, we should have a greater probability of achieving successful training and generalization. Individualized self-statements,

Kendall and Finch (1979) note, will most likely serve to engage the learner and foster transfer more than can self-statements that are supposedly universally applicable. The process of altering the content and instructional format of our programs to match the natural style and cultural context of our target populations could benefit from being a collaborative one, in which the input of the target individuals or cultural subgroups as consultants is actively sought, thereby increasing their feelings of partnership and sense of investment in the project, enhancing its acceptability and social validity, and potentially increasing the odds in favor of positive results. Unlike some articles of clothing, cognitive interventions present a case in which one size does not fit all.

One of the few cognitive behavioral studies to examine the impact of cultural variables is that of Robertson, Kendall, and Urbain (1980), in which no differences were found between high- and low-socioeconomic-status children in their degree of improvement following training. Nonetheless, the sizable body of research that has accumulated over the past two decades concerning social class, ethnic, and cultural differences in linguistic styles, maternal teaching strategies, and parent–child verbal interactions (e.g., Bernstein, 1965; Hess & Shipman, 1965) suggests that such differences might well account for part of the variance in the outcome of a verbally oriented procedure such as cognitive behavior modification. (See also Chapter 3 by Cohen and Schleser.) The importance of investigating the possible existence of such effects and of designing culturally and individually sensitive training curricula remains acute.

Supraindividual, Systems-level Change

Introduction to a Social Systems Orientation

Most cognitive behavioral interventions (even those having a preventive slant) have concentrated on individual target children, be they trained singly or in small groups. Such an orientation is understandable since most persons working in this area come from a background of research training in clinical (often child clinical) psychology and applied training in the traditional model of service delivery. Nonetheless, and though not wishing to undervalue the importance of individual-level interventions, we will suggest in this section the potential of supplementing our conventional approach with one that attends to supraindividual-level change. That is, our focus here will be on the potential of child cognitive behavior modification to bring about change in the numerous systems that affect the individual children in them. Although the bottom line of every child cognitive project is its effect, either direct or indirect, on youngsters, our emphasis in the present section is primarily on the group, organization, community, and society as units of intervention and analysis.

Several benefits can be envisioned as deriving from a systems-level perspective. First, through focusing on a given social system, be it a family, school, hospital, or community, we can hope to reach many more children (and more cost-effectively) than by intervening with individual youngsters in small groups. Second, an emphasis on social systems can help avoid or reduce the labeling of children that at times occurs with traditional child cognitive behavioral interventions, even those aimed at high-risk youngsters. Third, without a systems-level perspective, we are often left with a narrow, incomplete view of the effects of our interventions, since change in one part of a system might bring about change in another part of that system (or in another system, for that matter).

Fourth, and finally, there are many organizations and institutions already in place that significantly affect the lives of children and will undoubtedly continue to operate in the foreseeable future. By (a) analyzing such social systems to determine their current impact, (b) capitalizing on and allying ourselves with their strengths and beneficial aspects, and (c) attempting to help them improve where they may be acting to the detriment of youngsters' development, we can ideally aid them in functioning as positive forces. The following discussion will elaborate on these points.

Individual-level Interventions from a Systems Perspective

Before considering how child cognitive behavior modification could be intentionally utilized to effect system-level change, it may be instructive to examine how a social systems perspective can be valuable even in evaluating the outcome of interventions targeted at individuals or small groups. Several writers from a variety of viewpoints have recently called for the development of an "ecobehavioral psychology" (Lutzker, 1980; Willems, 1974, 1977) or "an experimental ecology of human development" (Bronfenbrenner, 1977). This perspective stresses the multidirectional interrelationships that exist between individuals and their social systems/environments, as well as relationships among social systems/environments; this being the case, such a perspective is quite congruent with the community model's ecological orientation discussed earlier.

For individual-level interventions, an ecobehavioral approach expands our view of the dependent and independent variables to be considered in planning and evaluating interventions. In designing projects, we need to take into account not only our intervention procedures but also possible forces that may serve to abet or hinder our efforts. Similarly, in examining the outcome of an intervention aimed at a particular youngster or at a group of target youngsters, we can gain a fuller understanding of the intervention's impact by gathering data on such issues as whether or not (a) "change in one or some behavior directly manipulated in one or some environments produces . . . changes in other behaviors in other environments" (Lutzker, 1980, p. 99); (b) there are unanticipated negative consequences of the intervention that, even if accompanied by positive results, may serve to raise doubts about the project's overall worth (Willems, 1974); and (c) change in the target children produces changes in significant others with whom they interact.

For illustrative purposes, we might apply the ecobehavioral perspective to a hypothetical cognitive behavioral intervention in which a group of impulsive elementary-school pupils is given training in verbal self-instruction twice weekly for a month in a corner of the school library. When designing the intervention, the trainer could, for example, observe and talk with the students' teachers to determine whether the latter's cognitive styles and instructional approaches would be compatible with the cognitive behavioral training and how the teachers could be recruited as resources rather than as obstacles in the project. Other significant natural change agents (e.g., family and peers) and their possible roles in the intervention could be similarly considered.

Following the actual month-long training, the trainer, rather than collecting data merely on a few selected variables for the target youngsters (e.g., the Matching Familiar Figures Test or academic measures), could attempt to look at the effect of the intervention on the following: (a) the target children's behavior (both scholastic and interpersonal) in the classroom and other school settings (e.g., playgound), (b) the behavior of the target children's teachers and of nontarget children (i.e., classmates), (c) the regular operation of the school (e.g., is the principal so impressed with the project that he or she wants to introduce the cognitive behavioral approach into all classes? Or has he or she concluded that it was a waste of time and that henceforth there shall be no further self-instructional training in the school?), (d) the target children's behavior at home and in the neighborhood, (e) the behavior of the target children's parents and siblings, (f) the relationship between changes occurring in one setting (e.g., the school) and those in another (e.g., the home), (g) the duration of behavior change, and (h) the consumer satisfaction of the target children, as well as that of significant others.

Such an exhaustive approach to outcome evaluation would (a) provide the trainer with a reasonably comprehensive estimate of the positive and negative results of the project, both for the target children and other natural change agents; (b) reveal whether the project created any impetus toward systems change; and (c) help determine the project's cost/benefit ratio, whether such programs should be mounted in the future, and, if so, how they might be modified to produce greater gains. While no single study can address the entire list of evaluation questions, the theoretical and practical contributions of individual-level cognitive behavioral projects will be enhanced by the extent to which they are able to include such questions within their purview.

While cognitive interventions have generally been remiss with respect to exploring the possible existence of higher-order indirect change, some operantly oriented behaviorists have begun to report intriguing results in this vein. Forehand and his colleagues (Forehand *et al.*, 1980; Humphreys, Forehand, McMahon, & Roberts, 1978), for instance, found that their training program for parents of noncompliant youngsters led to decreased sibling noncompliance and reduced parental depression, as well as producing the intended improvement in target children's behavior. One of the few reports in the child cognitive behavioral literature concerning the production of similar second-order effects was Peterson *et al.*'s (1980) finding that parents who participated in the training of their children in coping skills (before the youngsters' surgery) judged themselves to feel calmer and more competent and to be better able to handle their children's hospitalization than did parents in a control group.

Systems-level Interventions: Organizations, Communities, and Societies

In thinking about systems-level interventions, it is helpful to refer to Iscoe's (1974) notion of the "competent community." A competent community, according to Iscoe (1974, p. 608), "is one that utilizes, develops, or otherwise obtains resources, including . . . the resources of the human beings in the community itself" (a "community" being here defined by the geographical or psychological bonds of its members). Due to the sense of helplessness and powerlessness felt by many communities, they often do not realize their potential for competence. Consequently, community psychologists can perform a valuable function by helping communities learn additional strategies for coping with problems and by expanding communities' (and their members') "repertoire of possibilities and alternatives" to better enable them to acquire resources (Iscoe, 1974, p. 609). This concept of the competent community dovetails well with the community model's emphasis on seeking out and aiding in the development of strengths in the community as opposed to blaming victims for their difficulties (Rappaport *et al.*, 1975).

Applying these ideas to systems-level interventions, we might suggest that the role of such interventions should be to help communities and their institutions foster the development of competence in the persons and groups they comprise. As we hope the following illustrations will demonstrate, cognitive behavior modification procedures could play a useful part in the development of children's competence within the context of social systems change.

The school as an organizational entity provides one appropriate place to start when considering how society's institutions might better enhance youngsters' competence. For most child cognitive behavior modifiers, interventions in the schools have consisted primarily of training programs for individual pupils or small groups of youngsters viewed either as already possessing problem-solving deficits or (in a more preventive mode) as being at high risk for manifesting future deficits. Some encouraging steps have appeared, though, in the direction of incorporating cognitive behavioral training more smoothly into the routine of the schools. For example, Block's (1978) rational-emotive mental health program for high-risk high-school students was made a natural part of the students' school day by being defined as a course that met for 45 minutes each day for a full semester and for which students obtained one social science unit of credit. The development of sequential curricula in cognitive and self-control strategies (e.g., Bash & Camp, 1977; Wilson *et al.*, 1978a,b) provides another vehicle for schools to offer cognitive training as a regular part of the educational program, similar to spelling, reading, or arithmetic.

The existence of such curricula promotes positive movement toward the "routinizing" of cognitive training in the schools, in that they help facilitate and legitimate cognitive training as a "course" or activity potentially available to all pupils in a particular classroom, grade level, or school building; the stigmatizing effects that may occur when individual pupils are targeted for cognitive instruction can thereby be avoided. However, the setting-aside of part of the day for cognitive training still falls short of what might be achieved by conceptualizing the school as an organizational entity. If one regards cognitive self-instruction not as content matter (i.e., an end) but as an approach (i.e., a means) useful in learning almost any subject, then one can speculate as to whether one could "imbue the entire school curriculum and environment with the possibility of nurturing metacognitive skills" (Meichenbaum, 1980c, p. 29). Thus viewed, a cognitive problem-solving approach could be integrated into all coursework rather than being something that is reserved for the period from 10:00 to 10:45 A.M.

Verbal self-regulation procedures would seem to possess value not only in the study of academic areas but in such perhaps less obviously relevant subjects as physical education and health. In gym class, cognitive self-instruction and imagery techniques might well aid children in gaining proficiency in and deriving greater satisfaction from exercise activities that can be engaged in throughout one's life span (e.g., tennis, golf, swimming, and weightlifting). Health education might take similar good advantage of cognitive procedures by supplementing content presentation with instruction in how to manage one's life-style and achieve self-control in nutrition, smoking, etc. There are probably few, if any, components of the school curriculum in which a metacognitive orientation could not prove beneficial in some way. The successful application of this orientation would appear to depend more on the receptivity and creativity of school personnel than on any shortcomings of the metacognitive perspective itself.

In addition to school systems, there are numerous settings and organizations involving young people that seem suitable for the incorporation of cognitive strategies and self-management techniques. These include student councils, 4-H clubs, church youth groups, and scout troops—in fact, any organization whose aim, at least in part, is to assist children in becoming more self-reliant and better decision-makers.

If, in our consideration of social systems change, we move from the organizational level to the community and societal levels, we can begin to analyze the effects of pervasive, society-wide forces on child behavior in our culture. Although it might appear self-evident, it is perhaps sobering to realize that society, through such influences as the media and political rhetoric, already provides much cognitive instruction to children. A culture's language and imagery help determine not only what, but also how, its citizens (including its children) think. George Orwell (1950, pp. 77, 89) observed, "If thought corrupts language, language can also corrupt thought. . . . The slovenliness of our language makes it easier for us to have foolish thoughts." When language serves to hide or prevent clear thinking, commented Orwell, the result is frequently conformity and orthodoxy in both thought and behavior.

With this connection between popular language and cognitive development in mind, we note the need to obtain descriptive, naturalistic data so as to understand better the current effects of the media (e.g., television, movies, popular music) on the formation of youngsters' cognitive strategies and problem-solving approaches. We can then decide whether we are satisfied with these effects and, if we are not, how to exert pressure to modify them (Jason & Klich, 1980). Child cognitive behaviorists appear to be well qualified to participate in the data-gathering and interpretation process, providing useful information for and consultative assistance to child advocacy groups in our society.

It is perhaps ironic that it is public more than commercial television that has received attention from child cognitive behavioral theorists. In a critique of "Sesame Street," for instance, Meichenbaum and Turk (1972) argue that educational television programs for youngsters should contain more modeling of cognitive strategies and private speech by child and parent figures and other characters. They also recommend that self-verbalization by television characters be employed not just for cognitive but also for affective and motivational behaviors (e.g., self-evaluation, empathy, self-reinforcement). Similarly, Lutzker (1980) has recently advocated capitalizing on the potential modeling effects of public television to improve family functioning.

In light of its millions of child and teenage viewers, commercial television certainly merits no exemption from analysis by child cognitive behaviorists. From Saturday morning cartoons to evening "adult" programming to the ever-present advertisements, commercial television offers youngsters a continuing noncredit course in problem-solving and decision-making. Whether, after such coursework, the "graduates" achieve mastery of mature cognitive strategies is an open, and also to some extent empirical, question. One can only speculate on the cumulative effects of thousands of hours of hearing the verbalizations and watching the imagery contained in commercial television on the development of children's cognitive strategies and metacognitive processes.

SUMMARY

This chapter has addressed issues related to the locus of child cognitive behavioral interventions from the perspective of models of human services delivery. We began with an outline of the salient features of two approaches, referred to as the traditional and community models. Following this, the current status of child cognitive behavioral interventions was considered, with most work to date being judged as falling under the rubric of the traditional model. The authors then considered the potential implications of the community model for research and practice in child cognitive behavior modification. Locus of intervention (*where* we conduct our programs) was shown to be closely intertwined with the target levels and populations (the "who"), methodology and procedures (the "what"), time points (the "when"), staff and support personnel (the "how"), and target goals and behaviors (the "why") of intervention. Five aspects of a community-oriented intervention perspective were highlighted: (a) prevention and early intervention (b) paraprofessionals and natural change agents (c) the ecology of the natural environment (d) individual diversity and cultural relativism, and (e) supraindividual, systems-level change.

Incorporating "the community" and its related aspects as a construct into our conceptualizations and as an actuality into our interventions can, we believe, significantly broaden the scope and enhance the potency of our interventions. Communities and their institutions and populations are often "messy" and always challenging. They are, though, where our children are and, therefore, where the action is or ought to be.

7

Cognitive Training with Learning-Disabled Pupils

Barbara K. Keogh and Robert J. Hall

INTRODUCTION

Considering the broad array of symptoms and conditions that characterize children identified as exceptional, it is reasonable to hypothesize that learning-disabled children are likely candidates for cognitive training programs. Learning-disabled children learn many things well, yet show puzzling patterns of inconsistency in achievement and performance. Their school work may be satisfactory one day but dramatically inadequate the next; they may be deficient in reading but do average work in arithmetic; they may be attentive and task-directed at one moment, but erratic and distracted the next. It is these very inconsistencies that, although puzzling, provide the intuitive basis for the belief that learning-disabled children would profit from cognitive training techniques. Said directly, if learning-disabled children can learn and perform well in some situations, they may be helped through cognitive training to learn and perform well in many situations.

WHO IS LEARNING-DISABLED?

Before considering possible applications of cognitive training methods to learning-disabled children, however, the definitional uncertain-

Barbara K. Keogh • Special Education Research Program, Graduate School of Education, University of California, Los Angeles, California 90024. **Robert J. Hall** • Department of Educational Psychology, Texas A & M University, College Station, Texas 77843. Preparation of this chapter was supported in part by Project REACH, Contract #300-77-0306 between the Office of Special Education and the University of California, and by the Virginia Learning Disabilities Research Institute, Contract #300-80-0623 between the Office of Special Education and the University of Virginia.

ties that plague the field must be addressed. One of the major problems confronting the researcher or program planner working with learning-disabled children is to determine what defines the condition and to decide what criteria will be used for selection or identification. A number of definitional issues have been discussed (Hallahan & Bryan, 1981; Hallahan & Kauffman, 1976; Keogh, 1982) and a broad array of symptoms have been proposed as characterizing the condition. The diversity of presumably defining symptoms is well illustrated by data from the UCLA Marker Variable Project (Keogh, Major, Omori, Gándara, & Reid, 1980; Keogh, Major-Kingsley, Omori-Gordon, & Reid, 1982). In this work, the published literature on learning disabilities from 1970 through 1977 was systematically mapped and analyzed according to professional disciplines of the investigators (education, psychology, medicine, and related fields such as speech and hearing, optometry, occupational therapy, etc.) and according to age of subjects (CA 2–5, 6–12, 13+, and longitudinal or multiple-age samples). Definitional criteria were found to reflect the professional disciplines of investigators as well as the age of subjects. To illustrate: Almost 100 symptoms were found to describe learning-disabled subjects; moreover, these descriptors were frequently inconsistent and sometimes mutually exclusive. Investigators characterized learning-disabled children as hyperactive, in constant motion, fidgety and restless, or as underactive, slow moving, and easily tired; as distractible, impulsive, and overreactive, or as daydreaming and withdrawn; as aggressive, immature, and explosive, or as hypoactive and depressed. Given the diversity of symptoms it is not surprising that there are discrepant, even conflicting, findings from intervention studies.

DEFINING CHARACTERISTICS

Despite the broad array of symptoms and characteristics viewed as being relevant to learning disabilities, two important characteristics emerge as primary criteria for identification and selection. First, by definition, learning-disabled children must have intelligence within a normal range; second, they must be deficient or delayed in mastery of the usual academic tasks expected of children of comparable age and ability. Most professionals are uncomfortable with trying to put the discrepancy notion into a formula (Page, 1980) yet there is considerable agreement that both ability achievement are important in identifying learning-disabled pupils. Further, workable distinctions can be made among frankly retarded, emotionally disturbed, and learning-disabled children.

Consider: An impulsive, hyperactive child with an IQ of 65 and a reading score three years below grade level will be classified as mentally retarded. An impulsive, hyperactive child with a normal IQ and a reading score at grade level might be viewed as emotionally disturbed or behavior-disordered. Whatever the other symptoms or characteristics, children identified as learning-disabled must be within a normal ability range and below expectancy in achievement in school-related accomplishments such as reading or arithmetic. Despite other symptoms or characteristics, almost all definitions include normal ability and academic deficiency as inclusionary criteria.

It is important to note, too, that while diverse symptoms are proposed as characteristic of learning-disabled children, quite different theories have been proposed to explain the condition, and many perspectives on identification and intervention are advocated. Two contrasting views are illustrative. From the medical-neurological perspective, learning problems and the symptoms of hyperactivity, emotional lability, perceptual problems, and the like are considered as stemming from a common underlying neurological impairment. This point of view, epitomized by the early work of Strauss and his colleagues (Strauss & Kephart, 1947; Strauss & Lehtinen, 1947), has had an enormous impact on the field. It has lead to the involvement of medical and neurological professionals in the diagnosis and treatment of learning disabilities. The number of learning-disabled children receiving prescribed medication is testimony to the power of this position. The neurological perspective has also lead to a number of nonmedical intervention approaches, as for example, the sensory integration programs of Ayres and her followers (Ayres, 1972) and the educational intervention program of Cruickshank (Cruickshank, Bentzen, Ratzeburg, & Tannhauser, 1961). Both of these approaches involve intervention practices developed on the basis of presumed neurological impairment as the cause of learning disabilities.

In contrast to the neurological perspective, professionals with more educational or behavioral orientations propose that the setting, the nature of the instructional program, the pedagogical influences, the reinforcers, and the structure of the task to be learned are fundamental in understanding learning-disabled children and their problems (Adelman, 1971; Ayllon & Roberts, 1974; Lloyd, 1980; Lovitt, 1976). Rather than seeking underlying causes, these professionals attempt to analyze the task to be learned and to manipulate the behaviors and the environment in order to improve learning. Maladaptive behaviors are considered learned rather than stemming from neurological problems. Thus, the principles of learning theory are applied in an effort to bring about changes in performance.

Examination of the two positions yields some clear generalizations. First, the symptoms viewed as important may vary, but in all cases one of the major identifying parameters of learning disabilities is the ability–achievement discrepancy. Second, while describing the condition and providing direction for intervention, neither perspective explains the ability–achievement discrepancy. Consideration of this puzzling discrepancy, then, is important if we are to argue for the usefulness of cognitive training approaches for learning-disabled children.

AN INFORMATION-PROCESSING APPROACH

In earlier work, Hall (1979, 1980a) confronted directly the IQ–achievement discrepancy, basing his argument on an information-processing approach using Ann Brown's developmental model of memory. Since Brown's work is widely described and discussed (see Brown, 1975, 1981), only pertinent aspects of her model will be mentioned in this chapter.

In an important paper in 1975, Brown proposed three dimensions of memory: "knowing"—the knowledge system that forms a basis for cognition; "knowing about knowing"—the metamemorial processes, the knowledge and understanding individuals have of their own memory system; and, "knowing how to know"—the strategies an individual has available for purposeful memorization. Drawing on the work of Flavell (1971), Brown suggested that these three memory systems develop somewhat differently and that they exert different influences on particular learning requirements or tasks. Brown proposed, too, that memory tasks may be described along several dimensions. First, they may or may not require application of memorial strategies. For example, memory for unrelated pictures does not require active plans for acquisition and is relatively independent of retrieval strategies. Second, when a strategy is required for task solution, either a lack of strategy or a lack of application of strategy may lead to failure. Third, tasks may be semantic or episodic in nature. These distinctions deserve brief discussion because they lead directly to the issue of IQ–achievement discrepancy in learning-disabled children and to the possible utility of cognitive training programs as the intervention of choice.

In Brown's 1975 model the three aspects of memorial processing were related, but each addressed a somewhat different aspect of memory. The first, strategy–nonstrategy, suggested that learning tasks differ in their demands for cognitive processing, with a complex task requiring more refined memorial strategies or solutions than a simple task. The second distinction, episodic or semantic memory, suggested differences in memorial processing. *Semantic* referred to memory for meaningful, holistic units experienced in context; *episodic* referred to isolated, non-contextual memorial demands that often require exact recall—for instance, a spelling test. Brown suggested further that failure on memorial tasks may be due to mediation or production deficiencies. To demonstrate the distinction, when strategies are seemingly unavailable even after training, the child is said to have a mediation deficiency. This is in contrast to a production deficiency, in which the child has the strategies but does not generate them spontaneously or appropriately. In one case, the individual apparently does not have the appropriate strategies within his or her repertoire; in the second case, the individual has the strategies but does not apply them spontaneously. Common sense suggests that some individuals may be poor performers on memory and other cognitive tasks because they have "wired-in" or structural deficiencies that preclude development of a range of information-processing strategies. Yet considerable evidence argues against the structural hypothesis as an explanation for the poor educational performance of learning-disabled children. (Our view of what constitutes a production deficiency does not imply a presumed strategy deficit as has been argued by Turnure, Buium, & Thurlow, 1976, and Borkowski & Cavanaugh, 1979. Rather, we take the term to mean "failure to produce" and thus would agree with Turnure, Borkowski, and their colleagues that a production deficiency may be more appropriately viewed as an instructional deficiency, or a failure to provide children with efficient learning cues.)

The argument for a production rather than a mediation deficiency has already been advanced to explain the educational retardation of EMR children. In a series of studies, Campione and Brown (1977) have provided evidence that EMR children can be taught a range of problem-solving strategies that allow them to complete many problems successfully. The difficulty appears to be that the children do not spontaneously generate the strategies or apply them properly. The point of view proposed in this chapter is that problems in the generation and application of strategies are especially characteristic of learning-disabled children. In specific, it is proposed that learning-disabled pupils fail to generate effective processing strategies on school learning tasks, although other aspects of their learning and memorization are intact. Brown's early distinctions between strategy and nonstrategy, episodic and semantic, and production and mediation deficiency, while subsequently modified (Nelson & Brown, 1978), provide direction in explaining the IQ–achievement discrepancy that characterizes learning-disabled children.

IQ and Achievement

While IQ tests contain some culturally specific items, they also include a number of items that tap consensual information and skills—that is, knowledge that most individuals accrue through the process of living in a particular society. The tests weigh heavily understanding of language and vocabulary that characterize the child's everyday environment and frequently include problem-solving tasks that have examplars in real life. To illustrate, the WISC-R includes such items as "What should you do when you cut your finger?" and "How many legs does a dog have?" The point is that despite their potential cultural bias, IQ tests capture, in part at least, the knowledge and skills children have accrued through the process of living in their culture. Importantly, most of these skills have not been taught in a direct sense. As noted by Flavell (1976, 1977) and by the cross-cultural psychologists Scribner and Cole (1973) and Price-Williams and Gallimore (1980), such knowledge is for the most part incidental and informal. Children do not set out to learn the words needed for getting along in their everyday world in order to recall the words on demand; they do not purposefully learn selected information about their environment ("How many legs does a dog have?") in order to be ready to answer a question about dog's legs. Rather, this kind of learning occurs through interaction with the environment—through holistic, contextual, and redundant experience.

The theoretical notion that learning has both direct and indirect properties was articulated by Vygotsky (1978), who distinguished between spontaneous and scientific concepts. He suggested that, especially in the early years of development, children learn concepts and relationships through their natural and concrete experiences with their environments. Children organize, select, and recall on the basis of real-life interactions; they develop a broad repertoire of problem-solving skills that enables them to function within their immediate life situation. Consider either the massive language learning that has occurred by age 5 without formal instruction or the well-developed spatial organization of the preschooler. According to Vygotsky (1978), such perceptual and cognitive organization has developed from the natural interactions of child and environment. As suggested by Hall (1980a), these cognitive skills, applicable in a variety of situations including intelligence tests, represent Brown's (1975) semantic memory and are characteristic of the informal learnings talked about by anthropologists (Price-Williams & Gallimore, 1980).

In contrast to the naturally and incidentally learned concepts and skills that are reflected in performance on IQ tests, the child at school entrance is thrust into a formal learning setting. Learning is directed at selected content and is focused on development of skills that may have only tenuous ties to the child's real-life experiences. Learning is decontextualized, specific, organized in particular (even arbitrary) ways, and is directed at precise recall. Relative to the kinds of learning and skills mastered in the child's natural world, there is little redundancy and often little perceived relationship to other areas of experience. For example, the child's view of the distinction between correctly and incorrectly spelled words may be that it is entirely arbitrary and nonmeaningful (e.g., is it *girl* or *gril*? *recieve* or *receive*?). Achievement tests tap a broad array of specific, isolated learnings. Many school tasks are also episodic, tapping, in Vygotsky's term, "scientific concepts." These formal school learnings, as opposed to spontaneous, experience-based learnings, require active development and application of organizational and retrieval strategies. Order must be imposed in ways that allow for efficient processing of information for recall.

In sum, considering these distinctions in terms of Brown's 1975 model of memory, it is apparent that the kinds of learning and skills tapped by intelligence tests are, in part at least, tied to meaning and derived from experiences that are contextually based, often holistic, and learned for the most part incidentally or informally. In contrast, scientific or school learning, as reflected in achievement tests, is often decontextualized and specific, requiring the conscious application of memorial strategies that yield order and structure.

Applying this analysis to learning disabilities, it seems reasonable that Brown's distinctions are represented in the IQ–achievement discrepancy that characterizes these children. These distinctions may help explain some of these children's puzzling inconsistencies. That is, consistent with the notion of an IQ–achievement discrepancy, Brown (1975) has made a practical and theoretical distinction between strategic-episodic tasks (e.g., spelling tests requiring specific application of orthographic rules) and strategic-semantic tasks (e.g., vocabulary or comprehension tests requiring answers that capture the "gist" through manipulation of general information). Through their daily living, learning-disabled children have acquired the semantic learning and the functional skills that allow them to get along reasonably well within their home environments and to perform within a normal range on IQ tests. However, they have problems on tasks requiring production or generation of specific learning or memorial strategies that influence the efficient organization of input for retrieval and recall and thus are necessary for adequate performance in school.

Research Evidence

A number of investigators have provided evidence that learning-disabled children, selected on the basis of an IQ–reading level discrepancy, are indeed deficient or inconsistent in the generation and use of appropriate memorial or problem-solving strategies. Poor readers of normal ability have been found to perform poorly on memory tasks that require complex organizational and retrieval strategies, although doing adequately on simpler, less demanding tests (Bauer, 1979; Wong & Wong, 1977). Torgesen and Goldman (1977) report, too, that good and poor readers differ from adequate readers in the amount of verbal rehearsal used as well as the amount of recall on a memory task. Interestingly, differences between Torgesen and Goldman's groups were minimized when the task was varied to facilitate rehearsal. The following three studies, conducted through the UCLA Special Education program, are relevant to this point because they address directly the question of use of strategies by learning-disabled children.

Using Vygotsky's framework, Haight (1974) compared the performance of normally achieving, educationally handicapped (EH), and EMR children on a series of concept usage and concept formation tasks. The EH and EMR children performed similarly on the spontaneous concept usage test, with both groups generating fewer hypotheses than the normally achieving children. However, consistent with her prediction, Haight found that under instruction, the EH children learned to form new concepts and to solve the task as well as the normally achieving children, whereas the mentally retarded children performed at essentially the same level as in the unelaborated condition. Haight suggests that "normal intelligence quotients, the characteristic shared by educationally handicapped and normally achieving children, appear related to the ability to benefit from instruction" (p. xiv). Haight's work supports the view that learning-disabled children at school entrance have developed the concepts that are expressed in IQ, but lack efficient strategies for processing and retrieving information.

This approach was developed further by Robson (1977), who compared normally achieving and EH children on tests of categorical storage ability and on the children's use of categorical concepts to solve new problems. In his study, normally achieving and EH groups did not differ significantly on number of concepts stored or in the efficiency of their storage. However, on a 20-questions-type problem using the same storage categories, the EH children performed less well than did the normal achieving groups, apparently having difficulty in using the categories to solve the new problem. Of importance for this chapter, the educationally handicapped children in Robson's study improved in performance once the problem-solving task was organized categorically for them. Their performance equaled that of the normally achieving group when the task was structured to provide specific category cues.

In a further extension and direct test of the hypothesis that learning-disabled children do not generate adequate strategies for problem-solving, Hall (1979) used an associated clustering task, a sorting task, a 20-question-type game, and a transfer sorting task to measure different aspects of information storage and retrieval. He also provided different levels of instruction or cue elaboration to the control and experimental subjects. In the experimental condition, subjects were provided with elaborated instructions that cued solution strategies; in the control condition, subjects received only standard instructions. Learning-disabled and normally achieving children were found to differ in their spontaneous use of strategies. Importantly, these differences were minimized through strategic cuing instructions. On the associated clustering task, for example, learning-disabled children under the cued condition reached or exceeded the performance of the normally achieving control group. On the 20-questions task there was a large and significant difference between learning-disabled and normal achieving control groups (favoring the normal achievers), but no significant differences between cued normal and learning-disabled groups.

Interpreting these findings within Brown's 1975 model, it is our view that most learning-disabled children are not structurally deficient, and that they do not have generalized learning problems. Rather, we argue that their problems have to do with the specific organization of material for learning and in the nature of the strategies they generate to accomplish this. Therefore, learning-disabled children are likely targets for cognitive training programs based on strategy development and application. Before we proceed to research on cognitive training with learning-disabled children, it is important to consider briefly some issues and problems related to this approach.

UNRESOLVED ISSUES

In developing the theme that cognitive training is useful in improving the academic skills of learning-disabled pupils, clarification is required on a number of definitional issues. This section is not a disclaimer, but we hope to convey our sense of the complexity and confusion that accompany terms such as "learning disabilities" and "cognitive behavior modification."

First, while it is true that most definitions of learning disabilities highlight the IQ-achievement discrepancy, this criterion does little to delimit the range or the quality of skilled behaviors observable in classrooms or research samples containing learning-disabled pupils. Normal or above-normal IQ includes a broad spectrum of cognitive functioning. We would not expect, nor would we predict, that learning-disabled pupils with low average IQs (i.e., 80 to 90) would profit from elaborated instructions to the same degree as would learning-disabled pupils with higher IQs (i.e., 110 plus). Practically, this may mean shifts in focus and/or substance of cognitive training programs to reflect the quality and amount of skilled behaviors that learners spontaneously call up when working on given tasks in given environments (Keogh & Glover, 1980; Meichenbaum, 1980a, 1980c; O'Leary, 1980).

Related to the first issue is our suggestion that the concept of a learning disability is consistent with the theoretical distinction between semantic and episodic memories. We hasten to acknowledge that the terms "semantic" memory and "episodic" memory are no more precise than the term "learning disabilities." As Nelson and Brown (1978) note, "the two terms obviously mean different things to different people, and it is not at all clear that they in fact produce either an exhaustive or an exclusive classification" (p. 233). While these authors offer no hard-and-fast rules for applying the terms, they suggest an interpretation and urge "clarification through disambiguation" (p. 240). Nelson and Brown redefine episodic and semantic memory as follows:

> We favor a usage that distinguishes episodic as a form of memory input leading both to remembered autobiographical events ("the bear visited my tent") and to the formation of generalized event structures or scripts (what you expect to happen when you visit a restaurant) representing similar repetitive experiences or routines. We conceive of these generalized event structures as one component of an underlying conceptual memory and as the most important component for the young child. We would like to reserve the term semantic memory for storing of information about words and concepts represented in the language. (p. 240)

The revised definitions and the changed conceptualization of the relationship between semantic and episodic memory may provide direction in explaining the IQ–achievement discrepancy observed in learning-disabled pupils. With the introduction of the notion of an underlying conceptual memory, we might think of a memory continuum from episodic to semantic. For any given child interacting with a given task, conceptual memory acts as a filter and mixer, combining semantic information with episodic information according to task parameters perceived by the child. Thus, the episodic–semantic distinction may be recast to include terms such as event structures and scripts.

For example, WISC-R subtests such as Vocabulary, Information, and Comprehension include a number of items that tap consensual information and skills. Such knowledge is characteristic of informal learning and thus, we have argued, semantic memory. However, given that correct answers on those subtests are determined in part by gist and use in context, they also tell us something about the degree to which children call forth knowledge about personal events or repetitive experiences. If, by definition, the semantic memory system is freed from its experiential context, then as Nelson and Brown (1978) argue, information expressed in terms of event structures or scripts is more appropriately conceived of as part of episodic memory. The episodic–semantic distinction, then, may be defined as a distinction between levels or aspects within episodic memory.

It is to be expected that continuing work by memory theorists will lead to further changes in definitions and to even more insightful models. What is important for the student of learning disabilities is the heuristic value of the distinction between episodic and semantic memories, not the precise definitions. The competing development of general and specific knowledge bases as well as the transformation of specific knowledge to a general knowledge code remain at the core of the episodic–semantic distinction. Redefining terms elaborates but does not change the basic distinction. Thus, to account for the IQ–achievement discrepancy characteristic of learning-disabled pupils, notions of cognitive flexibility, learning through interaction with the environment, and amount and type of organization regularly imposed on academic tasks remain key concepts.

An additional point concerns the presence or absence of strategies. Merely acknowledging that a child fails to solve or to act efficiently on a problem due to the presence or absence of a strategy is misleading. Being "passive" or answering in a random fashion can be strategic if the child is aware that no response or a random resonse will cause a teacher or peer to provide information necessary for solving a problem. The point to be made is that strategy, too, is a nonspecific, global term. It refers to a continuum of organizational actions ranging from no response to a coordinated series of behaviors. Strategies systematically reduce the number of possible responses on a problem-solving task. In this regard, it may be useful to distinguish a strategy from what is strategic.

In our view, a *strategy* involves the manipulation of circumscribed information, whereas *strategic* refers to the more encompassing process of combining or recombining particular strategies into an overall plan of organization. It seems likely that specific strategies are similar in learning-disabled children and their normally achieving peers. It is the strategic organizational functions that differentiate the groups. At issue is whether the strategic organizational behavior will be appropriate and persistent enough to satisfy task demands. To say that a child fails to use a particular strategy or fails to be strategic suggests that teaching children how to use specific strategies or teaching children organizational plans generated by fiat (e.g., What is my problem?, etc.) may somehow provide the key that unlocks the door to a vast, well-integrated associative network of information. Yet, in the case of many learning-disabled children, this may be an inaccurate assumption. In pedagogical terms, some children may lack prerequisite knowledge or skills to which strategies can be applied. In addition, many learning-disabled children may have an inadequate array of specific strategies available to them. Recognition of individual differences among children in the breadth of their information and skills, in their repertoires of specific strategies, and in their more encompassing strategic abilities is important for intervenors setting up cognitive training programs. Such information may dictate both content and level of training procedures.

Cognitive training programs have been found to be effective when used with adults in stress-related situations (Meichenbaum, 1977). Most adults have well-integrated, well-developed cognitive systems; they are able to recognize the benefits of organization and are ready to seek those benefits by means of global programs based on self-questioning techniques. With children, however, particularly those with problems, the effects of a cognitive behavior modification approach are likely to interact with the level of skill possessed by the child. Moreover, level of skill is likely to covary with the quality of the child's verbalization, creating situations in which global self-instructional sets are not perceived by the child as useful. Children, at times unaware of their own skill levels, may interpret self-questions too literally. This may result in redundant processing of information and may lead to confusion, to reduced motivation, and to decrements in performance. We would argue that the ability to benefit from cognitive training programs may be a function of cognitive maturity. Thus, it is necessary for intervenors to adapt programs to the entering skills of less sophisticated participants.

Finally, there are ambiguities in the terms *cognitive training* and *cognitive behavior modification* (CBM). Both identify a perspective focusing on the "client's," as well as the educator's, internal dialogue (i.e., a "set of conscious self-statements and images"—Meichenbaum, 1980a, p. 87). As noted by Meichenbaum (1977), the CBM umbrella contains a number of subunits and has been applied to different areas: self-instruction, self-assessment, self-monitoring, self-evaluation, self-reinforcement (O'Leary, 1980; O'Leary & Dubey, 1979; Rosenbaum & Drabman, 1979); metacognition in relation to attentional processes (Loper, 1980; Loper, Hallahan, & Ianna, 1982; Miller & Bigi, 1979); reading comprehension (Meyers & Paris, 1978); self-control (Mischel, Mischel, & Hood, 1978); communication (Markham, 1977); and memory (Torgesen & Houck, 1980). Cognitive behavior modification is like a large city that expands its boundaries through annexation of suburbs. It becomes so diffuse and so spread-out that the concept of the city or its precise location gradually takes on less and less specificity. While there is little question that the term CBM is coming to encompass more and more territory, our knowledge of with whom and under what circumstances cognitive training techniques are most effective is still limited. We need to be impressed not by the global application of the term and its techniques but by the precision with which we can predict and explain the consequences of its use.

In summary, this section conveys how difficult it is to define and operationalize concepts such as cognitive behavior modification, learning disabilities, strategy, and episodic–semantic memory. Our task has been to develop a set of logical relationships and explanations linking the problems of learning-disabled pupils with cognitive training programs based on our sense of what these complex areas represent. Given the somewhat tenuous nature of these theoretical links, it is important to consider available evidence testing the effects of CBM procedures.

REVIEW OF RESEARCH

Keogh and Glover (1980) conclude their paper on generality and durability of cognitive training effects by pointing out that results to date obtained from cognitive training interventions "have been somewhat inconsistent and certainly not conclusive" (p. 80). Thus, they argue that prior to the establishment of a cognitive training programs in clinical or classroom settings, a number of points deserve attention. First, child characteristics such as cognitive and language skills may interact subtly but powerfully with program techniques. Second, number and breadth of training tasks may affect outcomes. Third, it is necessary to question the assumption that a child has the necessary prerequisite skills to solve a task. An organizational strategy may be of little use if the complement of subskills necessary for solving a task is deficient or incomplete. Finally, "the what and the when of outcomes need specification" (Keogh & Glover, 1980, p. 81), as goals may be differentially affected by interventions. The concerns expressed by Keogh and Glover are more practical than they are theoretical and thus provide a basis upon which programs directed at investigating the effects of cognitive training can be evaluated.

The purpose in this section is to examine the relative "generality and durability" of effects obtained from cognitive training programs applied to learning-disabled pupils. This selected literature is organized to consider training effects on impulsivity and on problem-solving skills.[1] Considerable evidence is drawn from ongoing work at the University of Virginia Learning Disabilities Research Institute and focuses on CBM procedures in educational settings. The reader is reminded of the broadness of the CBM-cognitive training definitions, since selected studies are representative of different positions on the cognitive behavioral continuum.

Modification of Impulsivity and Self-control

CBM procedures have been applied with children in the modification of impulsivity, an often-noted correlate and a sometimes hypothesized cause of learning disabilities (see Finch & Spirito, 1980, and Pressley, 1979, for discussion). The goal in most interventions has been the development of self-control. Kanfer (1970) notes that self-control involves inhibiting impulsive responses and substituting reflective behavior. Training studies designed to modify children's impulsivity have used normal children identified as impulsive on Kagan's Matching Familiar Figures Test (MFFT) (McKinney, 1975; Meichenbaum & Goodman, 1969b, 1971b; Nelson & Birkimer, 1978), clinical populations with impulsive behaviors (Bugental, Collins, Collins, & Chaney, 1978; Douglas, Parry, Marton, & Garson, 1976; Finch, Wilkinson, Nelson, & Montgomery, 1975; Moore & Cole, 1978; Palkes, Stewart, & Kahana, 1968), and learning-disabled children (Cullinan, Epstein, & Silver, 1977). Taken as a whole, the results of training studies are promising but not entirely consistent.

Verbal self-instruction procedures have been shown to be effective in modifying children's impulsive responses on the MFFT (Finch *et al.*, 1975; Nelson & Birkimer, 1978) and Porteus Mazes (Palkes *et al.*, 1968) when the training tasks were directly analogous to the pretest and posttest measures. Using verbal self-instruction techniques, Bender (1976) reported improvement on post-test performance for tasks similar to the match-to-sample training material, but found no transfer to the MFFT. While these studies illustrated the effectiveness of cognitive training procedures on particular aspects of impulsivity or self-control, as noted by Keogh and Glover (1980) and McKinney and Haskins (1980), they do not address critical questions of generality or durability, or consider the impact of changes in self-control on learning problems.

Some investigators have attempted to test the impact of CBM train-

[1]We wish to thank Anne Glover Wilcoxen for her help in preparation of this section of the chapter.

ing on outcomes not directly analogous to the training techniques. This of course allows some estimate of generalization. For example, Meichenbaum and Goodman (1971a) trained their "remedial class" of second-graders (children with behavior problems and/or low IQs) on a variety of activities ranging from simple sensorimotor tasks to more complex problem-solving tasks. Relative to comparison groups, the verbal self-instruction training group showed significantly improved performance on selected psychological processing measures; however, there were no significant differences among groups on attentiveness or appropriateness of behavior in the classroom. A four-week follow-up demonstrated persistence of effects, lending some support to the durability of training. Similar findings were reported by Moore and Cole (1978) with 8- to 12-year-old hyperactive boys. It appears that the generalization of verbal self-instruction training occurs when the training includes a variety of tasks, some of which resemble the generalization measures. In both the Meichenbaum and Goodman and the Moore and Cole studies, such a range of tasks was used. It is interesting to note that in both studies, generalization to tasks requiring similar psychological processing abilities occurred, but there was no impact on measures of classroom behavior.

Although the crux of learning-disabled children's problems is expressed in the IQ–achievement discrepancy already discussed, the social and behavioral problems of many learning-disabled children also contribute to their school difficulties. Possible modification of impulsive social behavior through verbal self-instruction techniques is therefore of interest. Snyder and White (1979) successfully decreased inappropriate classroom and social behaviors in severely behaviorally disordered adolescents through a verbal self-instruction program focused on class attendance, completion of social and self-care responsibilities, and control of impulsive social behavior. These behaviors were significantly modified through verbal self-instruction training, evidence consistent with changes in behavior reported by Bornstein and Quevillon (1976) and Kendall and Finch (1978). While promising, the impact of modifying impulsivity on learning and social behavior of learning-disabled children is not entirely clear, a point to be considered further in the next section.

On the basis of evidence to date, it is possible that generality and stability of change in self-control may be related to the length and intensity of training programs. Available studies differ markedly in this regard. Meichenbaum and Goodman (1971a) and Arnold and Forehand (1978) trained children in four or five 30-minute sessions over a two-week period; Snyder and White (1979) provided six 45-minute sessions for four weeks; and Bornstein and Quevillon's (1976) program involved a massed two-hour training session. In one of the few studies that failed to demonstrate stability of verbal self-instruction techniques (Cullinan *et al.*, 1977), the training was limited to one session of approximately 15 minutes. Apparently duration of training, along with content of training and the characteristics of the subjects, must be considered when assessing effectiveness of verbal self-instruction procedures.

Development of Problem-Solving Skills

While the primary application of CBM procedures with children has been in the development of self-control and the modification of impulsivity, a related application is the development of general problem-solving skills. The overall goal in these programs is the generation and development of mediating "thinking" skills that will enhance a child's overt problem-solving behavior. Modification of impulsivity is also included in many of these interventions. The programs tend to be highly structured and to include components of a problem-solving orientation, problem identification and definition, generation of alternative solutions, evaluation of the consequences of alternative solutions, and selective implementation of the most appropriate solution. The scope of problem-solving training programs is generally more extensive than that of the self-control training procedures previously described. Many programs require daily lessons extending over a period of two to four months, with training often conducted in small groups. A wide variety of procedures are employed including discussion, role-playing, modeling, and direct instruction. In some programs, verbal self-instruction and problem-solving strategies are combined.

The work of Douglas (Douglas, 1980; Douglas *et al.*, 1976) and her associates at McGill and the program by Camp and her colleagues (Camp, 1977, 1980; Camp, Blom, Hebert, & van Doornick, 1977) are illustrative of a problem-solving oriented cognitive training approach. Douglas focused on the development of self-control and teaching strategies for effective deployment and maintenance of attention. The training covered a three-month period in which hyperactive learning-disabled children were seen twice a week. Procedures included modeling, verbal self-instruction, general problem-solving training, and training on specific search, focusing, and attention deployment strategies. A variety of visual-motor, auditory-vocal, academic, and social tasks were employed. Parents and teachers were familiarized with the training techniques and encouraged to implement them at home and at school. Immediate and three-month post-test results indicated durable treatment effects. Although the training did not appear to affect performance on all measures of psychological processing, trained children were less impulsive and improved more on several reading tasks than did their control peers.

A second systematic and comprehensive cognitive training intervention programs is the "Think Aloud" program developed by Camp, Blom, Hebert, and van Doornick (1977). This program was designed to enhance self-control in aggressive second-grade boys and was implemented in 30 training sessions. Procedures included modeling and verbal self-instruction procedures similar to those of Meichenbaum and Goodman (1971a,b). These techniques were employed to teach subjects to deal with four basic questions: What is my problem? What is my plan? Am I using my plan? and How did I do? Shure and Spivack's (as described in Spivack, Platt, & Shure, 1976) problem-solving training procedures were also used. The training tasks included psychological processing tasks and interpersonal problem-solving games. Post-test comparisons showed significant improvement on several psychological processing tasks (e.g., prorated WISC performance IQ) and one measure of academic performance (WRAT reading scores) for the group receiving training relative to two control groups. The treatment group also generated significantly more solutions on an interpersonal problem-solving measure and improvement in selected aspects of classroom behavior as rated by teachers.

While the findings from these studies suggest some generalization of training to classroom behavior, academic skills, and psychological processing, the results are not entirely consistent and long-term persistence of effects over time is uncertain (see Keogh & Barkett, 1980, for detailed discussion). Cognitive training interventions emphasizing the development of problem-solving strategies appear to be more effective than interventions focusing on modification of impulsivity in producing durable and generalizable effects. Generalization of effects to educational skills in the Camp, Blom, Hebert, and van Doornick (1977) and Douglas *et al.* (1976) investigations is particularly encouraging. There are several possible explanations for these results. Problem-solving training programs are lengthier than interventions directed toward development of self-control, they employ a variety of training procedures, and they train a variety of skills. In addition, problem-solving strategy training teaches the child how to go about the process of problem solving. In contrast, impulse-control training assumes that the children will be able to use appropriate problem-solving strategies once they are able to focus their attention and monitor their behavior.

Educational Interventions

The bulk of the research on CBM applied to impulsivity and problem-solving has been relatively short-term and often laboratory- or clinic-based. While appealing, both the practicality and effectiveness of CBM problems for learning-disabled pupils in educational settings are uncertain. Evidence from an ongoing program of research at the Learning Disabilities Research Institute (LDRI) of the University of Virginia is, thus, directly relevant to this chapter. The LDRI was established in 1977 by a contract from the U. S. Department of Education, Bureau of Education for the Handicapped. Its mission was to develop empirically validated intervention procedures for working with learning-disabled children in the classroom and in the home. The Institute operated five self-contained, experimental classrooms for learning-disabled pupils in city and county elementary schools. Each classroom had one teacher, one teacher's aide, and 10 children. At the beginning of the 1980–1981 school year, the core sample contained 46 boys and 4 girls ranging in age from 85 to 141 months. Forty-one (82%) of the sample children were white and 9 (18%) were black. All children were from lower- to middle-income families, based on parent occupation. All subjects were selected from a larger pool of pupils who met district eligibility standards for placement as learning disabled. All children showed the IQ–achievement discrepancy already discussed. Ability, as determined by the WISC-R, was above the mentally retarded range ($\bar{X}$ = 95.22; SD = 10.05). Tested achievement in reading and/or math was less than or equal to 90% of measured ability (standard score comparisons). In addition, referring teachers were interviewed to identify those learning-disabled children who exhibited specific problems attending to task. No child had any known sensory or neurological problems, and no child was on medication. All classrooms used the Corrective Reading and Language System programs (published by Science Research Associates) as the core curricula (Lloyd, Epstein, & Cullinan, 1981).

Research Focus

From work in the areas of attention and memory (Hall, 1980b; Hallahan & Reeve, 1980), it has become apparent that learning-disabled pupils are at a "disadvantage in knowing how to go about engaging in tasks that require attention and memory skills" (Kauffman & Hallahan, 1979, p. 88). Therefore, researchers at the LDRI have continued to investigate the efficacy of various CBM procedures for improving the strategic behavior of learning-disabled pupils. In deference to the definitional issues outlined in the previous sections, the major LDRI research findings will be organized according to class of behavior or skill level affected. When we view CBM research along a continuum, three primary areas of focus can be identified. First, there has been investigation of "self-" techniques (e.g., self-instruction, self-recording, self-choice of treatment). These studies are primarily concerned with modifying overt behaviors related to improving children's attention to instruction. The assumption implicit in these studies is that if children appear to be on-task then they are in fact on-task.

A second group of studies has investigated the learning-disabled pupils' use of specific attack strategies or tactics. Children are taught prerequisite rote skills and then are trained to use task-specific strategies for manipulating the information they have learned. The strategies or tactics are then expanded into more generalizable algorithms, to test whether children effectively transfer attack strategies to problems on which they have received no training.

The third major area of investigation has focused on the transfer to generalization process. The aim in these studies has been to document the means by which learning-disabled pupils organize, select, and recall information relevant to problem-solving. Taken together, these studies represent a continuum of research ranging from investigation of overt, discrete behavior change to investigation of highly inferential changes in psychological processing behaviors. As one moves across the continuum, emphasis shifts from investigation of outcome or ends to investigation of process or means.

Self-studies

These studies explore the use of self-control techniques in the classroom. Glynn, Thomas, and Shee (1973) operationally defined four components of self-control: self-assessment, self-recording, self-determined reinforcement, and self-administered reinforcement. Together, self-assessment and self-recording are referred to as self-monitoring. In the Virginia LDRI, self-monitoring intervention procedures for "attention to task" function as externally imposed attention-cuing strategies. Pupils are first taught to monitor their own attending behaviors through self-assessment questions and then to record answers to their own questions. An audiotape recorder that emits low tones at random intervals is used to cue pupils when to ask themselves whether or not they are paying attention.

The effectiveness of this type of procedure has been tested using multiple-baseline designs with reversals. In each of the studies, subjects were between 8- and 11-years-old. Whenever possible, academic response data and on-task behavior were used as dependent measures. In addition, data reflecting teacher attention (praises and reprimands) to target subjects were collected during all phases of the studies. Specific findings are reviewed in Hallahan and Kneedler (1981). In general, the research has led to the following conclusions. (1) Self-recording results in increased on-task behavior and academic productivity (number of arithmetic problems answered and number of words written) (Hallahan, Lloyd, Kosiewicz, Kauffman, & Graves, 1979). (2) Backup reinforcers are not necessary. Effects were obtained on all studies done to date without benefit of backup reinforcers. (3) Cues (tones) and the act of recording are necessary elements. However, children can be "weaned" from reliance on cues (Heins, 1981) and from the recording response (Hallahan *et al.*, 1979; Lloyd, Hallahan, Kosiewicz, & Kneedler, 1980). (4) Minimal teacher time is required for administration, and other pupils are minimally disrupted by use of the procedure. Easiest implementation is during seat-work situations. It can, however, be used during small-group instruction. (5) Increased attention to task is maintained after all parts of the procedure are removed (Hallahan *et al.*, 1979; Heins, 1981). (6) The procedure appears to work best with pupils whose primary problem is attentional—that is, those children who have the tool skills necessary to complete their assignments successfully but who fail to apply them (Hallahan *et al.*, 1979; Heins, 1981). (7) There is some indication that there are "spillover" effects of increased attention to task from subjects directly treated in self-monitoring programs onto nontargeted pupils seated nearby (Kosiewicz, Hallahan, & Lloyd, 1981).

It should be noted that use of the self-monitoring procedures has not necessarily resulted in concommitant improvements in measures of academic achievement. These findings are consistent with those of Ferritor, Buckholdt, Hamblin, and Smith (1972) and Harris and Sherman (1974), who showed that reinforcing attentive behavior has little direct impact on academic performance. As Kazdin (1981) points out, "the importance of altering attentive behavior and minimizing mild levels of disruption from the standpoint of the students is unclear" (p. 46). Nevertheless, it might be argued that attention to task is a necessary but not sufficient condition for improved academic performance. Moreover, in the Virginia LDRI work to date, there has been no direct test of the long-term benefits of increased attention to task and/or increased academic productivity. Conceivably, positive changes in these two areas over time could promote more effective interactions between teacher and pupil and, thus, lead to systematic improvement in academic performance.

Academic Attack Strategy Training

This training represents an approach to instruction that is designed to teach children systematic ways to solve learning tasks. Children are taught a set of subskills and rules for combining the subskills in such a way that any problem in a specific subset of problems can be solved. Self-verbalization, self-monitoring, self-reinforcement, etc. are not required components of the training. For example, in beginning reading instruction, children are first taught the rote skill of saying sounds for letters. They then are taught a sounding-out strategy (tactic) for decoding. In basic multiplication, pupils first learn the rote skill of counting by numbers (e.g., recite "7, 14, 21 . . . 70"). Once the rote skills are mastered, pupils are taught a count-by strategy (tactic) to solve problems. To illustrate, in the problem $8 \times 7 = ?$, pupils would count by seven, eight times and write the eighth number said (56) in the answer space. To date, all LDRI studies using this technique have employed applied behavior analysis designs (i.e., single subject).

A more detailed explanation of the rationale and the training methods of academic attack strategies can be found in Lloyd (1980) and Lloyd, Saltzman, and Kauffman (1981). Results from the Virginia LDRI studies indicate that (1) These procedures are effective for teaching learning-disabled subjects (a) basic multiplication and division facts (Lloyd, Saltzman, & Kauffman, 1981) and (b) missing addend addition problems, as for example, $? + 7 = 15$ (Lloyd, Cameron, Cullinan, Kauffman, & Kneedler, 1981). (2) Small but consistent improvement in word-reading accuracy as compared with baseline performance was obtained from pupils taught to verbalize previously learned plans for decoding (Lloyd, Kneedler, & Cameron, 1982; see Lloyd, Kosiewicz, & Hallahan, 1982, for discussion of attack strategies in reading comprehension). Currently under investigation by Lloyd is the influence of types of arithmetic story problems on the solution processes of learning-disabled pupils. In this study, incomplete information is given and children are required to solve problems for the missing information. Algorithms for solving the problem must be produced by the child depending on the structure of the problem. Information derived from this study should provide insight into solution processes used by learning-disabled pupils and, thus, should help in designing effective procedures for teaching story problem-solving.

It is fair to point out that the long-term benefits of teaching attack strategies are unknown and that the process or circumstances under which a specific task strategy (tactic) takes on the more generalized properties (strategic behavior) are unclear. As Lloyd (1980) suggests, however, for learning disabled pupils,

> Task specific strategies appear to have a better chance of being successful than general strategies, at least with regard to academic learning. However, optimum effects will probably be obtained only when attack strategies for similar types of tasks (e.g., addition and multiplication) include identical steps for the parts of the operation that are identical. (p. 62)

Transfer to Generalization Studies

In this group of studies, the intent is to investigate the circumstances under which learning-disabled pupils generalize problem-solving strategies (tactics) into algorithms (strategic behaviors). The phrase *transfer to generalization* is meant to imply a continuing process, linking the facile knowledge of tool skills (e.g., decoding of sounds into words) to accessible skilled behaviors (e.g., correct spelling). A major question is, How many and what type of externally imposed constraints must be introduced to a training task before a child can make the final "cognitive leap" to generalization on some training task isomorph? Assumptions are made that information gets into the processing system, and that information already in the system (i.e., rote skills, knowledge of relationships) could, if retrieved, help children to identify and select among available strategic options. Both applied and experimental tasks have been used in the Virginia LDRI studies, and investigators have employed group designs with experimental and control subjects selected on the basis of specific levels of skill development or skill discrepancy.

The first set of studies, using laboratory-based tasks, addressed the problem of information organization. Hall (1979) demonstrated that learning-disabled pupils, trained to identify implicit categorical information in to-be-remembered word lists, could identify and then efficiently use the same categorical information on a different task (20 questions). Important to this demonstration of generalization was the elaborated instructions used in the experimental condition. Instructions introducing the abstract notion of categorization were anchored to information and knowledge of relationships well known by children. The idea was to provide a clear frame of reference for interpreting and encoding information, thereby increasing the probability that a specifically trained strategy would be more broadly applied (strategic behavior).

Zakreski (1982) attempted to replicate and extend these findings with similarly selected samples of learning-disabled and normally achieving pupils. In this work the notion of categorization was embedded in a familiar metaphor (detective game). The children were trained on a series of evidence-searching games (20 questions). They were then asked to recall words from an anonymous tipster (associative clustering task), and finally, to identify important clues (matrix solution task). Learning-disabled pupils in the experimental condition benefited dramatically from the training. They identified and used implicit categorical information across all tasks, recalling and clustering more words and asking more constraint-seeking questions than did learning-disabled control subjects. Learning-disabled experimental subjects in both studies were similar to their normally achieving peers in the flexible use of categorical information. Although Zakreski (1982) altered the training task and changed the sequence of the transfer tasks while using nonredundant, implicit categories, his findings were consistent with those of the earlier work, confirming that instructions must be elaborated through referents that are well known and overlearned.

The second series of studies, conducted by Gerber and Hall (1983, in press) at the Virginia LDRI, are centered around the applied task of spelling. Two major findings have emerged. First, the mere presence of well-established tool skills does not guarantee that they will be actively or appropriately used by learning-disabled pupils. Second, the sequence of acquisition for spelling skills is similar for normally achieving and learning-disabled pupils and is reflected in the quality of spelling errors produced by children. Because the sequence of acquisition is the same for the two groups, Gerber and Hall's (in press) analysis of orthographic problem-solving was derived from protocols from normally achieving children. Moreover, because the development of spelling skills in learning-disabled pupils parallels that in normally achieving pupils, it is possible to make point predictions about who should benefit from cognitive training programs designed to improve spelling quality. Thus far, researchers have shown that children with learning problems rarely produced spellings that are deviant, preliterate, or composed of random letter strings. Instead, their spellings reflected the intentional use of orthographic problem-solving strategies commensurate with their ability to spontaneously generate information about phonemic segmentation, sound–symbol correspondence, and application of morphographic rules. Second, learning-disabled pupils were appropriately confident of correct spellings and were fairly accurate in detecting their misspellings. However, despite awareness of errors, spontaneous self-correction attempts resulted in few improved or correct spellings. Gerber and Hall (in press) conclude,

> These analyses illustrate the degree to which spelling may be influenced by application of orthgraphic rules over and above knowledge of sound/symbol correspondence. Thus, they may reveal the degree to which spelling is influenced by general strategic abilities. (p. 37)

In another study-in-progress, Gerber and Hall (1983) asked learning-disabled pupils to spell a list of words and then to choose the correct spelling from eight variants. When asked to choose, many children identified either correct or nearly correct spellings. When asked to write the same words on paper, however, the children often produced spellings of far lower quality. Interviewed as to why they chose high-quality variants, children often were able to articulate specific orthographic rules (i.e., silent "e" to make the previous vowel long). Apparently these children have orthographic information that would be useful, but they fail to use that information systematically in appropriate situations. It was also apparent that when asked to produce spellings, the learning-disabled pupils typically failed to proofread their product or to determine where in the word they had uncertainty. Currently Gerber and Hall are in the data-collection phase of a training study that teaches children (1) to proofread their product; (2) to articulate where, if at all, they are uncertain about their product; (3) to produce alternative spellings from their knowledge of words and rules; and (4) to choose from the alternatives they have produced the best spelling for a target word. Preliminary results indicate that children with sufficient preskills (i.e., sound–symbol correspondence, knowledge about orthographic marking) do benefit from this training by producing more correct or better-quality incorrect spellings. In sum, a significant number of learning-disabled children show a marked discrepancy between what they know and what they can produce. Those children appear to be the ones who benefit most dramatically from a cognitive training program aimed at developing flexible access and use of information available to the learner.

IMPLICATIONS FOR EDUCATIONAL PRACTICE

It is appropriate to try to summarize what we know or think we know about cognitive behavior modification with learning disabled children. Because other applications of CBM procedures are discussed elsewhere in this volume, we will focus on implications for educational practice. First, it seems apparent that if the goal is to change overt, discrete, attending behaviors (i.e., on-task behavior), then self-monitoring techniques focused on self-assessment and self-recording can be effective. Furthermore, the durability of effects obtained from self-monitoring training has been impressive (Hallahan & Kneedler, 1981).

Although findings from self-monitoring research are replicable across elementary-age learning-disabled samples, we must acknowledge that the range of skilled behaviors affected by adoption of self-monitoring techniques is limited. "Looking like a learner" is not synonomous with learning. Improvement in productivity has not been clearly linked to improved skill acquisition or to more successful problem-solving. On the basis of the current evidence, it appears that self-monitoring techniques are most appropriately used by learning-disabled pupils who already possess the tool skills necessary for completing assignments. If the goal is to get children to attend to tasks for which they have demonstrated proficiency, then the self-monitoring aspects of CBM are likely to produce the desired result. If the goals are more complex, however, the problems of cognitive training increase and the impact of training is less certain. The notion that reduced impulsivity and increased attention to task result in improved achievement is probably too simple. Directed attention does not automatically generate organizational plans or solutions to problems. Thus, training techniques that improve behaviors only superficially associated with problem-solving will not necessarily produce changes in the processes by which children attempt to find solutions to academic problems.

Swanson's (1981) work illustrates the point. Looking at the effects of self-recording, tokens, and contingent free-time on learning-disabled children's reading comprehension performance, Swanson conducted three experiments using applied behavior analysis techniques. Results from Experiment I showed a clear effect of self-recording and token reinforcement on reduction of oral reading errors. At the same time, there were no concomitant increases in comprehension scores. In Experiment II, contingent free-time and self-recording increased independent silent reading, but again comprehension scores remained relatively unchanged. When comprehension was the specific target of contingent free-time and self-recording procedures, as in Experiment III, there were substantial improvements in measures of comprehension. Swanson concluded that comprehension performance is only minimally affected when treated as an untargeted dependent behavior. It should be noted that Swanson asked subjects to read passages that were matched to each child's reading level. Ninety-five percent of the comprehension questions requested literal information from the child. Thus, as in the Hallahan *et al.* (1979) work, children were asked to produce information consistent with their previously demonstrated level of skilled behavior, and they were able to produce "more of the same" when directly encouraged through use of token reinforcement and self-recording. In sum, it would appear that the effects of self-monitoring treatments, while somewhat limited in scope, can produce demonstrable changes in specifically targeted behaviors for which task demands are consistent with existing levels of skilled behavior.

Specification of skills and subskills is fundamental in training programs that are directed at improving learning-disabled pupils' educational performance. Research on academic attack strategy training at the Virginia LDRI, for example, centers on "making certain that the pupil knows how to perform a set of preskills that include all component behaviors required for successful use of the strategy and providing the pupil with a rule that specifies the sequence in which each preskill is to be employed" (Cullinan, Lloyd, & Epstein, 1981, p. 42). From a practical perspective, attack strategy work has provided valuable information about teaching technology. Knowledge of a task and the strategies appropriate to that task enables an intervenor to program effective instruction. This is by no means a minor demonstration, and it is consistent with the instructional approach outlined by Belmont and Butterfield (1977). The importance of this type of work is clearly apparent when one considers the savings, in teaching time and in time to learn, that accrue by not having to teach each item from a class of items. On the other hand, even in the Virginia LDRI work on arithmetic there is little evidence to document the acquisition of generalized skills—for instance, multiplication and division. Children clearly can acquire a specific strategy or tactic that can be used to solve problems similar in format and content. Whether these behaviors become "skilled" and thus separated from the parent tactic is as yet unclear. What is needed is evidence that academic attack strategy training improves the ability to apply flexibly and/or alter a tactic in accordance with the demands presented by some task isomorph. The point is well made by Brown (1978) in her commentary relating the instructional approach to the issue of generalization: "From our point of view, the aim of training is not to get children to perform more like adults on a single task, but to get them to think more like adults in a range of similar situations" (p. 138).

A closely related instructional question has to do with the subject areas appropriate as targets of training. Lloyd, Saltzman, and Kauffman (1981) argued that "any group of responses that can be reduced to a set of preskills and discriminated strategies is amenable to training similar to that used in these experiments" (p. 216). Based on work by a number of investigators, there are suggestions that structured strategy training can be applied to areas such as decoding (Samuels, 1981) and reading comprehension (Carnine, Prill, & Armstrong, 1978; Jenkins, Stein, & Osborn, 1981); however, the bulk of work has been with mathematics (Carnine, 1980; Cullinan *et al.*, 1981). Arithmetic may be a subject particularly suitable for analytic, elemental organization and, thus, especially amenable to training. A good test of the overall utility of academic attack strategy training will come with the application to academic subjects that tap children's abilities to use semantic, syntactic, homophonic, or analogical learning cues (e.g., reading comprehension and spelling).

Perhaps the most fundamental question in all cognitive training programs relates to generalization of effects. The generalization issue is complex, and interpretation of presumed program impact is sometimes muddled because of definitional differences held by different investigators. Consistent with Brown's (1978) interpretation, Borkowski and Cavanaugh (1979) suggested that there are differences between tests of maintenance and tests of generalization and that the processing requirements for generalization tasks are likely to vary along a continuum. In their terms:

> *Durability* or *maintenance* refers to the continued use of an acquired strategy on a task identical to that used during training. Only the specific to-be-learned materials are changed. In addition, prompts designed to evoke the trained strategy are usually not given. *Generality* requires not only a test with new materials but a change in task demands as well (Brown, 1978). Presumably the second task shares common features with the training task in terms of their processing requirements; however, the transfer task may require a modification in the specific form of the trained strategy for it to be applicable. (Campione & Brown, 1977, p. 572)

Given these definitions, it seems clear that a good deal of specific strategy training, and perhaps of other CBM research, demonstrates maintenance or durability rather than generalization. Most investigators have articulated a narrow definition of generalization and have demonstrated transfer to items drawn from the same class of items using essentially the same format. An important next step involves tests of the training within a broader definition of generalization.

Brown (1978) addressed one aspect of generalization when she urged the training of executive function skills in the hope that children would apply learned strategies to different tasks in different settings:

> Once we have trained mastery of a mnemonic skill in terms of the first two criteria, use and maintenance of the strategy, would it not be possible to intervene with some specific generalization training? For example, one could tell the child that the trained behavior could help him on a variety of similar tasks and that the trick is to know which ones. The child could then be exposed to a variety of prototypic tasks and the utility of the strategy in such situations demonstrated. At that point, far tasks could be considered, and the reason why the trained behavior would be inappropriate could be discussed and demonstrated. Finally, the child could be presented with a generalization test containing new prototypic and far tasks and his intelligent/unintelligent application of the strategy examined. (p. 139)

Generalization strategy training is particularly appealing for learning-disabled pupils given the ability–achievement distinctions already discussed. For the most part, research has generated more questions than answers, however. Inconsistencies in findings relate in part to definitional differences as noted earlier, but also may be due to program characteristics. While there are some guidelines on how generalization might be trained directly, the impact and interactions of training components are unclear. Most training packages include modeling by the experimenter, overt self-questioning routines, training of a parent strategy across a number of exemplars, explanation of the task to the child, and elaborated cues suggesting possible links among tasks. For example, in the Gerber and Hall work at the Virginia LDRI, each package follows guidelines outlined by Brown and Campione (1978), yet the procedures employed represent a shotgun approach to training. This makes it difficult to determine which (if any) aspect(s) of the training contributed to the observed effects. The differentiation and specification of the contribution of these training components to the overall impact is an important and necessary step in cognitive training research.

Several additional points deserve mention. Although basic research should not be constrained by what is practical, the microeconomics of the classroom (i.e., time to learn and time to teach) require the adoption of direct and efficient procedures. CBM procedures can be cumbersome, inefficient for some learners, and uneconomical for practical use in applied settings. In the mundane world, we seek optimal solutions under economic constraints (Gerber, 1981). Thus, we argue that the systematic approach for altering instructional antecedents proposed by Lloyd and his colleagues (Lloyd, Epstein, & Cullinan, 1981) is especially practical and useful for learning-disabled pupils in self-contained classrooms. Training of attack strategies is simple, economical, and generates predictable, albeit somewhat limited, consequences.

Conversely, transfer-to-generalization studies emanate from models of cognitive processing. Psychological processes are inferential and interactive; thus, models attempting to describe how information is processed tend to reflect complex cognitive systems. The inferential and complex nature of the topics under investigation translates into research that is high-risk, difficult to interpret, and often uncertain in terms of direct payoff. On the basis of previous work, however, two findings appear important. First, the probability of inducing elementary-age learning-disabled pupils to apply learned strategic routines flexibly across isomorphs is increased if training of strategic behavior is anchored to a referent well understood by the child. It would appear that this type of elaborated cueing takes advantage of the child's intact general knowledge base and his or her understanding of relationships.

Second, any cognitive training program that includes an external, overt self-monitoring routine must take into account the possible interaction of the training with the quality of skilled behavior already present in the child. That is, while the "one size fits all" concept of many training programs may be appropriate for modifying overt, discrete behaviors, it may well lead to equivocal or even decremental results when attempting to alter or refocus some complex processing behavior.

The Hall and Gerber studies in spelling suggest that the relative skill with which children regularly attempt to solve orthographic problems interacts with the instructional treatment. Training a child to approach and to evaluate strategically an orthographic problem requires that the child have some understanding of morphographic and syntactic rules. The more refined this rule-governed knowledge, however, the more likely it is that a child will spontaneously adopt self-checking procedures. Forcing children to interrupt their already streamlined self-checking routine by requiring them to demonstrate overtly their knowledge of the trained procedure may have differential consequences.

In summary, we began this chapter by suggesting that children with learning disabilities were good candidates for cognitive training programs that stress the formation of organizational plans and strategies. Although we have not been dissuaded from this point of view, it seems clear that implementation of any CBM program with learning-disabled pupils should follow a careful analysis of (1) the entering skill levels of children considered for treatment, (2) the target of the treatment (i.e., overt behavior, psychological process), (3) the outcome behavior expected to result from the treatment (i.e., rote skill transfer, broad-based strategic application), (4) whether or not the child has prerequisite skills necessary for participation in the treatment, and (5) whether or not the microeconomics of the classroom or laboratory can adequately support implementation of the planned training procedures.

Acknowledgments

We wish to thank Daniel Hallahan and the staff of the Virginia Learning Disabilities Research Institute for their willingness to share materials and ideas in the preparation of this chapter.

8

Cognitive Behavioral Interventions with Mentally Retarded Children

Thomas Whitman, Louis Burgio, and Mary Beth Johnston

INTRODUCTION

A number of theories of mental retardation have been advanced in recent years (cf. Mercer & Snell, 1977). These theories can be distinguished on various dimensions, the most basic of which is whether they attribute the differences between mentally retarded and normal functioning to a fundamental defect in cognitive structure of the individual or to normal polygenetic variation and adverse environmental conditions during the developmental period. These two models, referred to as the *defect* and *developmental* models (Zigler, 1967), lead to different predictions about task performance of mentally retarded and intellectually average individuals equated for developmental level (MA). Because of the diverse implications of these positions for theapeutic interventions, several specific theories from each paradigm will be briefly described.

The cognitive defect theorists focus on particular defective processes that they consider responsible for performance deficiencies of mentally retarded persons. These defects have been attributed to a deficiency in short-term memory activities (Ellis, 1970), to difficulty in organizing input material that detrimentally affects retrieval processes (Spitz, 1973, 1979), to difficulty in attending to the relevant dimensions of a stimulus (House & Zeaman, 1963; Zeaman & House, 1979), and to a dissociation between verbal and motor systems (Luria, 1963). Each theo-

Thomas Whitman, Louis Burgio, and Mary Beth Johnston • Department of Psychology, University of Notre Dame, Notre Dame, Indiana 46556.

ry proposes that the goal of habilitation is to compensate for the specific cognitive process that is operating inefficiently. For example, Ellis (1970) held that retarded children's deficiencies in short-term memory were due to their failure to use rehearsal strategies or to their employment of inadequate rehearsal strategies. Thus, Ellis recommended that retarded children be taught to use verbal and imagery rehearsal strategies to improve their performance on memory tasks.

In contrast to the defect theorists, the developmental theorists typically assume that there is no inherent qualitative difference between MA-matched intellectually average and mentally retarded individuals. Zigler (1967) held that the performance deficiencies of mildly mentally retarded individuals are related to motivational variables and that to overcome these deficits, a consistent experience of intensive social reinforcement is needed. Viewing cognitive functioning from a Piagetian perspective, Inhelder (1968) suggested that the problems of retarded persons are due to their fixation at an inferior level of intellectual organization, even though they are capable of more advanced cognitive functioning. She recommended that children be supplied with moderately challenging tasks to accelerate their cognitive structures toward more complex organization. According to operant developmental theorists, retarded persons have failed, because of their unique environmental experiences, to acquire the range of behaviors that other persons their age have mastered (Bigelow, 1977; Bijou, 1966). Operant theorists recommend the use of learning principles (i.e., reinforcement, punishment, extinction, stimulus control) to develop the deficient response repertoires of mentally retarded persons.

Clearly, both the defect and developmental paradigms for understanding the cognitive and adapative behavior of mentally retarded individuals have implications for educational planning. The operant model, focusing on specific behavior deficits and advocating a technology for remediating these deficits, has been systematically applied in the training of mentally retarded persons, especially the training of those who are severely and profoundly retarded. Behavior modification has transformed many institutions from custodial asylums into innovative training centers where mentally retarded children are taught to interact adaptively with their environment. Zigler's theory, derived primarily from studies of institutionalized mentally retarded persons, has provided a major impetus in the movement toward deinstitutionalization and has broadened the perspective of mental retardation researchers to include personality variables. The other theoretical orientations, both defect and developmental, are concerned primarily with cognitive variables. Only recently, with the growing interest in the modification of the cognitive functioning of mentally retarded children, has the potential of these theories for the education of retarded children been recognized.

Since the 1950s, basic researchers have examined cognitive processes in mildly and moderately retarded children (Borkowski & Cavanaugh, 1979). Initially, researchers studied performance deficits and methods for ameliorating these deficits by means of cognitive tasks that had little bearing on classroom activities. Concerned primarily with theoretical issues, they did not seek out the implications of their findings for the special-education classroom. Within the past decade, however, the interaction among cognitive researchers, applied psychologists versed in behavior modification, and educators has gradually increased.

THE COGNITIVE BEHAVIORAL INTERFACE

Lachman, Lachman, and Butterfield (1979) argued that within psychology the signs of a significant paradigmatic shift have recently become evident. Behaviorism enjoyed an unprecedented degree of allegiance in American experimental psychology during the 1940s, 1950s, and 1960s. Gradually, however, expanding bodies of research in information processing and psycholinguistics, growing dissatisfaction with behaviorism's ability to explain and/or modify complex human behavior, and the discovery of the work of Jean Piaget by American psychologists have contributed to a reevaluation of the adequacy of traditional behavioral conceptualizations concerning the modification of human behavior.

Faced with this challenge, many behavioral researchers and clinicians have been instrumental in the formulation of the area of cognitive behavior modification. The reasons for the development of this area are multiple. First, procedures based on operant learning principles have not proven as powerful as it was originally hoped they would be (Bellack & Hersen, 1977). While operant procedures have usually resulted in the desired changes in behavior, these changes have often been short-lived and confined to specific situations. Second, the behavioral rationales underlying several effective techniques have not been supported when subjected to careful empirical scrutiny (cf. Kazdin & Wilcoxon, 1976). Third, many behavioral scientists have adopted a social learning orientation based on the concept of reciprocal determinism (Bandura, 1977b, 1978), which views the individual not as a passive product of environmental influences but as an active participant in his or her own development. Within a short time, behavioral self-management, characterized by self-directed arrangement of external cues and consequences to facilitate a predetermined goal, has become a frequently implemented method of behavior change. Fourth, with the publication of Lloyd Homme's 1965 paper on *Coverants, the Operants of the Mind,* there began a reappraisal of radical behaviorism's neglect of private events (Mahoney & Arnkoff, 1978). Gradually, such constructs as internal speech and problem-solving strategies have become matters of concern, and the area of covert self-control has emerged.

The place of cognitive variables within the learning paradigm was the subject of much controversy during the first half of this century. This controversy became vigorous again during the late 1970s as a number of well-defined, empirically validated cognitive behavioral interventions emerged (Greenspoon & Lamal, 1978; Jaremko, 1979; Ledwidge, 1978, 1979; Locke, 1979; Mahoney & Kazdin, 1979; Meichenbaum, 1979b). The broader field of psychology was experiencing a "cognitive revolution" (Dember, 1974); the massive amount of data generated by growing numbers of cognitive researchers could no longer be ignored.

In view of the prominent position of both cognitive research and applied behavior analysis in the study of mental retardation, it is easy to understand why mental retardation specialists were, from the beginning, receptive to a cognitive behavioral interface. In contrast to the firm commitment to the learning paradigm that characterized the overall field of psychology, most theories within the specialty of mental retardation have been predominantly concerned with cognitive constructs. Moreover, there has been a history of basic cognitive research examining the validity of these constructs. In addition, because of considerable interest in cognitive variables generated by Jensen's (1969) controversial article on intelligence, new theories of intelligence have appeared (Campione & Brown, 1978; Sternberg, 1979) and the prospects of training intelligence have begun to be explored (Borkowski & Konarski, 1981). It is within the context of (1) increasing emphases on cognitive variables in general psychology and in behavior therapy, (2) the prominent place of both basic cognitive research and applied behavior analysis in the field of mental retardation, and (3) the growing interest in training intelligence that cognitive behavior therapy with mentally retarded persons has its roots.

While proponents of the various cognitive behavior modification approaches differ in the techniques they employ, they generally agree that human beings develop adaptive and maladaptive behavior through cognitive processes and that the goal of the cognitive behavioral clinician is to assess the individual's maladaptive cognitive processes and to arrange learning experiences that will alter these cognitions and their behavioral correlates (Mahoney & Arnkoff, 1978). Within specific therapy situations, individuals are taught to employ mediating responses (e.g., self-instructions, problem-solving algorithms) that exemplify general strategies for controlling behavior (Hobbs, Moguin, Tyroler, & Lahey, 1980)—strategies that will promote generalized behavioral change across situations and tasks. Because the focus of this training is on establishing the individual as the locus of control—in contrast to traditional behavior modification, in which external control is exerted on the person by others—cognitive behavioral interventions are viewed as enhancing both the individual's self-regulatory attributions and his or her skills. This would seem to be an especially appropriate goal for interventions with retarded children since they are typically viewed as being unable to control their own behavior (Kurtz & Neisworth, 1976), being in need of constant supervision (Mahoney & Mahoney, 1976), and being outer-directed in their problem-solving orientation (Balla & Zigler, 1979; Zigler, 1973).

COGNITIVE BEHAVIORAL INTERVENTIONS

Cognitive behavioral procedures used with retarded children can be classified in five catagories: self-regulation, problem-solving, cognitive strategy training, correspondence training, and self-instructional training. Although procedurally dissimilar, there is considerable overlap among these categories. The purpose of the following pages is to describe cognitive behavioral procedures that are implemented with mentally retarded children, to review research evaluating these procedures, and, finally, to present a framework within which further developments of this technology can be conceptualized, researched, and implemented.

Self-regulation

The ability of a child to regulate his or her own behavior involves the capacity to delay gratification through the use of certain self-control skills. The teaching of self-control skills is the goal of self-regulation training. When a behavior or set of behaviors is targeted for modification through the use of self-control procedures, the first step involves increasing the child's awareness of that behavior. This can be achieved by teaching the child self-monitoring skills; the child learns to identify a discrete occurrence of his or her behavior and to record that behavior accurately. Then, the child is taught to set an appropriate standard or goal for behavioral change. This standard can be based on social referents, the child's own past performance, or a combination of the two

(Bandura, 1977a). Next, the child is trained to evaluate his or her performance in relation to the standard. Finally, if the child's behavior compares favorably with the standard, the child is taught to reinforce him- or herself.

Research with mentally retarded children examining the various self-control components has fallen along two major lines of inquiry. The first type of research has examined whether retarded children are capable of acquiring self-control skills (cf. Litrownik & Steinfeld, 1982). This second type of research has assessed whether self-control programs can be utilized in applied settings to effect socially significant behavioral changes. This latter research has also attempted to establish the relative efficacy of self-control as compared with externally controlled behavior change procedures.

Analogue Studies

Since the utilization of self-control techniques requires retarded children to delay gratification, an important preliminary question is whether these children are capable of withstanding temporary discomfort for the prospect of long-term gain. Results of an early study by Mischel and Metzner (1962) indicated that a child's choosing to display self-control is related to his or her IQ. The lower a child's IQ, the lower the probability that he or she will postpone attainment of desired rewards. Morena and Litrownik (1974) reported that mildly retarded students were less likely than emotionally handicapped students to delay gratification. In contrast to these initially negative data, Litrownik and his colleagues found, in a series of studies, that moderately retarded adolescents do not always choose the immediate option in a delay-of-gratification paradigm; that their choice is determined, to some extent, by the reward option (Franzini, Litrownik, & Magy, 1978); that self-control behaviors by retarded adolescents in a workshop-setting increased when the participants had prior exposure to delay intervals before making a choice (Litrownik, Franzini, Geller, & Geller, 1977); and that moderately retarded adolescents can be taught to withstand delay intervals of increasing length (Franzini, Litrownik, & Magy, 1980).

Given that retarded children can be taught to delay their responses in situations that require self-control, the question of mentally retarded children's ability to learn such specific self-control skills as self-monitoring, standard setting, self-evaluation, and self-reinforcement merits exploration. The initial data regarding retarded children's ability to self-monitor were discouraging. In a study by Singer (1963), mildly retarded students were unable to report correctly scores they had obtained on a game-like task. Similarly, studies by Nelson, Lipinski, and Black (1976) and Zegiob, Klukas, and Junginger (1978) reported that retarded persons were extremely unreliable when monitoring their own behavior. Other investigators, however, have arrived at more optimistic conclusions. It has been demonstrated that, with training, moderately retarded children can monitor their behavior on a bead-chaining task (Litrownik & Freitas, 1980), while completing math problems (Mahoney & Mahoney, 1976), and during a bowling game (Litrownik, Freitas, & Franzini, 1978).

Setting performance standards and evaluating behavior in terms of these standards have been shown to facilitate performance for both intellectually average (Rosen, Diggory, & Welinsky, 1966) and retarded children (Rosen *et al.*, 1966; Warner & de Jung, 1971). Although some researchers (Rosen, Diggory, Floor, & Nowakiwska, 1971) doubted that retarded children could be trained to set appropriate standards for performance, Campione and Brown (1977) reported that, while the majority of the mentally retarded students they trained were unable to estimate realistically the number of pictures they could recall on a serial recall task, some older retarded students (MA = 8) became more realistic with additional experience and specific feedback. Employing a bowling task, Litrownik, Cleary, Lecklitner, and Franzini (1978) found that after being exposed to a model who set performance standards, trainable retarded children could adopt standards based initially on observations of others' performance and later on their own past performance. Brodsky, LePage, Quiring, and Zeller (1970), investigating whether mildly retarded children could adequately evaluate the correctness of their responses based on a predetermined performance standard, found that, before training, retarded children overestimated their level of correctness on a matching-to-sample task. After training that consisted of experimenter-administered feedback (contingent reinforcement of their responses), however, the accuracy of their performance evaluations increased.

In a study by Neisworth (1973), severely retarded children were taught to reward their own progress on a bead-stringing task. Although this program was originally established and monitored by adults, the children gradually took charge of the program without a decrement in performance. Litrownik, Lecklitner, Cleary, and Franzini (1978) taught retarded children to evaluate their own performance on a bead-stringing task and to administer contingently rewards that were fully accessible. Training consisted of instructions and prompting on both self-evaluative and self-reinforcement skills. Results indicated that the trained children correctly evaluated and rewarded themselves on the training task and on a transfer task. Only at a follow-up assessment, however, did the training group surpass the control group in the number of beads strung. The authors hypothesized that self-control skills must be applied over a relatively long period of time to effect a significant behavioral change.

Finally, Litrownik, Cleary, and Steinfeld (1978) attempted to teach moderately retarded children to use a comprehensive self-reinforcement routine that included self-monitoring, standard-setting, evaluation, and self-reward, Training consisted of taped and live demonstrations of appropriate skill performance. In addition, training was criterion-based and the children were expected to acquire the skills in small steps with the aid of prompts and reinforcement. The results indicated that moderately retarded children could acquire and accurately perform comprehensive self-reinforcement skills and that these skills could be maintained over time and transferred to another task. It was also found that the trained group outperformed a control group on the bead-stringing task.

In summary, research with mild and moderately retarded children suggests that, while they do not always spontaneously show self-regulatory skills, they can be taught to delay gratification, to monitor their performance reliably, to set realistic performance standards, and to evaluate accurately and reinforce contingently their performance in a laboratory task situation. Furthermore, several analogue studies have suggested that the acquisition of these skills facilitates the task performance of these mentally retarded children.

Applied Research

A number of investigations have indicated that self-monitoring can be used as a behavior change technique in applied settings. In this type of intervention, the children are trained in the self-monitoring alone. Nevertheless, the training had an effect on their behavior. Theorists claim that this "reactive effect" is due to the implicit contribution of additional self-control processes working unobtrusively in combination with the self-monitoring behavior (Kanfer, 1970; McFall, 1977). For example, Kanfer (1970) argued that during self-monitoring, the person observes the results of his or her performance, compares them against his or her personal performance standard, and then self-administers either covert reinforcement or punishment depending on the magnitude and direction of discrepancy between the observed performance and the standard. Regardless of the actual mechanism operating during self-monitoring, its efficacy as a behavioral change procedure with mentally retarded children in applied settings has been amply demonstrated

(Litrownik & Freitas, 1980; Nelson *et al.*, 1976; Nelson, Lipinski, & Boykin, 1978; Zegiob *et al.*, 1978).

Nelson *et al.* (1976) found that, in spite of initially low accuracy levels, retarded adolescents and adults could be taught to record negatively and positively valenced behaviors and that this recording reliably increased positively valenced behavior (talking) while not significantly influencing negatively valenced behavior (face-touching). In a similar study, Nelson *et al.* (1978) demonstrated that mildly retarded adolescents could be trained to increase appropriate verbalizations through a self-monitoring procedure. Of particular interest is their finding that both accurate and inaccurate self-monitors increased their appropriate verbalizations to comparable levels. Zegiob *et al.* (1978) also found that self-monitoring, even when inaccurately employed, decreased socially undesirable behavior in institutionalized mentally retarded adolescents. Finally, Zohn and Bornstein (1980) successfully utilized a self-monitoring procedure to increase work productivity of moderately retarded adults in a workshop setting. Both Zegiob *et al.* and Zohn and Bornstein found that their subjects could self-monitor for long periods of time with minimal external cues. Zegiob *et al.* demonstrated that self-monitoring behavior can be maintained for as long as six months.

The fact that both accurate and inaccurate self-monitoring had similar effects on behavior raises questions about the components of this intervention that are ultimately responsible for the behavior change achieved. Whatever the agent of change in these interventions, further research is merited because of the potential of self-monitoring for positively influencing the behavior of mentally retarded children.

Self-control techniques have also been used in conjunction with more traditional procedures. In a weight-reduction program, Rotatory, Fox, and Switzky (1980) devised a complex training package for mildly retarded adults including externally controlled monetary reinforcement for weight loss, self-monitoring of food intake, self-evaluation of performance, and contingent self-administration of positive or negative statements. The results, which suggested that this treatment package produced a modest weight loss for the treated individuals, were later replicated with moderately retarded adolescents (Rotatory & Fox, 1980). In this study, the adolescents continued to lose weight at a 35-week follow-up.

A number of studies have used self-control packages to maintain performance changes initiated through externally controlled procedures (Frederiksen & Frederiksen, 1975; Nelson *et al.*, 1976; Robertson, Simon, Pachman, & Drabman, 1979). Nelson *et al.* (1976) found that with adult retarded individuals, self-monitoring increased three target behaviors (conversation in the dining room, participation in activities, and keeping bedrooms tidy) beyond levels obtained when an externally controlled token system was in effect. Results by Frederiksen and Frederiksen (1975) showed that increases in on-task behavior and decreases in disruptive behavior that initially occurred during a teacher-evaluation and reinforcement phase of a program were maintained when the children were evaluating their own behavior with the teacher continuing to administer the reinforcement. In a similar study, Robertson *et al.* (1979) reduced the frequency of disruptive behaviors in a classroom of moderately retarded children through specific feedback and a token reinforcement program. In contrast to Frederiksen and Frederiksen, Robertson *et al.* successfully taught the children self-evaluation skills by reinforcing them for matching the teacher's evaluations of their behavior. The low levels of disruptive behaviors exhibited during the initial externally controlled phase of this study were maintained and were further reduced during the self-evaluation phase. These results were replicated with a similar population and similar behaviors by Shapiro and his colleagues (Shapiro & Klein, 1980; Shapiro, McGonigle, & Ollendick, 1980). One difference in the Shapiro and Klein program was that the children in their study were allowed to self-administer reinforcements (tokens) rather than having the reinforcements dispensed by the teacher. Also Shapiro *et al.* (1980), attempting to separate the effects of self-assessment and self-reinforcement training, found that some children displayed adequate self-regulatory behavior after only having been taught self-monitoring skills. Other children required training in both self-monitoring and self-reinforcement, while still others appeared incapable of learning any of the components necessary for successful self-regulation. These authors concluded that individual differences play a large role when retarded children learn self-control skills. In contrast to the studies discussed, Knapczyk and Livingston (1973) trained educable mentally retarded (EMR) children in self-recording and self-reinforcement skills to enhance their performance on a reading task. In a later phase of their study, the responsibility for a token procedure was assumed by the teacher. Results showed that the self-controlled and externally controlled token systems produced similar improvements in reading performance.

The only research reported in the mental retardation literature that directly compares self- and externally controlled intervention programs is a study conducted by Helland, Paluck, and Klein (1976). In this study, the productivity of trainable retarded adults and adolescents on a workshop task (collating papers) was examined under two reinforcement conditions. An external reinforcement group received experimenter compliments and material reinforcers for increasing production, while a self-reinforcement group was instructed in self-reinforcement (self-administered compliments and tangible rewards) for increased production. Results indicated that both groups improved performance on the collating task, with no apparent performance differences between the groups.

In general, then, research examining self-control programs with mildly and moderately retarded children in applied settings has determined that these children can be taught self-monitoring and self-reinforcement skills and that separately or in combination with external control procedures, these skills can effect and maintain behavioral change. Furthermore, although sparse, available data suggest that self-regulatory programs are as effective as externally administered programs. Particularly noteworthy is the fact that the behaviors of mentally retarded children that researchers have successfully modified using self-regulatory interventions (e.g., work productivity, weight-reduction, personal/social skills, classroom behavior) have considerable practical social ramifications for the children, a factor endorsing further efforts to develop these procedures.

Problem-Solving

Goldfried and Davison (1976) define problem-solving as an overt or covert process in which the problem-solver generates a variety of potentially effective responses to a problem situation and through which he or she learns to recognize and implement the most effective response. After the most productive response has been identified and implemented, it may be maintained by using self-control procedures such as those outlined in the previous section. With adults, problem-solving is generally taught in five stages (Goldfried & Davison, 1976). The stages include teaching the individual (1) to think of life as an ongoing process of solving problems, (2) to define completely and operationally a particular problem situation, (3) to generate a list of possible solutions to a specific problem, (4) to decide on a particular problem solution based on a prediction of the consequences of each solution and an evaluation of the utility of these in dealing with the problem (D'Zurilla & Goldfried, 1971), and (5) to implement the selected course of action, observe the consequences, and match the actual outcome against the anticipated outcome. If the match is satisfactory, the problem-solving process can be terminated; if not, the problem solver returns to earlier steps of the problem-solving procedure and repeats them until a satisfactory match is obtained.

While research suggests that mentally retarded individuals are deficient in problem-solving skills (Miller, Hale, & Stevenson, 1968; Smith, 1967; Stevenson, Hale, Klein, & Miller, 1968), little attention has been given to developing these skills in retarded children. Most studies do not attempt to train all of the steps of problem-solving delineated by Goldfried and Davison (1976); rather, they focus on developing specific components of the problem-solving algorithm. For example, in an attempt to teach problem-solving skills to retarded children, Ross and Ross (1973) devised a program to improve the children's ability (1) to listen to and understand the statement of a problem, (2) to identify the elements in the problem that would be helpful in solving it, (3) to see that many problems have more than one solution, and (4) to have confidence in their ability to offer adequate problem solutions. Training took place over a six-week period with small groups in which social problems were presented in a game-like context. A number of problem-solving behaviors (e.g., trading, combining available resources to meet a need, rearranging resources to remedy deficiencies) were introduced within the context of situations familiar to the children. The children alternated between (1) observing their peers and the experimenter generate problem solutions and (2) actively generating their own problem solutions. Results indicated that after training, children in the experimental group offered more problem solutions than children in a control group. Anecdotal evidence suggested that these skills generalized to the children's classroom. The success of this training package led to the development of a preschool- and primary-school curriculum to teach "brain-storming" skills to EMR children (Ross & Ross, 1974).

Hypothesizing that retarded children's inability to solve problems is related to a difficulty in attending to or in discriminating between relevant and irrelevant features of the problem, Ross and Ross (1979) developed another approach to problem-solving training. In this study, training consisted of presenting stories of social conflict to a small group of EMR children, after which the children were encouraged to discuss relevant and irrelevant dimensions of each problem. Procedures such as peer modeling, reinforcement, and frequent repetition were also used. Findings indicated that trained children were more successful than control-group children in understanding the relevant and irrelevant features of social conflict problems on a paper-and-pencil test. Again in this study, although no measures of transfer to everyday situations were taken, unsolicited reports from teachers suggested that there was generalization to a classroom setting.

Several researchers have investigated whether retarded children who have been supplied with several solutions to a problem can be taught to identify the best solution. Budoff and Corman (1976) helped a group of EMR children improve their performance on the Ravens Colored Progressive Matrices by training them to select the best alternative from those provided. Training involved presenting problems using a slide projector and allowing the group to solve the problems by drawing the elements from the various choices and visually determining which solution best completed the problem. The authors reported that training was most effective in improving, of the four subskills assessed by the Ravens Colored Matrices, the children's ability to reason by analogy. Unfortunately, in this study the description of the training procedures, called learning potential training, was not sufficient to allow an adequate evaluation or future replication.

Ross and Ross (1978) also attempted to teach EMR children to "select the best alternative." This training study, however, had considerable applied significance in that during training the children were confronted with a familiar social problem requiring some action or decision. The children were trained to participate in small-group discussions in a game-like atmosphere. Topics discussed included the concept of choice, norms for choosing one of several attractive alternatives, choices in emergency situations, and choices based on logic. Throughout all training sessions, tokens were awarded for good answers and for "trying hard." According to the results measured by a paper-and-pencil test, the trained children developed greater proficiency in selecting the best alternative and provided better rationales for their choices. The fact that this training program required 40 training sessions is an indication of how difficult the acquisition of evaluation skills is for EMR children. The authors argued, however, that the long-term social benefits for the children more than justified the time spent in training.

Problem-solving skills have also been used in combination with other training procedures to form complex training packages. In an uncontrolled case study, Schneider (1974) reported using problem-solving techniques as one component in a training package to teach impulse-control to aggressive retarded children. The problem-solving component of the package was intended to help the children imagine alternatives to aggressive behavior and their consequences. The treatment package, called the "turtle technique," included imagery training, relaxation techniques, token reinforcement, and other therapeutic procedures. Examples of various responses to frustrating situations were given and alternative solutions were discussed. The author argued that this training facilitated improved classroom behavior by the participants.

Research on problem-solving with mentally retarded children is in its initial stages. Thus far, studies have been directed at training components of the problem-solving algorithm outlined by Goldfried and Davison (1976); these studies have been almost entirely analogue studies with no empirical evidence for maintenance or generalization of the skills trained. The research has been limited to the educable retarded population. While the results do indicate that educable retarded children can be taught to generate several solutions to problem situations and to choose the best alternative when a series of alternatives is provided, the length of time required to teach such skills is long and the procedure tedious. Also, the relationship between the ability to generate and select alternatives and the ability to implement the chosen alternatives has not been explored. Although the teaching of global problem-solving strategies seems important because of the social benefit that would accrue to mentally retarded individuals from such training, efforts must also be directed toward ensuring that the social skills needed for effective problem-solving are within the children's repertoires if global problem-solving is to be successful.

Cognitive Strategy Training

As we have indicated, various theories of mental retardation have suggested that mentally retarded individuals manifest a number of cognitive deficiencies that are, to some extent, modifiable. Recently, cognitive psychologists have developed several models of intelligence (Campione & Brown, 1978; Sternberg, 1979) that have considerable heuristic value for identifying specific cognitive deficits in mentally retarded children and for designing systematic training programs for modifying these deficits (cf. Borkowski & Konarski, 1981). Thus, there is currently considerable interest in and optimism about instructional programs for training cognitive strategies in mentally retarded children (cf. Feuerstein, Rand, Hoffman, & Miller, 1980; Roberts, 1979; Taylor & Turnure, 1979).

Cognitive strategy training refers to interventions designed to teach children how to learn (cf. Brown & French, 1979). In this training, basic cognitive strategies are taught and children are helped to become aware of their own thought processes. When used with mentally retarded children, such strategy training attempts to compensate for existing deficits and to facilitate optimal cognitive development.

Past research comparing retarded and nonretarded children often revealed striking differences in performance on mediational tasks (cf. Borkowski & Wanschura, 1974). Turnure, Buium, and Thurlow (1976) suggested, however, that researchers were misguided in searching for mediational deficiencies in retarded children. Instead, Turnure *et al.* argued that researchers often have not provided retarded children with effective strategies for accomplishing tasks, thus producing children who are "instruction deficient." When mentally retarded children are provided with effective cognitive strategies, their performance on a variety of tasks improves. For example, Turnure *et al.* (1976) conducted an extensive investigation comparing mediational strategies. They investigated whether "what"- and "why"-type questions, which presumably activate semantic processing (cf. Craik & Tulving, 1975), could be instrumental in stimulating young children and EMR children to generate verbal responses that would function as effective mediators in enhancing acquisition and recall of paired associates. They compared labeling, sentence generation, sentence repetition, responses to "what"-type questions, and responses to "why"-type questions and found large performance differences in favor of the questioning groups. They concluded that semantic analysis induced by the questioning strategies was responsible for the differences among conditions for both mentally retarded and nonretarded individuals.

More recently, Kendall, Borkowski, and Cavanaugh (1980) trained EMR children to use and to generalize the Turnure *et al.* (1976) interrogative strategy to aid their learning of a paired-associate list. The key features of this instructional package were (1) active participation by the child, (2) extended training of the strategy, (3) semantic encoding of the to-be-learned material, (4) feedback on the strategy's value, (5) systematic introduction of the strategy's components, and (6) fading of the experimenter's involvement as the training progressed. The results indicated that EMR children could be taught to use, maintain, and, to a lesser extent, generalize an interrogative learning strategy.

Cognitive strategy training has been used to improve mentally retarded children's performance on a number of academic tasks. For example, Paris, Mahoney, and Buckhalt (1974) taught recall of information contained in short paragraphs by instructing retarded children to make up images corresponding to sentences that were read to them. The authors found that children trained in the use of imagery made more inferences and retained more information from the stories than children who did not receive imagery instruction. Taylor, Thurlow, and Turnure (1977) used a verbal elaboration strategy to facilitate vocabulary learning in mentally retarded children. In this study, the children were taught to use elaborations emphasizing relationships among two or more vocabulary words. Thurlow and Turnure (1977) developed a package of classroom materials to teach money, measurement, and time concepts using verbal elaboration procedures. Other researchers have used cognitive strategies to teach geography (Borkowski, Cavanaugh, & Reichart, 1978).

Certainly the most comprehensive cognitive strategy training program with EMR children is that developed by Reuven Feuerstein and his colleagues (Feuerstein, Rand, & Hoffman, 1979; Feuerstein *et al.*, 1980). Based on the cognitive psychology of Piaget, Feuerstein's argument is that mediated learning is the foundation on which higher order cognitive functioning is built and that, even as late as adolescence, significant modifications of cognitive deficiencies are possible. Cognitive deficiencies are conceptualized as occurring at one of three phases: input, elaboration, or output. Deficiencies occurring at the input phase are: blurred and sweeping perception; impulsive exploration; impaired verbal, spatial, temporal, and conservation concepts; and a lack of precision and accuracy. Major deficiencies noted during the elaboration phase include: an episodic grasp of reality, a lack of spontaneous comparative behavior, deficient planning, limited interiorization, and a general impaired need for logical evidence. At the output phase, the significant deficits involve: an insufficient need for precise and accurate communication, impulsive acting-out behavior, and trial-and-error responses.

The Instrumental Enrichment Program (IEP), devised by Feuerstein and his colleagues, attempts to compensate for cognitive deficits by exposing children to tasks designed to stimulate those cognitive functions identified as deficient. The IEP involves three to five hours of weekly instruction, in addition to regular classroom instruction, for approximately two to three years. Tasks are taught individually and in groups, and the students are active collaborators in defining immediate objectives and long-term goals. The teacher introduces a specific topic and clarifies the important concepts. As students work, the teacher reinforces appropriate behavior, provides information, and offers assistance when needed. Discussion follows, centering on an explanation of effective cognitive processes; the principles acquired during the lesson are then applied to academic and vocational studies and to general experiences in daily life, thereby enhancing generalization.

Preliminary results suggest that children who took part in the Feuerstein program improved their general intellectual functioning and their performance on specific cognitive tasks (spatial concepts, analytic perception, precision in performance of mental operations), on scholastic achievement, and on some measures of classroom interaction. These results were partially replicated by Arbitman-Smith and Haywood (1980), who reported that in the pilot year of their two-year program, EMR children exposed to the IEP significantly improved their scores on the Lorge-Thorndike IQ test.

The study of cognitive strategy training is relatively new, and systematic research is scarce. Much more research needs to be completed. Methodological rigor and ecological validity are extremely important dimensions of such research. Cognitive strategy training, more than research in self-regulation and problem-solving, is closely tied to both theories of mental retardation and models of intelligence and cognitive development. In addition, cognitive strategy training seems to be translatable into specific training programs to improve academic performance. Cognitive skill training, because of its roots in theory and its apparent potential for practically influencing the academic training of mentally retarded children, may provide the most promising area for the integration of cognitive theory and behavioral technology.

Correspondence Training

There is a growing body of research concerned with the relationship between what people say and what they do. Much of this research is based on the assumption that a correspondence exists between verbal and nonverbal behavior. The implication is that it may be possible to control nonverbal behavior by modifying verbal behavior. The appeal of this training procedure is related to the accessibility of an individual's verbal behavior and to the fact that with this training, motor behaviors may be maintained in situations that make it inconvenient or undesirable to monitor and reinforce these behaviors directly (Israel, 1978). Three different correspondence training procedures have been presented in the literature. In one type of program (say–do), the child is requested to state what he or she is going to do; subsequently the child is rewarded if his or her behavior corresponds to his or her stated intention (Israel, 1978). In a second type of correspondence training program (do–say), the child is asked to state what he or she has done previously and is rewarded for statements that accurately describe his or her behavior (Risley & Hart, 1968). Researchers have found empirical evidence that these two procedures yield similar results (Israel & O'Leary, 1973). The final correspondence procedure differs from the previous two in that it depends much less on the use of verbal cues. In this procedure, termed a "show–do" sequence (Whitman, Scibak, Butler, Richter, & Johnson, 1982), an instructor describes the correct performance of a target behavior. The child is then asked to show the instructor what the correct enactment of this behavior would look like in the setting in which it should occur. Then the child is given the opportunity to perform the target behavior. If the child actually emits the correct behavior, he or she is rewarded. In all of the correspondence procedures, if the child incorrectly states that he or she performed the target behavior, the instructor informs the child of the inaccuracy of his or her report and encourages the child to do better at the next opportunity. No reward is given when such noncorrespondence occurs.

Examination of the applied research literature suggests that the relationship between verbal and nonverbal behavior is complex. Kurtz, Neisworth, Goeke, and Hanson (1976) found that merely reinforcing normal children's anti-littering verbal statements resulted in increases in anti-littering behavior (e.g., picking up papers). In contrast, Brodsky (1967) failed to increase social behavior in an institutionalized mentally retarded female by reinforcing her stated intentions to emit such behavior. Similarly, Risley and Hart (1968) and Karoly and Dirks (1977) found with intellectually average children that merely reinforcing verbal behavior did not increase sharing and self-control behaviors, respectively. In both the Brodsky (1967) and Risley and Hart (1968) studies, however, prosocial behaviors did increase when reinforcement was delivered contingent upon matching the verbal report to the actual performance.

One explanation of these mixed results regarding the correspondence between verbal and nonverbal behavior may be found in the differing reinforcement histories of the children regarding correspondence between word and deed. For example, if a child has been reinforced for matching his or her verbal and nonverbal behavior, simply reinforcing and increasing the rate of verbal behavior should increase the corresponding nonverbal behavior for that child. Burron and Bucher (1978) tested this hypothesis with nonretarded children. They found that nonretarded children previously exposed to reinforcement for matching verbal and nonverbal behavior were more likely to show correspondence in a temptation situation than were children reinforced for noncompliance.

A series of studies conducted at the University of Notre Dame suggest that mentally retarded children can benefit from correspondence training implemented in classroom settings (Keogh, Whitman, Johnson, & Burgio, 1981; Scibak, Whitman, & Johnson, 1980; Whitman *et al.*, 1982). In the first of a three-study series, Whitman *et al.* (1982) examined whether correspondence training would reduce out-of-seat and talking-out behaviors in two EMR children and whether these changes would be maintained over time. At the beginning of each treatment session, the instructor carefully described for the children exactly what "staying in your seat" and "being quiet" meant and asked: "Are you going to stay in your seat today?" The children's target behaviors were observed for 20 minutes. At the end of the observation period, the instructor approached each child and made one of the following statements: "You said you were going to be quiet and/or stay in your seat and you did," or "You said you were going to be quiet (and/or stay in your seat) but you didn't, did you? Well, you'll have to try a little harder tomorrow." If the children's behavior were consistent with their verbalizations, they were reinforced. A withdrawal design with an eight-month follow-up was employed to assess the effects of correspondence training. Results suggested that the introduction of a "say–do" training sequence resulted in reliable decreases in out-of-seat and/or talking-out behavior with the two retarded children. Although treatment effects were maintained over an eight-month period for one child, behavioral change in the second was maintained for only three months.

In a similar project, Scibak *et al.* (1980) examined the efficacy of a say–do correspondence training package for modifying the rates of in-seat, quiet, and attentional behaviors in six educable retarded children. In this study, the direct effects of this treatment procedure were assessed through a multiple baseline design across subjects and behaviors. In addition, this project examined whether the training would produce generalized changes in appropriate classroom behavior; whether performance changes, initially brought about through correspondence training, could be maintained through the reinforcement of verbalizations only; and whether the maintenance procedure could be shifted from the experimenter to the teacher. The results demonstrated that correspondence training produced marked improvements in appropriate behavior of five of the six children. Furthermore, training effects were sustained during a maintenance and transfer period when only the children's verbal intentions to act appropriately were reinforced and when this procedure was faded from the experimenter to the classroom teacher.

Whitman *et al.* (1982) employed correspondence training to develop appropriate sitting posture in four EMR children during a math program. The correspondence training procedure used in this study differed from that employed in earlier studies both in the specificity of the verbal statements required during the "say" phase of the correspondence training and in the feedback given during the reinforcement phase. While in earlier studies often only a "yes" or a brief reply to questions was required during the "say" phase (e.g., Risley & Hart, 1968), the present study required each child to state his or her intention to emit four specific behavioral components that were defined as constituting proper sitting posture. Shaping and prompting were used to develop this chain of verbal responses. Feedback concerning the children's posture was also detailed, with the children being told specifically how they had or had not done what they said they would do. A multiple baseline across subjects design was used to assess the effects of the program. The results suggested that correspondence training was an extremely effective procedure for increasing appropriate sitting posture; each of the children showed rapid and extensive increases in proper sitting posture during a math program. Moreover, the effects were found to generalize to a handwriting exercise. The authors suggested that this generalization effect was related to the children's failure to discriminate the nature of the reinforcement contingencies. Consistent with the findings of Scibak *et al.* (1980), these changes were maintained when reinforcement was associated only with the child's statement of his or her intention to sit appropriately and when this procedure was faded from instructor to classroom teacher. Finally, the results suggested that for these educable retarded children, there was a direct and positive relationship between sitting posture, quantity of classwork completed, and accuracy of performance.

Correspondence training procedures as employed with normal and EMR children require a certain receptive and expressive linguistic ability on the part of the child; the child must be able to comprehend questions about his or her intention to behave in a certain fashion during training (say–do) or about how she or he behaved in the past (do–say). Furthermore, the child may, as in the last two studies, have to repeat detailed descriptions of behaviors during the say phase of training. Because of the importance of language facility in correspondence training, it is not clear whether actual speech is required for correspondence training to effect control over a child's nonverbal behavior. This question was also addressed by Whitman *et al.* (1982). In this study a correspondence procedure was developed for use with nonverbal retarded children for the purpose of increasing attending behavior. During correspondence training, the children were asked to show the experimenter how they were going to attend; subsequently they were reinforced if they did actually attend in that manner. If the children did not attend appropriately, they were given feedback by being shown how they should have behaved. An additional objective of this study was to determine whether attentional changes resulting from show–do correspondence training would be maintained during a maintenance and transfer phase when the children were reinforced only for showing what they were going to do. This procedure was initially administered by the experimenter and then faded to the teacher. The results indicated that correspondence training reliably increased the on-task behavior of the children during training, maintenance, and transfer. No marked changes on classwork assignments (math and phonics), however, were observed.

Keogh *et al.* (1981) used a complex correspondence training procedure to enhance listening skills in four children form an EMR class. Listening skills were defined behaviorally in terms of posture, eye contact, quiet behavior, and performance on a recall task. Following a say- and show–do correspondence training model, the children were required to both say and show how they were going to listen during task presentation. Results indicated that all children increased listening behavior during the training task and two of the four children demonstrated generalized listening behavior on untrained tasks. Only small changes in accuracy of recall were noted. In the opinion of the authors, the mixed nature of these generally positive results was in part a function of the difficulty of the recall tasks used and the stringent criteria imposed for listening behaviors.

As is the case with a number of interventions reviewed earlier in this chapter, research in the area of correspondence training is just beginning. The data suggest that it is an effective technique that can easily be implemented in natural settings to affect a range of behaviors. Particularly promising is its potential for achieving behavioral change in children with severely restricted verbal repertoires. Research needs to be done to explicate the range of behaviors responsive to correspondence training as well as the components of the training procedure (e.g., self-monitoring, reinforcement, overt and covert verbalization) that are most effective in producing behavioral change.

Self-instructional Training

Although usually conceptualized as two distinct therapeutic techniques, both correspondence training and self-instructional training utilize an individual's own verbal behavior to guide his or her nonverbal behavior. In a 1971 study with impulsive children, Meichenbaum and Goodman established that self-instructional training is useful for the remediation of certain clinical problems in children. In a series of studies (1969a,b, 1971b), they developed overall procedures for teaching self-instructions that have been replicated in subsequent studies. The training sequence proceeds in this way: (1) A proficient model completes a task while talking aloud, (2) the child performs the task assisted by the model's instructions, (3) the child rehearses the task while self-instructing aloud, (4) the child whispers the instructions as he or she completes the task, and finally (5) the child completes the task while guiding his or her performance through covert self-instruction. There are several important problem-solving skills included in the typical self-instruction routine: (1) problem definition ("What do I have to do?"); (2) attention to the task and response guidance ("Write slowly"); (3) standard setting, self-evaluation, and self-reinforcement ("Good, I did that one correctly"); and (4) skills for coping with errors ("Even if I made a mistake, I can fix it and go on"). In contrast to correspondence training, which usually focuses on relatively simple behaviors, self-instructional training is often employed with complex tasks that require multicomponent problem-solving strategies.

While early research on the efficacy of self-instructional programs focused on global behavioral problems, recent efforts have been directed at applying the self-instructional paradigm to the amelioration of specific academic deficits within a school environment. Self-instructional training has been used to reduce off-task behavior (Bornstein & Quevillon, 1976; Burgio, Whitman, & Johnson, 1980; Friedling & O'Leary, 1979) and to remediate deficits in handwriting (Robin, Armel, & O'Leary, 1975), reading comprehension (Bommarito & Meichenbaum, 1978), and math performance (Burns, 1972; Johnston & Whitman, 1980; Johnston, Whitman, & Johnson, 1980; Leon & Pepe, 1978; Wein & Nelson, 1978). Self-instruction has several advantages over other training procedures in that the intervention can be tailored to the needs of individual children and to the accomplishment of specific tasks. It maintains the child as the locus of control, readily incorporates sound teaching methods and goals, and focuses on the process as well as the product of the problem-solving procedure.

Optimism concerning self-instructional training with retarded children resulted from encouraging findings reported by Guralnick (1976) and Timlick and Norton (1978). Guralnick compared self-instructional training, modeling, and feedback for training mildly mentally retarded children to complete a complex perceptual discrimination task. Results showed that only the children given self-instructional training improved their accuracy on this task. Timlick and Norton (1978) compared the effectiveness of modeling and modeling plus verbal cues of various levels of abstraction on the concept-acquisition (measured by performance on the Leiter International Performance Scale) of noninstitutionalized moderately retarded children. Results indicated that the modeling plus self-verbalization conditions facilitated improved performance on the Leiter scale. Regrettably, this performance gain did not generalize to another measure.

Leon and Pepe (1978) were the first to use self-instruction as a strategy to remediate math deficits noted in learning-disabled and mentally handicapped children. They had teachers use one of two procedures for training math skills; the first procedure included traditional methods of teaching math (e.g., modeling, instruction, reinforced practice) while the second utilized self-instructional procedures. Although both procedures appeared to be effective remedial strategies, the authors reported that the self-instructional group showed greater generalization to math operations not directly taught and required less direct teaching time. Unfortunately, because a global diagnostic math test was employed to assess treatment gains, specific changes in skill level could not be determined.

A series of studies examining the efficacy of self-instructional training with retarded children was initiated at the University of Notre Dame (Burgio *et al.*, 1980; Johnston & Whitman, 1980; Johnston *et al.*, 1980; Levers, 1978). Levers (1978) developed a self-instructional package to increase attending behavior of three hyperactive mentally retarded children during a handwriting task. The self-instructions were designed to be short and simple so as to be easily learned by the children. As pointed out by Kazdin and Wilson (1978), it can be stated with greater certainty that a change in a target behavior is due to self-instruction if changes in self-instructional behavior precede or occur simultaneously with changes in the target behaviors. For this reason, the development and incidence of self-instructional behavior as well as on-task behavior were assessed in both the training and generalization settings. The results of the Levers study indicated that all three children learned the self-instructions and that increases in self-instruction were accompanied by corresponding increases in on-task behavior in the training environment. The educational significance of this training program was limited, however, because generalization of these effects to the classroom setting occurred for only one child and because no systematic changes in handwriting performance occurred in either the training or classroom settings.

Burgio *et al.* (1981) designed a self-instructional program aimed at increasing the attending behavior of two highly distractable EMR children in a training and two transfer situations. The effects of the training on three academic tasks were examined. While generally adhering to a self-instructional training format similar to that implemented by

Meichenbaum and Goodman (1971b), the Burgio *et al.* study contained a number of procedural modifications designed to augment the effectiveness of self-instructional training with mentally retarded children. For instance, before initiating the study, the target children were assessed to determine that the training was appropriate to their current level of achievement. It was established that each child had the ability to articulate the self-statements, that he or she understood what the verbalizations meant, and that the component motor responses were already in his or her response repertoires. In this regard, Higa, Tharp, and Calkins (1978) have shown that self-instruction is more likely to be successful when the target behavior is not entirely unfamiliar to the subjects. In addition, the children were reinforced only when their nonverbal behavior corresponded with their verbalizations.

As in the Levers (1978) study, the systematic application of learning principles, including shaping, fading, prompting, and contingent social reinforcement, was utilized to teach the self-instruction sequence and the corresponding motor behaviors. Furthermore, the children were not specifically directed to self-instruct covertly. Prior research has shown that with younger children, overt self-verbalization often leads to greater control over nonverbal behavior (Higa *et al.*, 1978; Meichenbaum & Goodman, 1969a). Thus, Burgio *et al.* argued that developmentally disabled children would benefit more from an overtly verbalized strategy.

After learning the self-instructions, the children were systematically and sequentially exposed to photo-slides of distracting situations, to audio distractors, and to "*in vivo*" distractors in the training setting. To facilitate generalization of the self-instructional training to the classroom setting, the distracting stimuli introduced into the training situation were chosen for their similarity to those actually present in the classroom. In order to inhibit attending to these distractors, the children were taught behavior-inhibiting self-instructions (e.g., "I'm not going to look; I'm going to keep doing my work"). Earlier research within the resistance-to-temptation paradigm (Patterson & Mischel, 1976) has demonstrated the utility of such self-statements. To facilitate generalization to the classroom and so that the children would more likely perceive the strategies as general procedures applicable to all academic tasks, they were encouraged to evoke classroom imagery in the training setting (Bornstein & Quevillon, 1976) and they were trained with the aid of multiple exemplars (Stokes & Baer, 1977).

The results of this project suggested that the training package produced direct and generalized changes in self-instructional behavior (see Figure 1). In addition, a decrease in off-task behavior occurred during math, printing, and an untrained phonics program in the one-to-one

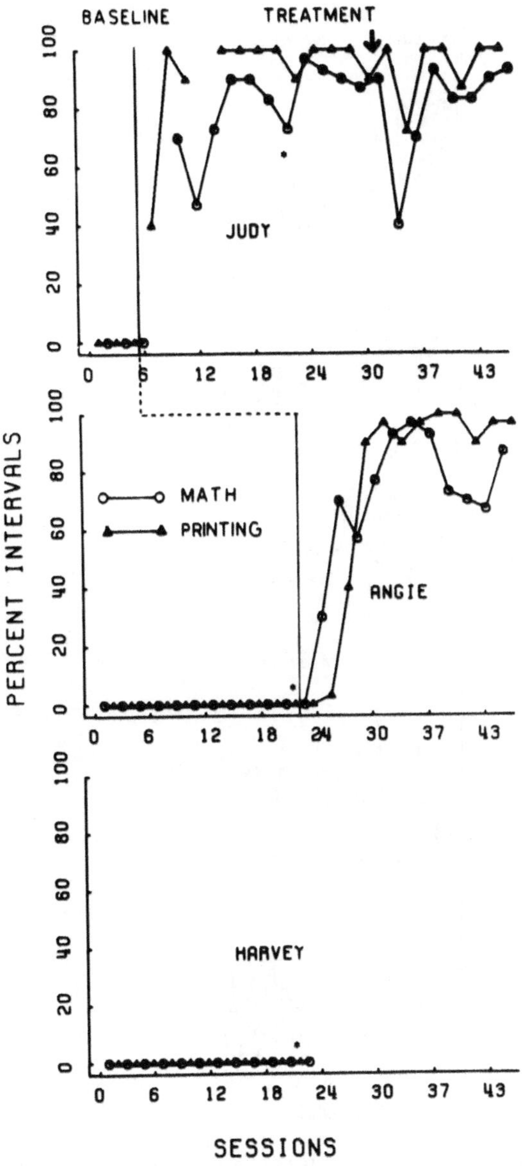

Figure 1. Percentage of intervals of self-instruction over sessions by the experimental subjects on the math (circles) and printing (triangles) tasks in the transfer I setting. (An asterisk designates a two-week school holiday when observations were not made. The arrow signifies the point at which training was faded out for Judy.)

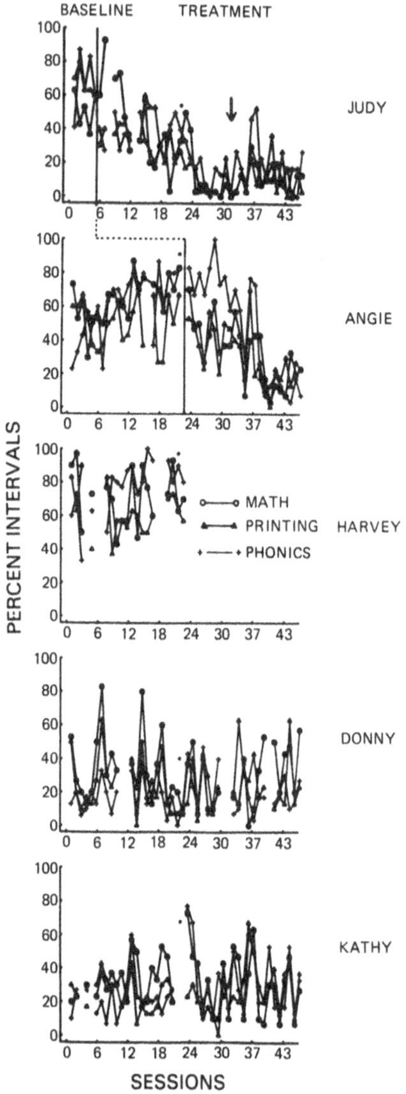

Figure 2. Percentage of intervals of off-task behavior over sessions by the experimental and criterion comparison subjects on the math (circles), printing (triangles), and phonics (crosses) tasks in the transfer II (classroom setting. (An asterisk designates a two-week school holiday when observations were not made. The arrow signifies the point at which training was faded out for Judy.)

and classroom generalization situations (see Figure 2). Once again, however, no reliable changes in academic performance were observed.

Besides the Levers (1978) and the Burgio *et al.* (1980) studies, other research (Ferritor, Buckholdt, Hamblin, & Smith, 1972) has shown that reduction of off-task behavior does not necessarily lead to increased proficiency on academic tasks. As Burgio *et al.* (1980) pointed out, if children do not possess certain requisite academic skills, it is unlikely that increasing attention will improve their accuracy on tasks requiring these skills.

In an attempt to improve the academic performance of EMR children, two additional studies were conducted (Johnston & Whitman, 1980; Johnston *et al.*, 1980). Both studies examined the effectiveness of self-instruction training program for teaching two specific and relatively complex math computation skills—addition with regrouping and subtraction with regrouping—academic skills that the subjects, children from special education classrooms, had failed to learn under normal classroom conditions. The self-instructions used in these studies were formulated after a careful task analysis of the math skills being taught, after attempts to ensure that children were familiar with the language used, and after determining that there was an easy correspondence between the words of the self-instruction and the motor behavior required to complete the task. Table 1 shows the instructions used to teach addition with regrouping. In the first study, a multiple baseline design across subjects and types of problem was utilized to assess the effects of the training procedure on rate and accuracy. For all three children, reliable and often marked increases in accuracy were evident during the respective training conditions (see Figures 3 and 4). Correlated but less pronounced increases in accuracy on addition and subtraction problems not requiring regrouping (a generalization measure) were apparent.

One difficulty associated with the Johnston *et al.* (1980) study concerned the inefficiency of a training procedure that required one-to-one teacher–student interaction, a condition that is time-consuming and difficult to implement extensively in the typical classroom. In a subsequent study, Whitman and Johnson (1983) examined the effectiveness of self-instruction training in teaching addition and subtraction with regrouping to mildly retarded children in a group setting. The results of this study clearly replicate those of the earlier Johnston *et al.* study, indicating that self-instructional training can be an effective procedure for teaching math skills to EMR children. Furthermore, these results demonstrated that self-instructional training can be implemented in a group setting, thereby making these procedures readily applicable to classroom environments.

Table 1. Example of Self-Instruction Training Sequence for Addition with Regrouping

Q. What kind of a problem is this? 36
+47

A. It's an add problem. I can tell by the sign.

Q. Now what do I do?

A. I start with the top number in the ones column and I add. 6 add 7 (*the child points to the 6 on the number line and counts down 7 spaces*) is 13. Thirteen has two digits. That means I have to carry. This is hard so I go slowly. I put the 3 in the ones column (*the child writes the 3 in the ones column in the answer*) and the 1 in the tens column (*the child writes the 1 above the top number in the tens column in the problem*).

Q. Now what do I do?

A. I start with the top number in the tens column. One add 3 (*the child points to the 1 on the number line and counts down 3 spaces*) is 4. 4 add 4 (*the child counts down 4 more spaces*) is 8 (*the child writes the 8 in the tens column in the answer*).

Q. I want to get it right so I check it. How do I check it?

A. I cover up my answer (*the child covers the answer with a small piece of paper*) and add again starting with the bottom number in the ones column. Seven add 6 (*the child points to the 7 on the number line and counts down 6 spaces*) is 13 (*the child slides the piece of paper to the left and uncovers the 3; the child sees the 1 which he/she has written over the top number in the tens column in the problem*). Got it right. 4 add 3 (*the child points to the 4 on the number line and counts down 3 spaces*) is 7. 7 add 1 (*the child counts down 1 more space*) is 8 (*the child removes the small piece of paper so that the entire answer is visible*). I got it right so I'm doing well.
(If, by checking his/her work, the child determines that he/she has made an error, he/she says, "I got it wrong. I can fix it if I go slowly." The child then repeats the self-instruction sequence starting from the beginning.)

The area of self-instructional training designed to remediate academic deficits of mentally retarded children is fertile for future research. The self-instructional training paradigm implemented in the studies reviewed involves a variety of procedures including instruction, self-instruction, verbal and nonverbal modeling, prompts, reinforcement, practice performing the target behaviors, correspondence between verbal and nonverbal behavior, specificity, imagery, and task-inhibiting and task-facilitating instructions. While some researchers have attempted to do component analysis studies (Wein & Nelson, 1978), it is still not possible to delineate which of these components are instrumental in producing change. In addition, future research should be conducted to determine subject characteristics that are particularly responsive to self-instructional training (cf. Higa *et al.*, 1978). Research also is needed to explicate the classes of academic behavior most amenable to modification by self-instruction. Finally, there is a need to compare self-instructional training with other instructional methods.

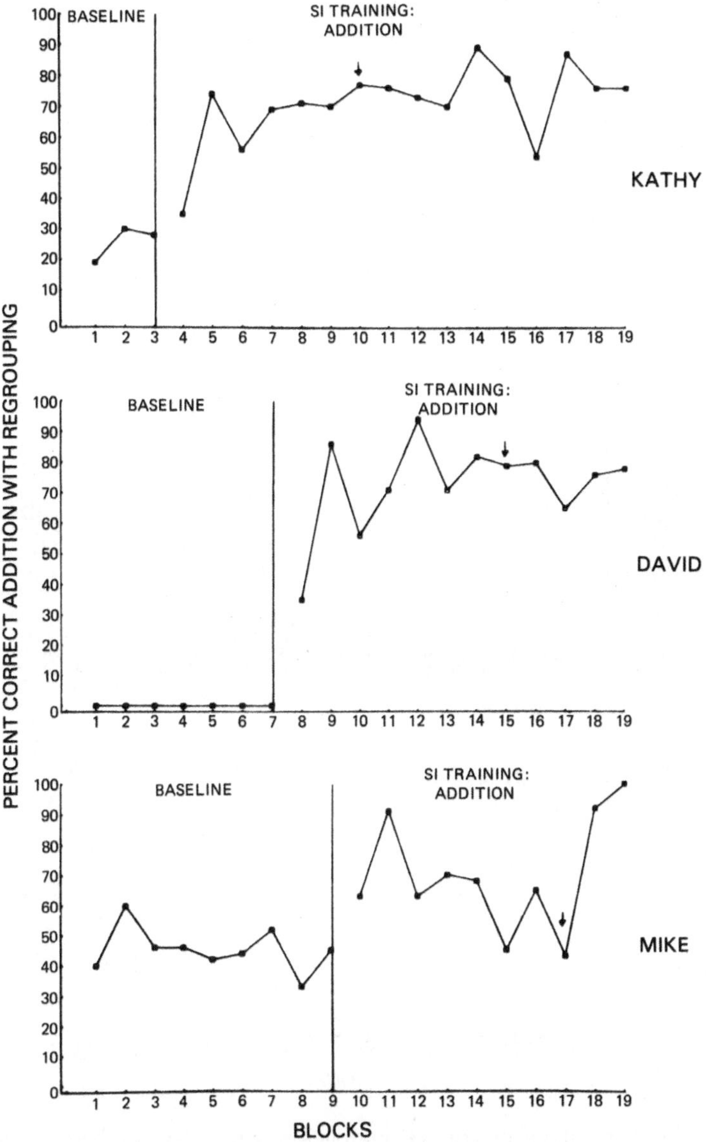

Figure 3. Percentage of correct addition-regrouping problems during the baseline and addition-regrouping conditions. (Arrows indicate when subtraction-regrouping training was initiated. SI, self-instruction.)

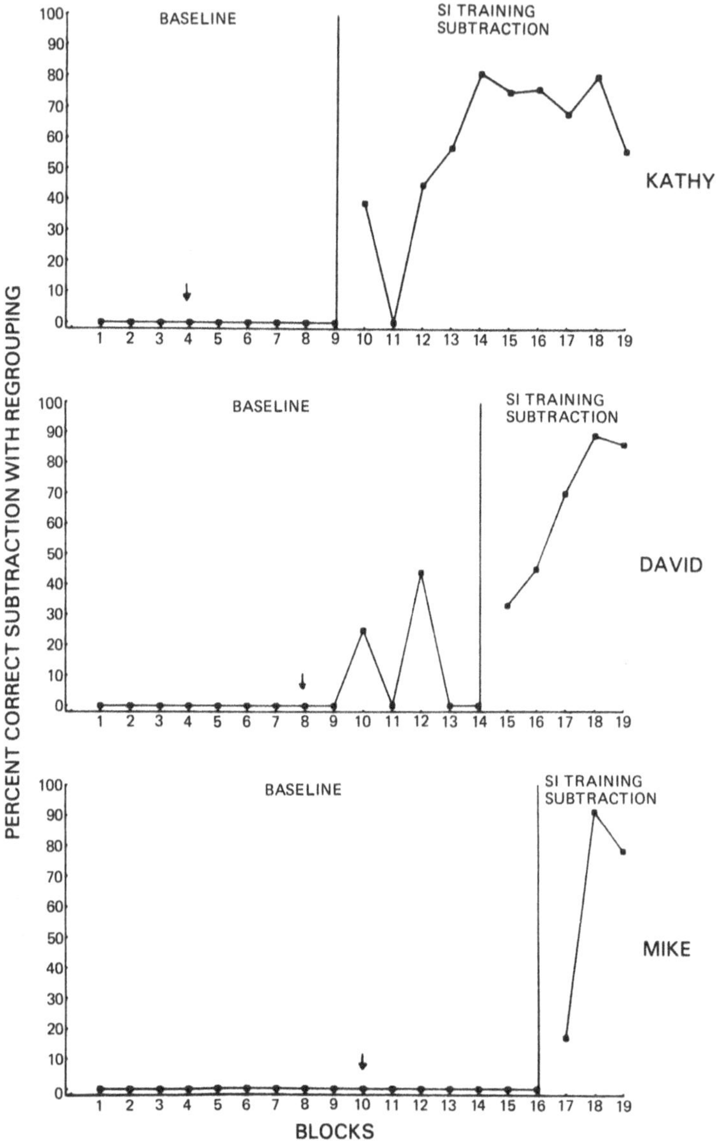

Figure 4. Percentage of correct subtraction-regrouping problems during the baseline and subtraction-regrouping training conditions. (Arrow indicates when addition-regrouping training was initiated. SI, self-instruction.)

CONCLUSION

As has become apparent over the course of this review, an impressive number of studies has been conducted within the last decade evaluating cognitive behavioral interventions with mentally retarded children. Results of this research suggest that mentally retarded individuals can learn such skills as self-monitoring, self-reinforcement, problem-solving, verbal elaboration strategies, and self-instruction, and that the acquisition of these skills often facilitates improved performance on a variety of tasks. Based on the results of these studies, there is increasing optimism within the scientific and educational communities concerning the promise of such programs.

Methodological problems in many of these studies, however, warrant a note of caution. First, it is not clear why mentally retarded children improve their performance during cognitive behavioral training programs. In the majority of studies reviewed, the acquisition of cognitive skills was not monitored but was inferred from the fact that, following training, beneficial changes occurred on tasks assumed to require cognitive mediation. As indicated earlier, in order to identify the processes effecting change, it is necessary to monitor the acquisition and use of the cognitive skills and to determine whether changes in cognitive skill are associated with changes in task performance (cf. Kendall & Hollon, 1981, for suggestions regarding assessment strategies for cognitive behavioral interventions). Second, in much of the research examined, performance changes occurred on laboratory tasks in controlled settings rather than on socially relevant tasks routinely occurring in natural environments. Thus, the social utility of many cognitive behavioral training programs remains undemonstrated. Although it is appropriate for research that is in the process of developing and refining a technology to be primarily analogue in nature, it is critical that researchers eventually demonstrate the ecological validity of the technology. Finally, while a considerable number of studies has been conducted evaluating different cognitive behavioral techniques, the total number of studies evaluating any specific technique remains small. Undoubtedly, this paucity results in part from the policy of professional journals to publish research examining innovative training techniques rather than studies that demonstrate, through direct and systematic replication, the applicability of existing approaches. The elusiveness of the processes responsible for behavioral change, the reality that much of the research is analogue, and the failure to conduct systematic evaluation of cognitive behavioral techniques mean that while these techniques show promise, they are not currently ready for widespread dissemination in schools and institutions.

In order to facilitate the process of developing and evaluating a cognitive behavioral technology for use with mentally retarded children, a model delineating the parameters that merit consideration needs to be articulated. At a minimum, such a model must take into account (1) the characteristics of the individuals with whom the technology is to be implemented (2) the nature of the tasks on which proficiency is desired and (3) the types of training procedures available. As will become evident in the forthcoming discussion of these parameters, these factors are not orthogonal but must be considered simultaneously.

As indicated earlier, there has been considerable and diverse theorizing about the nature of mental retardation. At present, there is little consensus about the specific deficiencies that constitute this disorder. Certain behavioral characteristics of mentally retarded children, however, should be taken into consideration when planning cognitive behavioral interventions. Because of the prominent place of language in cognitive behavioral strategies, it is important to note that retarded children often exhibit a language deficiency, that the level of this deficiency is correlated with the severity of retardation, and that there are striking individual differences with respect to this language deficiency. The existence of such individual differences means that it is important to complete a cognitive and behavioral assessment of language skills prior to program implementation. At a minimum, the level of language functioning of individuals engaged in cognitive behavioral programs should be evaluated so that training procedures can be designed to take this factor into account. If it is determined that a child has minimal expressive language skills, it may be necessary to employ a show–do rather than a say–do procedure in a correspondence training program or it may be expedient to simplify the language employed in a self-instructional program and to use words, grammatical structures, and vocabulary currently in the child's repertoire.

The importance of individual differences in cognitive structure was stressed by Piaget (1964), who considered skill acquisition to be dependent on preexisting cognitive structures capable of incorporating new learning. Based on similar reasoning, Borkowski and Konarski (1981) and Kahn (1977) pointed out the importance of cognitive readiness in curriculum planning and suggested that if a child's current cognitive level is ignored when developing training programs, the probability increases that such programs will fail. In order to minimize failure, program developers must be able to assess both the cognitive level of program participants and the types of cognitive skills required by specific tasks. In this model, training proceeds only after a match is made between student abilities and task demands. While the need for appropriate assessment is clear, adequate assessment tools are unfortunately, not readily available. Although Levine, Zetlin, and Langness's (1980) work with analysis of classroom curricula and Feuerstein's Learning Assessment Potential Device (Feuerstein *et al.*, 1979) represent important efforts, considerable work on assessment must be completed before good matches between student characteristics and task demands can be routinely made.

Besides language facility and cognitive level, a third subject variable that needs consideration in developing programs for mentally retarded children is the children's ability to attend to the task at hand. House and Zeaman (1963) postulate that inferior performance by mentally retarded individuals is related to an attentional deficit. They point out that performance can be improved through procedures that increase the saliency of the stimuli most relevant to problem solution. In contrast to this emphasis on stimulus manipulations, cognitive behavior therapists are interested in training attention through the use of covert cognitive strategies. From an operant perspective, these cognitive strategies may be seen as influencing target behaviors through highly complex, diverse, flexible sets of verbal cues. According to operant theory, cues that lead to appropriate discriminative responding are, by definition, influencing attentional processes (Skinner, 1953). The cognitive behavioral procedures described in this chapter can be viewed as attention-focusing or stimulus control procedures that are appropriately employed with mentally retarded children who have attentional problems.

A fourth individual-difference parameter involves personality variables. Balla and Zigler (1979) list personality characteristics frequently seen in mentally retarded individuals that deserve the attention of those planning cognitive behavioral interventions with this population. These authors describe mentally retarded children as having heightened motivation to interact with supportive adults, as having a low expectancy of success and a high expectancy of failure, as more responsive to tangible reinforcers than intangible ones, and as relying greatly on external cues to guide their behavior. These personality characteristics of mentally retarded children highlight the special importance of reinforcement in programs with this population. Reinforcement can play a variety of roles in a cognitive behavioral intervention with mentally retarded children. First, reinforcement assists the child to learn the intervention strategy. Second, differential reinforcement ensures that the intervention strategy will later cue specific target behaviors. Third, reinforcement motivates the child to continue to use the strategy he or she has learned.

In addition to consideration of the characteristics of the individuals with whom the technology is to be implemented, the nature of the task(s) on which proficiency is desired should be taken into account as influencing the development of cognitive behavioral interventions. Studies by Johnston *et al.* (1980) and Johnston and Whitman (1980) emphasize the usefulness of task analyses for developing self-instructional programs. As suggested earlier, within the operant framework, a cognitive behavioral technique can be thought of as a stimulus control procedure. Task proficiency is, then, a function of the adequacy of the cues provided. Assuming that the component behaviors required to perform a task are in a child's behavior repertoire, the objective in cognitive behavioral programs is to arrange cues in such a way that behaviors will occur in a task-facilitating sequence. The proper arrangement of cues can be arrived at by logical analysis of the task, by observation of proficient individuals performing the task, or by the researcher/clinician performing the target task and reflecting about the thoughts, images, and behaviors he or she employed to perform the task adequately (Meichenbaum, 1976).

How the target task is conceptualized in turn greatly influences the cognitive behavioral intervention planned. Initially, much of the cognitive behavioral research with mentally retarded children was focused on the development of fairly specific skills (e.g., self-monitoring, attending behavior, math problem-solving). Recently, however, there has been a growing interest in developing programs that facilitate generalized changes in problem-solving skills as well as improved performance on specific tasks.

Meichenbaum and Asarnow (1979) argued that the work of cognitive-developmental psychologists on metacognition is useful for understanding the processes underlying generalization and can serve as a guide for those developing cognitive behavioral programs. According to developmental researchers, metacognition is the subject's awareness of his or her own cognitive machinery and the way it works (Brown & Campione, 1978). It involves strategies such as self-monitoring, question asking, planning, and self-checking—strategies that facilitate problem-solving in a variety of contexts and on a variety of tasks. In cognitive behavioral terms, metacognition refers to the internal dialogue the child emits before, during, and after performing a task. Training to enhance metacognitive functioning involves the teaching of general problem-solving strategies. Deliberate training of these skills, argued Meichenbaum and Asarnow, will enhance treatment efficacy and the likelihood of treatment generalization (cf. Belmont & Butterfield, 1977; Borkowski & Cavanaugh, 1979; Campione & Brown, 1977; and Meichenbaum & Asarnow, 1979, for suggestions about how to enhance maintenance and generalization).

Recently, research has been done with intellectually average children (Kendall, 1981c; Kendall & Wilcox, 1980; Schlesser, Meyers, & Cohen, 1981) regarding the relative benefits of general problem solving-training and task-specific training. While some benefits of general problem-solving strategies have been documented, the data have not overwhelmingly supported this approach. Moreover, whether such strategies would benefit mentally retarded children remains to be demonstrated. It is likely that both general and specific approaches to teaching mentally retarded children have advantages. Which is most advantageous probably depends on the task demands, the skill level of the child, and the intellectual ability of the child. Ultimately, it seems that programs designed to include both specific and generalizable problem-solving strategies would be most effective.

In summary, optimism regarding the usefulness of cognitive behavior modification approaches to educating mentally retarded children appears justified. In particular, these approaches seem a promising means for integrating the achievements of cognitive psychologists, mental retardation specialists, and behavior modifiers so that mentally retarded children can learn complex self-control skills previously thought unattainable. Research findings indicate that mentally retarded children can learn well-planned cognitive behavioral intervention strategies and that these strategies can lead to improved task performance. Considerable research remains to be accomplished aimed at clarifying the processes responsible for the behavioral change achieved, demonstrating the ecological utility of these procedures, comparing the relative effectiveness of these programs, and delineating relevant person and task characteristics needing attention. As this research is completed, it is likely that cognitive behavioral procedures will evolve into an educationally effective technology that will facilitate intellectual and personal-social development in mentally retarded children.

9

Cognitive Behavior Modification with Psychotic Children

A BEGINNING

Alan J. Litrownik

INTRODUCTION

I am sure that many of you may be wondering how cognitive approaches could be applied to such a severely disturbed population. My first reaction to the appropriateness of such an approach was one of skepticism, but the conceptual understanding and application strategies that emerge from a cognitive social learning perspective are quite exciting.

Although I am pleased to have the opportunity to share my excitement, I should caution you, as I continually do myself, that I have not found *the answer*, but rather am taking part in what I believe is a further clarification and development of our thinking about psychotic children. In an attempt to facilitate the development of a more useful understanding and approach to the treatment of severely disturbed children, I will present (1) a brief discussion of the presenting problem—that is, childhood psychosis, including diagnostic and etiological issues; (2) a description of past and present intervention approaches and their limitations; (3) a conceptual model of self-management that will help guide the application of cognitive behavioral techniques; and finally (4) some examples of and suggestions for clinical application.

Alan J. Litrownik • Department of Psychology, San Diego State University, San Diego, California 92182.

THE PROBLEM: CHILDHOOD PSYCHOSIS

Diagnostic Confusion

Nowhere has there been more confusion over the years than that found when attempting to identify psychotic children. Even though Kanner first described 11 cases that he claimed represented a syndrome that could be distinguished from childhood schizophrenia in 1943, it has taken some 37 years for infantile autism to be accorded diagnostic status by the American Psychiatric Association (1980). Prior to the third edition of the Diagnostic and Statistical Manual (DSM-III), there was only one diagnostic category for psychotic kids—schizophrenia, childhood type.

In the 1960s, other classification systems from the World Health Organization (Rutter, Lebovic, Eisenberg, Sneznevsku, Sadoun, Brooke, & Lin, 1969) and the Group for the Advancement of Psychiatry (GAP, 1966) were proposed that differentiated among various subcategories of childhood psychoses (e.g., autism, symbiotic or interactional, disintegrative, schizophrenia) and/or developmental periods when psychoses emerged (e.g., infancy and early childhood, later childhood, adolescence). Since apparent schizophrenia in later childhood was distinguished from actual schizophrenia found in adults or adolescents, a new term, *schizophreniform*, was introduced in the GAP classification.

Following this lead, DSM-III has done away totally with the category of childhood psychoses, emphasizing that adult psychoses are not found in children. Instead, children who evidence severe qualitative abnormalities in their social and language development are categorized under Pervasive Developmental Disorders. Three subcategories are included: (1) infantile autism, (2) childhood onset, and (3) atypical. Although DSM-III has been criticized for its failure to base classification decisions on a single principle (e.g., etiology, syndrome, etc), it has been commended for explicitly describing behaviors characteristic of a particular category (Harris, 1979). For example, autism is identified as a behavioral syndrome that includes lack of responsiveness to other human beings, gross impairment in communicative skills, and bizarre responses to aspects of the environment (e.g., lack of cuddle, eye contact, play, etc), all developing within the first 30 months. Childhood onset disorders, formerly childhood schizophrenia, are described as developing after 30 months and before 12 years of age. This syndrome involves a gross and sustained disturbance in relations with people (e.g., lack of appropriate affect, social ineptitude, asociality, lack of peer relationships, and a lack of empathy with people in general). The third subcategory, atypical, is a catch-all for those who do not fit into the other two subcategories.

Although the effects of DSM-III and its descriptive approach remain to be seen, this long history of diagnostic confusion limits our understanding and treatment of the pervasive developmental disorders because of the questionable comparability of previously identified populations (Litrownik & McInnis, 1982; Piggott & Simson, 1975). It is also likely that different criteria will continue to be used in identifying and/or describing these children, in part as a result of (1) the reason or purpose of diagnosis or selection and (2) the complexity of these disorders (Schopler, 1978). Nevertheless, the focus on behavioral descriptions should facilitate our quest for both an understanding of and strategy for treating children with pervasive developmental disorders (Litrownik & McInnis, 1982; Lovaas, 1979).

Incidence and Prognosis

All of the pervasive developmental disorders are rare. For example, the incidence of autism has been estimated at anywhere from a low of 2 out of every 10,000 births (DSM-III) to a high of 12 per 10,000 births (Wing, 1979). While these estimates indicate that the incidence of autism is very low, a quick calculation shows that there are anywhere from 44,000 to 264,000 diagnosed autistic individuals in the United States alone!

This number becomes even more significant when it is recognized that these individuals are likely to require constant and close supervision throughout their lives. That is, the prognosis for the autistic person is extremely poor, with at least two out of three remaining severely impaired and in need of constant attention (DSM-III).

Etiological Perspectives

In the remainder of this chapter, I will focus on the subcategory of autism. While my focus will be on autism, the recommended cognitive behavioral approach can be adopted for use with other pervasive developmental disorders as well as other developmental disabilities (Litrownik, 1982; Litrownik & Steinfeld, 1982).

This section briefly reviews some of the conceptual frameworks that have been applied to autism in an attempt to understand this puzzling disorder. Based on these perspectives, specific deficits or dysfunctions that are primary to autism as well as identified etiological factors have been proposed.

Psychodynamic Framework

According to this perspective, autism is explained in terms of intrapsychic conflict. For example, Bettleheim (1967) claimed that the primary deficit in autism, failure in ego development, was a result of the child's parents unconsciously rejecting him or her. As a consequence of this unconscious desire not to have the child, parents fail to provide necessary stimulation during the periods when object relationships develop (birth to 6 months) and when language and locomotion begin to emerge (6 to 9 months). As a result of this lack of parental responsiveness, the child feels unable to control the external environment, fails to develop emotional attachments and speech and motor skills, and hence withdraws into a private fantasy world, attempting to impose some order and constancy through the insistence on sameness (Bettleheim, 1967; Sanders, 1975).

Behavioral Framework

The behavioral perspective requires a functional description and resultant understanding of autism (Koegel, Egel, & Dunlap, 1980; Lovaas, 1979); that is, problems are defined in terms of response deficits and/or excesses, and these deficits and excesses can be explained by how they are functionally related to antecedent and consequent events. This understanding of autism must be distinguished from the proposed etiological explanation that Ferster (1961) has presented. That is, it is possible to understand autism functionally while not adhering to Ferster's claim that autism develops because parents either completely ignore or deliver feedback intermittently to their child. In fact, Lovaas (1979) stated that even if a specific causal factor were identified (e.g., biological, etc.), it would not make any difference in how he treated the children. Treatment procedures are not designed to correct an underlying deficiency, but rather are aimed at "changing individual behaviors based on an analysis of the variables that might influence them" (Egel, Koegel, & Schreibman, 1980, p. 122).

Cognitive Social Learning Framework

This relatively recent perspective has evolved from the behavioral perspective, with the incorporation of cognitive and/or information-processing concerns along with a recognition that the individual is an active participant in the shaping of his or her environment and behavior (Bandura, 1977b, 1981; Kanfer, 1980; Karoly, 1977; Litrownik, 1982; Mahoney & Arnkoff, 1978; Meichenbaum & Asarnow, 1979). Most of the focus has been on trying to understand and clarify the role that thought and other person variables have in determining behavior (i.e., mechanisms of self-regulation).

The ability to regulate one's own behavior is a function, in part, of how an individual processes information. That is, the individual is seen as having much to say about resultant responses since a great deal happens between the occurrence of some external stimulation and the observation of a response. Specifically, the external stimulation undergoes selection, elaboration, and various transformations as it is prepared for retrieval and is then made available for immediate recall (Kail & Hagen, 1977). At least four levels have been identified where data processing deficits could exist: (1) sensory-receptor, (2) initial processing (e.g., selection and screening), (3) higher processing (e.g., organizing of information), and (4) executive (e.g., retrieval, response generation and selection) (Litrownik & McInnis, 1982; Yates, 1970).

Numerous processing deficits have been proposed to exist in autistic children. For example, there is some evidence to suggest that information may not excite appropriate receptor systems in autistic children (e.g., Rosenblum, Arick, Krug, Stubbs, Young, & Pelson, 1980; Student & Sohmer, 1978), or that if information does impinge on the receptors it may be distorted (e.g., Ornitz & Ritvo, 1968) or not selected for additional transformation and storage (e.g., Hermelin & O'Connor, 1970). Although most of this work is fragmented, focusing on specific levels of processing while ignoring the effects of other levels, these effects do offer a most promising direction of inquiry (see Litrownik & McInnis, 1982, for a review of this work and suggestions for systematically approaching information-processing in autistic children).

Biological Framework

Primary processing deficits identified by cognitive social learning theorists have been related to specific psychological and/or biological determinants. For example, specific areas of the cortex (e.g., hippocampus, reticular formation, left hemisphere) have been identified as possible sites of brain damage (Blackstock, 1978; Boucher, 1977; Hauser, DeLong, & Rosman, 1975; Rimland, 1964), while numerous biochemical abnormalities (e.g., dopamine, serotonin, enzymes, etc.) have similarly been implicated in the etiology of autism (see Piggott, 1979, and Porges, 1976, for reviews).

In summarizing the possible etiological explanations for autism, Rutter (1978) identified three general possibilities: (1) a specific medical condition, (2) biological causation without a single identifiable cause (as with cerebral palsy), and (3) a wide and heterogenous range of biological and psychosocial factors. Although it is far too early to settle on which it is, Rutter suggests (and many concur) that the second alternative seems to be most likely.

The Challenge

There is still a great deal of confusion surrounding study of the psychotic child. A variety of labels have been proposed as well as diagnostic criteria that serve different purposes. Etiological explanations and identified deficits similarly vary as a function of one's perspective and purpose. There is one area of agreement between clinicians and researchers: Children that evidence pervasive developmental disorders, specifically autism, are not likely to function independently as adults. The prognosis is poor because of severely limited cognitive and/or perceptual deficits, intellectual retardation, and a lack of social responsiveness.

Thus, large numbers of persons, anywhere from 30,000 to 185,000 identified as autistic in the United States alone, are likely to require constant care throughout their lives. In the United States the legislative branch of the government has recognized this need and mandated that these individuals receive appropriate services (e.g., Developmental Disabilities Act of 1975, Education for All Handicapped Act of 1975). The challenge with which providers of these services are now faced is one of developing interventions that meet the needs of the individuals, their caretakers, and the community in which they reside. In the design of interventions, effectiveness must be judged in terms of what is required to effect the change (i.e., cost) and what specific benefits result from the change (e.g., to the individual, caretaker, etc.).

Much research in the past 10 to 15 years has been conducted with the aim of developing a better understanding and treatment of autism and related disorders. As Schopler (1979) suggested, the challenge is to differentiate information of lasting significance from findings that are trivial and/or cannot be replicated. Such discriminations will not only help to identify appropriate intervention strategies but also should lead to specific suggestions for future research.

HISTORY OF INTERVENTION STRATEGIES

A historical review of treatment strategies applied to autistic children will necessarily be brief. It was only some 40 years ago that the syndrome was first delineated and only in the past 20 years that these children have been the target of specific interventions. These interventions have been based, for the most part, on the first two etiological perspectives described in the previous section.

Psychodynamic

Since this perspective sees the child as being disturbed as a result of rejecting parents, the first task of treatment is to remove the child from the home. Children are placed in residential treatment centers where the total milieu serves as the treatment. Staff are trained to respond to the child's every need and attempt to control or influence the environment (Bettleheim, 1967; Ruttenberg, 1971; Sanders, 1975). For example, Sanders (1975) described a case in which a child received a special helping of mashed potatoes at every meal because he said "mashed potatoes" when first visiting the kitchen.

Although Bettleheim (1967) has claimed that 42% of the autistic children who participated in this totally accepting and responsive treatment program made a "good" adjustment, the value of this approach remains questionable (see Litrownik, 1977; Lovaas, 1979; Wieland, 1971). First of all, the outcome reported by Bettleheim can be questioned because he himself subjectively evaluated the children and in over 65% of the 40 cases that he evaluated, the children had evidenced functional speech before age 5—that is, they had a good prognosis. In addition, the treatment was long term, costly, and not replicable, and the appropriateness of using psychoanalytic treatment procedures has been questioned because austistic children lack symbolic skills.

In defense of this approach, Ruttenberg (1978) has pointed out that psychoanalysis has never been advocated as a treatment for autism, but rather psychoanalytic concepts of child development have been used to understand (i.e., explain or interpret) treatment. Nevertheless, treatment effects are based on *post hoc* inferences that are determined by etiological assumptions, and there is still no good evidence indicating that this costly approach leads to meaningful change.

Behavioral

The other general treatment approach applied to autistic children is one based on the laws of learning. This behavioral approach received much of its impetus from the writings of Skinner (1953) and was championed by O. I. Lovaas in the 1960s (see Lovaas, 1968). The focus was an applied one, identifying problems (e.g., behavioral excesses and deficits) and designing specific interventions to modify these problems rather than trying to treat autism.

In contrast to the psychodynamic treatment strategy, this approach was extremely concrete. The task of treating autistic children was broken down into manageable units, for instance, eliminating tantrums and self-destructive responses, and developing verbal skills. Report of successful modification of specific behaviors were dramatic, and many heralded the introduction of the behavioral approach as a major treatment breakthrough (see Lovaas, 1979; Schopler, 1979).

As someone who had an opportunity to participate in some of this early work at UCLA, I can say that these were exciting times. Children who had been functionally mute were taught to communicate verbally, and those who had been physically restrained for their own protection (i.e., severely self-destructive) were released and had an opportunity to experience their surroundings. The changes were both dramatic and encouraging, but all of us tried to control our enthusiasm. After all, the focus was not on curing autism but rather on modifying specific response patterns. It was difficult, though, not to feel that some of the treated children were beginning to act like normal children. But these feelings were soon dispelled when a normally developing child was observed. They evidenced something—affect, spontaneity, etc.—that was missing in even the most advanced autistic child who participated in the program.

Not only were those of us who applied the laws of learning to the treatment of these autistic children painfully aware of the limited success, but we were also initially quite cautious since we did not want to mislead parents, professionals, etc. into thinking that a cure had been found. In any case, the children needed to acquire basic skills first and only then could higher-level activities (e.g., emotional, cognitive, etc.) become the focus. I, like other behavior modifiers, was comfortable with this rationale—don't worry about a cure but rather develop basic skills that might lead to further gains. It was too early to consider how these further gains might be accomplished since the children were just beginning to acquire lower-level skills (e.g., eye contact, imitation, etc.).

By the beginning of the 1970s it was no longer too early. The positive outcomes of behavior modification were well established and with similar clarity, its limitations were emerging. For example, specific responses were acquired, but the process was a slow one. Acquired skills were not maintained without continued application of the treatment nor were stimulus and response generalization observed. That is, it took a great deal of time and effort to teach the children to emit specific responses in the presence of specific cues, but the skills required to think, conceptualize, and adapt to life's demands were not observed (Lovaas, Koegel, Simmons, & Long, 1973; Ricks & Wing, 1975).

In addition, behavioral research began to focus on the acquisition of stimulus functions in autistic children as opposed to looking solely at response repertoires. These initial investigations (Lovaas, Litrownik, & Mann, 1971; Lovaas, Schreibman, Koegel, & Rehm, 1971) indicated that autistic children did not respond to environmental stimuli in the same way as did other children. These findings along with the emerging concern for possible processing deficits (e.g., faulty modulation of input, improper comprehension of sounds) suggested that behavioral programming was incomplete if it did not take likely cognitive and/or perceptual deficits into account.

CURRENT CLINICAL APPROACHES

The 1960s had been a period of conflict, specifically between behavioral and disease (e.g., psychodynamic, biological) perspectives as they related to treatment (Lovaas, 1979). By the 1970s the results of behavioral treatment applications had led to the general acceptance of this approach (see Schopler, 1979). The battle appeared to have been won, and those involved in the conflict were now able to admit that their approach had limitations. Thus, efforts to refine behavioral approaches responding to recognized limitations took place during the 1970s, resulting in currently accepted applied behavioral intervention strategies.

Behavioral

Proponents of this strategy continue to argue that an autistic child, or any disturbed child for that matter, can be understood and treated by focusing on antecedent and consequent events. Treatment from this perspective is not concerned with etiology nor is its objective one of treating the disorder. Rather, (1) specific problem behaviors that cut across diagnostic labels are identified and operationally defined, (2) variables that influence these behaviors are analyzed, and (3) these variables are systematically manipulated in order to obtain desired changes (Egel *et al.*, 1980; Koegel *et al.*, 1980; Lovaas, 1979).

Koegel and Lovaas (1978) pointed out that they have made every effort to understand and treat autistic children on a descriptive level. They cautioned against the introduction of hypothetical constructs and made the claim that they had avoided this pitfall with its attendant methodological and measurement problems. From this descriptive stance, Koegel *et al.* (1980) identified five general problem areas in autistic children that have been the focus of behavioral explanations and treatment: (1) physically disruptive behavior, (2) self-stimulatory behavior, (3) stimulus overselectivity, (4) lack of motivation, and (5) absence of generalization and maintenance of treatment gains. The general training approach that includes the systematic manipulation of variables influencing the operationally defined problem behavior has been further reduced to a specific discrete trial format. In this most basic training unit, four components have been identified: (1) a stimulus or instruction, (2) the child's response, (3) the therapist's response (i.e., consequence), and (4) the intertrial interval (Egel *et al.*, 1980; Koegel *et al.*, 1980).

Using this format, stimulus, consequence, and intertrial variables can be controlled by the therapist in an effort to increase or decrease a child's behavior. In the past several years much work has been conducted applying this format to the five problem areas identified above. As a result of this work Egel *et al.* (1980) claim that "the elimination of both many individual autistic behaviors and the diagnosis of autism itself appears to be possible for many autistic children at this time" (p. 142).

In the following sections I will present a critical review of some of the recent research in these areas that led to this claim as well as to the claim that over 50% of the autistic children treated were being "cured" (Koegel, 1979).

Stimulus Overselectivity

Stimulus overselectivity or overselective attention was first applied to describe the performance of autistic children some 12 years ago (Lovaas, Schreibman, Koegel, & Rehm, 1971). In this initial study it was found that autistic children appeared to have a difficult time responding to simultaneously presented cues. Subsequent studies suggested that this inability to respond to multiple-stimulus inputs occurred across multiple and single sensory modalities (see Litrownik & McInnis, 1982, for a review). In this series of studies conducted by Lovaas, Koegel, Schreibman, and their colleagues, the children were initially trained to a criterion on either a serial or simultaneous discrimination problem. For example, a bar-press response was required whenever a multiple-stimulus cue was presented in the serial discrimination studies. Training was discontinued once the child was making 90% of his or her bar-presses in the presence of the stimulus complex (e.g., light and tone). Then, components of the complex were presented individually (e.g., light, tone) interspersed among the training trials (e.g., light and tone). On the simultaneous problems, children were required to point to the correct stimulus complex (S+) when given a two-choice problem (S+ versus

S−). Assessment of stimulus control following acquisition of the discrimination included presentations of single-stimulus components of the S+ versus S− complexes on test trials. In all these studies, the investigators reported that autistic children were highly selective in their response to the multiple-cue complexes. That is, they failed to respond to all the stimuli when they were presented individually.

This descriptive deficit, stimulus overselectivity, was then called upon to explain the autistic child's failure to learn observationally, acquire speech, develop appropriate emotional responses, respond to social stimuli, and transfer prompted responses to appropriate environmental stimuli, and to explain the general failure of training efforts to generalize to other situations (see Lovaas, Koegel, & Schreibman, 1979). Based on these claims, overselectivity became the focus of remedial efforts. Two general strategies for remediation were identified: (1) treat overselectivity directly—that is, modify individuals so they are no longer overselective, and (2) take this deficit into account when designing treatments in order to circumvent the problem and/or take advantage of it.

Initial efforts to remediate this deficit directly were based on the observation that overselectivity was short-lived. Schreibman, Koegel, and Craig (1977) presented additional testing or probe trials to their autistic subjects and found that they were less likely to evidence overselectivity with this additional experience. A related remedial strategy was suggested by Koegel, Schreibman, Britten, and Laitinen (1979). They overtrained their autistic subjects on the multiple-cue disrimination problem before assessing overselectivity. When this overtraining included reinforcement on a partial (VR:3) as opposed to a continuous reinforcement schedule, responding to one component of the multiple cue and not the other (i.e., overselectivity) on nonreinforced probe trials decreased.

Another remedial technique was identified by Koegel and Schreibman (1977) when they found that autistic children could learn to respond to multiple-stimulus inputs in a conditional learning paradigm. Specifically, the children learned to respond (i.e., bar-press) to a combination of two cues (auditory plus visual) and not to the cues presented individually (auditory, visual). Since the children learned to respond to the multiple cue and not to the single cues, Koegel and Schreibman claimed that their overselectivity had been remediated.

The second general remedial strategy has led to the development of prompt-and-fade techniques that attempt to capitalize on the autistic child's restricted responding. Traditional prompt-and-fade approaches that included a stimulus not related to the discrimination (i.e., extrastimulus prompt) appeared to inhibit learning (Koegel & Rincover, 1976). It was assumed that stimulus overselectivity—the inability to respond to both the extrastimulus prompt and the discriminative stimulus—was responsible. A new within-stimulus prompt procedure was designed that made less attentional demand on the children. It included (1) an exaggeration of the feature differentiating the S+ and S−, (2) a gradual fading of this exaggerated feature, and finally (3) gradual inclusion of features in the two stimulus complexes that were irrelevant to the discrimination. Schreibman (1975) utilized this within-stimulus prompt procedure to teach a discrimination between nonmeaningful figures to her autistic subjects who had not acquired the discrimination when traditional extrastimulus prompts were used.

Rincover (1978) attempted to expand Schreibman's findings by (1) focusing on a more meaningful task (discriminating three-letter words) and (2) examining the effectiveness of prompts that included a feature found only in the S+ (distinctive feature) or in both the S+ and S− (nondistinctive feature). Eight autistic children were exposed to four prompt training procedures each: (1) within-stimulus distinctive, (2) within-stimulus nondistinctive, (3) extrastimulus distinctive, and (4) extrastimulus nondistinctive. For example, one of the discriminations included the words JAR (S+) and SON (S−). The distinctive feature prompt was the horizontal line in the J while the nondistinctive feature was the same lower curved line contained in both the letters J and S. When these features were extrastimulus prompts, the horizontal line or curved line was presented separately and above the letter J as opposed to being presented as an exaggerated feature within the letter (within-stimulus prompt). Actual prompt training involved six fading steps, from an exaggerated thickness to the same thickness as the rest of the letters. Using an extremely stringent criterion for success, Rincover (1978) reported that all of his eight subjects acquired the discrimination when a within-stimulus distinctive feature prompt was utilized, none with an extrastimulus nondistinctive prompt, one with the extrastimulus distinctive prompt, and four with the within-stimulus nondistinctive prompt. Although these results suggested that within-stimulus prompts that include a distinctive feature might be most efficacious in teaching two-choice discriminations, it should be noted that a subsequent assessment indicated that what the children had learned was trivial. That is, only the first letter of the three-letter word (e.g., J in JAR versus SON) controlled responding (Rincover, 1978).

In summarizing the area of research, Lovaas, Koegel, Schreibman, and their colleagues conclude that stimulus overselectivity appears to offer much promise, since it explains the lack of transfer and maintenance of treatment effects as well as other social and communicative deficits observed in autistic children. In addition, they proudly point to the methods of remediation that they claim have led to widespread behavior change (Egel *et al.*, 1980; Lovaas *et al.*, 1979).

Although some (e.g., Ross & Pelham, 1981) see this work as a "model of clinical research," questions about the significance of the described deficit and applied relevance of the proposed remedial strategies remain (see Gersten, 1980; Litrownik & McInnis, 1982). First, stimulus overselectivity was applied as a descriptive label, summarizing the apparent restricted responding of autistic children to multiple stimulus inputs in a particular experimental paradigm—that is, serial discrimination with multiple cues and single-cue probe trials (Lovaas, Schreibman, Koegel, & Rehm, 1971). With the accumulation of additional evidence for this descriptive deficit by these investigators and their colleagues (see Litrownik & McInnis, 1982, for a review) in the same experimental paradigm and in a simultaneous discrimination paradigm, stimulus overselectivity became established as an identifiable deficit and was given explanatory value. Many, if not all, of the severe behavioral deficiencies observed in autistic children were related to and in most cases explained by stimulus overselectivity (see Lovaas *et al.*, 1979). As a result, this term is no longer being used solely to describe observed performances of autistic children, but rather has acquired surplus meaning: It is now being used as a generalized explanatory deficit. All of this has occurred within a conceptual vacuum. That is, Koegel and Lovaas (1978) eschew the introduction of hypothetical constructs, such as "attention," into their thinking and hold fast to the claim that stimulus overselectivity refers to observed performances of autistic children.

The limitations of such a stance become obvious when one attempts to understand reports indicating that autistic children do not always evidence restricted responding (or stimulus control) to multiple cues (e.g., Anderson & Rincover, 1982; Crimmins & Romanczyk, 1978; Edwards, Shigley, & Edwards, 1976; Gersten, 1980; Litrownik, McInnis, Wetzel-Pritchard, & Filipelli, 1978; Prior & McGillivray, 1980; Schwartz & Johnson, 1981). These apparently contradictory findings are viewed as being inconsistent with the described deficit, stimulus overselectivity, and are either ignored or attacked (see Koegel & Lovaas, 1978). In fact, reports utilizing different experimental paradigms (e.g., match-to-sample, bidimensional probe trials) to assess stimulus control are not inconsistent, but rather serve to clarify the times at which restricted responding does or does not occur. That is, stimulus overselectivity is specific to the redundant relevant cue paradigm and is not a general deficit (Litrownik & McInnis, 1982).

Strong support for this claim comes from a follow-up of the children who participated in the Litrownik, McInnis, Wetzel-Pritchard, and Filipelli (1978) study. The seven autistic children, none of whom evidenced restricted responding on a four-dimension match-to-sample task, were first taught a simultaneous multiple-cue discrimination and if they acquired this discrimination, their responding to single-cue probe trials was observed (i.e., replication of Koegel & Wilhelm, 1973). Two of these children and 8 of 11 other potential subjects failed to reach the learning criterion within a reasonable number of training trials. Similar failures to train autistic children have been reported by those who have attempted to replicate the work of Koegel and his colleagues (see Gersten, 1980). The five children from the prior study who did acquire the discrimination all evidenced "stimulus overselectivity" on the probe trials—that is, consistent responding to one cue but not the other. Thus, the same autistic children were overselective in one paradigm and not in the other.

Based on these findings, some question about the significance of proposed remedial strategies emerges. For example, Koegel and Schreibman (1977) presented their autistic subjects with a conditional discrimination and found that the subjects learned to respond to a multiple-stimulus input. What they claim as a remedial approach is simply additional support for the claim that overselectivity is paradigm-specific. Other remedial attempts to modify overselectivity also appear to be trivial. That is, when first observed, overselectivity was found to be short-lived. Capitalizing on this, Schriebman *et al.* (1977) and Koegel *et al.* (1979), respectively, presented additional probe trials and overtraining on the initial discrimination and reported they had found another approach to treating overselectivity. Schreibman *et al.* (1977) did expose one child to a number of different simultaneous discrimination problems with single-component probe trials. After a number of sets, the child evidenced less overselectivity. In this single case, overselectivity in the redundant relevant cue paradigm was modified.

The other major approach to treatment has been to design more effective prompt procedures (Rincover, 1978; Schreibman, 1975). Not only has the relevance of such techniques been questioned (Gersten, 1980) but also we have been unsuccessful in two separate attempts to replicate the superiority of within-stimulus prompts that contain a distinctive feature, that is, Rincover's findings, in our lab (Richter, 1980; Zouzounis, Feldman, Gilbride, & Lancaster, 1980). In both studies it was found that autistic children either learned or did not learn the three-letter word discriminations regardless of the prompt procedure used. In summarizing these failures to replicate, Zouzounis *et al.* (1980) suggested that prompt training effectiveness is more likely a function of (1) the complexity of the task, (2) the child's learning history, and (3) general functioning level of the child, than of the particular prompt technique.

Motivation

Another area of concern has been the characteristic lack of motivation evidenced by autistic children (Egel, 1980). Although contemporary behavioral treatment approaches remain descriptive (Egel *et al.*, 1980; Koegel *et al.*, 1980), attempts to explain this observed motivational problem have relied on such theoretical constructs as learned helplessness (see Koegel & Egel, 1979).

Two general approaches to treating this lack of motivation have emerged. The first, based on the learned-helplessness explanation, focuses on developing individual competencies so that the child can come to control consequences. When translated into a specific treatment, this approach included prompting performance on a task until a criterion of 80% correct was attained (Koegel & Egel, 1979). Following this intervention, the subjects were presented with the same task, this time without prompts, and task-relevant behaviors were observed. In summarizing the results of this treatment, Koegel and Egel (1979) state that it was effective (i.e., greater task-relevant responses were obtained) when the subjects continued to perform the task correctly but not when they were incorrect.

The second approach aims at increasing the motivational value of applied reinforcers or consequences. For example, Egel (1980) reported that autistic children emitted lever-press responses more when a variety of consumable reinforcers were presented than with a single constant reinforcer. Rincover, Newsom, Lovaas, and Koegel (1977) reported that autistic children may be more responsive to a different class of reinforcers. Specifically, their austistic subjects worked longer and harder for contingent sensory stimuli (e.g., flickering light) than for consumables.

Based on this work, Egel (1980) has concluded that simple procedures for motivating autistic children have been identified. A critical appraisal of this work suggests that such a claim is premature, at best. On a descriptive level there is some question about the relevance of the first approach, prompting to a criterion of correctness, when (1) this proposed "new" treatment actually includes extrastimulus prompts that are supposedly not effective with autistic children (see previous section on stimulus overselectivity), (2) subsequent task-relevant responding occurs only when subjects continue to respond correctly, and (3) the effect is limited to the prompted task only (i.e., there is no evidence of task-relevant responses in other situations).

On a theorectical level (e.g., motivation, learned helplessness), the Koegel and Egel (1979) treatment appears to be extremely limited in its practical relevance. The same is true for the work aimed, thus far, at increasing the motivational value of applied reinforcers. That is, responses with little if any practical import (i.e., lever-press) have been maintained at high response strengths in laboratory settings. The applicability and generality of such procedures to relevant learning situations remain to be demonstrated.

Generalization and Maintenance

A variety of techniques based on learning principles have been developed and effectively applied in order to eliminate undesirable responses and teach appropriate ones (see Egel *et al.*, 1980, and Romanczyk, Kistner, & Plienis, 1982, for reviews). While specific behaviors have been modified, a continuing concern has been the lack of maintenance and generality of these changes (Litrownik, 1982; Lovaas *et al.*, 1973).

Applied behaviorists have been urged to program for transfer (Stokes & Baer, 1977). In response to these observed limitations and urgings, attempts have been made to understand the variables that influence generalization, and then, based on this understanding, to develop procedures that will promote generalization. The specific approaches identified include (1) expanding the program to include additional change agents (e.g., train parents), (2) expanding stimulus control (e.g., natural settings such as the classroom, home, etc.), (3) fading contingencies (e.g., withdraw extrinsic rewards and/or utilize intermittent reinforcement schedules), and (4) delaying reinforcer delivery, among others (Kazdin, 1978a).

All of these approaches have been applied in an attempt to foster maintenance and generalization. Reports indicate that these approaches, along with a focus on early identification and intervention, have resulted in superior maintenance but limited generality of behavior change (Egel *et al.*, 1980; Hayes, Rincover, & Solnick, 1980; Ross & Pelham, 1981). The problem remains; specific behaviors can be modified and maintained in specific situations when programmed, but general change does not occur (see Litrownik, 1982). It is quite possible that the lack of significant change is due to a focus at the molecular level (i.e., relationships between proximal responses and proximal stimuli), which is in most instances irrelevant to the business of living (Tyler, 1981).

Summary

In the early 1960s, when the behavioral approach first emerged, it encountered much resistance. The struggle to gain recognition and acceptance has been a long one, but it now appears that the battle has been won (see Schopler, 1979). One of the advantages of this victory has been the freedom to admit that behavioral approaches do have some limitations. In response to these admitted limitations, behavior modifiers have emphasized the importance of maintaining changes and insuring their generalization. As a result, the focus of recent interventions has been on programming generalization (e.g., involve parents) while recognizing that autistic children evidence restricted stimulus control (i.e., overselective attention).

Current behavioral interventions have evolved to the point at which we now have a better understanding of how autistic children function as well as how their behavior can be modified. Although these gains have been quite impressive, it appears that this perspective has taken us about as far as it can. In fact, the functional behavioral perspective has become even more rigid and insular (Hayes *et al.*, 1980). The hard line taken into battle 20 years ago has not wavered—the metaphor of man as a machine with unidirectional external determinants of behavior continues as the rallying cry (see Bandura, 1981, and Tyler, 1981, for a discussion). Setting of rigid boundaries and resultant specialization have been identified as "defense maneuvers designed to ward off challenges rather than meet them head on" (Tyler, 1981, p. 4).

As a result of such an insular stance, the functional behavioral understanding of autism is based on descriptive terms that have come to function as hypothetical constructs within a conceptual vacuum; complex presenting problems are simplified and dealt with superficially; the targets of modification are more likely to be determined by convenience than relevance (i.e., they are trivial); and interventions lead to the development of a reactive response repertoire as opposed to an active one (Hersen, 1981; Kazdin, 1978a; Litrownik, 1982; Staats, 1981). A number of current trends in psychology, including conceptual flexibility (Mahoney & Arnkoff, 1978), offer the promise of moving beyond this limited perspective. The remainder of this chapter will describe how these trends (e.g., reciprocal determinism, cognitions, self-regulation, etc.) can (1) lead to a better understanding of autism, (2) be conceptualized to direct specific interventions, and (3) actually be applied.

Cognitive Social Learning

The problems of stimulus overselectivity, motivation, and generalization and maintenance of change are viewed quite differently from a cognitive social learning perspective.

Stimulus Overselectivity

A recognition of recent advances made in understanding cognitive functioning helps to clarify the proposed information-processing deficits in autistic children as well as to suggest strategies for remediation. Litrownik and McInnis (1982) presented a working model of information-processing based on models previously proposed in order to understand normal cognitive processing as well as deficient processing in retarded persons and schizophrenic adults. A distinction was made between various attentional processes (e.g., selection of information on which to base responses, initial scanning of the environment and fixation on aspects of it) and parameters (e.g., breadth of attention) that define attentional processing.

It appears that multiple-cue simultaneous and serial discrimination paradigms with single-cue probe trials have assessed selective attention that is not only modifiable but is also controlled by higher processes (e.g., cognitive structures, learning sets, and meaningfulness of information). Paradigms other than these have either assessed the attentional parameter breadth of attention or attentional capacity (i.e., match-to-sample) or have assessed selective attention using different test or probe trials (i.e., bidimensional probe trials). Restricted responding has been observed in the former paradigms but not in the latter. As a result, relatively stable parameters of attentional processing do not appear to be deficient in autistic children. On the other hand, modifiable selection strategies in autistic children do show a developmental lag (Litrownik & McInnis, 1982; Litrownik, McInnis, Wetzel-Pritchard, & Filipelli, 1978; Schover & Newsom, 1976).

Butler and Rabinowitz (1981) offer a logical explanation for this observed developmental lag. First, they point out that solutions to multiple-component discrimination tasks can be based on each of the components individually or on a combination of the components (i.e., compound). Not only is there evidence indicating that the preferred solution (component or compound) is related to developmental level (i.e., younger children are more likely to utilize compound solutions), but also, within the same multiple-cue discrimination, some of the cues are utilized as individual components and some as part of a compound in order to solve the discrimination (Butler & Rabinowitz, 1981; Campione,

McGrath, & Rabinowitz, 1971). If assessment of stimulus control following acquisition of a multiple-cue discrimination problem includes presentations of single cues, the compounds used in the solution are destroyed. When this occurs the child will respond to individual cues that were solved on a component basis but not to those cues that were solved on a compound basis. The observed result is "stimulus overselectivity."

An example of just such a result was recently obtained in our laboratory (Zouzounis, 1981). Following the acquisition of a multiple-cue (light and tone) serial discrimination, David, a verbal 15-year-old autistic adolescent, responded to single presentations of the auditory cue but not to the visual cue. When questioned, he indicated that he had "noted" when the light went on by itself but did not respond because "the tone wasn't with it." Physiological measures (i.e., change in heart rate) confirm that he did in fact recognize and respond to the light. But since he apparently solved the discrimination by including light in a compound (light plus tone), he did not engage in an overt response when the light was presented during the probe trials. David did respond overtly (i.e., button-push) when the tone was presented alone, suggesting that his solution included the tone on a single-component basis.

The implications of such an understanding for treatment are extremely encouraging. House (1979) has demonstrated that the cognitive strategies used to solve multiple-cue discriminations can be easily modified in younger normal developing children. The promise of such an approach for modifying the cognitive strategies of autistic children comes from Schreibman *et al.*'s (1977) report that restricted responding of an autistic child diminished with repeated presentations of multiple-cue discrimination and single-probe test trials (e.g., learning set acquisition ensuring component solutions).

When one considers higher levels of processing and how they relate to overt performance on a task or problem, more appropriate targets for intervention can be identified, as in the example above. Another example relates to attempts to teach autistic children to discriminate between two three-letter words. The concept of "word" (meaningful string of letters) should be developed prior to discrimination training. This concept should by itself facilitate acquisition of the discrimination, precluding the need to utilize ineffective within-stimulus distinctive feature prompts that produce rote responding.

Motivation

From this perspective, concerns about motivational problems in autistic children go beyond the identification of effective external reinforcers and how to apply them (e.g., varied as opposed to constant reinforcers). Not only does the concept of "learned helplessness" suggest that children ought first to be taught how to perform a desired task, but it also directs efforts at developing adaptive internal processes (e.g., internal causal attribution, intrinsic rewards).

It is necessary to ensure that children can perform a specified task before they can learn that their performance is causally related to obtained outcomes. But these outcomes, whether they be external or internal, are not automatically linked to behaviors. If individuals do not have an internal causal attribution, then they are not likely to make the connection between behavior and its consequences (see Phares, 1973). The result is a failure on the part of these individuals to learn from experience.

Generalization and Maintenance

Causal attributions not only restrict acquisition but also limit the maintenance and generalization of changes accomplished through interventions (Davison & Vallins, 1969). Attempts to facilitate maintenance and generalization—that is, to develop an active adaptive individual—not only should consider causal attributions but also should move beyond limited behavioral approaches that fail to recognize that individuals can control their own behavior (see Bandura, 1981; Litrownik, 1982; Staats, 1981).

For example, we have all developed to a point at which we are able to get up in the morning and prepare ourselves to meet the requirements of the new day. Initially our every need was taken care of—feeding, washing, etc. But as we matured (i.e., gross and fine motor coordination), we began to take more responsibility for getting dressed and washed and eating breakfast. Now we set an alarm clock to ensure that we will rise at a given time, select the clothes that we should wear given the day's schedule, monitor the time, and evaluate what we have left to do in order to make decisions about how to procede (e.g., take a shower or just wash up, have eggs for breakfast or skip breakfast). These self-regulatory skills—monitoring, evaluating, and instructing—allow us to function independently and adaptively (see Litrownik, 1982).

Applied behavioral interventions have typically followed a three-step approach of teaching a skill (i.e., acquisition), developing proficiency, and then moving to self-initiation. Training usually stops after proficiency has been demonstrated, with the hope that self-initiation will follow. That hope has not been realized, so efforts have been made to facilitate maintenance and generalization. These efforts have not been successful, though evidence indicating that acquisition and proficiency can be developed continues to accumulate.

Reference to the above example of getting ready each morning to face the demands of the day helps (1) to explain why adaptive self-initiation has not resulted and (2) suggests an additional focus for intervention. Behavioral interventions have identified necessary self-help skills (e.g., washing, dressing, etc.) and have attempted to develop these skills. Once a subject is proficient at these skills, schedules of reinforcement, trainers, situations, etc., are manipulated in an attempt to generalize and maintain the changes. But this approach has resulted in robot-like progressions through an invariant series of skills without any evidence of adaptability. Adaptive application of these acquired skills has not been observed in autistic individuals because functional behaviorists have not recognized another class of skills—self-management, utilized by normally developing persons to determine when, where, and how to perform content skills (e.g., washing, dressing, etc.). These self-management skills (e.g., monitoring, evaluating, and cuing performance) develop in most of us without any specific training by our parents, as did the content skills. If autistic children have not acquired the content skills through normal developmental experiences and specific training is needed, it stands to reason that self-management skills will not develop following acquisition of content skills if they are not also specifically trained.

In focusing on self-management skills, it is also important to recognize that all behavior is a function of both environmental and organismic factors (see Bandura, 1981; Kanfer & Karoly, 1982). Thus, in the development of self-management skills in autistic children, it is possible to focus on increasing the amount of internal control exerted by them rather than developing children who function independent of any environmental controls.

The general approach to developing content skills such as getting dressed in the morning is also applicable to developing self-managing behavior. Specifically, the target skill is analyzed and broken down into smaller, more manageable steps, the individual is assessed, and training begins at the level of the individual's current performance and moves in gradual steps toward the targeted outcome. A variety of techniques can be utilized to develop either self-managing or content skills. These techniques—reinforcement, modeling, etc.—must be differentiated from the skills taught, while there must also be recognition that self-management and targeted skills can be taught through the same training techniques.

In the following sections, a working model of self-management that can guide training efforts is presented. A general approach to training, recommendations for how this training can be accomplished, and some specific examples based on this model follow.

Self-management: A Model

The first step in breaking down self-management into manageable units that can be applied to autistic children includes agreeing on a working model of what is involved in self-management. I've chosen to conceptualize (i.e., organize my thinking about) self-management in terms of general problem-solving (see Litrownik, 1982; Litrownik & Steinfeld, 1982). With this general model, a series of stages and skills or processes required at each stage can be identified. The first stage includes the identification of a problem and the recognition that something needs to be done to deal with it. According to Kanfer (1978), any disruption in the smooth flow of behavior can serve as a cue for problem-solving (i.e., identification). Thus, unexpected events, those that elicit arousal, and situations in general that place adaptive demands on an individual can all serve to identify a problem. Whether a problem is identified and the need to solve it recognized depends not only on the ability of the individual to self-monitor but also on the labeling of affect, attributions of control, and standards for performance among others. Thus, individuals in the same problem situations either may begin to deal adaptively with the situation or may fail to initiate the problem-solving process because the cues were not discriminated and/or the need to deal with the problem was not recognized.

After a problem is identified and the need to deal with it is recognized, a commitment must be made (Karoly, 1977). That is, a decision to spend the effort and energy necessary to solve the problem is required. The ability to make such a commitment is a function of an individual's performance attributions (Henker, Whalen, & Hinshaw, 1980) and anticipation of consequences (Fagen & Long, 1979). An individual who perceives a problem as being under his or her control (internal attribution), with the likelihood that a change will lead to some positive outcome, is likely to make a commitment. This commitment is typically stated in terms of a general standard or criterion for performance.

In the next stage, the individual begins to focus on the problem and possible solutions. Specifically, the individual appraises the problem and generates a number of possible solutions. Situational demands, individual capabilities, and available strategies or approaches to cope with the problem are identified. Based on this knowledge, a specific action routine is selected, requiring some cognitive evaluation of probable effects.

In the last stage, the selected plan or action routine is applied and monitored and its effectiveness is evaluated. This evaluation is based on the goals established during the commitment stage, with a positive outcome leading to continuance or discontinuance of the routine and a negative outcome resulting in a return to the previous stage so another possible solution can be identified and implemented.

A number of specific skills and operations that are required at each stage should be identified, operationalized, and broken down further. For example, much self-management training has focused on developing action routines or strategies to deal with specific problems.

Specific routines that have been identified include self-instructions, self-monitoring, self-evaluation, self-determined criteria for performance, self-reinforcement, self-punishment, relaxation, and distraction (O'Leary & Dubey, 1979; Rosenbaum & Drabman, 1979; Thoresen & Mahoney, 1974). In order to develop a given routine, specific components or skills that are involved should be identified. That is, the self-management routines must be further reduced to the level of specific skills required for a given routine. As an example, self-monitoring requires (1) observation of an individual's own behavior and/or consequence of his or her performance, (2) a discrimination between occurrence or nonoccurrence of the cue for (3) the self-recording response (see Litrownik & Freitas, 1980).

In sum, at each stage of the general problem-solving process, a number of specific skills or operations are required. These specific skills or operations can vary in the degree to which external or internal factors determine their occurrence. Thus, an individual may be quite adept at admitting that a problem exists with a minimum of external control (i.e., others telling the person that there is a problem) but at the same time be unable to commit him- or herself to solving the problem without external demands (e.g., a caretaker telling a child that he or she will have to learn to deal with name-calling on his or her own). The particular focus of a self-management training program necessarily depends on the repertoire of skills and abilities that an individual possesses. This repertoire is important in determining what content skills might be targeted as well as how training of the self-management process will proceed. If the content skills are already in the individual's repertoire, the focus of training should be on developing the self-management process (e.g., specific components, routines, and stages of problem-solving). On the other hand, if the targeted content skills are to be acquired, then training can either (1) focus on developing these first and then developing the self-management process or (2) attempt to develop the content and self-managing skills simultaneously (O'Leary & Dubey, 1979).

Self-management Training: Approaches

Since children with pervasive developmental disorders may evidence perceptual/cognitive, emotional/motivational, and personal/social deficits, many of the self-management training programs that have been developed for other populations are not appropriate (see Litrownik, 1982). That is, proposed deficits in psychotic children may preclude their benefiting, at least initially, from training aimed at developing symbolic verbal processes. These numerous and severe proposed deficits and the resultant limited expectations are most likely responsible for the very few reported attempts to utilize cognitive behavioral approaches with autistic children. Recent reports of the successful application of these techniques to populations of disturbed and/or retarded children suggest that if properly designed, self-management training programs can be effective with autistic children (e.g.,Holman & Baer, 1979; Litrownik, 1982; Litrownik & Steinfeld, 1982).

Successful training requires specification of what is to be acquired (i.e., problem-solving), analysis of specific skills required, and development of individual skills prior to combining them. Thus, training will necessarily involve small steps toward developing general problem-solving. Some of these smaller steps and specific skills included at these steps are identified in Table 1. For example, the initial training objective might be one of developing a routine or specific skills that allow a child to maintain his or her own appropriate behavior with a minimum of external control (e.g., self-reinforcement routine). In order to accomplish this end, specific prerequisite or readiness skills (e.g., appropriate task performance, discrimination between occurrence and nonoccurrence of appropriate task performance, etc.) and skills necessary for the routine (e.g., self-monitoring, standard-setting, self-evaluation, self-reward) need to be learned. Only then can these skills be combined to function as an effective self-management routine.

Depending on the individual's level of functioning, skills required for other problem-solving stages can be developed and eventually combined for rote application and then general application. In the selection or establishment of a program—that is, deciding what is to be acquired and how—a general six-step process can be applied (see Table 2). Following the initial assessment, content or to-be-controlled skills are identified and task-analyzed. It is during the third or next step that the problem-solving training objectives are identified and task-analyzed. After a more specific assessment that relates these objectives to current levels of functioning, training procedures that may include external (e.g., operant) or internal (e.g., covert) techniques are designed and

Table 1. Possible Progression of Objectives and Targets for Self-management Training

I. Develop prerequisite skills
Minimal skills (e.g., discriminations between work that is or is not finished) may need to be taught before beginning specific self-management training.

II. Skills necessary for routines
Routines or specific oprations that allow an individual to cope with a problem situation must be identified and task-analyzed.
The skills required for the application of a given routine are further analyzed and each skill is then developed individually.
For example, the self-reinforcement routine can be broken down into four component skills: (1) self-monitoring, (2) standard setting, (3) self-evaluation, and (4) self-reward. Each of these skills is developed separately, breaking them down into manageable smaller steps—for example, self-evaluation involves an initial discrimination between a performance that is greater than or equal to a standard *or* less than a standard, and a subsequent evaluation based on this discrimination.

III. Combine skills for a routine
After individual skills are acquired, they can be combined in order to function as a routine.
Initial applications will be for a specific task or setting, but with practice, general routine application can be programmed (e.g., other tasks and settings).

IV. Skills required for other problem-solving stages
Specific skills need to be identified and broken down into manageable training steps.
For example, developing skills in problem identification might involve labeling of affect and subsequent discriminations between these labels with some (e.g., fear) leading to problem identification and others (e.g., joy) not.

V. Combining skills for general problem-solving
After skills are developed, they can be combined, with the ultimate objective being the development of problem-solving.
An initial focus might be combining problem identification with the application of a routine. This would most likely include rote identification and implementation of the same routine initially, but subsequent training would focus on "selection" or the identification of the most appropriate routine available.

applied. In the next section, some applied examples will be presented in order to specify this general six-step process.

Self-management Training: Examples and Suggestions

The examples and suggestions that follow are based to a large extent on preliminary work that I am conducting in collaboration with the

Table 2. Six-step Process for Developing a Self-management Training Program

I. General assessment
   Identify general verbal, cognitive, social, etc. level of functioning.
   Consider potentially effective training techniques (e.g., contingency management, modeling, covert, etc.).

II. Specification of desired outcome
   Identify problem areas and specify targeted outcomes.
   The target may be a change in behavior (acquisition or elimination) or maintenance.
   Task analyze the targeted outcome if a change is desired, identifying steps that will lead to its development or elimination.

III. Identification of self-management process
   Determine which general problem-solving stages will be focused on and the specific skills to be developed (e.g., routines, problem identification, self-monitoring, etc.).
   Conduct a task analysis of these operations and/or skills.

IV. Second assessment
   Specific performance should be assessed as it relates to the targeted outcome (Step II) and self-management process to be developed (Step III).
   At this step, training needs are identified (i.e., what has to be taught).

V. Design the training program
   Specification of step-by-step procedures for developing skills and/or changing targeted outcomes.
   This includes the identification of specific training techniques, which may include external (e.g., physical prompts) and/or internal (e.g., covert modeling) methods.

VI. Evaluation
   Determine effectiveness of program. (Were the self-management skills acquired and applied appropriately, and did they result in the desired outcome?)
   This ongoing assessment is required for subsequent training decisions. (If effective, what should be developed next? If ineffective, how can the program be modified?)

professional staff (Drs. Elizabeth McInnis and Vera Bernard-Opitz) at Los Niños Center in San Diego. Our general strategy is one of introducing self-management training in the ongoing training program. The specific objective is to maximize independent performance through the application of self-monitoring and/or self-reinforcement routines to tasks (i.e., outcomes) that have been targeted for each child. The children targeted for such training thus far were not working independently or managing their own desirable or undesirable responses. For example, the targeted outcomes include (1) maintenance of accurate performance on cognitive tasks (e.g., math, reading, etc.) with a minimum of external monitoring, (2) elimination of an undesirable behavior (e.g., mouthing), and (3) acquisition of desirable response (e.g., speech).

Developing Routines. Specific skills required for a given routine must be identified and developed step by step. For example, the target behavior, mouthing, with one child has been of concern for well over a year. Various external, reward, response cost, and time-out procedures had been applied with negligible effects. Self-management training has begun, with this child having an opportunity to monitor his mouthing behavior by pressing one of two wrist counters. One counter has a happy face on it and is pressed when he has completed a scheduled activity (approximately 20–30 minutes) without mouthing (i.e., licking the palm of his hand), while the sad face counter is pressed when he has engaged in this undesirable response during the activity. Initially, the individual trainer responsible for monitoring the scheduled activity has been prompting correct recording (e.g., "You didn't mouth so you can press your happy counter"). There is some evidence suggesting that this procedure has led to a decrease in the frequency of this undesirable behavior. The next step is to begin developing self-observational skills, including a discrimination between sessions when mouthing has occurred and those when it has not occurred. This will be accomplished by allowing the child to indicate which wrist counter he believes should be pressed after the completion of a session. If correct, he will be socially reinforced (e.g., "That's right, you did/did not mouth.") and told either to "keep up the good work" or "try harder." If we find that this step is too difficult, we will break down the monitoring into smaller steps—for example, record every five minutes rather than at the completion of the session.

A second ongoing program has been implemented with a 14-year-old who two years previously had been almost totally nonverbal. During his stay at Los Niños he has developed verbal skills, though he continues to evidence articulation and sequencing problems as well as a lack of spontaneity and production of sentences. The targeted outcome has been the production of correctly sequenced three-word sentences during scheduled activities and structured conversational periods. A self-monitoring routine is being developed by first prompting the subject to press a wrist counter each time he produced a spontaneous sentence.

In order to evaluate the effectiveness of this first step, we compared verbal output during (1) self-monitoring periods with contingent rewards applied at the end of the session, (2) periods with contingent rewards only, and (3) periods without either contingent rewards or self-monitoring. The three treatments were randomly applied during the first three scheduled 20- to 30-minute activities of the day. Preceding each of the three activities, a five-minute conversational period was presented utilizing the same treatment.

The results of this preliminary evaluation indicate that there were more spontaneous verbalizations in the self-monitoring condition, while verbalizations in the other two conditions were more or less equivalent. Thus, there is some suggestion that training in the initial stages of self-monitoring can facilitate spontaneous verbalizations. Subsequent training will attempt to fade external prompts, allowing the subject to monitor without external controls.

In both of these examples, operant training techniques are being utilized to develop skills required for a specific routine, self-monitoring. A task analysis of this routine indicates that at least three skills are required: (1) self-observation, (2) discrimination between occurrence and nonoccurrence of targeted outcome, and (3) self-recording response. Our first objective has been the development of the self-recording response, or pressing the wrist counter. Subsequent training will focus on the first two steps of self-observation and discrimination training. Preliminary results of training suggest that self-recording can lead to increases in a desirable outcome (e.g., spontaneous speech) and decreases in an undesirable outcome (e.g., mouthing).

In another ongoing program, a self-reinforcement routine is being developed. Modeling, rehearsal, corrective feedback, and prompting procedures are being utilized to train specific skills required for this routine. For example, the child was first taught to monitor completion of a worksheet (e.g., math problems or phonics) and then the number of correctly completed problems on each sheet. The next steps included teaching the child to (1) evaluate his performance relative to an externally determined standard (i.e., number of pages completed with 80% accuracy in a three-minute period), (2) administer freely accessible rewards conditionally, and (3) set his own standard or criterion for performance.

At each step, the skills to be acquired were operationalized. For example, a standard was indicated by circling the number of pages to be completed, and the monitoring of performance included self-corrections of individual problems with pages checked when more than 80% were correct. This routine has been acquired and general application is now being programmed. Specifically, work periods will be lengthened, new math and phonic problems will be introduced, different tasks will be included, and application of the routine will move from an isolated to a class situation.

Some preliminary attempts have been made to teach self-instructional and relaxation routines to two children at Los Niños. Rote verbalization (e.g., "What is my problem?") and externally cued relaxation have been developed, but additional training that will lead to appropriate self-application of these skills is necessary. For example, self-cued relaxation needs to be developed so the child can apply this routine to a task or situation when told to do so, eventually without an external cue (i.e., when the need to relax is identified by the child).

An example of how self-cued relaxation can be developed in an autistic adult was described by Hughes and Davis (1980). Their 27-year-old male autistic subject was first taught to reduce his muscular activity, specifically, to lower the pitch of a tone emitted from an EMG biofeedback apparatus. Sessions included receipt of pennies for reductions in activity while the subject was reclining in a dimly lit room. During the next training phase, the subject sat upright in a chair and was verbally praised when he lowered the tone. The tone was presented at random times during the session so that response discrimination training took place. This discrimination was utilized to cue relaxation or a reduction in muscle activity in the next phase. Specifically, the subject was read a story and then asked to respond to 26 questions. He was told, "You got that question wrong" on 20 of the questions. Criticism such as this typically resulted in aggressive outbursts. The tone was turned on when he answered each question, and he was told to lower the tone. In the final phase, the EMG apparatus and resultant tone were removed. The to-be-controlled responses were verbal and physical aggression, which typically occurred when the subject was criticized. Relaxation paired with being criticized apparently reduced aggressive responses from 20 per session to approximately 5 per session.

While these preliminary reports are quite encouraging, much more work is needed before any claims of success can be made. At the same time that specific routines are being developed, it may also be appropriate to begin to focus on developing skills required for the other stages of problem-solving.

Skills Required for Other Problem-solving Stages. If individuals are to self-initiate the application of an acquired routine to a given problem situation, they must be able to identify when a problem exists. Training at this stage could focus on identifying cues that require some self-management action on the part of the individual. These cues might include any demands placed on a person to perform or any change in affect, or they could be more specific.

Self-application of a routine is not likely to follow problem identification without a commitment being made. This commitment requires anticipation of consequences and internal attributions. These internal attributions are necessary if an individual is to recognize the relationships between behaviors and outcomes—that is, contingencies. Thus internal attribution training with psychotic children can begin by giving them choices. A simple example is to give individuals an opportunity to select reinforcers that they would like to work for during a given session. Not only will such opportunities foster the development of internal attributions, but they can also be included in the development of "decision-making" skills. Thus, limited choices or options are presented initially, with later decisions requiring greater participation by the child. For example, infants are given few, if any, opportunities to make choices about what they will eat. The only control that they exert is in the form of how they respond to what has been placed in their mouths. The toddler, on the other hand, is often given a restricted number of options from which to choose: "Do you want Rice Krispies or Corn Flakes for breakfast?" Eventually the available options are not presented, and instead the child is asked, "What do you want for breakfast?"

A similar progression can be programmed when developing decision-making skills in autistic children. Additional visual cues can accompany presentation of options—for instance, a box of Corn Flakes and Rice Krispies—to ensure that the choices are understood, with these cues being faded along with stated options.

If a commitment to solve a problem is made, the next step is to appraise the situation and to assess and identify the problem demands and individual capabilities. Some suggestions for the kind of training that might be included at this step come from the work of Ross and Ross (1979). For example, at a very basic level psychotic children can be presented with a simple task, such as copying a design, and asked to identify what they would need to complete the task. In the identification of what would be needed, a number of objects (e.g., pencil, paper, doll, etc) could be presented, allowing the individual an opportunity to select from among them. The difficulty of the task can then be varied as a function of the number of distracting objects. More difficult tasks can also be presented, as appropriate to the individual's level of development. For example, a child who is to complete a page of math problems should learn to identify + and − signs and relate them to operations of addition and subtraction, respectively.

Routines appropriate for a given task are then selected and applied. The routines need to be developed initially and applied to specific classes of problems before the individual can be taught to select the appropriate routine. In the last example, a number of routines might be appropriately utilized to complete a page of math problems. For example, self-instructions would serve to cue the appropriate operation, while self-reinforcement could increase output. Finally, judgments about the appropriateness, usefulness, and general effectiveness of the solution or routine can be made, based on acquired self-evaluation skills.

SUMMARY AND CONCLUDING REMARKS

Children with pervasive developmental disorders come to professional service providers with severely impoverished behavioral repertoires and poor prognoses. In the prior two decades, traditional treatment interventions based on the psychodynamic perspective were supplanted by functional behavioral approaches. This change began in the 1960s and by the 1970s had progressed to the point at which operant technicians were able to admit that their techniques were limited.

After a decade of attempts to remedy these shortcomings, it is now apparent that this radical behavioral perspective has taken us about as far as it can. Our understanding of children with pervasive developmental disorders is restricted by the attempt to avoid internal constructs and, though responses can be modified, the result is an inflexible, dependent, and nonadaptable individual.

The next step toward better understanding and treatment of children is one that incorporates new findings from the area of cognitive social learning theory (e.g., triadic reciprocal determinism, information-processing). From this perspective it is recognized that the individual plays a vital role in determining his or her own behavior. The focus of training moves from *teaching disturbed children to engage in appropriate responses* to one of developing *appropriate individuals.*

This change in focus along with efforts to understand better how psychotic children process information led to specific explanations for described deficits (e.g., stimulus overselectivity) and suggestions for more appropriate interventions (e.g., develop problem-solving skills). These problem-solving skills develop in most of us, as do other skills, without any direct training, but this is not the case with severely disturbed children. They must be taught the simplest of skills, such as washing and getting dressed. It is logical to assume that if these basic skills have to be programmed, then problem-solving skills must also.

In order for such programming to begin, the skills involved in the problem-solving or self-management process must be identified. This chapter has presented a working model of self-management that helps direct these efforts. In addition, a general six-step process for developing training programs is offered, as are a number of specific training targets and some initial examples. The application of cognitive social learning theory to the understanding and treatment of psychotic children is just beginning. While initial reports are quite promising, much is still left to do.

10

Integrating Cognitive and Behavioral Procedures for the Treatment of Socially Isolated Children

Philip C. Kendall and Patricia Morison

INTRODUCTION

Social development in children remains a topic of interest to developmental psychologists, with a large literature devoted to understanding the ways in which adults influence and shape children's social behavior, both prosocial and aggressive. In recent years, however, there has been increased recognition of the importance of peer interaction in the process of a child's development (Hartup, 1979a; Lewis & Rosenblum, 1975). Experience with peers is seen as a necessary part of childhood socialization, providing an arena for sex-role learning, moral and cognitive development, mastery of aggressive impulses, and the achievement of general social competence (Hartup, 1976, 1979b). Similarly, much of the attention of mental health professionals concerned with childhood maladjustment has in the past focused on personality characteristics of the children, specific observable child behaviors, and relationships among the child's family members. However, there is a growing body of research suggesting that poor peer relations are a powerful predictor of

---

Philip C. Kendall and Patricia Morison • Department of Psychology, University of Minnesota, Minneapolis, Minnesota 55455. This chapter was prepared while the first author was a Fellow at the Center for Advanced Study in the Behavioral Sciences, Stanford, California. He is grateful for financial support provided by the National Institute of Mental Health (Grant No. 5-T32-MH14581-05), the John D. and Catherine T. MacArthur Foundation, and the University of Minnesota Quarter Leave System. Research support (NIMH Grant No. 1-RO-MH34623-01) also facilitated the preparation of this manuscript.

adult maladjustment (Cowen, Pederson, Babigian, Izzo, & Trost, 1973; Kohlberg, LaCrosse, & Ricks, 1972; Roff, 1961; Roff, Sells, & Golden, 1972).

It should be noted that the recent burgeoning of intervention studies focusing on childhood social isolation is typically attributed to data demonstrating the long-term consequences of social maladjustment in childhood (e.g., juvenile delinquency, Roff *et al.*, 1972; psychiatric disturbance, Cowen *et al.*, 1973; bad conduct military discharge, Roff, 1961). However, as Conger and Keane (1981) have pointed out, most of the predictive research focuses on sociometrically *rejected* children, who are often aggressive and disruptive, rather than on the withdrawn, shy child who is typically *ignored* sociometrically. Despite the lack of long-term predictive data on poor adult outcomes for shy, withdrawn children, treatment of this population is important for several reasons (Kendall, Hartup, & Cummings, 1983). For instance, in the short run, social skills treatments can ameliorate a skill deficit and improve overall adjustment by increasing friendship-making skills. Secondly, because friendships provide the context and the stimuli for the child's accomplishment of many cognitive, social, behavioral, emotional, and moral developmental tasks, interventions can have positive developmental consequences for withdrawn children.

Although the process of peer socialization is not entirely understood, one can readily imagine how early difficulties with peer interaction might initiate an irreversible pattern leading eventually to maladjustment. If children are denied (for whatever reasons) normal interactions with peers, they will have little opportunity for social learning, the development of social skills, and the establishment of friendship bonds. It is easy to imagine a snowball effect wherein children, initially isolated from peers, become increasingly unable to interact successfully as one aspect of the socialization process is denied them.

Social scientists with varying interests have individually recognized and described the important influences of interpersonal interaction on development (e.g., Bandura, 1969b; Flavell, 1963; Gough, 1948; Mead, 1934; Piaget, 1926). Although perhaps unique in its emphasis, the work of Harry Stack Sullivan illustrates the central role of peer relations in development. In *The Interpersonal Theory of Psychiatry* (1953) he discussed various phases of childhood and the distinctive contributions made by peer relations and friendships to each phase. For example, he discussed the importance of a "chum" or close friend of the same sex during the preadolescent era. Through this relationship, the child develops, for the first time, "a real sensitivity to what matters to another person" (p. 245). The absence of this "chumship" can have a lifelong impact on the capacity for interpersonal relations. In addition, Sullivan proposed that friendship and other aspects of peer relations are of potential therapeutic value. Successful negotiation of social relationships with peers can mitigate negative effects of a child's home and family. As the child enters school and the juvenile era, "the limitations and peculiarities of the home as a socializing influence begin to be open to remedy" (p. 227).

Thus, the identification and treatment of children who manifest primary difficulties in peer relationships seems of central importance to their subsequent adjustment. Interventions with these children should be aimed toward developing the cognitive and behavioral skills necessary to facilitate their reentry into the normal process of social development provided by the peer group. However, there is no one diagnostic group or type of child for whom these treatments are applicable. Some children in both clinic and educational settings may manifest poor peer relations as a primary problem. Difficulty with peers may, in addition, be a secondary feature of any one of a number of childhood behavior disorders. The third edition of the Diagnostic and Statistical Manual (American Psychiatric Association, 1980) (DSM-III) lists peer difficulties as an associated feature or complication of the Anxiety Disorders, Conduct Disorder, Attentional Deficit Disorders, and Language Disorders. Campbell and Paulauskas (1979), in a recent paper on peer relations in hyperactivity, suggested that adults, peers, and the hyperactive children themselves report impaired peer relations, although data illuminating the specific nature of each of the impairments are lacking. A recent investigation (Klein & Young, 1979) documented that hyperactive boys were perceived more negatively by peers on a classroom sociometric than were "active" boys from the same classrooms.

Children who experience difficulty with their peers, whether as a primary problem or secondary complication, might be expected to constitute a relatively large proportion of outpatient child clinic populations. And yet there exist few published reports of interventions specifically directed toward the alleviation of such difficulties in clinical populations. Most of the research reviewed in the present chapter comes from work with groups of normal children in schools, some of whom are reported by their teachers to be somewhat socially deviant. Nevertheless, many of these methods are applicable to the treatment of clinical populations, and this paper will attempt, first, to review such studies, and second, to extend their results to the cognitive behavioral treatment of clinical populations. Excluded from this review are studies that, although focusing on the facilitation of social interaction, treat children whose social isolation is secondary to a more severe disorder such as mental retardation or autism (e.g., Chennault, 1967; Lovaas,

Schaeffe, & Simmons, 1965; Strain & Timm, 1974; Whitman, Mercurio, & Caponigri, 1970).

ASSESSING THE NATURE OF THE PROBLEM

Since the available literature will suggest a variety of interventions that may be applied to children manifesting poor peer relations, the treatment chosen should depend in large part on a careful assessment of the exact nature of the child's social difficulties.[1] For example, consider the differences between children who are actively rejected by their peers and those who are neglected or ignored by their peers. The cognitive and behavioral deficits may vary widely between these two groups of children, requiring quite different intervention procedures for each.

Although much of the research relevant to this chapter has been conducted with children termed "socially isolated" or "withdrawn," the criteria used by various investigators to identify socially isolated children are sufficiently diverse to cast serious doubt on the homogeneity of this population. The selection criteria are generally based on one of three types of measures (or some combination thereof)—(a) teacher ratings of withdrawal, (b) sociometric assessment of a child's relative acceptance and/or rejection by the peer group, and (c) observational measures of frequency of interaction. The convergent validity of these measures can be questioned. For instance, it is not clear whether children assessed by a sociometric device as low in peer acceptance are the same children who are observed to interact infrequently with their peers. Little descriptive work exists to describe effectively the behaviors and symptoms of children identified by such methods. Data presented by Gottman (1977b) indicated the absence of a significant relationship between acceptance by peers and frequency of interaction ($r = -0.17$) for preschoolers. Thus, children selected as isolates on the basis of low levels of peer interaction do not seem to be the same children as those who are low in peer acceptance. Furthermore, the frequency of interaction shows a significant positive correlation with the amount of negative peer interaction and with rejection. Thus, it would appear that the higher the frequency of interaction with peers, the larger the proportion of that interaction is negative and the higher the child's level of rejection. Such data suggest that frequency of interaction may not be an accurate mea-

[1]The reader interested in assessments relevant for the larger area of "social skills" is referred to Hops and Greenwood (1981), Michelson, Foster, and Ritchey (1982), and Van Hasselt, Hersen, Whitehill, and Bellack (1979).

sure of the level of social acceptance. In sum, then, it appears that children identified as social isolates by these two methods (low sociometric acceptance or low frequency of interaction) may be different groups of children. Furthermore, most of the validational evidence relating poor peer relations to maladjustment has used sociometric, not observational, assessment of acceptance (e.g., Cowen, Pederson, Babigian, Izzo, & Trost, 1973; Roff *et al.*, 1972).

There is some evidence suggesting that children with low rates of interaction may have appropriate social behaviors in their repertoire but may merely emit them at a low rate (Keller & Carlson, 1974). Such children may avoid social interactions because of fear of aversive consequences (O'Connor, 1969, 1972), even exhibiting a phobia-like reaction to peers (Ross, Ross, & Evans, 1971). Others may be socially skilled yet spend most of their time interacting with adults (Allen, Hart, Buell, Harris, & Wolf, 1964). Evers-Pasquale and Sherman (1975) have suggested that withdrawn children exhibiting low rates of social interaction may have low expectancies for reinforcement for such interaction.

On the other hand, children rejected on a sociometric instrument may have deficient or maladaptive social skills. Unfortunately, there is little research to date documenting the actual social behaviors or social-skill deficits of children low in social acceptance on a sociometric instrument. Hartup, Glazer, and Charlesworth (1967) found that preschoolers who were less well liked by their peers were deficient in the giving and receiving of positive reinforcement. Using a sociometric measure with third- and fourth-graders, Gottman, Gonso, and Rasmussen (1975) identified "high-friends" children (i.e., those often chosen as a friend by classmates) and found them to give and receive more positive reinforcement. Furthermore, of the social cognitive skills assessed, referential communication accuracy (i.e., a child's ability to take a listener's informational needs into account when communicating) and "knowledge of how to make friends" discriminated high- and low-friends children, whereas a perspective-taking task and the ability to label emotions in facial expression did not.

Although there are some reasonably consistent bodies of data describing the cognitive and behavioral deficits correlated with certain childhood behavior disorders (e.g., children lacking self-control; Kendall & Williams, 1982; Little & Kendall, 1979), a more limited data base exists about either the behavioral or social cognitive correlates of children identified as having poor peer relations. Furthermore, few attempts have been made to discern different patterns of social difficulties with peers. It seems useful, however, to make a distinction, similar to that suggested by Strain, Cooke, and Apolloni (1976), between children with performance deficits and those with repertoire deficits. Lacking basic social skills, some children may have inappropriate or inadequate social repertoires. Other children may have appropriate skills in their social repertoires but may manifest a performance deficit in such a way that they have difficulty activating those skills and initiating social interaction. The nature of the deficits should, in large measure, determine the treatment methods employed.

The training studies that will be discussed tend to fall in one of two general categories. One body of research consists of attempts to facilitate and shape the actual social behaviors thought to be related to successful social interaction (e.g., sharing, question-asking, giving positive reinforcement, smiling). A second and relatively new approach focuses on training the social cognitive skills thought to underlie positive social interaction (e.g., perspective-taking skills, ability to infer emotions, social problem-solving). The former methods are more behavioral while the latter are more cognitive. Last, we will consider the cognitive behavioral treatment of socially isolated children. Cognitive behavioral approaches to treatment, in the general sense, are interventions that purposefully attempt to preserve the demonstrated efficiencies of behavior modification within a less doctrinaire context and to incorporate the cognitive activities of the client into the efforts to produce therapeutic change (Kendall & Hollon, 1979). More specifically, cognitive behavioral procedures with children can be described as an integration of behavioral and cognitive remedial efforts that focus on trying to teach children to think about their social world (Craighead, Wilcoxon-Craighead, & Meyers, 1978; Kendall, 1981b; Urbain & Kendall, 1980).

TYPES OF INTERVENTION

Social Reinforcement

It is a well-accepted fact, in both popular and professional circles, that social reinforcement from adults can be effective in increasing targeted social behaviors in young children. The literature is replete with examples. An oft-cited example illustrates how teacher attention made contingent on interaction with other children was effective in increasing rates of such interaction in a socially isolated 4-year-old (Allen *et al.*, 1964). An initially low rate of cooperative play was increased in a 5-year-old preschooler through the use of contingent adult social reinforcement (Hart, Reynolds, Baer, Brawley, & Harris, 1968). However reasonable the premise, the data are not conclusive regarding long-term effects. The lack of follow-up also makes it difficult to evaluate whether social interaction with peers is maintained in the absence of teacher attention. Several more recent studies that have employed adult shaping and reinforcement for social interaction suggest that the procedure does produce immediate increases in rates of social interaction, but that the gains are not retained at follow-up (Evers & Schwarz, 1973; O'Connor, 1972). Nevertheless, the contingent deployment of social reinforcement by adults is no doubt involved in the initiation or facilitation of social interactions among children and must be considered an important component of a treatment program for social isolates.

Priming Peers to Interact

Another technique that has been shown to facilitate an increase in the positive social behavior of isolated children is peer-priming. Strain (1977) trained a peer confederate to initiate play behavior and emit positive social behavior during individual play sessions with three behaviorally disordered preschoolers. Intervention phases consisting of confederate initiations increased the positive social behavior of all subjects involved. In addition, these positive social behaviors generalized to a classroom free-play period for two of the three subjects. Several other studies have suggested that a combination of priming peers, priming the subject, and providing teacher reinforcement can increase rates of social interaction in children with initially low rates (Baer & Wolf, 1970; Hops, Walker, & Greenwood, 1979; Walker & Hops, 1973). Kirby and Toler (1970) increased one 5-year-old's rate of interaction with other children by having the child pass out candy to his classmates. Through this procedure, social interaction was stimulated and was reinforced by positive reactions of peers to the target child.

Baer and Wolf (1970) have suggested that procedures such as teacher attention and priming are effective because they facilitate "entry into the natural community of reinforcement" provided by the preschool peer group. The authors state:

> A preschool is intrinsically a community of reinforcement contingencies which will shape and maintain an ever increasing repertoire of social behavior and will put that behavior under the control of peers. Thereby, the preschool creates generality of behavioral development, in that a child's peers will go with him into new environments and into the future. Thus, a preschool is a behavioral trap, the entry response to which is relatively simple, the behavioral consequences of which are relatively massive and general. (p. 324)

This notion provides a general framework for the goals of intervention with socially isolated children. Since the peer group itself contributes to social development in unique ways, the ultimate goal of therapeutic intervention should be to facilitate entry into the peer group. In some cases (as above) the child may possess the requisite skills and may only need assistance in having the opportunity to engage in them. In other cases the skills may need to be taught. It may be, however, that peers are the best teachers and the opportunity to interact positively with peers, as in the Strain (1977) study, can be instructive.

Providing Experiences with Peers

Through an examination of the effects of control groups engaging in unstructured play with peers, it appears that there is little direct evidence that socially isolated children will benefit from *unstructured* opportunities to interact with peers. Gains relative to treatment groups involving coached interaction are minimal (Jakibchuk & Smergilio, 1976; Keller & Carlson, 1974; Ladd, 1979; Oden & Asher, 1977). In contrast, providing the target child with the opportunity to play in pairs with *younger* children (with no structured instruction) has been found to increase the sociability of withdrawn preschoolers (Furman, Rahe, & Hartup, 1979). Based on the research documenting the rehabilitation of socially isolated monkeys through exposure to younger monkeys (Suomi & Harlow, 1972; see also Harlow & Mears, 1979), this study documented that play sessions in pairs with younger children increased the social behaviors of the older, withdrawn children more than did sessions with same-age pairs. Furman *et al.* (1979) suggest that the effectiveness of such a treatment may be due to a "leadership deficit" in the isolated children. The play sessions provide opportunities to be socially assertive; furthermore, such assertive behaviors are met with a higher probability of success when playing with a less mature child than with same-age children, such as those in the classroom.

Further support for these findings is found in the careful observational descriptions provided by Scarlett (1980) of the behaviors of nursery-school isolates. These isolates were significantly less likely than nonisolates to attempt to structure or influence the behavior of peers, even when engaged in interaction with them, supporting a "leadership deficit" hypothesis. Scarlett (1980) also found that isolates were more likely to interact with peers when in smaller and more structured groups of children.

Hops *et al.*, (1979) have included a "Joint Task" activity as one part of a multiple-component program for remediating social withdrawal in educational settings. Each target subject was assigned on a daily basis to work with a peer on a specific school-related task that required alternate verbal interaction (e.g., question-asking and responding). Hops *et al.*

suggested that this procedure is quite effective in increasing rates of interaction. Lilly (1971) provided poorly accepted elementary school children with the opportunity to work in small groups with popular peers over a period of five weeks. These small groups work on developing a magic show and making a film of it to be shown to the whole class. Treatment produced gains in acceptance for experimental subjects; however, these gains were not retained at six-week follow-up. Asher, Oden, and Gottman (1977) cited an example of an isolated child who seemed to gain a friend after she was given the opportunity to plan a puppet show with two peers and present it to the class. They suggested that being an "expert" at something valued by the peer group may enhance a child's acceptance.

Opportunities to interact with peers are essential in remediating deficits in social skills, but the exact nature of each opportunity seems important. It both seems reasonable and is consistent with the data to suggest that opportunities for interaction, being so vital to the therapeutic process, not be left to chance. Structured opportunities in which programmed experiences increase the likelihood of the intended outcome are the mandate.

Coaching Social Behaviors

One way to assure the existence of structure and insure the quality of interactions of children in groups is through the active participation of a teacher or therapist. Providing explicit instructions about strategies for social interaction, as well as other forms of coaching, have been employed in the treatment of socially deficient youngsters.

Instructions with rationale, demonstration, and practice with feedback were used to train four junior-high-school girls deficient in conversational skills (Minkin, Braukmann, Minkin, Timbers, Timbers, Fixsen, Phillips, & Wolf, 1976). The targeted behaviors were asking conversational questions and giving positive conversational feedback; these skills had previously been identified as reliable components of conversational skill. This coaching technique was effective in increasing the rates of the target behaviors. In addition, the subjects' conversational abilities after training were rated by adult judges as improved to a level higher than those of their junior-high-school peers. Although this study does suggest a method for improving conversational skills, it provides no indication of whether improvement in conversational skills enhanced the adjustment or peer acceptance of these "pre-delinquent" girls.

A "social-skills treatment package" consisting of instructions, feedback, behavior rehearsal, and modeling was applied to targeted social behaviors of four "unassertive" elementary-school children (Bornstein, Bellack, & Hersen, 1977). In a multiple-baseline design, the components of the package were applied sequentially to target behaviors such as increased eye contact, loudness of speech, and number of requests. Substantial increases in the targeted behaviors were reported for all four children; furthermore, independent global ratings of overall assertiveness gradually increased during training, with a sizable increase when treatment was directed toward increasing the number of requests.

In several studies employing groups of subjects, children low in social acceptance have been coached in the use and practice of specific social skills. For example, Oden and Asher (1977) selected third- and fourth-grade children who were infrequently chosen by their peers as companions to "play with" or "work with." The coaching intervention consisted of instructions from adults in social concepts, a game-playing session with peer partners to practice these concepts, and a postplay review with the coach. In a second condition (peer-pairing), subjects played the same games with peer partners but without coaching. In the control condition children played solitary games. Results indicated that the coached children improved on the "play with" sociometric measure, while the other groups remained unchanged. Unfortunately, the social concepts taught (participation, cooperation, communication, validation, support) were not measured directly, and thus it is difficult to discern whether target children were initially deficient in these areas. However, the authors have shown that specific instructions in social concepts are more effective at enhancing peer acceptance than is the opportunity for peer interaction alone.

Utilizing third-graders low in peer acceptance, Ladd (1979) embellished the procedure used by Oden and Asher (1977) through the addition of rehearsal and self-evaluation components of the coaching process. Three verbal social skills were selected for intervention and directly measured: asking questions of peers, leading peers (i.e., offering useful suggestions), and offering supportive statements. Treatment was effective in increasing question-asking and leading but not supportive statements, which were near zero at baseline and remained so. This finding suggests that there may be some social behaviors that are not appropriate for training at certain ages. Perhaps supportive verbal statements are not a part of the normal social repertoire of third-grade children. Additional measures indicated that trained children decreased in amounts of nonsocial behavior and received greater peer acceptance.

In a multiple-component treatment package (Hops *et al.*, 1979), coaching procedures were used to instruct low-interacting children in three types of social behavior: initiating interactions, responding to the initiations of peers, and maintaining the interactions ("keeping it going"). A second component of the program attempted to facilitate peer-group acceptance through a token reinforcement program with a group back-up reinforcer. A peer-pairing procedure in the classroom provided an opportunity for the practice of social skills. A fourth component involved training target children to self-report on their social behaviors. Although a full investigation of the treatment package is still being conducted, gains in social behavior have been demonstrated for a number of withdrawn children.

A study by Barton (1979) suggested the effective components of a program designed to facilitate sharing among preschoolers during cooperative play. A multiple-baseline design indicated that while instructions and modeling were not sufficient to enhance sharing, the added opportunity for rehearsal and practice of relevant skills resulted in increased sharing. This increase was further facilitated by in-session prompts and praise.

Several of the researchers engaged in the evaluation of coaching procedures have amended their interventions with interesting techniques. Hops *et al.* (1979) introduced a self-report procedure wherein the child and a chosen peer reported on social behaviors that had occurred during recess. Ladd (1979) also made an important addition to his treatment package by having children self-evaluate the effects on peers of newly learned social behaviors. This self-evaluation was thought to enable the children to modify their social behaviors in accordance with the responses of peers and the social norms of the particular environment.

The studies considered in this section suggest that social-skills coaching has some impact on increasing peer acceptance of third- and fourth-grade children. Treatment packages are typically quite complex (involving multiple-intervention components), making it difficult to determine the relative importance of the various phases of the coaching process. The need for component analyses notwithstanding, these studies suggest that a process consisting of instructions, practice with peers, feedback, and self-evaluation can be effective in teaching social behaviors.

Symbolic Modeling

Symbolic modeling, as a technique for facilitating social interaction in nursery-school children manifesting low rates of such interaction, has received substantial research attention. In an early study, O'Connor (1969) developed a film depicting a nonparticipating child joining in a series of progressively more active social interactions, with resulting reinforcing consequences. A narrative sound track described the social interactions being presented and their outcomes. Such modeling procedures are hypothesized to be effective by transmitting new social skills and extinguishing social fears and avoidance. After viewing the film, isolated preschool children have been found to increase their rates of social interaction to a level commensurate with that of nonisolates (Evers & Schwarz, 1973; O'Connor, 1969, 1972), while those viewing a control film about animals showed no change in social interaction rates. It should also be noted that the effects of the modeling film were not substantially enhanced by the addition of adult social reinforcement (Evers & Schwarz, 1973; O'Connor, 1972). More recently, however, Gottman (1977a) attempted to replicate these findings, while improving on some methodological weaknesses, and found no evidence for the effectiveness of O'Connor's (1969) symbolic modeling film when compared with a similar control film.

Modeling was combined with coaching, behavioral rehearsal, and feedback in a procedure designed to facilitate the social skills of low-acceptance elementary-school children (LaGreca & Santogrossi, 1980). On the basis of relevant literature, eight social-skill areas were selected for intervention (e.g., smiling, conversing). In addition, children received training in small groups rather than individually, which provided a "ready-made environment" in which to practice these skills and receive peer feedback. At the end of each weekly group session, children were given homework assignments that encouraged them to try out their new skills (e.g., "Greet a classmate at least once a day for the next week."). Results suggested that this training procedure was effective in improving the targeted social skills of these children (as assessed by structured interview, role-playing situations, and observations) but had no effect on sociometric ratings of acceptance.

Several authors (Evers & Schwarz, 1973; O'Connor, 1969) reported individual-subject data that indicate considerable variability in children's responses to the modeling film, with some subjects showing large gains and others demonstrating none. Evers-Pasquale and Sherman (1975) proposed that such differential responsiveness may be due to individual differences in the reward value placed on peer contact. They further hypothesized that the effect of a modeling film may be to induce change in a child's expectancy of positive reinforcement from peer interaction. If so, after viewing the film, children who place a high value on peer contact will be more likely to interact with peers than those isolates who are less peer-oriented. By developing a test to measure the reward value of peers, these authors were able to classify preschool children as peer-oriented or non-peer-oriented. After viewing the modeling film, peer-oriented subjects increased their rates of social interaction significantly more than did non-peer-oriented subjects. These results were replicated in a second study (Evers-Pasquale, 1978).

Variations in the characteristics of modeling films have also received research attention. Jakibchuk and Smergilio (1976) examined the effects of a self-speech sound track accompanying modeled social interactions. The 22 nursery-school-aged isolates were randomly assigned to one of four conditions. Two groups watched a series of videotapes depicting children displaying progressive change from solitary play to active participation with peers. The self-speech group watched these videotapes with a first-person description of the model's activities (e.g., "I would like to play with those children. But I'm afraid. . . . This is hard. But I'll try"). The narrative group watched the same videotapes accompanied by a conventional third-person narrative. Results demonstrated that children who heard the self-speech sound track increased to a level commensurate with nonisolates on all three dependent measures. Gains made by those hearing the third-person narrative were substantially less than those of the self-speech group and had disappeared at follow-up. Although the superiority of the self-speech group over the narrative group was expected, the lack of effectiveness of the third-person narrative film is inconsistent with other studies using these methods (e.g., Keller & Carlson, 1974; O'Connor, 1969, 1972). The authors themselves expressed surprise at the finding, but made a very reasonable suggestion—it might be influenced by the fact that a child's voice provided the third-person narrative in this study in contrast to the adult voice typically used.

Keller and Carlson (1974) developed four films that modeled one of the following socially reinforcing behaviors: initiation, smiling, token-giving, and physical contact signifying affection. The modeling procedure, produced increases in these socially reinforcing behaviors. However, the study also showed that the socially isolated preschoolers had access to these behaviors before treatment but simply emitted them at a lower rate than did nonisolates. Rather than teaching new social skills, symbolic modeling procedures seem to have the effect of disinhibiting low-frequency behaviors. Results of a number of training studies suggest, then, that symbolic modeling may be most judiciously employed when target children possess requisite skills yet exhibit deficits in their application and performance.

When evaluating the efficacy of symbolic modeling films, it is important to remember that the content of the film (i.e., the behaviors targeted for modeling) is being evaluated along with the specific technique of modeling; that is, a modeling film may show no effect, not because modeling *per se* is ineffective, but because the behaviors demonstrated are not germane to the deficits of the children. Similarly, a film such as O'Connor's (1969, 1972) may work, in part, because it focuses on the behaviors of approaching and joining in social interaction—behaviors that may be the central deficit in children with low interaction rates.

A recent study by Gresham and Nagle (1980) offered some support for the notion that the content of a particular intervention may contribute as much to its effectiveness as does the specific technique used to teach that content. In this study, the same set of target social skills was trained across groups of low-acceptance third- and fourth-grade children. However, the relative efficacy of modeling and coaching were compared as procedures for teaching those skills. In general, the two procedures were found to be equally effective in enhancing sociometric status and observed social behaviors. A combined modeling-coaching procedure produced effects similar to those of either procedure alone. There was some suggestive evidence, however, that coaching was more effective in reducing negative peer interaction, while modeling produced a greater impact by increasing positive peer interaction.

Results of these studies suggest that perhaps the clinician's choice between modeling or coaching procedure should depend on the pragmatic consideration of the target behaviors to be taught. Coaching, which is economically more feasible and practical in the clinician's office, may work well for behaviors such as smiling, question-asking, etc. It is more difficult for a clinician to demonstrate behaviors such as initiating interaction and joining in the activities of a group of children. Such behaviors, which are best demonstrated *by other children* and require groups of children interacting in natural situations, might be most effectively taught through modeling films.

Social Cognitive Interventions

A recent review of social cognitive problem-solving interventions with children (Urbain & Kendall, 1980) concluded that, while there are areas requiring more methodologically sound investigations, some encouraging results have been reported. The review covered training studies of interpersonal problem-solving, family problem-solving, verbally mediated self-control applied to social behavior, and social perspective-taking. While it was not the intent of that review to consider treatment effects for isolated or withdrawn children, several of the studies offer information concerning such children, and a more delimited consideration of these studies at this time seems warranted.

First, it is important to recognize that among developmental psychologists there has recently been a growing research effort devoted to understanding children's conceptions of their social world. The term "social cognition" refers to "the child's intuitive or logical representation of others, that is, how he [or she] characterizes others and makes inferences about their covert, inner psychological experiences" (Shantz, 1975, p. 1). Most of the research thus far has been concerned with acquiring a more complete picture of the child's cognitive development and with ascertaining how social cognitive abilities develop (see Shantz, 1975, for a review). Presumably, the way in which children think about others and about their social world influences their social behavior, and socially isolated children might be considered deficient in these cognitive skills.

Caution must be exercised, however, when considering the relevant literature on social cognitive interventions. First, a large majority of studies are conducted with samples of normal children. Treatments that enhance the skills of a "representative" sample of children are heuristically valuable, but direct application in clinical populations requires some extrapolation. Second, in those studies that include children with problems of adjustment, the identified problems were often those of the "externalizing" (acting-out, externalization-of-conflict) variety, as opposed to the "internalizing" (internalization-of-conflict) variety, which would include disorders associated with social withdrawal, isolation, anxiety, and depression. Although the results of the social cognitive intervention literature do not bear directly on the problem of social isolation, the suggested treatment methods have potential relevance to interventions with socially isolated children.

Evidence exists to suggest that socially maladjusted children may be deficient in social cognitive abilities. Chandler (1973) found a group of delinquent boys to be less skilled at taking the perspectives of another than were nondelinquents. Chandler, Greenspan, and Barenboim (1974) reported evidence of "persistent and age-inappropriate egocentric thinking" in a group of emotionally disturbed institutionalized children. That is, the disturbed children displayed deficits in their ability to view the world from outside their own point of view. Another study found that a group of clinic children manifesting primary interpersonal problems did more poorly than normal controls on tasks assessing reasoning about interpersonal relations and the resolution of interpersonal problems (Selman, Jaquette, & Lavin, 1977). In a series of investigations (Spivack & Shure, 1974; Spivack, Platt, & Shure, 1976), impulsive and inhibited children were found to differ from well-adjusted children in social problem-solving skills such as the ability to generate alternative solutions to social problems. In another investigation, popular third-

and fourth-grade children were found to be more adept than unpopular children on several of a battery of social cognitive measures (Gottman *et al.*, 1975).

Many of the social cognitive intervention efforts have been directed towards training children to improve role-taking skills. Role-taking, or perspective-taking, is typically considered to be the ability to see things from another's point of view when that point of view differs from one's own. Studies in this area have used several kinds of perspective-taking measures and examined several types of perspective-taking abilities: measures of visual-spatial role-taking (what does the other person see?), measures of communicative or cognitive role-taking (what is the other person thinking?), and affective role-taking (what is the other person feeling?) (Ford, 1979; Shantz, 1975; Urbain & Kendall, 1980). These tasks generally require the child to surpress his or her own point of view in order to describe another's (see also Kendall, Pellegrini, & Urbain, 1981).

Chandler (1973) used a task of role-taking requiring a child to tell a story depicted in a cartoon sequence and then tell the story again from the perspective of a bystander who has no knowledge of events depicted in a subset of the cartoons. Successful cognitive role-taking occurs when the child is able to restrict the privileged information from the perspective of the bystander. Delinquent boys (aged 11–13), low on role-taking performance, were enrolled in a training program involving the making of video films. Subjects developed skits about real-life problems and had the opportunity to enact each of the roles in different versions of the film. Reviewing the films provided feedback and a format for discussion of the social situations. Treatment subjects improved on the post-test measure of role-taking, and an 18-month follow-up showed a trend in the reduction of delinquent offenses for the treatment group.

A second study (Chandler *et al.*, 1974) employed a similar training program and the same measure of role-taking with institutionalized emotionally disturbed children who ranged in age from 8 to 15 years. In addition, a measure of referential communication was employed. Widely studied in cognitive development, referential communication tasks assess the child's ability to describe the relevant features of an object in such a way that a listener can select this object from a set of similar objects. The developmental literature on training referential communication skills has focused largely on the role of social cognitive conflict and modeling in enhancing referential communication performance (e.g., Ironsmith & Whitehurst, 1978; Lefebvre-Pinard & Reid, 1980; Shantz & Wilson, 1972). Most of these are laboratory studies and seem largely concerned with training the cognitive abilities related to encoding and discriminating task stimuli (Ford, 1979). Chandler *et al.* (1974), however, designed a series of games focused on enhancing children's ability to communicate information to each other and to assess the adequacy of their communications.

Thus, the study by Chandler *et al.* (1974) provides a comparison of role-taking training and referential communication training for emotionally disturbed youngsters. Both training groups were found to improve on measures of role-taking, while only the referential communication training produced improvement on a task of communication accuracy. The authors suggested that a particular hierarchiacal relation may exist between these two abilities, making role-taking necessary but not sufficient for referential communication accuracy.

Ianotti (1978) used a number of outcome measures to assess the effects of role-taking training on 6- and 9-year-old boys. The training procedure involved groups of five children assigned to play roles in stories. Children acted out solutions to story dilemmas; discussions centered on taking a perspective different from the child's own as well as on the emotional and cognitive aspects of that role in relation to the roles of other children in the group. Training increased performance on a role-taking task as well as a measure of altruism (donation of candy to a needy child). Measures of empathy and the use of aggressive solutions to interpersonal conflict were not affected by training.

Group sessions in which children are actively involved in role-playing social situations were used with eighth-graders in a study by Marsh, Serafica, and Barenboim (1980). Subjects were trained to integrate simultaneously the different perspectives of characters in a situation. Subjects then switched roles, and discussions centered on the different perspectives of the various story characters as well as the differences among interpretations of the same role. Training produced increases on a measure of the ability to analyze interpersonal problems. Other measures of social problem-solving and perspective-taking were not affected.

A training procedure designed according to a developmental model of perspective-taking produced increases on measures of perspective-taking for fourth- and fifth-graders who were initially below age norms for such abilities (Silvern, Waterman, Sobesky, & Ryan, 1979). Training involved viewing videotapes of interpersonal problems; in each tape, one character commits an error in perspective-taking and something goes "wrong" as a result. The developmental model was evident in that each successive problem required solution at a higher developmental level of perspective-taking. Subjects identify the error, discuss the consequences of such an error, and then reenact their own version of the situation. In addition to increased role-taking skills, treatment produced an increase on two items of a self-concept scale and a decrease on a scale of defensiveness. A control group consisting of unstructured peer-group interaction produced a similar decrease in defensiveness but no change on other measures.

The above three studies (Ianotti, 1978; Marsh *et al.*, 1980; Silvern *et al.*, 1979) demonstrate that age-appropriate training incorporating role-playing and discussion can facilitate performance on measures of social cognition. However, the generalization of such training to children's social behavior or adjustment, and to socially isolated children in particular, has not yet been demonstrated.

Several studies have incorporated both role-taking training and direct modification of social behavior into complex treatment packages. Gottman, Gonso, and Schuler (1976) chose target behaviors that had been previously documented to be deficient in unpopular children (Gottman *et al.*, 1975). These skills consisted of initiation of interaction, knowledge of ways of making friends, the distribution of positive reinforcement, and referential communication. Two isolated third-graders received social-skills training utilizing the combined techniques of a modeling film, explicit instruction, coaching, and practice with peers. As a control, two isolated children spent an equal amount of time with an adult but received no training. Treatment was effective in improving peer acceptance for the two experimental subjects; however, no change in the frequency of social interaction was noted. Although this study can be regarded only as a pilot project, it suggests the potential utility of a multifaceted treatment and the merit of focusing on the documented deficiencies of target children.

A series of training programs focusing on teaching the specific cognitive skills thought to be related to solving interpersonal problems have been reported (Spivack & Shure, 1974; Spivack *et al.*, 1976). These authors stated that their program does not focus on the content of thought, but rather on teaching children how to formulate plans and generate options in social problem solving. The ability to generate multiple solutions (alternative-solution thinking), to reason about possible consequences of a particular solution (consequential thinking), and to develop a logical plan to achieve a particular social goal (means–end thinking) are considered central in this intervention effort.

Although the research details are reported in a somewhat sketchy manner, these authors suggest that there is a direct link between these social problem-solving skills and behavior. For example, preschool children rated by their teachers as impulsive were significantly more deficient in the ability to generate alternative solutions than were their well-adjusted peers. More important for our present purposes, children classified as *inhibited* based on teacher ratings alone were found to be even more deficient. Training was reported to have had desirable effects on interpersonal cognitive problem-solving (Spivack & Shure, 1974), such as increased alternative-thinking and consequential thinking skills. The authors point out that both of these effects, but for different reasons, were particularly noteworthy among children initially identified as inhibited. The effects of training on the behavioral adjustment of the initially inhibited children indicated that 75% were rated as adjusted after treatment. Analysis of a separate measure of children's empathic interest and willingness to help others indicated that there was a significant increase in ratings of this behavior among the initially inhibited children. Unfortunately, data on the reliability of these measurements were not provided. Whereas the problem of post-treatment teacher ratings having been provided by nonblind participants is of much concern, follow-up ratings were provided by teachers who were blind to the children's previous experiences. Follow-up data indicated that the improvement was maintained over the period of several months.

A COGNITIVE BEHAVIORAL INTEGRATION

Fundamental to a cognitive behavioral intervention is the assessment of both the cognitive and behavioral factors related to the psychological problem under investigation (Kendall, 1981a). As we have seen, a frequency count of the amount of social interaction is not itself a sufficient criterion for the determination of social isolation. Although children's isolated and withdrawn patterns of behavior may result from a lack of social skills in their behavioral repertoires, such patterns may also result from a deficit in performance. Performance deficits are exemplified by children who have social skills but who fail to perform the behaviors in question. Why does a skilled child inhibit social interaction? What might be the nature of the child's internal evaluation of his or her social world that maintains such a lack of interaction? A careful examination of the manner in which the child cognitively processes social situations would facilitate appropriate decisions about therapeutic interventions. The first integration that is required, therefore, is in the employment of assessment procedures that evaluate both the cognitive and behavioral aspects of a child's performance (see also Kendall *et al.*, 1981).

The cognitive and behavioral approaches also can be integrated in the choice of intervention methods. Both the behavioral techniques and the social cognitive strategies have much to offer the mental health professional dealing with socially isolated children. The judicious utilization of cognitive *and* behavioral methods will maximize treatment efficacy.

The evidence reviewed herein has provided support for the utility of several behavioral strategies. For instance, the potency of adult social reinforcement, the value inherent in structured peer interactions, and the merits of behavioral coaching are fairly clear-cut. Add to this the efficacy of symbolic modeling as a procedure for behavioral disinhibition, and it is apparent that behavioral procedures cannot be ignored.

However, cognitive behavioral psychologists do not assume that these procedures directly alter children's behavior in a fashion that is independent of how each child thinks about events and event outcomes. Rather, the potency of the behavioral procedures is said to be mediated by the child's cognitive processing. An adult may provide social praise, but the child's cognitive processing of that experience may render the praise *non*rewarding. Whether or not the nonrewarding quality of praise for a particular child resulted from some excessive rewarding by an adult is not clear, but what remains clear, nevertheless, is that adult social praise can be nonrewarding. It is likely that the manner in which children process external contingencies determines, in part, the potency of these contingencies.

Behavioral treatment procedures can be substantially enhanced by addressing the cognitive processing associated with the behaviors being taught. A prime example emerges from the modeling literature. Modeling has been successfully employed to produce such diverse therapeutic and educational outcomes as the elimination of behavioral deficits, the reduction of inhibitions, and the facilitation of social behavior (Bandura, 1971a; Rosenthal & Bandura, 1978). An important differentiation concerns whether the model displayed "coping" or "mastery" behavior. A mastery model demonstrates ideal behavior; in the case of social withdrawal, successful interaction with other children would be portrayed. In contrast, a coping model initially demonstrates apprehension, but subsequently overcomes the deficit and performs effectively. For our purposes, the coping model would first appear shy, then approach other children, balk, approach them again, and finally interact with them. A number of studies have supported the superior efficacy of coping over mastery models (e.g., Kazdin, 1974; Meichenbaum, 1971a; Sarason, 1975). More importantly, Meichenbaum (1971a) has shown that models who provide a narrative of their self-verbalizations are superior to nonverbalizing models, the most effective modeling strategy being the coping model who verbalizes (e.g., "I can handle this") while demonstrating coping behaviors. Thus, behavioral modeling is enhanced by the inclusion of cognitive modeling.

The importance of considering the client's cognitive processing when working with socially isolated children can be illustrated through the following example. A group of children are on the playground, and the majority are involved in one of several small-group activities. For instance, five children are playing with a soccer ball, and four others are climbing on a tire-tree. The target child, physically capable but socially avoidant, is isolated. He appears to glance at, but not actively watch, the soccer players. An aide takes an interest in the child and suggests playing with them. "Come on, let's play too," says the aide while joining the game with a kick. The child turns away, not joining in the game and no longer paying attention to the activity.

The following example, in contrast, takes the child's cognitive processing into account. This aide also takes an interest in the child, walks over and stands next to him and watches the soccer players. The aide, thinking out loud, says, "Gee, they're really running around. Is it okay to do that?" (*Pause*) "Oh, this is recess, I forgot, I guess it's okay to run around, but what if they break something?" (*Pause*) "I guess that's not very likely, they play here all the time and haven't broken anything yet." (*Pause*) "Maybe I'll play too." (*Pause*) "No, they're better players than I am." (*Pause*) "But look there, that wasn't such a good kick, I could do that. I could just run around even if I don't kick it much at all. Maybe I will play for a few minutes."

In the first scenario the child was exposed to (yet another) someone who could easily join in. It's entirely possible that the child cognitively discounts such a model: "But that's easy for you to do" or "Yeah, but you know how to kick and I don't." It is this individual interpretation of the event that mediates the potential effectiveness of the modeling. By directly attending to cognitive processing factors, the second aide thinks through the process in a manner consistent with how the isolated child might interpret the situation. The model in the second case has produced a greater likelihood of the child's participating.

The recognition of the importance of an individual's cognitive processing of events raises a key question: What type of processing is being referred to? While cognitive processing plays a role in therapy across developmental levels, the type of cognitive processing can be seen to differ for adult and child clients. Cognitive behavioral interventions with children are *not* merely the simplification of the cognitive approaches employed for adults. It has been argued (Kendall, 1981b) that the nature of the cognitive problem associated with adult disorders can be classified as cognitive error. Beck, Rush, Shaw, and Emery (1979), Ellis (1962), Goldfried (1979), Mahoney (1977), and Meichenbaum (1977) (see also Kendall & Hollon, 1979) typically invoke illogical interpretations of the environment, irrational beliefs about personal performance abilities, inaccurate perceptions of everyday demands, and all-or-none categorical thinking of explanations of adult cognitive processing problems—all are cognitive *errors*. In contrast, the cognitive processing problems related to childhood disorders are typically cognitive *absences*. Often, the child fails to engage in the active information-processing activities of a problem-solver and fails to initiate the reflective thinking that can govern behavior. The central role of cognitive absences in problems of childhood is evident in acting-out, conduct disorders, and attentional and hyperactive problems. These behavior problems are all associated with an absence of self-control.

The likelihood that cognitive *errors* also play a part in problems of childhood increases when one considers the socially isolated and withdrawn child. Isolated behavior patterns may in some cases correspond to extensive self-criticism, inaccurate anticipation of rejection, and elaborate internal standards for success. Children lacking in perspective-taking skills may not be able to put themselves in another child's position and may therefore not recognize his or her performance as less than perfect. Here, as in the cognitive behavioral interventions for adults, the therapist must pay attention to the removal of dysfunctional cognitive processing. Thus, a cognitive behavioral treatment for socially isolated children would involve rewards, modeling, coaching, peer participation, and role-playing, as well as direct attention to the child's manner of cognitive processing.

Suggestions for Intervention Strategies

The therapeutic strategies used in both behavioral and social cognitive interventions are readily integrated for socially isolated children. The making, viewing, and reviewing of videotapes or films, common among studies of perspective-taking training, offer an ideal context for opportunities for role-switching and behavioral rehearsal. For instance, the task of the group could be to develop a skit related to making new friends. A new kid moves into the neighborhood and wants to make new friends. He or she ends up with friends. How did this happen? Such a task is highly desirable in this case because it is not only consistent with the needs of the socially isolated child, but also likely to be realistic for all children who may be involved in the training (e.g., nontarget peers). Moreover, it is the type of task used in interpersonal cognitive problem-solving assessment (means–end problem-solving; Shure & Spivack, 1972).

The treatment of socially isolated children can also incorporate self-instructional procedures. Although limited, this direction has already attracted some researchers (Gottman, Gonso, & Schuler, 1976; Jakibchuk & Smergilio, 1976). The utility of self-instructional procedures on social/interpersonal problem-solving tasks when modifying other forms of social behavior (e.g., lack of self-control; Kendall & Wilcox, 1980) also suggests its application for social isolates. It is possible that withdrawn children would benefit by learning to make a realistic and careful scrutiny of social situations and that use of the steps of self-instruction to think through a problem (e.g., problem identification, problem approach, generating alternatives) would facilitate their reaching a decision to participate. As noted earlier, socially withdrawn youngsters may be fraught with negative self-statements based on cognitive errors that inhibit them from participating in social events. Training in action-oriented self-statements may be desirable. For instance, "Should I play? No, I can't. Why not, I can give it a try. It won't kill me to try." The identification and subsequent removal of self-statements that interfere with social performance may be vital to the maintenance of behavior change. The focus here would be on the disconfirming of the isolates' negative thinking for those children exhibiting a performance deficit.

Groups can be very effectively utilized with this population. The nature of the deficit in socially isolated children concerns social (peer) interactions and, logically, the group provides an ideal context for its remedy. Trained peers who can stimulate interactions, adult leaders who can provide social reward, and the availability of multiple models who can demonstrate interactions are all components of small groups. Since coping models are desired, and since some of the literature points to the merits of mixed-age interactions, younger children who are also learning to interact would be valuable group members. Groups are advisable for perspective-taking experiences, role-play rehearsals, and basic opportunities to make friends.

A final recommendation concerns situational and conceptual specificity. Children, perhaps even more readily than adults, can learn to develop behavioral skills. Yet the entire behavior pattern being developed does not occur in a vacuum. The behaviors are learned in relation to specific situations, specific social situations in the case of isolated youngsters. The role of a particular peer group in fostering a given child's isolation may, in some cases, not lie with the child but rather with the peer group itself. Obvious examples exist in the cases of children singled out as "different" because of race, culture, handicap, or physical illness. Because little is known about the structure and norms of children's peer groups, however, other, not-so-obvious factors may cause a child's exclusion from the peer group and thus the appearance of being a social isolate. The treatment of isolated children would profit immensely from a recognition of the situational specificity of the behavioral deficits. More directly, interventions must include as an initial step the careful delineation of the situations in which the child is socially isolated. These situations, first and foremost, serve as the context of training.

Conceptual specificity parallels situational specificity. The concepts taught to children should be specific to each child's deficit and should be limited to one at a time. It would not be desirable to overwhelm any child with new concepts and new required behaviors, and it is necessary to exercise a greater degree of caution in regard to isolated children. Behavioral concepts must be presented gradually, unstressfully, and in a "coping" perspective. Only after success in specific situations and with specific concepts can the therapist build generalizable social skills.

Some of the literature on social-skills training in adults offers complementary advice. The integration of cognitive and behavioral procedures used with shy male college students, for example, makes use of peer-assisted role-playing, reflective thinking, rehearsal, and modification of internal thinking processes, and does so with an eye on specificity. Twentyman and McFall (1975) provide an excellent model. While their target problem (shyness) and target sample (college students) may be criticized as less than clinically relevant, the procedures of training can be praised. In order to preserve their contribution, their description of some of their social skills training procedures is reproduced below.

> The first treatment session concentrated on telephone skills. Subjects received training in five situations. The training sequence for each situation was as follows: (a) The subject heard a situation described and rehearsed responding covertly; (b) the tape-recorded responses of two "competent" male models in the same situation were presented; (c) coaching instructions were presented, with special attention given to the effective aspects of the models' responses; (d) the subject was instructed to think back to his response and consider how he might improve it; (e) the situation was presented again, and the subject rehearsed responding aloud; (f) a female assistant role played the interaction "live" with the subject over the intercom; and (g) the subject was given a chance to repeat the situation if he was not pleased with his response. In general, this training procedure provided subjects with modeling, coaching, and response rehearsal in an environment that minimized disruptive effects of overarousal; it also allowed each subject to proceed through training at his own pace. At the end of the first training session, the subject was given the name and telephone number of a female assistant with whom he had not interacted during the training session, and was instructed to phone her at a specific time and role play asking for a date.
>
> The training procedure in the second session was essentially the same as in the first session. This session, however, focused on social situations in which the subject would normally interact face-to-face with a woman. A

female assistant again role-played the face-to-face situations with the subject over the intercom. Presumably, the use of the intercom gradually prepared the subjects for the more difficult task of actual face-to-face interactions. At the end of the session subjects were again given a similar homework assignment.

In the first segment of the third training session, the telephone and face-to-face situations were reviewed. Then each subject was asked to describe two difficult social situations in which he would like to learn to respond more competently, and a slightly modified form of training was given for these: First, a female assistant read the situation, and the subject was given a chance to respond covertly, next, the subject was instructed to think about how he might improve his response, and then the female experimenter entered the subject's room and began playing the situation with him. Again, the subject was given the option of repeating a situation if he wished. (Twentyman & McFall, 1975, pp. 386–387)

Suffice it to say that an age-appropriate but equally systematic, approach integrating cognitive and behavioral training strategies is the current treatment of choice for socially isolated children.

Some General Considerations

The treatment strategies for socially isolated children that have been endorsed in this chapter are essentially guided, performance-based experiences with peers, with therapist attention directed toward each child's cognitive processing of events. Admittedly, this is a complex intervention. We recognize that the intervention strategies proposed herein are perhaps most accurately described as a treatment package. There are, indeed, a coordinated conglomerate of principles and procedures being suggested. At the present juncture, therefore, studies are needed to evaluate the effectiveness of such a treatment package. The treatment should be provided with all its components and experimentally contrasted with attention and test–retest controls. If and when such evidence demonstrates treatment efficacy, then dismantling studies or components analyses can be conducted to examine the aspects of the "package" most responsible for demonstrated successes (see also Kazdin & Wilson, 1978).

The application of self-instructional training to socially isolated children will contribute to advances along theoretical lines. To date, self-instructions have been posited as important in the control of impulsive behaviors (Kendall, 1977; Meichenbaum, 1977) and in this instance have been said to function in an inhibitory capacity, with the insertion of self-directed thought between stimulus and response resulting in a reduction of thoughless behavior. Self-instructional procedures thereby increase inhibitory control. To the extent that self-instruction is effective in decreasing social withdrawal, it can be said to function in a disinhibitory manner. Although direct tests are required of the types of effect capable of being produced through self-instruction training, evidence of the utility of such training with a different type of behavior problem will contribute to a theoretical analysis of the function of self-referent speech.

Developmental level (or simply age) is an important consideration that is directly implicated in the proper execution of the training procedures. First, the specific behaviors that are considered "socially skilled" differ at different levels of development. Specific behaviors that are successful in social interactions at age 5 are markedly different from those that are desirable at age 8. Moreover, not all adults respond to specific behavior from younger and older children in an identical manner. Therefore, not only is the importance of developmental level illustrated, but also the limits of training only specific skills should be emphasized. The inclusion of cognitive strategies in child psychotherapy is vital, but one must again recognize and take into consideration the developmental level of target children. Before age 5 or 6, for instance, self-instructions may not be desirable additions to treatment. A child before this age may not be at the developmental level when an analysis of such internal self-referent speech is beneficial. As a result, younger children should be exposed to heavier doses of peer-initiated interactions, structured play opportunities, adult social praise, and coping models. Although there is a paucity of data addressing social isolation during adolescence, the increased influence of the peer group during this developmental period is likely to render individuals especially vulnerable to social rejection. Furthermore, self-statements are likely to become more elaborated and to exercise greater influence on adolescents than on younger children. A clear call for research on the treatment of social isolation in adolescence is in order.

Last, we turn full circle and return to the issue of assessment. Two general points require consideration: (a) assessment guiding treatment and (b) levels of assessment in treatment-outcome evaluation.

The distinction that seems to be most promising for treatment is that distinguishing performance deficits from repertoire deficits. Performance deficits refer to children who have difficulty behaving in social contexts but, on assessment, evidence social skills. This type of isolation may be precipitated by avoidance (fear of aversive consequences) and/or a lack of expectancy of positive consequences. The literature suggests that peer-priming in structured sessions, social reinforcement, and modeling are viable procedures. In effect, each is intended to disinhibit social behavior. Yet another performance-deficit problem involves the withdrawn child who possess social skills but does not take the time to analyze and/or fails to recognize the appropriate situation for their development.

Repertoire deficits reflect an absence of social skills or the presence of maladaptive social behaviors. Socially isolated children in this category might benefit most from coached behavioral rehearsal, directive feedback, and rewarded practice with peers. Teaching such specific behavioral skills as smiling, giving positive reinforcement, and initiating interactions become important. Perspective-taking and interpersonal problem-solving are social cognitive skills requiring attention.

A joint assessment of social behavior and social cognition may provide the best information for treatment planning. There is some suggestion, for example, that although hyperactive children are rated as more poorly adjusted socially, they do not differ from age-mates in cognitive role-taking skills (Paulauskas & Campbell, 1979). Thus, although these children seem to be able to differentiate perspectives in a controlled experimental setting, teacher reports suggest that they are unable to put their social reasoning ability to use in their environment. Because of high levels of stimulation and stress, these children may act in an automatic and less mature manner. Interventions with these children could focus on learning to recognize and use social reasoning in appropriate contexts. Other children may actually be deficient in social cognitive skills, and with them, interventions aimed at teaching social reasoning would be more appropriate. Selman *et al.*, (1977) reported that within a group of disturbed children, there were some who had adequate social reasoning skills yet still had difficulty with peers. They suggested that conditions of stress may influence the capacity of these children to use their social reasoning skills, while other children manifest aberrant reasoning. Certainly treatment implications are different.

Kendall *et al.* (1981) have recently argued that since one of the most important characteristics of any assessment procedure is its ability to reflect accurately therapeutic changes, therapy evaluations should include assessments at both *specifying* and *impact* levels. That is, certain assessments are designed to determine, when the treatment worked, exactly what changed. What exact skills did the child acquire? What specific behaviors were observed to change? Naturalistic observations and tests of specific cognitive abilities would serve well as specifying level assessments.

Impact level assessments seek to reflect therapeutic changes that were noticed by raters blind to treatment conditions. How does the recently treated child behave toward peers, teachers, and parents? Has the child gained friends and become more accepted by the peer group? Parent and teacher ratings and sociometric instruments are desirable measures for assessing the overall impact of treatment.

SUMMARY

Following a discussion of the nature of the problem, several types of intervention for socially isolated children were described and reviewed. These intervention strategies included social reinforcement, peer-priming, peer interaction, behavioral coaching, symbolic modeling, and social cognitive procedures. A cognitive behavioral integration was proposed and outlined and some relevant issues were considered.

If it has achieved its ultimate goal, this paper has demonstrated that a multiplicity of reasons may exist to account for a child who is often seen playing alone, seemingly without friends. Careful and systematic consideration of the causes of social isolation is critical to its successful treatment. Observational assessment of the child as she or he plays and works with peers, and sociometric ratings to determine the nature of peer evaluations (e.g., is the child rejected or merely ignored?) provide necessary information. Rejection by peers may result from something as simple as thumb-sucking (Furman, 1980) or odd clothes to more complex uncooperative and hostile behavior. A child who appears withdrawn may indeed have avoidant fears of interaction with other children or, alternatively, may be somewhat shy in groups, yet have close friendships with individual peers. Social cognitive tasks, psychological tests, and role-playing exercises can be used to assess the social skills possessed by a child and to choose target skills for intervention. Gathering extensive assessment data will facilitate not only the understanding of a child's isolation and the design of treatment, but also the evaluation of a child's improvement. And although increases in social skills such as conversing or social cognitive abilities such as role-taking are desirable, the ultimate goal of intervention with socially isolated children is entry into the social world of the peer group. Evidence of greater acceptance by peers and increased inclusion in their activities becomes the ultimate test of therapeutic intervention.

11

Childhood Stress and Anxiety

INDIVIDUALIZING COGNITIVE BEHAVIORAL STRATEGIES IN THE REDUCTION OF MEDICAL AND DENTAL STRESS

Barbara G. Melamed, Avigdor Klingman, and Lawrence J. Siegel

INTRODUCTION

Fears are a common problem of normal childhood. As many as 9 out of 10 children develop specific fears sometime during their early years (Lapouse & Monk, 1959; MacFarlane, Allen, & Honzik, 1954). These fears take many forms and include fears of physical injury (e.g., being kidnapped, having an operation), natural events (e.g., storms, the dark), and social and achievement situations (e.g., exams, class recitations) (Miller, Barrett, Hampe, & Noble, 1972).

Childhood fears are often quite transient in nature and tend to dissipate with age (MacFarlane *et al.*, 1954). Therefore, all fearful or anxious behaviors may not warrant professional intervention. Seriously distressing or debilitating fears, however, such as school phobia, often necessitate therapeutic interventions.

Miller, Barrett, and Hampe (1974) provided a useful set of criteria for judging the dysfunctional nature of anxiety responses. They suggest that anxiety states warrant consideration for treatment when they (1) are

The authors' contributions to this chapter should be considered equal.

Barbara G. Melamed • Department of Clinical Psychology, College of Health Related Professions, University of Florida, Gainesville, Florida 32610. **Avigdor Klingman** • Department of Counseling, University of Haifa, Haifa, Israel. **Lawrence J. Siegel** • Department of Clinical Psychology, College of Health Related Professions, University of Florida, Gainesville, Florida 32610. The authors wish to acknowledge the support of the National Institute of Dental Research through grant DE-05305.

out of proportion to the demands of the situation, (2) cannot be explained or reasoned away, (3) are beyond voluntary control, (4) lead to avoidance of the feared situation, (5) persist over an extended period of time, (6) are unadaptive, and (7) are not age- or stage-specific.

Normal children who are exposed to a stressful situation can develop maladaptive fears, particularly when they do not have adequate coping skills. Almost all children are exposed to medical and dental procedures. Such experiences as hospitalization for surgery, diagnostic procedures such as cardiac catheterization, and restorative dental treatment can be highly stressful events for children. Children encounter numerous distressing experiences in medical and dental settings, including pain and discomfort, exposure to an unknown and unfamiliar environment, loss of control, and separation from parents. As a result, many fear-related behaviors often become associated with such settings.

The purpose of this chapter is to review cognitive behavioral methods for reducing stress, and thereby anxiety, in children undergoing medical and dental procedures. Medical and dental settings provide an opportunity to investigate anxiety and fear in the naturally occurring environment of the child. While the focus of this chapter is on treating medical and dental fear-related behaviors, the assessment and treatment approaches presented below are applicable to numerous anxiety states of childhood. Extensive reviews of cognitive behavioral procedures for treating a broad array of anxiety-related disorders in children are available (cf. Gelfand, 1978; Johnson & Melamed, 1978; Richards & Siegel, 1978; Ross, 1981).

RESPONSE TO MEDICAL STRESSORS: A PROTOTYPE FOR ANXIETY MANAGEMENT

Each day thousands of children undergo medical and dental procedures. An ecological approach to the study of childhood fears and their treatment in medical and dental settings is possible because of naturally occurring stressful experiences associated with medical and dental interventions. Children cannot readily avoid medical and dental treatment when it is necessary because adults typically determine when the treatment occurs. As a result, escape or avoidance behaviors are impracticable and the child must encounter the stressful procedure.

Medical and dental settings provide relatively controlled environments in which stressful stimuli that elicit anxiety-related behaviors are more easily identifiable. Children also typically have repeated contact with medical and dental procedures. Such situations provide an opportunity to study the effects of repeated exposure to these experiences and to evaluate the long-term efficacy of cognitive behavioral interventions in reducing the distress of medical and dental treatment. Finally, because the stressful stimuli in these settings are more readily recognizable, it is possible to *prevent* extreme negative emotional responses by teaching the child adaptive coping skills. Such anxiety-provoking experiences can provide the basis for the development of effective coping responses that can lead to mastery behavior (Bandura, 1977b; Murphy, 1962).

Importance of Prevention

Because medical and dental procedures represent stressful situations for many children, the potential for preventing fears and maladaptive behaviors exists, especially since these stressful events are relatively predictable. There is considerable research support for the importance of preventing stress and anxiety in children undergoing medical and dental treatment. For example, there is evidence that high levels of pre- and postoperative anxiety can impede recovery from surgery (Dumas, 1963; Janis, 1958; Skipper & Leonard, 1968).

Several studies of severe dental fears among children (Sermet, 1974; Shaw, 1975) have found a large number of traumatic dental experiences and a greater incidence of somatic disturbances in children with extreme fear as compared with nonfearful children. Similarly, children who reported greater dental fears were found to be more disruptive during treatment and to have more general behavior problems than low fearful children (Melamed, Yurcheson, Fleece, Hutcherson, & Hawes, 1978).

The occurrence of earlier experience with doctors and surgery is related to increased dental anxiety (Martin, Shaw, & Taylor, 1977). It may also be true that children who are afraid of dentists may generalize and show protest behavior with pediatricians. Furthermore, there is some evidence to indicate that children may become increasingly sensitized to repeated dental visits (Venham, Bengston, & Cipes, 1977), suggesting that intervention during the early phases of dental treatment may prevent subsequent stress. Finally, a preventive approach to the stress of dental treatment in children is supported by the literature, which indicates that dental fears in adults may be learned in childhood (Kleinknecht, Klepac, & Alexander, 1973).

PREREQUISITES OF COPING

A thorough assessment of the child's level of functioning and a careful determination of the behaviors required of the child during medical or dental procedures must be made prior to any cognitive behavioral treatment. For example, during dental treatment, the child must remain cooperative, maintain good chair behavior, and tolerate some level of discomfort. In addition to assessing the goals established by the health-care-provider, one must also consider the child's perspective. A child may sit quietly in the dental chair, but if he or she becomes terrified during a restorative treatment session, it is unlikely that he or she will cooperate during subsequent visits.

In order to select an appropriate cognitive behavioral program, it is important to identify what the child must know to manage the stressful medical or dental procedures effectively. For example, Cohen and Lazarus (1979) have identified four types of information that can be provided to patients, including (1) information about the reasons for a particular medical treatment, (2) information describing in detail the necessary medical procedures, (3) information about the sensations or side effects of treatment, and (4) information about specific coping strategies to use during stressful events.

Any program to facilitate a child's adjustment to medical procedures must build on the strengths and skills already in the child's repertoire. It is therefore important to evaluate the child's previous learning history in similar stress-related situations. How has the child responded to past medical procedures? What is the child's expectations about his or her ability to manage or control these stressful events? Some evidence suggests that children's previous experience with medical or dental treatment can affect their subsequent responses to cognitive behavioral intervention programs (Melamed *et al.*, 1978; Siegel, 1977).

Nature of the Stressor

The literature on dental fears pinpoints fear of injections (shots), drilling, and choking as prominent features of the situation that elicit much self-report of anxiety (Kleinknecht *et al.*, 1973). In younger children, those with high anxiety to these items were most disruptive during restorative treatment (Cuthbert & Melamed, 1982).

A taxonomy that clarifies which aspects of a stressful situation are most likely to present difficulties will lead to coping procedures specific to these fear-evoking events. An increased focus on relevant features will optimize transfer of coping strategies.

Individual Characteristics

Another important set of considerations in the assessment of fears and the selection of an intervention program are the individual characteristics of the child. Most intervention methods are presented to all target children in a similar manner, with the assumption that they will benefit equally from exposure to the same program. Little research attention has been devoted to identifying factors that indicate which children will respond the most favorably to a particular stress-reduction procedure (Siegel, 1976). There is considerable evidence in the adult literature that individual styles of coping with stress-related information can influence the extent to which a patient benefits from a stress-preparation procedure (Andrew, 1970; Auerbach, Kendall, Cuttler, & Levitt, 1976; DeLong, 1971; Shipley, Butt, Horwitz, & Farbry, 1978; Shipley, Butt, & Horwitz, 1979).

Within a cognitive behavioral framework, anxiety or fear is regarded as a multidimensional construct. Fear can be manifested in three basic response systems. First, fear may be expressed at a cognitive level, through verbal self-report of thoughts and feelings of apprehension. Second, fear may also be expressed at an overt behavioral level, through responses that are directed at escaping from or avoiding the stressful situation. Finally, fear can be manifested as physiological responses that indicate a high state of arousal (e.g., rapid heart rate and breathing).

Because anxiety or fear represents a complex pattern of responses, it is important to assess as many of these response systems as possible. Furthermore, since the three response modalities do not always show change at the same rate or in a consistent manner across systems for the same individual (Hodgson & Rachman, 1974), it is useful to assess concurrently all the dimensions of anxiety to ensure maximum treatment effectiveness. For example, a child may report after treatment that he or she no longer "feels" anxious, but may continue to engage in avoidance behaviors and remain highly disruptive during a dental or medical procedure. Therefore, no one response domain should be regarded as the primary index of fear. Rather, the interrelations among the three response systems should be evaluated in an effort to assess the fear-related responses more accurately and to discover the best predictors of therapeutic change.

INTERVENTION

Several cognitive behavioral methods have been used to reduce the stress and anxiety associated with medical and dental procedures. Four techniques have been used primarily with children, including information approaches, modeling procedures, systematic desensitization, and coping-skills training. Cognitive behavioral approaches to fear reduction employ various means to help children control their stress reactions: (1)

providing accurate information to reduce the uncertainty, (2) gradually exposing the individual to increasingly great anxiety-evoking stimuli to facilitate extinction of the fear response, and (3) providing new or alternative response patterns to allow the individual to manage the stressful event more effectively.

Most intervention strategies with children undergoing medical procedures have combined several of these approaches in the same program. In addition, these procedures have been provided in the context of support and encouragement from others. As a result, it has been difficult to evaluate which component or combination of components is responsible for treatment effects.

In addition, the treatment packages tend to be presented to all children without consideration for the specific factors that may contribute to the child's difficulty in handling the stressful experience. For example, is the child anxious merely because he or she lacks information? Does the child lack the specific skills to function effectively in the situation? Do negative cognitions lead to anticipatory stress reactions? Do conditioned emotional responses leading to excessive visceral arousal contribute to the avoidance behaviors? Unfortunately, few attempts have been made to match the intervention procedures to the specific factors that elicit or maintain the child's stress reactions in medical and dental settings.

REVIEW OF INTERVENTION METHODS

Information

The preparation of children for medical procedures through providing preparatory information about what will happen is one intervention to reduce the stress often associated with hospitalization, medical procedures, and dental treatment. Procedural information as a means of reducing psychological stress consists of descriptions relating to the physical setting, personnel, and sequence of events to be experienced and may include some justifications for the procedures (e.g., Langer, Janis, & Wolfer, 1975; Peterson & Ridley-Johnson, 1980). The primary purpose of procedural information is to impart information to the child that will (a) correct any misinformation that he or she might have, (b) help the child to master the experiences by anticipating events and procedures, and (c) enhance understanding of the meaning and purpose of the procedure. Several studies have examined the effects of procedural information (e.g., Chapman, 1970; Herbertt & Innes, 1979; Skipper & Leonard, 1968; Vernon & Bigelow, 1974); patients receiving such data scored slightly better than controls on indexes of recovery.

J. E. Johnson (1975), Johnson, Rice, Fuller, and Endress (1978), and Fuller, Endress, and Johnson (1978) suggest that preparatory information that is presented from the experiencing patient's vantage point and that includes sensory information will lead to a better overall adjustment in medical settings. Information that included sensory description was found to facilitate coping with threatening events in the laboratory (Johnson, 1973) as well as in some health-care settings (Johnson & Leventhal, 1974; Johnson *et al.*, 1978). Siegel and Peterson (1980) found that children who were given a description of typical feelings, sights, and sounds that they would experience during dental treatment demonstrated better physiological and psychological adjustment than did a placebo control group.

It has been proposed that preparatory information is effective because it (a) suggests to the patient that such experiences are normal and are not signs of threat (Lazarus, 1968; Staub & Kellett, 1972); (b) allows the patient to form a more detailed and more accurate image of the impending event and thereby to achieve more cognitive control over the threat; (c) increases, through cognitive control, the person's ability to select purposefully and rehearse mentally coping strategies that already exist in his or her repertoire (Meichenbaum, Turk, & Burstein, 1975); and (d) provides a desensitizing experience that may extinguish some conditioned fear responses (Shipley *et al.*, 1978).

Modeling

In modeling (Bandura, 1977b; Rosenthal & Bandura, 1978), an observer is exposed to a model or models (live, filmed, videotaped, or imagined) performing behaviors and receiving the consequences that occur to the behavior. Laboratory and clinical evidence demonstrated the powerful influence of observational mechanisms and showed that fearful observers profit from viewing others perform threatening activities (Mahoney, 1974; Rosenthal & Bandura, 1978). Successful applications of modeling techniques for treatment of phobic children's fears were documented (Bandura & Menlove, 1968; Bandura, Grusec, & Menlove, 1967; Jones, 1924a; Kornhaber & Schroeder, 1975; Ritter, 1968).

Modeling procedures were also employed and empirically evaluated as preventive interventions to reduce realistic fears and avoidance behavior in medical settings. Children were exposed to various aspects of the feared situation through the eyes of another child (or other children) going through the medical procedure or before dental restorations

(Machen & Johnson, 1974; Melamed, Hawes, Heiby, & Glick, 1975; Melamed *et al.*, 1978; White, Akers, Green, & Yates, 1974), or before hospitalization and elective surgery (Ferguson, 1979; Melamed & Siegel, 1975; Melamed, Meyer, Gee, & Soule, 1976; Peterson & Shigetomi, 1981; Vernon, 1973).

For example, Vernon and Bailey (1974) used a 12-minute motion picture showing several children going through an entire sequence of mock anesthesia procedure. The models were shown responding calmly to the induction, not expressing emotion apart from an occasional smile. It was presented to children undergoing minor elective operations shortly before they left for the operating room. These children were judged to be significantly less upset than controls while waiting to enter the operation room as well as while being readied for induction. Melamed and her colleagues (Melamed *et al.*, 1978) presented children who were to undergo dental restoration brief videotapes using child models going through steps that a dental restorative visit comprises—reception of the patient, the dental examination, the injection of local anesthetic, the preparation of the tooth, the placing and carving of the restoration, and the dismissal of the patient. They found that overall, a peer-model videotape was superior to a demonstration (no model) preparatory videotape in reducing disruptive behavior. Roberts, Wurtele, Boone, Ginther, and Elkins (1981) studied a preventive program for the reduction of nonpatient children's fears of hospitals and medical procedures. The experimental group viewed a 30-minute slide and audiotape show that depicted the children going through various medical procedures and was narrated by child models. The control group viewed an unrelated slide show. The experimental group exhibited a significant reduction in self-reported medical fears compared with the control group, and the differences were found to be maintained at a two-week follow-up assessment.

Cautela (Cautela, Flannery, & Hartey, 1974) has suggested that modeling may be implemented on a covert basis. In such a procedure, patients can be directed in the imaginal and symbolic rehearsal of the appropriate desired behavior. Chertock and Bornstein (1979), who examined the efficacy of this procedure in the treatment of children's dental fears, asked children to imagine visually 10 standardized scenes hierarchically arranged from least to most anxiety-provoking. Subjects were instructed to close their eyes and relax as scenes were presented verbally. This research failed to show the superiority of covert modeling over a no-model treatment control procedure. Children's ability to carry out these instructions varied, however, with one-third of the subjects being unable actually to visualize the scenes.

Participant modeling is another version of the modeling procedure. In this procedure, the client observes the model perform the desired response and is then guided by the model to rehearse actively and practice the modeled behavior either during the modeling presentation itself or at periods following the demonstration (Bandura, Blanchard, & Ritter, 1969; Lewis, 1974; Ritter, 1968, 1969). Participant modeling has been shown to be an effective treatment for fear-related problems in several controlled outcome studies and is one of the most powerful treatment techniques available for phobic problems.

The use of more than one model was found to enhance the modeling effect (Bandura, 1977b). The use of peer models was found to be more effective than the use of adult models (Kornhaber & Schroeder, 1975). The use of peer models similar to the observer in age, sex, and race was found to be beneficial for children hospitalized for minor surgery (Melamed *et al.*, 1976). Girls have been shown to model a boy model's behavior more often than boys will model girls' behavior (Nicholas, McCarter, & Heckel, 1971), and black subjects tend to imitate white models more than they will a black model (Neeley, Heckel, & Leichtman, 1973). Thus, presenting diverse (boys, girls, young, old, black, and white) peer models is likely to increase treatment effects.

The affect of the model's behavior has also been addressed. Narration by the model (or models) in a filmed modeling further enhances identification with the model. Rachman (1972) has postulated that models who are observed to overcome their fears and acquire mastery gradually appear to be more effective in producing reduction of fear in the observer. The relative efficacy of coping versus mastery models is difficult to evaluate because of differing uses of these terms in various studies (M. A. Bruch, 1978; Klorman, Hilpert, Michael, LaGana, & Sveen, 1980; Kornhaber & Schroeder, 1975; Meichenbaum, 1971a). Coping models are assumed to be more similar to the fearful child than mastery models and may enhance imitation.

The content of the film *Ethan Has an Operation* provides an example of how the various components of modeling can be selected to present appropriate models. This film portrays a youngster who hesitantly approaches a big hospital, goes through preoperative procedures displaying some anxiety, narrates his own feelings, is provided with specific information about the procedure he is to go through, encounters a rewarding atmosphere, talks to other children who describe their own experiences, and goes home in the same manner by which he arrived to show that no adverse consequences have occurred (Melamed & Siegel, 1975).

Systematic Desensitization

Desensitization (Wolpe, 1958) is another intervention approach that is used in the medical setting. Children and adults have been treated successfully through exposure, either in imagination or in reality, to medical events and concerns. The basic procedure is to train the patient in a response antagonistic to anxiety and then gradually expose the patient to a hierarchy of anxiety-producing stimuli.

This procedure may be used when patients exhibit extreme fear of even minor medical procedures. Nimmer and Kapp (1974) presented a multifaceted program for the treatment of injection phobia. Turnage and Logan (1974) used a similar program to treat a severe case of hypodermic-needle phobia. Katz (1974) described the rapid treatment of a hemodialysis phobia in an adolescent patient.

The use of desensitization procedure as a preparatory intervention was suggested by Machen and Johnson (1974), who studied preschool children not previously exposed to dental procedures. The children were exposed to a hierarchy of anxiety-producing stimuli presented gradually during a 30-minute session. Stimuli that produced the least anxiety were presented first, and higher-anxiety-evokers were presented as the subjects were able to tolerate them. Because the injection of local anesthetic, dental drilling, and exposure to the dental operatory were found to be high-anxiety stimuli, and prophylaxis and radiographs relatively low-anxiety stimuli (Howitt & Stricker, 1965); the items used to represent these events, in order of presentation from least to most anxiety evoking, were prophylaxis, mirror and explorer, rubberdam clamp, rubberdam, copalite, X-ray film, hand-piece, anesthetic syringe, dental chair, light, water and air syringes, and hand-piece. The children were exposed to this hierarchy in an ordinary room and were introduced to the operatory itself only at the end of the session. Although desensitization is a promising approach, more research is needed in this area to determine its effectiveness as a preparatory technique. It might be possible to construct standardized, easily administered hierarchies for many common medical or dental fears. The use of systematic desensitization would be a primary choice when the child does show a visceral component of anxiety or for a child who exhibits extreme avoidance responses that are likely to interfere with the treatment.

Self-control

A recent approach that can be applied to the treatment and the prevention of children's fears is the use of self-control procedures. Mahoney (1974) described self-control as change in overt or covert behavior that is relatively independent of external forces. It is often conceptualized as individual, internally produced responses to conflict situations in which several alternative behaviors are simultaneously available (Hartig & Kanfer, 1973; Kanfer, 1977; Thoresen & Coates, 1976).

Strategies of self-control generally involve self-observation, environmental planning, and behavioral programing (Mahoney & Thoresen, 1974). These strategies basically involve the same systematic manipulation of environmental events as that in externally managed behavioral procedures, but they teach the client how to initiate these events and take responsibility for their control.

Several studies have demonstrated the effectiveness of various self-control training programs with children (Meichenbaum, 1977; Meichenbaum & Goodman, 1971b; Palkes, Stewart, & Kahana, 1968). Studies supporting the use of self-control methods to reduce anxiety were conducted mostly with adult populations. These studies investigated such methods as self-directed desensitization (Rosen, Glasgow, & Barrera, 1976), guided participant modeling (Moss & Arend, 1977), self-directed performance (Bandura, Jeffrey, & Gajdos, 1975), anxiety-management training (Suinn & Richardson, 1971; Thompson, Griebstein, & Kuhlenschmidt, 1980), self-control desensitization (Goldfried & Goldfried, 1977), individualized covert modeling (Harris & Johnson, 1980), self-control relaxation (Goldfried & Trier, 1974), training in heart-rate control (Gatchel, Hatch, Watson, Smith, & Gass, 1977), training in cue-controlled relaxation (Russell, Miller, & June, 1975), and self-control of cognitions that elicit anxiety (Ellis, 1973; Goldfried & Goldfried, 1975). A comprehensive critical review of the studies using these procedures is presented by Rosenbaum and Merbaum (in press). One study focused on children who were afraid of the dark (Kanfer, Karoly, & Newman, 1975). In this study, one group (competence group) of children were taught self-instructions that included such sentences as "I am a brave boy; I can handle myself in the dark." Another group was taught about nonaversive aspects of being in the dark, and a third group was taught to repeat a neutral nursery rhyme. Children in the competence group were able to remain longest in the dark, while children in the neutral group remained in the dark for the shortest period. Although this study has some limitations and should be considered preliminary (Johnson & Melamed, 1978), self-control methods seem to have potential for increasing the child's belief in his or her ability to cope with an anxiety-arousing situation and in motivating children to follow through on a prevention program.

There have been few attempts in the research literature to assess directly individual differences in self-control. Kendall and Wilcox (1979) developed a self-control rating scale to be used by teachers. Rosenbaum (1980) developed a self-report instrument to assess individual tendencies to apply self-control methods to the solution of behavioral problems, and Rimon (1980) developed a similar instrument to be used with children.

The recent focus in cognitive behavioral approaches has led to the development of coping-skills training packages. In such procedures, the individual is taught active skills to be used for dealing with aversive situations. Such packages include cognitive skills (Barrios & Shigetomi, 1979, 1980; Meichenbaum & Asarnow, 1979), which are assumed to be easily adapted to diverse situations (e.g., relaxation, imagery training, self-instruction, and selective attention and distraction). Comprehensive coping-skills training packages are described by Goldfried (1973), Richardson and Suinn (1973), and Meichenbaum and Cameron (1973).

Meichenbaum (1975, 1977) described stress inoculation training procedures. Operationally, the program involves three phases: (a) education, providing the patient with a conceptual framework in lay terms to enable him or her to understand the nature of his or her responses to stressful events; (b) rehearsal, providing the patient with a variety of coping techniques to employ at each of the various stages of the coping process; and (c) suggesting that the patient practice his or her coping skills under various stressful conditions. For example, Meichenbaum (1974a) used self-statements as cognitive coping to be employed in the rehearsal phase in four stages: to prepare for a stressor, to confront and handle a stressor, to cope with the feeling of being overwhelmed, and to reinforce self-statements.

Coping-skills training procedures with children were studied during psychological preparation for invasive medical and dental procedures. Siegel and Peterson (1980) provided preschool children about to undergo their first dental restorations with a coping-skills training package that included relaxation, pleasant imagery, and calming self-talk. Another group of children received sensory information pertaining to the dental treatment session. In comparison to a no-treatment control group, children receiving coping-skills training as well as children receiving sensory information displayed fewer disruptive behaviors and less physiological arousal, were more cooperative, and were rated as being less anxious.

Peterson and Shigetomi (1981) assigned children scheduled for tonsillectomies to experimental groups presented with either information alone, a modeling film, cognitive behavioral coping skills, or a combination of film and coping skills. The coping techniques condition included instructions in cue-controlled relaxation, distracting mental imagery, and comforting self-talk. Results from this study tended to indicate that the coping-skills groups experienced less distress and were more cooperative during the hospital experience than the information alone or modeling film group, and that coping procedures were more effective than the modeling-only condition on some of the observational measures. Zastowney, Kirschenbaum, and Meng (in press) used Meichenbaum's (1975) stress inoculation rationale for parent-assisted training in coping skills.

Self-control procedures often have overlapping methods that make the procedures hard to compare for the effective ingredient. It is also frequently not clear whether the patient has actually acquired the specific coping skill. Few studies have attempted to measure process changes such as self-reported or physiological change during the treatment itself. One final problem is that retrospective self-reports of children are often unreliable.

Parents as Therapists

Parent-training with common childhood behaviors is a recent and growing development in the field of child therapy (e.g., Arnold, 1978). Involvement of parents in an instrumental role may facilitate the role of parents as "coping coaches" in assisting their children to cope during primary as well as secondary prevention (e.g., Berkowitz & Graziano, 1972). Some investigators have focused on the parents of hospitalized children, particularly mothers, as primary agents of intervention in facilitating children's adjustment to the hospital.

A series of studies by Skipper and Leonard (1968) and Skipper, Leonard, and Rhymes (1968) studied the effects of an intervention program with mothers on their child's response to hospitalization for minor elective surgery. In the experimental intervention, a supportive and reassuring nurse provided the mother with information about the hospital routines and medical procedures and informed the mother of her role in caring for her child in the hospital. Numerous physiological and behavioral measures indicated that the experimental-group children exhibited less emotional distress, more rapid physical recovery, and fewer behavioral disturbances than did children in the control group, which provided no special intervention programs for the mother. Mahaffey (1965) reported similar results.

Several programs have been developed in which both the child and parents have received joint preparatory intervention (Ferguson, 1979; Peterson & Shigetomi, 1981; Visintainer & Wolfer, 1975; Wolfer & Visintainer, 1975; Zastowney *et al.*, in press). Peterson and Shigetomi (1981) treated parents and their children together; the family received one of the following interventions: (a) preoperative information through a puppet show, (b) cognitive and behavioral coping procedures introduced by puppets, (c) filmed modeling, or (d) coping plus filmed modeling procedure. Parents actively assisted their children in practicing these techniques and mothers rated themselves as more satisfied with the hospital experience when they actively participated than when they did not.

Zastowney *et al.* (in press) assigned parent–child dyads to information, anxiety-reduction, or coping-skills presurgical preparatory interventions. All groups received information about procedure through a puppet film. In the anxiety-reduction group, parents also learned procedures to reduce their own distress (e.g., relaxation). Parents in the coping-skills group learned how to help their children use coping self-talk and related techniques. The results indicated that the anxiety-reduction and coping-skills groups significantly reduced children's self-reported fears compared with the information group. In addition, of the three groups, the coping-skills group displayed the fewest maladaptive behaviors before, during, and after hospitalization.

Additional research is needed to address more clearly the role played by parental preparation and to assess more accurately the respective contributions of parent preparation alone, concurrent parent and child preparation, and child preparation alone.

INDIVIDUALIZING INTERVENTION

Much of the surgery preparation literature is predicated on the assumption that a child's anxiety over the hospital experience comes from fears of (1) separation from the family, (2) pain or discomfort, and (3) unknown factors regarding medical procedures. As we have reported, information packages that are in use attempt to include features of the impending event, sensations to be expected, successful coping strategies, and reassurances. Although it is recognized that not all children are equally vulnerable to hospital stress and that younger children are thought to be at greater risk, preparation is rarely selective. We have recently questioned the wisdom of the nonselective approach (Melamed, Robbins, & Graves, 1982). Apart from the inefficiency of nonselectivity—many children show few adverse effects of the hospital experience—some studies have found that younger children may fail to benefit from information or may even become increasingly anxious if a great deal of information is imparted or if this information is given far in advance of the actual hospitalization (Ferguson, 1979; Melamed *et al.*, 1976). Often, a child with previous experience facing a minor stressor (such as restorative dental treatment involving anesthetic injection) does not gain any additional benefit from pretreatment preparation (Klorman *et al.*, 1980; Melamed & Siegel, 1980).

Age

Many of the treatment studies of comparative therapy packages have failed to assess the actual acquisition of the information presented. Different children may learn varying amounts from these interventions. Age, conceptual ability, and cognitive style influence information processing. By ignoring these individual differences, research has failed to identify the factors that would best predict a given child's response to a particular treatment approach. Manipulation checks of the patients' behavioral rehearsal of new coping techniques or the use of them during the medical intervention are often lacking. Although there is much in the child development literature regarding differences in children's abilities to process and remember information, age and conceptual level of development are often neglected in the analysis of treatment differences. (See Chapter 3, Cohen & Schleser.) The child's memory is influenced by the cognitive operations available (Ginsburg & Opper, 1979; Piaget, 1952). Research by Morrison, Holmes, and Haith (1974), Sheingold (1973), and Schwantes (1979) demonstrated age differences in children's abilities to encode and process new information. Younger children get less information from videotape modeling (Melamed, 1982), are less able to restate their imagery during modeling rehearsal (Chertok & Bornstein, 1979), and benefit less from verbal explanation than from a visual videotape prior to hospitalization (Ferguson, 1979). Puppet-therapy approaches (Cassell, 1965) might help by enabling the preoperational child to manipulate concrete objects, which may have more emotional meaning for them than the various nontactile approaches.

Another difficulty with many of the packages is that they may present material at a level that is not congruent with the child's conceptual belief regarding illness. There is extensive evidence that children of different ages have different conceptions of the causes of illness (Campbell, 1975; Peters, 1978; Simeonsson, Buckley, & Monson, 1979). Nagy (1951) studied children between 3 and 12 years of age and found that children under 6 based their cause–effect connection on the temporal continuity between events (e.g., milk-drinking preceded illness; therefore milk caused sickness), while children 6 and 7 years of age cited unspecified infections, and 8- to 10-year-olds understood that microorganisms cause illness. Thus, if you explain that masks are worn in surgery to keep germs away, children under 7 have little with which to connect that fact in their logical thought.

Children also have different ways of defending against threatening events. Findings with adults suggest that when a child who tends to deny being concerned is presented with information that necessitates admitting concern, anxiety may be heightened rather than reduced (Kendall, 1983; Shipley *et al.*, 1978). Burstein and Meichenbaum (1979) found that children who were high in defensiveness tended to play less with hospital-relevant toys prior to surgery than did their less defensive peers. Knight, Atkins, Eagle, Evans, Finkelstein, Fukushima, Katz, and Weiner (1979) found that children who were using denial as their primary defense style tended, when threatened with hospital details, to show higher cortisol-production rates than did those children who were utilizing a variety of defenses including intellectualization and isolation. Siegel (1981) reported that in structured interviews with 8- to 12-year-old children, both the flexibility and the number of coping strategies listed by the children related to adaptive adjustment in the hospital. Therefore, before deciding on the type of information to present, one should assess the child's usual style of coping with threat. While children who intellectualize may want to hear every detail of the coming experience, children who deny may do best with little or no information.

Previous Experience

The effects of previous experience on the childs' ability to benefit from preparation are documented. Melamed *et al.* (1978) demonstrated that children with previous experience and children with no previous experience need different types of preparatory exposure. Other researchers have demonstrated a lack of effectiveness of videotape modeling with children returning for dental treatment (Klorman *et al.*, 1980) and for repeated surgery (Melamed & Siegel, 1980). In order to understand the interaction of previous experience with anticipation of the new impending event, we must assess the quality of the prior experience, the accuracy of expectation regarding the current situation, and the abilities of the individual in self-control or coping strategies. Information provided by preparatory packages may be learned better if the child has a meaningful framework in which to encode the information (Waters & Waters, 1979). However, if an aversive previous experience gives the child negative associations to the situations depicted in the preparation, sensitization may occur unless the child is taught and practices more appropriate responses. Martin *et al.* (1977) found that children who had had previous medical or surgical experiences responded more negatively to anesthetic injection during dental treatment than did those without prior experience.

Individual Difference Factors in Surgery Preparation

The task of the psychologist in trying to reduce anxiety, therefore, should go beyond merely providing information. Further requirements include analyzing the child's capabilities, specifying what aspects of the procedure are likely to be threatening, clarifying the physicians' or dentists' expectations requiring cooperation, and selecting a preparation format that is congruent with the child's characteristics and the behaviors to be learned.

Our current research emphasis attempts to identify the individual characteristics that affect children's readiness to acquire information about impending events such as hospitalization and dental restorative treatments. In order to evaluate the amount of information acquired from the preparation program, we typically look at the child's cognitive functioning and arousal level and at observer ratings of their anxiety and uncooperativeness. The effect of information on the child's performance during the stressful event is assessed by measures taken during the treatment, health-care providers' evaluation of cooperation, and the mother's evaluation of the child's reaction. In addition, we are developing inventories to assess the child's ability for self-control (Klingman & Rosenbaum, 1981) in the face of fear through practice of the coping techniques provided. The relationship between predisposing personality styles (such as defensiveness) and ability for self-control is also studied because it is associated with acquisition and utilization of preparatory information. In the evaluation of the benefit of a preparatory package used at Shands Teaching Hospital, a description of the findings on the preparation of 42 children ages 4–17 for elective surgery provided support for the importance of age, previous experience, and arousal level in processing information. Children were assigned either to a hospital slide-tape[1] preparation or a hospital-unrelated control film condition. These groups were matched in overall age, sex, race, type of surgery, and previous experience.

Children were shown the film or slide-tape on the afternoon or

[1]The slide-tape "You're Going to Have an Operation" (1977) was produced by Natalie Small, Learning Resources Center, J. Hillis Miller Health Center, University of Florida, Gainesville, Florida.

Table 1. Time of Assessment

	Baseline	Prefilm	During film	Post-film	Operating room	One month after discharge
Heart rate	X	X	X	X		
Palmar Sweat Index	X	X		X		
Peabody Picture Vocabulary Test		X				
Hospital Fears Rating Scale		X		X		
Observer rating of anxiety		X		X		
Operating room behavior rating					X	
Hospital information test				X		X

evening prior to surgery on the day of hospital admission. By this time, the child had received a blood test and a brief examination by the nurse or doctor, during which blood pressure was taken. Table 1 shows measures taken and the time of assessment. (For purposes of brevity, the slide-tape will sometimes be referred to as a film hereafter.)

In addition to baseline measurement, heart rate (HR) and Palmar Sweat Index (PSI) were taken immediately before and after film preparation. The Hospital Information Test is a 20-item questionnaire designed to assess the amount of information children have about general hospital procedures related to surgery. The items are general, although the slide-tape hospital preparation was used to formulate pertinent questions. The retest reliability was 0.73, $p < 0.01$.

In order to evaluate the effects of hospital preparatory material above and beyond those of general knowledge, this test was administered to both the experimental and control film groups immediately following film presentation. An estimate of intellectual ability (Peabody Picture Vocabulary Test) was administered in order to make sure that performance on the information test was not biased by verbal ability. Other measures selected have been used in previous research on film modeling effectiveness. In addition, several measures of postoperative recovery were taken from the medical chart and through posthospital questionnaires filled out by the parent 4–6 weeks after hospital discharge.

The results indicated that children presented with a hospital-relevant slide-tape acquired more information about the impending events than did those children who did not receive this preparation, $t\ (40) = 2.55$, $p < 0.02$. Children who received relevant information got over 80% correct on the Hospital Information Test, compared with 66% for those who did not.

When the effects of age and previous experience were examined, it was clear that not every child was benefiting to the same extent. Figure 1 shows that regardless of type of preparation, older children between the ages of 8 and 17 had significantly more information than younger children, $t\ (40) = 5.8$, $df = 40$, $p < 0.001$. Older children who saw the hospital-relevant preparation significantly enhanced their knowledge relative to the older children in the group that did not receive the relevant preparation, $t = 3.7$, $df = 28$, $p < 0.001$.

Effects of previous experience are seen in Figure 2. Children with previous experience who were given hospital-relevant preparation got significantly more information correct than did children with previous experience who did not receive the relevant preparation ($t = 4.6$, $df = 20$, $p < 0.001$). Children without previous experience, however, did not

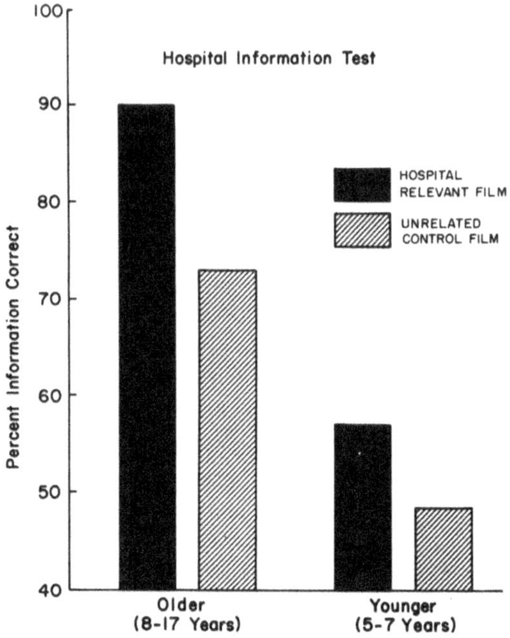

Figure 1. Percentage of information correct as a function of age, after exposure to hospital-relevant or -unrelated film.

show a greater percentage of information correct after viewing the hospital-relevant film than those who saw the control film. Thus, for children with no previous experience, information was not being encoded.

There were also differences in the physiological responses of children. Figure 3 shows that those seeing the hospital-relevant film exhibited significantly greater heart-rate increase pre- to postfilm than did children shown a hospital-unrelated control film ($t = 1.99$, $df = 40$, $p < .06$). Children who saw the hospital-relevant film also showed significantly greater reduction in palmar sweating pre- to post-film than did children shown the unrelated control film ($t = 2.67$, $df = 34$, $p < .02$). This decrease in palmar sweating occurred primarily in those children with no previous experience. Figure 4 reveals that children with no previous experience who viewed the hospital-relevant film showed significantly greater reduction in palmar sweating than did those children with previous experience who also viewed the hospital-relevant film, t $(df = 13) = 2.13$, $p < 0.05$.

The decrease in palmar sweating for the children with no previous experience may reflect their desensitization to being provided with new information about the hospital. The direction of change supported the

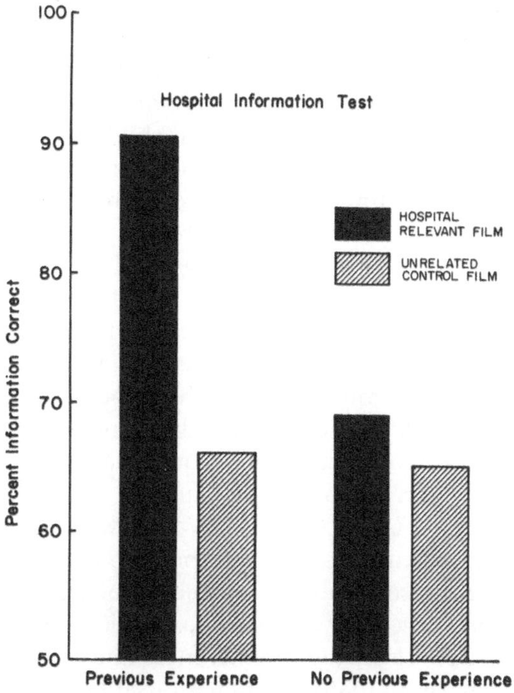

Figure 2. Percentage of information correct as a function of previous surgery experience, after exposure to hospital-relevant or -unrelated film.

notions that moderate levels of activation (i.e., increased heart rate) are facilitative of "work of worry" or other mechanisms of coping with stressors. Children with lower palmar sweating levels prior to viewing the film were also rated by observers as higher in anxiety ($r = -0.59$, $p < 0.03$), suggesting, as others have, that a certain degree of alertness or arousal facilitates information acquisition. These interpretations of the findings may be premature, but they certainly point out the importance of considering individual arousal differences.

Our data suggest that having more information about impending events also positively affects the child's adjustment and recovery. Compared with children who had less information prior to the actual surgery, children with more information were rated by their mothers as adjusting better to the hospital experience ($r = -0.54$, $p < 0.01$) and having fewer posthospital behavior problems ($r = -0.46$, $p < 0.01$; Peterson Behavior Problem Checklist).

Our results support the hypothesis that having information about impending events does facilitate hospital recovery. However, the age of the child and the previous surgery history are important considerations in deciding how information should be presented. In evaluating a slide-tape preparation for children between the ages of 5 and 17 who were in the hospital for elective surgery, it was found that children had to be 8 years of age or older to receive more information from the hospital-related material than from the unrelated film exposure. The children who had had prior surgery experience were able to recognize more information correctly after the presentation. These results are consistent with those of the literature in child development. Piaget's theory would predict that the children who have reached the concrete operational stage of development, usually around 7–8, have greater ability to abstract and encode material presented to them than younger children. Greater cognitive scanning ability is noted with advancing age (Schwantes, 1979). It follows that previous experience would make the material presented in the slide-tape format more familiar and hence easier to encode, particularly for the younger children (Waters & Waters, 1979).

Regarding physiological findings, our interpretation is speculative in that the meanings of increases or decreases in arousal are not clearly defined. The heart-rate increase after exposure to hospital-relevant material may in fact simply reflect greater attentiveness and activation. In terms of the theories suggesting that moderate arousal facilitates infor-

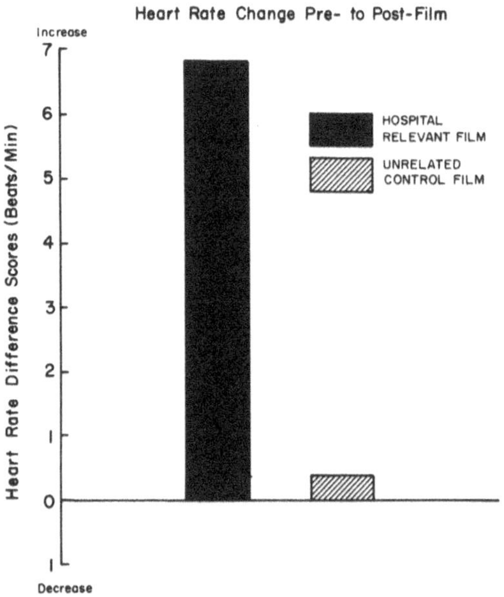

Figure 3. Mean change in heart rate pre- to post-film as a function of exposure to hospital-relevant slide-tape or hospital-unrelated film.

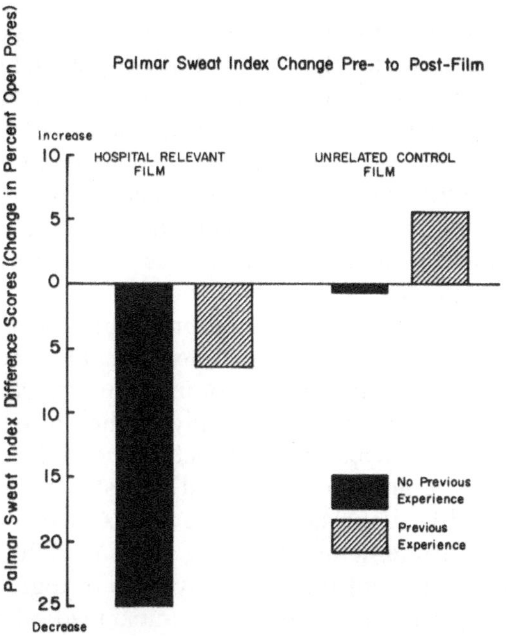

Figure 4. Mean change in Palmar Sweat Index as a function of previous surgery experience in a group after exposure to hospital-relevant or -unrelated film.

mation acquisition (Lacey, 1967), the palmar sweat decrease in children without prior experience (who were also likely to be younger) may indicate that these children were underaroused. More systematic research looking at changes in physiology during information-processing needs to be carried out.

In conclusion, it is important to individualize the preparatory package. We must first assess whether the child is likely to understand and benefit from the material, in terms of his or her previous experience, age, and anxiety levels. In addition, we have looked at two child variables, defensiveness style and self-report of self-control, as moderating factors in information-processing. Preliminary data (Unger, 1982) revealed that low-defensive children acquired more information from a preparatory videotape prior to dental treatment than did high-defensive children.

FUTURE RESEARCH DIRECTIONS

The careful identification of high-risk factors that may make children more vulnerable to adverse effects of hospitalization is prerequisite to considering whom to prepare. The area of psychological preparation provides an ideal arena for the study of developmental effects on children's information-processing during fear-evoking situations. The ideal research paradigm will allow for the evaluation of the interaction of individual subject characteristics with various treatment components in order to optimize the matching of appropriate pairs. The research discussed in the preceding section evaluated the effect on information acquisition of different subject characteristics in order to evaluate the efficacy of a specific slide-tape preparation.

While various cognitive behavioral procedures have been effective in reducing the stress of medical treatment, maintenance of the treatment effects may be an important factor in evaluating cost–benefit considerations. The cost of creating and applying the procedures, the flexibility of the procedures across different patients, and the effectiveness of the preparation program across repeated stressful medical and dental procedures should be important considerations in the selection of an optimal treatment strategy for alleviating stress in children. Currently, there are few investigations of the effectiveness of cognitive behavioral procedures for reducing stress beyond an initial medical or dental experience (cf. Siegel & Peterson, 1981). Further research is clearly needed in this area.

Also needed is an ecological assessment of children's self-generated coping strategies while undergoing stressful procedures. By building on the skills of children who function optimally under stressful conditions, it may be possible to develop more effective preparation programs that take into consideration children's preferred coping styles (Siegel, 1983).

Over the course of most intervention programs, children receive various types of information and instruction. Few studies, however, have investigated whether children actually understand and/or recall the material that has been presented to them or whether, in fact, they actually use the strategies they have been taught. Examination of these process variables would benefit future interventions.

Finally, research needs to identify the therapeutic components of the various treatment packages. Because there is considerable overlap among the various cognitive behavioral procedures discussed in this chapter (e.g., they all provide some type of information in the context of a supportive relationship), it is not surprising to find that numerous studies report equal effectiveness in reducing stress. By identifying the relative contribution of the various components of these packages, we will be able to develop maximally effective stress-reduction procedures for children.

This chapter invites the reader to address the old questions of who needs preparation, how to prepare the individual, and what works, in terms of research hypotheses. These questions may shed light on a whole array of individual considerations that predict optimal preparation. Thus, instead of speculating as to the relative effectiveness of modeling, behavioral rehearsal, and desensitization, one may address the question in another way so that the individual's need in a specific situation prompts a clear choice of one method over another based on empirical data. This data base comes from both developmental psychology laboratories and clinical studies. Cognitive factors have a definite place in the evaluation of behavioral methods, in that they are an integral part of the individual's response to stress, information-processing, and self-appraisal of competence.

Acknowledgments

We gratefully acknowledge the contributions of Drs. James Talbert, Bradley Rogers, Farhot Moazam, and Dixon Walker, who participated as surgeons; Dr. Shirley Graves, for pediatric anesthesiology; Drs. Carroll Bennett, Clem Hill, Sterling Ronk, and Frank Courts, as dentists; Natalie Small and Patricia Cluff, as pediatric patient educators; Stephanie Smith, Jan Faust, and Jesus Fernandez, for data collection; Rochelle Robbins, who participated in the earlier conceptualization of this research; and Julie Dardick, for manuscript preparation. Mitzi Dearborn, M.A., was largely responsible for coordination and data analysis. The hospital and nursing staff of pediatric surgery units at Shands Teaching Hospital supported the research effort.

12

Aggression

Bonnie W. Camp and Roberta Shockley Ray

In writing this chapter we have three purposes. The first is to provide a selective review of the literature on behavioral interventions with aggressive children, including a survey of contingency-management and cognitive behavioral approaches. Our second purpose is to present the Think Aloud program, a self-instructional procedure incorporating cognitive modeling and interpersonal problem-solving components aimed at functional control of overt aggressive behavior through the training of verbal mediational processes. Third, and finally, we consider the current status of cognitive behavioral approaches with aggressive children, discussing issues in the evaluation of treatment effectiveness conceptually related to the purposes and procedures of cognitive behavior modification.

AGGRESSION: A CLINICALLY SIGNIFICANT PROBLEM

Physical aggression, non-compliance, destructiveness, verbal combativeness, and negative relationships with peers and adults are defining characteristics of conduct disorder. Empirical approaches to classification consistently identify conduct disorder as a major dimension of childhood psychopathology. This factor, often characterized as aggression accompanied by disturbed social relationships, emerges in studies of normal and treatment populations across the ages of childhood, from preschool through adolescence (Achenbach & Edelbrock, 1978; Miller, 1972; Quay, 1979).

Bonnie W. Camp • Department of Pediatrics and Psychiatry, University of Colorado Medical School, Denver, Colorado 80262. **Roberta Shockley Ray** • Department of Psychology, University of Denver, Denver, Colorado 80208.

Conduct disorders represent an especially important target for early intervention because of their frequency, persistence, and association with serious adolescent and adult psychopathology. Although estimates of prevalence are difficult to specify due to variance in defining criteria and sampling procedures across studies, reports generally suggest that the incidence of conduct disorder in clinical populations is relatively high (Achenbach & Edelbrock, 1978; Miller, 1972; Robins, 1966). In a study of referrals to child guidance clinics, Gilbert (1957) found aggression to be the second most frequent referral complaint (after school failure) for all school-age children. Conduct problems, unlike the age-specific problems of anxiety and social withdrawal, tend to be relatively stable over time. Aggression, noncompliance, and poor social relationships identified in 6- to 10-year-old children tend to persist into adolescence where they are accompanied by school failure and delinquency (Gersten, Langner, Eisenberg, Simcha-Fagen, & McCarthy, 1976; Glick, 1972; Lefkowitz, Eron, Walder, & Huesman, 1977). Finally, conduct disorders in childhood also are associated with serious adult pathologies, including psychoses, alcoholism, and criminal behavior (Conger & Miller, 1966; Robins, 1979).

CONTINGENCY MANAGEMENT AND COGNITIVE BEHAVIORAL APPROACHES TO AGGRESSION

The frequency, stability, and prognostic significance of aggressive behavior make it a logical target for the efforts of behavior therapists. Two promising approaches derived from a social learning orientation define a continuum of behavioral intervention efforts described in the clinical literature of the 1970s.

The first general approach, environmental contingency management, is typified by programs for training parents in differential consequation of prosocial and aggressive behaviors. Parent training programs for dealing with aggressive, noncompliant, and socially disruptive behaviors are supported by data establishing at least short-term treatment efficacy. The current literature is concerned with maintenance and generalization of treatment effects and with the design of well-controlled comparative and parametric studies. Two extensions of contingency management approaches, self-administered contingencies and social skills training approaches, share with parent training the emphasis on observable aggressive behavior as the appropriate target and on contingency management as the primary treatment technique.

The second major behavioral approach to treatment of aggression is cognitive behavior modification. Considerable evidence supports the notion that mediational processes may be important determinants of learning and performance. Cognitive behavior therapy encompasses a variety of techniques aimed at modifying behavior by intervening at the level of mediational processes presumed to regulate overt behavior. A variety of techniques have been applied to a wide range of adult problem behaviors. In children, the majority of interventions have been based on cognitive modeling, cognitive social problem-solving, and self-instructional approaches. Work with aggressive children has used these techniques to teach the appropriate use of cognitive strategies as mediators of behavior. Although the use of cognitive behavioral strategies with aggressive populations has a shorter history than do the contingency management approaches, and clinical utility is not yet adequately established, several programs provide promising preliminary results and suggest the need for a series of careful clinical trials.

Although contingency management approaches and cognitive behavioral techniques provide conceptual and practical contrasts, they are not necessarily competing treatment orientations. These approaches derive from different conceptualizations of the basis of conduct problems, aim at different treatment targets, and utilize somewhat different techniques to accomplish therapeutic change. Interestingly, each approach has suggested that components of the other might be employed to promote the maintenance and generalization of treatment gains. To date, no single study has contrasted parent training and self-instructional techniques as exemplars of different approaches to the amelioration of aggressive behavior in children, nor have many studies made use of components of the two approaches in a single treatment package.

The following is a brief review of the current clinical studies representing a contingency-management/cognitive mediation continuum of social learning approaches.

Parent Training

The development of parent training procedures has been based largely on the behavioral analysis of interaction in families of children displaying high rates of social aggression. These observational studies suggest that "coercive" systems are characterized by high rates of aversive interchange and by ineffective parental consequation of both aggressive and prosocial behaviors (see Patterson, 1976; Wahler, Berland, Coe, & Leske, 1977).

An extensive literature on parent training provides description of intervention programs and presents data on short-term efficacy (Forehand & Atkeson, 1977; Graziano, 1977; Reisinger, Ora, & Frangia, 1976). Patterson and his colleagues have conducted research in parent training programs over the last decade. Their program emphasizes the development of the parents' skills in positive social and token consequation of prosocial behaviors and in the use of time-out or response-cost contingencies for social aggression. Individual and group meetings with parents include training in monitoring targeted behaviors, applying social learning concepts to the writing of behavioral change programs to be implemented in the home, and the use of staff modeling and coaching as well as participant rehearsal to ensure the acquisition of contingency management skills. Over the course of training, parents gradually assume more of the responsibility for development of change programs and the evaluation of their effectiveness; project staff gradually assume the role of consultants. A treatment manual is available (Patterson, Reid, Jones, & Conger, 1975).

Outcome data describing the parent-training program at the Oregon Social Learning Center support the effectiveness of this contingency management approach in decreasing the frequency of coercive behaviors in young conduct-disordered children (Patterson, 1982). Significant reductions in deviant child behavior, as measured by direct observations and parental report, have been found in a series of studies. Patterson and Fleischman (1979), for example, describe a sample of fifty families in which 84% of the referred children were observed to function within the normative range for coercive behaviors in nonproblem children. This level of treatment effect was found at the conclusion of treatment and after one year of followup assessment.

Although outcome studies conducted by other parent-training groups have replicated these effects (e.g., Baum & Forehand, 1981), there also have been several instances of failure to observe significant treatment gains (Bernal, Klinnert, & Schultz, 1980; Eyberg & Johnson, 1974; Ferber, Keeley, & Shemberg, 1974) or maintenance of treatment gains relative to a control group (Kent & O'Leary, 1976). Although the need for controlled group studies frequently has been discussed in this literature, relatively few have been reported (e.g., Alexander & Parsons, 1973; Christophersen, Barnard, Ford, & Wolff, 1976).

Self-management of Contingencies

Self-management strategies have been taught to children as a method of promoting long-term behavior change. The current literature emphasizes teaching various components of self-management (evaluation, criterion-setting, self-reinforcement) as a maintenance-enhancing follow-up to successful operant intervention programs, such as classroom token economies designed to increase on-task behavior or academic performance while decreasing disruptive classroom behavior (Bolstad & Johnson, 1972).

The study by Turkewitz, O'Leary, and Ironsmith (1975) illustrates this approach. Self-evaluation of academic and social behaviors was taught as a means of withdrawing an active token program while maintaining treatment gains of an experimenter-directed token economy. Following the training, in which accurate self-evaluations were reinforced, the children's reports showed greater correspondence with the experimenter's evaluation of their academic or social behavior. Although this training in self-evaluation effectively maintained behavioral gains in the experimental classroom, the effects of the self-management training did not generalize to the regular classroom. The investigators attributed this lack of generalization to their failure to ensure that the new behaviors would be reinforced in the classroom (for severely disturbed children) and to the absence of peer models for appropriate responding.

Controversy continues (Jones, Nelson, & Kazdin, 1977) regarding the extent to which self-reinforcement effects may be meaningfully separated from environmental contingencies that confound these studies, especially in the absence of data regarding long-term maintenance or across-settings generalization.

Social Skills Training

Social skills training is based on an assumption that behavior problems are an outgrowth of specific social interactional skill deficiencies. The majority of social skill assessment and intervention programs have been directed at the amelioration of social withdrawal or isolation in children experiencing low levels of peer acceptance (Gottman, 1977b). Aggressive children, who may experience considerable peer rejection, have only recently become a target population for social skills training (Bornstein, Bellack, & Hersen, 1980; Elder, Edelstein, & Narick, 1979).

Bornstein *et al.* (1980), described a treatment program including prompting, feedback, modeling, instruction, and rehearsal to train discrete, appropriately assertive social interactional skills. Brief treatment (three sessions per skill) of four highly aggressive pre-adolescents produced gains in social skills maintained over a period of six months for three of the subjects. Evidence of generalization to the ward setting was quite inconsistent. Elder *et al.* (1979), reporting on a similar social skills training program for institutionalized aggressive adolescents, demonstrated generalization of improved skills to untrained role-play situations, accompanied by inconsistent generalization to the ward environment.

Social skill training for aggressive children has been limited thus far to a series of case studies. Prior to the further development of prosocial skill curricula and design of group studies with appropriate controls, assessment studies should be directed at further specification of the nature of the social skill deficit pattern in aggressive children. The work of Selman (1976) and Chandler (1973) on social role-taking provides a needed developmental perspective to complement the operant and modeling training techniques.

Cognitive Modeling

This approach adds a cognitive component to training in appropriate coping behaviors through symbolic modeling. The cognitive model, usually an adult or peers, demonstrates discrete overt coping behaviors enhanced by verbalization of a strategy or rationale.

The case series presented by Goodwin and Mahoney (1975) illustrates the application of a cognitive modeling approach to reducing aggressive behaviors. Three boys, referred to an outpatient program for treatment of aggressive, destructive classroom behaviors participated in a verbal taunting game over a four-week period. Following baseline assessment of classroom behavior and coping responses during the taunting game, the subjects viewed a film in which the model coped with verbal assaults by calm nonaggressive behavior and the use of covert self-instructions (dubbed into the tape). No significant changes in coping responses were observed in the taunting game that followed the first viewing of the tape. During the second viewing of the tape, the experimenter pointed out and discussed the modeled coping statements and each subject was asked to verbalize the coping responses he could recall. This addition of coaching and rehearsal increased significantly the frequency of coping responses observed in an immediately subsequent and a one-week post-treatment taunting session. Classroom observational data, on treated subjects only, demonstrated an increase in appropriate (nonaggressive, nondisruptive) classroom behaviors. Although the case study design does not permit definitive conclusions regarding the effective component or the necessity of including coaching and rehearsal, the results of this often-cited pilot study suggest further trials of cognitive modeling with socially aggressive subjects. There have been no reported follow-up studies utilizing cognitive modeling as the primary approach to teaching active coping skills for aggression-inducing social situations.

Interpersonal Cognitive Problem-Solving Approaches

Cognitive social problem-solving approaches have evolved from D'Zurilla and Goldfried's (1971) specification of components of the problem-solving process and from the extensive work of Spivack and Shure (1974) on the assessment and training of problem-solving skills in children.

Spivack and Shure's data suggest that aggressive or impusive children exhibit deficits in generating alternative solutions to interpersonal problem situations. Although some data suggest that their two-month classroom training program enhanced alternative thinking and produced concommitant changes in classroom ratings of behavioral adjustment, these data pertain principally to normal preschool and kindergarten populations. The efficacy of the training program in appropriately controlled studies of aggressive populations remains to be established. The availability of assessment devices and the specification of curriculum should encourage such clinical trials. The Think Aloud program presented in the next section of this paper incorporates concepts from the work of Spivack and Shure.

A number of procedures for reducing classroom aggression have included problem-solving components directed at the development of alternatives to aggression. In a classic study, Chittenden (1942) used role-playing and discussion of prosocial alternative responses in a doll-play conflict situation. The 10 nursery-school children who received this individual problem-solving treatment were selected on the basis of observed high rates of aggression and low rates of cooperative play. Following a series of 11 15-minute training sessions, the children showed significant decreases in observed classroom aggression, and this was maintained at a one-month follow-up. Post-treatment increases in cooperative behavior were not maintained. Failure to include observations of the no-treatment control group in posttreatment assessment makes it impossible to establish definitively that observed changes were due specifically to training.

In the briefest demonstration treatment found, Zahavi and Asher (1978) established that a single 10-minute individual instruction session with a teacher (focusing on consequences of and alternatives to aggression) was effective in reducing aggression in preschool children as contrasted with an untreated group of aggressive children. Although an untreated control group was included and blind observers collected the data, no follow-up data were collected to provide information on the duration or generalization of effect.

Robin, Schneider, and Dolnick (1976) described the Turtle Technique, which is a multicomponent procedure, including problem-solving, designed to alter aggressive responding in young children. The turtle response of withdrawing from the aggression-eliciting situation and assuming a posture incompatible with physical aggression is taught by modeling and prompting. Muscle relaxation is taught as a response for coping with the "tension" presumed to accompany situational cues for aggression. The third, problem-solving component of the program is the generation of prosocial alternatives to aggression. This program was implemented by classroom teachers in two classrooms for the emotionally disturbed. Significant decrements in observed aggression were found for the 11 children treated. No data were presented on other class members or on the use of prosocial alternative responding relative to reliance on the withdrawal component of the turtle response. This is an excellent example of the need to present data on the components of a complex response.

Self-instructional Techniques

The application of basic research on the ability of the child to use covert verbalization to control overt behavior can be traced to Meichenbaum's development of a self-instructional training program for impulsive children (Meichenbaum, 1977; Meichenbaum & Goodman, 1971b). Developmental theory (e.g., Luria, 1961; Vygotsky, 1962) and a diversity of laboratory and naturalistic studies of the influence of private speech on behavior have combined to provide the basis for clinical applications of self-instructional techniques (Cole & Kazdin, 1980; Kendall, 1977).

The clinical aim of self-instructional training is the development of internalized speech that the child uses to control overt behavior. Self-instructional training programs typically expose the child to a cognitive model who performs tasks while instructing aloud on how to approach the task, provides directions for attending to salient aspects of the task, and delivers self-reinforcement for successful task completion. The child first is trained to self-instruct aloud, then to fade self-instructions to a whisper, and finally, to use covert speech to guide overt behavior.

Subject populations for studies of the effectiveness of self-instructional training commonly have consisted of children defined as impulsive on the basis of their performance on the Matching Familiar Figures Test (Kagan, 1966). Although Quay (1979) reports that aggressive children have a more impulsive cognitive style than normal or withdrawn children, studies of impulsive children typically have not provided data that would allow the reader to determine whether the subjects also could be considered socially aggressive. Absence of adequate subject description also applies to clinical populations variously labelled as hyperactive, delinquent, learning disabled, and emotionally disturbed (e.g., Bugental, Whalen, & Henker, 1977; Douglas, Parry, Marton, & Garson, 1976; Kendall & Finch, 1978; Williams & Akamatsu, 1978). The recent development of a Self-Control Rating Scale (Kendall, Zupan, & Braswell, 1981) and the continued use of established behavior rating scales by some investigators should further the goal of adequate subject description.

Recent investigations of self-instructional training have focused on school-problem populations referred for treatment (Kendall & Wilcox, 1980; Urbain & Kendall, 1980), investigated the contribution of contingency management components such as response cost (Forman, 1980a), and included measurement of overt performance outside the training situation (Camp, 1980; Forman, 1980a). Clearly, researchers in this area are interested in clinical applications as well as in comparative studies and multilevel evaluation strategies.

The most programmatic work in cognitive behavior modification with aggressive children has been the development of the Think Aloud program by Camp and her colleagues (Camp, 1980; Camp & Bash, 1981; Camp, Blom, Hebert, & van Doorninck, 1977). This multi-component training package, based on an assessment of the mediational skills of aggressive boys, utilizes self-instructional and interpersonal problem-solving techniques. The next section describes the development, training procedures, and evaluation of the Think Aloud program as applied to the treatment of aggressive boys.

THINK ALOUD

Development

Since aggressive behavior, especially in young children, often appears to reflect the absence of regulating processes, one would expect that mediational activity would be characteristically deficient in aggressive children and that training that helps them to produce mediating verbalizations will result in decreased aggressive behavior as well as increased prosocial behavior. In some ways, however, it is a long way from this formulation to the actual design of a cognitive behavior modification treatment program for aggressive boys. First, one must determine whether cognitive deficits are present and if so, how they are revealed. If cognitive deficits are present, one must also determine how mediational activity in aggressive children differs from the norm. With answers to these questions, one should then be able to determine how to normalize the cognitive behavior of aggressive boys. Only then can one properly address the question of whether normalizing cognitive behavior will lead to a decrease in aggressive behavior and/or an increase in prosocial behavior.

Early work with aggressive boys showed that they differed from normal boys not only in behavior but in cognitive skills as well. In young boys, however, the cognitive differences were not the same as those reported for older aggressive and delinquent youths. Whereas older aggressive boys tended to show characteristic deficits in verbal as compared to nonverbal intelligence (Camp, 1966; Prentice & Kelly, 1963), the young aggressive boys showed adequate verbal skills but deficient nonverbal performance relative to their normal counterparts (Camp, 1977; Camp, Zimet, van Doorninck & Dahlem, 1977). In addition, they were more impulsive and tended to talk more, with more emphasis on task-irrelevant speech during problem-solving.

It seemed, then, that a cognitive behavior modification program for young aggressive boys not only should address the content of self-statements but also needed to promote the boys' spontaneous use of self-guiding speech when confronted with both cognitive and social problems. Merely inhibiting a behavior, for example, is not likely to lead to more desirable behavior unless there is a repertory of alternatives that can be substituted. The Think Aloud program was designed to address both of these issues.

The content of the program included

1. Using verbalization to inhibit first responses in a problem situation
2. Developing an organized approach to problem-solving
3. Increasing the repertory of alternative response solutions
4. Developing language for understanding cause and effect
5. Developing a repertory of evaluation skills
6. Using both cognitive/impersonal problems and social/ interpersonal problems

The following elements were included in hope of promoting the spontaneous use of skills:

1. Adult modeling of cognitions
2. Stimulating overt verbalization of child's thoughts, followed by fading to covert levels

3. Promoting independence in the use of these skills
4. Promoting generalization by applying the skills to many contexts within the program
5. Providing verbal transitions to promote generalizations to real-life situations

Description of Program

In the hope of providing for a wider dissemination as a preventive as well as a treatment tool, Think Aloud was designed as a psychoeducational training program that could be carried out by teachers. In this spirit, a training manual was prepared, with lesson plans including specific materials and dialogues, to cover approximately 40 sessions. These lessons begin with the use of "Copy Cat" to ensure imitation of both words and actions and proceed to developing the use of four questions to organize one's approach to problem-solving, promoting thinking of alternative answers to questions, and gradually breaking with Copy Cat to develop independent verbalization of plans, self-monitoring, and evaluation.

Figure 1 shows a dialogue from the second lesson that illustrates the use of Copy Cat.

On subsequent tasks, the child is asked to play Copy Cat while the teacher models ways of thinking through a problem and coping with mistakes. Then the child is asked to work through a problem on his or her own. Cue pictures are also introduced to help the child remember and answer four questions: What is my problem? How can I do it? Am I following my plan? How did I do?

Once the basic strategy of modeling and verbalizing an organized approach to problem-solving has been applied successfully to several cognitive problems such as puzzles, mazes, and matrices, social problems are introduced. These are modeled closely on the work of Shure and Spivack (Shure & Spivack, 1974a; Spivack & Shure, 1974) and provide a sequence of lessons that move through the following stages:

1. Practice with identifying and expressing feeling and the basic language of cause and effect—that is, why — because, if — then, what might happen next?
2. Practice developing alternative solutions to social problems.
3. Practice developing alternative ideas about consequences of actions.
4. Establishing a repertory of evaluation skills.
5. Analysis of problems into solutions, consequences, and evaluation of each choice.

TEACHER: *(The Ralph cue pictures and pages of shapes should be in a folder on the table. The crayons should be out of sight.)*
Let's play Copy Cat again. Remember you have to say* what I say and do what I do.* If I point my finger,* you point your finger.* (*Continue with Copy Cat for about 30 seconds, emphasizing "do what I do" with gestures.*)

CHILDREN: ____________________

TEACHER: Good copying. Today I'm going to show you a new way of working on problems. I call it thinking out loud because we say out loud what our brain is thinking. What do I call this way of solving problems?

CHILDREN: ____________________

TEACHER: We'll start with a very easy problem. You probably would not think of it as a problem. But we're going to pretend it is like a problem we have to solve. Later on we will do lots harder problems and then this thinking out loud will really help. To teach you to think out loud we'll use Copy Cat.

Coloring Shapes

TEACHER: (*Give the children and yourself the pages of shapes to be colored. Select the circle with a fat border first.*)
We each have a paper with some shapes on it. The problem (Classroom teacher's name) gave us is to color the first circle the best we can without going outside the line. You pick a crayon and I'll pick one.

CHILDREN: ____________________

TEACHER: Let's learn to think out loud to help us do this paper. You be copy cats. You must copy what I say and do. Let's try it.
(*Hold the crayon high in the air.**) I'm going to think out loud.* What is my problem?* I am supposed to color this circle* without going outside the line.* How

(*continued*)

Figure 1. *(Continued)*

> can I do it?* I'll go slowly.* I'll be careful.* I'll outline the circle first.* Then I can go faster in the middle.* That's my plan.* Here I go.* (*Begin coloring.**)
> (*The children may become so intent on coloring that they fail to copy. Remind them as often as necessary, Where are my copy cats?*)
>
> *Children copy statements and gestures.

Figure 1. Example of Copy Cat Script. (From *Think Aloud: Increasing Social and Cognitive Skills—A Problem-Solving Program for Children* [*Primary Level*] by B. W. Camp and M. A. S. Bash, Champaign, Ill.: Research Press, 1981. Copyright 1981 by Research Press. Reprinted by permission.)

Figure 2 gives an excerpt from the first lesson introducing interpersonal problem-solving.

Although much of the material in social lessons was an adaptation of Shure and Spivack's work with younger children, some lessons went beyond the Shure and Spivack work to address issues specifically important to aggressive children. This was especially true of material dealing with evaluating the consequences of actions in social situations. One lesson sets out some standard criteria for evaluating consequences to determine whether an action was a "good idea" or "not a good idea." Others deal specifically with the issues of Safety, Fairness, Feelings, and Effectiveness. An excerpt from the Fairness lesson is presented in Figure 3.

Once social problems have been introduced, these are interspersed with increasingly complex cognitive problems that either emphasize following complex directions using negative commands or require independent thinking, often physically at some distance from the teacher. Aside from simply increasing the difficulty of the material by using more complex mazes, matrices, or design building, several lessons make increasingly difficult demands for linguistic control over nonverbal behavior. An example dealing with complex mixed categorization is presented in Figure 4.

In addition to the Think Aloud Program Guide (Camp & Bash, 1981), interested readers may consult Camp and Bash (1980) and Bash and Camp (1980) for further discussion of materials in the program.

TEACHER:	On the next problem you'd better wear your detective hats because you will be looking for more clues. You'll look for clues in pictures of people. (*Lay out four Understanding Our Feelings pictures: 1, 2, 3, and 4. Point to the smiling boy.*) Is this boy smiling?
CHILDREN:	________________
TEACHER:	Yes, this boy is smiling. (*Point to the sad boy.*) Is this boy smiling?
CHILDREN:	________________
TEACHER:	No, this boy is not smiling. Now, both of you point to a picture of a boy who is not smiling.
CHILDREN:	________________
TEACHER:	Show me a person who is not mad.
CHILDREN:	________________
TEACHER:	Point to the mad boy. This boy is frowning. He probably feels mad. (Point to the smiling boy.) This boy is smiling. He probably feels happy. If this boy feels happy, and this boy feels mad (*point to respective pictures*), then they do not feel the same way. They have different feelings. (*Point to the smiling boy and laughing man.*) Do these people have the same feelings or do they have different feelings?
CHILDREN:	________________
TEACHER:	Yes, they are both smiling. They probably feel the same way. (*Point to the laughing man.*) If this man is laughing, then is he feeling happy or is he feeling sad?
CHILDREN:	________________
TEACHER:	Yes, he is probably feeling happy. (*Put your hands on your head.*) Where are my hands?
CHILDREN:	________________
TEACHER:	How can you tell? You can see them with your ______. Now, close your eyes and keep them closed. (*Put your hands on your hips.*) Where are my hands now?
CHILDREN:	________________
TEACHER:	You can't be sure because you cannot see with your

(*continued*)

Figure 2. *(Continued)*

TEACHER (*cont.*):
eyes closed. Now open your eyes. Now tell me where my hands are.

CHILDREN: ________________

TEACHER: How can you tell? You can see with your ______. Can you see with your eyes closed?

CHILDREN: ________________

TEACHER: Can we see with our ears?

CHILDREN: ________________

TEACHER: No, we cannot see with our ears. What can we do with our ears?

CHILDREN: ________________

TEACHER: Yes, we can hear with our ears. I am laughing. (*Demonstrate.*) Am I happy or am I sad?

CHILDREN: ________________

TEACHER: How can you tell I feel happy?

CHILDREN: ________________

TEACHER: (*If the response is "You're laughing," ask*) How can you tell I'm laughing? Did you see me with your eyes?

CHILDREN: ________________

TEACHER: Did you hear me with your ears?

CHILDREN: ________________

TEACHER: Yes, you can tell two ways that I am happy: You can see me laughing and you can hear me laughing. Let's pretend I cannot hear you (*plug ears*). I can only see you. What would you do so I know you are happy? Show me.

CHILDREN: ________________

TEACHER: Yes, I can tell you are happy—you are (*smiling*). What would you do to show me you feel sad? Remember I can only see you.

CHILDREN: ________________

TEACHER: I can tell you feel sad because you are (*crying*). What would you do to show me you are angry.

CHILDREN: ________________

TEACHER: Oh yes, I can tell by your face you feel angry. You are scowling. If you are scowling, you probably feel mad.

(*continued*)

Figure 2. (*Continued*)

TEACHER (*cont.*):
Good, now let's pretend I cannot see you. (*Cover eyes.*) I can only hear you. How would you let me know you are happy?

CHILDREN: ____________________

TEACHER: (*When children produce an audible response, say*) Yes, I can tell you are happy. I can hear you laughing. How would I know you are sad if I can only hear you?

CHILDREN: ____________________

TEACHER: (*Any attempt at audible sobbing or sniffling deserves empathetic recognition, such as*) You must be unhappy or sad. I can hear you crying. Very good. How would I know you feel angry? Recognize as above. If the children cannot sound angry, give a demonstration and ask them to try it.

CHILDREN: ____________________

TEACHER: (*Lay out three additional pictures: 5, 6, and 7. Ask Child 1*) Point to two people who feel the same way. You may record the appropriateness of the child's response on the Identifying Emotions Recording Form.

CHILD 1: ____________________

TEACHER: How do they feel?

CHILD 1: ____________________

TEACHER: How can you tell?

CHILD 1: ____________________

TEACHER: Yes, you can see them with your eyes. (*Ask Child 2*) Point to two people who feel different ways. (*Record*).

CHILD 2: ____________________

TEACHER: How do they feel?

CHILD 2: ____________________

TEACHER: How can you tell he or she is sad (or happy or mad)?

CHILD 2: ____________________

TEACHER: (*Ask Child 1*) Point to someone who feels different than this child. (*Points to mad boy. Record.*)

CHILD 1: ____________________

TEACHER: (*Ask Child 2*) Who feels the same as this lady? (*Points to the mother with a baby. Record.*)

(*continued*)

Figure 2. *(Continued)*

CHILD 2:	____________________
TEACHER:	If the children have trouble with this activity, practice more comparisons, which are suggested on the Recording Form.
	We have two different ways to know how someone feels. We can (*point to eyes*) _______ or we can _______ (*point to ears if necessary*). How can you tell when your teacher is happy?
CHILDREN:	____________________
TEACHER:	How can you tell when your friend is angry?
CHILDREN:	____________________
TEACHER:	How do you let your family know you are sad?
CHILDREN:	____________________
TEACHER:	We will practice being detectives often. We will look carefully for clues that tell us how people feel.

Figure 2. Excerpt from initial lesson preparing for interpersonal problem-solving. (From *Think Aloud: Increasing Social and Cognitive Skills—A Problem-Solving Program for Children* [*Primary Level*] by B. W. Camp and M. A. S. Bash, Champaign, Ill.: Research Press, 1981. Copyright 1981 by Research Press. Reprinted by permission.)

Outcome Research

There have been five controlled studies with the Think Aloud program for individual and/or pairs of aggressive boys in first and second grade. With the exception of 14 boys selected for deviance on the Walker (1970) checklist, subjects for these trials were all selected by teacher report of aggressive behavior using Miller's (1972) School Behavior Checklist. The first study selected boys who were two or more standard deviations above the population mean on the Aggressive Scale, and subsequent studies used subjects who scored one-and-one-half or more standard deviations above the mean.

Each study has included, as a minimum, measures of cognitive change and teacher ratings of classroom behavior. Some trials have included behavior observations, and most have used an adaptation of the Preschool Interpersonal Problem Solving (PIPS) test (Shure & Spivack, 1974b) as a post-test only. With each trial, different questions have been addressed by changing the research design, measures used, compari-

TEACHER: (*The Ralph cue pictures should be on the table or wall as reminders to the children, and the "Safe" sign should be posted in the room. The fairness pictures and the "Fair" and "Not Fair" signs should be in a folder on the table, and the two puppets should be close at hand but out of sight. The bag of riddles, the recording form, and the pencil should be out of sight.*) Yesterday we learned one way to decide if doing something is a good idea or not. (*Review the safety criterion briefly.*) Today we are going to learn a second way to judge what is happening in pictures. (*Present the picture of a girl on a bike. Point to her.*)

This girl wanted to ride a bike so she took Teresa's bike away from her. Is it a good idea or not to grab something from someone?

CHILDREN: ____________________

TEACHER: Why is it not a good idea?

CHILDREN: ____________________

(*continued*)

Figure 3. *(Continued)*

TEACHER:	So it is not a good idea to take something from others because it is not fair. What did the girl on the bike want?
CHILDREN:	____________
TEACHER:	What could she say or do that would be fair so she can ride the bike?
CHILDREN:	____________

Figure 3. Excerpt from script for Fairness Lesson. (From *Think Aloud: Increasing Social and Cognitive Skills—A Problem-Solving Program for Children [Primary Level]* by B. W. Camp and M. A. S. Bash, Champaign, Ill.: Research Press, 1981. Copyright 1981 by Research Press. Reprinted by permission.)

sons selected for examination, or content of the program to address different issues.

In the first trial (Camp, Blom, Hebert, & van Doorninck, 1977), 24 aggressive boys were assigned randomly to either an experimental (Think Aloud) or a no-treatment control group. Pre- and post- measures were also made on a comparison group of normal boys. These measures included the aggressive and prosocial scales of the School Behavior Checklist, modified to reflect change, and a battery of cognitive tests that had previously been shown to discriminate between normal and aggressive boys (Camp, 1977; Camp & Bash, 1981). Scores on the cognitive tests were weighted according to results from the prior discriminate function analysis and summed to achieve a single score (d-score) for each boy. This score can be viewed as a measure of how much each boy's cognitive pattern resembled the pattern typical of aggressive boys as opposed to the pattern typical of normal boys.

Figure 5 shows the changes in cognitive pattern that occurred in each group. Prior to treatment, d-scores for the Think Aloud group and the Aggressive Control group were similar to each other and close to the mean for aggressive boys. The d-score for the normal boys was different from those of the other two groups and close to the mean for normal boys. Following treatment, the d-score for Think Aloud boys dropped to a level similar to that of normal boys and different from that of boys in the Aggressive Control group, who changed only slightly. This indicated normalization in the cognitive pattern of boys in the Think Aloud group but not in the Aggressive Control group. Teacher ratings of classroom behavior also showed that Think Aloud boys improved signifi-

TEACHER: Now we'll change the problem again. I will still say four words. If one of the words is "ball" alone, do not clap. If one of the words is a color name alone, do not clap. If I say the word "ball" and a color, do clap. I'll try a couple to see how it works. What is my problem? I'm supposed to clap if I hear both the word "ball" and a color name. How can I do it? I'll listen to all four words. If I hear "ball" I'll hold up a finger on my left hand. (*Raise left index finger.*) If I hear a color word, I'll hold up a finger on my right hand. (*Demonstrate.*) If I have both fingers up, I'll clap. (*If possible ask an older student or an adult to read the four words on the Auditory Inhibition Recording Form, Step Three, Line 1. Otherwise use a tape you have prepared before the lesson. Model using your plan. After the words are read, say,*) I only have the color finger up, because I did not hear the word "ball." So I won't clap. How did I do? My plan worked. Raising my finger made it easy to remember what I heard.

HELPER (*Read the four words in Line 2 of Step Three.*)

TEACHER: (*Model the plan again.*) Both fingers are raised because I heard "ball" and "purple," so I can clap. Now it is your turn. Your problem is to clap after I say four words if you hear "ball" and a color word. Let me hear you think out loud.

CHILD: ____________________

TEACHER: Read each item from Step Three. You may record the child's responses. If the child errs on "silver" or "white" items, repeat them at the end of the list. If he or she errs again, ask him or her to name all the colors he or she can. If he or she includes white and silver, repeat those items from Step Three.

CHILD: ____________________

Recording Form

				PE NPE IM
	Step Three			Verbalizations
1. friend	bag	BROWN	super	
2. apple	BALL	run	PURPLE	

(*continued*)

Figure 4. *(Continued)*

3. catch	ORANGE	inside	record
4. swallow	RED	BALL	under
5. SILVER	pencil	divide	BALL
6. edge	lick	print	BALL
7. smile	balloon	GREEN	close
8. BALL	tighten	WHITE	fly

Total Errors ______

Figure 4. Script for Auditory Inhibition Game and Recording Form. (From *Think Aloud: Increasing Social and Cognitive Skills—A Problem-Solving Program for Children* [*Primary Level*] by B. W. Camp and M. A. S. Bash, Champaign, Ill.: Research Press, 1981. Copyright 1981 by Research Press. Reprinted by permission.)

cantly more than aggressive controls on prosocial behavior. Both Think Aloud and control boys improved in aggressive behavior, but the differences between them were not significant.

The program was revised to strengthen social problem-solving portions by including, among other things, two boys working together during each lesson. This was first piloted on a small group of 14 boys (selected as deviant on the Walker checklist) and then utilized in a larger study comparing Think Aloud with the Great Expectations program, a self-esteem-building program conceptualized as an attention-control program (Camp, 1980; Camp & Bash, 1981). Sixty-three aggressive boys were assigned randomly to participate in either Think Aloud or Great Expectations for daily one-half hour sessions over eight weeks. Instructors in both programs were 34 initially naïve teachers and teacher aides.

Short-term cognitive changes in this trial were similar to those in the first trial but not as dramatic. However, Think Aloud significantly helped to stabilize the cognitive pattern of boys who were initially classified as having a cognitive pattern resembling normal boys. In the Great Expectations program, these "cognitively normal" boys shifted toward the "cognitively aggressive" pattern. Cognitively aggressive boys in the Think Aloud program shifted toward the normal pattern but not enough to be significantly different from Great Expectations boys. However, a 6- to 12-month follow-up showed an increasing improvement in cognitive pattern among Think Aloud boys that differed from Great Expectations boys at the 0.06 level of confidence. On classroom teacher ratings, both Think Aloud and Great Expectations boys showed significant improvement in prosocial behavior. They differed significantly from each other

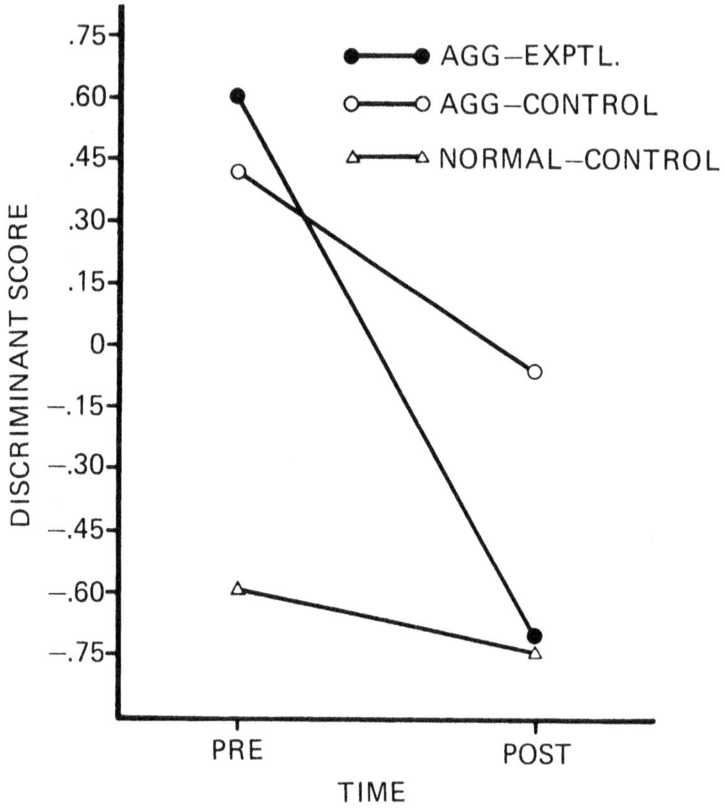

Figure 5. Pre- and post- discriminant scores shown for aggressive-experimental, aggressive-control, and normal-control groups. (From "'Think Aloud': A Program for Developing Self-control in Young Aggressive Boys" by B. W. Camp, G. E. Blom, F. W. Hebert, and W. J. van Doorninck, *Journal of Abnormal Child Psychology*, 1977, *5*, 157–159. Copyright 1977 by Plenum Press. Reprinted by permission.)

in the amount of improvement in aggressive behavior, with the Great Expectations group superior to the Think Aloud group, but neither group differed significantly from a composite group of untreated controls.

Behavior observations in the classroom, however, differed somewhat from teacher ratings. Discriminant function analysis of behavior observations correctly identified program membership of 47/63 boys, though none of the univariate analysis showed significant differences between the groups. It was difficult to describe the exact nature of the differences in behavioral pattern between the two groups because there seemed to be a suppressor relationship between two of the variables contributing most to the discriminant function. Judging by the size and direction of standardized discriminant coefficients, these results appeared to show that Think Aloud boys engaged in a variety of "deviant" behaviors while on-task. These deviant behaviors tended to be vocalizing, making noise, fidgeting, and getting out of seat. Great Expectations boys were more likely to be participating and tended to show no deviant behavior while on-task, but when they showed deviant behavior, it was in the form of hostility and physical contact with others. This suggested that Think Aloud boys were using Think Aloud techniques in the classroom and were channeling aggressive impulses into less socially disruptive forms of behavior.

Despite teacher ratings of short-term improvement by children, overall teacher ratings of deviance were not changed by either program on long-term follow-up. The last controlled trial was therefore undertaken as a refresher program in Think Aloud to be given to both Think Aloud and Great Expectations graduates (Camp, 1980; Camp & Bash, 1981). It was conceived as the most powerful program possible at that time because it employed an experienced instructor, individualization of the program content, and further refinement of procedures to improve the impact of social lessons. This refresher was provided individually to 22 graduates of Think Aloud and 22 graduates of Great Expectations, three times weekly for one month. The most important comparisons were between boys judged to make good progress in the refresher program and boys judged to make moderate or poor progress. These judgments of progress represented the Think Aloud instructor's assessment of the quality of each boy's performance in the refresher program itself and served as the basis for separating boys into two groups, Good Progress and Poor Progress (included moderates). Regular classroom teachers completed the Conners Hyperkinetic Scale (1969) and the Schaefer-Aaronsen Preschool and Primary Classroom Behavior Scale (1966) prior to the boys' beginning the refresher program and again after they completed it. Boys in the Good Progress group showed improvement on Schaefer-Aaronsen scales of extraversion and friendliness and on the Conners Hyperactivity Scale, while boys in the Poor Progress group showed no change or got worse. Furthermore, the degree of improvement in the Good Progress boys was sufficient to indicate behavior in the normal range on the one scale (Conners), with normative data for comparison. Improvement on the Schaefer-Aaronsen task-oriented scale was also present in the Good Progress group, but interpretation of this finding is somewhat attenuated by the fact that they were worse at the beginning of the program. Cognitive changes with the refresher program were less dramatic. However, achieving a normal cognitive pattern prior to beginning the refresher course predicted Good Progress group membership for Think Aloud graduates. None of the measures predicted response of the Great Expectations graduates to the refresher program.

EVALUATION ISSUES

The cognitive behavioral intervention literature of the past decade reflects a pattern of development in research designs that has been common to all therapy areas. The earliest and largest number of reports are case studies or case series, sometimes using multiple-baseline strategies (e.g., Goodwin & Mahoney, 1975; Robin *et al.*, 1976). Comparisons of a cognitive behavioral strategy group to no-treatment control groups or in designs allowing for the assessment of nonspecific treatment effects are rare in studies of clinical populations. Camp has provided data on the Think Aloud program at both levels of evaluation design, comparing Think Aloud to no-treatment control groups of aggressive and normal children (Camp, Blom, Hebert, & van Doorninck, 1977) and to a nonspecific contrast program, Great Expectations (Camp, 1980; Camp & Bash, 1981).

The literature on aggression includes few true comparative studies. Forman's (1980a) contrast of self-instructional and response-cost procedures for altering aggressive classroom behavior is a welcome exception. To date there have been no studies providing direct comparison of cognitive behavioral approaches and contingency management programs utilizing parents as primary treatment agents.

Two recent studies directed at a broad spectrum of classroom behavior problems, rather than aggressive behavior specifically, illustrate a growing interest in comparative and parametric research on cognitive approaches. Urbain and Kendall (1980) contrasted the effectiveness of two social cognitive approaches (problem-solving and social perspective-taking) and contingency management. Kendall and Wilcox (1980) utilized a parametric design to assess the relative effectiveness of concrete and conceptual variants in self-instructional training. They found stronger effects for conceptual (not problem-specific) training.

Comparative studies are needed to answer questions regarding essential components of cognitive behavioral interventions and the relative strength of types of programs. At a simpler level, however, there are still major problems in establishing clinical utility of any program, that is, whether a program produces clinically significant effects that generalize over time to new situations. Some of the following issues are particularly important in evaluating the clinical utility of cognitive behavioral approaches with aggressive children: program objectives, subject characteristics, outcome measures, program design, and treatment duration.

Program Objectives

All training programs with disturbed children may be classified according to how well they serve the dual role of ameliorating a problem and preventing later problems—that is, as both treatment and secondary prevention (e.g., Berlin, 1972). Development of appropriate evaluation criteria for a specific program will depend on the extent to which the purpose of the program is preventive or therapeutic and on the target behaviors it proposes to change.

Typically, it is implicitly or explicitly assumed that any program designed for children with aggressive behavior problems has the primary target of decreasing aggressive behavior. Although this is certainly an agreeable outcome for everyone else, it may be short-sighted for many aggressive children and even detrimental to some (i.e., those for whom aggressive behavior is the only defense in a miserable environment). Studies on older aggressive and delinquent boys and men have demonstrated characteristic cognitive deficits that appear related to treatability and recidivism. This characteristic pattern of cognitive deficits consists of educational underachievement (Graham & Kamano, 1958; United States General Accounting Office Report, 1977), less adequate performance on verbal than performance scales of the Wechsler (Camp, 1966; Prentice & Kelly, 1963), deficiencies in impulse control, ego development, and abstract thinking (Giora, 1975; Megargee, 1971; Staub, 1971a).

Although the presence of aggressive behavior disorders at age 5–8 years is associated with later delinquency (Glick, 1972), the cognitive pattern and academic achievement of aggressive boys at this age does not show the characteristics described. The pattern in this younger group of aggressive boys differs from that of normal boys but not in the same way as it does later on (Camp, 1977; Camp, Zimet, van Doorninck, & Dahlem, 1977). Furthermore, longitudinal studies of aggressive behavior problems have indicated that family disharmony is a principle contemporaneous instigator of aggressive behavior in school (Eron, Walder, & Lefkowitz, 1971). In the long run, however, cognitive competence and acceptance of parental values are more predictive of which young aggressive boys will still be aggressive 10 years later (Lefkowitz *et al.*, 1977). The present studies at least raise the point that if long-lasting clinical effects are to be expected, it may be equally or more important to improve cognitive behavior in young aggressive boys than it is to decrease their aggressive behavior. Often this issue of cognitive effects has been ignored, even in cognitive behavior modification programs.

Clarification of program objectives is closely related to the selection of outcome measures, discussed in more detail later. At this point, however, it is worth noting that even when the program objective is to improve social behavior in aggressive boys, it is important to clarify whether improvement means increased prosocial behavior, decreased aggressive behavior, or both. These behaviors are not simple opposites, though investigators have often tended to make this assumption. Where both sets of behaviors have been measured (e.g., Camp, 1980; Camp & Bash, 1981; Camp, Blom, Hebert, & van Doorninck, 1977; Chittenden, 1942), it has become evident that programs may have differential effects on prosocial and aggressive behavior in both short-term and long-term follow-up.

Subject Characteristics

The clinical subject population for cognitive behavior studies, even within the descriptive category of aggression, remains a heterogeneous lot. A few case studies have included subjects referred to mental health facilities for treatment of social aggression (Goodwin & Mahoney, 1975; McCullough, Huntsinger, & Nay, 1977). Others have included children referred for in-school counseling or special class placements (Forman, 1980a; Robin *et al.*, 1976). The largest number, however, have been children rated as aggressive on classroom behavior checklists (Camp & Bash, 1981; Camp, Blom, Hebert, & van Doorninck, 1977) or "nominated" as aggressive by a teacher within a normal classroom.

Regardless of referral status, what seems especially important for the understanding of the clinical utility of the cognitive behavior procedures being investigated is a multiple-measure description of the population. This would provide data on cognitive deficiencies *and* overt social aggression, obtained from standardized assessment instruments available to all investigators. There has been a great increase in the number of studies on clinical populations. It is important that our understanding of complex and often disparate results be increased by adequate subject description, so that subject comparability across studies can be assessed.

In addition, program evaluation will be greatly improved by specifying client characteristics that relate to treatment outcome. Two studies from the literature on parental contingency control of aggression suggest that there are identifiable characteristics of aggressive children or their families that moderate the effectiveness of operant approaches. Reid and Patterson (1976) considered the frequency of observed aggressive, antisocial behaviors in a sample of children referred for treatment. They found a subsample, described as aggressive but displaying low rates of observed aggression. The treatment outcome (as measured by decrease in antisocial behavior) for these clients was less favorable, although their pattern of stealing, lying, and fire-setting was clearly predictive of continued adjustment problems. As a result of this analysis, it has been suggested that home observations precede the decision to treat and that consideration be given to the possibility that parent training procedures may not be the treatment of choice unless a clinically significant level of social aggression is observed. Along the same line, Wahler (1980) identified a family constellation associated with lower probability of success in parent training. This "insular" family is characterized by low income level and inadequate social supports for the primary caregiver, often a single mother. Wahler suggested that this family should be considered high risk and that attempts at change should be directed at enhancing the mother's social support system prior to any attempts to engage in parent training.

Presumably, cognitive behavior therapy faces a similar problem. In early trials with Think Aloud, results were expected to be achieved through mere exposure to the program. Later, it was recognized that only a very powerful program could be expected to produce enough positive change in enough people to achieve group differences. Another factor, described by Bergin (1971) as the phenomenon of a "deterioration effect" from treatment, was considered in later trials. This factor tends to show up when subjects are analyzed into "improved" and "nonimproved" groups. When a similar distinction between "good progress" and "poor progress" was made for children in a Think Aloud trial, highly significant differences were demonstrated in independent assessments of regular classroom behavior and to a lesser extent, in academic tests. These differences were all the more convincing because the groups did not differ in initial ratings; "poor progress" children showed no change or worsening pre- to post-treatment, while "good progress" children showed enough improvement to be considered "normal" in some instances.

Another effort to assess the influence of individual differences on the outcome of Think Aloud training included attempts to predict response to the program by separating participants on the basis of some preprogram variable not used in selection of participants. For this purpose, a cognitive test profile score, the "d-score" (see Camp & Bash, 1981, for derivation), was derived from a battery of tests administered to a reference group of aggressive and normal boys. In early trials with Think Aloud when program delivery was tightly controlled, aggressive boys with aggressive profiles showed significant changes in cognitive profile. A later study evaluating the response to the Think Aloud program, delivered by 19 teachers in the process of training, showed that aggressive boys with an "aggressive" cognitive profile did not have significant changes in this profile immediately following either Think Aloud or the control program. Furthermore, aggressive boys who were in the control program and who had a "normal" cognitive profile deteriorated, while similar boys in the Think Aloud program retained their "normal" cognitive profile or improved. On long-term follow-up, however, boys in the Think Aloud program showed progressive "normalization" of their cognitive pattern after termination of the program. Furthermore, those Think Aloud graduates with a normal pattern 6 to 12 months later had the best response to a refresher course.

These studies illustrate how subclasses within a clinical population may respond differently at different times to treatment in different hands even though the overall trend is similar. In addition, researchers would also profitably consider how different classroom or family environments affect the aggressive child with newly gained self-instructional and problem-solving skills. A classroom or family environment that actively discourages prosocial behavior and reinforces aggression may directly compete with the child's newfound skill in considering alternatives and their consequences. Generalization to a setting that will provide negative consequences for utilization of new cognitive skills should not be expected. Data from the operant-systems analyses of aggression-producing families suggest that these systems may not be supportive of new cognitive skills. Perhaps a comparative study would show that, at least in the coercive family system, a combination of parent training and cognitive behavior modification would be more effective than either singly, whereas in the supportive family or classroom, the treatments would be more equally effective. This also raises basic questions about the extent to which a supportive environment is an important facet of maintained treatment effects.

Outcome Measures

The need for multiple indexes of treatment outcome is by now well established in therapy research. The practical utility of using standardized, widely available assessment instruments is receiving some acknowledgment in recent behavioral studies. Measures of clinical significance or social validity (Forehand, Wells, & Griest, 1980; Kazdin, 1977b; Wolf, 1978) are commonly suggested adjuncts to tests of statistical significance. Concern with programming for and adequately measuring generalization across time, response modes, and settings is a commonly repeated theme of methodological critiques in operant and cognitive behavioral journals (Cole & Kazdin, 1980; Stokes & Baer, 1977; Wahler, Berland, & Coe, 1979).

The very recent cognitive behavioral studies, especially those dealing with applications to clinical populations, are more likely to include multiple indexes of effect and to provide data on maintenance and generalization. Studies of nonclinical populations, on the other hand, have seldom provided data on outcome indexes other than the target test response or on follow-up measures across settings or response modes.

Although desirable, the use of multiple outcome measures can also be somewhat confusing. One way to reduce this confusion is to organize and order the various measures along a generalization gradient of increasing "distance" from the program. For example, the first level in such a gradient could be evidence of proficiency with the program. This type of evaluation might represent little more than having an independent examiner assess the adequacy of a child's response to a problem similar to that used in the program. Although essential for establishing a causal link between skills developed in the program and change in other behavior, this level of evaluation is typically either ignored or emphasized to the exclusion of other levels. For the Think Aloud program, this level of evaluation was accomplished through use of a modified version of the Preschool Interpersonal Problem Solving Tests (PIPS) (Shure & Spivack, 1974b). Used as a post-test only, this was almost a direct measure of competency in the type of social problem-solving taught in the program. As expected, Think Aloud boys in all trials were consistently superior to controls on the two most important scores, number of alternative solutions produced and amount of irrelevant, repetitive talk.

These findings established that boys had learned the program, but they also raised questions for further analysis. Think Aloud boys gave more alternative solutions but these included more instances of aggressive solutions. This suggested that the program needed strengthening to go beyond development of alternative thinking to more emphasis on constructive alternatives. It was not until the third trial with Think Aloud as a classroom program (seventh revision) that a significant increase in nonaggressive alternatives was demonstrated among Think Aloud graduates.

The second level in the generalization gradient might require that cognitive change be demonstrated either on tasks different from those used in a program or in the criterion/target-problem setting. This level could take forms such as improved performance on cognitive tests reflecting spontaneous application of skills developed in the program or evidence of increased use of self-instruction when coping with a classroom problem. As mentioned previously, this level or evaluation may be particularly important for programs designed to assist aggressive children; even among recent programs (e.g., Forman, 1980a; Robin *et al.*, 1976), few have provided this type of data. However, considerable effort went into developing a measure for evaluating this type of effect of the Think Aloud program. Since this measure has been somewhat controversial, it seems worth discussing in some detail.

Most studies of treatment effects have reported a collection of univariate analyses on group means and have then attempted to reason about change in individual children from changes in group means. Since changes in group means seldom reflect the changes in individual children, this procedure is often misleading. When one has "more variables than subjects," there may even be problems in knowing how to interpret changes in group means themselves. Consequently, it is imperative that some method be developed for combining scores so that the pattern of change in individual children can be examined.

Such a measure was developed for differentiating the cognitive pattern of aggressive boys from normal boys using discriminant function analysis. This analysis produced a combination of test scores for each boy that yielded the best differentiation between the groups. This combination score, or discriminant score, could then be used to determine how close an individual boy was to the discriminant score mean of aggressive boys or the discriminant score mean of the normal boys. If the d-score was closer to the mean of aggressive boys, the boy was classified as "cognitively aggressive"; if the d-score was closer to the mean for normal boys, the boy was classified as "cognitively normal." Reviewers reporting on early work with the Think Aloud program (Craighead, Wilcoxin-Craighead, & Meyers, 1978; Hobbs, Moguin, Tyroler, & Lahey, 1980) overlooked or misunderstood need for and use of such a profile score. Hobbs *et al.*, for example, criticized Camp, Zimet, van Doorninck, and Dahlem (1977) for "using more variables than subjects," as though Camp and her colleagues were doing the usual series of univariate or multivariate analyses. They failed to recognize that these variables were merely used to calculate a *single* score with weights derived from the above-mentioned discriminant function analysis. Although results were reported for each variable for those readers interested in individual measures, data analysis emphasized changes in the summary d-score as presented in Figure 5. When changes in this d-score occurred, it was also possible to describe the direction of change as normalizing or becoming more aggressive.

Criticism of this d-score has also been presented by Koretz (1979), who attempted to show that Camp's method for differentiating between groups of aggressive and normal boys only capitalized on chance difference that would not stand up under cross-validation. Koretz's arguments were, however, partly based on a misinterpretation of the published data and some incorrect assumptions about data not reported in the published paper. Nevertheless, available data were examined to determine whether Koretz's prediction was correct. In the initial sample of aggressive and normal boys used to derive the d-score, there was 79%–82% correspondence between groupings based on sample selection criteria and grouping based on cognitive pattern (d-score). In a subsequent sample of aggressive boys, this percentage slipped only to 70%. According to Koretz's prediction, this percentage should have been nc greater than chance.

The d-score derived by Camp is perhaps an awkward beginning, but it represents an effort to combine multiple cognitive measures in a way that may be used to characterize an individual child's functioning before and after a treatment program. Further efforts in this direction, however, should help to establish better methods for measuring at this second level of generalization.

Once one has established changes in cognitive functioning, the next (third) level in the generalization gradient might involve cognitive and/or social behavior changes in a naturalistic setting where adult prompting, signaling, and supervision are present. The regular classroom is such a setting. Data from this source could include such measures as teacher ratings of cognitive (e.g., grades) and social behavior *and* naturalistic behavior observations by independent observers. Blind assessment is especially important at this level.

Most would agree that a major jump in the generalization gradient comes between the second level (effects on cognitive tests) and this third level (effects on cognitive/social behavior in the classroom). However, some change at this stage seems necessary to establish clinical validity for most programs. And indeed, most recent studies have provided such data. Yet, few studies of aggressive children have presented both observational and teacher rating data. Again, the Think Aloud program stands alone in this regard (Camp & Bash, 1981). As one might expect, when both teacher ratings and behavior observations were done, there was some discrepancy between results of the teacher ratings and the behavior observations. The behavior observations were difficult to interpret but seemed to indicate more difference between Think Aloud graduates and graduates of a comparison program than did the teacher ratings.

Another aspect of evaluation at this level concerns the way in which clinical significance, as opposed to mere statistical significance, is assessed. One approach involves collecting normative data in the criterion setting and then determining whether treatment brings subjects to the performance level of peers who are assumed to be functioning adaptively. The second approach uses the evaluation of referral agents, such as teachers and parents, regarding the impact of the training program on target behaviors. Although this second approach has sometimes taken the place of collecting data on the child's behavior, only Camp (Camp, 1980; Camp, Zimet, van Doorninck, & Dahlem, 1977) and Kendall and Wilcox (1980) have provided normative data by which to evaluate the effectiveness of their self-instructional programs with aggressive boys.

The fourth level in the generalization gradient might involve demonstration of cognitive or social behavior changes in naturalistic settings where adult direction and supervision are negligible. A good example of such behavior would be peer interactions on the playground. Assessment can be approached somewhat through teacher ratings of social behavior and peer nominations, but anecdotes often remain the major source of information on this point (e.g., Bash & Camp, 1980). Developing unobtrusive measures for assessing improvement at this level is particularly challenging for investigators of aggressive behavior, but to date almost nothing has been done.

The fifth level in the generalization gradient would require that program effects be maintained over time and across many situations. This is particularly critical to answering questions of clinical utility, yet many promising techniques have provided data only for end of treatment (e.g., Forman, 1980a; Goodwin & Mahoney, 1975; Robin *et al.*, 1976). Long-term (6–12 months) follow-up of boys in the Think Aloud program found little evidence of any program impact on global ratings of behavior. Part of the explanation for this seemed to be the insensitivity of the teacher rating scale in use at the time, but part of the explanation was that the original program was probably too weak to produce long-term effects at this level (Camp, 1980; Camp & Bash, 1981).

An important long-term change, was, however, shown in a progressive trend toward normalization of the cognitive pattern in Think Aloud boys that continued after termination of the original program. This difference between Think Aloud boys and boys in the control program Great Expectations was significant at the 0.06 level of confidence and resulted partly from the fact that boys in the Great Expectations program showed deterioration in their cognitive pattern with the passage of time. No other reports of long-term effects on cognitive or social behavior of aggressive boys have been located.

Program Design

The specificity of behavior therapy techniques makes the precise description of treatment approaches possible. The limitations of journal publication often discourage detailed specification of the independent variable. Investigators must be encouraged to make treatment manuals available, including details of training tasks, procedures for carrying out various components, and length/frequency of sessions. A book such as this should encourage this type of detailed description of clinical procedures. Accurate replications of treatment packages will be necessary, especially if lengthy, multicomponent treatments are to be adequately evaluated. Detailed manuals are also necessary to an understanding of the diversity of treatments that may be included within a complex self-instructional/problem-solving approach; this understanding is essential for the design of meaningful dismantling studies aimed at determining effective ingredients and for the construction of more effective and efficient interventions. Treatment manuals are available for a few of the intervention strategies reviewed here (e.g., for the Turtle Technique—Robin *et al.*, 1976—and for Think Aloud—Camp & Bash, 1981).

With greater specification of effective ingredients in various intervention programs, it seems likely that cross-fertilization between contingency management and cognitive behavior modification programs will increase. Stokes and Baer (1977) have suggested that operant therapists consider various self-control strategies as treatment elements to be included at the initiation of a contingency management program. Self-evaluation and self-reinforcement procedures have been used as treatment elements in several classroom token economies (Bolstad & Johnson, 1972; Turkewitz *et al.*, 1975). In general, however, operant clinicians, whom Krantz (1971) has accused of living in a closed system without much awareness of developmental research or alternative treatment strategies, have not looked to the more "purely" cognitive behavior therapies for additions to their treatment packages with aggressive children.

Cognitive behavioral clinicians, on the other hand, have found it useful to include response-cost contingencies in self-instructional treatment packages for impulsive (Kendall, 1977) and aggressive children (Forman, 1980a). This operant component has been effective in producing reductions in disruptive behaviors. In fact, a recent study by Forman (1980a) suggests that response cost alone may be as effective as a self-instructional procedure, at least in the reduction of disruptive classroom behavior. It should be noted, however, that this study did not provide data on the "take" of the self-instructional package—that is, whether the children learned and used the self-instructional procedures. Camp and colleagues (Camp & Bash, 1981) have struggled with the problem of curbing various interfering behaviors such as silliness and hyperactivity in the Think Aloud program, but their efforts have largely culminated in procedures that encourage the use of incompatible behavior. Perhaps introducing a response-cost contingency would be more effective in decreasing disruptive behavior during the program and would additionally lead to a greater decrease in aggressive behavior in the classroom.

Treatment Duration

Length of treatment in the studies reviewed here varies from a single 10-minute training session per child (Zahavi & Asher, 1978) to 40 one-half hour sessions (Camp & Bash, 1981; Camp, Blom, Hebert, & van Doorninck, 1977). The mean length of treatment in cognitive behavioral approaches reviewed by Ledwidge (1978) was 9.1 (S.D.=5.92) sessions with a range of 4–26. It is instructive to contrast these figures with the treatment duration data presented by Patterson, Cobb, and Ray (1973), which indicated that parent contingency management training averaged 31.4 hours per family.

Although efficiency of treatment is an admirable goal, the general conclusion that cognitive behavioral approaches have shown little utility in their application to clinical populations should take into account that the studies done to date have generally been very brief treatments, often designed only to consider the possibility of change and not to discover the best treatment package for durable results. Under these circumstances, the likelihood of clinically significant change in a long-standing pattern of deviant child–environment interaction or the child's failure to learn use of language to mediate motor behavior seems slight indeed. In addition to the total time and length of treatment differences between effective social learning programs and some of the cognitive behavioral "demonstrations," the contingency management training programs have commonly used either planned or performance-based booster shots or short refresher courses.

The Think Aloud program is conducted in 40 sessions over a period of two months. This program length is comparable to the parent-training programs of Patterson and colleagues and to the length of problem-solving curricula such as those proposed by Shure and Spivack. Additionally, one Think Aloud study looked at the effects of a brief refresher course. As mentioned previously, children who made "good progress" in this program showed significant improvement in classroom behavior, while children who responded poorly to the refresher program deteriorated or showed no change.

Significant changes in complex problem behavior should not be expected to appear in a durable and generalizable fashion overnight. Approaches such as those represented by Chittenden (1942), Goodwin and Mahoney (1975), Pitkanen (1974), and Robin *et al.* (1976) perhaps deserve replication within designs that would allow study of the relationship of variations in length of training to duration of effect. Since a number of the brief-treatment studies made no attempt to evaluate the maintenance of treatment effects, it is not possible to say that lengthier treatment would produce more durable effects. However, the preliminary results produced in these studies should be replicated in studies that include follow-up data and provide for the possibility of varying treatment lengths as an important parameter of the treatment package.

SUMMARY

The frequency, stability, and prognostic significance of aggressive behavior make it a logical target for the efforts of behavior therapists. Cognitive behavioral modification approaches to this problem represent part of a continuum of procedures that include parent training in contingency management, self-management of contingencies, social skills training, cognitive modeling, interpersonal cognitive problem-solving, and self-instruction techniques. The procedures addressed have ranged from brief, one-trial, single-case studies demonstrating that a procedure briefly alters one type of behavior to complex packages, exemplified by the Think Aloud program, that address both cognitive and social behavior problem replicated in groups of aggressive children and that involve assessment of short-term gains, long-term gains, and response to a refresher program. Several other promising procedures were identified as needing replication within designs that would allow more in-depth evaluation of the program's clinical utility.

Although any definitive assessment of the clinical utility of cognitive behavioral interventions aimed at the prevention or remediation of aggressive behavior disorders is premature, it does seem clear that sufficient preliminary data are available on multicomponent programs, including cognitive modeling, problem-solving, and self-instructional procedures, to warrant continuation of clinical studies. Conclusions regarding clinical utility will be easier to review meaningfully if investigators carefully specify both the purpose of the program and subject characteristics, provide procedural manuals that permit replication of training techniques, design studies to answer substantive questions of specific locus-of-treatment effect, assess clinical significance of findings, and provide data on generalization of effect across response modes, time, and setting. Think Aloud is a model of the data-based development and evaluation of a cognitive behavioral intervention program. The series of evaluation studies presented here and in progress represent a research program aimed at the establishment of preventive-remedial utility. While a number of major evaluation questions remain for the Think Aloud program, the questions addressed thus far provide an example of the consideration of major evaluation issues within the context of a clinically relevant cognitive training program.

13

Cognitive Behavioral Interventions with Delinquents

Robert E. Kennedy

THE DELINQUENCY PROBLEM

Crimes committed by adolescents and, increasingly, by preadolescent children constitute a major part of the current crime problem in the United States. In 1976, for example, persons between ages 11 and 18, who represented about 12% of the population, committed 34% of the robberies, 52% of the burglaries, 53% of the car thefts, and 17% of the forcible rapes and aggravated assaults that were reported to police and subsequently accounted for by arrests (Federal Bureau of Investigation, 1977). About 35% of imprisoned male felons have spent some time as adolescents in training schools and other institutions for delinquents, and a much higher percentage have had some contact with a juvenile court (Allen & Simonsen, 1978), so that even the very high crime rates just cited for adolescents underestimate the amount of crime that might be prevented by effective treatments for "juvenile delinquency."

Another estimate of the size of the problem of juvenile delinquency is the number of persons involved. In 1977, over 650,000 persons under 18 years old spent time in training schools or other secure facilities or lived in community placements such as group homes; an even larger number were under probation or parole supervision (Hindelang, Gottfredson, & Flanagan, 1981). Some of these adolescents were in custody because they had committed offenses that would not have been illegal had they been adults (so-called "status offenses"). However, most had

Robert E. Kennedy • Department of Psychology, Davidson College, Davidson, North Carolina 28036.

been arrested for at least one act that would have been a serious misdemeanor or a felony if committed by an adult.

THE NEED FOR COGNITIVE BEHAVIORAL INTERVENTIONS

Nonbehavioral counseling, education, and vocational training programs have failed to show consistently positive effects on the post-treatment behavior of delinquents (cf. Lipton, Martinson, & Wilks, 1975). In contrast, institutional and individual programs based on operant learning principles have produced improvements during treatment in delinquents' rule-following behavior, achievement in academic and vocational training programs, and other important behaviors. Among the impressive post-treatment results of these programs have been reductions in police contacts, arrests, and convictions among the treated delinquents (cf. Burchard & Harig, 1976; Davidson & Seidman, 1974). However, reports of noncooperation and resistance to such programs by delinquents are not uncommon (cf. Holt & Hobbs, 1979). More importantly, when follow-up comparisons between treatment and control groups have been extended for periods longer than a year or two, the recidivism rates of the behavioral treatment groups have often risen to approximately the same levels as those of control subjects (cf. Davidson & Seidman, 1974; McCombs, Filipczak, Friedman, & Wodarski, 1978). Also, comparisons of operant programs with other special programs for delinquents, rather than with conventional institutional treatments, have not consistently shown behavioral programs to be superior in their long-term effects (e.g., Cavior & Schmidt, 1978; Jesness, 1975).

Problems with generalization and maintenance of the positive effects of these and other operant programs (cf. Keeley, Shemberg, & Carbonell, 1976) have led to frequent suggestions that behavioral programs should emphasize the teaching of self-regulatory skills and adaptive thinking processes that might promote the post-treatment maintenance of behavioral improvements and facilitate their generalization to environments outside the treatment setting (e.g., Kazdin, 1980; Meichenbaum, 1977; Stokes & Baer, 1977). In fact, many of the studies described below have provided evidence that such "cognitive behavioral" interventions can facilitate behavior change among delinquents participating in operant programs (e.g., Seymour & Stokes, 1976; Snyder & White, 1979) and can by themselves produce behavioral change that generalizes to nontreatment settings and appears to be maintained even after quite extended follow-up periods (e.g., Klein, Alexander, & Parsons, 1977; Sarason, 1978).

TARGET BEHAVIORS IN COGNITIVE BEHAVIORAL INTERVENTIONS

Research has produced a long list of behavioral and cognitive differences between delinquents and nondelinquents and thereby suggested a large variety of possible target behaviors for interventions with delinquents. However, the target behaviors of the early operant programs for delinquents were restricted for the most part to academic skills and conformity to institutional or familial rules. A basic assumption of these programs was that if delinquents learned to succeed academically and to follow rules they would be better able to gain reinforcement for nondelinquent behavior in the natural environment. Unfortunately, even quite substantial changes in delinquents' rule-following behavior and academic achievement have not always been followed by long-term declines in their recidivism rates (e.g., Cohen & Filipczak, 1971).

A major target of more recent behavioral programs has been delinquents' apparent deficiencies in social skills, especially the skills necessary to resolve interpersonal conflict situations in an adaptive, nonaggressive manner. Many attempts to improve delinquents' social skills have concentrated on teaching them specific overt behaviors, often for use in particular situations (e.g., Werner, Minkin, Minkin, Fixsen, Phillips, & Wolf, 1975). In contrast, the cognitive behavioral interventions described in this chapter have been designed to teach generalized skills involving the use of mediational responses that can help the delinquent develop and maintain adaptive overt social behavior. The four main types of mediational responses emphasized in these interventions have been (1) interpersonal problem-solving behaviors, which are cognitive skills involved in the generation of possible responses to interpersonal problems and the choice of the most desirable solution; (2) self-instructional control of impulsive behavior, which has been used not only to improve delinquents' social skills but also to reduce problem behaviors such as stealing; (3) self-management skills, the set of responses by which individuals regulate their own behavior through the self-presentation of consequences that are contingent on their own evaluations of whether their behaviors have met relevant self-imposed goals or standards (cf. Bandura, 1978); and (4) perspective-taking, which is the capacity to infer or predict the cognitive and emotional responses of other persons and which several theorists have identified as an important component of moral judgment and behavior (cf. Hogan, 1973). Discussion of each of these target behaviors will include a short introduction to the general theory and research on that group of skills and a review of the evidence for a deficit in such skills among delinquents. However, the emphasis in the discussion of each area will be on specific attempts at training delinquents in these skills and on the evidence for the effectiveness of such training.

INTERPERSONAL PROBLEM-SOLVING SKILLS

Many theorists have maintained that a major source of many of the antisocial behaviors of delinquents and adult criminals is a deficit in the skills necessary for responding to interpersonal problem or conflict situations in an adaptive, nonaggressive manner (e.g., Bandura, 1973; Sarason, 1979; Toch, 1969). Much of the research investigating this hypothesized deficit has focused on overt behaviors (e.g., Kirchner, Kennedy, & Draguns, 1979), and a large number of studies have been devoted to training delinquents and adult criminals in specific overt social skills (cf. Kennedy, 1981). However, there is substantial evidence that many delinquents also have deficiencies in some of the cognitive responses to interpersonal problems that have been found to increase a person's chances of producing successful solutions to such problems.

Models of Interpersonal Problem-Solving

The models of interpersonal problem-solving (IPS) that have been used most frequently in the assessment and training of problem-solving skills are those of D'Zurilla and Goldfried (1971) and of Spivack and his colleagues at Hahnemann Hospital (Spivack, Platt, & Shure, 1976). Although these two models are basically similar, differences between them in some significant details have implications for training in IPS skills.

D'Zurilla and Goldfried (1971), generalizaing from problem-solving research in cognitive, social, and industrial psychology, described successful problem-solving as a five-step process: (1) a general orientation or "set" to perceive an interaction between persons as a problem to be solved, with the "set" including the inhibition of immediately available but possibly maladaptive (i.e., impulsive) responses; (2) problem definition and formulation; (3) generation of alternatives; (4) decision-making, involving the estimation of the probable consequences of the alternative responses generated in Step 3 and a choice of the response that has the consequences with the best combination of desirability and probability; and (5) verification, or evaluation of the outcome of the response chosen during decision making and of the desirability of going back to an earlier stage in the process if the outcome is not satisfactory. D'Zurilla and Goldfried suggested that one important strategy for increasing the chances of producing a successful solution is to produce a large number of possible solutions during the generation of alternatives stage before moving on to decision-making; this hypothesis has been supported by subsequent research (D'Zurilla & Nezu, 1980).

The second model of IPS, developed by Spivack *et al.* (1976), includes some processes that are not found or are present only implicitly in D'Zurilla and Goldfried's (1971) model. In addition to sensitivity to interpersonal problems, ability to generate solutions ("alternative thinking"), and tendency to anticipate possible consequences of actions, Spivack *et al.* identified three other components of adaptive problem-solving: (1) "causal thinking," or the analysis of interpersonal behavior in cause-and-effect terms; (2) "means–end thinking," or the ability to generate specific step-by-step means by which a problem solution or goal can be reached; and (3) "perspective-taking," or the ability to view a problem situation from the perspective of other persons involved in it.

IPS Deficits in Delinquents

The Hahnemann group has developed methods of assessing these hypothesized component skills and has found deficits in specific IPS behaviors among various groups of children, adolescents, and adults characterized by diverse maladaptive behaviors (cf. Spivack *et al.*, 1976). When the Hahnemann group has compared the skills of nondelinquent adolescents with those of incarcerated adolescent heroin addicts (Platt, Scura, & Hannon, 1973) or with groups of adolescents exhibiting behaviors associated with delinquency (Platt, Spivack, Altman, Altman, & Peizer, 1974; Spivack & Levine, 1963), the nondelinquents have consistently shown higher skill levels on tests of three different IPS abilities: means–end thinking, alternative thinking, and perspective-taking. In these studies, means–end thinking was measured by variations of the Means-Ends Problem Solving Procedure (MEPS—Platt & Spivack, 1975), in which the subject is asked to fill in the steps by which the central character in each of a series of stories describing interpersonal problems gets from a given beginning to a given end. The "delinquent" adolescents in the studies by Platt, Spivack, and their colleagues (Platt *et al.*, 1973, 1974; Spivack & Levine, 1963) gave responses showing (1) less awareness of possible obstacles and of the passage of time, and (2) poorer articulation of the individual steps in the problem-solving process. Relative to the normal controls, these adolescents also gave fewer discrete relevant alternative solutions to a series of interpersonal problems constituting the test of alternative thinking (cf. Spivack *et al.*, 1976), and, when subjects were asked to retell from each character's point of view four stories that they had produced in response to Thematic Apperception Test cards, the delinquents were poorer at coordinating all the characters' points of view, suggesting a deficiency in perspective-taking.

The deficits in component problem-solving skills found among delinquent and acting-out adolescents in the Hahnemann studies may account for a more general problem-solving deficit shown by 14- to 17-year-old delinquents studied by Freedman and her colleagues (Freedman, Rosenthal, Donahoe, Schlundt, & McFall, 1978). These investigators gave to groups of delinquents, nondelinquent adolescent "good citizens," and adolescent "leaders" an "Adolescent Problem Inventory" composed of 44 problem situations chosen and refined using Goldfried and D'Zurilla's (1969) recommendations for the behavioral analysis of social competence. Even when subjects were asked to describe the "best way" someone could solve a problem rather than the way they would actually respond themselves, the delinquents gave problem-solving responses that were rated by judges as significantly less adaptive than those given by the nondelinquent groups. However, when given the opportunity to choose the "best" response from among five alternatives provided by the researchers, the delinquents made choices that were not significantly different in rated competence from those of the nondelinquent groups. These results, like those of the Hahnemann studies, suggest that delinquents as a group may not be deficient in the ability to discriminate among adaptive and nonadaptive solutions to interpersonal problems when they are provided with such solutions but that they are deficient in their ability to generate competent responses on their own. Several attempts to remedy this type of deficiency by cognitive behavioral interventions have produced not only improvements in IPS skills but long-term reductions in delinquent behavior.

Training Delinquents in IPS Skills

Training Delinquents as Individuals

Sarason and Ganzer (1973) devised two related programs for incarcerated delinquents aged 15 to 18 years that attempted to increase their "awareness of what constitutes socially acceptable and effective behavior" (p. 442). In one program, groups of four or five boys each met for one hour per week for 15 weeks with two graduate student group leaders who role-played competent ways of responding to interpersonal situations that had been identified by boys in previous groups as being problems for them. After the leaders' role-playing, the group participants were asked to imitate the modeled behaviors while role-playing the situations themselves. In the second program, the same problem situations were discussed by the group leaders and participants, with the leaders commenting on the adaptiveness of responses suggested by the boys and attempting to provoke discussion of related situations but providing no actual modeling of competent responses. Although these programs did not attempt to teach covert IPS skills in a very explicit way and although the modeling program emphasized the acquisition of overt behaviors, Sarason (1978) later described the programs as an attempt to affect the delinquents' "information-processing" activities. Also, it is obvious from detailed descriptions of the modeling scripts and the discussion format that in both programs considerable emphasis was placed on behaviors such as recognizing problem situations, inhibiting impulsive responses, generating alternatives, and predicting consequences of possible responses (Sarason, undated).

Sarason (1978) followed the treatment-group members and a group of untreated controls for almost five years after the end of the program. By that time, 48% of the control group had become recidivists, compared with only 23% of each of the treatment groups. The recidivism rate of the treatment groups was also significantly lower than the base rate of recidivism shown by the cumulative population of the instituion where the programs took place. These results are impressive because of the length of the follow-up, the size of the comparison groups (64 boys in each), and the relatively small cost of the programs in professional time. However, the lack of a difference in recidivism between the two treatment groups is somewhat surprising for two reasons. First, other follow-up data from this study indicated that, compared with discussion alone, the modeling treatment produced better long-term recall of the purpose and content of treatment, more frequent conscious applications of the behaviors learned, and greater subjective estimates of benefit from treatment (Sarason, 1978). Second, other comparisons of similar modeling and discussion groups have tended to show that modeling produces greater immediate behavioral change (Block, 1978; Ollendick & Hersen, 1979; Scopetta, 1972; Snyder & White, 1979). Given these latter results and the superiority of Sarason and Ganzer's modeling program on measures other than recidivism, modeling of problem-solving may usually be expected to produce greater treatment effects than discussion alone.

Social skills and problem-solving programs similar to that of Sarason and Ganzer (1973) have been included in comprehensive behavioral programs for delinquents (e.g., Thoresen, Thoresen, Klein, Wilbur, Becker-Haven, & Haven, 1979) and for adolescents at high risk for delinquency (e.g., Filipczak, Archer, & Friedman, 1980). These programs have produced promising short-term results but have not included research to determine the contribution of problem-solving training or of its individual components to these positive results.

Training Delinquents and Their Families

Many of the situations that had been identified by Sarason and Ganzer's (1973) pilot subjects as presenting problems involved conflict between the boy and his family. Such family conflict has long been recognized as contributing to the development of delinquent behavior (e.g., Patterson & Reid, 1970), and several programs have been developed to train delinquents and their parents to use IPS skills in the resolution of disagreements and disputes.

Kifer, Lewis, Green, and Phillips (1974), for example, trained three parent–delinquent pairs (two mother–daughter pairs and one father–son pair, with youths aged 13 to 17 years) in the use of decision-making and negotiating skills. Each training session had three phases. At the beginning of the session, the parent and child role-played a hypothetical parent–child conflict situation described to them by the trainers. After this role-play phase, the trainers gave the participants a written description of the situation that they had just role-played, a list of possible response options for both the parent and the child in that situation, and a list of possible consequences of each of the alternative responses. Trainers and clients then discussed which response options were likely to lead to which consequences and added other optional responses and consequences if any occurred to them. When the consequences of all proposed responses had been identified, both the parent and the child were asked to select his or her preferred response to the situation on the basis of its probable consequences. The third phase of the session then began, with the parent and child again role-playing the situation, starting with each person's presenting his or her preferred option. During this role-play, trainers used instructions and feedback to increase the pair's use of three negotiation behaviors: (1) "complete communication," the statement of one's position in terms of what one wants or thinks regarding the situation, followed by a request that the other person respond to this position or state his own; (2) "identification of issues," explicit identification of points of conflict in the situation; and (3) "suggestion of options," statements suggesting alternative courses of action that might resolve the conflict. Kifer *et al.* (1974) did not refer to D'Zurilla and Goldfried's (1971) model of problem-solving, but their program obviously included training in several of the component processes identified in that model: problem definition and formulation, generation of alternatives, identification of consequences, and choice of response based on desirability of its consequences.

Kifer *et al.* (1974), using a multiple-baseline design across subject pairs, found that the negotiation behaviors of each pair increased dramatically after the introduction of training and reached preset success criteria after an average of five training sessions. Comparisons of behavioral observations in the home made before and after treatment showed substantial increases in each pair's use of negotiation behaviors and in the frequency of conflict-resolution responses. This appeared to be encouraging evidence for the generalization of training effects to the home, but the self-reports of 12 mother–son and 12 mother–daughter dyads (with adolescents aged 11 to 14) who participated in a quite similar program with an even greater emphasis on a problem-solving approach to conflict resolution indicated little or no generalization of treatment effects (Robin, Kent, O'Leary, Foster, & Prinz, 1977). Little and Kendall (1979) have suggested that the inconsistency between these results and those of Kifer *et al.* may have been produced by the insensitivity of Robin *et al.*'s self-report measure to actual behavioral changes. However, it seems equally if not more plausible to attribute Kifer *et al.*'s positive generalization results to their subjects' possible "reactivity" to the behavioral observations (cf. Kent & Foster, 1977), especially since Kifer *et al.*'s home observations were not naturalistic but involved parent–child discussions that were elicited and somewhat structured by the observers (Kifer *et al.*, 1974, p. 358).

The work of Alexander and Parsons (1973) has provided stronger evidence for the generalization of the effects of problem-solving training with 13- to 16-year-old male and female delinquents and their families. These investigators used modeling and behavioral rehearsal to teach 46 families a general process of problem-solving that emphasized clear communication, presentation of alternative solutions, and negotiation leading to reciprocally satisfying resolutions. This program led not only to the successful acquisition of the problem-solving skills by the families but a lower recidivism rate after 6 to 18 months among the treated delinquents than among control group families who received client-centered therapy, psychodynamic therapy, or no treatment. An equally important result of the program was that during a follow-up period of up to 3½ years the siblings of the delinquents in the families that had received problem-solving training had significantly fewer contacts with juvenile courts than did the siblings of delinquents in the control groups (Klein *et al.*, 1977).

A replication of Alexander and Parsons's (1973) original program, using a different therapist for each family, examined the relationship of treatment outcome with treatment process measures and the skill levels of the individual therapists (Alexander, Barton, Schiavo, & Parsons, 1976). The problem-solving training with a group of 21 male and female delinquents aged 13 to 16 and their parents produced a recidivism rate that was similar to that found in the original study, but Alexander *et al.* (1976) found that recidivism was quite high among delinquents whose families had made little progress in changing problem-solving interactions during therapy sessions. On the other hand, there were no recidivists during the follow-up period of 12 to 15 months among the delinquents whose families had changed their interactional style substantially during treatment. Further, although the families' progress in therapy was not related to ratings of their communicative effectiveness during the first treatment session, treatment progress was highly correlated with *a priori* assessments of the individual therapists' skills in "structuring" (directiveness and self-confidence) and relationship-building (affect–behavior integration, warmth, and humor). These clinically important results add to previous evidence with "contingency contracting" (Stuart & Lott, 1972) that even in the relatively structured family programs used by behavior therapists variations in therapist behavior can have significant effects on treatment outcome.

Summary and Comments

Results of both individual and family programs providing training in IPS skills have suggested that such programs represent an effective and efficient type of treatment for many delinquents. The effects of Sarason and Ganzer's (1973) program on the long-term recidivism of relatively high-risk delinquents, the replication by Alexander and his colleagues of the results of their original program, and their finding that its effects generalize to the siblings of participating delinquents are even more impressive when compared with the generally weak and transient effects usually produced by other short-term treatments of delinquents (cf. Lipton *et al.*, 1975).

Treatment efficiency and effectiveness might be even greater with programs that provided assessment of the separate component skills of effective problem-solving and gave individuals training in the particular skills in which they showed the most pronounced deficiencies. For example, research on the IPS deficiencies of delinquents indicates that a deficiency in generation of alternatives may be more common among them than a deficiency in choosing the most adaptive response from among the alternatives generated (e.g., Freedman *et al.*, 1978; Platt *et al.*, 1973). Training emphasizing the generation of adaptive alternatives might thus be more effective with many delinquents than a more general, less focused type of training. The Hahnemann group has already developed a variety of measures and training exercises for the IPS component skills that could be readily adapted to such an individualized treatment approach (Spivack *et al.*, 1976).

SELF-INSTRUCTIONAL CONTROL OF IMPULSIVE BEHAVIOR

Several prominent theories of delinquency assume that the antisocial behavior of many delinquents stems in large part from a serious deficit in impulse control (e.g., Glueck & Glueck, 1974). Such a deficit would seem to be a natural target for a cognitive behavioral approach to the treatment of delinquency, since among the most frequently reported cognitive behavioral interventions have been programs in which normal, impulsive, hyperactive, or aggressive young children have been trained to control their impulsive behavior by giving themselves appropriate self-instructions (cf. Craighead, Wilcoxon-Craighead, & Meyers, 1978; Hobbs, Moguin, Tyroler, & Lahey, 1980; Urbain & Kendall, 1980).

Impulse Control Deficits among Delinquents

Research comparing the impulsivity of delinquents and nondelinquents has not always found a relative deficit in impulse control among the delinquents. However, there is considerable evidence that adolescents identified variously as "psychopathic," "sociopathic," or "conduct-disorder" delinquents have more difficulty controlling impulsive behavior than do either nondelinquents or other delinquent groups (cf. Quay, 1979). Delinquents in this psychopathic group tend to be institutionalized more often, to present greater discipline problems within institutions, and to have higher rates of recidivism than delinquents in other diagnostic groups (Sarason & Ganzer, 1973; Quay, 1979). Since some of the apparently more severe delinquent behavior of adolescents in the psychopathic group may be related to their problems with impulse control, an intervention that could remedy this type of deficit might be quite effective in reducing problem behavior among this large group. The relative success of the few reported attempts to train delinquents in the use of self-instructions suggest that self-instruction training might be one such program.

Self-instruction Training with Delinquents

One study that provided only equivocal evidence that self-instruction training can help delinquents learn to control their impulsive behavior was reported by Williams and Akamatsu (1978), who attempted to replicate Meichenbaum and Goodman's (1971b) success in teaching children to reduce their impulsive behavior on a laboratory task by modeling the use of self-instruction to go slowly and be careful. These investigators found that their treatment group of male and female incarcerated delinquents showed greater improvements than a no-treatment control group not only on a training task—the Matching Familiar Figures test (Kagan, 1966)—but also on a generalization task—the picture arrangement task of the Wechsler Intelligence Scale for Children. However, an attention control group showed post-treatment gains as large as those of the self-instruction group. Williams and Akamatsu (1978) did not interpret these findings as a failure to demonstrate the effectiveness of self-instruction training, since the attention control group actually received what they called "minimal modeling" cues, including instructions to "go slowly" (p. 287). But their results do not provide strong evidence that training in self-instructions was actually responsible for the improvement shown by the treatment group.

The clinical potential of self-instruction training with delinquents was suggested by the results of a case study reported by McCullough, Huntsinger, and Nay (1977), who taught a 16-year-old boy with a long history of aggressive outbursts at home and at school to use "thought-stopping," a form of self-instruction (Wolpe, 1969), to control the subvocal cursing that was first in a chain of covert responses to conflict situations that led eventually to the boy's overt aggressive behavior. McCullough *et al.* also taught the boy to relax his body when it became tense during an interaction and to walk away from a conflict when he felt in imminent danger of losing his temper. This combination of treatments apparently produced a dramatic decrease in the number and the severity of the boy's outbursts. Unfortunately, however, an attempt by Huntsinger (1976) to use this same type of training with 12- to 16-year-old male delinquents incarcerated in a state training school produced no post-treatment differences in aggressive behavior within the institution among the treatment group, a discussion-only attention control group, and a nontreated control group.

Self-instruction training produced more positive results in a study by Snyder and White (1979), who trained five aggressive delinquents to use adaptive self-verbalizations to control their behavior in a residential behavior modification program. During the first phase of the group training, Snyder and White introduced the concept of private speech and tried to show, through their own examples and through examples supplied by the subjects, how private speech can control overt behavior. In the second phase of the training, the task of the group was to identify the self-verbalizations that accompanied behaviors considered undesirable in the residential program. In addition to the situation, self-verbalization, and behavior involved, the group also tried to identify the probable consequence of the behavior. The next phase included discussion of the self-defeating aspects of these self-verbalizations and an attempt to replace them, through modeling, covert modeling, and role-playing, with more adaptive self-verbalizations that included a statement of the contingencies in the situation, the demands of the task, and self-reinforcement for success. For example, one undesirable self-verbalization identified by the group occurred in response to a cottage counselor's saying in the morning, "Time to get up." The maladaptive self-verbalization in response to this situation was "The hell with that, this feels good" (p. 230), the maladaptive behavior was staying in bed, and the consequence was losing token points. The adaptive self-verbalization that the delinquents learned was "Already, damn. It feels good to stay in bed, but if I get up I'll get points I need for cigarettes. OK just open my eyes, sit up. Good I made it" (p. 231). The adaptive behavior was getting out of bed, and the consequences were getting points and avoiding confrontation with the counselor. The last phase of treatment involved discussion of subjects' attempts to apply the self-monitoring, self-verbalization, and self-reinforcement skills learned in the group to their actual behavior in the residential program. The subjects were given social reinforcment when they reported improvements in problem-situation behaviors. Also, when they reported failure instead of success, the subjects were trained to use coping statements to decrease frustration and maintain motivation. The group leaders first tried to point out the self-defeating nature of such negative covert responses to failure as "What do I care, get out of bed when they say so. Screw it! They can take their self-talk and stick it" (p. 231). Modeling and role-playing were then used to develop more adaptive self-verbalizations such as, "OK, so I didn't get out of bed. Everybody blows it now and then. I have been doing better and all I need to do is keep trying. I can still get enough points to go to a movie this weekend" (p. 231).

Snyder and White had chosen the five subjects for their treatment group, five subjects for a discussion-only attention control group, and five subjects for a no-treatment group from among male and female delinquents aged 14 to 17 who did not seem to be responding positively to the residential treatment program. During the four-week treatment period and a six-week follow-up, all the groups showed some reductions in (1) their absences from academic classes, (2) their failures to complete social and self-care responsibilities, and (3) their impulsive behaviors (e.g., drug-taking, physical aggression, stealing, or destruction of property). However, these changes were significantly greater in the group trained in self-instructions than in either of the control groups, with the treatment group reducing all three classes of undesirable behaviors by well over 50%.

Summary and Comments

Training in the use of self-instructions to control impulsive behavior would seem a potentially valuable intervention with delinquents, since deficits in impulse control are apparently common among a subgroup of delinquents whose behaviors seem more resistant than those of other delinquents to more conventional types of treatment. Although the evidence for the effectiveness of self-instruction training with delinquents is slight and inconsistent, Snyder and White's (1979) results do suggest that teaching delinquents to give themselves more adaptive instructions can lead to substantial improvements in their behavior, at least within the context of an ongoing residential token program. Future research is obviously needed to determine whether self-instruction training can have an effect on delinquents' behavior after they leave such a program and whether such training can be effective as a noninstitutional treatment for delinquents.

SELF-MANAGEMENT SKILLS

Self-instructional control of impulsive behavior is only one component of the set of behaviors involved in the process that cognitive behavioral theorists have called "self-management," "self-regulation," or "self-control" (e.g., Bandura, 1978; Mahoney & Arnkoff, 1978). According to Bandura (1978), self-regulatory behavior also involves (1) goal- or standard-setting, (2) self-observation of behavior, (3) self-evaluation or the comparison of self-observed behavior with a goal or standard, and (4) the self-presentation of overt or covert positive consequences (self-reinforcement) or negative consequences (self-punishment). Bandura (1977a) has also identified perceived "self-efficacy," or a person's perception of the probability that he or she can successfully execute a behavior, as an important influence on the self-regulation of behavior.

Numerous studies have shown that children and adolescents can be trained successfully to use each of these self-regulatory behaviors (cf. O'Leary & Dubey, 1979). Such self-management interventions generally have been as effective as externally administered programs in controlling and changing target behaviors and have on occasion led to generalization and maintenance results seldom produced by equivalent externally controlled programs. Drabman Spitalnik, and O'Leary (1973), for example, rewarded disruptive 9- and 10-year-old boys in a remedial reading program for self-evaluations that matched external evaluations made by their teacher. After accurate self-evaluation had been established, Drabman *et al.* gradually faded out the matching contingency and for 12 days allowed the boys to award themselves token system points solely on the basis on their own evaluations. Despite the opportunity to reward themselves noncontingently, the boys contined to make self-evaluations that closely matched the now-surreptitious teacher evaluations. Not only were improvements in behavior maintained in the reading program during this period, but they generalized to times of the school day when the token program was not in effect. An earlier study with disruptive adolescents in a psychiatric hospital school had found similar maintenance of behavioral change when students switched either from a positive reinforcement program or from a response cost program, both of which were based on teacher evaluations, to an equivalent type of program in which consequences were determined by the students' own evaluations of their behavior (Kaufman & O'Leary, 1972).

Self-management Skill Deficits in Delinquents

The evidence for deficits in self-management skills among delinquents is for the most part indirect. For example, delinquents in general, and again psychopathic delinquents in particular, have shown less ability than nondelinquents to delay gratification in laboratory studies in which they have been given a choice between a small immediate reward and a larger but delayed reward (e.g., Unikel & Blanchard, 1973). The behavior of delinquents in such studies reflects a generalized unwillingness to delay gratification that is usually attributed to the low expectations of delinquents about their chances for achieving such minimal conventional goals as graduating from high school and finding decent work (cf. Sarason, 1978) and from their consequent devaluation of these goals (e.g., Stein, Sarbin, & Kulik, 1968). Low expectations of achieving conventional goals could also account for the tendency of delinquents to spend more time than nondelinquents thinking about immediate goals and less about future goals (e.g., Landau, 1975), to be more willing than nondelinquents to apply negative labels to themselves (e.g., Wodarski, Feldman, & Pedi, 1975), and to express a more external generalized locus of control (e.g., Beck & Ollendick, 1976). Not only do delinquents tend to be more external in perceived locus of control than nondelinquents, but among delinquents themselves external locus of control has been found to be related to a higher number of delinquent offenses both before and after participation in a residential token economy (Ollendick, Elliott, & Matson, 1980).

The implication of all this research is the not-uncommon suggestion that a major goal of treatment programs for delinquents should be to increase their expectations that they can achieve conventional goals through socially acceptable behavior. Training in educational, vocational, and social skills that provides numerous success experiences may be the most effective method of increasing such expectations and decreasing delinquents' external locus of control (Bandura, 1977a). In fact, Eitzen (1975) presented evidence that the Achievement Place program (Fixsen, Phillips, Phillips, & Wolf, 1976), which provides social skills training and reinforces academic success, produces among its participants a movement toward a more internal perceived locus of control and an increase in "self-esteem." However, the Achievement Place program itself provides some training in self-management skills (e.g., Fixsen, Phillips, & Wolf, 1973), and other studies of various types of self-management training with delinquents strongly suggest that they can facilitate the effects of staff-administered reinforcement programs, especially with delinquents who initially do not respond well to this type of program.

Self-management Training with Delinquents

Goal-Setting

A laboratory study by Gagne (1975) has provided evidence for the potential utility of training delinquents to set realistic goals for themselves. In this study, male delinquents aged 13 to 16 who were asked to set explicit trial-by-trial goals for their performance on a learning task performed significantly better than delinquents who did not set such goals. This performance-facilitating effect of goal-setting has been utilized in individualized academic programs for both adult criminals and delinquents (cf. Ayllon & Milan, 1979), but it seems that neither in these nor in any other behavioral programs for delinquents have attempts been made to train goal-setting as a generalized mediational skill.

Self-observation and Self-evaluation

Two studies have produced evidence that making reinforcement contingent on delinquents' own evaluations of their behavior can add to the effectiveness of conventional token programs. Seymour and Stokes (1976) asked four 14- to 18-year-old adolescent girls in a maximum-security institution to self-record both a full range of work behaviors in a day-long education program and appropriate behaviors during vocational training sessions. Self-recorded behaviors were rewarded by tokens used in a staff-directed token economy that had proved ineffectual in controlling the behavior of these particular girls. Reinforcement contingent on self-recorded behavior led to substantial increases in work and appropriate vocational training behaviors for three of the four girls, changes that were maintained during short follow-up periods when token reinforcement was withdrawn but the girls continued their self-recording.

Wood and Flynn (1978), working with 10- to 15-year-old delinquent males in a residential program modeled on Achievement Place, compared the maintenance of improved room-cleaning behavior produced by a staff-administered token program with that produced by tokens given on the basis of self-recorded behavior. During the initial phases of the self-recording program, a reinforced matching procedure similar to that used by Drabman *et al.* (1973) was used to ensure the accuracy of the boys' self-recording but was quickly faded when they reached a preset criteria for accuracy. Both the external reinforcement and the self-recording programs were withdrawn after 25 days of treatment, and room-cleaning behavior was observed for the next 60 days. Although the number of boys in each treatment ($n = 3$) was too small to allow reliable statistical evaluation of the results, the self-recording condition appeared to produce superior maintenance, since the boys in that group maintained a level of room-cleaning behavior close to the level that they had displayed when receiving reinforcement, while the behavior of the boys in the external token program decreased to a level closer to the one that they had displayed during the initial baseline than the one that they displayed during treatment.

This first withdrawal phase was followed by a 40-day period in which all the boys self-recorded their behavior and received tokens contingent on their self-reports. The final phase of the study was a third baseline of 22 days during which all the boys maintained their behavior at a level quite close to that shown during the second treatment phase. During all the periods when the boys were receiving tokens for self-reported behavior but their self-reports were not being overtly checked, they nevertheless maintained a high level of agreement with staff observations made without their knowledge.

Self-reinforcement

Cognitive social learning theory assumes that in the studies just reviewed the maintenance of behavior change following withdrawal of external reinforcers was produced at least in part by "self-evaluative consequences in the form of self-satisfaction, self-pride, self-dissatisfaction, and self-criticism" (Bandura, 1978, p. 350). However, neither Seymour and Stokes (1976) nor Wood and Flynn (1978) seem to have included explicit training in covert reinforcement as part of their program. The possible utility of such training with delinquents is apparent, however, in a case study reported by Stumphauzer (1976), describing the treatment of compulsive stealing in a 12-year-old girl.[1] Stumphauzer began by training the girl, through imaginal role-playing, to shift her attention from the usual kinds of things she stole to other interesting objects and activities, with this shift followed by covert self-reinforcing statements such as, "'I'm proud of myself'" (p. 266). After several sessions of such training, Stumphauzer had the girl begin self-monitoring her own stealing behavior and using self-reinforcing statements when she refrained from stealing. Finally, actual counting of stealing incidents was replaced by daily self-evaluations and self-reinforcement in the girl's own words, such as, "'I have done so well . . . that I did not think to steal,'" and, later in treatment, "'At the store I look for what I'm supposed to and not things that will get my interest'" (pp. 266–267). This treatment, combined with family contracting that included monetary and social reinforcers for refraining from stealing, apparently eliminated the girl's reported stealing, which did not recur during an 18-month follow-up.

Stumphauzer's (1976) treatment might not have produced such dramatic results with most delinquents, since the girl described in his case study had advantages that many delinquents do not: good grades and an interest in school, basically prosocial attitudes, and very motivated and cooperative parents. On the other hand, the girl's stealing was not a minor problem, since she had been stealing almost daily for five years and since, when she was referred for treatment, she was stealing not only at home and in school but also in stores, putting her in imminent danger of becoming involved with juvenile authorities.

Self-management Training Combined with Other Treatments

Other behavioral programs for delinquents have included elements of self-management training in more comprehensive treatment pack-

[1]Most cognitive behavioral interventions designed to reduce antisocial behavior in children have focused on verbal and physical aggression (cf. Little & Kendall, 1979; Urbain & Kendall, 1980). Stealing, on the other hand, has seldom been an explicit target behavior in either operant or cognitive interventions. This relative neglect may be an important oversight, since young children who steal seem much more likely to commit serious juvenile offenses during adolescence than children whose main behavior problem is aggression (Moore, Chamberlain, & Mukai, 1979).

ages. Snyder and White's (1979) self-instructional training program, for example, contained explicit training in making self-reinforcing statements as part of the self-instructions. Also, the coping statements that were taught as adaptive responses to failure emphasized realistic self-evaluation ("Everybody blows it now and then. I have been doing better") and goal-setting ("All I need to do is keep trying. I can still get enough points to go to a movie this weekend").

Gross, Brigham, Hopper, and Bologna (1980) included training in principles of behavior modification, self-management skills, and interpersonal problem-solving in their program for noninstitutionalized male and female delinquents aged 12 to 16 years. They required each adolescent to complete one project involving the modification of someone else's behavior and another involving modification of his or her own behavior. This training was followed by decreases in teacher- and parent-rated problem behaviors and by increases in the youths' school grades. These improvements were maintained during a two-month follow-up period.

Schwitzgebel and Kolb (1964) reported more impressive results for an apparently simple procedure in which delinquents aged 15 to 21 with a history of many arrests were paid to come to a storefront in their neightborhood two or three times per week and talk for an hour into the microphone of a tape recorder. Compared with a no-treatment control group, the young men who received between 9 and 10 months of this "treatment" had 49% fewer arrests, spent 49% less time incarcerated, and had a 22% lower recidivism rate during a three-year follow-up. Schwitzgebel and Kolb attributed these positive results in part to their having overtly reinforced with monetary bonuses any attempts by the delinquents during their conversations to "explore feelings and solutions [to problems] and to expand their capacity for self-direction," which was defined as the "ability of a person, through planning, to control his own reinforcers" p. 303). Such attempts at problem-solving and self-direction were the only behaviors overtly reinforced during the project besides punctual attendance at the sessions.

Summary and Comments

Only a few attempts at direct training of delinquents in self-management skills have been reported, and most of these have combined such training with other treatments, so that it is difficult to evaluate the independent effects of the self-management training itself. The results of three of these studies, however, suggest that such training can enhance the effects of a residential operant program on delinquents' behavior, at least within the program itself, and that providing delinquents with the skills and the opportunity to manage their own behavior may be an effective way to reduce the resistence and noncooperation with which some delinquents respond to externally administered programs (Seymour & Stokes, 1976; Snyder & White, 1979; Wood & Flynn, 1978).

A residential program such as Achievement Place would be an ideal setting for systematically testing the effects of training delinquents in each of the component skills of self-management. An individual or group could be gradually moved from a staff-administered program to one that was for the most part self-managed, through the step-by-step substitution of self-recording for external observation, self-evaluation for staff evaluation, individually determined performance standards for externally imposed standards, and covert self-reinforcement for tangible reinforcers. Many operant programs actually employ a version of this process to wean residents from highly structured reinforcement systems (e.g., Fixsen *et al.*, 1976). The evidence reviewed above suggests that specific training in self-management skills during this fading process might facilitate the maintenance of the treatment effects it is designed to produce.

PERSPECTIVE-TAKING SKILLS

One long-standing theory of antisocial behavior maintains that some persons are able to violate other people's rights with little compunction or guilt because of an inability or failure to assume the perspective or point of view of the persons whose rights they are violating. This theory has been presented in different forms by a long series of personality theorists and social psychologists (e.g., Gough, 1948; Hogan, 1973; Mead, 1934; Sarbin, 1954). But most of the evidence that antisocial behavior is actually associated with deficits in perspective-taking has come from studies based on Piagetian theory.

Piaget (1928, 1962a) introduced the idea that children's social behavior is affected by their degree of egocentrism or inability to take another persons' point of view. However, a subsequent deluge of research, which began in the 1960s (e.g., Feffer & Gourevitch, 1960; Flavell, Botkin, Fry, Wright, & Jarvis, 1968), has produced skepticism that perspective-taking can be considered a unitary construct. This research has found generally low or nonsignificant correlations among measures of cognitive perspective-taking (making inferences about another person's thoughts or about the information he or she has about a situation), affective perspective-taking (making inferences about another person's internal emotional responses), and perceptual perspective-taking (making inferences about another person's visual perception of objects) (cf. Ford, 1979). Nevertheless, this research has also provided evidence that at least cognitive and affective perspective-taking are related to important social behaviors. For example, affective perspective-taking in young children has been found to be correlated positively with measures of cooperation and other prosocial behaviors (e.g., D. W. Johnson, 1975). Cognitive perspective-taking apparently correlates fairly highly with maturity of moral judgment (cf. Jurkovic, 1980) and with peer group status and classroom adjustment (e.g., Burka & Glenwick, 1978). Egocentrism, or low perspective-taking ability, among the boys in Burka and Glenwick's (1978) study was associated with learning difficulties and high levels of aggressive behavior.

Most attempts to train children or adults to take the perspective of others have involved some form of *role-reversal* or role-switching, in which a person repeatedly role-plays with a trainer or with other members of a group an interchange between persons that usually involves conflict or disagreement. Instead of playing the same "character" during each role-play of the situation, the person switches roles between role-plays and takes the part of a different character during the next simulation. In the context of disagreements and negotiations among adults, such training has been found to reduce hostility between opponents and increase acceptance of the possible validity of opposing positions (Johnson, 1971). Training programs with children have been successful in increasing performance on conventional measures of perspective-taking ability, and, while changes in perspective-taking have not always been accompanied by changes in other social behaviors (Urbain & Kendall, 1980), several studies have found that perspective-taking training can produce clinically important changes in behavior. For example, Feshbach (1978) found that when aggressive third- to fifth-grade children were given both role-switching experience accompanied by discussion of the feelings of characters in the role-played situations and direct training and practice in identifying emotions, they showed greater reductions in aggression ratings than did children in an attention-control group who were trained in nonsocial problem-solving.

Perspective-taking Deficits among Delinquents

Direct evidence for the link between perspective-taking deficits and antisocial behavior has come from a growing number of studies reporting that samples of delinquents and of adult prisoners score lower on various perspective-taking tasks than do noncriminal comparison groups or age-appropriate norms (e.g., Chandler, 1973; Kennedy,

Kirchner, & Draguns, 1980; Little, 1979; Platt *et al.*, 1973; Rotenberg, 1974; Widom, 1976). Most of the tasks used in these studies were designed as measures of cognitive perspective-taking but deficits in affective perspective-taking have also been found among both delinquents (Rotenberg, 1974) and adult criminals (Kennedy *et al.*, 1980).

Deficits in perspective-taking, like deficits in impulse control and delay of gratification, have been found to be most pronounced among the groups of delinquents and adult criminals labeled "psychopathic" (Jurkovic & Prentice, 1977; Kennedy, Kirchner, & Draguns, 1979). Psychopathic individuals also have been reported to show physiological responses to distress cues from other persons that are weaker than those of nonpsychopaths (House & Milligan, 1976) and to expect to experience less negative reactions to harming disliked others and to view such behavior as more self-congruent than nonpsychopaths (Klass, 1980). Thus, even if psychopathic delinquents learned effective problem-solving, impulse control, and self-management skills, they still might readily violate other persons' rights when they thought such antisocial behavior was to their advantage. The presumed effect of perspective-taking training, on the other hand, is to deter the delinquent from antisocial behavior by a heightened appreciation of his or her potential victim's point of view and by a concomitant increase in negative reactions to the victim's distress. Such training might therefore be especially valuable for the treatment of psychopathic and other delinquents whose antisocial behavior is unaffected by other treatments.

Perspective-taking Training with Delinquents

The strongest evidence for the usefulness of perspective-taking training with delinquents comes from a study by Chandler (1973), who paid 30 young delinquents between the ages of 11 and 13 to take part in a 10-week "film workshop" in a storefront in their neighborhood. Half of these boys received perspective-taking training in which groups of 5 boys each developed brief skits about real-life situations involving persons their own age, with each skit having one part for each boy in the group. The boys role-played and videotaped each of these skits as many times as it took for each boy to play each of the parts. All the videotapes were viewed by the group at the end of each set, ostensibly in an effort to improve the skits. The other 15 boys took part in attention control training groups in which they made cartoon and documentary films about their own neighborhood but could not use themselves as subjects or actors.

An assessment prior to treatment had indicated that the cognitive perspective-taking of the delinquent boys was comparable to that of nondelinquent children about half their age and was considerably inferior to that of a group of nondelinquent boys of the same age from the same neighborhood. After treatment, however, the boys who had received perspective-taking training scored much closer to age-appropriate norms, showing greater improvement in perspective-taking than either the attention control group or a no-treatment group. The treatment group also had almost 50% fewer "known delinquencies" than the control groups during an 18-month follow-up.

Few other attempts at explicit training in perspective-taking with delinquents have been reported. Little (1979) attempted to replicate Chandler's (1973) study with institutionalized girls aged 13 to 16 but found that her treatment group did not improve significantly more in perspective-taking or earn more points in a token system than did an attention control group. However, various methodological problems with this study (e.g., sample size, sample selection) limit the interpretability of its results. Perhaps more significant than this single failure to replicate Chandler's (1973) results is the striking fact that some of the most successful problem-solving and self-instructional training programs described above provided participants with considerable experience in role-switching during the role-playing of personally relevant situations (e.g., Kifer *et al.*, 1974; Sarason & Ganzer, 1973; Snyder & White, 1979). Role-switching experience was obviously not considered a crucial element in these programs, usually being mentioned only in passing in descriptions of the treatments. However, Chandler's (1973) results suggest that such experience might play an important but heretofore unnoticed role in the effectiveness of these programs.

Summary and Comments

There is considerable evidence both for the relationship between antisocial behavior and a deficit in perspective-taking activity and for the effectiveness of role-switching in increasing perspective-taking among nondelinquent children. Given this evidence and the positive results of Chandler's (1973) training program, it is quite surprising that so few additional attempts to increase delinquents' perspective-taking have been reported. Chandler (1973) himself may have discouraged attempts at replication when he warned that his training could have reduced his treatment group's police contacts not because it reduced their antisocial behavior but because it increased their ability to avoid getting caught for such behavior by police. This warning, although perhaps partly facetious, points to some important theoretical questions regarding perspective-taking training and delinquency.

The most important of these questions is the identity of the process that mediates between an increase in perspective-taking and the presumed reduction in delinquent behavior. As Chandler (1973) indirectly pointed out, increased perspective-taking *per se* would not necessarily prevent antisocial behavior. One possible mediating process is a perspective-taking-induced increase in empathic emotional responses to others' distress, since high levels of such responses have been found to be negatively correlated with aggression (Mehrabian & Epstein, 1972) and positively correlated with altruistic behavior (Krebs, 1975). Another possibility is that increased perspective-taking ability or activity leads to increases in the maturity of delinquents' moral judgments (cf. Jurkovic, 1980). Of course, it is possible that both of these processes, and others as well, are involved.

Identification of the processes that mediate between changes in perspective-taking and decreases in antisocial behavior could have important implications for such training. For example, if it were found that training-induced increases in empathic emotional responses are related to decreases in antisocial behavior, components that enhance such increases could be added to the training. In fact, Feshbach (1978) found that perspective-taking training that included several experiences focused specifically on attending to others' emotions led to somewhat greater reductions in aggression among her subjects than did a program focusing strictly on cognitive perspective-taking. Replication of Feshbach's treatments using older, delinquent children and including measurement of training-induced changes in empathic responses, maturity of moral judgment, and other possible mediating processes might provide information of both theoretical and clinical importance.

AN INDIVIDUALIZED APPROACH TO INTERVENTIONS WITH DELINQUENTS

The research reviewed above has identified several important cognitive behavioral deficits that seem to be common among delinquents or particular groups of delinquents. With the exception of training in problem-solving skills, however, the cognitive behavioral interventions designed to remedy these deficits have not produced enough evidence for their effectiveness to warrant firm conclusions about their usefulness as treatments for delinquents. Nonetheless, there is certainly enough supporting evidence for the effectiveness of each type of intervention reviewed here to encourage future research and attempts to apply these interventions in clinical settings.

Both clinical applications and research analysis of these interventions would benefit from an emphasis on the assessment and treatment of the separate component skills involved in problem-solving behavior, self-instructional control of behavior, self-management, and perspective-taking. In most of the treatment studies reviewed above, a treatment package with several components was used with undifferentiated groups of delinquents that may have included individuals who actually had only mild deficits, or no deficits at all, in some or even all of the various skills being taught. This type of research may be efficient in establishing the effectiveness of a general type of intervention, but both research and clinical practice are likely to benefit from an early replacement of such relatively indiscriminate use of multiple-component intervention packages with investigations of the effect of training in specific component skills on the behavior of persons who are particularly deficient in those skills. Especially in clinical applications of cognitive behavioral interventions with delinquents, it is important to provide individuals with training in those specific skills for which they have the greatest need.

Most attempts to match individual delinquents with appropriate specific treatments have used classification systems based on statistical analysis of self-report and observational data or on theoretical notions about the sources of antisocial behavior (cf. Quay, 1979). This method of assigning individuals to treatments is actually not a great improvement over indiscriminate use of a single treatment with all delinquents, since it still ignores the particular individual's specific pattern of behavioral strengths and deficits. For example, several studies cited above showed that psychopathic delinquents as a group have a higher rate of impulse control and perspective-taking deficits than do nonpsychopathic delinquents. However, such results do not indicate that all delinquents labeled psychopathic have such deficits or that none of the delinquents in other subgroups suffer from poor impulse control or perspective-taking. It is not surprising, therefore, that efforts to "individualize" treatment based on even well-validated classification systems have not been overwhelmingly successful (e.g., Beker & Heyman, 1972; Cavior & Schmidt, 1978).

Several behavioral clinicians have recently pointed out that designing a treatment for an individual solely on the basis of the diagnostic label most appropriate for his or her behavior is unlikely to produce a maximally effective treatment program (e.g., Craighead, 1980; Hersen,

1981; Lazarus, 1976). Instead, these authors suggest, the design of an individualized treatment should include (1) assessment of the person's specific excesses and deficits in overt behaviors and covert mediational processes, and (2) the selection of particular interventions designed to remedy the specific problems identified during the assessment. Lazarus (1976) further suggested that these interventions be applied, when possible, in an order dictated by the severity of the effects on the individual's life of each of his or her problem behaviors.

Applying such an individualized approach to the treatment of a particular delinquent would involve assessment of the person's academic achievement and skills, overt social skills, and his or her skills in the mediational processes discussed in this chapter. An individualized treatment program would begin with training in those skills in which the delinquent had the most severe deficits, followed by systematic progression to training in less severely deficient skills. In some cases, training in only one or two skills might suffice to produce substantial changes in a delinquent's behavior, whereas a long series of training experiences might be needed before another person's antisocial behavior was effectively controlled. This approach would provide individualized treatment programs, but it does not require individualized training since the research reviewed in this chapter indicates that training in many of the relevant cognitive behavioral skills can be done quite effectively in groups. It could also include problem-solving training for the delinquent and his or her parents when assessment indicated high levels of conflict in the family.

The assessment procedures necessary for such an individualized program would probably be more extensive and time-consuming than the more conventional procedures used for classification purposes in juvenile corrections. But reliable procedures for the assessment of the specific skills that are the targets of cognitive behavioral interventions are becoming more common and more readily available (cf. Kendall & Hollon, 1981; Spivack *et al.*, 1976). The results of many of the programs reviewed above in which delinquents have been trained in cognitive behavioral skills suggest that the extra time and effort involved in an individualized approach might be well rewarded by improvements in the behavior of the delinquents involved.

14

Preventive Interventions for Children

COGNITIVE BEHAVIORAL PERSPECTIVES

Daniel S. Kirschenbaum and Arnold M. Ordman

WHY PREVENTION?

Two central problems have been recognized by many clinical researchers and practitioners during the past two decades. First, despite increased utilization of effective paraprofessional resources (Durlak, 1980), the proliferation of community mental health centers and crisis intervention programs (Rappaport, 1977), and the burgeoning self-help movement (Glasgow & Rosen, 1978), we still have inadequate helping resources relative to identified numbers of personal and social problems (e.g., Albee, 1967; Glidewell & Swallow, 1969; Meyers, Craighead, & Meyers, 1974; President's Commission on Mental Health, 1978; Zax & Cowen, 1976). Second, the limited services that are available are still used infrequently and ineffectively by large segments of society in great need of assistance (Cowen, 1978; Lorion, 1978). For example, in a recent large-scale survey, Langer, Gersten, Greene, Eisenberg, Herson, and McCarthy (1974) noted that nearly twice as many impoverished inner-city children, compared with their less destitute urban peers, experienced "psychiatric or emotional disorders great enough to interfere markedly with their role functioning or incapacitate them" (p. 117).

Of the many proposed solutions to the dilemma of inadequate helping services, the one that has become increasingly popular is the idea that we should greatly accelerate our work in *prevention*. Prevention has featured prominently in calls to arms pertaining to, among other areas,

Daniel S. Kirschenbaum and Arnold M. Ordman • Department of Psychology, University of Wisconsin–Madison, Madison, Wisconsin 53706.

behavioral medicine (e.g., Stachnik, 1980), ecology (e.g., Martin & Osborne, 1980), and individual and community-wide psychological distress (e.g., Bloom, 1968; Cowen, 1973, 1977, 1980; Meyers *et al.*, 1974). The present chapter also focuses on prevention. Yet, unlike previous expositions (see, also, Kent & Rolf, 1979; Klein & Goldston, 1977), our emphasis is on large-scale prevention programs for children that have included cognitive behavioral methods and goals. The rationale for this focus is that community-wide impact probably requires community-wide intervention (Caplan, 1964; Rappaport, 1977) and, as will be discussed in more detail in subsequent sections, cognitive behavioral approaches hold the most promise as foundational procedures for effective preventive programs (Craighead, Wilcoxon-Craighead, & Meyers, 1978; Durlak, 1977; Glenwick & Jason, 1980; Kirschenbaum, Pedro-Carroll, & DeVoge, 1983; Martin & Osborne, 1980; Meyers *et al.*, 1974; Nietzel, Winett, MacDonald, & Davidson, 1977).

Prevention: Definitions and Perspectives

> Imagine that you are out for a picnic on a pleasant spring day with a group of friends. You have just set out a checkered tablecloth with all manner of your favorite foods. You have situated yourself by the bank of a river, and as you are about to bite into a sandwich a cry is heard from the river. "Help, help!" the screamer yells. Putting down your sandwich you tear off your shoes and clothes and dive in to rescue a drowning victim, apply artificial respiration, and prepare to return to your picnic. Suddenly two people call out "help, help!" You dive in again and pull them out one on each arm. But as you return there are three or four others calling for help. Again you return, but this time, tired and overwhelmed by several people at once, you let a few slip away. Again, now in larger numbers, people call for help, but you cannot handle very many. You are only one person and you don't even swim very well yourself. Your friends don't swim at all, but as they watch you one has a bright idea. "Why not go upstream and find out who is pushing these people in?" (recounted by Rappaport, 1977,p. 632—origin unknown)

Prevention is the idea that problems can be stopped at their points of origin. That idea, when translated into action, has saved countless millions of lives through preventive medical efforts (Stachnik, 1980). Gerald Caplan's book, *Principles of Preventive Psychiatry* (1964), brought the concept to the mental health profession and provided us with some key definitions. According to Caplan, *tertiary prevention* is the reduction of problems in an entire community (i.e., large-scale amelioration) by intervening with people who have serious problems in living. *Secondary prevention* is reducing the rate of problems in a community (again an emphasis on large-scale efforts) primarily by intervening at the early stages of problem development—for instance, working with large numbers of children who evidence mild to moderate problems in living. Finally, *primary prevention*, is the lowering of the rate of problems in living in a community "by counteracting harmful circumstances before they have a chance to produce illness" (Caplan, 1964, p. 26).

Caplan's definitions have been expanded and clarified in recent years. The clarifications help delineate the nature of "community" (Martin & Osborne, 1980; Chapter 1), argue for increased attention to populations at high risk (Goldston, 1977), and specify diverse preventive interventions that have been and could be implemented (Bloom, 1968; Cowen, 1977, 1980; Jason, 1980a). For example, Cowen (1980) described methods of "wooing primary prevention" in a 2 × 2 × 2 matrix: "content direction" (health, maladjustment) × "intentionality: prime focus" (mental health, non-mental-health dependent variables) × "type of study" (programmatic, relational, i.e., experimental or correlational).

In the elaborated language of prevention, the concepts most relevant to the present focuses are primary and secondary prevention programs for children that attempt to improve health or decrease maladjustment, that affect "mental health" variables, and that are experimental in design. Specifically, we will review primarily large-scale interventions that have included cognitive behavioral goals and therapies and that were targeted at children at "high risk" for developing serious problems in living. These programs, whether labeled primary prevention (Goldston, 1977) or early secondary prevention (Cowen, 1967), hold great promise.

It has become very clear in recent years that early identification of children at "high risk" is both feasible (e.g., Cowen, Pederson, Babigian, Izzo, & Trost, 1973; Watt & Lubensky, 1976) and efficiently and effectively accomplishable (e.g., Cowen, Dorr, Clarfield, Kreling, McWilliams, Pokracki, Pratt, Terrell, & Wilson, 1973; Dorr, Stephens, Pozner, & Klodt, 1980; Durlak, Stein, & Mannarino, 1980; Kirschenbaum, Marsh, & DeVoge, 1977). However, we have not yet empirically, theoretically, or pragmatically established which goals and methods should be utilized specifically for which children. In the next sections, we consider the potential goals for large-scale preventive interventions and then review several of the more promising methods that have been used in recent years to reach those goals.

Cognitive Behavioral Goals for Preventive Programs

Nearly everyone around "Joey," teachers, parent, school staff, and day care center staff, referred to him literally as a "monster." His routine *daily* ac-

> tivities consisted of attacking other children, attacking teachers, kicking, screaming, biting, pinching, growling, tearing up nearly every other child's work, and lying on his back and sliding around the room. Data gathered in a classroom observation corroborated Joey's excessive acting out behaviors. Not surprisingly, in the self-portrait drawn by Joey during the child assessment interview he portrayed himself as a Dracula-like monster and labeled the picture accordingly. (Kirschenbaum *et al.*, 1983)

> "Laura" was very timid, and she related poorly to her classmates. Some boys "picked on" Laura in class. Others often tried to trip her. Yet Laura never complained about this abuse. In some ways, she seemed retarded though the teacher doubted this because her reading level approached average. Laura enjoyed talking with the teacher and always seemed to want to be close to her. When other children were around the teacher's desk, however, Laura withdrew and typically stood alone and detached behind the group. Laura rarely spoke to her peers. For example, when the children were doing art work, Laura would rather tear paper by hand than ask another child to hand her a pair of scissors. (Cowen, Trost, Lorion, Door, Izzo, & Isaacson, 1975, p. 252)

The two behavior patterns illustrated above by the cases of "Joey" and "Laura" are the two patterns most clearly and consistently identified by both prospective-longitudinal studies of childhood predictors of adult dysfunctioning (e.g., Cowen, Dorr, Clarfield, Kreling, McWilliams, Pokracki, Pratt, Terrell, & Wilson, 1973; Spivack & Swift, 1977; Victor & Halverson, 1976) and by retrospective analyses (e.g., Robins, 1966; Roff, Knight, & Wertheim, 1976; Watt & Lubensky, 1976; Watt, Stolorow, Lubensky, & McClelland, 1970). Although various descriptors have been used to label them, one pattern is an acting-out or aggressive one (e.g., "Joey") and the other is an immature-moody-withdrawn constellation (e.g., "Laura"). These patterns have been sex-linked in several studies (e.g., Victor & Halverson, 1976; Watt & Lubensky, 1976) with "high risk" boys typically seeming "cheerless, emotional, and *actively* maladjusted, and girls seeming calm, immature, and *quietly* maladjusted (Watt & Lubensky, 1976, p. 372)." Of course, with the relaxation of behavioral sex roles witnessed in recent years (see Maccoby & Jacklin, 1974), these sex differences may become increasingly blurred over time.

One of the things that the acting-out and immature-withdrawn behavioral patterns have in common is that they are both considered indicators of personal and social incompetence (Anderson & Messick, 1974). Altering each pattern, however, may require different interventions (cf. Durlak, 1980; Kirschenbaum, 1979; Lorion, Cowen, & Caldwell, 1974). Nonetheless, improving children's personal and social competence seems to be a parsimonious general goal statement in programs that seek to provide before-the-fact primary prevention or ameliorative early secondary prevention (Cowen, 1977, 1980; Kirschenbaum, DeVoge, Marsh, & Steffen, 1980; Zigler & Trickett, 1978).

Personal and social competence may be defined as those coordinated sets of behaviors that help people adapt effectively within the context of their social environments and that can be enhanced through experience (cf. Anderson & Messick, 1974; Kirschenbaum *et al.*, 1983). This definition is only "relatively" operational because it does not specify "adapt effectively." Rather than spending the remainder of this chapter in yet another definitional struggle, let us assume that effective adaptation in children is measurable through multimodal assessment of personal, social, and academic skills in such settings as schools, playgrounds, and homes. In other words, let us assume that teacher ratings, parent ratings, peer ratings, psychological testing, achievement testing, and behavioral observations can reliably distinguish effective from ineffective adaptation in a variety of settings.

Among the skills that *seem,* based on an initial review of the literature, to meet the definition proposed for personal and social competence are social (or interpersonal) problem-solving, empathy or social cognition (differentiation of feeling states in others), self-management (self-control, self-regulation), and self-efficacy (positive self-esteem in many situations, internal locus of control—particularly for children other than primary-graders) (Kirschenbaum *et al.*, 1983). Social problem-solving includes well-defined components that can be improved in children through structured feedback and specific instructional game-playing and other procedures (e.g., Allen, Chinsky, Larcen, Lochman, & Selinger, 1976; Blechman & Olson, 1975; Gesten, Flores de Apodaca, Rains, Weissberg, & Cowen, 1979; Shure & Spivack, 1978; Spivack & Shure, 1974; Weissberg, Gesten, Carnrike, Toro, Rapkin, Davidson, & Cowen, 1981; Weissberg, Gesten, Rapkin, Cowen, Davidson, Flores de Apodaca, & McKim, 1981). Empathy (and related social cognitive constructs) can be improved through instruction, modeling, and contingency management procedures (e.g., Chandler, 1973; Fry, 1966, 1969; Gottman, Gonso, & Schuler, 1976; Shantz & Wilson, 1972; Staub, 1971b; Stokes, Fowler, & Baer, 1977; Walker & Hops, 1973). Children's self-management skills have also shown dramatic improvements as a function of a variety of interventions including self-instruction (Finch, Wilkinson, Nelson, & Montgomery, 1975; Kendall & Finch, 1976, 1978; Kendall & Wilcox, 1980; Meichenbaum & Goodman, 1971), forced delay (Heider, 1971; Kagan, Pearson, & Welch, 1966), modeling (Debus, 1970; Denney, 1972; Robin, Schneider, & Dolnick, 1976), external contingency management (O'Leary & O'Leary, 1977), and self-regulated contingency management (O'Leary & Dubey, 1979; Rosenbaum & Drabman, 1979). In a similar vein, improving a variety of positive self-reactions (e.g., self-efficacy, internality in locus of control) has also been accomplished using a variety of procedures (deCharms, 1979; Lefcourt, 1976, 1979).

Social problem-solving, empathy, self-management, and self-efficacy appear to meet one of the definitional requirements of personal/social competencies. These behaviors seem modifiable (based on a preliminary review of the literature). Close scrutiny of the specific effects of specific interventions does, however, indicate that we are a long way from understanding which interventions improve which of the proposed competencies for which children (Craighead *et al.*, 1978; Hobbs, Moguin, Tyroler, & Lahey, 1980; Urbain & Kendall, 1980. It is also vitally important to realize that each of the proposed competencies seems partially, but not necessarily clearly, related to overall social adaptation or adjustment (see Hopper & Kirschenbaum, in press; Humphrey & Kirschenbaum, 1981; Lefcourt, 1976; Shantz, 1975; Spivack & Shure, 1974; Weissberg, Gesten, Cornrike, Toro, Rapkin, Davidson, & Cowen, 1981; Weissberg, Gesten, Rapkin, Cowen, Davidson, Flores de Apodaca, & McKim, 1981). Thus, questions raised by previous reviewers and similar issues considered in subsequent sections of this chapter indicate that, based on current information, we can only tentatively accept the proposed competencies as potentially useful candidates for improvement in preventive interventions. We must be ready and willing to change the goals and methods of preventive programs as empirical evidence accumulates that clarifies the adaptive consequences of the proposed competencies and that demonstrates more efficient and effective ways of improving these competencies.

Meanwhile, it is necessary to proceed with the difficult business of prevention. Progress in increasing our knowledge about how to accomplish the arduous sociopolitical process of conducting large-scale early intervention programs (see Cowen, 1978; Kirschenbaum *et al.*, 1983; Meyer, 1975; Muñoz, Snowden, & Kelly, 1979) cannot wait for increased understanding of personal/social competence. Both types of information are vital to the success of prevention programing and both can develop concurrently. Thereby, researchers and community practitioners can create an exciting cybernetic system that may well be capable of advancing the lofty goals of prevention.

COGNITIVE BEHAVIORAL PREVENTIVE INTERVENTIONS: SOCIAL PROBLEM-SOLVING, STRESS INOCULATION, AND MULTICOMPONENT INTERVENTIONS

Accepting the general goal of improving children's competencies as a desirable first step for preventive programs leads to considering several potential courses of action (Barrios & Shigetomi, 1980; Bloom, 1968;

Cowen, 1977, 1980). Examples of three of the most promising types of interventions will be presented here. First, one could attempt to improve one type of personal/social competence that seems pivotal—that is, that has the greatest likelihood of producing generalized effects across situations and accelerating or maintaining effects over time. Many interventionists view social problem-solving as a pivotal social competency. Accordingly, we will review the research on the effects of large-scale interventions designed to increase this competency and, thereby, improve many children's adaptation. A second tactic was termed the "milestone approach" by Bloom (1968). This approach involves administering an intervention to people at a critical point in their lives. By definition, crises are times when our usual problem-solving strategies are ineffective. Therefore, people in crises are often amenable to considering new styles of adaptation (Caplan, 1964). Although few large-scale cognitive behavioral studies using the milestone approach have been reported, we will consider the findings obtained in both large- and small-scale attempts to improve children's competencies at highly stressful times in their lives—for example, stress innoculation programs administered prior to dental treatment and prior to surgery. Finally, the approach to administering large-scale multicomponent interventions will be considered by presenting a detailed analysis of one such program, Cincinnati's Social Skills Development Program. We will examine its results in view of studies that directly compared behavioral preventive programs with other types of interventions.

Social Problem-Solving Interventions

Examiner: What if your classmate Johnny was playing with a really nifty truck?
What could you do to get to play with it?
Tell me all of the things you could do.
Andy: –Ask for it.
–Ask, pretty please, can I have it.
–Ask him if I could have my turn now.
–Give him money for it.
–Say, I'll let you come to my birthday party.
–Snatch it away.
–Hit him and take it when he's on the ground.
–Tell him you'll be his best friend if he lets you play with it.
(Adapted from Shure and Spivack, 1974a)

"Andy" showed evidence of rather good social problem-solving skills by suggesting so many alternatives to the "peer problem." George Spivack, Myrna Shure, and their associates have developed a variety of assessment devices and detailed training manuals to measure and teach three major types of social problem-solving (SPS) skills.

The first type of SPS skill, illustrated in "Andy's" responses above, is called alternative thinking, frequently assessed in preschoolers through the Preschool Interpersonal Problems Solving (PIPS) Test (Shure & Spivack, 1974b). Alternative thinking is the ability to generate numerous alternative solutions to interpersonal problems. The second SPS skill is called means-end thinking and is often measured by the Means-Ends Problem Solving Test (MEPS; Platt, Spivack, & Bloom, 1971). Means-end thinking is the step-by-step planning necessary to reach a desired interpersonal goal. Such planning involves the ability to foresee and circumvent potential obstacles as well as the awareness that goals usually cannot be attained immediately. A final SPS skill, consequential thinking, is the awareness of consequences that could occur as a result of following particular courses of action. According to Spivack and his associates, SPS skills tap the processes, rather than the specific content areas, that children use in thinking through interpersonal problems.

Beyond the appealing and logical nature of the SPS concepts, probably the most exciting thing about SPS skills is that evidence gathered by Spivack, Shure, and associates at Hahnemann Medical College indicates that SPS skills may be pivotal social competencies. Social problem-solving skills relate significantly to social adjustment in preschoolers and primary-grade children, according to some studies (e.g., Larcen, Spivack, & Shure, 1972; Shure, Newman, & Silver, 1973; Spivack & Shure, 1975). For example, Shure, Spivack, and Powell (1972) found that preschoolers who were rated by their teachers as "acting out" or "withdrawn" demonstrated significantly less alternative thinking than did those children whose ratings suggested healthy adjustment. In another study, Shure and Spivack (1972) compared 10- to 12-year-olds in special classes for the emotionally disturbed with children of the same age in normal classes and found that the well-adjusted children exhibited more means-end thinking. Before jumping on the SPS bandwagon, however, let us take a closer look at, and then comparatively examine, the large-scale studies conducted on SPS skills by researchers at the Hahnemann Medical College, the University of Connecticut, and the University of Rochester.

Hahnemann Medical College

The largest-scale evaluation study of Spivack and Shure's SPS training included 219 children (Spivack & Shure, 1974). One hundred and thirteen preschool children from 20 "Get Set" classes in Philadelphia were trained, while 106 children served as controls. Teachers conducted daily 5- to 20-minute training sessions for 12 consecutive weeks. A structured game format was used to teach both SPS skills and "prerequisite skills" such as how to pay attention and identify emotions. Children were rated pre- and post-treatment by their teachers and classified as impulsive (acting-out), inhibited (withdrawn), or adjusted. (The criteria for categorizing children were not specified.) Teachers also rated children's popularity, initiative, and independence. The PIPS test (Shure & Spivack, 1974b) was used to assess differential changes in SPS skills.

The data indicated that the training was very successful in improving SPS skills. The trained group significantly increased the number of alternative solutions suggested, and this increase was not due to increased extraneous talk. The trained group also decreased the extent of coercive or forceful solutions they suggested. This was particularly apparent for the impulsive subgroup. Consequential and cause-and-effect thinking were also improved. The children initially rated as inhibited and impulsive showed the greatest improvement on the PIPS test measures.

The teachers who conducted the training also evaluated student classroom behavior. Fifty percent of the impulsive children were rated by their teachers as adjusted after treatment. Only 21% of the control children improved. Seventy-five percent of the inhibited children were rated as adjusted after training, compared with 35% of the controls. The teachers' ratings also indicated that the initially inhibited children who received training increased the frequency with which they showed concern for others. Teachers also thought that girls who were in the program and who were initially rated as either impulsive or inhibited increased their peer popularity. Teacher ratings of initiative and autonomy increased in all three subgroups of children who received training.

Spivack and Shure attempted to relate the changes they observed in problem-solving ability to the teacher-rated improvements. They compared trained children whose classification changed from impulsive or inhibited to adjusted with those who remained unadjusted. They found that those who improved on the teacher ratings increased their alternative thinking more than those children who remained unchanged. Differences between the groups on consequential thinking bordered on significance ($p < 0.06$) and causal thinking ratings did not differentiate the groups.

The strongest evidence that the training program was effective comes from follow-up data gathered after the preschool children had entered kindergarten the next year. At this time some of the children were rated by their new teachers, who were blind to their training status. Findings showed that 30 of 36 trained children who had improved their behavioral rating maintained that improvement at follow-up. Of the 58 trained children who were rated at the end of training as adjusted, 86% maintained that rating at follow-up, compared with 66% in the control group. Also, trained children maintained their improved ability to generate alternative solutions to problems and to conceptualize consequences. Finally, 93% percent of trained children who were rated as adjusted on both the pre- and post-test maintained that rating at follow-up, compared with 63% of the control children. Spivack and Shure also reported that individual differences in IQ did not contribute to the program's effectiveness.

University of Connecticut

Allen *et al.* (1976) conducted a large-scale primary prevention project for third- and fourth-grade children. Their theoretical model combined components of the Spivack and Shure project with D'Zurilla and Goldfried's (1971) schematic problem-solving model. Allen *et al.* divided their problem-solving curriculum into six units: (1) a general orientation that used group problem-solving and brainstorming, and fostered the attitude that most problems are solvable; (2) identification and definition of problems and establishment of short- and long-term goals; (3) generation of alternative solutions; (4) consideration of the relevant consequences or obstacles that are possible for any given solution to a problem; (5) elaboration of solutions and step-by-step means to achieve goals; and (6) integration of the above-mentioned steps.

Six classes containing a total of 150 children (average age = 9.0 years) received the training. Classroom teachers and aides conducted 24 30-minute lessons in problem-solving over a 12-week period. The teachers used classroom exercises, small-group activities, reinforcement, role-playing, and six narrated modeling videotapes, and in general, emphasized active participation by students.

To assess problem-solving skills, Allen *et al.* used a modified version of Shure and Spivack's MEPS test. This problem-solving measure involved reading the child five hypothetical problem situations with successful outcomes and asking the child to tell how the protagonist solved the problem. For example, here is one such problem situation:

> Joyce had just moved into the neighborhood. She didn't know anyone and felt very lonely. The story ends with Joyce having many good friends and feeling at home in the neighborhood. What happens in between Joyce's moving in and feeling lonely, and when she ends up with many good friends? (p. 97)

Twenty-six randomly selected students were also tested to see how many alternative solutions they generated in a "real-life" situation. This contrived situation involved having the experimenter tell the child that the testing room was occupied and asking the child to help the experimenter solve the problem. Other outcome measures included self-esteem (Coopersmith, 1967), locus of control (Nowicki & Strickland, 1973), level of aspiration, and sociometric status. A modified version of the Walker Problem Behavior Identification Checklist (Walker, 1970) was used to assess teachers' ratings of adjustment. Allen *et al.* had language arts teachers, rather than classroom teachers, do the ratings, in an attempt to minimize expectancy effects resulting from knowledge of which children were receiving treatment.

The findings of the Connecticut group showed that, for the most part, the students learned the major components of the program. The problem-solving data indicated that the trained children generated significantly more alternative solutions and "elaborations" at post-treatment than at baseline. Training also resulted in a greater number of subjects generating a solution to all five problems. However, a large percentage (47%) of students failed to generate a single solution and this tendency did not discriminate between the groups. Improvements in problem-solving were unrelated to IQ, age, sex, or differential teacher effectiveness. Unfortunately, McClure, Chinsky, and Larcen (1978) found that the adaptive changes shown by experimental subjects (e.g., alternative thinking) did not persist at a four-month follow-up.

Regarding outcome measures of adjustment, the groups did not differ in self-esteem, level of aspiration, teacher's ratings, or on peer sociometric scores. On the other hand, the trained children became significantly more "internal" in locus of control than did the controls, a change generally associated with improved adaptation (Lefcourt, 1976).

University of Rochester

A third ambitious series of large-scale primary prevention projects using SPS skill training as their basis have been conducted by researchers of the University of Rochester (Gesten *et al.*, 1979; Weissberg, Gesten, Cornrike, Toro, Rapkin, Davidson, & Cowen, 1981; Weissberg, Gesten, Rapkin, Cowen, Davidson, Flores de Apodaca, & McKim, 1981). In 1976–1977, Gesten *et al.* (1979) conducted a 17-lesson program for second- and third-grade suburban children. The Rochester program was modeled after the Spivack and Shure (1974) and Allen *et al.* (1976) paradigms (cf. D'Zurilla & Goldfried's, 1971). The program consisted of five units: (a) recognition of feelings, (b) problem-sensing and identification, (c) generation of alternative solutions, (d) consideration of consequences, and (e) generalization to real-life problems and persistence in problem-solving.

The Gesten *et al.* (1979) study utilized two treatment groups and one control group. One treatment group (three classes) received the full 17-lesson program and the other received only 5 videotaped lessons of the full program. The classroom teachers conducted the program with the help of undergraduate aides. The results were similar to those reported by Allen *et al.* (1976). The children in the full program improved their SPS skills (alternative solution and consequential thinking) more than the controls or brief treatment group. However, despite differential SPS skill acquisition, there were no group differences on any of the postprogram adjustment measures, including peer sociometric and teacher ratings of competencies and problems.

In 1977–1978 Weissberg, Gesten, Rapkin, Cowen, Davidson, Flores de Apodaca, and McKim (1981) tried to bolster the Gesten intervention by increasing the number of lessons from 17 to 52, thus lengthening the program from two to four months. There were 243 second- to fourth-grade children in the project, half of whom served as controls. The children went to either a low-income urban school or a suburban middle-SES school. The teachers conducted half-hour problem-solving lessons four times a week.

The study of Weissberg and colleagues addressed three questions: (a) Does training improve SPS skills? (b) Does it enhance behavioral adjustment? (c) Are SPS skill and adjustment gains related? The results, consistent with previous research, answer the first question affirmatively. Program children improved significantly more than controls on the SPS skills of problem identification, alternative thinking and consequential thinking. They also attempted more solutions to and persisted longer in a contrived real-life problem situation. (The contrived problem situation was one in which the child was offered money by the experimenter to go into another room and get a black magic marker from a same-sexed peer. The peer was a confederate who politely refused to give the marker to the child. The child was told by the experimenter that the marker was needed for a project that they would work on and was also given standardized prompts if necessary.) The answer to the enhancement of adjustment question is less clear. On measures of the children's self-esteem, anxiety, and sociometric status, there were no differences between groups. However, the program did lead to improved teacher adjustment ratings for the suburban but not the urban children. The final question that Weissberg *et al.* investigated concerned the relationship of SPS skill and adjustment gains. The authors reported generally insignificant correlations between SPS skills and rating of adjustment, raising questions as to what the suburban teachers were responding to when they rated the children's adjustment differentially improved.

Weissberg, Gesten, Carnrike, Toro, Rapkin, Davidson, and Cowen (1981) conducted an even more intensive prevention program during 1978–1979. This program, built on the preceding one, involved 332 trained children and 231 controls. The children were second-, third-, and fourth-graders from either suburban or urban schools. Of the total of 563 students, 267 children were randomly selected to be tested on SPS skills and 69 were post-tested in a contrived behavioral problem situation. The teachers conducted the program and also rated the adjustment of all students both pre- and post-treatment.

The 1978–1979 program differentially improved the experimental group's alternative solution thinking (means-end and consequential thinking were not assessed). In the contrived behavioral test, the trained children also attempted more alternative solutions and required fewer prompts. In addition, trained children relative to controls expressed greater confidence in their interpersonal problem-solving ability on a 12-item scale. Teacher-rated adjustment, but not peer sociometric ratings, indicated greater improvement for both urban and suburban program children on summed competency and problem behavior scores, global ratings of adjustment and likability, and on the shy-anxious problem scale. However, teacher ratings of adjustment gains were unrelated to SPS skill acquisition. The authors qualified the interpretation of these positive findings by pointing out that, on the pre-test, control and experimental groups were equivalent only on global ratings of adjustment and likability.

Summary, Evaluation, and Conclusions

Virtually all of the SPS training programs have been successful in teaching children most of the major components of that particular problem-solving approach. It is apparent that children aged 4–12 can learn SPS skills when that acquisition is measured by their responses to hypothetical problem situations. More impressive are the findings of the Rochester and Connecticut programs that there appears to be a generalization of some of these skills to contrived behavioral tests. Since children appear to learn SPS skills, the key question becomes, Does this training lead to improved adjustment?

The most optimistic findings have come from the Hahnemann group. They found that, for preschoolers, training led to improved teacher ratings of adjustment and that there was a positive relationship between SPS skill-acquisition and improvements in adjustment. Unfortunately, with older children the results have been more inconclusive. A very recent report of a somewhat smaller-scale study by the Rochester group (Winer, Hilpert, Gesten, Cowen, & Subin, 1982) found no relationship between adjustment and SPS measures among kindergarteners. Allen *et al.*'s (1976) intervention with third- and fourth-graders had no effect on teacher or peer ratings, self-esteem, or level of aspiration. In fact, their solitary positive finding of increased internality among the children in the program relative to controls disappeared at a four-month follow-up (McClure *et al.*, 1978). Gesten *et al.* (1979) failed to find adjustment gains in second- and third-graders as assessed by peer and teacher ratings. Finally, Weissberg, Gesten, Carnrike, Toro, Rapkin, Davidson, and Cowen (1981) and Weissberg, Gesten, Rapkin, Cowen, Davidson, Flores de Apodaca, and McKim (1981) also reported rather minimal effects of SPS training on adjustment and, once again, no relationship between SPS skill-acquisition and ratings of adjustment.

Methodological issues can be raised in this literature pertaining to an over-reliance on potentially biased teacher ratings (see Shuller & McNamara, 1976) and some restrictions in modalities of assessment (see Cowen, 1978; Kirschenbaum *et al.*, 1980; Zigler & Trickett, 1978). For the most part, however, the studies were conducted carefully and elaborately. For example, exceptionally clear specification of the independent variables through detailed training manuals is a consistently laudable feature in all of these programs. Thus, a more fundamental question remains focal: Why is it that while SPS programs can teach children SPS skills, these skills often do not improve adjustment and are rarely correlated with adjustment gains?

Although Spivack, Platt, and Shure (1976) presented a large body of literature linking SPS skills to the quality of social adjustment, several studies, in addition to those conducted recently by the Connecticut and Rochester groups, provide evidence that calls into question the assumption that SPS skills are pivotal social competencies. Hodge (1979) found that none of the SPS skills differentiates second- to fourth-grade children rated by their peers and teachers as withdrawn, aggressive, and competent. In a concurrent study, Ordman (1979) found that Hodge's second- to fourth-graders could, however, be differentiated on the basis of classroom behavior as measured by independent observers. Hopper and Kirschenbaum (in press) reported findings with sixth graders similar to those of Hodge. These studies accentuate the importance of examining variations in problem-solving responses within populations that have not been previously identified as deviant—the normal population versus the extreme groups approach.

Hodge (1979) and Hopper and Kirschenbaum (in press), as well as Daut (1979) in a similar study, found that competent children are not clearly differentiated by the typical SPS measures from their less adaptive peers. Perhaps a different methodology is needed to discover pivotal personal and social competencies. Gottman's work (e.g. Gottman, 1977a,b; Gottman, Genso, & Rasmussen, 1975) is a good example of a progression of assessment studies in which behavioral deficiencies in unpopular children were identified. Gottman and his colleagues investigated the relationship among social skills, interactional styles, and popularity in third- and fourth-graders. Using individual testing, they found that popular children had a greater knowledge of how to make friends and performed better on a referential-communication task compared with their unpopular peers. They also found that, relative to unpopular children, popular children distributed and received more positive reinforcement, daydreamed less, and used different strategies when attempting to enter a peer group. These assessment studies are exemplary in several respects including the use of a well-validated criterion such as sociometric status to determine reference groups and the use of multiple assessment techniques including thorough and detailed naturalistic observation to determine social skill deficits. This research then formed the basis of successful treatment packages for unpopular children (Gottman, Gonso, & Schuler, 1976).

In sum, it appears that despite the intuitive appeal of SPS skills, making their acquisition the core element for prevention programs directed at children in primary grades or older is a gamble that is not paying off. Of course, the jury is still out until refinements in methodology (cf. Gottman *et al.*, 1975; Hopper & Kirschenbaum, in press) and follow-up assessments are completed. Nonetheless, the technology of conducting large-scale interventions has been improved by this work, and that knowledge will undoubtedly *advance* the cause of prevention.

Stress Inoculation

Ask any parents about their child's first dental appointment or first admission to a hospital, and it is likely that they will relate clear anecdotal documentation showing how stressful those experiences can be. Empirical evidence is consonant with many parents' impressions. Children frequently suffer maladaptive responses to hospitalization (e.g., Cassell, 1965; Prugh, Staub, Sands, Kirschenbaum, & Lenihan, 1953), and postoperative anxiety and other behavior problems often impede recovery (e.g., Dumas, 1963; Skipper & Leonard, 1968). Fear of dentistry is also a major concern, particularly when it is estimated that 12 million

Americans avoid dental treatment (Friedson & Feldman, 1958; Gale & Ayer, 1969). In summary, with respect to the present discussion, it is clear that dental and surgical treatments are crises or milestones that afford excellent opportunities to teach children self-control and self-efficacy competencies. Accordingly, we will review the results of dental and hospital stress inoculation studies with children and then present a summary and evaluation of them.

Reducing Dental Fears

> The 13-minute experimental videotape showed an initially fearful 4-year-old black child experiencing a typical dental procedure with a sensitive and friendly dentist. The child was shown coping with his anxiety and clearly discovering that there was nothing to fear. The child model was verbally reinforced for this cooperation and was given a toy at the end of the procedure. (Melamed, Hawes, Heiby, & Glick, 1975, p. 798)

Melamed and her colleagues (Melamed, Weinstein, Hawes, & Katin-Borland, 1975; Melamed, Hawes, Heiby, & Glick, 1975) conducted a series of projects demonstrating that filmed modeling can effectively reduce children's fearful behavior during dental treatment. Melamed, Weinstein, Hawes, and Katin-borland (1975) assigned 14 children to either a modeling or control condition, matching for age, sex, race, and initial level of fear on the children's Fear Survey Schedule (Scherer & Nakamura, 1968). The film described above was shown to the experimental subjects prior to their having a tooth filled.

The results indicated that the children who viewed the peer modeling film received lower fear ratings by the dentists and independent observers. The observers were not aware of the group assignment. Relative to the control group, the experimental group also reported less fear on the Fear Survey Schedule immediately prior to treatment and engaged in fewer disruptive behaviors during the dental treatment.

The results of a second project (Melamed, Hawes, Heiby, & Glick, 1975) replicated the results of the previous study using a control group that viewed a film unrelated to dental treatment. In the second experiment, the Palmar Sweat Index (Johnson & Dabbs, 1967) was added as a measure of physiological arousal, and the authors reported a "trend" (statistically unspecified) for the experimental group to show less physiological arousal than the control group during treatment.

Melamed (1979) subsequently investigated factors that influence the videotapes' effectiveness. This study involved 80 4- to 11-year-old children who were assigned to conditions, balancing for age, sex, race, previous dental experience, and initial self-reported fear on the children's Fear Survey Schedule. Assessments were collected during the children's first visit to the clinic for standard prophylaxis and examination and during their second visit a week later for restorative treatment. When the children returned to the clinic, they were shown one of the videotapes immediately before their restorative treatment. Melamed compared videotapes of a dentist and assistant describing and demonstrating procedures with videotapes of the same procedures using a 7-year-old model who remained cooperative and fearless throughout. The auditory tracks were the same in both conditions. She found that the peer modeling videotapes reduced anxiety more than the demonstration of the same procedures without peer modeling. Children who viewed the peer-model rather than the no-model videotape had less self-reported anxiety prior to the dental treatment, exhibited fewer disruptive behaviors, and were rated as less anxious by observers.

Klorman, Hilpert, Michael, LaGana, and Sveen (1980) performed a series of experiments that examined the effectiveness of modeling on 106 children with prior dental treatment experience and on 30 children without prior pedodontic experience. The children viewed either a control film or a videotape of a "coping" (gradually becoming less fearful) or a mastery (fearless) model receiving a filling (cf. Meichenbaum, 1971a). A postvideotape interview indicated that the children correctly perceived the differences between the coping and mastery models. Observations by independent observers indicated that for the inexperienced patients, both modeling films were successful relative to the control film in significantly reducing the children's disruptive behavior during dental treatment. On the other hand, the experienced patients, who were rated as more cooperative than the inexperienced patients, appeared unaffected by the modeling intervention. Dentists' reports of cooperativeness and autonomic arousal yielded no significant differences between experimental groups.

Preparation for Surgery

Melamed and Siegel (1975) demonstrated the generalizability of the modeling approach when they used it to prepare children for surgery. Thirty children with no prior history of hospitalization were randomly assigned to experimental and control groups. The experimental group saw a film entitled "Ethan Has An Operation." The film portrays a 7-year-old white male coming to the hospital with his parents and going through admission, preoperative blood test, and talks with the surgeon and anesthesiologist. Ethan is a coping model who shows some fear but then copes with it. The film also depicts anesthesia-induction and Ethan experiencing discomfort in the recovery room. Ethan narrates the film and is shown going home with his parents after the operation. The children in the control group saw a film unrelated to the hospital. All of the children received preoperative preparation from the hospital staff, which included familiarizing them with procedures and locations in the hospital and answering questions.

The results indicated that the children who received this modeling treatment were better prepared for surgery, compared with controls. The authors utilized measures of the cognitive, behavioral, and physiological dimensions of fear (see Lang, 1971). They found that the experimental group showed less physiological arousal, both pre- and post-operation, as measured by the Palmar Sweat Index. The experimental children showed fewer behavioral indexes of anxiety pre- and postoperation as assessed by behavioral observations. The children who viewed the model also appeared to be less anxious on measures of self-reported fear. Furthermore, the parents of the control children rated them on a behavior problem checklist as having increased behavior problems in the four weeks post-hospitalization, while this did not occur in the experimental group. These findings are particularly impressive when one considers that both groups did get a relatively thorough pre-operative preparation from the hospital staff.

Peterson and Shigetomi (1981) reported an experiment designed to test whether the addition of coping skills training added potency to preparation that already included either information or modeling. Specifically, all of the children (2.5- to 10.5-year-old tonsillectomy patients) were provided with information about hospital procedures through a puppet show and a tour. The puppet show also provided the coping model of a puppet who expressed his initial fear and eventual adaptive behavior. The tour and puppet show constituted the preparation for the information-only treatment group. Children in the information-plus-self-coping condition were introduced to each of three coping skill techniques by the puppet. The techniques were cue-controlled relaxation (Russell & Sipich, 1973), distractive imagery (e.g., Lazarus & Abramovitz, 1962), and comforting self-talk (Meichenbaum & Goodman, 1971b). The children practiced the use of these procedures. Parents received a booklet describing the techniques and were asked to record the number of times the child practiced each technique. The parents were instructed to train their child in the use of the procedures at home and to prompt the child to use them in the hospital. Children in the information-plus-coping-skills-plus-film model group also viewed Melamed's "Ethan Has An Operation." To complete the 2 × 2 design, (coping skills—no coping skills × film–no film), a final group received information and viewed the film but received no training in coping skills.

Ratings by nurses and laboratory technicians who were unaware of group assignment indicated that during painful procedures such as blood tests and preoperative injections, the children in the coping-plus-modeling condition were the least anxious and most cooperative. Parental and independent observer ratings following surgery showed that the coping groups were less anxious and more cooperative than the other groups. The parents who participated in the coping skills groups also rated themselves as feeling more calm and competent than the other parents. However, as the authors noted, several of the findings were nonsignificant or only marginally so, including, for example, no significant contrasts between the best coping group and one of the comparison groups (information-only) and no group differences on child self-report measures.

Summary, Evaluation, and Conclusions

The Melamed *et al.*, Klorman *et al.*, and Peterson and Shigetomi prevention experiments are promising demonstrations of the potential use of behavioral techniques to reduce pain, stress, and anxiety. It appears that both modeling and coping skills training can benefit children in the specific situation for which they were devised (i.e., dental treatment or surgery). The noteworthy success demonstrated by Peterson and Shigetomi's (1981) coping-plus-modeling intervention provides encouragement to preventionists interested in using the milestone approach to build competencies (e.g., Barrios & Shigetomi, 1979, 1980). A recent and remarkably similar presurgical stress inoculation study by Zastowny, Kirschenbaum, and Meng (in press) essentially replicated Peterson and Shigetomi's finding in that a coping skills training procedure proved superior to anxiety-reduction and information interventions. If these interventions actually enhance the development of key personal and social competencies, further research should reveal maintenance and generalization of effects over time and across other stressful and, perhaps, nonstressful situations.

There are at least two points about the success of the dental and surgical projects that have implications for facilitating the development of social problem-solving and other preventive interventions. Both the SPS skill projects and the stress inoculation approaches shared the goal of helping children learn how to solve or cope with stressful situations. First, the techniques utilized in stress inoculation—modeling, self-controlled relaxation, and, to a lesser extent, self-instructional training—have established a firm empirical history of effectiveness with children (Bandura, 1969a; Hobbs *et al.*, 1980). The SPS skill literature is on much weaker ground when claiming that training children in ways to solve hypothetical problems will generalize to actual interpersonal problem situations. Thus, this contrast demonstrates the value of developing a sound empirical foundation to techniques in prevention programs. A second implication is derived from the findings indicating that helping children utilize situation-specific action plans seems particularly promising. Emphasis on *doing*, rather than primarily thinking about, problem-producing situations may produce more rapid and permanent skills enhancement (cf. Bandura, 1977a; Leventhal, 1974).

Multicomponent Interventions

Cincinnati's Social Skills Development Program

The programs that come closest to actual community-wide interventions are the large-scale multicomponent programs that have developed following the Cowen and associates' model (Cowen *et al.*, 1975). During the past two decades, Rochester's Primary Mental Health Program (PMHP) has become the national prototype for early intervention. This program has, through a series of intensive national workshops and more than 150 publications, spawned approximately three dozen "offspring" that, collectively, serve over 120,000 pupils (Cowen, Davidson, & Gesten, 1980). In this section we will review the functioning and evaluation data from one of the more well-established PMHP offspring, Cincinnati's Social Skills Development Program (SSDP) (Kirschenbaum, 1979; Kirschenbaum *et al.*, 1983).

Staffing and Assessments. SSDP developed from a one-school pilot project in 1973 to a seven-school program by 1975 (for historical details see Kirschenbaum *et al.*, 1983). It utilizes the four structural emphases of the PMHP school-based model for conducting early secondary prevention: (1) focus on young children (primary-graders), (2) systematic mass screening to identify large numbers of children at risk for developing more serious problems later in their lives, (3) use of paraprofessionals to expand greatly the available person resources, and (4) use of alternative roles for professionals, again to expand greatly the available person resources—in other words, emphasis on training and supervision of paraprofessionals and consultation instead of primary emphasis on direct service delivery. Like its Rochester predecessor, SSDP is also school-based because the school offers many advantages over other locations for conducting such a program in preventive interventions—it becomes part of an established learning center, uses a central location, and increases systems-wide interactions (see Allen *et al.*, 1976; Cowen *et al.*, 1975).

Although SSDP has changed in both staffing patterns and other relevant dimensions in recent years, the core program has remained relatively constant during the past ten years. The core program consists of staffing each predominantly inner-city school with one full-time MA-level professional team leader, one full-time paraprofessional, and three to six part-time paraprofessionals (primarily students and some nonstudent volunteers). All staff are selected by program administrators for interpersonal skills such as warmth, verbal fluency, and general comfort in social exchanges (cf. Cowen, Dorr, & Pokracki, 1972). Staff salaries, overhead, and other costs have come from a variety of funding sources over the years, with the mainstays being the City of Cincinnati Health Department and Community Development funding (HUD). The Board of Education of the City of Cincinnati contributes more than ample cooperation, rent-free space, furniture, and related services.

Cincinnati's SSDP is the first large-scale early intervention program that bases its screening, assessment, intervention, and evaluation on a social competence model (Kirschenbaum, 1979). In screening and assessment, SSDP systematically gathers data about children's problems as well as their competencies through referrals, screening interviews with teachers, and a variety of formal ratings by teachers (see Table 1 for a summary and Kirschenbaum *et al.*, 1983, for details). One of the screening instruments that has been used in SSDP and continues to be the most widely utilized tool for mass screening in similar programs deserves special mention here. The instrument, entitled the "AML," consists of 11 behaviorally keyed problems rated for frequency by teachers, for example, *a*cting-out, *m*oodiness, and *l*earning problems (Cowen, Dorr, Clarfield, Kreling, McWilliams, Pokracki, Pratt, Terrel, & Wilson, 1973). Its validity has been well established for preschoolers (Carberry & Handal, 1980), primary-graders (Bower, 1960; Cowen, Dorr, Clarfield, Kreling, McWilliams, Pokracki, Pratt, Terrel, & Wilson, 1973; Durlak *et al.*, 1980; Levine, 1977; Lorion & Cowen, 1978; Van Fleet & Kannegieter, 1969), and children in intermediate grades (Dorr *et al.*, 1980). In SSDP in particular, it was shown that having teachers complete AML ratings on all primary grade children (one minute per child) increased the number of apparently high-risk children who were identified by more than 100% over the number identified by referral alone (Kirschenbaum, Marsh, & DeVoge, 1977).

After selection of 15%–25% of the primary-grade population in each

Table 1. Summary of the Social Skills Development Program's Method of Conducting Mass Screening and Assessment[a]

Mass screening
1. Gather referrals from principals, teachers, parents, and school staff
2. Conduct screening interviews with teachers[b]
3. Conduct behavioral observations in classroom and free-play settings
4. Obtain ratings from teachers (Gesten, 1976; Lorion *et al.*, 1975)
5. Selection (from generally about 100 initial possibilities to 40 for therapy, 40 for consultation)

Assessment
1. Child-specific teacher interview
2. Family assessments
3. Child interview
4. Establish and distribute behavioral goals

[a]This process described SSDP mass screening and assessment as it was performed in 1977–1978 (see Kirschenbaum *et al.*, 1983, for details).
[b]The screening interview process eliminated the usefulness of having teachers complete AMLs on each child (cf. Kirschenbaum, Marsh, & DeVoge, 1977; Kirschenbaum *et al.*, 1979).

school, target children are assigned to services in the following approximate percentages: 50% to group therapy, 10% to individual therapy, 3% to individual and group therapy, and 37% to teacher and parent consultation only (no direct therapy). All children in therapy conditions also receive assistance indirectly through advice, discussion, and suggestions for change provided to their parents and teachers—that is, consultation. Team leaders (and their supervisors) assign children to individual therapy generally if the child seems particularly deficient in social competencies. Some of the children receive only consultation services, largely because of limitations in staff size and the availability of space.

Interventions. Unlike the Rochester Program (PMHP), which primarily employs individual "companionship" therapy, SSDP emphasizes the improvement of children's social competence through structured group therapy and consultation. The end-product of the screening and assessment procedures is the formation of specific behavioral goals for each child. School teams select behavioral goal statements from among a list of 88 possibilities that were developed by the entire staff (Kirschenbaum, Klei, Brown, & DeVoge, 1979). As shown in Table 2, the statements are subsumed by 10 general goal statements (listed in the staff's rank-ordered preferences in Table 2). After selecting several appropriate goal statements for a child ($M = 7$; Kirschenbaum, 1979), the school team distributes a copy of the child's "Goals Information Sheet"

Table 2. Sample Goal Statements from the Social Skills Development Program's Goals Information Sheet[a]

Goal statements	Comments about progress
A. To improve positive self-image:	
To increase the frequency of behaviors that require risk-taking in the group (e.g., volunteering to be first in a new game, asking peers to play)	
To increase the frequency of making realistic positive statements about oneself	
B. To increase understanding of others:	
To increase accurate expression (through words, acting-out in role-playing, drawing, puppet play, posters, etc.) of various roles (i.e., expected behaviors in different settings such as home, school, church, street)	
C. To increase understanding of self:	
To increase accurate description of one's behavior (e.g., skills, physical assets and limitations)	
To increase accurate description of one's feelings	
D. To improve ability to help others understand self (ability to express self):	
To increase the frequency and accuracy, and clarity (details) of descriptions of feelings ideas, values, beliefs and life events through words, role-play, puppet play, drawing, poster-making, etc.	
E. To improve self-control:	
To increase the amount of time spent (at one sitting) at a given task or game (particularly when the task is somewhat unpleasant or tedious)	
To plan a given activity or task with increased clarity and specificity	
F. To improve problem-solving skills:	
To increase suggested number of alternative solutions that could solve a given interpersonal problem or conflict	
G. To increase understanding and ability to express feelings about family relationships and issues:	
To increase recognition and expression of how the family changes because of death, divorce, remarriage, new births, and so on	

(*continued*)

Table 2. (*Continued*)

Goal statements	Comments about progress
To increase accurate expression of who is in family and how each member is related to self	
H. To increase understanding and ability to express feelings about special issues (including: death, divorce, drugs, hospitalization, moving, new baby, race, and sex):	
To increase clarity and accuracy in describing special issues and feelings about them	
To decrease avoidance of expressing self about particularly sensitive issues (e.g., "death" for child whose grandfather died recently), i.e., decreased latency in talking about a sensitive issue when it is mentioned	
I. To improve creative abilities:	
To increase the frequency of use of creative materials and games (arts and crafts, music, dance, fantasy games)	
To increase the originality (unusualness) of creative products	
J. To improve academic skills:	
To increase the frequency of use of reading, writing, and arithmetic during play (e.g., putting titles on paintings; using cue words to prompt listening or sharing)	
To increase vocabulary	

[a]From "A nonexperimental, but useful, evaluation of a therapy/consultation early intervention program" by D. S. Kirschenbaum, R. Klei, J. Brown, and J. DeVoge, in *Evaluation in practice: A sourcebook of program evaluation studies from mental health care systems in the United States* (G. Landsberg, W. Neigher, R. Hammer, C. Windle, and R. Woy, editors), Washington, D.C.: Government Printing Office, 1979. Copyright 1979 by the National Institute of Mental Health. Reprinted by permission.

to teachers, parents, and the school principal. Follow-up contacts with teachers, principals, and parents clarify the individualized goal statements, begin individualized consultative treatment plans, and further ensure that stigmatizing labels are not used and that no record of the children's involvement with SSDP will appear in the children's school record.

The therapy groups, the primary and most expensive intervention, are conducted by pairs of staff members. Children's goal statements help determine the specific content of the groups (4–5 children per group), but almost all groups include the following sequence of five events: (a) group discussion, (b) structured group activity designed to improve specific goal-related social competencies (e.g., Spivack & Shure, 1974, exercises; Chandler, 1973, empathy training procedures; see Kirschenbaum, Bane, Fowler, Klei, Kuykendahl, Marsh, & Pedro, 1976, for details), (c) individual activities, (d) clean-up, (e) snack and wrap-up discussion (Kirschenbaum, Pedro, & DeVoge, 1977). Children in therapy receive a mean of 27 therapy sessions (range = 3–70). Some children, 10–20 per school, also receive therapy services during the summer months; 10%–15% of the target children receive more than one year of direct helping services.

All primary-grade teachers and parents receive consultation about the children in SSDP. Teachers receive at least 12 contacts per year and parents receive at least 4. The contacts range in scope and specificity from developing cooperative supportive relationships to devising specific contingency management systems (e.g., Kirschenbaum & Pedro-Carroll, 1979; Kirschenbaum *et al.*, 1983—the case of "Joey"). The consultative contacts are provided more often and more intensely to teachers and parents of children who receive both therapy and consultation interventions compared with children who receive only consultation services.

Evaluations. Assessment of the efficacy of SSDP has included case studies (e.g., Kirschenbaum & Pedro-Carroll, 1979), nonexperimental analyses of reactions from teachers and staff (Kirschenbaum *et al.*, 1979), and experimental investigations using a multimethod approach to assess general adaptation (adjustment) and social competencies (Kirschenbaum, 1979; Kirschenbaum *et al.*, 1980). Generally, the data present SSDP as an effective strategy to enhance the adaptive functioning of many inner-city children who were identified as "high risk." The specific effects of the program, particularly as assessed in the experimental studies, however, suggest that several modifications are in order to maximize effectiveness.

Kirschenbaum (1979) examined the effects of SSDP over a one-year period on three groups of children from the seven inner-city schools that housed SSDP compared with "high-risk" children selected from two demographically similar control schools. The three SSDP groups were Therapy 1 ($n = 58$), Therapy 2 ($n = 101$), and Consultation ($n = 114$). The SSDP staff nonrandomly assigned 10%–20% of their target children to Therapy 1. These children, viewed as especially needy, received both therapy and consultation services. Random assignment placed the remaining target children in Therapy 2 (the same therapy and consultation treatment as in Therapy 1) or Consultation (consultation only). Based on small-group discussions with SSDP staff (similar to the "screening interviews" conducted in SSDP schools), primary-grade teachers in the control schools selected 4–6 children per class as Controls ($n = 65$).

The groups were similar in age ($\bar{X} = 7.35$, SD = 1.3) and sex (58.5% boys, 41.5% girls). Although socioeconomic comparisons indicated that all nine school communities were equally impoverished (e.g., 78% of the children in the nine schools were on a free-lunch program), more white children (predominantly Appalachian) and fewer black children were in SSDP than among the controls—SSDP: 58.1% black/41.9% white versus Control: 80.3% black/19.7% white ($p < 0.001$). Thus, race was used as a covariate.

Using race and preintervention teacher ratings on Gesten's (1976) competency-oriented Health Resources Inventory (HRI) and on Lorion *et al.*'s (1974) problem-oriented Classroom Activity Rating Scale (CARS) as covariates, differential improvement in adaptation between groups was examined through analyses of covariance. Teachers rated children in all three SSDP groups, compared with controls, as improved in competence (HRI ratings) but not improved in problem behaviors (CARS ratings). Therapy 2 and Consultation groups, which were initially better adjusted than Therapy 1 according to teacher ratings, improved significantly more than Therapy 1 on several factors of the HRI. The results were not qualified by interactions due to age or sex.

Although the findings provide some global support for the efficacy of SSDP, they did raise some difficult questions. Children who were initially less well adjusted benefited least (cf. Durlak, 1980); teachers rated no improvements in problem behaviors; and Therapy 2 children, who received the most extensive and expensive helping services, changed to the same extent as did Consultation children, the recipients of diminished services. More specific outcome measures, for example, tests of social skills and behavioral observations, appeared warranted to examine the source of these findings. Such assessments might have been better able to detect more sensitively specific changes in behavior as a function of SSDP participation (cf. Ordman, 1979; Zigler & Trickett, 1978).

Kirschenbaum *et al.* (1980) reported a more specific evaluation of the effects of SSDP over the same one-year period that Kirschenbaum (1979) investigated. In the 1980 paper, three assessment modalities were employed. First, in Study 1, individual tests of social skills afforded pre- to post- comparisons between Therapy 2 ($n = 55$) and Consultation ($n = 44$) on several competencies: empathy, social problem-solving, and locus of control. (Recall that Therapy 2 and Consultation groups were formed randomly and were, therefore, equivalent samples.) Second, data available from children's school records permitted comparison among all SSDP groups ($N = 224$) of pre- versus postintervention assessment of lateness, absenteeism, performance on standardized reading-readiness tests, and report-card grades. Third, trained observers recorded the frequency of 11 categories of behaviors (including task-irrelevant, task-relevant, and prosocial behaviors using the Social Competence Classroom Behavioral Observation System—Kirschenbaum, Steffen, & D'Orta, 1978) to examine pre- to post- behaviors in small samples of therapy children ($n = 8$), consultation children ($n = 7$), and nontarget comparison children ($n = 7$). Therapy children were expected to outperform consultation children on all assessments at post-intervention.

Therapy, compared with consultation, increased children's skill at distinguishing between various feelings (the most basic of the empathy measures, Study 1; see Urberg & Docherty, 1976), increased their externality in locus of control (Study 1), and increased the frequency of their cooperative interactions with teachers and maintained a higher frequency of appropriate solitary behavior (Study 3). It is important to note that externality was significantly correlated with all other indexes of adjustment in this study (cf. Phares, 1973; Tolor, Tolor, & Blumin, 1977). On the other hand, although both therapy and consultation groups improved their report-card grades over time, consultation children showed significantly greater gains on this measure. In addition, therapy and consultation were not differentiated on any of the remaining assessments (e.g., accurate empathy, social problem-solving).

These results generally suggest that therapy led to some benefits relative to consultation, but the differences among the groups were noticeably smaller than anticipated. Recall that therapy children received a much more elaborate set of interventions than did consultation children. Although consultation may have been more potent than expected (see Kirschenbaum *et al.*, 1979), it seems parsimonious to suggest that therapy had less impact than it could have had. The less-than-optimal findings reported in the 1980 evaluation, in the evaluation based on ratings by teachers (Kirschenbaum, 1979), and in all similar early intervention programs (see Allen *et al.*, 1976; Cowen *et al.*, 1975; Kellam, Branch, Agrawa, & Ensminger, 1975; Sandler, Duricko, & Grande, 1975) clearly indicate that more powerful interventions may be required to produce more dramatic effects with large numbers of "high-risk" children.

Toward More Potent Early Intervention Programs: Behavioral versus Nonbehavioral Programs

Among the potential methods of increasing the potency of preventive programs relative to the approaches used in many multicomponent interventions (e.g., Cowen *et al.*, 1975; Kellam *et al.*, 1975; Kirschenbaum *et al.*, 1983) are increasing their length, increasing their structure, and relying more on behavioral techniques. The Weissberg *et al.* program (Weissberg, Gesten, Carnrike, Toro, Rapkin, Davidson, & Cowen, 1981; Weissberg, Gesten, Rapkin, Cowen, Davidson, Flores de Apodaca, & McKim, 1981) illustrates the effects of increasing length and structure. Weissberg *et al.*, relative to Gesten *et al.* (1979), increased the number and duration of their SPS lessons, from 17 in two months to 52 in four months. While the more intensive program differentially improved adjustment ratings, neither evaluation found relationships between gains in adjustment ratings and acquisition of skills taught in the programs.

The use of behavioral techniques in large-scale preventive programs holds great promise for improving the efficiency and effectiveness of such efforts (Durlak, 1977). Behavioral approaches have demonstrated their usefulness in a wide range of situations (including predental and presurgical stress inoculation, as noted previously). In addition, professionals, paraprofessionals, teachers, and parents can learn how to utilize cooperatively and effectively behavioral technologies to teach specific competencies (see Kazdin, 1975). Of greatest import to the present considerations, several relatively large-scale studies have compared the efficacy of behavioral and nonbehavioral approaches in the context of early intervention programs (Durlak, 1980; Durlak & Gillespie, 1980; Fo & O'Donnell, 1974; Jason & Ferone, 1978; Jason, Ferone, & Anderegg, 1979).

One of the most carefully controlled large-scale intervention studies that compared behavioral and nonbehavioral interventions was reported by Durlak (1980). Two types of group treatment, behavioral (n = 51) and supportive relationship (n = 42), were compared to each other and to a no-treatment control group (n = 26). Teachers completed a behavior problem checklist and 15% of first-, second-, and third-graders, the children with the highest ratings of maladjustment, were recruited for the experiment.

The group leaders, who worked in pairs, were graduate students in psychology or volunteers. The intervention was divided into two 10-week sessions. All of the children in the treatment groups participated in the first session, and those who needed further help, in the judgment of the group leaders, continued into the second 10 weeks. The groups, composed of 5 to 8 children, were conducted once a week for one hour.

Both behavioral and relationship treatment groups utilized the same set of group activities (games and exercises) during each session. In the behavioral group, the leaders developed programs using token and social contingencies aimed at fostering target behavior that was opposite and incompatible with the child's typical dysfunctional classroom behavior. In the relationship treatment group, leaders attempted to establish warm, trusting, and empathic relationships by active listening and empathic responding. Particular attention was paid to the children's expressions of feelings, conflicts, and wishes. Care was taken to ensure that the group leaders in both conditions had equal expectancies concerning treatment efficacy.

After the first 10-week session, the results indicated that the behavioral treatment led to the greatest improvements on teacher-rated adjustment. The children in the relationship groups did better than the no-treatment controls but not as well as the behavioral group. This finding is supported by the number of children whose treatment was terminated after the first 10-week session, 47% for the behavioral groups and 29% for the relationship groups. The results of the evaluation after the second 10-week session revealed that those children who had been terminated after the first session maintained their gains in teacher ratings. No outcome measures were collected for the controls at this time. A comparison of teacher ratings for children in the behavioral and relationship treatments after the second session revealed that the behavioral treatment was significantly superior on seven out of eight measures. The data also suggested that both types of interventions were least helpful for the children whom teachers had initially rated as the most maladjusted.

This study supports the notion (see Durlak, 1977) that behavioral interventions are superior to relationship therapy when treating children in the schools. One of the obvious weaknesses of this investigation is its dependency on teacher ratings and group leaders' discretion as the outcome measures. Accordingly, Durlak and his associates have replicated and extended this investigation in order to compare more thoroughly behavioral and relationship approaches.

Durlak and his associates substantially extended Durlak's earlier work (1977, 1980) in a series of three one-year programs conducted in Carbondale, Illinois. To summarize their results briefly, in the first year of their program (Durlak & Mannarino, 1980), they found that maladjusted children in a 10-week behavioral program ($n = 49$) significantly reduced their disruptive behavior as measured by independent observers relative to a relationship control group ($n = 49$). Teacher ratings of maladjustment did not differentiate the groups. The results of the second year of the Carbondale project (Durlak & Gillespie, 1980) indicated that, while the children receiving behavioral treatment exhibited far more inappropriate classroom behavior compared with their nonprogram peers prior to treatment, the rates of problem behavior were nearly identical for the two groups at post-treatment. The third-year project (Durlak & Gillespie, 1980) replicated the findings of the previous studies and in addition found that social-plus-token-reinforcement was more effective than social reinforcement alone in reducing inappropriate classroom behavior.

Three other studies are consistent with Durlak's finding of the increased effectiveness of programs that incorporate behavioral principles. Fo and O'Donnell (1974) recruited adult nonprofessionals to work one-on-one as "buddies" for a small number of children between 11 and 17 years of age who were referred to the project for a wide range of problems including truancy and classroom disruption. The youngsters were randomly assigned to one of four conditions: (a) relationship ($n = 5$); (b) social approval, in which the relationship (i.e., social approval) was contingent on the performance of the desired behavior ($n = 7$); (c) social and material reinforcement, which was the same as social approval but with $10 per month also contingent on desired behavior ($n = 7$); and (d) no-treatment control ($n = 7$).

The results clearly showed that the social and social-material contingency conditions increased attendance, the major dependent measure in the study. The relationship and control conditions had no effect on truancy. Six additional children with assorted other behavioral problems such as fighting and not doing homework were placed in the social-material reinforcement condition, and a significant reduction in the frequency of the targeted problem behavior was observed.

Jason and Ferone (1978) compared behavioral and process consultations as methods of intervening with acting-out first-graders. One teacher was given consultations regarding behavior modification principles such as ignoring disruptive behaviors and actively attending to appropriate ones, while another teacher was given a process consultation that consisted of support, clarification, and reflective responses from the consultant in an attempt to help the teacher understand and resolve classroom problems. Each teacher (both female) identified the four children in her class with the most serious acting-out problems.

Fifteen weeks of behavioral observation data were collected for each of the four most disruptive children in each classroom. Behavior was observed for four weeks of baseline, seven weeks of treatment, and four weeks of follow-up. The behavioral data indicated that the children in the class that received behavioral consultation significantly reduced (by 27%) their disruptive behavior, and that this improvement was maintained during follow-up. No behavioral changes were noted for the children in the process condition. Jason and Ferone also found that the teacher in the behavioral, but not the process, condition increased the percentage of time that she paid attention to the desirable behaviors of the target children. Teachers also filled out the Classroom Adjustment Rating Scale (Lorion, Cowen, & Caldwell, 1975). According to this outcome measure, children in both conditions significantly improved (cf. Durlak & Gillespie, 1980). This finding is at odds with the observational data and points out the inherent weakness of using biased teacher ratings. If teachers are involved in providing treatment or are not blind to conditions, they are prone to be overly positive in their evaluations. It is also interesting to note that the improvements made by the children in the behavioral condition did not occur until midway through the series of consultations, when specific individualized programs for each child were discussed with the teachers.

Jason *et al.* (1979) conducted a second evaluation of classroom interventions that was similar to the previous study but also included ecological consultation and no-treatment control conditions. The goal of the ecological consultation was to help the teachers change the structure of their classes to facilitate the appropriate behavior of the disruptive children. Alterations of the traditional classroom format included the extension use of small groups arranged according to ability. Steps were also taken to ensure that none of the groups had more than one problem child.

There was one first- and one third-grade class in each of the four conditions. Each teacher identified four or five disruptive "target" children whose behavior was evaluated. Target children were monitored during four-week baseline, eight-week treatment, and four-week follow-up periods. The results, consistent with their previous findings, indicated that significant reductions in observed and teacher-rated behavioral problems occurred only in the classes provided with behavioral consultation. Target children in the control and ecological classes did not change, while the children in the process condition actually increased the frequency of their problem behaviors.

In sum, behavioral techniques appear more effective than less structured and less directive "relationship" approaches. The effects are consistent despite variations across studies in service-deliverers, location, and method of intervention (i.e., individual or group therapy or consultation). Furthermore, use of behavioral observation data as the major dependent variable adds to the validity of these studies relative to some of the previous preventive research—that is, effects resulting from expectancies or biases are reduced (Shuller & McNamara, 1976). It seems, therefore, that lengthy, structured, and behavioral procedures may enhance the effectiveness of large-scale multicomponent interventions.

SUMMARY AND CONCLUSIONS

The idea of prevention applied to problems in living is certainly one of the most exciting solutions posed for the long-standing dilemma of inadequate matching between mental health needs and services. The marriage of cognitive behavioral concepts with community psychology holds great promise for the development of goals and programs that may, eventually, help prevent serious problems in living from developing in large numbers of people. In the present chapter, we described the improvement of children's personal and social competencies as a potentially important goal for preventive programs. We then reviewed three examples of large-scale preventive interventions based on cognitive behavioral principles and directed at the enhancement of children's competencies. The examples illustrated three different but related approaches to improve personal and social competencies in programs that approximated community-wide efforts in scope (i.e., sample sizes were generally over 100).

Attempts to improve one set of "pivotal" competencies, social problem-solving skills, were shown to be carefully and elaborately executed. Although some findings in the SPS literature are promising, in general it seems that SPS skills may not be vital tools for enhancing children's adapation. On the other hand, the use of cognitive behavioral stress inoculation procedures exemplifies the promise of the "milestone" approach to prevention. Finally, multicomponent community interventions were described by presenting an analysis of Cincinnati's Social Skills Development Program. The results of evaluations of SSDP, especially when considered in light of evidence pointing to the relative superiority of behavioral over relationship techniques, suggests that lengthy, structured, and behavioral procedures should be incorporated in early intervention programs.

The present literature review almost writes its own conclusions. The emerging interchange between cognitive behavioral approaches and community psychology has extended from industrial and ecological concerns (e.g., reducing littering; see Meyers *et al.*, 1974), to large-scale preventive approaches for children. Although cognitive behaviorism and community psychology have vastly different origins and orientations (see Glenwick & Jason, 1980; Nietzel *et al.*, 1977; Rappaport, 1977), it is now abundantly clear that both traditions can benefit from interaction with each other. Cognitive behavioral technology can improve the assessment (e.g., Gottman *et al.*, 1975; Shuller & McNamara, 1976) and effectiveness of preventive approaches with children (e.g., Durlak, 1980; Jason *et al.*, 1979). Concurrently, use of community psychology principles greatly facilitates the implementation of large-scale cognitive behavioral interventions with children (see Kirschenbaum *et al.*, 1983; Reppucci & Saunders, 1974; Saunders & Reppucci, 1978). As the data reviewed here suggest, there is now every reason to expect that the relationship between cognitive behaviorism and community psychology should continue to develop in a healthy symbiosis, perhaps culminating in the achievement of the vitally important "glittering" goals of primary prevention.

Acknowledgments

The authors gratefully acknowledge Joe Durlak, Lenny Jason, and Roger Weissberg for cordially providing many useful and important prepublication drafts of their work. Also, the patient, efficient, and professional work of Cris Virgin and Judy Markgraf, who transformed our rough draft into an attractive manuscript, is sincerely appreciated.

References

Abikoff, H. Cognitive training interventions in children: Review of a new approach. *Journal of Learning Disabilities*, 1979, *12*, 123–135.

Achenbach, T. M. The Child Behavior Profile: I. Boys aged 6 through 11. *Journal of Consulting and Clinical Psychology*, 1978, *46*, 478–488. (a)

Achenbach, T. M. Psychopathology of childhood: Research problems and issues. *Journal of Consulting and Clinical Psychology*, 1978, *46*, 759–776. (b)

Achenbach, T. M., & Edelbrock, C. S. The classification of child psychopathology: A review and analysis of empirical efforts. *Psychological Bulletin*, 1978, *85*, 1275–1301.

Achenbach, T. M., & Edelbrock, C. S. The Child Behavior Profile: II. Boys aged 12–16 and girls aged 6–11 and 12–16. *Journal of Consulting and Clinical Psychology*, 1979, *47*, 223–233.

Achenbach, T. M., & Edelbrock, C. S. Behavioral problems and competencies reported by parents of normal and disturbed children aged four through sixteen. *Monographs of the Society for Research in Child Development*, 1981, *46*(1, Serial No. 188).

Adelman, H. S. The not so specific learning disability population. *Exceptional Children*, 1971, *37*, 528–533.

Ainsworth, M. D. S., & Bell, S. M. Attachment, exploration and separation: Illustrated by the behavior of one-year-olds in a strange situation. *Child Development*, 1970, *41*, 49–67.

Ainsworth, M. D. S., Blehar, N., Waters, E., & Wall, S. *Patterns of attachment: A psychological study of the strange situation*. Hillsdale, N.J.: Lawrence Erlbaum Associates, 1978.

Albee, G. W., The relation of conceptual models to manpower needs. In E. L. Cowen, E. A. Gardner, & M. Zax (Eds.), *Emergent approaches to mental health problems*. New York: Appleton-Century-Crofts, 1967.

Alexander, J. F. Defensive and supportive communication in normal and deviant families. *Journal of Consulting and Clinical Psychology*, 1973, *40*, 223–231.

Alexander, J. F., & Parsons, B. Short-term behavioral intervention with delinquent families: Impact on family process and recidivism. *Journal of Abnormal Psychology*, 1973, *81*, 219–225.

Alexander, J. F., Barton, C., Schiavo, R. S., & Parsons, B. V. Systems-behavioral intervention with families of delinquents: Therapist characteristics, family behavior, and outcome. *Journal of Consulting and Clinical Psychology*, 1976, *44*, 656–664.

Alexander, J. F., Haas, L. J., Klein, N. C., & Warburton, J. R. *Functional family therapy*. Paper presented at the annual meeting of the Western Psychological Association, Honolulu, May 1980.

Allen, G. J., Chinsky, J. M., Larcen, S. W., Lochman, J. E., & Selinger, H. V. *Community psychology in the schools.* Hillsdale, N.J.: Lawrence Erlbaum Associates, 1976.
Allen, H. E., & Simonsen, C. E. *Corrections in America: An introduction.* Encino, Calif.: Glencoe, 1978.
Allen, K. E., Hart, B., Buell, J. S., Harris, F. R., & Wolf, M. M. Effects of social reinforcement on isolate behavior of a nursery school child. *Child Development,* 1964, *35,* 511–518.
American Psychiatric Association. *Diagnostic and statistical manual of mental disorders* (3rd ed.). Washington, D.C.: Author, 1980.
Anderson, L., Fodor, I., & Alpert, M. A comparison of methods for training self-control. *Behavior Therapy,* 1976, *7,* 649–658.
Anderson, N. *The role of stimulus variables in "overselective" attention in autistic children.* Paper presented at the 12th annual meeting of the Association for the Advancement of Behavior Therapy, Chicago, November 1978.
Anderson, N., & Rincover, A. The generality of overselectivity in developmentally disabled children. *Journal of Experimental Child Psychology,* 1982, *34,* 217–230.
Anderson, S., & Messick, S. Social competency in young children. *Developmental Psychology,* 1974, *10,* 282–293.
Andrew, J. Recovery from surgery, with and without preparatory instruction for three coping styles. *Journal of Personality and Social Psychology,* 1970, *15,* 223–226.
Anthony, E. J. Children at risk from divorce: A review. In E. J. Anthony & C. Kopernik (Eds.), *The child in his family: Children at psychiatric risk.* New York: Wiley, 1974.
Aponte, H. J., & VanDeusen, J. M. Structural family therapy. In A. S. Gurman & D. P. Kniskern (Eds.), *Handbook of family therapy.* New York: Brunner/Mazel, 1981.
Appel, L. F., Cooper, R. G., McCarrell, N., Sims-Knight, J., Yussen, S. R., & Flavell, J. H. The development of the distinction between perceiving and memorizing. *Child Development,* 1972, *43,* 1365–1381.
Arbitman-Smith, R., & Haywood, H. C. Cognitive education for learning disabled adolescents. *Journal of Abnormal Child Psychology,* 1980, *8,* 51–64.
Armentrout, J. A. Parental child-rearing attitudes and preadolescents' problem behaviors. *Journal of Consulting and Clinical Psychology,* 1971, *37,* 278–285.
Arnold, J. E., Levine, A. G., & Patterson, G. R. Changes in sibling behavior following family intervention. *Journal of Consulting and Clinical Psychology,* 1975, *43,* 683–688.
Arnold, L. E. (Ed.). *Helping parents help their children.* New York: Brunner/Mazel, 1978.
Arnolds, S. C., & Forehand, R. A comparison of cognitive training and response cost procedures in modifying cognitive styles of impulsive children. *Cognitive Therapy and Research,* 1978, *2,* 183–187.
Asch, S. E. Studies in the principles of judgments and attitudes: II. Determination of judgments by group and ego standards. *Journal of Social Psychology,* 1940, *12,* 433–465.
Asher, S. R., Oden, S. L., & Gottman, J. M. Children's friendships in school settings. In L. Katz (Ed.), *Current topics in early childhood education* (Vol. 1). Norwood, N.J.: Ablex Publishing, 1977.
Auerbach, S. M., Kendall, P. C., Cuttler, H. F., & Levitt, N. R. Anxiety, locus of control, type of preparatory information, and adjustment to dental surgery. *Journal of Consulting and Clinical Psychology,* 1976, *44,* 809–818.
Ault, R. L. Problem solving strategies of reflective, impulsive, fast accurate, and slow inaccurate children. *Child Development,* 1973, *44,* 259–266.
Ayllon, T., & Milan, M. *Correctional rehabilitation and management: A psychological approach.* New York: Wiley, 1979.

Ayllon, T., & Roberts, M. D. Eliminating discipline problems by strengthening academic performance. *Journal of Applied Behavior Analysis*, 1974, *7*, 71–76.

Ayres, A. J. *Sensory integration in learning disorders.* Los Angeles: Western Psychological Services, 1972.

Baer, D. M., & Wolf, M. M. The entry into natural communities of reinforcement. In R. Ulrich, T. Stachnik, & J. Mabry (Eds.), *Control of human behavior: From cure to prevention.* Glenview Ill.: Scott, Foresman, 1970.

Baer, D. M., Wolf, M. M., & Risley, T. R. Some current dimensions of applied behavior analysis. *Journal of Applied Behavior Analysis*, 1968, *1*, 91–97.

Baldwin, A. L. *Theories of child development* (2nd ed.). New York: Wiley, 1980.

Balla, D., & Zigler, E. Personality development in retarded persons. In N. R. Ellis (Ed.), *Handbook of mental deficiency, psychological theory and research.* Hillsdale, N.J.: Lawrence Erlbaum Associates, 1979.

Balswick, J. O., & Macrides, C. Parental stimulus for adolescent rebellion. *Adolescence*, 1975, *10*, 253–266.

Bandura, A. *Principles of behavior modification.* New York: Holt, Rinehart & Winston, 1969. (a)

Bandura, A. Social-learning theory of identification processes. In D. Goslin (Ed.), *Handbook of socialization theory and research.* Chicago: Rand McNally, 1969. (b)

Bandura, A. Psychotherapy based upon modeling principles. In A. E. Bergin & S. L. Garfield (Eds.), *Handbook of psychotherapy and behavior change.* New York: Wiley, 1971. (a)

Bandura, A. Vicarious and self-reinforcement processes. In R. Glaser (Ed.), *The nature of reinforcement.* New York: Academic Press, 1971. (b)

Bandura, A. *Aggression: A social learning analysis.* Englewood Cliffs, N.J.: Prentice-Hall, 1973.

Bandura, A. Self-efficacy: Toward a unifying theory of behavioral change. *Psychological Review*, 1977, *84*, 191–215. (a)

Bandura, A. *Social learning theory.* Englewood Cliffs, N.J.: Prentice-Hall, 1977. (b)

Bandura, A. The self system in reciprocal determinism. *American Psychologist*, 1978, *33*, 344–358.

Bandura, A. In search of pure unidirectional determinants. *Behavior Therapy*, 1981, *12*, 30–40.

Bandura, A., & Menlove, F. L. Factors determining vicarious extinction of avoidance behavior through symbolic modeling. *Journal of Personality and Social Psychology*, 1968, *8*, 99–108.

Bandura, A., & Walters, R. H. *Social Learning and personality development.* New York: Holt, Rinehart & Winston, 1963.

Bandura, A., Ross, D., & Ross, S. A. Transmission of aggressive models. *Journal of Abnormal Social Psychology*, 1961, *63*, 572–582.

Bandura, A., Gruse, J. E., & Menlove, F. L. Vicarious extinction of avoidance behavior. *Journal of Personality and Social Psychology*, 1967, *5*, 16–23.

Bandura, A., Blanchard, I. B., & Ritter, B. The relative efficacy of desensitization and modeling approaches for inducing behavioral, affective and attitudinal change. *Journal of Personality and Social Psychology*, 1969, *13*, 173–199.

Bandura, A., Jeffrey, R. W., & Gajdos, E. Generalizing change through participant modeling with self-directed mastery. *Behavioral Research and Therapy*, 1975, *13*, 141–152.

Barker, R. G. *Ecological psychology: Concepts and methods for studying the environment of human behavior.* Stanford, Calif.: Stanford University Press, 1968.

Barkley, R., Copeland, A., & Sivage, C. A self-control classroom for hyperactive children. *Journal of Autism and Developmental Disorders*, 1980, *10*, 75–89.

Barnett, C., Leiderman, P., Grostein, R., & Klaus, M. Neonatal separation: The maternal side of interactional deprivation. *Pediatrics*, 1970, *45*, 197.

Barrett, D. E. *A Re-examination of the relationship between aggression and prosocial behavior in children*. Paper presented at the fourth Biennial Southeastern Conference on Human Development, Nashville, Tenn., April 26, 1976.

Barrios, B. A., & Shigetomi, C. C. Coping-skills training for the management of anxiety: A critical review. *Behavior Therapy*, 1979, *10*, 491–522.

Barrios, B. A., & Shigetomi, C. C. Coping-skills training: Potential for the prevention of fears and anxieties. *Behavior Therapy*, 1980, *11*, 431–439.

Barton, E. J. *A further analysis of the importance of modeling in developing sharing*. Paper presented at the biennial meeting of the Society for Research in Child Development, San Francisco, March 1979.

Bash, M. A., & Camp, B. W. Training teachers in the Think Aloud classroom program. In G. Cartledge & J. Milburn (Eds.), *Teaching social skills to children: Innovative approaches*. New York: Pergamon Press, 1980.

Bates, E. *Language and context: The acquisition of pragmatics*. New York: Academic Press, 1976.

Bateson, G., Jackson, D. D., Haley, J., & Weakland, J. Toward a theory of schizophrenia. *Behavioral Science*, 1956, *1*, 251–264.

Bauer, R. H., Memory, acquisition, and category clustering in learning disabled children. *Journal of Experimental Child Psychology*, 1979, *27*, 365–383.

Baum, C. G., & Forehand, R. Long term follow-up assessment of parent training by use of multiple outcome measures. *Behavior Therapy*, 1981, *12*, 643–652.

Beakel, N., & Mehrabian, A. Inconsistent communications and psychopathology. *Journal of Abnormal Psychology*, 1969, *74*, 126–130.

Beck, A. T. *Cognitive therapy and the emotional disorders*. New York: International Universities Press, 1976.

Beck, A. T., Rush, A. J., Shaw, B. F., & Emery, G. *Cognitive therapy of depression*. New York: Guilford Press, 1979.

Beck, S. J., & Ollendick, T. H. Personal space, sex of experimenter, and locus of control in normal and delinquent adolescents. *Psychological Reports*, 1976, *38*, 383–387.

Beker, J., & Heyman, D. D. A critical appraisal of the California differential treatment program. *Criminology*, 1972, *10*, 3–59.

Bell, R. Q. Parent, child, and reciprocal influences. *American Psychologist*, 1979, *34*, 821–826.

Bellack, A. S., & Hersen, M. *Behavior modification: An introductory textbook*. Baltimore, Md.: Williams & Wilkins, 1977.

Belmont, J., & Butterfield, E. The instructional approach to developmental cognitive research. In R. Kail & J. Hagen (Eds.), *Perspectives on the development of memory and cognition*. Hillsdale, N.J.: Lawrence Erlbaum Associates, 1977.

Bem, S. The role of comprehension in children's problem-solving. *Developmental Psychology*, 1970, *2*, 351–358.

Bender, N. N. Self-verbalization versus tutor verbalization in modifying impulsivity. *Journal of Educational Psychology*, 1976, *88*, 347–354.

Berenda, R. W. *The influence of the group on judgments of children*. New York: King's Crown Press, 1950.

Bergin, A. E. The evaluation of therapeutic outcomes. In A. E. Bergin & S. L. Garfield (Eds.), *Handbook of psychotherapy and behavior change*. New York: Wiley, 1971.

Berkowitz, B. Y., & Graziano, A. M. Training parents as behavior therapists: A review. *Behavior Research and Therapy*, 1972, *10*, 297–317.

Berlin, I. N. Prevention of mental and emotional disorders of childhood. In B. B. Wolman (Ed.), *Manual of child psychopathology*. New York: McGraw-Hill, 1972.

Bernal, M. E., Klinnert, M. D., & Schultz, L. A. Outcome evaluation of behavioral parent training and client-centered parent counseling for children with conduct problems. *Journal of Applied Behavior Analysis*, 1980, *13*, 677–691.

Berndt, T. J. Developmental changes in conformity to peers and parents. *Developmental Psychology*, 1979, *15*(6), 608–616.

Bernstein, B. A socio-linguistic approach to social learning. In J. Gould (Ed.), *Penguin survey of the social sciences*. New York: Penguin, 1965.

Bettleheim, B. *The empty fortress*. New York: Free Press, 1967.

Bigelow, G. The behavioral approach to retardation. In T. Thompson & J. Grabowski (Eds.), *Behavior modification of the mentally retarded*. New York: Oxford University Press, 1977.

Bijou, S. W. A functional analysis of retarded development. In N. R. Ellis (Ed.), *International review of research in mental retardation* (Vol. 1). New York: Academic Press, 1966.

Blackstock, E. G. Cerebral asymmetry and the development of early infantile autism. *Journal of Autism and Childhood Schizophrenia*, 1978, *8*, 339–351.

Blanchard, E. B., Bassett, J. E., & Koshland, E. Psychopathy and delay of gratification. *Criminal Justice and Behavior*, 1977, *4*, 265–271.

Blechman, E. A., & Olson, D. H. The family contract game: Description and effectiveness. In D. H. Olson (Ed.), *Treating relationships*. Iowa City, Iowa: Graphic Publishing, 1975.

Blechman, E. A., Olson, D. H., & Hellman, I. D. Stimulus control over family problem-solving behavior: The family contract game. *Behavior Therapy*, 1976, *7*, 686–692.

Block, J. Parents of schizophrenic, neurotic, asthmatic, and congenitally ill children. *Archives of General Psychiatry*, 1969, *20*, 659–674.

Block, J. B. Effects of a rational-emotive mental health program on poorly achieving, disruptive high school students. *Journal of Counseling Psychology*, 1978, *25*, 61–65.

Block, J. H., Block, J., & Morrison, A. *Parental agreement-disagreement on child rearing orientations and gender-related personality correlates in children*. Unpublished manuscript, University of California at Berkeley, 1980.

Bloom, B. L. The evaluation of primary prevention programs. In L. M. Roberts, N. S. Greenfield, & M. H. Miller (Eds.), *Comprehensive mental health: The challenge of evaluation*. Madison: University of Wisconsin Press, 1968.

Bloom, B. L. *Community mental health: A general introduction*. Monterey, Calif.: Brooks/Cole, 1977.

Bloom, B. L. Social and community interventions. *Annual Review of Psychology*, 1980, *31*, in press.

Bolstad, O., & Johnson, S. Self-regulation in the modification of disruptive classroom behavior. *Journal of Applied Behavior Analysis*, 1972, *5*, 443–454.

Bommarito, J., & Meichenbaum, D. *Enhancing reading comprehension by means of self-instructional training*. Unpublished manuscript, University of Waterloo, 1978.

Borke, H. Chandler & Greenspan's "ersatz egocentrism": A rejoinder. *Developmental Psychology*, 1972, *7*, 107–109.

Borkowski, J. G., & Cavanaugh, J. C. Maintenance and generalization of skills and strategies by the retarded. In N. R. Ellis (Ed.), *Handbook of mental deficiency, psychological theory and research*. Hillsdale, N.J.: Lawrence Erlbaum Associates, 1979.

Borkowski, J. G., & Konarski, E. A. Educational implications of efforts to train intelligence. *Journal of Special Education*, 1981, *15*, 289–3015.

Borkowski, J. G., & Wanschura, P. B. Mediational processes in the retarded. In N. R. Ellis (Ed.), *International review of research in mental retardation* (Vol. 7). New York: Academic Press, 1974.

Borkowski, J. G., Cavanaugh, J. C., & Reichart, G. J. Maintenance of children's rehearsal strategies: Effects of children's amount of training and strategy form. *Journal of Experimental Child Psychology*, 1978, *26*, 288–298.

Bornstein, M. R., Bellack, A. S., & Hersen, M. Social-skills training for unassertive children: A multiple-baseline analysis. *Journal of Applied Behavior Analysis*, 1977, *10*, 183–195.

Bornstein, M., Bellack, A. S., & Hersen, M. Social skills training for highly aggressive children: Treatment in an inpatient psychiatric setting. *Behavior Modification*, 1980, *4*, 173–186.

Bornstein, P. H., & Quevillon, R. P. The effects of a self-instructional package on overactive preschool boys. *Journal of Applied Behavior Analysis*, 1976, *9*, 179–188.

Boucher, J. Alternation and sequencing behavior, and response to novelty in autistic children. *Journal of Child Psychology and Psychiatry* 1977, *18*, 67–72.

Bowen, M. The use of family theory in clinical practice. *Comprehensive Psychiatry*, 1966, *7*, 345–374.

Bowen, M. Theory in the practice of psychotherapy. In P. J. Guerin, Jr. (Ed.), *Family therapy: Theory and practice*. New York: Gardner Press, 1976.

Bower, E. M. *Early identification of emotionally disturbed children in school*. Springfield, Ill.: Charles C Thomas, 1960.

Bower, G. H. Cognitive psychology: An introduction. In W. H. Estes (Ed.), *Handbook of learning and cognitive process* (Vol. 1). Hillsdale, N.J.: Lawrence Erlbaum Associates, 1975.

Bower, G. H. Contacts of cognitive psychology with social learning theory. *Cognitive Therapy and Research*, 1978, *2*, 123–146.

Bowlby, J. *Attachment and loss* (Vol. 1): *Attachment*. New York: Basic Books, 1969.

Brainerd, C. *Piaget's theory of intelligence*. Englewood Cliffs, N.J.: Prentice-Hall, 1978.

Bransford, J. D. *Human cognition: Learning, understanding, and remembering*. Belmont, Calif.: Wadsworth Publishing, 1979.

Brazelton, T. B., Tronick, E., Adamson, L., Als, H., & Wise, S. Early mother-infant reciprocity. *Parent-infant interaction*. Ciba Foundation 33. New York: Elsevier Scientific Publishing, 1975.

Bridges, K. M. B. The study of social development in early infancy. *Child Development*, 1933, *4*, 36–49.

Brigham, T. A. Self-control. In T. A. Brigham & A. C. Catania (Eds.), *Handbook of applied behavior research: Social and instructional processes*. New York: Halsted, 1978.

Briscoe, R. V., Hoffman, D. K., & Bailey, J. S. Behavioral community psychology: Training a community board to problem solve. *Journal of Applied Behavior Analysis*, 1975, *8*, 157–168.

Brodsky, G. The relation between verbal and nonverbal behavior change. *Behavior Research and Therapy*, 1967, *5*, 183–191.

Brodsky, G., LePage, T., Quiring, J., & Zeller, R. Self-evaluative responses in adolescent retardates. *American Journal of Mental Deficiency*, 1970, *74*, 792–795.

Bronfenbrenner, U. Toward an experimental ecology of human development. *American Psychologist*, 1977, *32*, 513–531.

Bronson, W. Peer-peer interaction in the second year of life. In M. Lewis & L. A. Rosenblum (Eds.), *Friendship and peer relations*. New York: Wiley, 1975.

Brooks-Gunn, J., & Lewis, M. Early social knowledge: The development of knowledge about others. In H. McGurk (Ed.), *Issues in childhood social development*. London: Methuen, 1978.

Brooks-Gunn, J., & Lewis, M. Affective exchanges between normal and handicapped infants and their mothers. In T. Freed & A. Fogel (Eds.), *Emotion and interaction: Normal and high risk infants*. Hillsdale, N.J.: Erlbaum, 1982a.

Brooks-Gunn, J., & Lewis, M. The development of the self. In C. Kopp & N. Krokaw (Eds.), *Developmental psychology*. Reading, Mass.: Addison-Wesley, 1982b.

Brooks-Gunn, J., & Lewis, M. Temperament and affective interaction in handicapped infants. *Topics in Early Childhood*, in press.

Brooks-Gunn, J., & Matthews, W. S. *He & she: How children develop their sex-role identity*. Englewood Cliffs, N.J.: Prentice-Hall, 1979.

Brown, A. L. The development of memory: Knowing, knowing about knowing, and knowing how to know. In H. W. Reese (Ed.), *Advances in child development and behavior* (Vol. 10). New York: Academic Press, 1975.

Brown, A. L. Knowing when, where, and how to remember: A problem of metacognition. In R. Glaser (Ed.), *Advances in instructional psychology*. Hillsdale, N.J.: Lawrence Erlbaum Associates, 1978.

Brown, A. L. Metacognitive development and reading. In R. J. Spiro, B. Bruce, & W. F. Brewer (Eds.), *Theoretical issues in reading comprehension*. Hillsdale, N.J.: Lawrence Erlbaum Associates, 1981.

Brown, A. L., & Campione, J. C. Permissible inference from the outcome of training studies in cognitive development research. *The Quarterly Newsletter of the Institute for Comparative Human Development*, 1978, *2*, 46–53.

Brown, A., & French, L. The zone of potential development: Implications for intelligence testing in the year 2000. *Intelligence*, 1979, *3*, 253–271.

Brown, A., Campione, J., & Murphy, M. Maintenance and generalization of trained metamnemonic awareness of educable retarded children. *Journal of Experimental Child Psychology*, 1977, *24*, 191–211.

Brown, A. L., Smiley, S. S., Day, J. D., Townsend, M. A. R., & Lawton, S. C. Intrusion of a semantic idea in children's comprehension and retention of stories. *Child Development*, 1977, *48*, 1454–1466.

Bruch, H. *The golden cage*. Cambridge, Mass.: Harvard University Press, 1978.

Bruch, M. A. Type of cognitive modeling, imitation of modeled tactics, and modification of test anxiety. *Cognitive Therapy and Research*, 1978, *2*, 147–164.

Budoff, M., & Corman, L. Effectiveness of a learning potential procedure in improving problem-solving skills of retarded and nonretarded children. *American Journal of Mental Deficiency*, 1976, *81*, 260–264.

Bugental, D. B., Whalen, C. K., & Henker, B. Causal attributions of hyperactive children and motivational assumptions of two behavior-change approaches: Evidence for an interactionist position. *Child Development*, 1977, *48*, 874–884.

Bugental, D. B., Collins, S., Collins, L., & Chaney, L. A. Attributional and behavioral changes following two behavior management interventions with hyperactive boys: A follow-up study. *Child Development*, 1978, *49*, 247–250.

Bugental, D. B., Love, L. R., & Kaswan, J. W. Videotaped family interaction: Differences reflecting presence and type of child disturbance. *Journal of Abnormal Psychology*, 1972, *79*, 285–290.

Buhler, C. *The first year of Life*. New York: John Day, 1930.

Burchard, J. D., & Harig, P. T. Behavior modification with juvenile delinquency. In H.

Leitenberg (Ed.), *Handbook of behavior modification and behavior therapy*. Englewood-Cliffs, N.J.: Prentice-Hall, 1976.

Burgess, R. L., Burgess, J. J., & Esveldt, K. C. An analysis of generalized imitation. *Journal of Applied Behavior Analysis*, 1970, *3*, 39–46.

Burgio, L. D., Whitman, T. L., & Johnson, M. R. A self-instructional package for increasing attending behavior in educable mentally retarded children. *Journal of Applied Behavior Analysis*, 1980, *13*, 443–459.

Burka, A. A., & Glenwick, D. S. Egocentrism and classroom adjustment. *Journal of Abnormal Child Psychology*, 1978, *6*, 61–70.

Burns, B. The effect of self-directed verbal commands on arithmetic performance and activity level of urban hyperactive children. (Doctoral dissertation, Boston College, 1972). *Dissertation Abstracts International*, 1972, *33*, 1782B. (Microfilm No. 72-22, 884)

Burstein, S., & Meichenbaum, D. The work of worrying in children undergoing surgery. *Journal of Abnormal Child Psychology*, 1979, *7*(2), 121–132.

Burron, D., & Bucher, B. Self-instructions as discriminative cues for rule-breaking or rule following. *Journal of Experimental Child Psychology*, 1978, *26*, 46–57.

Butler, G., & Rabinowitz, M. An investigation of factors contributing to the apparent overselective responding of mentally retarded children. *Child Development*, 1981, *52*, 430–442.

Byng-Hall, J. Symptom bearer as marital distance regulator: Clinical implications. *Family Process*, 1980, *19*, 355–365.

Camp, B. W. WISC performance in acting out and delinquent children with and without EEG abnormality. *Journal of Consulting Psychology*, 1966, *30*, 350–353.

Camp, B. W. Verbal mediation in young aggressive boys. *Journal of Abnormal Psychology*, 1977, *86*, 145, 153.

Camp, B. W. Two psychoeducational treatment programs for young aggressive boys. In C. K. Whalen & B. Henker (Eds.), *Hyperactive children—The social psychology of identification and treatment*. New York: Academic Press, 1980.

Camp, B. W., & Bash, M. A. Think Aloud: Improving self-control through training in problem-solving. In D. P. Rathjen & J. P. Foreyt (Eds.), *Social competence: Intervention for children and adults*. New York: Pergamon Press, 1980.

Camp, B. W., & Bash, M. A. S. *Think Aloud: Increasing social and cognitive skills—a problem-solving program for children (Primary level)*. Champaign, Ill.: Research Press, 1981.

Camp, B. W., Blom, G. E., Hebert, F., & Van Doorninck, W. J. "Think aloud": A program for developing self-control in young aggressive boys. *Journal of Abnormal Child Psychology*, 1977, *5*, 157–169.

Camp, B. W., Zimet, S. G., van Doorninck, W. J., & Dahlem, N. W. Verbal abilities in young aggressive boys. *Journal of Educational Psychology*, 1977, *69*, 129–135.

Campbell, J. Illness as a point of view. The development of children's concepts of illness. *Child Development*, 1975, *46*, 92–100.

Campbell, S. B. Mother-child interaction in reflective, impulsive, and hyperactive children. *Developmental Psychology*, 1973, *8*, 341–349.

Campbell, S. B., & Paulauskas, S. Peer relations in hyperactive children. *Journal of Child Psychology and Psychiatry*, 1979, *20*, 233–246.

Campione, J. C., & Brown, A. L. Memory and metamemory development in educable mentally retarded children. In R. W. Kail & J. W. Hagen (Eds.), *Perspectives on the development of memory and cognition*. Hillsdale, N.J.: Lawrence Erlbaum Associates, 1977.

Campione, J. C., & Brown, A. L. Toward a theory of intelligence: Contributions from research with retarded children. *Intelligence*, 1978, *2*, 279–304.

Campione, J. C., McGrath, M., & Rabinowitz, F. M. Component and configurational learning in children: Additional data. *Journal of Experimental Psychology*, 1971, *88*, 137–139.

Caplan, G. *Principles of preventive psychiatry*. New York: Basic Books, 1964.

Carberry, A. T., & Handal, P. J. The use of the AML scale with a headstart population: Normative and validational studies. *American Journal of Community Psychology*, 1980, *8*, 353–364.

Carey, W. B. A simplified method for measuring infant temperament. *Journal of Pediatrics*, 1970, *77*, 188–194.

Carey, W. B. Measuring infant temperament. *Journal of Pediatrics*, 1972, *81*, 414.

Carnine, D. W. Preteaching versus concurrent teaching of the component skills of a multiplication problem-solving strategy. *Journal for Research in Mathematics Education*, 1980, *11*, 375–379.

Carnine, D. W., Prill, N., & Armstrong, J. *Teaching slower performing students general case strategies for solving comprehension items*. Eugene, Oreg.: University of Oregon Follow Through Project, 1978.

Carver, R. P. Two dimensions of tests: Psychometric and edumetric. *American Psychologist*, 1974, *29*, 512–518.

Cassell, S. Effects of brief puppet therapy upon the emotional responses of children undergoing cardiac catheterization. *Journal of Consulting and Clinical Psychology*, 1965, *29*, 1–8.

Catania, A. C. The myth of self-reinforcement. *Behaviorism*, 1975, *3*, 192–199.

Cautela, J. R., Flannery, R. B., & Hartey, S. Covert modeling. *Behavior Therapy*, 1974, *5*, 494–502.

Cavanaugh, J. C., & Borkowski, J. G. Searching for metamemory-memory connections: A developmental study. *Developmental Psychology*, 1980, *16*, 441–453.

Cavior, H. E., & Schmidt, A. A test of the effectiveness of a differential treatment strategy at the Robert F. Kennedy Center. *Criminal Justice and Behavior*, 1978, *5*, 131–139.

Chandler, M. J. Egocentrism and anti-social behavior: The assessment and training of social perspective-taking skills. *Developmental Psychology*, 1973, *9*, 326–332.

Chandler, M. J., Greenspan, S., & Barenboim, C. Assessment and training of role-taking and referential communication skills in institutionalized emotionally disturbed children. *Developmental Psychology*, 1974, *10*, 546–553.

Chapman, J. S. Effects of different nursing approaches on psychological and physiological responses. *Nursing Research*, 1970, *5*, 1–7.

deCharms, R. Personal causation and perceived control. In L. C. Perlmuter & R. A. Monty (Eds.), *Choice and perceived control*. Hillsdale, N.J.: Lawrence Erlbaum Associates, 1979.

Chase, W. G., & Simon, H. A. Perception in chess. *Cognitive Psychology*, 1973, *4*, 55–81.

Chennault, M. Improving the social acceptance of unpopular educable mentally retarded pupils in special classes. *American Journal of Mental Deficiency*, 1967, *72*, 455–458.

Chertok, S. L., & Bornstein, P. H. Covert modeling treatment of children's fears. *Child Behavior Therapy*, 1979, *1*, 249–255.

Chittenden, G. E. An experimental study in measuring and modifying assertive behavior in young children. *Monographs of the Society for Research in Child Development*, 1942, *VII*(1, Serial No. 31).

Christophersen, R. E., Barnard, J., Ford, D., & Wolff, M. The family training program: Improving parent/child interaction patterns. In L. A. Hamerlynck, L. C. Handy, & E. J. Mash (Eds.), *Behavior Modification and families. II: Applications and developments*. New York: Brunner/Mazel, 1976.

Cichetti, D., & Sroufe, L. A. An organizational view of affect: Illustration from the study of

Down's syndrome infants. In M. Lewis & L. Rosenblum (Eds.), *The development of affect*. New York: Plenum Press, 1978.

Clarfield, S. P. The development of a teacher referral form for identifying early school maladaptation. *American Journal of Community Psychology*, 1974, *2*, 100–210.

Clark, D. B., & Baker, B. L. *Training parents of developmentally disabled children: Prediction of follow-up outcome*. Paper presented at the annual meeting of the American Psychological Association, New York, August 1979.

Cobb, J. A. The relationship of discrete classroom behaviors to fourth-grade academic achievement. *Journal of Educational Psychology*, 1972, *63*, 74–80.

Cohen, F., & Lazarus, R. S. Coping with the stress of illness. In G. C. Stone, F. Cohen, & N. Adler (Eds.), *Health psychology*. San Francisco: Jossey-Bass, 1979.

Cohen, H. L., & Filipczak, J. *A new learning environment*. San Francisco: Jossey-Bass, 1971.

Cohen, R., & Meyers, A. W. The generalization of self-instructions. In B. Gholson & T. L. Rosenthal (Eds.), *Applications of cognitive-developmental theory*. New York: Academic Press, in press.

Cohen, R., Schleser, R., & Meyers, A. Self-instructions: Effects of cognitive level and active rehearsal. *Journal of Experimental Child Psychology*, 1981, *32*, 65–76.

Cohen, S., & Przybycien, C. A. Some effects of sociometrically selected peer models on the cognitive style of impulsive children. *Journal of Genetic Psychology*, 1974, *124*, 213–220.

Cohen, S. E., & Beckwith, L. Preterm infant interaction with the caregiver in the first year of life and competence at age two. *Child Development*, 1979, *50*, 767–776.

Cole, C., & Morrow, W. R. Refractory parent behaviors in behavior modification training groups. *Psychotherapy: Theory, Research and Practice*, 1976, *13*, 162–169.

Cole, J. K., & Magnussen, M. G. Family situation factors related to remainers and terminators of treatment. *Psychotherapy: Theory, Research and Practice*, 1967, *4*, 107–109.

Cole, P. M., & Kazdin, A. E. Critical issues in self-instruction training with children, *Child Behavior Therapy*, 1980, *2*, 1–23.

Combs, M. L., & Slaby, D. A. Social-skills training with children. In B. B. Lahey & A. E. Kazdin (Eds.), *Advances in clinical child psychology* (Vol. 1). New York: Plenum Press, 1977.

Condon, W. S., & Sander, L. W. Neonate movement is synchronized with adult speech: Interactional participation and language acquisition. *Science*, 1974, *183*, 99.

Cone, J. D. Confounded comparisons in triple response mode assessment research. *Behavioral Assessment*, 1979, *1*, 85–96.

Conger, J. C., & Keane, S. P. Social skills intervention in the treatment of isolated or withdrawn children. *Psychological Bulletin*, 1981, *90*, 478–495.

Conger, J. J., & Miller, W. C. *Personality, social class, and delinquency*. New York: Wiley, 1966.

Conners, C. K. A teacher rating scale for use in drug studies with children. *American Journal of Psychiatry*, 1969, *126*, 884–888.

Conners, C. Ratings scales for use in drug studies in children. *Pharmacotherapy Bulletin*, 1973, 24–84.

Coopersmith, S. *The antecedents of self-esteem*. San Francisco: W. H. Freeman, 1967.

Copeland, A. P. The relevance of subject variables in cognitive instructional programs for impulsive children. *Behavior Therapy*, 1981, *12*, 520–529.

Cowen, E. L. An overview and directions for future work. In E. L. Cowen, E. A. Gardner, & M. Zax (Eds.), *Emergent approaches to mental health problems*. New York: Appleton-Century-Crofts, 1967.

Cowen, E. L. Social and community interventions. *Annual Review of Psychology*, 1973, *24*, 423–472.

Cowen, E. L. Baby-steps toward primary prevention. *American Journal of Consulting and Clinical Psychology*, 1977, *5*, 1–22.

Cowen, E. L. Some problems in community program evaluation research. *Journal of Consulting and Clinical Psychology*, 1978, *46*, 792–806.

Cowen, E. L. The wooing of primary prevention. *American Journal of Community Psychology*, 1980, *8*, 258–284.

Cowen, E. L., Dorr, D., & Pokracki, F. Selection of nonprofessional child-aids for a school mental health project. *Community Mental Health Journal*, 1972, *8*, 220–226.

Cowen, E. L., Dorr, D., Clarfield, S. P., Kreling, B., McWilliams, S. A., Pokracki, F., Pratt, D. M., Terrell, D. L., & Wilson, A. The AML: A quick screening device for early detection of school maladaptation. *American Journal of Community Psychology*, 1973, *1*, 12–35.

Cowen, E. L., Pederson, A., Babigian, H., Izzo, L. D., & Trost, M. A. Long-term follow-up of early detected vulnerable children. *Journal of Consulting and Clinical Psychology*, 1973, *41*, 438–446.

Cowen, E. L., Trost, M. A., Lorion, R. P., Dorr, D., Izzo, L. D., & Isaacson, R. V. *New Ways in school mental health*. New York: Human Sciences Press, 1975.

Cowen, E. L., Gesten, E. L., Boike, M., Norton, P., Wilson, A. B., & DeStefano, M. A. Hairdressers as caregivers. I. A descriptive profile of interpersonal help-giving involvements. *American Journal of Community Psychology*, 1979, *7*, 633–648.

Cowen, E. L., Davidson, E. R., & Gesten, E. L. Program dissemination and the modification of delivery practices in school mental health. *Professional Psychology*, 1980, *11*, 36–47.

Craddock, C., Cotler, S., & Jason, L. A. Primary prevention immunization of children for speech anxiety. *Cognitive Therapy and Research*, 1978, *2*, 389–396.

Craighead, W. E. A brief clinical history of cognitive-behavior therapy with children. *School Psychology Review*, 1982, *11*, 5–13.

Craighead, W. E. Away from a unitary model of depression. *Behavior Therapy*, 1980, *11*, 122–128.

Craighead, L. W., Brownell, K. D., & Horan, J. J. Behavioral interventions for weight reduction and smoking cessation. In W. E. Craighead, A. E. Kazdin, & M. J. Mahoney (Eds.), *Behavior modification: Principles, issues, and applications* (2nd Ed.). Boston: Houghton Mifflin, 1981.

Craighead, W. E., Wilcoxon-Craighead, L. W., & Meyers, A. W. New directions in behavior modification with children. In M. Hersen, R. M. Eisler & P. M. Miller (Eds.), *Progress in behavior modification* (Vol. 6). New York: Academic Press, 1978.

Craighead, W. E., Kazdin, A. E., & Mahoney, M. J. *Behavior modification: Principles, issues, and applications* (2nd ed.). Boston: Houghton Mifflin, 1981.

Craighead, W. E., Meyers, A. W., Craighead, L. W., & McHale, S. M. Issues in cognitive-behavior therapy with children. In M. Rosenbaum, C. M. Franks, & Y. Jaffe (Eds.), *Perspectives on behavior therapy in the eighties*. New York: Springer Publishing, 1982.

Craik, F. I. M., & Tulving, E. Depth of processing and the retention of words in episodic memory. *Journal of Experimental Psychology: General*, 1975, *104*, 268–294.

Crimmins, D. B., & Romanczyk, R. G. *Stimulus overselectivity in psychotic children*. Unpublished paper, SUNY, Binghampton, 1978.

Cronbach, L. J. *Essentials of psychological testing*. New York: Harper & Row, 1970.

Cruickshank, W. M., Bentzen, F. H., Ratzburg, F. H., & Tannhauser, M. T. *A teaching method for brain-injured and hyperactive children*. New York: Syracuse University Press, 1961.

Cullinan, D., Epstein, M. H., & Silver, L. Modification of impulsive tempo in learning-disabled pupils. *Journal of Abnormal Child Psychology*, 1977, *5*, 437–444.

Cullinan, D., Lloyd, J., & Epstein, M. H. Strategy training: A structured approach to arithmetic instruction. *Exceptional Education Quarterly*, 1981, *2*(1), 41–49.

Cunningham, T. R., & Tharp, R. G. The influence of settings on accuracy and reliability of behavioral observations. *Behavioral Assessment*, 1981, *3*, 67–78.

Cuthbert, M. I., & Melamed, B. G. A screening device: Children at risk for dental fears and management problems. Manuscript submitted for publication, 1982.

Damon, W. *The social world of the child*. San Francisco: Jossey-Bass, 1977.

Daut, R. *The development of a situation specific measure of social skill for third- and fourth-grade children*. Unpublished doctoral dissertation, University of Wisconsin, Madison, 1979.

Davidson, W. S., & Seidman, E. Studies of behavior modification and juvenile delinquency: A review, methodological critique and social perspective. *Psychological Bulletin*, 1974, *81*, 998–1011.

Davison, G. C., & Vallins, S. Maintenance of self-attributed and drug-attributed behavior of change. *Journal of Personality and Social Psychology*, 1969, *11*, 25–33.

Debus, R. L. Effects of brief observation of model behavior on conceptual tempo of impulsive children. *Developmental Psychology*, 1970, *2*, 22–32.

DeLange, J. M., Lanham, S. L., & Barton, J. A. Social skills training for juvenile delinquents: Behavioral skill training and cognitive techniques. In D. Upper & S. Ross (Eds.), *Behavior group therapy*. Champaign, Ill.: Research Press, 1981.

Dell, P. F. Researching the family theories of schizophrenia: An exercise in epistemological confusion. *Family Process*, 1980, *19*, 321–335.

DeLong, R. Individual differences in patterns of anxiety arousal, stress relevant information and recovery from surgery. (Unpublished doctoral dissertation, University of California, Los Angeles, 1970.) *Dissertation Abstracts International*, 1971, *32*, 445B.

Dember, W. N. Motivation and the cognitive revolution. *American Psychologist*, 1974, *29*, 161–168.

Denney, D. R. Modeling effects upon conceptual style and cognitive tempo. *Child Development*, 1972, *43*, 105–119.

Dielman, T. E., Barton, K., & Cattell, R. B., Relationships among family attitudes and child rearing practices. *Journal of Genetic Psychology*, 1977, *10*, 105–112.

Diener, C. I., & Dweck, C. S. An analysis of learned helplessness: Continuous changes in performance, strategy, and achievement cognitions following failure. *Journal of Personality and Social Psychology*, 1978, *36*, 451–462.

Dimsdale, J. E., & Moss, J. Short term calectolerance response to psychological stress. *Psychological Medicine*, 1980, *42*, 493–497.

Doane, J. A. Family interaction and communication deviance in disturbed and normal families: A review of research. *Family Process*, 1978, *17*, 357–376.

Dohrenwend, B. P., & Dohrenwend, B. S. *Social status and psychological disorder*. New York: Wiley, 1969.

Dorr, D., Stephens, J., Pozner, R., & Klodt, W. Use of the AML scale to identify adjustment problems in fourth-, fifth-, and sixth-grade children. *American Journal of Community Psychology*, 1980, *8*, 341–352.

Douglas, V. I. Treatment and training approaches to hyperactivity: Establishing internal or external control. In C. K. Whalen & B. Henker (Eds.), *Hyperactive children—The social psychology of identification and treatment*. New York: Academic Press, 1980.

Douglas, V. I., Parry, P., Marton, P., & Garson, C. Assessment of a cognitive training program for hyperactive children. *Journal of Abnormal Child Psychology*, 1976, *4*, 389–410.

Drabman, R. S., Spitalnik, R., & O'Leary, K. D. Teaching self-control to disruptive children. *Journal of Abnormal Psychology*, 1973, *82*, 10–16.

Drake, D. M. Perceptual correlates of impulsive and reflective behavior. *Developmental Psychology*, 1970, *2*, 204–212.

Drillien, C. M. *The growth and development of the prematurely-born infant*. Baltimore, Md.: Williams & Wilkins, 1964.

Druker, J. F., & Hagen, J. W. Developmental trends in the processing of task-relevant and task-irrelevant information. *Child Development*, 1969, *40*, 371–382.

Dumas, R. G. Psychological preparation for surgery. *American Journal of Nursing*, 1963, *63*, 52–55.

Duncan, P. Parental attitudes and interactions in delinquency. *Child Development*, 1971, *42*, 1751–1765.

Durfee, J. T., & Lee, L. C. *Infant-infant interaction in a day care setting*. Paper presented at the American Psychological Association meetings, Montreal, August 1973.

Durlak, J. A. Description and evaluation of a behaviorally oriented school-based preventive mental health program. *Journal of Consulting and Clinical Psychology*, 1977, *6*, 48–52.

Durlak, J. A. Comparative effectiveness of paraprofessional and professional helpers. *Psychological Bulletin*, 1979, *86*, 80–92.

Durlak, J. A. Comparative effectiveness of behavioral and relationship group treatment in the secondary prevention of school maladjustment. *American Journal of Community Psychology*, 1980, *8*, 327–340.

Durlak, J. A., & Gillespie, J. F. *Developing preventive mental health services for school children*. Paper presented at the Midwestern Psychological Association meeting, St. Louis, May 1980.

Durlak, J. A., & Gillespie, J. F. *Assessing the applied significance of treatment effects in a school-based preventive mental health program*. Paper presented at the meeting of the Midwestern Psychological Association, Minneapolis, May 1982.

Durlak, J. A., & Mannarino, A. P. *Behavioral vs. relationship treatment in the secondary prevention of school maladjustment*. Manuscript submitted for publication, 1980.

Durlak, J. A., Stein, M. A., & Mannarino, A. P. Behavioral validity of a brief teacher rating scale (the AML) in identifying high-risk acting-out schoolchildren. *American Journal of Community Psychology*, 1980, *8*, 101–115.

Dweck, D. S. The role of expectations and attributions in the alteration of learned helplessness. *Journal of Personality and Social Psychology*, 1975, *31*, 674–685.

D'Zurilla, T. J., & Goldfried, M. R. Problem solving and behavior modification. *Journal of Abnormal Psychology*, 1971, *78*, 107–126.

D'Zurilla, T. J., & Nezu, A. A study of the generation-of-alternatives process in problem-solving. *Cognitive Therapy and Research*, 1980, *4*, 67–72.

Edwards, C. P., & Lewis, M. Young children's concepts of social relations: Social functions and social objects. In M. Lewis & L. Rosenblum (Eds.), *The child and its family: The genesis of behavior* (Vol. 2). New York: Plenum Press, 1979.

Edwards, J. L., Shigley, R. H., & Edwards, R. P. A case report of an autistic boy: Selective responding to components of bidimensional visual and auditory stimuli. *Journal of Autism and Childhood Schizophrenia*, 1976, *6*, 139–146.

Egel, A. L. The effects of constant vs varied reinforcer presentation on responding by autistic children. *Journal of Experimental Child Psychology*, 1980, *30*, 455–463.

Egel, A. L., Koegel, R. L., & Schreibman, L. Review of educational-treatment procedures for autistic children. In L. Mann & D. A. Sabatino (Eds.), *The fourth review of special education*. New York: Grune & Stratton, 1980.

Egeland, B. Training impulsive children in the use of efficient scanning techniques. *Child Development*, 1974, *45*, 165–171.

Eitzen, D. S. The effects of behaviour modification on the attitudes of delinquents. *Behaviour Research and Therapy*, 1975, *13*, 295–299.

Elardo, P. T., Caldwell, B. M., & Webb, R. *An examination of the relationship between role-taking and social competence.* Paper presented at the Southeastern Conference on Human Development, Nashville, Tenn., April 1976.

Elder, J. P., Edelstein, B. A., & Narick, M. N. Adolescent psychiatric patients: Modifying aggressive behavior with social skills training. *Behavior Modification*, 1979, *3*, 161–178.

Ellis, A. *Reason and emotion in psychotherapy.* New York: Lyle Stuart, 1962.

Ellis, A. *Humanistic psychotherapy.* New York: McGraw-Hill, 1973.

Ellis, N. R. Memory processes in retardates and normals. In N. R. Ellis (Ed.), *International review of research in mental retardation* (Vol. 4). New York: Academic Press, 1970.

Emery, R. E. *Interparental conflict and child behavior problems: A review.* Unpublished manuscript, State University of New York at Stony Brook, 1981.

Emery, R. E., & O'Leary, K. D. *Children's perceptions of marital discord as related to behavior problems of boys and girls.* Paper presented at the annual meeting of the Association for the Advancement of Behavior Therapy, San Francisco, December 1979.

Erickson, R. C. Outcome studies in mental hospitals: A review. *Psychological Bulletin*, 1975, *82*, 519–540.

Erikson, E. H. *Childhood and society.* New York: Norton, 1950.

Eron, L. D., Walder, L. O., & Lefkowitz, M. M. *Learning of aggression in children.* Boston: Little, Brown, 1971.

Everett, P. B. A behavioral approach to transportation systems management. In D. S. Glenwick & L. A. Jason (Eds.), *Behavioral community psychology: Progress and prospects.* New York: Praeger Publishers, 1980.

Evers, W. L., & Schwarz, J. C. Modifying social withdrawal in preschoolers: The effects of filmed modeling and teacher praise. *Journal of Abnormal Child Psychology*, 1973, *1*, 248–256.

Evers-Pasquale, W. L. The Peer Preference Test, a measure of reward value: Item analysis, cross validation, concurrent validation, and replication. *Journal of Abnormal Child Psychology*, 1978, *6*, 175–188.

Evers-Pasquale, W., & Sherman, M. The reward value of peers: A variable influencing the efficacy of filmed modeling in modifying social isolation in preschoolers. *Journal of Abnormal Child Psychology*, 1975, *3*, 179–189.

Eyberg, S. M., & Johnson, S. M. Multiple assessment of behavior modification with families: Effects of contingency contracting and order of treated problems. *Journal of Consulting and Clinical Psychology*, 1974, *42*, 594–606.

Eysenck, H. J. (Ed.). *Behavior therapy and the neuroses.* New York: Pergamon Press, 1960.

Eysenck, H. J. *The effects of psychotherapy.* New York: International Science Press, 1966.

Fagen, S. A., & Long, N. J. A psychoeducational curriculum approach to teaching self-control. *Behavioral Disorders*, 1979, *4*, 68–82.

Fagot, B. *Aggression in toddlers.* Paper presented at the Infancy Study Conference, New Haven, March 1980.

Fagot, B. I. *Preschool sex stereotyping: Effect of sex of teacher vs. training of teacher.* Paper presented at the Society for Research in Child Development meetings, New Orleans, March, 1977.

Federal Bureau of Investigation. *Uniform crime reports.* Washington, D.C.: U.S. Department of Justice, 1977.

Feffer, M. H. The cognitive implications of role taking behavior. *Journal of Personality*, 1959, *27*, 152–168.

Feffer, M. H., & Gourevitch, V. Cognitive aspects of role taking in children. *Journal of Personality*, 1960, *28*, 383–396.

Feinberg, H., & Roberts, R. N. *Conceptual versus concrete self instructional training in the learning disability classroom*. Manuscript submitted for publication, 1983.

Felner, R. D., Jason, L. A., Moritsugu, J. N., & Farber, S. (Eds.). *Preventive psychology: Theory, research, and practice in community settings*. New York: Pergamon Press, 1983.

Ferber, H., Keeley, S. M., & Shemberg, K. M. Training parents in behavior modification. Outcome of and problems encountered in a program after Patterson's work. *Behavior Therapy*, 1974, *5*, 415–419.

Ferguson, B. F. Preparing young children for hospitalization: A comparison of two methods. *Pediatrics*, 1979, *64*, 656–664.

Ferreira, A. J., & Winter, W. D. Family interaction and decision making. *Archives of General Psychiatry*, 1965, *13*, 214–223.

Ferreira, A. J., & Winter, W. D. Information exchange and silence in normal and abnormal families. *Family Process*, 1968, *7*, 251–276.

Ferritor, D. E., Buckholdt, D., Hamblin, R. L., & Smith, L. The noneffects of contingent reinforcement for attending behavior on work accomplished. *Journal of Applied Behavior Analysis*, 1972, *5*, 7–17.

Ferster, C. B. Positive reinforcement and behavioral deficits of autistic children. *Child Development*, 1961, *32*, 437–456.

Ferster, C. B., & DeMeyer, M. K. The development of performance in autistic children in an automatically controlled environment. *Journal of Chronic Diseases*, 1961, *13*, 312–345.

Ferster, C. B., & DeMyer, M. K. A method for the experimental analysis of the behavior of autistic children. *American Journal of Orthopsychiatry*, 1962, *32*, 89–98.

Ferster, C. B., Nurnberger, J. I., & Levitt, E. B. The control of eating. *Journal of Mathematics*, 1962, *1*, 87–109.

Feshbach, N. D. *Empathy training: A field study in affective education*. Paper presented at the American Educational Research Association meeting, Toronto, March 1978.

Feuerstein, R., Rand, Y., & Hoffman, M. *The dynamic assessment of retarded performers*. Baltimore, Md.: University Park Press, 1979.

Feuerstein, R., Rand, Y., Hoffman, M., & Miller, R. *Instrumental enrichment: An intervention program for cognitive modifiability*. Baltimore, Md.: University Park Press, 1980.

Field, T. (Ed.). *Infants born at risk: Behavior and development*. New York: S. P. Medical & Scientific Books, 1979.

Field, T., Ting, G., & Shuman, H. H. The onset of rhythmic activities in normal and high-risk infants. *Developmental Psychobiology*, 1979, *12*, 97–100.

Field, T., Dempsey, J., & Shuman, H. Developmental follow-up of pre- and post-term infants. In S. Friedman & M. Sigman (Eds.), *Preterm birth and psychological development*. New York: Academic Press, 1981.

Filipczak, J., Archer, M., & Friedman, R. M. In-school social skills training: Use with disruptive adolescents. *Behavior Modification*, 1980, *4*, 243–263.

Finch, A. J., & Montgomery, L. E. Reflection-impulsivity and information seeking in emotionally disturbed children. *Journal of Abnormal Child Psychology*, 1975, *3*, 47–51.

Finch, A. J. Jr., & Spirito, A. Use of cognitive training to change cognitive processes. *Exceptional Education*, 1980, *1*(1), 31–39.

Finch, A., Wilkinson, M., Nelson, W., & Montgomery, L. Modification of an impulsive cognitive tempo in emotionally disturbed boys. *Journal of Abnormal Child Psychology*, 1975, *3*, 49–52.

Fixsen, D. L., Phillips, E. L., & Wolf, M. M. Achievement Place: Experiments in self-government with pre-delinquents. *Journal of Applied Behavior Analysis*, 1973, *6*, 31–57.

Fixsen, D. L., Phillips, E. L., Phillips, E. A., & Wolf, M. M. The teaching-family model of group home treatment. In W. E. Craighead, A. E. Kazdin, & M. J. Mahoney (Eds.), *Behavior modification: Principles, issues, and applications*. Boston: Houghton-Mifflin, 1976.

Flavell, J. *The development of role-taking and communication skills in children*. New York: Wiley, 1968.

Flavell, J. H. *The developmental psychology of Jean Piaget*. Princeton, N.J.: Van Nostrand Reinhold, 1963.

Flavell, J. H. Developmental studies of mediated memory. In H. W. Reese & L. P. Lipsett (Eds.), *Advances in child development and behavior* (Vol. 5). New York: Academic Press, 1970.

Flavell, J. H. First discussants' comments: What is memory development the development of? *Human Development*, 1971, *14*, 272–278.

Flavell, J. H. Metacognitive aspects of problem-solving. In L. B. Resnick (Ed.), *The nature of intelligence*. Hillsdale, N.J.: Lawrence Erlbaum Associates, 1976.

Flavell, J. H. *Cognitive development*. Englewood Cliffs, N.J.: Prentice-Hall, 1977.

Flavell, J. H., & Wellman, H. M. Metamemory. In R. V. Kail & J. W. Hagen (Eds.), *Perspectives on the development of memory and cognition*. Hillsdale, N.J.: Lawrence Erlbaum Associates, 1977.

Flavell, J. H., Beach, D. R., & Chinsky, J. M. Spontaneous verbal rehearsal in a memory task as a function of age. *Child Development*, 1966, *37*, 283–299.

Flavell, J. H., Botkin, P. T., Fry, C. L., Wright, J. W., & Jarvis, P. E. *The development of role-taking and communication skills in children*. New York: Wiley, 1968.

Flavell, J. H., Friedrichs, A. G., & Hoyt, J. D. Developmental changes in memorization processes. *Cognitive Psychology*, 1970, *1*, 324–340.

Fo, W. S., & O'Donnell, C. R. The buddy system: Relationship and contingency conditions in a community intervention program for youth with professionals as behavior change agents. *Journal of Consulting and Clinical Psychology*, 1974, *42*, 163–169.

Ford, M. E. The construct validity of egocentrism. *Psychological Bulletin*, 1979, *86*, 1169–1188.

Forehand, R., & Atkeson, B. M. Generality of treatment effects with parents as therapists: A review of assessment and implementation procedures. *Behavior Therapy*, 1977, *8*, 575–593.

Forehand, R., & Atkeson, B. M. Behavior modification with severely disturbed children. In W. E. Craighead, A. E. Kazdin, & M. J. Mahoney (Eds.), *Behavior modification: Principles, issues and applications* (2nd ed.). Boston: Houghton Mifflin, 1981.

Forehand, R., Wells, K. C., & Griest, D. L. An examination of the social validity of a parent training program. *Behavior Therapy*, 1980, *11*, 488–502.

Forman, S. G. A comparison of cognitive training and response cost procedures in modifying aggressive behavior of elementary school children. *Behavior Therapy*, 1980, *11*, 594–600.

Forman, S. G. Stress management training: Evaluation of effects on school psychological services. *Journal of School Psychology*, 1981, *19*, 233–241.

Forman, S. G. Stress management for teachers: A cognitive-behavioral program. *Journal of School Psychology*, 1982, *20*, 182–187.

Foster, S. L., & Ritchey, W. L. Issues in the assessment of social competence in children. *Journal of Applied Behavior Analysis*, 1979, *12*, 625–638.

Fox, N., & Lewis, M. The role of maturation and experience in preterm infant development. In J. J. Gallagher (Ed.), *New directions in special education*. San Francisco: Jossey-Bass, 1981.

Frank, G. H. The role of the family in the development of psychopathology. *Psychological Bulletin*, 1965, *64*, 191–205.

Franzini, L. R., Litrownik, A. J., & Magy, M. A. Immediate and delayed reward preferences of TMR adolescents. *American Journal of Mental Deficiency*, 1978, *82*, 406–409.

Franzini, L. R., Litrownik, A. J., & Magy, M. A. Training adolescent TMRs in delay behavior. *Mental Retardation*, 1980, *18*, 45–47.

Fredericks, L. E. Teaching of hypnosis in the overall approach to the surgical patient. *American Journal of Clinical Hypnosis*, 1978, *20*, 175–183.

Fredericksen, L. W., & Frederiksen, C. B. Teacher-determined and self-determined token reinforcement in a special education classroom. *Behavior Therapy*, 1975, *6*, 310–314.

Freedman, B. J., Rosenthal, L., Donahoe, C. P., Schlundt, D. G., & McFall, R. M. A social-behavioral analysis of skill deficits in delinquent and nondelinquent adolescent boys. *Journal of Consulting and Clinical Psychology*, 1978, *46*, 1448–1462.

Freund, A., & Dann, S. An experiment in group upbringing. *Psychoanalytic Study of the Child, Vol. VI*, 1952, 127–168.

Friedling, C., & O'Leary, S. G. Effects of self-instructional training on second- and third-grade hyperactive children: A failure to replicate. *Journal of Applied Behavior Analysis*, 1979, *12*, 211–219.

Friedson, E., & Feldman, J. J. The public looks at dental care. *Journal of the American Dental Association*, 1958, *57*, 325–335.

Fry, C. L. Training children to communicate to listeners. *Child Development*, 1966, *37*, 675–685.

Fry, C. L. Training children to communicate to listeners who have varying listener requirements. *Journal of Genetic Psychology*, 1969, *114*, 153–166.

Fullard, W., & Reiling, A. M. An investigation of Lorenz's "babyness." *Child Development*, 1976, *47*, 1191–1193.

Fuller, S. S., Endress, M. P., & Johnson, J. E. The effects of cognitive and behavioral control on coping with an aversive health examination. *Journal of Human Stress*, 1978, *4*, 18–25.

Furman, W. Promoting social development: Developmental implications for treatment. In B. B. Lahey & A. E. Kazdin (Eds.), *Advances in clinical child psychology* (Vol. 3). New York: Plenum Press, 1980.

Furman, W., Rahe, D. F., & Hartup, W. W. Rehabilitation of socially withdrawn preschool children through mixed-age and same-age socialization. *Child Development*, 1979, *50*, 915–922.

Furstenberg, F. F. *Children's names and paternal claims: Bonds between unmarried fathers and their children.* Undated.

Gagne, E. E. Effects of immediacy of feedback and level of aspiration statements on learning tasks for delinquent youngsters. *Journal of Abnormal Child Psychology*, 1975, *3*, 53–60.

Gale, E., & Ayer, N. M. Treatment of dental phobias. *Journal of the American Dental Association*, 1969, *73*, 1304–1307.

Ganzer, V. J., & Sarason, I. G. Variables associated with recidivism among juvenile delinquents. *Journal of Consulting and Clinical Psychology*, 1973, *40*, 1–5.

Garner, D. M. Body image in anorexia nervosa. *Canadian Journal of Psychiatry*, 1981, *26*, 224–227.

Gartner, A., & Riessman, F. *Self-help in the human services.* San Francisco: Jossey-Bass, 1977.

Garvey, C., & Hogan, R. Social speech and social interaction: Egocentrism revisited. *Child Development*, 1973, *44*, 562–568.

Gassner, S., & Murray, E. J. Dominance and conflict in the interactions between parents of normal and neurotic children. *Journal of Abnormal Psychology*, 1969, *74*, 33–41.

Gatchel, R. J., Hatch, J. P., Watson, P. J., Smith, D., & Gass, E. Comparative effectiveness of voluntary heart rate control and muscular relaxation as active coping skills for reducing speech anxiety. *Journal of Consulting and Clinical Psychology*, 1977, *45*, 1033–1100.

Gelfand, D. M. Social withdrawal and negative emotional states. In B. B. Wolman, J. Egan, & A. O. Ross (Eds.), *Handbook of treatment of mental disorders in childhood and adolescence*. Englewood Cliffs, N.J.: Prentice-Hall, 1978.

Gelfand, D. M., & Hartmann, D. P. Behavior therapy with children: A review and evaluation of research methodology. *Psychological Bulletin*, 1968, *69*, 204–215.

George, J. M., Scott, D. S., Turner, S. P., & Gregg, J. M. The effects of psychological factors and physical trauma on recovery from oral surgery. *Journal of Behavioral Medicine*, 1980, *3*, 291–310.

Gerber, M. M. Economic considerations for "appropriate" education for exceptional children. *Exceptional Education Quarterly*, 1981, *2*(2), 49–57.

Gerber, M. M., & Hall, R. J. *Development of orthographic problem-solving strategies in learning disabled children*. Paper presented at the meeting of the American Educational Research Association, Los Angeles, April 1981.

Gerber, M. M., & Hall, R. J. Development of spelling in learning disabled and normally achieving children. *Monographs of the Society for Research in Learning and Remedial Education*, 1983, *1*(1).

Gerber, M. M., & Hall, R. J. Spelling errors of attentionally disordered learning disabled children. *Learning Disability Quarterly*, in press.

Gersten, J. C., Langer, T. S., Eisenberg, J. B., Simcha-Fagen, O., & McCarthy, E. D. Stability and change in types of behavioral disturbance of children and adolescents. *Journal of Abnormal Child Psychology*, 1976, *4*, 111–127.

Gersten, R. M. In search of cognitive deficit in autism: Beyond the stimulus overselectivity model. *Journal of Special Education*, 1980, *14*, 47–65.

Gesten, E. L. A health resources inventory: The development of a measure of the personal and social competence of primary grade children. *Journal of Consulting and Clinical Psychology*, 1976, *44*, 775–786.

Gesten, E. L., Flores de Apodaca, R., Rains, M. H., Weissberg, R. P., & Cowen, E. L. Promoting peer related social competence in young children. In M. W. Kent & J. E. Rolf (Eds.), *The primary prevention of psychopathology: Social competence in children*. Hanover, N.H.: University Press of New England, 1979.

Gilbert, G. M. A survey of "referral problems" in metropolitan child guidance centers. *Journal of Clinical Psychology*, 1957, *13*, 37–42.

Gilmore, J. B. Play: A special behavior. In R. N. Haber (Ed.), *Current research in motivation*. New York: Holt, Rinehart & Winston, 1966.

Ginsburg, H., & Opper, S. *Piaget's theory of intellectual development*. Englewood Cliffs, N.J.: Prentice-Hall, 1969.

Giora, Z. *Psychopathology: A cognitive view*. New York: Gardner Press, 1975.

Glasgow, R. E., & Rosen, G. M. Behavioral bibliotherapy: A review of self-help behavior therapy manuals. *Psychological Bulletin*, 1978, *85*, 1–23.

Glenwick, D. S., & Barocas, R. Training impulsive children in verbal self-control by use of natural change agents. *Journal of Special Education*, 1979, *13*, 387–39.

Glenwick, D. S., & Jason, L. A. (Eds.). *Behavioral community psychology: Progress and prospects*. New York: Praeger Publishers, 1980.

Glenwick, D. S., & Stevens, E. Vertical supervision. In A. K. Hess (Ed.), *Psychotherapy supervision*. New York: Wiley, 1980.

Glick, S. J. First follow-up study of Glueck Table to identify predelinquents at school entrance. In S. Glueck & E. Glueck (Eds.), *Identification of pre-delinquents*, New York: Medical Book Corporation, 1972.

Glidden, L. M. Developmental effects in free recall learning. *Child Development*, 1977, *48*, 9–12.

Glidewell, J. C., & Swallow, C. S. *The prevalence of maladjustment in elementary schools: A report prepared for the Joint Commission on the Mental Health of Children*. Chicago: University of Chicago Press, 1969.

Glueck, S., & Glueck, E. *Of crime and delinquency*. Springfield, Ill.: Charles C. Thomas, 1974.

Glynn, E. L., Thomas, J. D., & Shee, S. M. Behavioral self-control of ontask behavior in an elementary classroom. *Journal of Applied Behavior Analysis*. 1973, *6*, 105–113.

Goldfried, M. R. Reduction of generalized anxiety. Through a variant of systematic desensitization. In M. R. Goldfried & M. Merbaum (Eds.), *Behavior change through self-control*. New York: Holt, Rinehart & Winston, 1973.

Goldfried, M. R. Anxiety reduction through cognitive-behavioral intervention. In P. C. Kendall & S. D. Hollon (Eds.), *Cognitive-behavioral interventions: Theory, research, and procedures*. New York: Academic Press, 1979.

Goldfried, M. R., & Davison, G. C. *Clinical behavior therapy*. New York: Holt, Rinehart & Winston, 1976.

Goldfried, M. R., & D'Zurilla, T. J. A behavioral-analytic model for assessing competence. In C. D. Spielberger (Ed.), *Current topics in clinical and community psychology* (Vol. 1). New York: Academic Press, 1969.

Goldfried, M. R., & Goldfried, A. P. Cognition change methods. In F. H. Kanfer & A. P. Goldstein (Eds.), *Helping people change*. New York: Pergamon Press, 1975.

Goldfried, M. R., & Goldfried, A. P. Importance of hierarchy content in the self-control of anxiety. *Journal of Consulting and Clinical Psychology*, 1977, *43*, 124–134.

Goldfried, M. R., & Kent, R. N. Traditional versus behavioral personality assessment: A comparison of methodological and theoretical assumptions. *Psychological Bulletin*, 1972, *77*, 409–420.

Goldfried, M. R., & Merbaum, M. (Eds.). *Behavior change through self-control*. New York: Holt, Reinhart & Winston, 1973.

Goldfried, M. R., & Trier, C. S. Effectiveness of relaxation as an active coping skill. *Journal of Abnormal Psychology*, 1974, *83*, 348–353.

Goldiamond, I. Self-control procedures in personal behavior problems. *Psychological Reports*, 1965, *17*, 851–868.

Goldston, S. E. Primary prevention: A view from the federal level. In G. W. Albee & J. M. Joffee (Eds.), *Primary prevention of psychopathology* (Vol. 1). Hanover, N.H.: University Press of New England, 1977.

Goodwin, S. E., & Mahoney, M. J. Modification of aggression through modeling: An experimental probe. *Journal of Behavior Therapy and Experimental Psychiatry*, 1975, *6*, 200–202.

Gottman, J. The effects of a modeling film on social isolation in pre-school children: A methodological investigation. *Journal of Abnormal Child Psychology*, 1977, *5*(1), 69–79. (a)

Gottman, J. M. Toward a definition of a social isolation in children. *Child Development*, 1977, *48*, 513–517. (b)

Gottman, J., Gonso, J., & Rasmussen, B. Social isolation, social competence and friendship in children. *Child Development*, 1975, *46*, 709–718.

Gottman, J., Gonso, J., & Schuler, P. Teaching social skills to isolated children. *Journal of Abnormal Child Psychology*, 1976, *4*, 179–197.

Gottman, J., Notarius, C., Markman, H., Bank, S., Yoppi, B., & Rubin, M. E. Behavior exchange theory and marital decision making. *Journal of Personality and Social Psychology*, 1976, *34*, 14–23.
Gough, H. G. A sociological theory of psychopathy. *American Journal of Sociology*, 1948, *56*, 359–366.
Graham, E. E., & Kamano, D. Reading failure as a factor in the WAIS subtest patterns of youthful offenders. *Journal of Clinical Psychology*, 1958, *14*, 302–305.
Graham, H. Smoking in pregnancy: The attitudes of expectant mothers. *Social Science and Medicine*, 1976, *10*, 399–405.
Graziano, A. M. *Behavior therapy with children*. Chicago: Aldine, 1971.
Graziano, A. M. Parents as behavior therapists. In M. Hersen, R. M. Eisler, & P. M. Miller (Eds.), *Progress in behavior modification* (Vol. 4.). New York: Academic Press, 1977.
Graziano, A. M., & Mooney, K. C. Family self-control instruction for children's nighttime fear reduction. *Journal of Consulting and Clinical Psychology*, 1980, *48*, 206–213.
Greenspoon, J., & Lamal, P. A. Cognitive behavior modification—Who needs it? *Psychological Record*, 1978, *28*, 343–351.
Greenwood, C. R., Walker, H. M., Todd, N. M., & Hops, H. Selecting a cost-effective screening device for the assessment of preschool social withdrawal. *Journal of Applied Behavior Analysis*, 1979, *12*, 639–652.
Gresham, F. M. Social skills training with handicapped children: A review. *Review of Educational Research*, 1981, *51*, 139–176.
Gresham, F. M., & Nagle, R. J. Social skills training with children: Responsiveness to modeling and coaching as a function of peer orientation. *Journal of Consulting and Clinical Psychology*, 1980, *48*, 718–729.
Gross, A. M., Brigham, T. A., Hopper, C., & Bologna, N. C. Self-management and social skills training: A study with predelinquent and delinquent youths. *Criminal Justice and Behavior*, 1980, *7*, 161–184.
Group for the Advancement of Psychiatry, Committee on Child Psychiatry. *Psychopathological disorders in childhood: Theoretical considerations and a proposed classification*. GAP Report No. 62, New York, June 1966.
Guralnick, M. J. Solving complex discrimination problems: Techniques for the development of problem solving strategies. *American Journal of Mental Deficiency*, 1976, *81*, 18–25.
Gurin, G., Veroff, J., & Feld, S. *Americans view their mental health: A nationwide survey*. New York: Basic Books, 1960.
Gurman, A. S. Contemporary marital therapies. A critique and comparative analysis of psychoanalytic, behavioral and systems theory approaches. In T. J. Paolino Jr. & B. S. McGrady (Eds.), *Marriage and marital therapy*. New York: Brunner/Mazel, 1978.
Gurman, A. S., & Kniskern, D. P. Research on marital and family therapy: Progress, perspective and prospect. In S. L. Garfield & A. E. Bergin (Eds.), *Handbook of psychotherapy and behavior change: An empirical analysis* (2nd ed.). New York: Wiley, 1978.
Gutman, H. G. *The black family in slavery and freedom: 1850–1925*. New York: Vintage Press, 1977.
Haight, S. B. *A comparison of concept usage and concept formation in educationally handicapped and normal achieving children*. Unpublished doctoral dissertation, UCLA, 1974.
Haley, J. Marriage therapy. *Archives of General Psychiatry*, 1963, *8*, 213–234.
Haley, J. Testing parental instructions to schizophrenic and normal children: A pilot study. *Journal of Abnormal Psychology*, 1968, *73*, 559–565.
Hall, R. J. *An information processing approach to the study of learning disabilities*. Unpublished doctoral dissertation, UCLA, 1979.

Hall, R. J. An information processing approach to the study of exceptional children. In B. K. Keogh (Ed.), *Advances in special education* (Vol. 2): *Perspectives on application*. Greenwich, Conn.: JAI Press, 1980. (a)

Hall, R. J. Cognitive behavior modification and information-processing skills of exceptional children. *Exceptional Education Quarterly*, 1980, (*1*), 9–15. (b)

Hallahan, D. P., & Bryan, T. H. Learning disabilities. In J. M. Kauffman & D. P. Hallahan (Eds.), *Handbook of special education*. Englewood Cliffs, N.J.: Prentice-Hall, 1981.

Hallahan, D. P., & Kauffman, J. M. *Introduction to learning disabilities*. Englewood Cliffs, N.J.: Prentice-Hall, 1976.

Hallahan, D. P., & Kauffman, J. M. *Exceptional children: Introduction to special education*. Englewood Cliffs, N.J.: Prentice-Hall, 1978.

Hallahan, D. P., & Kneedler, R. D. Attacking the strategy deficits of learning disabled children: Research of self-monitoring. *Exceptional Education Quarterly*. 1981, *2*(3), 72–83.

Hallahan, D. P., & Reeve, R. E. Selective attention and distractibility. In B. K. Keogh (Ed.), *Advances in special education* (Vol. 1). Greenwich, Conn.: JAI Press, 1980.

Hallahan, D. P., Lloyd, J., Kosiewicz, M. M., Kauffman, J. M., & Graves, A. W. Self-monitoring of attention as a treatment for a learning disabled boy's off-task behavior. *Learning Disabilities Quarterly*, 1979, *2*(3), 24–32.

Harbin, H. T. Episodic dyscontrol and family dynamics. *American Journal of Psychiatry*, 1977, *134*, 1113–1116.

Harlow, H. F. Love in infant monkeys. *Scientific American*, July 1959, 68–74.

Harlow, H. F. Age-mate or peer affectional system. In D. S. Lehrman, R. A. Hinde, & E. Shaw (Eds.), *Advances in the study of behavior* (Vol. 2). New York: Academic Press, 1969.

Harlow, H. F., & Mears, C. *The human model: Primate perspectives*. New York: Wiley, 1979.

Harris, G., & Johnson, S. B. Comparison of individualized covert modeling, self-control desensitization, and study skills training for alleviation of test anxiety. *Journal of Consulting and Clinical Psychology*, 1980, *48*, 186–194.

Harris, S. L. DSM-III—Its implications for children. *Child Behavior Therapy*, 1979, *1*, 37–46.

Harris, V. W., & Sherman, J. A. Homework assignments, consequences, and classroom performance in social studies and mathematics. *Journal of Applied Behavior Analysis*, 1974, *7*, 505–419.

Hart, B. M., Reynolds, N. J., Baer, D. M., Brawley, E. R., & Harris, F. R. Effect of contingent and noncontingent social reinforcement on the cooperative play of a preschool child. *Journal of Applied Behavior Analysis*, 1968, *1*, 73–76.

Hartig, M., & Kanfer, F. The role of verbal self-instructions in children's resistance to temptation. *Journal of Personality and Social Psychology*, 1973, *25*, 259–267.

Hartman, L. The preventive reduction of psychological risk in asymptomatic adolescents. *American Journal of Orthopsychiatry*, 1979, *49*, 121–135.

Hartup, W. Peer interaction and social organization. In P. H. Mussen (Ed.), *Carmichael's manual of child psychology* (Vol. 2). New York: Wiley, 1970.

Hartup, W. W. Peer interaction and the behavioral development of the individual child. In E. Schopler & R. Reichler (Eds.), *Psychopathology and child development*. New York: Plenum Press, 1976.

Hartup, W. W. Peer relations and the growth of social competence. In M. W. Kent & J. E. Rolf, (Eds.), *The primary prevention of psychopathology: Promoting social competence and coping in children* (Vol. 3). Hanover, N.H.: University Press of New England, 1979. (a)

Hartup, W. W. The social worlds of childhood. *American Psychologist*, 1979, *34*, 944–950. (b)

Hartup, W. W., Glazer, J. A., & Charlesworth, R. Peer reinforcement and sociometric status. *Child Development*, 1967, *38*, 1017–1024.

Hauser, S. L., DeLong, G. R., & Rosman, P. Pneumographic findings in the infantile autism syndrome: A correlation with temporal lobe disease. *Brain*, 1975, *98*, 667–688.

Havertape, J. F., & Kass, C. E. Examination of problem solving in learning disabled adolescents through verbalized self instructions. *Learning Disability Quarterly*, 1978, *1*, 94–99.

Hawkins, R. P. Who decided that was the problem? Two stages of responsibility for applied behavior analysis. In W. S. Wood (Ed.), *Issues in evaluating behavior modification*. Champaign, Ill.: Research Press, 1975.

Hay, W. M., Hay, L. R., & Nelson, R. O. The effects of social versus academic contingencies on attending behavior and academic performance. *Behavior Therapy*, 1977, *8*, 431–441.

Hayes, S. C., Rincover, A., & Solnick, J. V. The technical drift of applied behavior analysis. *Journal of Applied Behavior Analysis*, 1980, *13*, 275–285.

Hedberg, A. G., & Schlong, A. Eliminating fainting by school children during mass inoculation clinics. *Nursing Research*, 1973, *22*, 352–353.

Heider, E. R. Information processing and the modification of an "impulsive conceptual tempo." *Child Development*, 1971, *42*, 1276–1281.

Heins, E. D. *A components analysis of cues to self-record in a treatment procedures for increasing attention to task.* (Technical Report No. 35.) Charlottesville, Va.: University of Virginia Learning Disabilities Research Institute, 1981.

Helland, C. P., Paluck, R. J., & Klein, M. A comparison of self and external reinforcement with the trainable mentally retarded. *Mental Retardation*, 1976, *14*, 22–23.

Heller, K., & Monahan, J. *Psychology and community change*. Homewood, Ill.: Dorsey Press, 1977.

Henker, B., Whalen, C. K., & Hinshaw, S. P. The attributional contexts of cognitive intervention strategies. *Exceptional Education Quarterly*, 1980, *1*, 17–30.

Herbertt, R. M., & Innes, J. M. Familiarization and preparatory information in the reduction of anxiety in child dental patients. *Journal of Dentistry for Children*, 1979, *46*, 319–323.

Hermelin, B., & O'Connor, N. *Psychological experiments with autistic children*. London: Pergamon Press, 1970.

Hersen, M. Limitations and problems in the clinical application of behavioral techniques in psychiatric settings. *Behavior Therapy*, 1979, *10*, 65–80.

Hersen, M. Complex problems require complex solutions. *Behavior Therapy*, 1981, *12*, 15–29.

Hess, R. D., & Shipman, V. C. Early experience and the socialization of cognitive modes in children. *Child Development*, 1965, *36*, 869–886.

Hetherington, E. M., Stouwie, R. J., & Ridberg, E. H. Patterns of family interaction and child-rearing attitudes related to three dimensions of juvenile delinquency. *Journal of Abnormal Psychology*, 1971, *78*, 160–176.

Higa, W. R., Tharp, R. G., & Calkins, R. P. Developmental verbal control of behavior: Implications for self-instructional training. *Journal of Experimental Child Psychology*, 1978, *26*, 489–497.

Hinde, R. A. *The biological basis of human social behavior*. New York: McGraw-Hill, 1974.

Hinde, R. A. Interactions, relationships, and social structure. *Man*, 1976, *11*, 1–17.

Hindelang, M. J., Gottfredson, M. R., & Flanagan, T. J. *Sourcebook of criminal justice statistics*. Washington, D.C.: U.S. Department of Justice, 1981.

Hobbs, N. Helping disturbed children: Psychological and ecological strategies. *American Psychologist*, 1966, *21*, 1105–1115.

Hobbs, N. *Helping disturbed children: Psychological and ecological strategies, II: Project Re-ED,*

Twenty years later. Nashville, Tenn.: Vanderbilt Institute for Public Policy Studies, 1979.

Hobbs, S. A., Moguin, L. E., Tyroler, M., & Lahey, B. B. Cognitive behavior therapy with children: Has clinical utility been demonstrated? *Psychological Bulletin,* 1980, *87,* 147–165.

Hodge, J. D. *Interpersonal-cognitive problem-solving of primary grade children demonstrating the dimensions of behavioral adjustment identified within the normal range of functioning.* Unpublished doctoral dissertation, University of Wisconsin, Madison, 1979.

Hodgson, R., & Rachman, S. Desynchrony in measures of fear. *Behavior Research and Therapy,* 1974, *12,* 319–326.

Hoffman, L. Deviation amplifying processes in natural groups. In J. Haley (Ed.), *Changing families: A family therapy reader.* New York: Grune & Stratton, 1971.

Hoffman, M. L. Developmental synthesis of affect and cognition and its implications for altruistic motivation. *Developmental Psychology,* 1975, *11,* 607–622.

Hogan, R. Moral conduct and moral character. *Psychological Bulletin,* 1973, *79,* 217–232.

Holman, J., & Baer, D. M. Facilitating generalization of on-task behavior through self-monitoring of academic tasks. *Journal of Autism and Developmental Disorders,* 1979, *9,* 429–446.

Holt, M. M., & Hobbs, T. R. Problems of behavioral interventions with delinquents in an institutional setting. In A. J. Finch & P. C. Kendall (Eds.), *Clinical treatment and research in child psychopathology.* New York: Spectrum, 1979.

Homme, L. Perspectives in psychology: Control of coverants, the operants of the mind. *Psychological Record,* 1965, *15,* 501–511.

Hopper, R., & Kirschenbaum, D. S. *Social problem-solving skills and social competence in preadolescent children.* Paper presented at the meeting of the American Psychological Association, New York, September 1979.

Hopper, R., & Kirschenbaum, D. S. Social problem-solving and social competence in preadolescents: Is inconsistent problem-solving problematic? *Developmental Psychology,* in press.

Hops, H., & Greenwood, G. R. Social skills deficits. In E. J. Mash & L. G. Terdal (Eds.), *Behavioral assessment of childhood disorders.* New York: Guilford Press, 1981.

Hops, H., Walker, H. M., & Greenwood, C. R. PEERS: A program for remediating social withdrawal in school. In L. A. Hamerlynck (Ed.), *Behavioral systems for the developmentally disabled: I. School and family environments.* New York: Brunner/Mazel, 1979.

House, B. J. Attention to components or compounds as a factor in discrimination transfer performance *Journal of Experimental Child Psychology,* 1979, *27,* 321–331.

House, B. J., & Zeaman, D. Miniature experiments in the discrimination learning of retardates. In L. P. Lipsitt & C. C. Spiker (Eds.), *Advances in child development and behavior* (Vol. 1). New York: Academic Press, 1963.

House, T. H., & Milligan, W. L. Autonomic responses to modeled distress in prison psychopaths. *Journal of Personality and Social Psychology,* 1976, *34,* 556–560.

Howitt, J. W., & Stricker, G. Sequential change in response to dental procedures. *Journal of the American Dental Association,* 1965, *70,* 70–74.

Hudson, L. M. On the coherence of role-taking abilities: An alternative to correlational analysis. *Child Development,* 1978, *49,* 223–227.

Hughes, H., & Davis, R. Treatment of aggressive behavior: The effect of EMG response discrimination biofeedback training. *Journal of Autism and Developmental Disorders,* 1980, *10,* 193–202.

Humphrey, L. L., & Kirschenbaum, D. S. Self-control and perceived social competence in preschool children. *Cognitive Therapy and Research,* in press.

Humphreys, L., Forehand, R., McMahon, R., & Roberts, M. Parent behavioral training to modify child noncompliance: Effects on untreated siblings. *Journal of Behavior Therapy and Experimental Psychiatry*, 1978, *9*, 235–238.

Huntsinger, G. M. *Teaching of self-control of verbal and physical aggression to juvenile delinquents*. Unpublished manuscript, Virginia Commonwealth University, 1976.

Ianotti, R. J. Effects of role-taking experiences on role-taking, empathy, altruism and aggression. *Developmental Psychology*, 1978, *14*, 119–124.

Inhelder, B. *The diagnosis of reasoning in the mentally retarded*. New York: Chandler Publishing, 1968.

Ironsmith, M., & Whitehurst, G. J. How children learn to listen: The effects of modeling feedback styles on children's performance in referential communication. *Developmental Psychology*, 1978, *14*, 546–554.

Iscoe, I. Community psychology and the competent community. *American Psychologist*, 1974, *29*, 607–613.

Israel, A. C. Some thoughts on correspondence between saying and doing. *Journal of Applied Behavior Analysis*, 1978, *11*, 271–275.

Israel, A. C., & O'Leary, K. D. Developing correspondence between children's words and deeds. *Child Development*, 1973, *44*, 575–581.

Jackson, D. D. Family rules—Marital quid pro quo. *Archives of General Psychiatry*, 1965, *12*, 589–584.

Jacob, T. Family interaction in disturbed and normal families: A methodological and substantive review. *Psychological Bulletin*, 1975, *82*, 33–65.

Jakibchuk, Z., & Smergilio, V. L. The influence of symbolic modeling on the social behavior of preschool children with low levels of social responsiveness. *Child Development*, 1976, *47*, 838–841.

Janis, I. L. *Psychological stress*. New York: Wiley, 1958.

Jaremko, M. E. Cognitive behavior modification: Real science or more mentalism? *Psychological Record*, 1979, *29*, 547–552.

Jason, L. A. Behavioral approaches to prevention in the schools. In R. Price, J. Monahan, B. C. Bader, & R. F. Ketterer (Eds.), *Prevention in community mental health: Research, policy, and practice*. New York: Sage Publications, 1980. (a)

Jason, L. A. *Teaching competencies in a clinical-child preventive intervention*. Paper presented at the annual meeting of the Midwestern Psychological Association, St. Louis, May 1980. (b)

Jason, L. A., & Burrows, B. Transition training for high school seniors. *Cognitive Therapy and Research*, 1983, *7*, 79–91.

Jason, L., & Ferone, L. Behavioral versus process consultation interventions in school settings. *American Journal of Community Psychology*, 1978, *6*, 531–540.

Jason, L. A., & Glenwick, D. S. Future directions: A critical look at the behavioral community approach. In D. S. Glenwick & L. A. Jason (Eds.), *Behavioral community psychology: Progress and prospects*. New York: Praeger Publishers, 1980. (a)

Jason, L. A., & Glenwick, D. S. An overview of behavioral community psychology. In D. S. Glenwick & L. A. Jason (Eds.), *Behavioral community psychology: Progress and prospects*. New York: Praeger Publishers, 1980. (b)

Jason, L. A., & Klich, M. *Intervening to alter inappropriate advertising in the media*. Paper presented at the meeting of the Association for the Advancement of Behavior Therapy, New York, November 1980.

Jason, A. J., Ferone, L., & Anderegg, T. Evaluating ecological, behavioral, and process consultation interventions. *Journal of School Psychology*, 1979, *17*, 103–115.

Jenkins, J. R., Stein, M. L., & Osborn, J. R. What next after decoding? Instruction and research in reading comprehension. *Exceptional Education Quarterly*, 1981, *2*(1), 27–39.

Jensen, A. R. How much can we boost IQ and scholastic achievement? *Harvard Educational Review*, 1969, *39*, 1–123.

Jesness, J. F. Comparative effectiveness of behavior modification and transactional analysis programs for delinquents. *Journal of Consulting and Clinical Psychology*, 1975, *43*, 758–779.

Jessor, R., & Jessor, S. Theory testing in longitudinal research on marihuana use. In D. Kandel (Ed.), *Longitudinal research on drug use: Empirical findings and methodological issues*. Washington, D.C.: Hemisphere-Wiley, 1978.

Johnson, D. W. Role reversal: A summary and review of the research. *International Journal of Group Tensions*, 1971, *4*, 318–334.

Johnson, D. W. Affective perspective-taking and cooperative disposition. *Developmental Psychology*, 1975, *11*, 869–870.

Johnson, J. E. Effects of accurate expectation about sensations on the sensory and distress component of pain. *Journal of Personality and Social Psychology*, 1973, *27*, 261–275.

Johnson, J. E. Stress reduction through sensation information. In E. G. Sarason & C. D. Speilberger (Eds.), *Stress and anxiety* (Vol. 2). New York: Wiley, 1975.

Johnson, J. E., & Dabbs, J. M. Enumerations of active sweat glands: A simple physiological indicator of psychological changes. *Nursing Research*, 1967, *16*, 273–276.

Johnson, J. E., & Leventhal, H. Effects of accurate expectations and behavioral instructions on reactions during a noxious medical examination. *Journal of Personality and Social Psychology*, 1974, *29*, 710–718.

Johnson, J. E., Rice, V. H., Fuller, S. S., & Endress, M. P. Sensory information, instruction in a coping strategy, and recovery from surgery. *Research in Nursing and Health*, 1978, *1*, 4–17.

Johnson, S. B., & Melamed, B. G. The assessment and treatment of children's fears. In B. Lahey & A. Kazdin (Eds.), *Advances in child clinical psychology*. New York: Plenum Press, 1978.

Johnson, S. M., & Lobitz, G. K. The personal and marital adjustment of parents as related to observed child deviance and parenting behaviors. *Journal of Abnormal Child Psychology*, 1974, *2*, 193–207.

Johnston, M., & Whitman, T. *Teaching addition and subtraction to educable retarded children: Self-instructional training in a group setting*. Paper presented at the meeting of the Association for the Advancement of Behavior Therapy, New York, 1980.

Johnston, M. B., Whitman, T. L., & Johnson, M. R. Teaching addition and subtraction to mentally retarded children: A self-instructional program. *Applied Research in Mental Retardation*, 1980, *1*, 141–160.

Jones, M. C. The elimination of children's fears. *Journal of Experimental Psychology*, 1924, *7*, 382–390. (a)

Jones, M. C. A laboratory study of fear: The case of Peter. *Journal of Genetic Psychology*, 1924, *31*, 308–315. (b)

Jones, R. R., Reid, J. B., & Patterson, G. R. Naturalistic observation in clinical assessment. In P. McReynolds (Ed.), *Advances in psychological assessment* (Vol. 3). San Francisco: Jossey-Bass, 1975.

Jones, R. T., Nelson, R. E., & Kazdin, A. E. The role of external variables in self-reinforcement. *Behavior Modification*, 1977, *1*, 147–178.

Jurkovic, G. J. The juvenile delinquent as a moral philosopher: A structural-developmental perspective. *Psychological Bulletin*, 1980, *88*, 709–727.

Jurkovic, G. J., & Prentice, N. M. Relation of moral and cognitive development to dimensions of juvenile delinquency. *Journal of Abnormal Psychology*, 1977, *86*, 414–420.

Kagan, J. Reflection-impulsivity: The generality and dynamics of conceptual tempo. *Journal of Abnormal Psychology*, 1966, *71*, 17–24.

Kagan, J. "Commentary," in T. Zelniker & W. E. Jeffrey, Reflective and impulsive children: Strategies of information processing underlying differences in problem solving. *Monographs of the Society for Research in Child Development*, 1976, *41*(168, Serial no. 5).

Kagan, J., & Moss, H. *Birth to maturity*. New York: Wiley, 1962.

Kagan, J., Rosman, B. L., Day, D., Albert, J., & Phillips, W. Information processing in the child: Significance of analytic and reflective attitudes. *Psychological Monographs*, 1964 (Whole No. 578).

Kagan, J., Pearson, L., & Welch, L. Modifiability of an impulsive tempo. *Journal of Educational Psychology*, 1966, *57*, 359–365.

Kahn, J. V. Cognitive training of severely and profoundly retarded children. In M. A. Thomas (Ed.), *Developing skills in severely and profoundly handicapped children: Very special children series*. Reston, Va.: Council for Exceptional Children, 1977.

Kail, R. *The development of memory in children*. San Francisco: W. H. Freeman, 1979.

Kail, R. V., & Hagen, J. W., (Eds.). *Perspectives on the development of memory and cognition*. Hillsdale, N.J.: Lawrence Erlbaum Associates, 1977.

Kane, J. S., & Lawler, E. E. Methods of peer assessment. *Psychological Bulletin*, 1978, *85*, 555–586.

Kanfer, F. H. Self-regulation: Research, issues, and speculations. In C. Neuringer & J. L. Michael (Eds.), *Behavior modification in clinical psychology*. New York: Appleton-Century Crofts, 1970.

Kanfer, F. H. The maintenance of behavior by self-generated stimuli and reinforcement. In A. Jacobs & L. B. Sachs (Eds.), *The psychology of private events*. New York: Academic Press, 1971.

Kanfer, F. The many faces of self-control, or behavior modification changes its focus. In R. B. Stuart (Ed.), *Behavioral self-management*. New York: Brunner/Mazel, 1977.

Kanfer, F. H. Self-management: Strategies and tactics. In A. P. Goldstein & F. H. Kanfer (Eds.), *Maximizing treatment gains: Transfer enchancement in psychotherapy*. New York: Academic Press, 1978.

Kanfer, F. H. Self-management methods. In F. H. Kanfer & A. P. Goldstein (Eds.), *Helping people change*. New York: Pergamon Press, 1980.

Kanfer, F. H., & Karoly, P. Self-control: A behavioristic excursion into the lion's den. *Behavior Therapy*, 1972, *3*, 398–416.

Kanfer, F. H., & Karoly, P. The psychology of self-management: Abiding issues and tentative directions. In P. Karoly & F. H. Kanfer (Eds.), *Self-management and behavior change: From theory to practice*. New York: Pergamon Press, 1982.

Kanfer, F., Karoly, P., & Newman, A. Reduction of children's fear of the dark by competence-related and situational threat-related verbal cues. *Journal of Consulting and Clinical Psychology*, 1975, *43*, 251–259.

Kanner, L. Autistic disturbances of affective contact. *Nervous Child*, 1943, *2*, 217–250.

Karoly, P. Behavioral self-management in children: Concepts, methods, issues and directions. In M. Hersen, R. Eisler, & P. Miller (Eds.), *Progress in behavior modification* (Vol. 5). New York: Academic Press, 1977.

Karoly, P., & Dirks, M. J. Developing self control in preschool children through correspondence training. *Behavior Therapy*, 1977, *8*, 398–405.

Kassinove, H., Crisci, R., & Tiegerman, S. *Journal of Community Psychology*, 1977, *5*, 266–274.

Katz, R. C. Single session recovery from a hemodialysis phobia: A case study. *Journal of Behavior Therapy and Experimental Psychiatry*, 1974, *5*, 205–206.
Kauffman, J. M., & Hallahan, D. P. Learning disability and hyperactivity (with comments on minimal brain dysfunction). In B. B. Lahey & A. E. Kazdin (Eds.), *Advances in clinical child psychology* (Vol. 2). New York: Plenum Press, 1979.
Kaufman, K. F., & O'Leary, K. D. Reward, cost, and self-evaluation procedures for disruptive adolescents in a psychiatric hospital school. *Journal of Applied Behavior Analysis*, 1972, *5*, 293–309.
Kaye, K. Toward the origin of dialogue. In H. R. Schaffer (Ed.), *Studies on mother-infant interaction*. New York: Academic Press, 1972.
Kazdin, A. E. Covert modeling, model similarity, and reduction of avoidance behavior. *Behavior Therapy*, 1974, *5*, 325–340.
Kazdin, A. E. *Behavior modification in applied settings*. Homewood, Ill.: Dorsey Press, 1975.
Kazdin, A. Artifact, bias and complexity of assessment: The ABCs of reliability. Journal of Applied Behavior Analysis, 1977, *10*, 141–150. (a)
Kazdin, A. E. Assessing the clinical or applied importance of behavior change through social validation. *Behavior Modification*, 1977, *1*, 427–452. (b)
Kazdin, A. E. The application of operant techniques in treatment, rehabilitation, and education. In S. L. Garfield & A. E. Bergin (Eds.), *Handbook of psychotherapy and behavior change: An empirical analysis* (2nd ed.). New York: Wiley, 1978. (a)
Kazdin, A. E. *History of behavior modfication: Experimental foundations of contemporary research*. Baltimore, Md.: University Park Press, 1978. (b)
Kazdin, A. E. Fictions, factions, and functions of behavior therapy. *Behavior Therapy*, 1979, *10*, 629–654.
Kazdin, A. E. *Behavior modification in applied settings* (2nd ed.). Homewood, Ill.: Dorsey Press, 1980.
Kazdin, A. E. Behavior modification in education: Contributions and limitations. *Developmental Review*, 1981, *1*, 34–57.
Kazdin, A. E., & Wilcoxon, L. A. Systematic desensitization and nonspecific treatment effects: A methodological evaluation. *Psychological Bulletin*, 1976, *83*, 729–758.
Kazdin, A. E., & Wilson, G. T. *Evaluation of behavior therapy: Issues, evidence, and research strategies*. Cambridge, Mass.: Ballinger, 1978.
Keeley, S. M., Shemberg, K. M., & Carbonell, J. Operant clinical intervention: Behavior management or beyond? Where are the data? *Behavior Therapy*, 1976, *7*, 292–305.
Keeney, T. J., Canizzo, S. R., & Flavell, J. H. Spontaneous and induced verbal rehearsal in a recall task. *Child Development*, 1967, *38*, 953–966.
Kellam, S. G., Branch, J. D., Agrawal, K. C., & Ensminger, M. E. *Mental health and going to school: The Woodlawn program of assessment, early intervention and evaluation*. Chicago: University of Chicago Press, 1975.
Kellam, S. G., Brown, C. H., & Fleming, J. P. *The prevention of teenage substance use: Longitudinal research and strategy*. Chicago, Ill.: Social Psychiatry Study Center, 1982.
Keller, M. F., & Carlson, P. M. The use of symbolic modeling to promote social skills in preschool children with low levels of social responsiveness. *Child Development*, 1974, *45*, 912–919.
Kelly, J. G. The mental health agent in the urban community. In *Urban America and the planning of mental health services*. New York: Group for Advancement of Psychiatry, 1964.
Kelly, J. G. Qualities for the community psychologist. *American Psychologist*, 1971, *26*, 897–903.

Kendall, C., Borkowski, J. G., & Cavanaugh, J. C. Metamemory and the transfer of an interrogative strategy by EMR children. *Intelligence,* 1980, *4,* 255–270.

Kendall, P. C. On the efficacious use of verbal self-instructional procedures with children. *Cognitive Therapy and Research,* 1977, *1,* 331–341.

Kendall, P. C. Assessment and cognitive-behavioral interventions: Purposes, proposals, and problems. In P. C. Kendall & S. D. Hollon (Eds.), *Assessment strategies for cognitive-behavioral interventions.* New York: Academic Press, 1981. (a)

Kendall, P. C. Cognitive-behavioral interventions with children. In B. B. Lahey & A. E. Kazdin (Eds), *Advances in clincial child psychology* (Vol. 4). New York: Plenum Press, 1981. (b)

Kendall, P. C. One-year follow-up of concrete versus conceptual cognitive-behavioral self-control training. *Journal of Consulting and Clinical Psychology,* 1981, *49,* 748–749. (c)

Kendall, P. C. Stressful medical procedures: Cognitive-behavioral strategies for stress management and prevention. In D. Meichenbaum, & M. E. Jaremko (Eds), *Stress reduction and prevention.* New York, Plenum Press, 1983.

Kendall, P. C., & Finch, A. J. Jr. A cognitive-behavioral treatment for impulse control: A case study. *Journal of Consulting and Clinical Psychology,* 1976, *44,* 852–857.

Kendall, P. C., & Finch, A. J. A cognitive-behavioral treatment for impulsivity: A group comparison study. *Journal of Consulting and Clinical Psychology,* 1978, *46,* 110–118.

Kendall, P. C., & Finch, A. J. Jr. Developing nonimpulsive behavior in children: Cognitive-behavioral strategies for self-control. In P. C. Kendall & S. D. Hollon (Eds.), *Cognitive-behavioral interventions: Theory, research, and procedures.* New York: Academic Press, 1979.

Kendall, P. C., & Hollon, S. D. (Eds.). *Cognitive-behavioral interventions: Theory, research, and procedures.* New York: Academic Press, 1979.

Kendall, P. C., & Hollon, S. D. Cognitive-behavioral interventions: Overview and current status. In P. C. Kendall & S. D. Hollon (Eds.), *Cognitive-behavioral interventions: Theory, research, and procedures.* New York: Academic press, 1979.

Kendall, P. C., & Hollon, S. D. Assessing self-referent speech: Methods in the measurement of self-statements. In P. C. Kendall & S. D. Hollon (Eds.), *Assessment strategies for cognitive behavioral interventions.* New York; Academic Press, 1981.

Kendall, P. C., & Korgeski, G. P. Assessment and cognitive-behavioral interventions. *Cognitive Therapy and Research,* 1979, *3,* 1–21.

Kendall, P. C., & Wilcox, L. E. Self-control in children: Development of a rating scale. *Journal of Consulting and Clinical Psychology,* 1979, *47,* 1020–1029.

Kendall, P. C., & Wilcox, L. E. Cognitive-behavioral treatment for impulsivity: Concrete versus conceptual training and non-self-controlled problem children. *Journal of Consulting and Clinical Psychology,* 1980, *48,* 80–91.

Kendall, P. C., & Williams, C. L. Behavioral and cognitive behavioral approaches to outpatient treatment with children. In W. E. Craighead, A. E. Kazdin, & M. J. Mahoney (Eds.), *Behavior modification: Principles, issues, and applications* (2nd ed.). Boston, Mass.: Houghton Mifflin, 1981.

Kendall, P. C., & Williams, C. L. Assessing the cognitive and behavioral components of children's self-management. In P. Karoly & F. Kanfer (Eds.), *Self-management and behavior change: From theory to practice.* New York: Pergamon Press, 1982.

Kendall, P. C., & Zupan, B. A. Individual versus group application of cognitive-behavioral self-control procedures with children. *Behavior Therapy,* 1981, *12,* 344–359.

Kendall, P. C., Pellegrini, D. S., & Urbain, E. S. Approaches to assessment for cognitive-behavioral interventions with children. In P. C. Kendall & S. D. Hollon (Eds.), *Assessment strategies and cognitive-behavioral interventions.* New York: Academic Press, 1981.

Kendall, P. C., Zupan, B. A., & Braswell, L. Self-control in children: Further analyses of the Self-Control Rating Scale. *Behavior Therapy*, 1981, *12*, 667–681.

Kendall, P. C., Hartup, W. W., & Cummings, L. *Developmental treatment of childhood social withdrawal* (NIMH Grant Application). University of Minnesota, 1983.

Kennedy, B. A., & Miller, D. J. Persistent use of verbal rehearsal as a function of information about its value. *Child Development*, 1976, *47*, 566–569.

Kennedy, R. E. *Social skills training in corrections*. Unpublished manuscript, Davidson College, 1981.

Kennedy, R. E., Kirchner, E. P., & Draguns, J. G. *Perspective-taking in adult criminal psychopaths*. Unpublished manuscript, Pennsylvania State University, 1979.

Kennedy, R. E., Kirchner, E. P., & Draguns, J. G. *Perspective-taking, socialization, and moral judgment in adult criminals and noncriminal controls*. Unpublished manuscript, Pennsylvania State University, 1980.

Kent, M. W., & Rolf, J. E. (Eds.). *Primary prevention of psychopathology* (Vol. III): *Social competence in children*. Hanover, N.H.: University Press of New England, 1979.

Kent, R. N., & Foster, S. L. Direct observational procedures: Methodological procedures in naturalistic settings. In A. R. Ciminero, K. S. Calhoun, & H. E. Adams (Eds.), *Handbook of behavioral assessment*. New York: Wiley, 1977.

Kent, R. N., & O'Leary, K. D. A controlled evaluation of behavior modification with conduct problem children. *Journal of Consulting and Clinical Psychology*, 1976, *44*, 586–596.

Kent, R., O'Leary, K. D., Diament, C., & Dietz, A. Expectation biases in observational evaluation of therapeutic change. *Journal of Consulting and Clinical Psychology*, 1974, *42*, 774–780.

Keogh, B. K. Research in learning disabilities: A view of status and need. In J. P. Das, R. Mulcahey, & T. Wall (Eds.), *Learning disabilities*. New York: Plenum Press, 1982.

Keogh, B. K., & Barkett, C. J. An educational analysis of hyperactive children's achievement problems. In C. Whalen & B. Henker (Eds.), *Hyperactive children: The social ecology of identification and treatment*. New York: Academic Press, 1980.

Keogh, B. K., & Glover, A. T. The generality and durability of cognitive training effects. *Exceptional Education Quarterly*, 1980, *1*(1), 75–82.

Keogh, B. K., Major, S. M., Omori, H., Gándara, P., & Reid, H. B. Proposal markers in learning disabilities research. *Journal of Abnormal Child Psychology*, 1980, *8*(1), 21–31.

Keogh, D., Whitman, T., Johnson, M., & Burgio, L. *Increasing listening skills in four educably mentally retarded boys through correspondence training*. Paper presented at the meeting of the Association for Behavior Analysis, Milwaukee, 1981.

Keogh, B. K., Major-Kingsley, S. M., Omori-Gordon, H., & Reid, H. B. *A system of marker variables for the field of learning disabilities*. Syracuse, New York: Syracuse University Press, 1982.

Kerr, M. E. Family systems theory and therapy. In A. S. Gurman & D. P. Kniskern (Eds.), *Handbook of family therapy*. New York: Brunner/Mazel, 1981.

Kifer, R. E., Lewis, M. A., Green, D. R., & Phillips, E. L. Training predelinquent youths and their parents to negotiate conflict situations. *Journal of Applied Behavior Analysis*, 1974, *7*, 357–364.

Kim, N. S. Cognitive-behavioral treatment for students' adaptation to academic major departments and improvement of academic performances. *Behavior Therapy*, 1980, *11*, 256–262.

Kirby, F. D., & Toler, H. C. Modification of preschool isolate behavior: A case study. *Journal of Applied Behavior Analysis*, 1970, *3*, 309–314.

Kirchner, E. P., Kennedy, R. E., & Draguns, J. G. Assertion and aggression in adult offenders. *Behavior Therapy*, 1979, *10*, 452–471.

Kirschenbaum, D. S. Social competence intervention and evaluation in the inner city: Cincinnati's Social Skills Development Program. *Journal of Consulting and Clinical Psychology*, 1979, *47*, 778–780.

Kirschenbaum, D. S., & Pedro-Carroll, J. L. Helping teachers utilize classroom behavioral observation data: A case study using the teacher feedback form. *Behavioral Engineering*, 1979, *5*, 155–160.

Kirschenbaum, D. S., Bane, S., Fowler, R., Klei, B., Kuykendahl, K., Marsh, M. E., & Pedro, J. L. *Social Skills Development Program: Handbook for helping*. Cincinnati, Ohio: Health Department, 1976.

Kirschenbaum, D. S., Marsh, M. E., & DeVoge, J. B. The effectiveness of a mass screening procedure in an early intervention program. *Psychology in the Schools*, 1977, *14*, 400–406.

Kirschenbaum, D. S., Pedro, J. L., & DeVoge, J. B. A questionnaire for the process analysis of social skills oriented group therapy with children. *Journal Supplement Abstract Service Catalog of Selected Documents in Psychology*, 1977, *7*, 42, Ms. 1474. (Abstract)

Kirschenbaum, D., Steffen, J., & D'Orta, C. An easily mastered social competence classroom behavioral observation system. *Behavioural Analysis and Modification*, 1978, *2*, 314–322.

Kirschenbaum, D., Klei, R., Brown, J., & DeVoge, J. A nonexperimental, but useful, evaluation of a therapy/consultation early intervention program. In G. Landsberg, W. Neigher, R. Hammer, C. Windle, & R. Woy (Eds.), *Evaluation in practice: A sourcebook of program evaluation studies from mental health care systems in the United States*. Washington, D.C.: Government Printing Office, 1979.

Kirschenbaum, D. S., DeVoge, J. B., Marsh, M. E., & Steffen, J. J. Multimodal evaluation of therapy vs. consultation components in a large inner city early intervention program. *American Journal of Community Psychology*, 1980, *8*, 587–602.

Kirschenbaum, D. S., Pedro-Carroll, J. L., & DeVoge, J. B. A social competency model meets an early intervention program: Description and evaluation of Cincinnati's Social Skills Development Program. In D. F. Ricks & B. S. Dohrenwend (Eds.), *Origins of psychopathology*. New York: Cambridge University Press, in press.

Klahr, D. Goal formation, planning, and learning by pre-school problem solvers or: "My socks are in the dryer." In R. S. Siegler (Ed.), *Children's thinking: What develops?* Hillsdale, N.J.: Lawrence Erlbaum Associates, 1978.

Klahr, D., & Wallace, J. G. *Cognitive development: An information processing approach*. Hillsdale, N.J.: Lawrence Erlbaum Associates, 1976.

Klass, E. T. Cognitive appraisal of transgression among sociopaths and normals. *Cognitive Therapy and Research*, 1980, *4*, 353–367.

Klaus, M. H., & Kennel, J. Mothers separated from their newborn infants. In M. H. Klaus & A. A. Faranoff (Eds.), *Care of the high risk neonate*. Philadelphia: W. B. Saunders, 1977.

Klein, A. R., & Young, R. D. Hyperactive boys in their classroom: Assessment of teacher and peer perceptions, interactions, and classroom behaviors. *Journal of Abnormal Child Psychology*, 1979, *7*, 425–442.

Klein, D. C., & Goldston, S. E. (Eds.). *Primary prevention: An idea whose time has come*. Washington, D.C.: DHEW Publication No. (ADM) 77–447, 1977.

Klein, M. M., & Shulman, S. Behavior problems of children in relation to parental instrumentality-expressivity and marital adjustment. *Psychological Reports*, 1980, *47*, 11–14.

Klein, N. C., Alexander, J. F., & Parsons, B. V. Impact of family systems intervention on recidivism and sibling delinquency: A model of primary prevention and program evaluation. *Journal of Consulting and Clinical Psychology*, 1977, *45*, 469–474.

Kleinknecht, R., Klepac, R., & Alexander, L. Origins and characteristics of fear in dentistry. *Journal of the American Dental Association*, 1973, *86*, 842–848.

Klesges, R. C., Sanchez, V. C., & Stanton, A. L. Obtaining employment in academia: The hiring process and characteristics of successful applicants. *Professional Psychology*, 1982, *13*, 577–586.

Klingman, A., & Rosenbaum, H. *Children's Self-Control Scale.* Unpublished paper, University of Haifa, Haifa, Israel, 1981.

Klorman, R., Hilpert, P., Michael, R., LaGana, C., & Sveen, O. Effects of coping and mastery modeling on experienced and inexperienced pedodontic patient's disruptiveness. *Behavior Therapy*, 1980, *11*, 156–168.

Knapczyk, D. R., & Livingston, G. Self-recording and student teacher supervision: Variables within a token economy structure. *Journal of Applied Behavior Analysis*, 1973, *6*, 481–486.

Knight, R., Atkins, A., Eagle, C., Evans, N., Finkelstein, J. W., Fukushima, D., Katz, J., & Weiner, H. Psychological stress, ego defenses, and cortisol production in children hospitalized for elective surgery. *Psychosomatic Medicine*, 1979, *41*, 40–49.

Kobasigawa, A. Utilization of retrieval cues by children in recall. *Child Development*, 1974, *45*, 127–134.

Koegel, R. L. Discussant. In L. Schreibman (Chair), *Current research on education of autistic children.* Symposium presented at the 13th annual Association for the Advancement of Behavior Therapy Convention, San Francisco, December 1979.

Koegel, R. L., & Egel, A. L. Motivating autistic children. *Journal of Abnormal Psychology*, 1979, *88*, 418–426.

Koegel, R. L., & Lovaas, O. I. Comments on autism and stimulus overselectivity. *Journal of Abnormal Psychology*, 1978, *87*, 563–565.

Koegel, R. L., & Rincover, A. Some detrimental effects of using extra stimuli to guide learning in normal and autistic children. *Journal of Abnormal Child Psychology*, 1976, *4*, 59–71.

Koegel, R. L., & Schreibman, L. Teaching autistic children to respond to simultaneous multiple cues. *Journal of Experimental Child Psychology*, 1977, *24*, 299–311.

Koegel, R. L., & Wilhelm, H. Selective responding to the components of multiple cues by autistic children. *Journal of Experimental Child Psychology*, 1973, *15*, 442–453.

Koegel, R. L., Schreibman, L., Britten, K., & Laitinen, R. The effects of schedule of reinforcement on stimulus overselectivity in autistic children. *Journal of Autism and Developmental Disorders*, 1979, *9*, 383–397.

Koegel, R. L., Egel, A. L., & Dunlap, G. Learning characteristics of autistic children. In W. Sailor, B. Wilcox, & L. Brown (Eds.), *Methods of instruction with severely handicapped students.* Baltimore: Brookes, 1980.

Kohlberg, L., Yaeger, J., & Hjertholm, E. Private speech: Four studies and a review of theories. *Child Development*, 1968, *39*, 691–736.

Kohlberg, L., LaCrosse, J., & Ricks, E. The predictability of adult mental health from childhood behavior. In B. B. Wolman (Ed.), *Manual of child psychopathology.* New York: McGraw-Hill, 1972.

Koretz, D. Validity shrinkage in psychopathology research: An example of the need for caution. *Journal of Abnormal Psychology*, 1979, *88*, 328–333.

Korner, A. F., & Thoman, E. B. Visual alertness in neonates as evoked by maternal care. *Journal of Experimental Child Psychiatry*, 1970, *10*, 67–78.

Kornhaber, R., & Schroeder, H. Importance of model similarity on extinction of avoidance behavior in children. *Journal of Consulting and Clinical Psychology*, 1975, *43*, 601–607.

Kosiewicz, M. M., Hallahan, D. P., & Lloyd, J. *Self-monitoring of attention in an LD classroom: Across subject generalization.* (Technical Report No. 34.) Charlottesville, Va.: University of Virginia Learning Disabilities Research Institute, 1981.

Krantz, D. L. The separate worlds of operant and non-operant psychology. *Journal of Applied Behavior Analysis,* 1971, *4,* 61–70.

Krasner, L. Behavior modification—values and training: The perspective of a psychologist. In C. M. Franks (Ed.), *Behavior therapy: Appraisal and status.* New York: McGraw-Hill, 1969.

Krebs, D. Empathy and altruism. *Journal of Personality and Social Psychology,* 1975, *32,* 1134–1146.

Kreutzer, M. A., Leonard, C., & Flavell, J. H. An interview study of children's knowledge about memory. *Monographs of the Society for Research in Child Development,* 1975, *40*(1, Serial No. 159), 1–58.

Kubany, E. S., & Sloggett, B. B. A coding procedure for teachers. *Journal of Applied Behavior Analysis,* 1973, *6,* 339–344.

Kupke, T. E., Calhoun, K. S., & Hobbs, S. A. Selection of heterosocial skills: II. Experimental validity. *Behavior Therapy,* 1979, *10,* 336–346.

Kurtz, P. D., & Neisworth, J. T. Self-control possibilities for exceptional children. *Exceptional Children,* 1976, *42,* 212–217.

Kurtz, P. D., Neisworth, J. T., Goeke, K., & Hanson, M. Training verbal-nonverbal correspondence. *Journal of Applied Social Psychology,* 1976, *6,* 314–321.

Kyriacou, C., & Sutcliffe, J. Teacher stress: A review. *Educational Review,* 1977, *29,* 299–306.

Lacey, J. Somatic response patterning of stress. In M. Appley & R. Trumbull (Eds.), *Psychological stress: Issues in research.* New York: Appleton-Century-Crofts, 1967.

Lachman, R., Lachman, J., & Butterfield, E. *Cognitive psychology and information processing: An introduction.* New Jersey: Lawrence Earlbaum Associates, 1979.

Ladd, G. W. *Social skills and peer acceptance: Effects of a social learning method for training verbal social skills.* Paper presented at the biennial meeting of the Society for Research in Child Development, San Francisco, March 1979.

LaGreca, A. M., & Santogrossi, D. A. Social skills training with elementary school students: A behavioral group approach. *Journal of Consulting and Clinical Psychology,* 1980, *48,* 220–227.

Lahey, B. B., & Drabman, R. S. Behavior modification in the classroom. In W. E. Craighead, A. E. Kazdin, & M. J. Mahoney (Eds.), *Behavior modification: Principles, issues, and applications* (2nd ed.). Boston, Mass.: Houghton Mifflin, 1981.

Lamb, M. (Ed.). *The role of the father in child development.* New York: Wiley, 1976.

Landau, S. F. Future time perspective of delinquents and non-delinquents. *Criminal Justice and Behavior,* 1975, *2,* 22–29.

Lang, P. J. The application of psychophysical methods to the study of psychotherapy and behavior modification. In A. E. Bergin & S. L. Garfield (Eds.), *Handbook of psychotherapy and behavior change.* New York: Wiley, 1971.

Langer, E. J., Janis, I. E., & Wolfer, J. A. Reduction of psychological stress in surgical patients. *Journal of Experimental Social Psychology,* 1975, *11,* 155–165.

Langer, T. S., Gersten, J. C., Greene, E. L., Eisenberg, J. G., Herson, J. H., & McCarthy, E. D. Treatment of psychological disorders among urban children. *Journal of Consulting and Clinical Psychology,* 1974, *42,* 170–179.

Lapouse, R., & Monk, M. Fears and worries in a representative sample of children. *American Journal of Orthopsychiatry,* 1959, *29,* 803–818.

Larcen, S. W., Spivack, G., & Shure, M. *Problem-solving thinking and adjustment among dependent-neglected pre-adolescents.* Paper presented at the meeting of the Eastern Psychological Association, Boston, 1972.

Law Enforcement Assistance Agency. *Statistics for corrections.* Washington, D.C.: U.S. Government Printing Office, 1979.

Lazarus, A. A. *Multi-modal behavior therapy.* New York: Springer Publishing, 1976.

Lazarus, A. A. *In the mind's eye.* New York: Rawson Associates Publishers, 1977.

Lazarus, A., & Abramovitz, A. The use of "emotive imagery" in the treatment of children's phobias. *Journal of Mental Science,* 1962, *108,* 191–195.

Lazarus, R. S. Emotions and adaptation: Conceptual and empirical relations. In W. J. Arnold (Ed.), *Nebraska Symposium on Motivation* (Vol. 16). Lincoln: University of Nebraska Press, 1968.

Ledwidge, B. Cognitive behavior modification: A step in the wrong direction? *Psychological Bulletin,* 1978, *85,* 353–375.

Ledwidge, B. Cognitive behavior modification or new ways to change minds: Reply to Mahoney and Kazdin. *Psychological Bulletin,* 1979, *56,* 1050–1053.

LeFave, M. K. Correlates of engagement in family therapy. *Journal of Marital and Family Therapy,* 1980, *6,* 75–81.

Lefcourt, H. M. *Locus of control: Current trends in theory and research.* Hillsdale, N.J.: Lawrence Erlbaum Associates, 1976.

Lefcourt, H. M. Locus of control for specific goals. In L. C. Perlmuter & R. A. Monty (Eds.), *Choice and perceived control.* Hillsdale, N.J.: Lawrence Erlbaum Associates, 1979.

Lefebvre-Pinard, M., & Reid, L. A. A comparison of three methods of training communication skills: Social conflict, Modeling and conflict-modeling. *Child Development,* 1980, *51,* 179–187.

Lefkowitz, M. M., Eron, L. D., Walder, L. O., & Huesman, L. R. *Growing up to be violent.* New York: Pergamon Press, 1977.

Leon, J. A., & Pepe, H. *Self-instructional training: Cognitive behavior modification as a resource room strategy.* Unpublished manuscript, Illinois State University, 1978.

Lerner, R. M., & Spanier, G. B. *Child influences on marital and family interaction: A life-span perspective.* New York: Academic Press, 1978.

Leventhal, H. Attitudes: Their nature, growth, and change. In C. Nemeth (Ed.), *Social psychology: Classic and contemporary integrations.* Chicago: Rand McNally, 1974.

Levers, S. R. *Increasing task-related behavior in "hyperactive" children through the use of a self-instructional procedure.* Unpublished manuscript, University of Notre Dame, 1978.

Levine, H., Zetlin, A., & Langness, L. Everyday memory tasks in classrooms for TMR learners. *Quarterly Newsletter of the Laboratory of Comparative Human Cognition,* 1980, *2,* 1–6.

Levine, M. Sex differences in behavior ratings: Male and female teachers rate male and female pupils. *American Journal of Community Psychology,* 1977, *5,* 347–353.

Levitt, E. The results of psychotherapy with children: An evaluation. *Journal of Consulting Psychology,* 1957, *21,* 189–196.

Levitt, E. Psychotherapy with children: A further evaluation. *Behavior Research and Therapy,* 1963, *1,* 45–51.

Lewis, M. State as an infant-environment interaction: An analysis of mother-infant interaction as a function of sex. *Merrill-Palmer Quarterly,* 1972, *18,* 95–121.

Lewis, M. The social network systems model: Toward a theory of social development. In T. Field (Ed.), *Review in human development.* New York: Wiley, 1982.

Lewis, M., & Brooks-Gunn, J. Self, other and fear: Infants' reactions to people. In M. Lewis & L. Rosenblum (Eds.), *The origins of fear: The origin of behavior* (Vol. 2). New York: Wiley, 1974.

Lewis, M., & Brooks-Gunn, J. *Social cognition and the acquisition of self.* New York: Plenum Press, 1979.

Lewis, M., & Coates, D. L. Mother-infant interactions and cognitive development in twelve-week-old infants. *Infant Behavior and Development*, 1980, *3*, 95–105.

Lewis, M., & Michalson, L. *Children's emotions and moods: Development, theory and measurement*. New York: Plenum, 1983.

Lewis, M., & Rosenblum, L. (Eds.). *Friendship and peer relations: The origins of behavior* (Vol. 4). New York: Wiley, 1975.

Lewis, M., & Sullivan, M. *Imitation in the first six months of life: Phenomenon in the eye of the beholder*. Manuscript submitted for publication.

Lewis, M., Young, G., Brooks, J., & Michaelson, L. The beginning of friendship. In M. Lewis & C. Rosenblum (Eds.), *Friendship and peer relations*. New York: Wiley, 1975.

Lewis, S. A comparison of behavior therapy techniques in the reduction of fearful and avoidance behavior. *Behavior Therapy*, 1974, *5*, 648–655.

Liben, L. S. Evidence for developmental differences in spontaneous seriation and its implication for past research on long-term memory improvement. *Developmental Psychology*, 1975, *11*, 121–125.

Liben, L. S. Memory from a cognitive-developmental perspective: A theoretical and empirical review. In W. Overton & J. Gallagher (Eds.), *Knowledge and development* (Vol. 1). New York: Plenum Press, 1977.

Liberman, R. P., Wallace, C., Teigen, J., & Davis, J. Interventions with psychotic behaviors. In K. S. Calhoun, H. E. Adams, & K. M. Mitchell (Eds.), *Innovative treatment methods in psychopathology*. New York: Wiley, 1974.

Liebman, R., Minuchin, S., & Baker, L. The use of structural family therapy in the treatment of intractable asthma. *American Journal of Psychiatry*, 1974, *131*, 535–540.

Liem, J. H. Effects of verbal communications of parents and children: A comparison of normal and schizophrenic families. *Journal of Consulting and Clinical Psychology*, 1974, *42*, 438–450.

Lilly, M. S. Improving social competence of low sociometric status, low achieving students. *Exceptional Children*, 1971, *37*, 341–347.

Linehan, K. S., & Rosenthal, T. L. Current behavioral approaches to marital and family therapy. *Advances in Behaviour Research and Therapy*, 1979, *2*, 99–143.

Lipton, D., Martinson, R., & Wilks, J. *The effectiveness of correctional treatment*. New York: Praeger Publishers, 1975.

Little, V. L. *The relationship of role-taking ability to self-control in institutionalized juvenile offenders*. (Doctoral dissertation, Virginia Commonwealth University, 1978). *Dissertation Abstracts International*, 1979, *39* 2992B. (University Microfilms No. 78-22, 701)

Little, V. L., & Kendall, P. C. Cognitive-behavioral interventions with delinquents: Problem-solving, role-taking, and self-control. In P. C. Kendall & S. D. Hollon (Eds.), *Cognitive behavioral interventions: Theory, research, and procedures*. New York: Academic Press, 1979.

Litrownik, A. J. Childhood psychosis. In J. F. Calhoun, J. R. Acocella, & L. D. Goodstein (Eds.), *Abnormal psychology: Current perspectives* (2nd ed.). New York: CRM/Random House, 1977.

Litrownik, A. J. Special considerations in the self-management training of the developmentally disabled. In P. Karoly & F. H. Kanfer (Eds.), *Self-management and behavior change: From theory to practice*. New York: Pergamon Press, 1982.

Litrownik, A. J., & Freitas, J. L. Self-monitoring in moderately retarded adolescents: Reactivity and accuracy as a function of valence. *Behavior Therapy*, 1980, *11*, 245–255.

Litrownik, A. J., & McInnis, E. T. Cognitive and perceptual deficits in autistic children: A model of information processing, critical review, and suggestions for the future. In J.

J. Steffen & P. Karoly (Eds.), *Autism and severe psychopathology: Advances in child behavioral analysis and therapy* (Vol. 2). Lexington, Mass.: D. C. Heath, 1982.

Litrownik, A. J., & Steinfeld, B. I. Developing self-regulation in retarded children. In P. Karoly & J. J. Steffen (Eds.), *Improving children's competence: Advances in child behavioral analysis and therapy* (Vol. 1). Lexington, Mass.: D. C. Heath, 1982.

Litrownik, A. J., Franzini, L. R., Geller, S., & Geller, M. Delay of gratification: Decisional self-control and experience with delay intervals. *American Journal of Mental Deficiency*, 1977, *82*, 149–154.

Litrownik, A. J., Cleary, C. P., Lecklitner, G. L., & Franzini, L. R. Self-regulation in retarded persons: Acquisition of standards for performance. *American Journal of Mental Deficiency*, 1978, *83*, 86–89.

Litrownik, A. J., Cleary, C. P., & Steinfeld, B. I. *Self regulation in mentally retarded persons: Acquisition and effects of self-reinforcement.* Unpublished manuscript, San Diego State University, 1978.

Litrownik, A. J., Freitas, J. L., & Franzini, L. R. Self-regulation in retarded persons: Assessment and training of self-monitoring skills. *American Journal of Mental Deficiency*, 1978, *82*, 499–506.

Litrownik, A. J., Lecklitner, G. L., Cleary, C. P., & Franzini, L. R. *Acquisition of self-evaluation and self-reward skills and their effects on performance.* Unpublished manuscript, San Diego State University, 1978.

Litrownik, A. J., McInnis, E. T., Wetzel-Pritchard, A. M., & Filipelli, D. L. Restricted stimulus control and inferred attentional deficits in autistic and retarded children. *Journal of Abnormal Psychology*, 1978, *87*, 554–562.

Lloyd, J. Academic instruction and cognitive behavior modification: The need for attack strategy training. *Exceptional Education Quarterly*, 1980, *1*(1), 53–63.

Lloyd, J., Hallahan, D. P., Kosiewicz, M. M., & Kneedler, R. D. *Self-assessment recording: Two comparisons of reactive effects on attention to task and academic productivity.* (Technical Report No. 29) Charlottesville, Va.: University of Virginia Learning Disabilities Research Institute, October 1980.

Lloyd, J., Cameron, N. A., Cullinan, D., Kauffman, J. M., & Kneedler, R. D. *Addition strategy training with learning disabled children* (Technical Report No. 40). Charlottesville: University of Virginia Disabilities Research Institute, 1981.

Lloyd, J., Epstein, M., & Cullinan, D. Direct teaching for learning disabilities. In J. Gottlieb & S. F. Strickhart (Eds.), *Current theories and research in learning disabilities.* Baltimore, Md.: University Park Press, 1981.

Lloyd, J., Saltzman, N. J., & Kauffman, J. M. Predictable generalization in academic learning as a result of preskills and strategy training. *Learning Disability Quarterly*, 1981, *4*, 203–216.

Lloyd, J. W., Hallahan, D. P., Kosiewicz, M. M., & Kneedler, R. D. Reactive effects of self-assessment and self-recording on attention to task and academic productivity. *Learning Disability Quarterly*, 1982, *5*, 216–227.

Lloyd, J., Kneedler, R. D., & Cameron, N. The effects of verbal self-guidance on word reading accuracy. *Reading Improvement*, 1982, *19*, 84–89.

Lloyd, J., Kosiewicz, M. M., & Hallahan, D. P. Reading comprehension: Cognitive training contributions. *School Psychology Review*, 1982, *11*, 35–41.

Lobitz, G. K., & Johnson, S. M. Normal versus deviant children. A multimethod comparison. *Journal of Abnormal Child Psychology*, 1975, *3*, 353–374.

Locke, E. A. Behavior modification is not cognitive and other myths: A reply to Ledwidge. *Cognitive Therapy and Research*, 1979, *3*, 119–125.

Loper, A. B. Metacognitive development: Implications for cognitive training. *Exceptional Educational Quarterly*, 1980, *1*, 1–8.

Loper, A. B., Hallahan, D. P., & Ianna, S. O. Meta-attention in learning disabled and normal students. *Learning Disability Quarterly*, 1982, *5*, 29–36.

Lorenz, K. Z. Die Angeborenen Formen möglicher Erfahrung. *Zeitschrift fur Tier psychologie*, 1943, *5*, 235–409.

Lorion, R. P. Socioeconomic status and psychotherapy. In S. L. Garfield & A. E. Bergin (Eds.), *Handbook of psychotherapy and behavior change* (2nd ed). New York: Wiley, 1978.

Lorion, R. P., & Cowen, E. L. Referral to a school mental health project: A screening note. *American Journal of Community Psychology*, 1978, *6*, 247–251.

Lorion, R. P., Cowen, E. L., & Caldwell, R. A. Problem types of children referred to a school-based mental health program: Identification and outcome. *Journal of Consulting and Clinical Psychology*, 1974, *42*, 491–496.

Lorion, R. P., Cowen, E. L., & Caldwell, R. A. Normative and parametric analyses of school maladjustment. *American Journal of Community Psychology*, 1975, *3*, 291–301.

Lovaas, O. I. A behavior therapy approach to the treatment of childhood schizophrenia. In J. P. Hill (Ed.), *Minnesota Symposium on Child Psychology*. Minneapolis: University of Minnesota Press, 1967.

Lovaas, O. I. A program for the establishment of speech in psychotic children. In H. N. Sloane & B. D. MacAulay (Eds.), *Operant procedures in remedial speech and language training*. Boston: Houghton Mifflin: 1968.

Lovaas, O. I. Contrasting illness and behavioral models for the treatment of autistic children: A historical perspective. *Journal of Autism and Developmental Disorders*, 1979, *9*, 315–323.

Lovaas, O. I., Schaeffer, B., & Simmons, J. Q. Building social behavior in autistic children by use of electric shock. *Journal of Experimental Research in Personality*, 1965, *1*, 99–109.

Lovaas, O. I., Litrownik, A., & Mann, R. Response latencies to auditory stimuli in autistic children engaged in self-stimulatory behavior. *Behavior Research and Therapy*, 1971, *9*, 39–49.

Lovaas, O. I., Schreibman, L., Koegel, R., & Rehm, R. Selective responding by autistic children to multiple sensory input. *Journal of Abnormal Psychology*, 1971, *77*, 211–222.

Lovaas, O. I., Koegel, R., Simmons, J. Q., & Long, J. S. Some generalization and follow-up measures on autistic children in behavior therapy. *Journal of Applied Behavior Analysis*, 1973, *6*, 131–166.

Lovaas, O. I., Koegel, R. L., & Schreibman, L. Stimulus overselectivity in autism: A review of research. *Psychological Bulletin*, 1979, *86*, 1236–1254.

Love, L. R., & Kaswan, J. *Troubled children: Their families, schools and treatments*. New York: Wiley, 1974.

Love, L. R., Kaswan, J., & Bugental, D. B. Differential effectiveness of three different clinical interventions for different socioeconomic groupings. *Journal of Consulting and Clinical Psychology*, 1972, *39*, 347–360.

Lovitt, T. C. Thomas C. Lovitt. In J. Kauffman & D. P. Hallahan (Eds.), *Teaching children with learning disabilities: Personal perspectives*. Columbus, Ohio: Charles E. Merrill, 1976.

Lozoff, B., Brittenham, G. M., Trause, M. A., Kennell, J. H., & Klaus, M. H. The mother-newborn relationship: Limits of adaptability. *Journal of Pediatrics*, 1977, *91*, 1–12.

Luria, A. The directive function of speech in development. *Werd*, 1959, *18*, 341–352.

Luria, A. R. *The role of speech in the regulation of normal and abnormal behaviors*. New York: Liverwright, 1961.

Luria, A. R. Psychological studies in mental deficiency in the Soviet Union. In N. R. Ellis (Ed.), *Handbook of mental deficiency*. New York: McGraw-Hill, 1963.

Lutzker, J. R. Deviant family systems. In B. B. Lahey & A. E. Kazdin (Eds.), *Advances in clinical child psychology* (Vol. 3). New York: Plenum Press, 1980.

Maccoby, E. E., & Jacklin, C. N. *The psychology of sex differences.* Stanford, Calif.: Stanford University Press, 1974.

MacDonald, K. R., Hedberg, A. G., & Campbell, L. M. A behavioral revolution in community mental health. *Community Mental Health Journal,* 1974, *10,* 228–235.

Macfarlane, A. Olfaction in the development of social preferences in the human neonate. In *Parent-infant interaction* (Ciba Foundation Symposium 33). New York: Associated Scientific Publishers, 1975.

Macfarlane, A. *The psychology of childbirth.* Cambridge, Mass.: Harvard University Press, 1977.

Macfarlane, J., Allen, L., & Honzik, M. *A developmental study of the behavioral problems of normal children.* Berkeley: University of California Press, 1954.

Machen, J., & Johnson, R. Desensitization, model learning, and the dental behavior of children. *Journal of Dental Research,* 1974, *53,* 83–89.

Mahaffey, P. R. The effects of hospitalization on children admitted for tonsillectomy and adenoidectomy. *Nursing Research,* 1965, *14,* 12–19.

Mahoney, M. J. *Cognition and behavior modification.* Cambridge, Mass.: Ballinger, 1974.

Mahoney, M. J. Reflections on the cognitive-learning trend in psychotherapy. *American Psychologist,* 1977, *32,* 5–13.

Mahoney, M. J., & Arnkoff, D. B. Cognitive and self-control therapies. In S. L. Garfield & A. E. Bergin (Eds.), *Handbook of psychotherapy and behavior change: An empirical analysis* (2nd ed.). New York: Wiley, 1978.

Mahoney, M. J., & Kazdin, A. E. Cognitive behavior modification: Misconceptions and premature evaluation. *Psychological Bulletin,* 1979, *86,* 1044–1049.

Mahoney, M. J., & Mahoney, K. Self-control techniques with the mentally retarded. *Exceptional Children,* 1976, *42,* 338–339.

Mahoney, M., & Thoresen, C. *Self-control: Power to the person.* Monterey, Calif.: Brooks/Cole, 1974.

Mahoney, M. J., Kazdin, A. E., & Lesswing, N. J. Behavior modification: Delusion or deliverance? In C. M. Franks & G. T. Wilson (Eds.), *Annual review of behavior therapy, theory and practice.* New York: Brunner/Mazel, 1974.

Malamuth, Z. N. Self-management training for children with reading problems: Effects on reading performance and sustained attention. *Cognitive Therapy and Research,* 1979, *3,* 279–289.

Margolin, G. The reciprocal relationship between marital and child problems. In J. P. Vincent (Ed.), *Advances in family intervention, assessment and theory. An annual compilation of research.* Greenwich, Conn.: JAI Press, 1981.

Markham, E. M. Realizing that you don't understand: A preliminary investigation. *Child Development,* 1977, *48,* 986–992.

Marsh, D. T., Serafica, F. C., & Barenboim, C. Effect of perspective-taking training on interpersonal problem solving. *Child Development,* 1980, *51,* 140–145.

Martin, B. Brief family intervention: Effectiveness and the importance of including the father. *Journal of Consulting and Clinical Psychology,* 1977, *45,* 1002–1010.

Martin, G. L., & Osborne, J. G. (Eds.), *Helping in the community: Behavioral applications.* New York: Plenum Press, 1980.

Martin, R. B., Shaw, M. A., & Taylor, P. P. The influence of prior surgical experience on the child's behavior at the initial dental visit. *Journal of Dentistry for Children,* 1977, *14,* 443–447.

Masangkay, Z. S., McCluskey, K. A., McIntyre, C. W., Sims-Knight, J., Vaughn, B. E., &

Flavell, J. H. The early development of inferences about the visual percepts of others. *Child Development*, 1974, *45*, 357–366.
Mash, E. J., & Mercer, B. J. A comparison of the behavior of deviant and non-deviant boys while playing alone and interacting with a sibling. *Journal of Child Psychology and Psychiatry*, 1979, *20*, 197–207.
Masten, A. S. Family therapy as a treatment for children: A critical review of outcome research. *Family Process*, 1979, *18*, 323–335.
Masters, J. C., & Santrock, J. W. Studies in the self-regulation of behavior: Effects of contingent cognitive and affective events. *Developmental Psychology*, 1976, *12*, 334–348.
Masters, J. C., Felleman, E. S., & Barden, R. C. Experimental studies of affective states in children. In B. B. Lahey & A. E. Kazdin (Eds.), *Advances in child clinical psychology* (Vol. 4). New York: Plenum Press, 1981.
Masur, E. F., McIntyre, C. W., & Flavell, J. H. Developmental changes in apportionment of a study time among items in a multitrial free recall task. *Journal of Experimental Child Psychology*, 1973, *15*, 237–246.
Matekunas, M. N. Parent–child similarity in reflection-impulsivity (Doctoral Dissertation, Purdue University, 1972). *Dissertation Abstracts International*, 1973, *33*, 4493B. (University Microfilm No. 73–6062.)
Matteson, R. Adolescent self-esteem, family communication, and marital satisfaction. *Journal of Psychology*, 1974, *86*, 35–47.
Matthews, W. S. Conduites sociales et conduites d'agression: Etude differentielle des comportements relationnels des enfants en fonction le leur status sociometrique. (Social and aggressive behaviors and their relation to the sociometric status of preschool-age children.) Unpublished thesis, Université de Paris, 1972.
Matthews, W. S. Sex and familiarity effects upon the proportion of time young children spend in spontaneous fantasy play. *Journal of Genetic Psychology*, 1978, *133*, 9–12.
Matthews, W. S. Sex role perception, portrayal, and preference in the fantasy play of young children. *Sex Roles*, 1981, *7*, 979–987.
McAmmond, D. M., Davidson, P. O., & Kovitz, D. M. A comparison of the effects of hypnosis and relaxation training on stress reaction in a dental situation. *American Journal of Clinical Hypnosis*, 1971, *13*, 233–242.
McClure, L., Chinsky, J., & Larcen, S. Enhancing social problem-solving performance in an elementary school setting. *Journal of Educational Psychology*, 1978, *70*, 504–513.
McCombs, D., Filipczak, J., Friedman, R. M., & Wodarski, J. S. Long-term follow-up of behavior modification with high-risk adolescents. *Criminal Justice and Behavior*, 1978, *5*, 21–35.
McCord, W., McCord, J., & Howard, A. Familial correlates of aggression in nondelinquent male children. *Journal of Abnormal and Social Psychology*, 1961, *62*, 79–93.
McCullough, J. P., Huntsinger, G. M., & Nay, W. R. Case study: Self-control treatment of aggression in a 16-year-old male. *Journal of Consulting and Clinical Psychology*, 1977, *45*, 322–331.
McFall, R. M. Behavioral training: A skill acquisition approach to clinical problems. In J. T. Spence, R. Carson, & J. Thibaut (Eds.), *Behavioral approaches to therapy*. Morristown, N.J.: General Learning Press, 1976.
McFall, R. M. Parameters of self-monitoring. In R. B. Stuart (Ed.), *Behavioral self-management: Strategies, techniques and outcomes*. New York: Brunner/Mazel, 1977.
McGee, C., Kauffman, J., & Nussen, J. Children as therapeutic change agents: Reinforcement intervention paradigms. *Review of Educational Research*, 1977, *47*, 451–477.
McKim, M. K., *Natural determinants of change in cognitive tempo*. Paper presented at the

biennial meeting of the Society for Research in Child Development, San Francisco, 1979.

McKinney, J. D. Problem-solving in reflective and impulsive children. *Journal of Educational Psychology*, 1975, *67*, 807–820.

McKinney, J. D., & Haskins, R. Cognitive training and the development of problem-solving strategies. *Exceptional Education*, 1980, *1*(1), 41–51.

Mead, D. E., & Campbell, S. S. Decision-making and interaction by families with and without a drug-abusing child. *Family Process, 1972, 11*, 487–498.

Mead, G. *Mind, self, and society*. Chicago: University of Chicago Press, 1934.

Megargee, E. I. The role of inhibition in the assessment and understanding of violence. In J. L. Singer (Ed.), *The control of aggression and violence*. New York: Academic Press, 1971.

Mehrabian, A., & Epstein, N. A measure of emotional empathy. *Journal of Personality*, 1972, *40*, 525–543.

Meichenbaum, D. Examination of model characteristics in reducing avoidance behavior. *Journal of Personality and Social Psychology*, 1971, *17*, 298–307. (a)

Meichenbaum, D. *The nature and modification of impulsive children*. Paper presented at the biennial meeting of the Society for Research in Child Development, Minneapolis, 1971. (b)

Meichenbaum, D. *Cognitive behavior modification*. Morristown, N.J.: General Learning Press, 1974. (a)

Meichenbaum, D. Self-instructional strategy training: A cognitive prosthesis for the aged. *Human Development*, 1974, *17*, 273–280. (b)

Meichenbaum, D. Self-instructional methods. In F. H. Kanfer & A. P. Goldstein (Eds.), *Helping people change*. New York: Pergamon Press, 1975.

Meichenbaum, D. A cognitive-behavior modification approach to assessment. In M. Hersen & A. S. Bellack (Eds.), *Behavioral assessment*. New York: Pergamon Press, 1976.

Meichenbaum, D. *Cognitive-behavior modification: An integrative approach*. New York: Plenum Press, 1977.

Meichenbaum, D. *Cognitive behavior modification newsletter* (No. 4). Waterloo, Canada: University of Waterloo Press, 1979. (a)

Meichenbaum, D. Cognitive behavior modification: The need for a fairer assessment. *Cognitive Therapy and Research*, 1979, *3*, 127–132. (b)

Meichenbaum, D. Teaching children self-control. In B. B. Lahey & A. E. Kazdin (Eds.), *Advances in child clinical psychology* (Vol. 2). New York: Plenum Press, 1979. (c)

Meichenbaum, D. Cognitive behavior modification with exceptional children: A promise yet unfulfilled. *Exceptional Education Quarterly*, 1980, *1*(1), 83–88. (a)

Meichenbaum, D. A cognitive-behavioral perspective on intelligence. *Intelligence*, 1980, *4*, 271–283. (b)

Meichenbaum, D. *Teaching thinking: A cognitive-behavioral perspective*. Paper presented at the NIE-LROC conference on thinking and learning skills, Pittsburgh, October 1980. (c)

Meichenbaum, D., & Asarnow, J. Cognitive-behavior modification and metacognitive development: Implications for the classroom. In P. C. Kendall & S. Hollon (Eds.), *Cognitive-behavioral interventions: Theory, research, and procedures*. New York: Academic Press, 1979.

Meichenbaum, D., & Cameron, R. Training schizophrenics to talk to themselves: A means of developing attentional controls. *Behavior Therapy*, 1973, *4*, 515–534.

Meichenbaum, D., & Goodman, J. The developmental control of operant motor responding by verbal operants. *Journal of Experimental Child Psychology*, 1969, *7*, 553–565. (a)

Meichenbaum, D., & Goodman, J. Reflection-impulsivity and verbal control of motor behavior. *Child Development*, 1969, *40*, 785–707. (b)

Meichenbaum, D., & Goodman, J. *The nature and modification of impulsive children: Training impulsive children to talk to themselves.* Paper presented at the meeting of the Society for Research in Child Development, Minneapolis, April 1971. (a)

Meichenbaum, D. H., & Goodman, J. Training impulsive children to talk to themselves: A means of developing self-control. *Journal of Abnormal Psychology*, 1971, *77*, 115–126. (b)

Meichenbaum, D., & Goodman, J. Critical questions and methodological problems in studying private speech. In G. Zivin (Ed.), *Development of self-regulation through private speech.* New York: Wiley, 1979.

Meichenbaum, D. H., & Turk, L. Implications of research on disadvantaged children and cognitive-training programs for educational television: Ways of improving "Sesame Street." *Journal of Special Education*, 1972, *6*, 27–42.

Meichenbaum, D., Turk, D., & Burstein, S. The nature of coping with stress. In I. G. Sarason & C. D. Spielberger (Eds.), *Stress and anxiety* (Vol. 2). New York: Wiley, 1975.

Melamed, B. G. Behavioral approaches to fear in dental settings. In M. Hersen, R. M. Eisler, & P. M. Miller (Eds.), *Progress in behavior modification* (Vol. 7). New York: Academic Press, 1979.

Melamed, B. G. Reduction of medical fears: An information processing analysis. In J. Boulougouris (Ed.), *Learning theory approaches to psychiatry.* New York: Wiley, 1982.

Melamed, B. G., & Siegel, L. J. Reduction of anxiety in children facing hospitalization and surgery by use of filmed modeling. *Journal of Consulting and Clinical Psychology*, 1975, *43*, 511–521.

Melamed, B. G., & Siegel, L. J. *Behavioral medicine: Practical applications in health care.* New York: Springer Publishing, 1980.

Melamed, B. G., Hawes, R. R., Heiby, E., & Glick, J. Use of filmed modeling to reduce uncooperative behavior of children during dental treatment. *Journal of Dental Research*, 1975, *54*, 779–801.

Melamed, B., Weinstein, D., Hawes, R., & Katin-borland, M. Reduction of fear-related dental management problems with use of filmed modeling. *Journal of the American Dental Association*, 1975, *90*, 822–826.

Melamed, B. G., Meyer, R., Gee. C., & Soule, L. The influence of time and type of preparation on children's adjustment to hospitalization. *Journal of Pediatric Psychology*, 1976, *1*, 31–37.

Melamed, B. G., Yurcheson, R., Fleece, E. L., Hutcherson, S., & Hawes, R. Effects of film modeling on the reduction of anxiety-related behaviors in individuals varying in levels of previous experience in stress situation. *Journal of Consulting and Clinical Psychology*, 1978, *46*, 1357–1367.

Melamed, B. G., Robbins, R. L., & Graves, S. Preparation for surgery and medical procedures. In D. Russo & J. Varni (Eds.), *Behavioral pediatrics: Research and practice.* New York: Plenum Press, in press.

Melamed, B. G., Bennett, C. G., Ross, S. L., Bush, J. P., Hill, C., Ronk, S., Courts, F., & Jerrell, G. *The effect of dentist reinforcement strategies on pediatric patient compliance and fear.* Manuscript submitted for publication.

Meltzoff, A. N., & Moore, M. K. *Neonate imitation: A test of existence and mechanism.* Paper presented at the meeting of the Society for Research in Child Development, Denver, 1975.

Mercer, C. D., & Snell, M. E. *Learning theory research in mental retardation: Implications for teaching.* Columbus, Ohio: Charles E. Merrill, 1977.

Messer, S. B. Reflection-impulsivity: A review. *Psychological Bulletin*, 1976, *83*, 1026–1052.

Meyer, W. R. The politics of evaluation research: The Peace Corps. *Journal of Applied Behavioral Science*, 1975, *11*(3), 261–280.
Meyers, A. W., Craighead, W. E., & Meyers, H. H. A behavioral-preventive approach to community mental health. *American Journal of Community Psychology*, 1974, *2*, 275–286.
Meyers, M., & Paris, S. Children's metacognitive knowledge about reading. *Journal of Educational Psychology*, 1978, *70*, 680–690.
Michelson, L., Foster, S. L., & Ritchey, W. L. Social-skills assessment of children. In B. B. Lahey & A. E. Kazdin (Eds.), *Advances in clinical child psychology* (Vol. 4). New York: Plenum Press, 1981.
Milan, M. A., & Long, C. K. Crime and delinquency: The last frontier? In D. S. Glenwick & L. A. Jason (Eds.), *Behavioral community psychology: Progress and prospects*. New York: Praeger Publishers, 1980.
Miller, L. C. School Behavior Check List: An inventory of deviant behavior for elementary school children. *Journal of Consulting and Clinical Psychology*, 1972, *38*, 134–144.
Miller, L. C., Barrett, C., Hampe, E., & Noble, H. Factor structure of childhood fears. *Journal of Consulting and Clinical Psychology*, 1972, *39*, 264–268.
Miller, L. C., Barrett, C. L., & Hampe, E. Phobias of childhood in a prescientific era. In A. Davids (Ed.), *Child personality and psychopathology: Current topics*. New York: Wiley, 1974.
Miller, L. K., Hale, G. A., & Stevenson, H. W. Learning and problem solving by retarded and normal Ss. *American Journal of Mental Deficiency*, 1968, *72*, 681–690.
Miller, P. H., & Bigi, L. The development of children's understanding of attention. *Merrill-Palmer Quarterly*, 1979, *25*, 235–250.
Miller, S. P., & Shada, E. T. Preparatory information and recovery on open-heart surgery patients. *Heart & Lung*, 1978, *7*, 487–493.
Minkin, N., Braukmann, C. J., Minkin, B. L., Timbers, G. D., Timbers, B. J., Fixsen, D. L., Phillips, E. L., & Wolf, M. M. The social validation and training of conversational skills. *Journal of Applied Behavior Analysis*, 1976, *9*, 127–139.
Minuchin, S. *Families and family therapy*. Cambridge, Mass.: Harvard University Press, 1974.
Minuchin, S., Baker, L., Rosman, B. L., Liebman, R., Milman, L., & Todd, T. C. A conceptual model of psychosomatic illness in children. *Archives of General Psychiatry*, 1975, *32*, 1031–1038.
Minuchin, S., Rosman, B. L., & Baker, L. *Psychosomatic families*. Cambridge, Mass.: Harvard University Press, 1978.
Mischel, W. Processes in delay of gratification. In L. Berkowitz (Ed.), *Advances in experimental social psychology* (Vol. 7). New York: Academic Press, 1974.
Mischel, W., & Metzner, R. Preference for delayed reward as a function of age, intelligence, and length of delay interval. *Journal of Abnormal and Social Psychology*, 1962, *64*, 425–431.
Mischel, W., Mischel, H., & Hood, S. *The development of effective ideation to delay gratification*. Unpublished manuscript, Stanford University, 1978.
Mishler, E. G., & Waxler, N. E. Family interaction processes and schizophrenia: A review of current theories. *Merrill-Palmer Quarterly*, 1965, *11*, 269–315.
Moely, B. E., Olson, F. A., Halwes, T. G., & Flavell, J. H. Production deficiency in young children's clustered recall. *Developmental Psychology*, 1969, *1*, 26–34.
Moore, D. R., Chamberlain, P., & Mukai, L. H. Children at risk for delinquency: A follow-up comparison of aggressive and children who steal. *Journal of Abnormal Child Psychology*, 1979, *7*, 345–355.

Moore, S., & Updegraff, R. Sociometric status of preschool children related to age, sex, nurturance-giving, and dependency. *Child Development*, 1964, *35*, 519–524.

Moore, S. F., & Cole, S. O. Cognitive self-mediation training with hyperkinetic children. *Bulletin of the Psychonomic Society*, 1978, *12*, 18–20.

Moos, R. H. *The Social Climate Scales: An overview*. Palo Alto, Calif.: Consulting Psychologists Press, 1974.

Morena, D. A., & Litrownik, A. J. Self-concept in educable mentally retarded and emotionally handicapped children: Relationships between behavioral and self-report indices and an attempt at modification. *Journal of Abnormal Child Psychology*, 1974, *2*, 281–292.

Morrison, F. J., Holmes, D. L., & Haith, M. M. A developmental study of the effects of familiarity on short term visual memory. *Journal of Experimental Child Psychology*, 1974, *18*, 412–425.

Moss, M. K., & Arend, R. A. Self-directed contact desensitization. *Journal of Consulting and Clinical Psychology*, 1977, *45*, 730–738.

Mossige, A., Petterson, R. B., & Blakar, R. M. Egocentrism and inefficiency in the communication of families containing schizophrenic members. *Family Process*, 1979, *18*, 405–425.

Mowrer, O. H., & Mowrer, W. M. Enuresis—A method for its study and treatment. *American Journal of Orthopsychiatry*, 1938, *8*, 436–459.

Moynahan, E. D. The development of knowledge concerning the effect of categorization upon free recall. *Child Development*, 1973, *44*, 238–246.

Mueller, E., & Brenner, J. The growth of social interaction with a toddler play group: The role of peer experience. *Child Development*, 1977, *48*, 854–861.

Mueller, E., & Lucas, T. A developmental analysis of peer interaction among toddlers. In M. Lewis & L. Rosenblum (Eds.), *Friendship and peer relations: The origins of behavior* (Vol. 4). New York: Wiley, 1975.

Mullinix, S. D., & Galassi, J. P. Deriving the content of social skills training with a verbal response components approach. *Behavioral Assessment*, 1981, *3*, 55–66.

Munoz, R. F., Snowden, L. R., & Kelly, J. G. (Eds.). *Social and phychological research in community settings*. San Francisco: Jossey-Bass, 1979.

Murphy, L. *The widening world of childhood*. New York: Basic Books, 1962.

Murrell, S. A., & Stachowiak, J. G. Consistency, rigidity, and power in the interaction patterns of clinic and nonclinic families. *Journal of Abnormal Psychology*, 1967, *72*, 265–272.

Myerson, W. A., & Hayes, S. C. Controlling the clinician for the client's benefit. In J. E. Krapf, & E. A. Vargas (Eds.), *Behaviorism and ethics*. Kalamazoo, Mich.: Behaviordelia, 1978.

Nagy, M. Children's ideas of the origin of illness. *Health Education Journal*, 1951, *9*, 6–12.

Napier, A. Y., & Whitaker, C. A. *The family crucible*. New York: Harper & Row, 1978.

Neeley, J., Heckel, R., & Leichtman, H. The effects of race of model and response consequences to the model on imitation of children. *Journal of Social Psychology*, 1973, *89*, 225–231.

Neimark, E. E. Intellectual development during adolescence. In F. D. Horowitz (Ed.), *Review of child development research* (Vol. 4). Chicago: University of Chicago Press, 1975.

Neisworth, J. T. *Independence training with severely retarded children*. Unpublished research report, Pennsylvania State University, 1973.

Nelson, K., & Brown, A. L. The semantic-episodic distinction in memory development. In P. A. Ornstein (Ed.), *Memory development in children*. Hillsdale, N.J.: Lawrence Erlbaum Associates, 1978.

Nelson, R. O. The use of intelligence tests within behavioral assessment. *Behavioral Assessment,* 1980, *2,* 417–423.

Nelson, R. O. Realistic dependent measures for clinical use. *Journal of Consulting and Clinical Psychology,* 1981, *49,* 168–182.

Nelson, R. O., & Bowles, P. E. The best of two worlds—observations with norms. *Journal of School Psychology,* 1975, *13,* 3–9.

Nelson, R. O., & Hayes, S. C. Some current dimensions of behavioral assessment. *Behavioral Assessment,* 1979, *1,* 1–16.

Nelson, R. O., Lipinski, D. P., & Black, J. L. The reactivity of adult retardates' self-monitoring: A comparison among behaviors of different valances and a comparison with token reinforcement. *Psychological Record,* 1976, *26,* 189–201.

Nelson, R. O., Hay, L. R., & Hay, W. M. Comments on Cone's "Relevance of reliability and validity for behavioral assessment." *Behavior Therapy,* 1977, *8,* 427–430.

Nelson, R. O., Lipinski, D. P., & Boykin, R. A. The effects of self-recorders training and the obtrusiveness of the self-recording device on the accuracy and reactivity of self-monitoring. *Behavior Therapy,* 1978, *9,* 200–208.

Nelson, W. J., & Birkimer, J. C. Role of self-instruction and self-reinforcement in the modification of impulsivity. *Journal of Consulting and Clinical Psychology,* 1978, *46,* 183.

Nelson, W. M. III., Finch, A. J. Jr., & Hooke, J. F. Effects of reinforcement and response-cost on cognitive style in emotionally disturbed boys. *Journal of Abnormal Psychology,* 1975, *84,* 426–428.

Nichol, G., Cohen, R., Meyers, A. W., & Schlesser, R. Generalization of self-instruction training. *Journaal of Applied Developmental Psychology,* 1982, *3,* 205–215.

Nicholas, K., McCarter, R., & Heckel, B. Effects of race and sex on the imitation of television models. *Journal of Social Psychology,* 1971, *85,* 315–318.

Nietzel, M. T., Winett, R. A., MacDonald, M. L., & Davidson, W. S. *Behavioral approaches to community psychology.* New York: Pergamon Press, 1977.

Nimmer, W. H., & Kapp, R. A. A multiple impact program for the treatment of an injection phobia. *Journal of Behavioral Therapy and Experimental Psychiatry,* 1974, *5,* 257–258.

Norcross, J. C., & Prochaska, J. O. A national survey of clinical psychologists: Characteristics and activities. *Clinical Psychologist,* 1982, *35*(1), 5–8.

Nowicki, S., & Strickland, B. R. A locus of control scale for children. *Journal of Consulting and Clinical Psychology,* 1973, *40,* 148–155.

Nuckolls, K. B., Cassel, J., & Kaplan, B. H. Psychosocial assets, life crisis, and the prognosis of pregnancy. *American Journal of Epidemiology,* 1972, *95,* 431–441.

O'Connor, M. The effect of role-taking training on role-taking and social behaviors in young children. *Social Behavior and Personality,* 1977, *5,* 1–11.

O'Connor, R. D. Modification of social withdrawal through symbolic modeling. *Journal of Applied Behavior Analysis* 1969, *2,* 15–22.

O'Connor, R. D. The relative efficacy of modeling, shaping, and the combined procedures for the modification of social withdrawal. *Journal of Abnormal Psychology,* 1972, *79,* 327–334.

Oden, S., & Asher, S. R. Coaching children in social skills for friendship making. *Child Development,* 1977, *48,* 495–506.

Ojemann, R. H. Incorporating psychological concepts in the school curriculum. *Journal of School Psychology,* 1967, *5,* 195–204.

Ojemann, R. H., Levitt, E., Lyle, W., & Whiteside, M. F. The effects of a "causal" teacher training program and certain curricular changes on grade school children. *Journal of Experimental Education,* 1955, *24,* 95–114.

O'Leary, K. D., & O'Leary, S. G. *Classroom management: The successful use of behavior modification* (2nd ed.). New York: Pergamon Press, 1977.

O'Leary, K. D., Kaufman, K. F., Kass, R. E., & Drabman, R. S. The effects of loud and soft reprimands on the behavior of disruptive students. *Exceptional Children*, 1970, *37*, 145–155.

O'Leary, S. G. A response to cognitive training. *Exceptional Education Quarterly*, 1980, *1*, 89–94.

O'Leary, S. G., & Dubey, D. R. Applications of self-control procedures by children: A review. *Journal of Applied Behavior Analysis*, 1979, *12*, 449–465.

Oleinick, M. S., Bahn, A. K., Eisenberg, L., & Lilienfeld, A. M. Early socialization experiences and intrafamilial environment. *Archives of General Psychiatry*, 1966, *15*, 344–353.

Ollendick, T. H., & Hersen, M. Social skills training for juvenile delinquent. *Behaviour Research and Therapy*, 1979, *17*, 547–554.

Ollendick, T. H., Elliott, W., & Matson J. L. Locus of control as related to effectiveness in a behavior modification program for juvenile delinquents. *Journal of Behavior Therapy and Experimental Psychiatry*, 1980, *11*, 259–262.

Olson, D. H. Marital and family therapy: Integrative review and critique. *Journal of Marriage and the Family*, 1970, *32*, 501–538.

Olson, D. H. Empirically unbinding the double bind: Review of research and conceptual reformulations. *Family Process*, 1972, *11*, 69–94.

Oltmanns, T. F., Broderick, J. E., & O'Leary, K. D. Marital adjustment and the efficacy of behavior therapy with children. *Journal of Consulting and Clinical Psychology*, 1977, *45*, 724–729.

Ordman, A. *Peer relations and withdrawn children*. Unpublished master's thesis, University of Wisconsin, Madison, 1979.

Ornitz, E. M., & Ritvo, E. R. Perceptual inconsistency in early infantile autism. *Archives of General Psychiatry*, 1968, *18*, 76–98.

Orwell, G. Politics and the English language. In G. Orwell *Shooting an elephant and other essays*. New York: Harcourt, Brace & Company, 1950.

Palkes, H., Stewart, M., & Kahana, B. Porteus maze performance of hyperactive boys after training in self-directed verbal commands. *Child Development*, 1968, *39*, 817–826.

Paris, S. G., & Carter, A. Y. Semantic and constructive aspects of sentence memory in children. *Development Psychology*, 1973, *9*, 109–113.

Paris, S. G., & Lindauer, B. K. The role of inference in children's comprehension and memory for sentence. *Cognitive Psychology*, 1976, *8*, 217–227.

Paris, S. G., & Upton, L. R. Children's memory for inferential relationships in prose. *Child Development*, 1976, *47*, 660–668.

Paris, S. G., Mahoney, G. J., & Buckhalt, J. A. Facilitation of semantic integration in sentence memory of retarded children. *American Journal of Mental Deficiency*, 1974, *78*, 714–720.

Patterson, C. J., & Mischel, W. Effects of temptation-inhibiting and task-facilitating plans on self-control. *Journal of Personality and Social Psychology*, 1976, *33*, 209–217.

Patterson, G. R. Changes in status of family members as controlling stimuli: A basis for describing treatment process. In L. A. Hamerlynck, L. C. Handy, & E. J. Mash (Eds.), *Behavior change: Methodology, concepts, and practice*. Champaign, Ill.: Research Press, 1973.

Patterson, G. R. The aggressive child: Victim and architect of a coercive system. In E. J. Mash, L. A. Hamerlynck, & L. C. Handy (Eds.), *Behavior modification and families*. New York: Brunner/Mazel, 1976.

Patterson, G. R. *A social learning approach to family intervention. 3. Coercive family process.* Eugene, Oreg.: Castalia, 1982.
Patterson, G. R., & Fleishman, M. J. Maintenance of treatment effects: Some considerations concerning family systems and follow-up data. *Behavior Therapy*, 1979, *10*, 168–185.
Patterson, G. R., & Hops, H. Coercion, a game for two: Intervention techniques for marital conflict. In R. E. Ulrich & P. Mountjoy (Eds.), *The experimental analysis of social behavior.* New York: Appleton-Century-Crofts, 1972.
Patterson, G. R., & Reid, J. B. Reciprocity and coercion: Two facets of social systems. In C. Neuringer & J. Michaels (Eds.), *Behavior modification in clinical psychology.* New York: Appleton-Century-Crofts, 1970.
Patterson, G. R., Cobb, J. A., & Ray, R. S. A social engineering technology for retraining the families of aggressive boys. In H. E. Adams & I. P. Unikel (Eds.), *Issues and trends in behavior therapy.* Springfield, Ill.: Charles C. Thomas, 1973.
Patterson, G. R., Reid, J. B., Jones, R. R., & Conger, R. E. *A social learning approach to family intervention. I. Families with aggressive children.* Eugene, Oreg.: Castalia Press, 1975.
Paulauskas, S. L., & Campbell, B. G. Social perspective-taking and teacher ratings of peer interaction in hyperactive boys. *Journal of Abnormal Child Psychology*, 1979, *7*, 483–493.
Peed, S., Roberts, M., & Forehand, R. Evaluation of the effectiveness of a standardized parent training program in altering the interaction of mothers and their noncompliant children. *Behavior Modification*, 1977, *1*, 323–350.
Perri, M. G., & Richards, C. S. An investigation of naturally occurring episodes of self controlled behaviors. *Journal of Counseling Psychology*, 1977, *24*, 178–183.
Peters, B. M. School-aged children's beliefs about causality of illness: A review of the literature. *Maternal Child Nursing Journal*, 1978, *7*, 143–154.
Peterson, L., & Ridley-Johnson, R. Pediatric hospital responses to survey on pre-hospital preparation for children. *Journal of Pediatric Psychology*, 1980, *5*, 1–7.
Peterson, L., & Shigitomi, C. The use of coping techniques to minimize anxiety in hospitalized children. *Behavior Therapy*, 1981, *12*, 1–14.
Peterson, L., Hartman, D. P., & Gelfand, D. M. Prevention of child behavior disorders: A lifestyle change for child psychologists. In P. O. Davidson & S. M. Davidson (Eds.), *Behavioral medicine: Changing health life-styles.* New York: Brunner/Mazel, 1980.
Phares, E. J. *Locus of control: A personality determinant of behavior.* Morristown, N.J.: General Learning Press, 1973.
Phillips, E. L., Phillips, E. A., Fixsen, D. L., & Wolf, M. M. *The teaching-family handbook.* Lawrence: University of Kansas Printing Service, 1972.
Piaget, J. *The language and thought of the child.* New York: Harcourt, Brace, 1926.
Piaget, J. *Judgement and reasoning in the child.* New York: Harcourt, Brace, 1928.
Piaget, J. *The origins of intelligence in children* (M. Cook, Trans.). New York: International Universities Press, 1952. (Originally published, 1936.)
Piaget, J. *The moral judgment of the child.* New York: Collier Books, 1962. (a)
Piaget, J. *Play dreams and imitation in childhood.* New York: W. W. Norton, 1962. (b)
Piaget, J. Development and learning. *Journal of Research in Science Teaching*, 1964, *2*, 176–186.
Piaget, J., & Inhelder, B. *The child's conception of space.* London: Routledge & Kegan Paul, 1956.
Piaget, J., & Inhelder, B. *Memory and intelligence.* New York: Basic Books, 1973.
Pick, A. D., Frankel, D. G., & Hess, V. L. Children's attention: The development of selectivity. In E. M. Hetherington (Ed.), *Review of child development research* (Vol. 5). Chicago: University of Chicago Press, 1975.

Piggott, L. R. Overview of selected basic research in autism. *Journal of Autism and Developmental Disorders*, 1979, *9*, 199–218.

Piggott, L. R., & Simson, C. B. Changing diagnosis of childhood psychosis. *Journal of Autism and Childhood Schizophrenia*, 1975, *5*, 239–245.

Pitkanen, L. The effect of simulation exercises on the control of aggressive behavior in children. *Scandanavian Journal of Psychology*, 1974, *15*, 169–177.

Platt, J. J., & Spivack, G. *Manual for the Means-Ends Problem-Solving procedure (MEPS).* Philadelphia: Hahnemann Medical College & Hospital, Department of Mental Health Sciences, 1975.

Platt, J. J., Spivack, G., & Bloom, M. *Means-ends problem-solving procedure (MEPS): Manual and tentative norms.* Philadelphia: Department of Mental Health Sciences, Hahneman Medical College and Hospital, 1971.

Platt, J. J., Scura, W., & Hannon, J. R. Problem-solving thinking of youthful incarcerated heroin addicts. *Journal of Community Psychology*, 1973, *1*, 278–281.

Platt, J. J., Spivack, G., Altman, N., Altman, D., & Peizer, S. B. Adolescent problem-solving thinking. *Journal of Consulting and Clinical Psychology*, 1974, *42*, 787–793.

Porges, S. W. Peripheral and neurochemical parallels of psychopathology: A psychophysiological model relating autonomic imbalance to hyperactivity, psychopathy, and autism. In H. W. Reese (Ed.), *Advances in child development and behavior* (Vol. 11). New York: Academic Press, 1976.

Porter, B., & O'Leary, K. D. Marital discord and childhood behavior problems. *Journal of Abnormal Child Psychology*, 1980, *8*, 287–295.

Porteus, S. D. *The Maze Test: Recent advances.* Palo Alto, Calif.: Pacific Books, 1955.

Prentice, N., & Kelly, F. J. Intelligence and delinquency: A reconsideration. *Journal of Social Psychology*, 1963, *60*, 327–337.

President's Commission on Mental Health. *Report to the President*, (Vol. I). Washington, D.C.: U.S. Government Printing Office, 1978.

Pressley, M. Increasing children's self-control through cognitive interventions. *Review of Educational Research*, 1979, *49*, 319–370.

Price-Williams, D., & Gallimore, R. The cultural perspective. In B. K. Keogh (Ed.), *Advances in special education* (Vol. 2): *Perspectives on application.* Greenwich, Conn.: JAI Press, 1980.

Prior, M., & McGillivray, J. The performance of autistic children on three learning set tasks. *Journal of Child Psychology and Psychiatry*, 1980, *21*, 313–323.

Prugh, D. G., Staub, E. M., Sands, H. H., Kirschenbaum, R. M., & Lenihan, E. A. A study of the emotional reactions of children and families to hospitalization and illness. *American Journal of Orthopsychiatry*, 1953, *23*, 70–106.

Quay, H. C. Classification. In H. C. Quay & J. S. Werry (Eds.), *Psychopathological disorders of childhood.* New York: Wiley, 1979.

Rachman, S. J. Clinical applications of observational learning, imitation, and modeling. *Behavior Therapy*, 1972, *3*, 379–397.

Rappaport, J. *Community psychology: Values, research, and action.* New York: Holt, Rinehart & Winston, 1977.

Rappaport, J. In praise of paradox: A social policy of empowerment over prevention. *American Journal of Community Psychology*, 1981, *9*, 1–25.

Rappaport, J., Davidson, W. S., Wilson, M. N., & Mitchell. A. Alternatives to blaming the victim or the environment: Our places to stand have not moved the earth. *American Psychologist*, 1975, *30*, 525–528.

Reese, H. W. Verbal mediation as a function of age level. *Psychological Bulletin*, 1962, *59*, 502–509.

Rehm, L. P. (Ed.). *Behavior therapy for depression*. New York: Academic Press, 1981.
Reid, J. B., & Patterson, G. R. Follow-up analyses of behavioral treatment program for boys with conduct problems. A reply to Kent. *Journal of Consulting and Clinical Psychology*, 1976, *44*, 299–302.
Reisinger, J. J., Frangia, G. W., & Hoffman, E. H. Toddler management training: Generalization and marital status. *Journal of Behavior Therapy and Experimental Psychiatry*, 1976, *7*, 335–340.
Reisinger, J. J., Ora, J. P., & Frangia, G. W. Parents as change agents for their children: A review. *Journal of Community Psychology*, 1976, *4*, 103–123.
Reppucci, N. D., & Saunders, J. T. The social psychology of behavior modification naturalistic settings. *American Psychologist*, 1974, *29*, 649–660.
Richter, M. *Effectiveness of stimulus fading techniques with autistic children*. Unpublished master's thesis, San Diego State University, 1980.
Richards, C. S., & Seigel, L. J. Behavioral treatment of anxiety states and avoidance behaviors in children. In D. Marholin (Ed.), *Child behavior therapy*. New York: Gardner, 1978.
Richardson, F. C., & Suinn, R. M. A comparison of traditional systematic desensitization, accelerated massed desensitization, and anxiety management training in the treatment of mathematics anxiety. *Behavior Therapy*, 1973, *4*, 212–218.
Ricks, D. M., & Wing, L. Language, communication, and the use of symbols in normal and autistic children. *Journal of Autism and Childhood Schizophrenia*, 1975, *5*, 191–221.
Riessman, F. The 'helper' therapy principle. *Social Work*, 1965, *10*, 27–32.
Rimland, B. *Infantile autism*. New York: Appleton-Century-Crofts, 1964.
Rimland, B. Death knell for psychotherapy? *American Psychologist*, 1979, *34*, 1972.
Rimon, D. *Children's assessment to their self-control: Development of a scale*. Unpublished master's thesis, Tel-Aviv University, 1980.
Rincover, A. Variables affecting stimulus fading and discriminative responding in psychotic children. *Journal of Abnormal Psychology*, 1978, *87*, 541–553.
Rincover, A., Newsom, C. D., Lovaas, O. I., & Koegel, R. L. Some motivational properties of sensory stimuli in psychotic children. *Journal of Experimental Child Psychology*, 1977, *24*, 312–323.
Riopelle, A. J. (Ed.). *Animal problem solving*. Baltimore, M.d.: Penguin, 1967.
Risley, T., & Hart, B. Developing correspondence between the nonverbal and verbal behavior of preschool children. *Journal of Applied Behavior Analysis*, 1968, *1*, 267–281.
Riskin, J., & Faunce, E. E. An evaluative review of family interaction research. *Family Process*, 1972, *11*, 365–455.
Ritter, B. The group desensitization of children's phobias. *Behavior Research and Therapy*, 1968, *6*, 1–6.
Ritter, B. The use of contact desensitization demonstration plus participation, and demonstration alone in the treatment of acrophobia. *Behavior Research and Therapy*, 1969, *7*, 157–164.
Roberts, M. *Rectory Paddock School*. Kent, England: Paddock School, 1979.
Roberts, M. C., Wurtele, S. K., Boone, R. R., Ginther, G., & Elkins, P. D. Reduction of medical and psychological fears by use of modeling: A preventive application in a general population of children. *Journal of Pediatric Psychology*, 1981, *6*, 293–300.
Roberts, R. N. Private speech in academic problem-solving: A naturalistic perspective. In G. Zivin (Ed.), *The development of self-regulation through private speech*. New York: Wiley, 1979.
Roberts, R. N. Naturalistic assessment for classroom intervention: Speech and motor behavior as predictors of academic competence. *Behavioral Assessment*, 1981, *3*, 15–30.

Roberts, R. N., & Dick, M. L. Self control in the classroom: Theoretical issues and practical applications. In T. R. Kratochwill (Ed.), *Advances in school psychology* (Vol. 2). Hillsdale, N.J.: Lawrence Erlbaum, 1982.

Roberts, R. N., & Mullis, M. *A component analysis of self-instructional training.* Paper submitted for publication, 1983.

Roberts, R. N., & Tharp, R. G. A naturalistic study of school children's private speech in an academic problem-solving task. *Cognitive Therapy and Research,* 1980, *4,* 341–352.

Robertson, D., & Keeley, S. *Evaluation of a mediational training program for impulsive children by a multiple case study design.* Paper presented at the annual convention of the American Psychological Association, New Orleans, August 1974.

Robertson, L., Kendall, P. C., & Urbain, E. S. *A multistudy analysis of the role of socioeconomic status (SES) in cognitive-behavioral treatments with children.* Unpublished manuscript, University of Minnesota, 1980.

Robertson, S. J., Simon, S. J., Pachman, J. S., & Drabman, R. S. Self-control and generalization procedures in a classroom of disruptive retarded children. *Child Behavior Therapy,* 1979, *1,* 347–362.

Robin, A. L., Armel, S., & O'Leary, K. D. The effects of self-instruction on writing deficiencies. *Behavior Therapy,* 1975, *6,* 178–187.

Robin, A., Schneider, M., & Dolnick, M. The turtle technique: An extended case study of self-control in the classroom. *Psychology in the Schools,* 1976, *13,* 449–453.

Robin, A. L., Kent, R., O'Leary, D., Foster, S., & Prinz, R. An approach to teaching parents and adolescents problem-solving communication skills: A preliminary report. *Behavior Therapy,* 1977, *8,* 639–643.

Robins, L. N. *Deviant children grown up: A sociological and psychiatric study of sociopathic personality.* Baltimore: Williams & Wilkins, 1966. (Reprinted by Robert E. Krieger Publishing, Huntington, New York, 1974.)

Robins, L. N. *Sturdy childhood predictors of adult outcomes: Replications from longitudinal studies.* Paper presented at the American Psychopathological Association Meeting, 1978.

Robins, L. N. Follow-up studies. In H. C. Quay & J. S. Werry (Eds.), *Psychopathological disorders of childhood.* New York: Wiley, 1979.

Robson, G. M. *Problem solving strategies in learning disabled and normal achieving children.* Unpublished doctoral dissertation, UCLA, 1977.

Roff, J. D., Knight, R., & Wertheim, E. A factor-analytic study of childhood symptoms antecedent to schizophrenia. *Journal of Abnormal Psychology,* 1976, *85,* 543–549.

Roff, M. Childhood social interactions and young adult bad conduct. *Journal of Abnormal and Social Psychology,* 1961, *63,* 333–337.

Roff, M., Sells, S. B., & Golden, M. M. *Social adjustment and personality development in children.* Minneapolis: University of Minnesota, 1972.

Rogers, C. R. *Client-centered therapy.* Boston: Houghton Mifflin, 1951.

Rogers-Warren, A., & Baer, D. Correspondence between saying and doing: Teaching children to share and praise. *Journal of Applied Behavior Analysis,* 1976, *3,* 335–354.

Rogoff, B., Newcombe, N., & Kagan, J. Planfulness and recognition memory. *Child Development,* 1974, *45,* 972–977.

Romanczyk, R. G., Kistner, J. A., & Plienis, A. Self-stimulatory and self-injurious behavior: Etiology and treatment. In J. J. Steffen & P. Karoly (Eds.), *Autism and severe psychopathology: Advances in child behavioral analysis and therapy* (*Vol.* 2). Lexington, Mass.: D. C. Heath, 1982.

Rosen, G. M., Glasgow, R. E., & Barrera, M. A controlled study to assess the clinical efficacy of totally self-administered systematic sensitization. *Journal of Consulting and Clinical Psychology,* 1976, 44, 208–217.

Rosen, M., Diggory, J. C., & Werlinsky, B. E. Goal-setting and expectancy of success in institutionalized and noninstitutionalized mental subnormals. *American Journal of Mental Deficiency*, 1966, *71*, 249–255.

Rosen, M., Diggory, J. C., Floor, L., & Nowakiwska, M. Self-evaluation, expectancy, and performance in the mentally subnormal. *Journal of Mental Deficiency Research*, 1971, *15*, 81–95.

Rosenbaum, M. A schedule for assessing self-control behaviors: Preliminary findings. *Behavior Therapy*, 1980, *11*, 109–121.

Rosenbaum, M. S., & Drabman, R. S. Self-control training in the classroom: A review and critique. *Journal of Applied Behavior Analysis*, 1979, *12*, 467–485.

Rosenbaum, M., & Merbaum, M. Self-control of anxiety and depression: An evaluative review of treatments. *Clinical Behavior Therapy Review*, in press.

Rosenblum, S. M., Arick, J. R., Krug, D. A., Stubbs, E. G., Young, N. B., & Pelson, R. O. Auditory brainstem evoked responses in autistic children. *Journal of Autism and Developmental Disorders*, 1980, *10*, 215–225.

Rosenthal, T. L., & Bandura, A. Psychological modeling: Theory and practice. In S. L. Garfield & A. E. Bergin (Eds.), *Handbook of psychotherapy and behavior change* (2nd ed.). New York: Wiley, 1978.

Rosenthal, T. L., & Zimmerman, B. J. *Social learning theory and cognition*. New York: Academic Press, 1978.

Ross, A. O. *Psychological disorders of children*. New York: McGraw-Hill, 1980.

Ross, A. O. *Child behavior therapy: Principles, procedures and empirical basis*. New York: Wiley, 1981.

Ross, A. O., & Lacey, H. M. Characteristics of terminators and remainers in child guidance treatment. *Journal of Consulting Psychology*, 1961, *25*, 420–424.

Ross, A. O., & Pelham, W. E. Child psychopathology. *Annual Review of Psychology*, 1981, *32*, 243–278.

Ross, D. M., & Ross, S. A. Cognitive training for the EMR child: Situational problem-solving and planning. *American Journal of Mental Deficiency*, 1973, *78*, 20–26.

Ross, D. M., & Ross, S. A. *The pacemaker primary curriculum*. Belmont, Calif.: Fearon, 1974.

Ross, D. M., & Ross, S. A. Cognitive training for EMR children: Choosing the best alternative. *American Journal of Mental Deficiency*, 1978, *82*, 598–601.

Ross, D. M., & Ross, S. A. Cognitive training for the EMR child: Language skills prerequisite to relevant-irrelevant discrimination tasks. *Mental Retardation*, 1979, *17*, 3–7.

Ross, D. M., Ross, S. A., & Evans, T. A. The modification of extreme social withdrawal by modification with guided practice. *Journal of Behavior Therapy and Experimental Psychiatry*, 1971, *2*, 273–279.

Ross, E. S., & Karoly, P. *Verbal self-control in children: An investigation of mother-child communication patterns*. Paper presented at the annual convention of the Association for Advancement of Behavior Therapy, Atlanta, December 1977.

Rotatory, A. F., & Fox, R. The effectiveness of a behavioral weight reduction program for moderately retarded adolescents. *Behavior Therapy*, 1980, *11*, 245–255.

Rotatory, A. F., Fox, R., & Switzky, H. A multicomponent behavioral program for achieving weight loss in the adult mentally retarded person. *Mental Retardation*, 1980, *18*, 31–33.

Rotenberg, M. Conceptual and methodological notes on affective and cognitive role taking (sympathy and empathy): An illustrative experiment with delinquent and nondelinquent boys. *Journal of Genetic Psychology*, 1974, *125*, 177–185.

Rubin, Z. *Friendship*. Cambridge, Mass.: Harvard University Press, 1980.

Russell, R. K., & Sipach, J. F. Cue-controlled relaxation in the treatment of test anxiety. *Journal of Behavior Therapy and Experimental Psychiatry*, 1973, *4*, 47–49.

Russell, R. K., Miller, D. E., & June, L. N. A comparison between group systematic desensitization and cue-controlled relaxation in the treatment of test anxiety. *Behavior Therapy*, 1975, *6*, 172–177.

Ruttenberg, B. A. A psychoanalytic understanding of infantile autism and its treatment. In D. W. Churchill, G. D. Alpern, & M. K. DeMeyer (Eds.), *Infantile autism*. Springfield, Ill.: Charles C. Thomas, 1971.

Ruttenberg, B. A. Aversives only as a last resort. *Journal of Autism and Childhood Schizophrenia*, 1978, *8*, 106–107.

Rutter, M. Parent-child separation: Psychological effects on the children. *Journal of Child Psychology and Psychiatry*, 1971, *12*, 233–260.

Rutter, M. *Helping troubled children*. New York: Plenum Press, 1975.

Rutter, M. Diagnosis and definition of childhood autism. *Journal of Autism and Childhood Schizophrenia*, 1978, *8*, 139–161.

Rutter, M., Lebovic, S., Eisenberg, L., Sneznevsku, A. V., Sadoun, R., Brooke, E., & Lin, T. A tri-axial classification of mental disorder in childhood. *Journal of Child Psychiatry*, 1969, *10*, 41–61.

Rutter, M., Yule, B., Quinton, D., Rowlands, O., Yule, W., & Berger, M. Attainment and adjustment in two geographical areas: III—Some factors accounting for area differences. *British Journal of Psychiatry*, 1974, *125*, 520–533.

Rutter, M., Graham, P., Chadwick, O. F. D., & Yule, W. Adolescent turmoil: Fact or fiction? *Journal of Child Psychology and Psychiatry*, 1976, *17*, 35–56.

Samuels, S. J. Some essentials of decoding. *Exceptional Education Quarterly*, 1981, *2*,(1), 11–25.

Sander, L. W., Julia, H. L., Stechler, G., & Burns, P. Continuous 24-hour interactional monitoring in infants reared in two caretaking environments. *Psychosomatic Medicine*, 1972, *34*, 270.

Sanders, J. An autistic child in residential treatment. *Reiss-Davis Clinic Bulletin*, 1975, *12*, 97–106.

Sandler, I. N., Duricko, A., & Grande, L. Effectiveness of an early secondary prevention program in an inner-city elementary school. *American Journal of Community Psychology*, 1975, *3*, 23–32.

Santa-Barbara, J., & Epstein, N. B. Conflict behavior in clinic families: Preasymptotic interactions and stable outcomes. *Behavioral Science*, 1974, *19*, 100–110.

Sarason, I. G. *Transcripts of modeling scenes and description of discussion format*, undated. (Manuscript available from I. G. Sarason, Department of Psychology, University of Washington, Seattle, Washington, 98105.)

Sarason, I. G. Test anxiety and the self-disclosing model. *Journal of Consulting and Clinical Psychology*, 1975, *43*, 148–153.

Sarason, I. G. A cognitive social learning approach to juvenile delinquency. In R. D. Hare & D. Schalling (Eds.), *Psychopathic behaviour: Approaches to research*. New York: Wiley, 1978.

Sarason, I. G., & Ganzer, V. J. Modeling and group discussion in the rehabilitation of juvenile delinquents. *Journal of Counseling Psychology*, 1973, *20*, 442–449.

Sarbin, T. R. Role theory. In G. Lindzey (Ed.), *Handbook of social psychology*. Cambridge, Mass.: Addison-Wesley, 1954.

Satir, V. *Conjoint family therapy: A guide to theory and technique* (Rev. ed.). Palo Alto, Calif.: Science & Behavior Books, 1967.

Saunders, J. T., & Reppucci, N. D. The social identity of behavior modification. In M.

Hersen, R. Eisler, & P. Miller (Eds.), *Progress in behavior modification* (Vol. 6). New York: Academic Press, 1978.

Sawin, D. B., & Parke, R. D. Development of self-verbalized control of resistance to deviation. *Developmental Psychology*, 1979, *15*, 120–127.

Scarlett, W. G. Social isolation from agemates among nursery school children. *Journal of Child Psychology and Psychiatry*, 1980, *12*, 231–240.

Schaefer, E. E., & Aaronson, M. R. *Classroom behavior inventory: Preschool to primary*. Bethesda, Md.: National Institute of Mental Health, 1966.

Schaeffer, E. S., & Bayley, N. Maternal behavior, child behavior, and their inter-correlations from infancy through adolescence. *Manual of Social Research in Child Development*, 1963, Serial No. 87–28, No. 3.

Schaffer, H. R. *The growth of sociability*. Harmondsworth, England: Penguin, 1971.

Scherer, M., & Nakamura, C. A fear survey schedule for children (FSS-FC): A factor analytic comparison with manifest anxiety (CMAS). *Behavior Research and Therapy*, 1968, *6*, 173–182.

Schlesser, R. S., Meyers, A. W., & Cohen, R. Generalization of self-instructions: Effects of general versus specific content, active rehearsal, and cognitive level. *Child Development*, 1981, *52*, 335–340.

Schlesser, R., Meyers, A. W., Thackwray, D., & Cohen, R. *Generalizations of self-instructions in impulsive fourth graders: Effects of discovery versus fading*. Paper presented at the annual meeting of the Association for the Advancement of Behavior Therapy, Toronto, November 1981.

Schopler, E. On confusion in the diagnosis of autism. *Journal of Autism and Childhood Schizophrenia*, 1978, *8*, 137–138.

Schopler, E. Editorial: Special issue on behavioral research. *Journal of Autism and Developmental Disorders*, 1979, *9*, 311–314.

Schopler, E., & Loftin, J. Thought disorders in parents of psychotic children: A function of test anxiety. *Archives of General Psychiatry*, 1969, *20*, 174–181.

Schover, L. R., & Newsom, C. D. Overselectivity, developmental level, and overtraining in autistic and normal children. *Journal of Abnormal Child Psychology*, 1976, *4*, 289–298.

Schneider, M. R. Turtle technique in the classroom. *Teaching Exceptional Children*, 1974, *6*, 22–24.

Schreibman, L. Effects of within-stimulus and extra-stimulus prompting on discrimination learning in autistic children. *Journal of Applied Behavior Analysis*, 1975, *8*, 91–112.

Schreibman, L., Koegel, R. L., & Craig, M. S. Reducing stimulus overselectivity in autistic children. *Journal of Abnormal Child Psychology*, 1977, *5*, 425–436.

Schuham, A. I. Power relations in emotionally disturbed and normal family triads. *Journal of Abnormal Psychology*, 1970, *75*, 30–37.

Schuham, A. I. Activity, talking time and spontaneous agreement in disturbed and normal family interaction. *Journal of Abnormal Psychology*, 1972, *79*, 68–75.

Schwantes, F. M. Cognitive scanning process in children. *Child Development*, 1979, *50*, 1136–1143.

Schwarz, J. C., & Zuroff, D. C. Family structure and depression in female college students: Effects of parental conflict, decision-making power, and inconsistency of love. *Journal of Abnormal Psychology*, 1979, *88*, 398–406.

Schwartz, S., & Johnson, J. H. *Psychopathology of childhood*. New York: Pergamon Press, 1981.

Schwitzgebel, R., & Kolb, D. A. Inducing behavior change in adolescent delinquents. *Behavior Research and Therapy*, 1964, *1*, 297–304.

Scibak, J., Whitman, T., & Johnson, M. *Increasing appropriate classroom behavior in educable retarded children*. Paper presented at the meeting of the Association for the Advancement of Behavior Therapy, New York, 1980.

Scopetta, M. *A comparison of modeling approaches to the rehabilitation of institutionalized male adolescent offenders implemented by paraprofessionals* (Doctoral dissertation, University of Miami, 1972). *Dissertation Abstracts International*, 1972, *33*, 2822B. (University Microfilms No. 72-31, 901.)

Scribner, S., & Cole, M. Cognitive consequences of formal and informal education. *Science*, 1973, *182*, 553–559.

Sears, R. R. Influence of methodological factors in doll-play performance. *Child Development*, 1947, *18*, 190–197.

Sears, R. R., Maccoby, E. E., & Levin, H. *Patterns of child rearing*. Evanston, Ill.: Row, Petersen, 1957.

Seidman, E., & Rappaport, J. The educational pyramid: A paradigm for research, training, and man-power utilization in community psychology. *American Journal of Community Psychology*, 1974, *2*, 119–130.

Selman, R. L. Toward a structural analysis of developing interpersonal relations concepts: Research with normal and disturbed preadolescent boys. In A. D. Pick (Ed.), *Minnesota Symposium on Child Psychology* (Vol. 10). Minneapolis: University of Minnesota Press, 1976.

Selman, R. L., Jaquette, D., & Lavin, D. R. Interpersonal awareness in children: Toward an integration of developmental and clinical child psychology. *American Journal of Orthopsychiatry*, 1977, *47*, 264–274.

Sermet, O. Emotional and medical factors in child dental anxiety. *Journal of Child Psychology and Psychiatry*, 1974, *15*, 313–321.

Seymour, F. W., & Stokes, T. F. Self-recording in training girls to increase work and evoke staff praise in institution for offenders. *Journal of Applied Behavior Analysis*, 1976, *9*, 41–54.

Shantz, C. U. The development of social cognition. In E. M. Hetherington (Ed.), *Review of child development research* (Vol. 5). Chicago: University of Chicago Press, 1975.

Shantz, C. U., & Wilson, K. Training communication skills in young children. *Child Development*, 1972, *43*, 693–698.

Shapiro, A. K. Placebo effects in medicine, psychotherapy, and psychoanalysis. In A. E. Bergin & S. L. Garfeild (Eds.), *Handbook of psychotherapy and behavior change*. New York: Wiley, 1971.

Shapiro, E. S., & Klein, R. D. Self-management of classroom behavior with retarded/disturbed children. *Behavior Modification*, 1980, *4*, 83–97.

Shapiro, E. S., McGonigle, J. J., & Ollendick, T. H. An analysis of self-assessment and self-reinforcement in a self-managed token economy with mentally retarded children. *Applied Research in Mental Retardation*, 1980, *1*, 227–240.

Shaw, O. Dental anxiety in children. *British Dental Journal*, 1975, *139*, 134–139.

Sheingold, K. Developmental differences in intake and storage of visual information. *Journal of Experimental Child Psychology*, 1973, *16*, 1–11.

Shepherd, M., Oppenheim, A. N., & Mitchell, S. Childhood behaviour disorders and the child-guidance clinic: An epidemiological study. *Journal of Child Psychology and Psychiatry*, 1966, *7*, 39–52.

Sherif, M., Harvey, O. J., White, B. J., Hood, W. R., & Sherif, C. W. *Intergroup conflict and cooperation*. Norman, Okla.: University Book Exchange, 1961.

Shipley, R. H., Butt, J. M., Horwitz, B., & Fabry, J. Preparation for a stressful medical procedure: Effect of amount and prestimulus exposure and coping style. *Journal of Consulting and Clinical Psychology*, 1978, *46*, 499–507.

Shipley, R. H., Butt, J. H., & Horwitz, E. A. Preparation to experience a stressful medical examination: Effects of repetitious videotape exposure on coping style. *Journal of Consulting and Clinical Psychology*, 1979, *47*, 485–492.

Shuller, D. Y., & McNamara, J. R. Expectancy factors in behavioral observation. *Behavior Therapy*, 1976, *7*, 519–527.

Shure, M. B., & Spivack, G. Means-ends thinking, adjustment, and social class among elementary school-aged children. *Journal of Consulting and Clinical Psychology*, 1972, *38*, 348–353.

Shure, M. B., & Spivack, G. *A mental health program for kindergarten children: Training script*. Philadelphia: Department of Mental Health Sciences, Hahnemann Community Mental Health/Mental Retardation Center, 1974. (a)

Shure, M. B., & Spivack, G. *Preschool interpersonal problem-solving (PIPS) test: Manual*. Philadelphia: Department of Mental Health Sciences, Hahnemann Community Mental Health/Mental Retardation Center, 1974. (b)

Shure, M. B., & Spivack, G. *Problem-solving techniques in childrearing*. San Francisco: Jossey-Bass, 1978.

Shure, M. B., & Spivack, G. Interpersonal cognitive problem solving and primary prevention: Programming for preschool and kindergarten children. *Journal of Clinical Child Psychology*, 1979, *2*, 89–94.

Shure, M. B., & Spivack, G. Interpersonal problem solving as a mediator of behavioral adjustment in preschool and kindergarten children. *Journal of Applied Developmental Psychology*, 1980, *1*, 29–44.

Shure, M. B., & Spivack, G., & Powell, L. *A problem-solving intervention program for disadvantaged preschool children*. Paper presented at the meeting of the Eastern Psychological Association, Boston, 1972.

Shure, M. B., Newman, S., & Silver, S. *Problem-solving thinking among adjusted, impulsive, and inhibited head start children*. Paper presented at Eastern Psychological Association, Washington, D.C., 1973.

Siegel, L. J. Preparation of children for hospitalization: A selected review of the research literature. *Journal of Pediatric Psychology*, 1976, *1*, 26–30.

Siegel, L. J. *Therapeutic modeling as a procedure to reduce the stress associated with medical and dental procedures*. Paper presented at the meeting of the Association for Advancement of Behavior Therapy, Atlanta, December 1977.

Siegel, L. J. *Naturalistic study of coping strategies in children facing medical procedures*. Paper presented at the meeting of the Southeastern Psychology Association, Atlanta, 1981.

Siegel, L. J. Hospitalization and medical care of children. In C. E. Walker & M. C. Roberts (Eds.), *Handbook of clinical child psychology*. New York: Wiley, 1983.

Siegel, L. J., & Peterson, L. Stress reduction in young dental patients through coping skills and sensory information. *Journal of Consulting and Clinical Psychology*, 1980, *48*, 785–787.

Siegel, L. J., & Peterson, L. Maintenance effects of coping skills and sensory information on young children's response to repeated dental procedures. *Behavior Therapy*, 1981, *12*, 530–535.

Siegel, L. J., Dragovich, S. L., & Marholin, D. The effects of biasing information on behavioral observations and rating scales. *Journal of Abnormal Child Psychology*, 1976, *4*, 221–223.

Siegler, R. S. *Children's thinking: What develops?* Hillsdale, N.J.: Lawrence Erlbaum Associates, 1978. (a)

Siegler, R. S. The origins of scientific reasoning. In R. S. Siegler (Ed.), *Children's thinking: What develops?* Hillsdale, N.J.: Lawrence Erlbaum Associates, 1978. (b)

Silvern, L. E., Waterman, J. M., Sobesky, W., & Ryan, V. L. Effects of a developmental model of perspective taking training. *Child Development*, 1979, *50*, 243–246.

Simeonsson, R., Buckley, L., & Monson, L. Conceptions of illness casuality in hospitalized children. *Journal of Pediatric Psychology*, 1979, *4*, 77–84.

Singer, R. V. *Incidental intentional learning in retarded and normal children*. Unpublished doctoral dissertation, Michigan State University, 1963.

Skinner, B. F. *Science and human behavior*. New York: Free Press, 1953.

Skipper, J. K., & Leonard, R. C. Children, stress, and hospitalization: A field experiment. *Journal of Health and Social Behavior*, 1968, *9*, 275–287.

Skipper, J., Leonard, R. C., & Rhymes, J. Child hospitalization and social interaction: An experimental study of mothers' feelings of stress, adaptation, and satisfaction. *Medical Care*, 1968, *6*, 496–506.

Smith, M. L., & Glass, G. V. Meta-analysis of psychotherapy outcome studies. *American Psychologist*, 1977, *32*, 752–760.

Smith, R. M. Creative thinking abilities of educable mentally handicapped children in the regular grades. *American Journal of Mental Deficiency*, 1967, *71*, 571–575.

Snyder, J. J. Reinforcement analysis of interaction in problem and nonproblem families. *Journal of Abnormal Psychology*, 1977, *86*, 528–535.

Snyder, J. J., & White, M. H. The use of cognitive self-instruction in the treatment of behaviorally disturbed adolescents. *Behavior Therapy*, 1979, *10*, 227–235.

Spitz, H. H. Consolidating facts into the schematized learning and memory system of educable retardates. In N. R. Ellis (Ed.), *International review of research in mental retardation* (Vol. 6). New York: Academic Press, 1973.

Spitz, H. H. Beyond field theory in the study of mental deficiency. In N. R. Ellis (Ed.), *Handbook of mental deficiency, psychological theory and research*. Hillsdale, N.J.: Lawrence Erlbaum Associates, 1979.

Spivack, G., & Levine M. *Self-regulation in acting-out and normal adolescents*. Washington, D.C.: National Institute of Health, 1963. (Report M-4531)

Spivack, G., & Shure, M. B. *Social adjustment of young children: A cognitive approach to solving real-life problems*. San Francisco: Jossey-Bass, 1974.

Spivack, G., & Shure, M. B. *Maternal childrearing and the interpersonal cognitive problem-solving ability of four-year-olds*. Paper presented at the meeting of the Society for Research in Child Development, Denver, 1975.

Spivack, G., & Swift, M. High risk classroom behaviors in kindergarten and first grade. *American Journal of Community Psychology*, 1977, *5*, 385–397.

Spivack, G., Platt, J. J., & Shure, M. B. *The problem-solving approach to adjustment*. San Francisco: Jossey-Bass, Inc., 1976.

Sroufe, L. A., & Waters, E. Attachment as an organizational construct. *Child Development*, 1979, *50*, 971–975.

Staats, A. W. Paradigmatic behaviorism, unified theory, unified theory construction methods, and the Zietgeist of separatism. *American Psychologist*, 1981, *36*, 239–256.

Stachnik, T. J. Priorities for psychology in medical education and health care delivery. *American Psychologist*, 1980, *35*, 1–8.

Stanton, M. D., & Todd, T. C. *Structural family therapy with heroin addicts: Some outcome data*. Paper presented at the meeting of the Society of Psychotherapy Research, June 1976.

Staub, E. The learning and unlearning of aggression. In J. L. Singer (Ed.), *The control of aggression and violence*. New York: Academic Press, 1971. (a)

Staub, E. The use of role playing and induction in children's learning of helping and sharing behavior. *Child Development*, 1971, *42*, 805–816. (b)

Staub, E., & Kellett, D. S. Increasing pain tolerance by information about aversive stimuli. *Journal of Personality and Social Psychology*, 1972, *21*, 198–203.

Stein, K. B., Sarbin, T. R., & Kulik, J. A. Future time perspective: Its relation to the socialization process and the delinquent role. *Journal of Consulting and Clinical Psychology*, 1968, *32*, 257–264.

Steinglass, P. The conceptualization of marriage from a systems theory perspective. In T. J. Paolino, Jr. & B. S. McGrady (Eds.), *Marriage and marital therapy*. New York: Brunner/Mazel, 1978.

Stern, D. *The first relationship: Infant and mother*. Cambridge, Mass.: Harvard University Press, 1977.

Sternberg, R. J. The nature of mental abilities. *American Psychologist*, 1979, *34*, 214–230.

Stevenson, H. W., Hale, G. A., Klein, R. E., & Miller, L. K. Interrelations and correlates in children's learning and problem solving. *Monographs of the Society for Research in Child Development*, 1968, *33*(7, Serial No. 123).

Stokes, T. F., & Baer, D. M. An implicit technology of generalization. *Journal of Applied Behavior Analysis*, 1977, *10*, 349–367.

Stokes, T. F., Fowler, S. A., & Baer, D. M. *Training preschool children to recruit natural communities of reinforcement*. Paper presented at the meeting of the American Psychological Association, San Francisco, August 1977.

Strain, P. S. An experimental analysis of peer social initiations on the behavior of withdrawn preschool children: Some training and generalization effects. *Journal of Abnormal Child Psychology*, 1977, *5*, 445–455.

Strain, P., & Timm, M. A. An experimental analysis of social interaction between a behaviorally disordered preschool child and her classroom peers. *Journal of Applied Behavior Analysis*, 1974, *7*, 583–590.

Strain, P. S., Cooke, T. P., & Apolloni, T. *Teaching exceptional children: Assessing and modifying social behavior*. New York: Academic Press, 1976.

Strauss, A. A., & Kephart, N. C. *Psychopathology and education of the brain-injured child* (Vol. 2): *Progress in theory and clinic*. New York: Grune & Stratton, 1947.

Strauss, A. A., & Lehtinen, L. E. *Psychopathology and education of the brain-injured child*. New York: Grune & Stratton, 1947.

Strodtbeck, F. L. Husband-wife interaction over revealed differences. *American Sociological Review*, 1951, *16*, 468–473.

Stuart, R. B., & Lott, L. A. Behavioral contracting with delinquents: A cautionary note. *Journal of Behavior Therapy and Experimental Psychiatry*, 1972, *3*, 161–169.

Student, M., & Sohmer, H. Evidence from auditory nerve and brainstem evoked responses for an organic brain lesion in childhood with autistic traits. *Journal of Autism and Childhood Schizophrenia*, 1978, *8*, 13–20.

Stumphauzer, J. S. Elimination of stealing by self-reinforcement of alternative behavior and family contracting. *Journal of Behavior Therapy and Experimental Psychiatry*, 1976, *7*, 265–268.

Suinn, R. M., & Richardson, R. Anxiety management training: A nonspecific behavior therapy for anxiety control. *Behavior Therapy*, 1971, *2*, 498–510.

Sullivan, H. S. *The interpersonal theory of psychiatry*. New York: W. W. Norton, 1953.

Suomi, S. J., & Harlow, H. F. Social rehabilitation of isolate-reared monkey. *Developmental Psychology*, 1972, *6*, 487–496.

Swanson, L. Modification of comprehension deficits in learning disabled children. *Learning Disability Quarterly*, 1981, *4*, 189–202.

Taylor, A. M., & Turnure, J. E. Imagery and verbal elaboration with retarded children:

Effects on learning and memory. In N. Ellis (Ed.), *Handbook of mental deficiency, psychological theory and research* (2nd ed.). Hillsdale, N.J.: Lawrence Erlbaum Associates, 1979.

Taylor, A., Thurlow, M., & Turnure, J. Vocabulary development of educable retarded children. *Exceptional Children*, 1977, *43*, 444–450.

Thomas A. & Chess, S. *Temperament and development*. New York: Brunner/Mazel, 1977.

Thompson, J. G., Griebstein, M. G., & Kuhlenschmidt, S. Effects of EMG biofeedback and relaxation training in the prevention of academic underachievement. *Journal of Counseling Psychology*, 1980, *27*, 97–106.

Thoresen, C., & Coates, J. Behavior self-control: Some clinical concerns. In M. Thoresen, R. *Modification* (Vol. 2). New York: Academic Press, 1976.

Thoresen, C. E., & Mahoney, M. J. *Behavioral self-control*. New York: Holt, Rinehart & Winston, 1974.

Thoresen, K. E., Thoresen, C. E., Klein, S. B., Wilbur, C. S., Becker-Haven, J. F., & Haven, W. G. Learning House: Helping troubled children and their parents change themselves. In J. S. Stumphauzer (Ed.), *Progress in behavior therapy with delinquents*. Springfield, Ill.: Charles C. Thomas, 1979.

Thurlow, M., & Turnure, J. Children's knowledge of time and money: Effective instruction for the mentally retarded. *Education and Training of the Mentally Retarded*, 1977, *12*, 203–212.

Timlick, C., & Norton, R. *The effects of modeling and verbal cues on concept acquisition of moderate retardates*. Unpublished manuscript, University of Winnipeg, 1978.

Toch, H. *Violent men*. Chicago: Aldine, 1969.

Tolor, A., Tolor, B., & Blumin, S. S. Self-concept and locus of control in primary-grade children identified as requiring special educational programming. *Psychological Reports*, 1977, *40*, 43–49.

Toner, I. J., Moore, L. P., & Ashley, P. K., The effect of serving as a model of self-control on subsequent resistance to deviation in children. *Journal of Experimental Child Psychology*, 1978, *26*, 85–91.

Torgesen, J., & Goldman, T. Verbal rehearsal and short-term memory in reading disabled children. *Child Development*, 1977, *48*(1), 56–60.

Torgesen, J. K., & Houck, D. G. Processing deficiencies of learning disabled children who perform poorly on the Digit Span Test. *Journal of Educational Psychology*, 1980, *72*, 141–160.

Traub, A. C., & Orbach, J. Psychophysical studies of body-image: The adjustable body-distorting mirror. *Archives of General Psychiatry*, 1964, *11*, 53–66.

Turkewitz, H., O'Leary, K. D., & Ironsmith, M. Generalization and maintenance of appropriate behavior through self-control. *Journal of Consulting and Clinical Psychology*, 1975, *43*, 577–583.

Turnage, J. R., & Logan, D. L. Treatment of a hypodermic needle phobia by in vivo systematic desensitization. *Journal of Behavior Therapy and Experimental Psychiatry*, 1974, *5*, 67–69.

Turnure, J. E., Buium, N., & Thurlow, M. L. The effectiveness of interrogatives for promoting verbal elaboration productivity in young children. *Child Development*, 1976, *47*, 851–855.

Twentyman, C. T., & McFall, R. M. Behavioral training of social skills in shy males. *Journal of Consulting and Clinical Psychology*, 1975, *43*, 384–395.

Tyler, L. E. More stately mansions—Psychology extends its boundaries. *Annual Review of Psychology*, 1981, *32*, 1–20.

Ullman, L. P., & Krasner, L. (Eds.). *Case studies in behavior modification.* New York: Holt, Rinehart & Winston, 1965.

Unger, M. *The defensiveness of children in relation to recall of information from a modeling videotape presentation.* Unpublished master's thesis, University of Florida, 1982.

Unikel, I. P., & Blanchard, E. B. Psychopathy, race, and delay of gratification by adolescent delinquents. *Journal of Nervous and Mental Disease,* 1973, *156,* 57–60.

United States General Accounting Office Report. *Learning disabilities: The link to delinquency should be determined, but school do should more now.* Washington, D.C.: U.S. Government Printing Office, 1977. (GGD-76–97)

Urbain, E. S., & Kendall, P. C. Review of social-cognitive problem-solving interventions with children. *Psychological Bulletin,* 1980, *88,* 109–143.

Urberg, K. A., & Docherty, E. M. Development of role-taking skills in young children. *Developmental Psychology,* 1976, *12,* 198–206.

Van Fleet, P., & Kannegieter, R. *Investments in prevention: The prevention of learning and behavior problems in young children.* San Francisco: PACE I. D. Center, 1969.

Van Hasselt, V. B., Hersen, M., Whitehill, M. B., & Bellack, A. S. Social skill assessment and training for children: An evaluative review. *Behavior Research and Therapy,* 1979, *17,* 413–437.

Varni, J. W., & Henker, B. A self-regulation approach to the treatment of three hyperactive boys. *Child Behavior Therapy,* 1979, *1,* 171–192.

Venham, L., Bengston, D., & Cipes, M. Preschool child's response to sequential dental visits. *Journal of Dental Research,* 1977, *56,* 454–459.

Vernon, D. T. A. Use of modeling to modify children's responses to natural potentially stressful situations. *Journal of Applied Psychology,* 1973, *58,* 351–356.

Vernon, D. T. A., & Bailey, W. C. The use of motion pictures in the psychological preparation of children for induction of anesthesia. *Anesthesiology,* 1974, *40,* 68–72.

Vernon, D. T. A., & Bigelow, D. A. Effects of information about a potentially stressful situation on responses to stress impact. *Journal of Personality and Social Psychology,* 1974, *29,* 50–59.

Victor, J. B., & Halverson, C. F. Behavior problems in elementary school children: A follow-up study. *Journal of Abnormal Child Psychology,* 1976, *4,* 17–29.

Vincent, J. P., Weiss, R. L., & Birchler, G. R. A behavioral analysis of problem solving in distressed and nondistressed married and stranger dyads. *Behavior Therapy,* 1975, *6,* 475–487.

Vincze, M. The social contacts of infants and young children reared together. *Early Child Development and Care,* 1971, *1,* 99–109.

Visintainer, M. A., & Wolfer, J. A. Psychological preparation for surgical pediatric patients: The effect on children's and parent's stress responses and adjustment. *Pediatrics,* 1975, *5,* 646–655.

Vogel, E. F., & Bell, N. W. The emotionally disturbed child as the family scapegoat. In N. W. Bell & E. F. Vogel (Eds.), *A modern introduction to the family.* New York: Free Press, 1968.

Vygotsky, L. S. *Mind in society: The development of higher psychological processes* (M. Cole, V. John-Steiner, S. Scribner, & E. Souberman, Eds.). Cambridge, Mass.: Harvard University Press, 1978.

Vygotsky, L. *Thought and language.* New York: Wiley, 1962.

Wahler, R. G. Some structural aspects of deviant child behavior. *Journal of Applied Behavior Analysis,* 1975, *8,* 27–42.

Wahler, R. G. The insular mother: Her problems in parent-child treatment. *Journal of Applied Behavior Analysis*, 1980, *13*, 207–219.

Wahler, R. G., & Fox, J. J. Solitary toy play and time out. A family treatment package for children with aggressive and oppositional behavior. *Journal of Applied Behavior Analysis*, 1980, *13*, 23–39.

Wahler, R. G., Berland, R. M., Coe, T. D., & Leske, G. Social systems analysis: Implementing an alternative behavioral model. In A. Rogers-Warren & S. F. Warren (Eds.), *Ecological perspectives in behaviors analysis*. Baltimore, Md.: University Park Press, 1977.

Wahler, R. G., Berland, R. M., & Coe, T. D. Generalization processes in child behavior change. In B. B. Lahey & A. E. Kazdin (Eds.), *Advances in clinical child psychology* (Vol. 2). New York: Plenum, 1979.

Waite, L. H., & Lewis, M. *Early imitation with several models: An example of socio-affective development*. Paper presented at the meeting of the Society for Research in Child Development, San Francisco, March 1979.

Waldrop, M. F., & Halverson, L. F. Jr. Intensive and extensive peer behavior: Longitudinal and cross-sectional analyses. *Child Development*, 1975, *46*, 19–26.

Walker, H., & Hops, H. The use of group and individual reinforcement contingencies in the modification of social withdrawal. In I. L. Hamerlynck, L. Handy, & E. Mash (Eds.), *Behavior change: Methodology, concepts, and practice*. Champaign, Ill.: Research Press, 1973.

Walker, M. *Walker problem behavior identification checklist manual*. Los Angeles: Western Psychological Services, 1970.

Warner, D. W., & de Jung, J. E. Effects of goal setting upon learning in educable retardates. *American Journal of Mental Deficiency*, 1971, *75*, 681–684.

Wasik, B. H., & Loven, M. D. Classroom observational data: Sources of inaccuracy and proposed solutions. *Behavioral Assessment*, 1980, *2*, 211–227.

Waters, H. S., & Waters, E. Somatic processing in children's free recall: The effects of context and meaningfulness on encoding variability. *Child Development*, 1979, *50*, 735–746.

Watson, D. L., & Hall, D. L. *Self-control of hyperactivity*. Unpublished manuscript, Pupil Services Division, La Mesa-Spring Valley School District, 1977.

Watson, J. B. *Behaviorism*. Chicago: University of Chicago Press, 1924.

Watson, J. B., & Rayner, R. Conditioned emotional reactions. *Journal of Experimental Psychology*, 1920, *3*, 1–14.

Watt, N. F. Patterns of childhood social development in adult schizophrenics. *Archives of General Psychiatry*, 1978, *35*, 160–170.

Watt, N. F., & Lubensky, A. W. Childhood roots of schizophrenia. *Journal of Consulting and Clinical Psychology*, 1976, *44*, 363–375.

Watt, N. F., Stolorow, R. D., Lubensky, A. W., & McClelland, D. C. School adjustment and behavior of children hospitalized for schizophrenia as adults. *American Journal of Orthopsychiatry*, 1970, *40*, 637–657.

Watzlawick, P., Beavin, J. H., & Jackson, D. D. *Pragmatics of human communication*. New York: W. W. Norton, 1967.

Watzlawick, P., Weakland, J., & Fisch, R. *Change: Principles of problem formation and problem resolution*. New York: W. W. Norton, 1974.

Wein, K., & Nelson, R. *The effects of self-instructional training on arithmetic problem solving skills*. Unpublished manuscript, University of North Carolina at Greensboro, 1978.

Weinrich, R. J. *Inducing reflective thinking in impulsive, emotionally disturbed children*. Unpublished doctoral thesis, Virginia Commonwealth University, 1975.

Weissberg, R. P., Gesten, E. L., Carnike, C. L., Toro, P. A., Rapkin., B. D., Davidson, E.,

& Cowen, E. L. Social problem-solving skills training: A competence-building intervention with 2nd–4th grade children. *American Journal of Community Psychology*, 1981, *9*, 411–424.

Weissberg, R. P., Gesten, E. L., Rapkin, B. D., Cowen, E. L., Davidson, E., Flores de Apodaca, R., & McKim, B. The effects of social problem-solving on the problem-solving skills and adjustment of 3rd grade children. *Journal of Consulting and Clinical Psychology*, 1981, *49*, 251–261.

Wellisch, D. K., Vincent, J., & Ro-Trock, G. K. Family therapy versus individual therapy: A study of adolescents and their parents. In D. H. L. Olson, (Eds.), *Treating relationships*. Lake Mills, Iowa: Graphic Publishing Company, 1976.

Werner, J. S., Minkin, N., Minkin, B. L., Fixsen, D. L., Phillips, E. L., & Wolf, M. M. "Intervention Package": An analysis to prepare juvenile delinquents for encounters with police officers. *Criminal Justice and Behavior*, 1975, *2*, 55–83.

Werry, J. S. Developmental hyperactivity. *Pediatric Clinics of North America*, 1968, *15*, 581–599.

White, S. H. Evidence for a hierarchial arrangement of learning processes. In L. P. Lipsett & C. C. Spiker (Eds.), *Advances in child development and behavior* (Vol. 2). New York: Academic Press, 1965.

White, W., Akers, J., Green, J., & Yates, D. Use of imitation in the treatment of dental phobia in early childhood: A preliminary report. *Journal of Dentistry for Children*, 1974, *41*, 106–110.

Whitehead, L. Sex differences in children's responses to family stress: A re-evaluation. *Journal of Child Psychology and Psychiatry*, 1979, *20*, 247–254.

Whiting, B., & Edwards, C. P. A cross-cultural analysis of sex differences in the behavior of children aged three through eleven. *Journal of Social Psychology*, 1973, *91*, 171–188.

Whitman, T., & Johnston, M. Teaching addition and subtraction with regrouping to educable mentally retarded children: A group self-instructional training program. *Behavior Therapy*, 1983, *14*, 127–143.

Whitman, T., Mercurio, J. R., & Caponigri, V. Development of social responses in two severely retarded children. *Journal of Applied Behavior Analysis*, 1970, *3*, 133–138.

Whitman, T., Scibak, J., Butler, K., Richter, R., & Johnson, M. Improving classroom behavior in mentally retarded children through correspondence training. *Journal of Applied Behavior Analysis*, 1982, *15*, 545–564.

Widom, C. S. Interpersonal and personal construct system in psychopaths. *Journal of Consulting and Clinical Psychology*, 1976, *85*, 330–334.

Wieland, I. H. Discussion of treatment approaches. In D. W. Churchill, G. D. Alpern, & M. K. DeMeyer (Eds.), *Infantile autism*. Springfield, Ill.: Charles C. Thomas, 1971.

Wild, C. M., Shapiro, L. N., & Abelin, T. Sampling issues in family studies of schizophrenia. *Archives of General Psychiatry*, 1974, *30*, 211–215.

Willems, E. P. Behavioral technology and behavioral ecology. *Journal of Applied Behavior Analysis*, 1974, *7*, 151–165.

Willems, E. P. Steps toward an ecobehavioral technology. In A. Rogers-Warren & S. F. Warren (Eds.), *Ecological perspectives in behavior analysis*. Baltimore, Md.: University Park Press, 1977.

Williams, D. Y., & Akamatsu, T. J. Cognitive self-guidance training with juvenile delinquents: Applicability and generalization. *Cognitive Therapy and Research*, 1978, *2*, 285–288.

Williams, P. D. Preparation of school-age children for surgery: A program in preventive pediatrics—Philipines. *International Journal of Nursing Studies*, 1980, *17*, 107–119.

Wilson, C. F., Hall, D. L., & Watson, D. L. *Teaching educationally handicapped children self-*

control: Teacher's manual, Grades 1, 2, 3. San Diego, Calif.: Department of Education, San Diego County, 1978. (a)

Wilson, C. F., Hall, D. L., & Watson, D. L. *Teaching educationally handicapped children self-control: Teachers manual. Grades 7, 8.* San Diego, Calif.: Department of Education, San Diego County, 1978. (b)

Wilson, G. T., & O'Leary, K. D. *Principles of behavior therapy.* Englewood Cliffs, N.J.: Prentice-Hall, 1980.

Winer, J., Hilpert, P., Gesten, E. L., Cowen, E. L., & Subin, W. E. The evaluation of a kindergarten social problem-solving program. *Journal of Primary Prevention,* 1982, *2,* 412–420.

Winett, R. A. An emerging approach to energy conservation. In D. S. Glenwick & L. A. Jason (Eds.), *Behavioral community psychology: Progress and prospects.* New York: Praeger Publishers, 1980.

Wing, L. *Diagnosing early childhood autism.* Paper presented at the annual meeting of the National Society for Autistic Children, San Jose, Calif., June 1979.

Wodarski, J. S., Feldman, R. A., & Pedi, S. J. Labeling by self and others: The comparison of behavior among "anti-social" and "pro-social" children in an open community agency. *Criminal Justice and Behavior,* 1975, *2,* 258–275.

Wolf, M. M. Social validity: The case for subjective measurement or how applied behavior analysis is finding its heart. *Journal of Applied Behavioral Analysis,* 1978, *11,* 203–214.

Wolfer, J. A., & Visintainer, M. A. Pediatric surgical patients and parents' stress responses and adjustment. *Nursing Research,* 1975, *4,* 244–255.

Wolfer, J. A., & Visintainer, M. A. Pediatric surgical patients' and parents' stress responses and adjustment as a function of psychological preparation and stress point nursing care. *Nursing Research,* 1979, *24*(4), 244–255.

Wolff, S., & Acton, W. P. Characteristics of parents of disturbed children. *British Journal of Psychiatry,* 1968, *114,* 593–601.

Wolpe, J. *Psychotherapy by reciprocal inhibition.* Stanford, Calif.: Stanford University Press, 1958.

Wolpe, J. *The practice of behavior therapy.* New York: Pergamon Press, 1969.

Wood, R., & Flynn, J. M. A self-evaluation token system *versus* an external evaluation token system alone in a residential setting with predelinquent youths. *Journal of Applied Behavior Analysis,* 1978, *11,* 503–512.

Wong, B., & Wong, R. Recall and clustering of verbal materials among normal and poor readers. *Bulletin of the Psychonomic Society,* 1977, *10*(5) 375–378.

Wright, J. *The Kansas reflection-impulsivity scale for preschoolers: A manual for users.* St. Ann, Mo.: Lemcel, 1972.

Yando, R. M., & Kagan, J. The effect of teacher tempo on the child. *Child Development,* 1968, *39,* 27–34.

Yando, R., Seitz, V., & Zigler, E. *Imitation: A developmental perspective.* Hillsdale, N.J.: Lawrence Erlbaum Associates, 1978.

Yates, A. J. *Behavior therapy.* New York: Wiley, 1970.

Youniss, J. The nature of social development: A conceptual discussion of cognition. In H. McGurk (Ed.), *Issues in childhood and social development.* London: Methuen, 1978.

Youniss, J. *Parents and peers in social development.* Chicago: University of Chicago Press, 1980.

Yussen, S. R., & Levy, V. M. Developmental changes in predicting one's own span of short-term memory. *Journal of Experimental Child Psychology,* 1975, *19,* 502–508.

Zahavi, S., & Asher, S. R. The effect of verbal instructions on preschool children's aggressive behavior. *Journal of School Psychology,* 1978, *16,* 146–153.

Zakraski, R. S. *Effects of context and training in the generalization of a cognition strategy by normally achieving of learning disabled boys.* Unpublished doctoral dissertation, University of Virginia, 1982.

Zastowny, T. R., Kirschenbaum, D. S., & Meng, A. L. Coping skills training for children: Effects on distress before, during and after hospitalization for surgery. *Journal of Consulting and Clinical Psychology,* in press.

Zax, M., & Cowen, E. L. *Abnormal psychology: Changing conceptions.* New York: Holt, Rinehart & Winston, 1972.

Zax, M., & Cowen, E. L. *Abnormal psychology: Changing conceptions* (2nd ed.). New York: Holt, Rinehart & Winston, 1976.

Zax, M., & Specter, G. A. *An introduction to community psychology.* New York: Wiley, 1974.

Zeaman, D., & House, B. J. A review of attention theory. In N. R. Ellis (Ed.), *Handbook of mental deficiency, psychological theory and research.* Hillsdale, N.J.: Lawrence Erlbaum Associates, 1979.

Zegiob, C., Klukas, N., & Junginger, J. Reactivity of self-monitoring procedures with retarded adolescents. *American Journal of Mental Deficiency,* 1978, *83,* 156–163.

Zelniker, T., & Jeffrey, W. E. Reflective and impulsive children: Strategies of information processing underlying differences in problem solving. *Monographs of the Society for Research in Child Development,* 1976, *41*(168, Serial no. 5.).

Zigler, E. Familial mental retardation: A continuing dilemma. *Science,* 1967, *155,* 292–298.

Zigler, E. The retarded child as a whole person. In D. K. Routh (Ed.), *The experimental psychology of mental retardation.* Chicago: Aldine, 1973.

Zigler, E., & Trickett, P. K. IQ, social competence, and evaluation of early childhood education programs. *American Psychologist,* 1978, *33,* 789–798.

Zivin, G. (Ed.). *The development of self regulation through private speech.* New York: Wiley, 1979.

Zohn, C. J., & Bornstein, P. H. Self-monitoring of work performance with mentally retarded adults: Effects upon work productivity, work quality, and on-task behavior. *Mental Retardation,* 1980, *18,* 19–25.

Zouzounis, J. A. *Developmental assessment of attentional processes in normals and autistics: Cardiac and behavioral responses to relevant redundant cues.* Unpublished master's thesis, San Diego State University, 1981.

Zouzounis, J. A., Feldman, G. I., Gilbride, K. E., & Lancaster, E. A. *Effects of stimulus fading procedures on overselectivity in autistic children.* Paper presented at the annual meeting of the Western Psychological Association, Honolulu, May 1980.

Zussman, J. U. Situational determinants of parental behavior: Effects of competing cognitive activity. *Child Development,* 1980, *51,* 792–800.

Author Index

Subject Index